A
HERO
FOR
OUR TIME

Other books by Ralph G. Martin

Jennie: The Life of Lady Randolph Churchill—
The Romantic Years: 1854–1895

Jennie: The Life of Lady Randolph Churchill—
The Dramatic Years: 1895–1921

Cissy

The Woman He Loved: The Story of the Duke and Duchess of Windsor

Skin Deep—A Novel

Boy from Nebraska

The Best Is None Too Good

The Bosses

Ballots and Bandwagons

World War II: A Photographic Record of the War in the Pacific from
Pearl Harbor to V-J Day

The Wizard of Wall Street

The G.I. War

A Man for All People

Lincoln Center for the Performing Arts

President from Missouri—A Juvenile

WITH ED PLAUT:

Front Runner, Dark Horse

WITH MORTON D. STONE:

Money, Money, Money

WITH RICHARD HARRITY:

Eleanor Roosevelt: Her Life in Pictures

The Human Side of FDR

Man of the Century: Winston Churchill

Man of Destiny: Charles De Gaulle

The Three Lives of Helen Keller

World War II: A Photographic Record of the War in Europe from
D-Day to V-E Day

A HERO FOR OUR TIME

*An Intimate Story of
the Kennedy Years*

RALPH G. MARTIN

MACMILLAN PUBLISHING COMPANY

New York

Macmillan Publishing Company
866 Third Avenue, New York, N.Y. 10022
Collier Macmillan Canada, Inc.

Library of Congress Cataloging in Publication Data
Martin, Ralph G., 1920–
A hero for our time.
1.   Kennedy, John F. (John Fitzgerald), 1917–1963.
2.   Kennedy family.   3.   Presidents—United States—
Biography.   I.   Title.
E842.M343   1983   973.922'092'4   [B]   83-9352
ISBN 0-02-580880-X

10   9   8   7   6   5   4   3   2   1

Designed by Jack Meserole

Printed in the United States of America

Unless otherwise noted, all photographs in this book
are courtesy of the John F. Kennedy Library, Boston, Massachusetts.

For my dear friends:

Gabriela and Howard Byrne, Ed Cunningham, Ida Epton, Shirley and Paul Green, Ruth and Larry Hall, Alaine Krim, Nancy and Ed Plaut, Guyo Tajiri, Ruth and Len Tropin, and Harriett and John Weaver

And in memory of:

Jack Danby, Herb Lyons, Joe McCarthy, Richard Paul, and Stan Swinton

CONTENTS

Contents

III

The Path to Power

IV

A Year of Crisis

V

The Growth of a President

Contents

VI

The Times of Trial

VII

The Myth and the Magic

A
HERO
FOR
OUR TIME

PROLOGUE

It was a cool September midnight in 1959 at Logan airport in Boston, and the Convair at the edge of the runway was set apart and silent. Inside, all was dark except a spacious compartment in the rear. It had a couch that opened into a bed, and two chairs, one of which was riveted to the floor. In it, the candidate sat, brooding over some papers, his face weary. As John Fitzgerald Kennedy stood up to shake my hand, his eyes looked quizzical and he had the slightest trace of a smile, a voice almost mocking when he said, "I heard you were going to do a hatchet job on me."

That was why, obviously, Kennedy had called our previous publisher urging him to cancel our contract negotiations—and he did. We had to move to another publisher, who was not so easily intimidated. At that point, Kennedy changed his mind and decided to see us.

"It's just a book to you," he said in a voice that had some fury in it—the most passion I would ever see in him—"but to me, it's my life, my whole future."

Ed Plaut and I were then co-authoring a book on presidential campaign techniques called *Front Runner, Dark Horse.* I assured him we were coming in clean, that we simply wanted to write an honest book. He looked at me as if he were examining me for nits or wrinkles, and then calmed quickly.

In the course of the conversation, Kennedy threw in another query. "I understand you don't like Bobby?"

I told him I had never met Bobby. "I know Bobby rubs some

people the wrong way," he said, "but you'll like him when you get to know him."

I never got to know Bobby, but I did get to know Jacqueline Kennedy.

She was quiet, shy, and pregnant. I had not talked to her much on the campaign plane because this was a political book and I knew she was not much interested in politics. But there was a time in Indianapolis—Kennedy was making a speech we both had heard several times, and so I suggested we go somewhere and talk. We went to the airport for lunch, and then onto the plane so that we could be more comfortable. There were just the two of us, and she mixed the drinks and we talked for the rest of the afternoon.

The campaigning was too hectic and her husband was too busy to talk much to her, or to listen, and that afternoon on the plane may have been a kind of release for her. As we drank and talked, she lost the whispery quality in her voice that might have come from Miss Porter's School. She said with some anger and much passion, "I wish Jack wouldn't call me 'Jackie.' How I hate that name! My name is Jacqueline. *My name is Jacqueline!*"

Like her husband, she could calm quickly after an outburst. I had not expected to like her very much, but I did. I found her a highly intelligent, very sensitive young woman with a full awareness of the public world into which she was now moving at such speed. It was not a pattern she would have selected, but it was part of her husband, and so she would somehow make it part of herself.

Jacqueline Kennedy must have worried a great deal during those months before our book appeared. She must have had "morning after" concerns about things she had told me that could have been sensationalized so easily. When the book was published—without any of her revelations—her quiet gratitude may have been one of the reasons she answered a national magazine query about her favorite books that year and listed ours among them.

That book was primarily political, but this one is more about magic.

I

*Let the Word
Go Forth . . .*

"I was having dinner with Jack and Jackie and a man named Smith and his wife," remembered editor-artist William Walton. "Smith was a Republican and ambassador to Cuba, and his wife, Flo, was a former girl friend of Jack's. This was January 1957, and the Smiths were going to the Eisenhower inaugural and they were all dressed up in evening clothes. The rest of us were just sitting around in our everyday clothes to watch the inaugural on television.

"Jack and Jackie and I talked about this often, because only four years later—*four years later*—we were the ones going to the Kennedy inaugural."

The Passing of the Torch

John Fitzgerald Kennedy had had the gift of much in his life: much wealth, good looks, much excitement, fun, luck, satisfaction. He had tested his courage in war, and proved it. He had faced the threat of death, and passed it. He knew of his attraction to women, and loved it. Now, he had come closer to the hub of power, and wanted it. He would become not only the most powerful man in the world but an almost impossible myth. And the lingering question always would be: how much of the myth was real?

*   *   *

Flying from Palm Beach to Washington in January 1961, John F. Kennedy was scribbling a new opening for his inaugural address on a pad of yellow paper. He was slouched behind his desk, sipping a glass of milk and taking an occasional bite of a medium-rare fillet.

He read a few pages aloud, then expressed some doubts about the long introduction.

"It's tough. The speech to the Massachusetts legislature went so well. It's going to be hard to meet that standard. What I want to say is that the spirit of the Revolution is still here, still a part of this country." He put the speech away and began talking about the Eisenhower budget, which he felt was unrealistically balanced. He worried that all the red ink would be blamed on the new administration. He then discussed his Cabinet and seemed very pleased.

The new President would become "the most prayed-for man in the world," the Reverend Billy Graham told the press after golfing with Kennedy in Palm Beach. The *Boston Globe* gave him an even more elevated office with a printing error that referred to him as "Saint John Kennedy." Family and intimates quickly tabbed him "Saint John." But his friend and aide Dave Powers felt he needed more deflating. When Kennedy asked Powers to get him his usual breakfast, Powers told him, "Get it yourself. You're not president yet." His chauffeur, former Senate policeman John L. "Muggsy" O'Leary, was similarly informal. "For God's sake, get going or we're gonna be late!"

More respectful was Robert Frost, whom John Kennedy had asked to read a poem at his inauguration. "If you can bear at your age the honor of being made President of the United States," the old poet replied, "I ought to be able at my age to bear the honor of taking some part in your inauguration."

In pre-inaugural days the Kennedys' Georgetown house looked like the nerve center of a convention. "It was so crowded," Jacqueline remembered, "that I could be in the tub, and then find that Pierre Salinger was holding a press conference in my bedroom."

"She loosens Jack up, deflates him when he gets overserious or pompous," said Charles Bartlett, an old friend and a Washington correspondent for the *Chattanooga Times*. She would serve teaspoons with soup, and play records of Fred Astaire dancing. She sent William Walton a telegram when he was made Deputy Grand Marshal of the inaugural parade: WILL YOU WEAR BLUE JEANS A BIT TOO TIGHT YOUR TRADEMARK OR OLD CORDUROY JACKET IN WHICH YOU GREETED MRS. LA GUARDIA IN NEW YORK?

Kennedy had told Bartlett that he planned to curb his womanizing ways in the White House. "He was sitting right in this chair," Bartlett said, "when he told me he was going to keep the White House white." At the same time, however, Kennedy had arranged to have his pretty, obliging stewardess, Janet des Rosiers, put on the payroll of the White House secretarial staff.

Only eight years before, in 1953, Jacqueline Kennedy had been a reporter covering the inaugural for the *Washington Times-Herald*, shivering on the cold curb across the street from the White House, watching Mamie Eisenhower jump up and clap her hands and blow a kiss to the West Point cadet choir when they sang, "Mamie, the First Lady in the Land." She had interviewed Mamie's niece, who told her: "A girl in my class said when my uncle's President, I should tell my teacher to give me good marks or he'd throw her off the school board." She remembered what a workman had told her of Mrs. Eisenhower. "She's a prisoner of the Secret Service for the next four years." And first-grader Tricia Nixon had said of her father, "He's always away. If he's famous, why can't he stay home?" In her article on that inaugural, Jacqueline wrote, "Mamie's lively laughter could be heard far back in the crowd . . . while Mrs. Truman sat stolidly with her gaze glued on the blimp overhead through most of the ceremony."

Now Mrs. Eisenhower would look for the blimps.

Bill Walton had known both Kennedys before they had known each other. A ruggedly handsome man, Walton had been a war correspondent and a magazine editor, and was now an artist.

Walton explained, "I was acceptable to Jack as a constant companion at this time because I had no ties, no connections, no family—my kids had grown up, and I was divorced. Besides, I didn't want anything from him. I wasn't pushing any particular project, I didn't have any candidates for office, and I didn't want any office myself."

On the day before the inauguration, Walton received a call from Alice Roosevelt Longworth. "What are you going to do with the President at your home all day?" Walton thought she was joking until he queried Kennedy's secretary, Evelyn Lincoln. "Oh yes, we were going to call you," she said.

It seemed that Jacqueline Kennedy had issued an ultimatum to her husband. "Jackie told him that, if he expects her to move to the White House tomorrow, he's got to clear out of the house with everybody so she can get things arranged for moving." Kennedy and Mrs. Lincoln soon arrived with the Secret Service, and took over. The phone rang constantly for Mrs. Lincoln, so Walton found himself answering the doorbell. Kennedy had stacked the day with necessary appointments. There was everybody from Ted Sorensen's family from Nebraska to Chief of Staff General Lemnitzer. There was also the new head of the Federal Aviation Administration, Najeeb Hallaby, who whispered to his friend Walton, "Aren't you going to introduce me to the President?"

Ben Bradlee of *Newsweek* and columnist Rowland Evans joined them for lunch, which was awkward because other newspapermen were waiting in the streets and would resent two of their peers selected for this honor. So, after lunch, Bradlee and Evans exited by climbing over the fence in the backyard.

"Do you have a typewriter?" Kennedy asked. Walton had an old portable and he typed up the announcements for the presidential appointments while Kennedy puffed on a borrowed cigar and worked on the exact wording.

Kennedy left at four to dress for the evening's pre-inaugural balls. Rosemarie Sorrentino was at the house with Kenneth, from Lilly Daché in New York, to do Jackie's hair. "And it was a madhouse, I can tell you," Sorrentino said. "I still remember, she introduced me as her hairdresser and said, 'Jack, Rosemarie also does Marilyn Monroe's hair.' He looked up, and the first thing he said was, 'Is Marilyn Monroe really as temperamental as everyone says she is?' "

"And then it started to snow about four-thirty," Walton said. "Very, very heavily. Jack assigned me a car and a driver, but we got stuck about three blocks from my house and I went back home. Jack called later to say that they couldn't pick me up at my house because of the snow but they would wait for me at their house. They were six blocks away. By then it was a real snowstorm. I got all dressed up and put on my big boots and walked in that very, very, deep unplowed snow and got there exhausted. The only area that had been cleared was from their house to Constitution Hall, and as we drove by we saw all kinds of snowbound people, some of them lighting bonfires to keep warm, and Jack said, 'Turn on the car light so they can see Jackie.'

"Jackie looked absolutely lovely. And she sat forward so everybody could see her, and Jack and I sat back, and I saw that he was reading something, and I asked what it was. 'Jefferson's second inaugural,' he said, 'and it's better than mine.'

"When we got to the concert hall, there were very few people there. A busload of musicians was stuck somewhere, other entertainers still hadn't arrived, and there were only a few hundred people and a handful of musicians. We sat in the box up front. Finally, the musicians started playing and they put on a partial program for an hour. Then we went from there to the Frank Sinatra gala. There were more people there and that ball lasted a long time."

Sinatra later joined the Kennedy family in a downtown restaurant to entertain them at a small family party that lasted into the early morning hours.

An exhausted Jacqueline, still recovering from the birth of her son, went home about eleven. To save her strength, she had not gone to the Young Democrats' Dance or the Governors' Reception or the Reception for Distinguished Women, where she would have had to greet forty-five hundred guests. Nor did she attend the reception honoring Vice-President and Mrs. Johnson, whom she had quietly referred to as "Colonel Cornpone and his little Pork Chop."

The blizzard brought with it a kind of festival madness. "It was gay—the way a city becomes when a blizzard falls on it and everybody feels helpless anyway and perfect strangers embrace and everybody becomes friends and sings and jumps in the snow," conductor Leonard Bernstein remembered. Bernstein and Bette Davis were among those stranded in limousines that couldn't move. They commandeered a police car, which drove along the sidewalks between trees to take them to the armory ball where they were scheduled to entertain. Many of the performers went on unwashed and unchanged and un-black-tied.

"It made the occasion more exciting actually than it might have been," said Bernstein.

Bernstein later saw Kennedy dancing with someone he knew and cut in. Kennedy, though surprised, recovered quickly, "but the girl was furious. . . ."

During the evening, labor leader James Carey called Kennedy "Jack," then thought about it and smiled. "That may be the last time I'll be able to call you 'Jack.' Tomorrow it will be 'Mr. President.' "

Shortly after 8:00 PM, the night before the inauguration, Kennedy was told, "The President is calling the President-elect." Since the weather was so miserable, Eisenhower said to Kennedy, would the Kennedys like to come into the White House for coffee before driving out to the inaugural ceremony?

Waiting for the Kennedys in the Red Room the next morning were the Eisenhowers, the Nixons, the Johnsons, and leaders of the Senate and the House of Representatives. A half-hour later, the President and the President-elect, cordial and still chatting, emerged for their ride together down Pennsylvania Avenue in the bubbletop Lincoln.

President Eisenhower wore his silk topper; Kennedy carried his.

Kennedy had listened to the advice of the eighty-four-year-old president *pro tempore* of the Senate, Senator Carl Hayden of Arizona, who told inaugural chairman Ed Foley: "Ed, tell that young fella he should wear a cutaway coat and silk hat. I want him to come down looking like a President."

On the morning of Inauguration Day, Kennedy needed a new collar for his formal shirt. His driver, Muggsy, brought one and it didn't fit. "Call my father and see if he has one I can wear," Kennedy said. They rummaged around and finally found one.

*   *   *

Jacqueline stood there in the White House hall looking a little lost. Finally she saw her husband's military aide and went to him. "No one's told me what I'm supposed to do. I just don't know. Jack's told me nothing."

The aide whispered to Kennedy, who then asked him to find a private room for Jacqueline and himself. "I need five minutes."

That done, he told his aide, "All right, see that this thing runs, and keep it moving. Tell me where we go next and what we're gonna do."

Inevitably, the ceremony ran behind schedule. Waiting in a small chamber near the rotunda, Kennedy saw television reporter Nancy Dickerson and she came over to talk. For those moments, he did not want to be alone. When all was ready, he went onto the windswept platform, shook hands with former President Truman, and sat next to Eisenhower. They had an animated discussion about the crucial importance of weather forecasters on World War II's D-Day. It was 12:13 PM and technically he had been President since noon, even though he had not yet taken the oath of office.

"I knew it would be long," the new President said afterwards about Richard Cardinal Cushing's invocation, "but halfway through I was saved by the thought that here is Kennedy, the first Catholic president being inaugurated, and Cardinal Spellman is having to watch it on television." The Kennedys were unhappy with Cardinal Spellman. Three weeks before the election, Spellman had met Nixon at the airport and had paraded through Manhattan with him.

It was twenty-three degrees, the wind whipping the paper in his hands as eighty-six-year-old poet Robert Frost tried to read some of his poetry, the sun blinding him. Vice-President Johnson jumped up and tried to shade the paper with his hat, but the old poet faltered, to the embarrassed titters of the crowd. The most anguished face on the platform was that of the new First Lady. Finally the poet stood up proudly and said he would recite something else without reading:

> . . . Such as we were we gave ourselves outright
> The deed of gift was many deeds of war
> To the land vaguely realizing westward,
> But still unstoried, artless, unenhanced,
> Such as she was, such as she will become.

Kennedy finally arose to the fanfare, removed his black topcoat on that frigid Friday, and stepped forward with Chief Justice Earl Warren to repeat the oath of office over a family Bible, his voice crisp and clear. His youth—his forty-four years—no longer mattered. "When your hand's on the Bible, you're the most powerful man in the world." Kennedy later admitted that his hand might have slipped off the Bible while he concentrated on the oath.

When Jacqueline covered the Eisenhower inauguration for the *Washington Times-Herald,* she noted that "Ike planted a kiss on Mamie's cheek right after taking the oath."

At her own husband's inauguration, a great many observed that he did not kiss her after taking the presidential oath.

Then slowly, dramatically, he read his thirteen-hundred-word inaugural speech:

"Let the word go forth from this time and place, to friend and foe alike, that the torch has been passed to a new generation of Americans. . . ."

A regional manager of Bristol-Myers afterwards told a reporter, "When he talked about that torch, my hand was right out there. I was ready to do whatever he asked me to do."

Kennedy continued: "Ask not what your country can do for you—ask what you can do for your country."

House Speaker Sam Rayburn said: "That speech he made out there was better than anything Franklin Roosevelt said at his best—it was better than Lincoln. I think—really think—that he is a man of destiny."

"I was so proud of Jack," Jacqueline said after the inaugural. "There was so much I wanted to say! But I could scarcely embrace him in front of all those people. So I remember I just put my hand on his cheek and said, 'Jack, you were so wonderful!' "

Before the parades began, Kennedy had a cup of tomato soup, some lobster Newburg, and garlic bread. In the old Supreme Court chamber of the Capitol, he also signed the nomination papers for his ten Cabinet appointees and UN Ambassador Adlai Stevenson. The White House doorman brought them blankets while they sat on the cold reviewing stand. Mrs. Kennedy accepted hers but Kennedy refused his. Nor did she wait until the bitter end, but he did. So did most of the shivering crowd of seven hundred fifty thousand.

As he sat there, he was most moved by the float showing his old PT boat, his former crew saluting him as they passed. He told his aide he did not want to be left alone and he wasn't. He talked seriously to the head of the Atomic Energy Commission about getting more scientists, and at one point pulled out of the crowd his old friend Eddie McLaughlin and introduced him to Chief Justice Warren. "Eddie's done extremely well, Mr. Chief Justice."

"You haven't done too goddamn badly yourself, Mr. President," Eddie replied.

As the Chief Justice left, the new President took a good look at Eddie's full-figured wife and asked, "Is all that up front really *you?*"

*   *   *

Shortly before noon, a White House truck parked in front of 3307 N Street. Among the things carried into the truck were Caroline's rocking horse and baby John's white wicker bassinet, bedecked with dotted Swiss and pink ribbon.

"Mrs. Kennedy always knew exactly where she wanted everything placed, and she seldom changed her mind," said Mrs. Adele Murphy, head of Residential Services, Inc. Even before Inauguration Day, some of the Kennedy furniture had been moved quietly into White House storage rooms.

In a White House car behind the truck were Jacqueline's social secretary, Tish Baldrige, and Jacqueline's maid, Providencia "Provie" Parades. With them, in protective plastic, was Jacqueline's inaugural ball gown of white satin and chiffon.

Everything had been timed.

Kathleen Bouvier said, "As the inaugural parade began, we rose every half-minute to applaud. Not only because it was so marvelous, but because it was standing up so frequently that kept us from freezing to death."

The proud Kennedy father sat in the front row, and he and his son had much to talk about: "This is what I've been looking forward to for a long time." It was rumored, but not confirmed, that the retarded Rosemary Kennedy watched her brother's presidential inauguration from a private limousine. His mother told Jack how pleased she was to have seen him at early morning Mass, "starting his presidency by offering it his mind and heart, and expressing his hopes and fears to Almighty God, and asking His blessing as he began his great duties."

*   *   *

Two hundred Bouviers, Auchinclosses, Lees, and Kennedys collected in the State Dining Room of the White House after the parade. At an earlier luncheon for the families at the Mayflower Hotel—hosted by the President's father—the social conversation seemed strained. It was much the same at the White House.

Joseph Kennedy was strangely glum and moody. Perhaps he was thinking of his son Joe. At the lunch and reception afterwards, a feeling of tension could be felt between people with very different backgrounds of taste and wealth and politics and class.

Edith Beale, who shared a Bouvier grandfather with Jacqueline, sidled over to Joseph Kennedy and told him that she and his son Joe had met at a dance in 1938. "I fell in love with him immediately," she told him. She had hoped to marry him, and she might have been the First Lady—if he had not been killed. Joseph Kennedy listened sadly, and quickly moved away.

Mrs. Auchincloss reported that Jacqueline was upstairs resting. "She has five balls to go to tonight." Wouldn't she come down just to make an appearance, just to say hello and wave? "We're her family." Her mother shrugged her shoulders. A Secret Service man then came to get Michel Bouvier. He was not only Jacqueline's godfather and her father's nephew, but almost like an older brother. As many observed, Michel looked remarkably like Jacqueline's father, who had died two years before— the same eyes and chin and body frame, and even the same pencil-line mustache. Michel stayed with Jacqueline upstairs for a half hour, then returned to say that Jacqueline was resting and would not appear. The party was soon over.

It was dark before Jack returned to the White House to drink a daiquiri, get warm, and change clothes for the evening festivities.

Five visiting queens had slept in that wide bed hung with pink curtains, but none of that mattered much at this moment of Inauguration Day because Jacqueline felt too weak to get up to dress for dinner. "I just didn't have one bit of strength left and felt absolutely panicked. What could I do? Somehow I managed to get in touch with Dr. Travell." Dr. Janet Travell hurried from the presidential reviewing stand, diagnosed the problem as painful leg cramps and exhaustion, and prescribed a single rust-colored pill called Dexedrine.

It worked. When she came down the stairway to the Red Room, where her husband was waiting to take her to the inaugural balls, she wore a sheath of white chiffon, the bodice sparkling with brilliants, all of it veiled in a gossamer cape that fell to the floor. She stood poised in the doorway, wearing her white kid gloves with twenty pearl buttons, and her husband reacted like the hero of a modern romance novel. He stared and said, "Darling, I've never seen you look so lovely." Fortunately, the day before, Jacqueline had arranged for her portable bar to be brought from the Georgetown house, stocked with bottles of his favorite, Dom Perignon. Then her husband toasted her in champagne.

*   *   *

The tradition was rich. Thomas Jefferson had invited well-wishers to the White House and was nearly crushed by the crowd. Andrew Jackson issued an open invitation and twenty thousand arrived for his spiked orange punch and ice cream, smashing glasses, trampling on waiters, and wrecking the carpets. At the Madison ball, windows had to be broken to let in air, and Dolley Madison complained that she couldn't dance on the crowded floor because of her elaborate Paris headdress. President Madison confided that he "would rather be in bed." Presbyterians James Polk and Woodrow Wilson had no inaugural balls because they did not dance—for religious reasons. Rutherford Hayes was sworn in secretly after a disputed election. Warren G. Harding wanted an inaugural ball, but the country's economic plight was too serious. It was Franklin D. Roosevelt who brought the balls back with all their excitement and glamour. But nobody equaled the lavishness of President James Buchanan, a bachelor bon vivant who provided 400 gallons of oysters, 500 quarts of chicken salad, 60 saddles of mutton, 8 rounds of beef, 75 hams, and 500 quarts of jellies. In contrast, Truman provided 6 salads, most of them green, and a dish of truffles and mushrooms. The most noteworthy souvenir of the Eisenhower balls was a footprint a guest found on the back of her gown—between her shoulders.

There were five balls that night, and the President moved fast, always walking ahead of his wife. When an aide later mentioned that the First Lady was having trouble keeping up with him, his answer was almost too casual, "Well, she'll just have to walk faster." Overheard by others was the comment, "Jackie's too young to be First Lady. . . . Can you imagine kiddy-cars in the East Room?"

Only the President and Jacqueline didn't dance at any of the balls, primarily because of security problems. As it was, the crowd crushed towards them to be as close as possible, simply standing and staring.

Some song lyrics Kennedy liked were:

> Big John, now everyone is glad
> Your home will be that big white pad.

After the third ball, at 1 AM, Jacqueline told her husband she had had enough. "I want to go back."

"Mac will take you."

The last time Air Force aide Godfrey McHugh had escorted her to the White House he was a major and she was an inquiring photographer going to a staff dance. Now she was the First Lady, asking him, "Are you going to work hard for the President or are you going to continue to be a playboy?"

"You know damn well I'm not a playboy," he answered.

The President seemed to relax more after his wife had left. A Boston friend later pointed at several invited actresses and said to Kennedy, "You're not going over the wall the first night at the White House, are you?"

The presidential caravan left the final ball behind the accompanying motorcycle police, and drove quietly through the narrow streets of Georgetown, pulling up at one of the houses on Dumbarton Avenue. The President walked up the steps alone, rang the doorbell, and waited more than a minute before someone finally opened it.

"Joe heard the doorbell but wouldn't go to the door because it was so late," Susan Alsop recalled. "Finally he went and there was the President. He was just very keyed up and wanted to talk."

"I hadn't planned a house party," columnist Joseph Alsop said. "I just told a few people that there'd be a bottle of champagne at my house after the inaugural ball—if the lights were on. I'd gone and forgotten to tell my people to turn the lights off. So I got home from the ball, bored to death, and the lights were blazing and there were all these people hammering at the door. Somehow the word had passed around that I was having a party. And then more and more people came. Well, there wasn't *anything* to eat—not even an egg. I did have someone coming from abroad a bit later, a friend of ours, and I was having a big party for this friend and I did have some terrapin saved up for that. So out came the terrapin and I heated that up and then I got out some more champagne. Oh, we had an awful lot of people by then.

"Then, suddenly, on this extremely sordid scene, the bell rang again and I went to the door. There was this whole block, lights ablaze in everybody's windows, and there was this Secret Service escort looking like a military cortege, and there was this young man with snow in his hair who said he heard I was having a party and he didn't want to go to bed yet, and I said, 'Come on in.'

"Jackie had been bone-tired and desperate to go to bed and he was suddenly all alone. They'd moved into the White House that day and the place was like a barn. Every single pretty thing belonging there had been put in the cellar. He couldn't even get a nightcap, and he didn't want to be alone, and so here he was.

"So he came in and everybody made much of him. I gave him the terrapin but he didn't like it. Most people don't at first, do they? But somebody made a toast and he drank the champagne and he seemed gay.

"I was so busy housekeeping, I had no idea how many people came and went. He stayed an hour or so and I think he had a good time. It was a helluva mess to clean up afterwards. . . ."

At 3:22 AM, the President of the United States emerged, puffing a cigar, and went back to his big new white house.

II

The Young Years

You must think of him as this little boy, sick so much of the time, reading in bed, reading history, reading the Knights of the Round Table, reading Marlborough. For Jack, history was full of heroes. Jack had this hero idea of history.

—JACQUELINE KENNEDY

Growing Up Kennedy

The Colemans and the Kennedys were next-door neighbors in the Kennedy compound in Hyannis Port and owned a wedge-shaped piece of land in common. The elder Coleman was a Republican who never liked the Kennedys. But Nancy Coleman and the Kennedy kids were close. They considered her an extra sister. She was always asked to sail with them ("when they needed extra ballast," she said, laughing), swim and dance with them.

"A long long time ago," Nancy Coleman said, "we would sit in our house and look at that big Kennedy house and know that *somebody* in that big house was going to be President of the United States. We didn't know whether it was going to be Big Joe or Little Joe or Jack, but we knew it was going to be somebody in there."

"Nobody knows the Kennedys good," said Patsy Mulkern, who worked hard in the early Kennedy campaigns. "They don't let you know them good. That's one thing about them. You hear people all day long telling you how close they were to Kennedy. Nobody was close to him."

"The Kennedys are the most interesting family in history since the Bonapartes," Alice Roosevelt Longworth said.

There were those who claimed the Kennedys were arrogant. Arrogance, however, implies condescension. This was not their style. Call it ego, certainly. Call it the power of money, of course. Call it ambition, and why not? But arrogance is a hard word. It does not fit well with John Kennedy's self-deprecating laughter, or Bob Kennedy's early shyness, or Ted Kennedy's easy familiarity, or the hard-working charity of the Kennedy women.

If they sometimes assumed superiority—and they did—and if they showed impatience, friends felt it was a mixture of self-confidence plus a sense of purpose. "Us against the world." They were taught early that they were a tribe. If one shut you out, they all did. Fight the common enemy, even if the enemy was right. It seemed true that they preferred each other's company to everyone else's.

That's what made them so intriguing—they didn't seem to need anyone else. When they were together, they seemed all alike. You had to get them apart to see how different they were. It looked as if they lived off each other. "We liked each other more than we liked other people, but I suppose that's natural," Eunice remarked. No Kennedy would tell other Kennedys things they didn't want to hear. Each of them would rather have another Kennedy say, "Nice play!" than get a compliment from the pope or the president. Yet each tried desperately to beat the other. "Come on, let's have another game. . . . Let's play another point." They hated to lose. They believed, "winning isn't everything; it's the only thing."

That came from their father.

The surprise was that they were all rich enough to become wandering wastrels or alcoholics, but instead devoted themselves to public service and public responsibility.

That came from their mother.

What propelled them into prominence was that they seemed to fill a national need for celebrities in the same way that the

Royal Family filled a need for the British. Partly, the Kennedys were the created creatures of our press. Their handsome faces and fascinating lives sold papers and magazines, and this feeding fed on itself. But the basic material was there—the excitement, the shimmering dream.

It was more than a state of mind, or a life-style, or a national philosophy. It was part of a national need for hope. Fenced in by a wall of small expectations, the average American family saw in the Kennedys the idealized world of the American dream.

In American history, only a few distinguished families have trained their children for political careers. The Adams family, the Lodges, the McCormacks, and the Kennedys in Massachusetts; the Tafts in Ohio; the Byrds in Virginia; the Longs in Louisiana; the Wagners and the Roosevelts in New York.

Why did the Kennedy sons succeed politically while the Roosevelt sons failed?

Certainly President Roosevelt had the same understanding of power and knew how to use it. But Roosevelt did not use that power for his sons in the driving way that Joe Kennedy did. Perhaps it was because he was already President and Joe Kennedy never would be. Eleanor Roosevelt once confessed that she had had to make a choice between her husband and her children. She decided that her husband needed her more, to be his legs, ears, eyes, and conscience. When she helped him, she knew she was serving her country and the world.

Franklin D. Roosevelt, Jr., revealed that he had to make an appointment to see his parents. He told of seeing his father on an important personal problem. While he talked, his father never stopped working at his desk. When young Franklin finished telling his trouble, his father simply said, "Glad you could drop by." End of interview.

"You know," Kennedy told Steve Smith, "when I was just trying out for the freshman team for some of those swimming meets, my Dad was always there. He was *always* there. He did the same for all his kids."

His father was a one-man cheering section: "My business is my family and my family is my business."

Joseph Patrick Kennedy, Sr., was a man of sheer, unmitigated gall with a tight, dry mind. He looked like a powerful bald eagle with blue eyes that took on the color of an icy lake when they turned from warmth to hate. Straight and spare, he had a prominent chin, wore old-fashioned spectacles, gestured animatedly with a bright alertness, and could pour on enormous charm whenever he wanted. He had a firm handshake and a trigger temper, and he liked to laugh. He was, he said, one of the twenty richest men in America, worth some $400 million. He understood power. "Let me see any other motive in the people who command." He understood Wall Street. "I always said that with enough inside information and unlimited credit, you are sure to go broke." He was the world's richest bootlegger, and he didn't drink; he was one of the greatest speculators, but he hated gambling with cards or horses. His friend Morton Downey insisted that Joseph Kennedy had not missed a first-Friday communion in twenty-seven years.

Joseph came from the backwater of East Boston where his father made barrels on the docks. He then was a saloon keeper, later a political boss. He remembered overhearing one of his father's friends telling how he voted 128 times on election day. Nor did he ever forget a description of the cobblestoned streets of Beacon Hill, home of Boston's Brahmins. "Those aren't cobblestones; those are Irish heads." When a newspaper described Kennedy as a Boston Irishman, he said, "I was born here. My children were born here. What the hell do I have to do to be an American?"

Joseph Kennedy made his own rules. His classmates of 1912 at Harvard remember how he caught the ball at the end of the Harvard-Yale game and ran off the field with it—instead of following tradition and handing it to the captain.

"I was on a plane with him when I was a kid," said Franklin D. Roosevelt, Jr., of Joseph Kennedy, "and he was telling me foul stories in loud language until a woman behind us leaned forward and said she would appreciate it if he would have the decency to keep quiet in a place where other people couldn't walk away from him if they didn't want to listen. He simply laughed and went right on. I think Jack's father was one of the most evil, disgusting men I have ever known. Oh, I know he was a financial genius but he was a rotten human being. He once called in my brother Jimmy to work out a deal with Ballantines, and Jimmy went and worked out the whole deal, then had trouble just getting old man Kennedy to even pay his expenses. And Kennedy made a pile out of that one."

His office at 230 Park Avenue in New York City was not the office of a multimillionaire magnate. It was no more than twelve by fourteen feet, with a thin partition on one side, a worn carpet, an old desk, a battered couch, and only one window, looking south. It reminded one of a remark by a highly success-ful advertising executive who said, "I can afford *not* to have a mink coat."

Publisher William Randolph Hearst advised Joe Kennedy that the handicap of being a rich man's child was that there was little natural inclination to try hard. He warned him not to leave each of his children million-dollar trust funds.

"If you make them independent, they won't need you," he said. "They'll leave you."

"If I thought that would happen, then I'd be a lousy father," Kennedy answered.

"But then there's the myth about my father putting a million dollars in trust for each of us in order to enable us to go into public life," John Kennedy once said. "Well, that was in 1929, and he was speculating pretty hard and his health wasn't too good, and *that* was the reason he did it. There was no other reason."

"My father is one of the greatest men in the world," John Kennedy told his neighbor Larry Newman, "and one of the most misunderstood. They all knock him, but you've got to think of what he's done. How many people do you know who have done what he has?"

"The real measure of success is to get a family that does as well as mine," the father mused in a quiet moment.

Once the young Kennedys were all sprawled around the Hyannis lawn, stretched out on chaise lounges, sipping Cokes, sunning. Suddenly the Kennedy chauffeur appeared with the word that their father was landing at the airport and he was going to pick him up.

Almost instantly the scene changed. Everybody scrambled. They started playing tennis, football, readying the sailboat.

When their father arrived, he surveyed the scene. He liked to see them all busy.

And they knew it.

The family competition?

"That's overrated," John Kennedy insisted. "We played together and we played against each other in sports and there's always the desire of a younger brother or sister to show up an older one on something, but it was never more than that. Drive, yes; competition, no. Although I will say he'd ride our asses pretty hard if we lost in the sailing races."

He put them alone in sailboats when they were so small you couldn't see their heads from the shore. He also kept them on a tight allowance. Jack Kennedy had to write a letter explaining that he wanted his allowance raised from forty to seventy-five cents a week so that he could buy Boy Scout equipment, "things that will last for years. . . ." Robert Kennedy had a newspaper route and used his father's Rolls-Royce to make deliveries. Once, much later, when the father reduced one of his daughters to tears by bawling her out for spending too much money, it was John Kennedy who broke the mood by saying, "Well, Dad, the obvious solution is that you'll have to work harder."

The old man was the wheel around which everything turned.

When he was in the residence, the neighbors could set their clocks by his habits. Every morning at 11:45, he and his wife headed for the beach to swim. They swam a prescribed number of strokes before they both got out at the same time to head for the house for a single drink before lunch. It was all timed, punctual.

Sunday, as neighbor Sancy Newman remembered it, was special, "a mob scene, but very organized. The family would say grace before the meal, as always, and Mrs. Kennedy would discuss the morning's church sermon. Her husband would then try to steer the general discussion into a free-for-all, encouraging everybody to say something. When one of his children asked a question—no matter how simple or stupid it seemed—the Ambassador went to great lengths to answer it. If necessary, one of the younger ones would get an encyclopedia. But if a guest raised a point, the Ambassador gave it short shrift."

"We didn't have opinions in those days," John Kennedy recalled. "They were mostly monologues by my father . . . well, not monologues, you know. Later the discussions included us more, but mostly about personalities, not debates on issues and things. I never had any particular interest in political subjects in those days. It was mostly talk about some of the personalities that my father ran into and some of those he brought home. When I was a little older, there was a certain amount of discussion with my brothers and with my father, but it was conversational, never organized."

His school roommate, Kirk Lemoyne Billings, remembered of the Kennedy tabletalk that the old man "was so interesting that you wanted to read and study so that you could take part. I remember the way the children slowly did. He would encourage them to disagree with him completely, and of course they later did disagree with him."

"The truth is that they couldn't possibly be around the old man without getting interested in damn near everything," recalled a visitor. "The old man has opinions on everything. Some are sound, some are preposterous. But everything he says tends to be stimulating. You can't sit there and not care what he is saying. You find yourself thinking, 'The old boy's pretty damn smart,' or you realize his premise is full of holes and you can't wait for him to pause, so you can tell him why you think he's wrong. And he will listen to you, probably not agree with you, but he will be attentive to what you're saying."

"He disciplined Jack like a Jesuit," said Boston friend Norman McDonald. "When the father was around, Jack couldn't invite any friends he wanted to their summer home in Hyannis Port. He had to submit a guest list and schedule to his father, and could invite only people who were useful."

During summers, all the Kennedy children were required to read an hour a day, and the books had to be approved by their parents.

If he could be unprincipled, tactless, mean, and even vicious, this redheaded, freckle-faced man was always a concerned father.

"Don't let me lose confidence in you again," he wrote seventeen-year-old Jack after a bad school report, "because it will be pretty nearly an impossible task to restore it. . . . You have the goods. Why not try to show it? . . . Pay a little more attention to penmanship. Mine has always been pretty bad . . . but yours is disgraceful. . . .

"Now, Jack, I don't want to give the impression that I am a nagger, for goodness knows I think that is the worst thing any parent can be. After long experience in sizing up people, I definitely know you have the goods and you can go a long way. Now, aren't you foolish not to get all there is out of what God has given you? . . . I will not be disappointed if you don't turn out to be a real genius, but I think you can be a really worthwhile citizen with good judgment and good understanding."

The father insisted that he never played favorites, but when any of his children lost any kind of competition, he always told them, "Joe would have won. . . ."

Joseph Patrick Kennedy, Jr., was the golden boy. Taller, broader, handsomer, more charming than his younger brothers, he was the natural student, the natural athlete. "Joe was clearly the kind of man his father would have liked to have been," claimed Harvey Klemmer—the Ambassador's aide in London— who knew them both well. "Joe was no intellectual but he was sharper than Jack, brighter, quicker, the kind of witty extrovert who made a party by entering a room."

Professor Harold Laski of the London School of Economics called Joe "adorably unsophisticated . . . took criticisms with disarming friendliness . . . was always anxious to know . . . that smile that was pure magic . . . and submitted . . . to relentless teasing about his determination to be nothing less than President of the United States."

Joe was also a bit of a bully, quick-tempered, sometimes even cruel, the kind of kid who could shove somebody aside so he could catch the ball.

At Choate, Jack was nicknamed "Ratface." He was a skinny boy with glasses, an unstable back, and plagued by so much sickness that his brother Bobby wrote, "If a mosquito bit Jack, the mosquito would die."

The sibling rivalry was strong. In a letter to his parents, Jack wrote from Choate in December 1931, when he was fourteen and Joe sixteen:

"When Joe came home he was telling me how strong he was and how tough. The first thing he did to show me how tough he was was to get sick so that he could not have any Thanksgiving dinner. Manly Youth. He was then going to show me how to Indian wrestle. I then threw him over on his neck. Did the sixth former lick him. Oh Man he was all blisters, they almost paddled the life out of him. He was roughhousing in the hall . . . a sixth former caught him . . . and all the sixth formers had a swat or two. What I wouldn't have given to be a sixth former."

"Joe had more personality than Jack maybe, but Jack had more charm," his sister Eunice said. "Joe was physically bigger and stronger, but Jack perhaps had the higher I.Q. I remember when he was about seven they gave him an I.Q. test, and Mother told me afterwards how exceptionally high it was. I think he was brighter than the rest of us. He used to read a lot more."

"I never had that drive at Choate. I was just a drifter there," Jack reminisced years later. "I didn't work particularly hard."

Jack, who had to cram to get grades, had a friend throw him passes after practice until it was too dark to see the ball. His brother Joe tried to talk him out of football "because you just don't weigh enough and you're going to get yourself banged up."

* * *

A neighbor described a weekly night downstairs in the Kennedy basement projection room in Hyannis Port where they showed the latest films for family and friends. Preceding the main feature was the Pathé News, then a sing-along.

"It was terrible," Sancy Newman said. "The Kennedys had the worst voices in the world, and they all joined in, even Papa Joe, and loud! Nobody in that house could carry a note. Horrendous!"

The patriarch sat in the back on a wicker seat, with a seat on each side of him, while everybody else sat up front. Servants often came in and sat along the sides. Rose Kennedy invariably came in late and usually also sat on the side. She was never known to sit in one of the wicker chairs alongside her husband. Joe Kennedy reserved them for the prettiest girls in the room. He would always call out a name of one of the neighbor girls. It was not an invitation any of them relished because it became a well-circulated fact that anyone sitting alongside Joe Kennedy could expect to get her pretty bottom pinched, and often. One young woman ruefully showed her friends that her bottom had been pinched black and blue.

He was always highly conscious that his millions were not old enough to be respectable. "But it was respectable enough. Ben Bradlee recalled, "When Cardinal Cushing needed a hundred-thousand-dollar guarantee to insure two football teams playing in Boston for a charity, he called Joe Kennedy, and Joe said, 'Sure,' just like that."

In a quiet time of reflection, Joe Kennedy told a friend, "Six or seven times in my life, the pendulum swung my way. If it hadn't fallen favorably to me, life could be quite a bit different."

One of those times was his marriage to Rose Fitzgerald, daughter of his father's political rival, Mayor "Honey Fitz."

"Rose is my flower, Rose is my name, rose is my color," she would say.

She was eighteen in 1908 when she spent a year in a teaching convent in Holland, studying the piano. She later substituted as hostess for her shy mother when her father was Mayor of Boston. "I married for love," she said, "but got money as a bonus." Asked about some of her ecstasies, she replied, "Oh, little things like getting my first mink coat, reading in the newspaper that my husband was worth fifty, or was it a hundred million dollars."

And what was her greatest tragedy, a neighbor asked.

"Rosemary's lobotomy."

The neighbor persisted: But what about all the assassinations and fatal accidents?

"They were all acts of God," Rose Kennedy insisted. "With Rosemary, the decision was man-made."

Religion was her core.

"At the dinner table, she would ask the children if they knew why the priest was wearing purple vestments instead of black that morning," her husband said, "and she would explain it to them." She also drilled them on the catechism and the liturgy of the Mass, and waited at the bottom of the stairs on Sunday morning to hand each of the girls white gloves and a prayer book as they raced away for Sunday Mass.

She didn't want them "to be snotty like a lot of other rich summer kids."

"There were so many of them [children], I don't know how much real love each one of them got in their childhood," *Look* reporter Laura Bergquist said. "Certainly they got very little love from their mother, Rose. I mean, she was very strict and very correct and a faithful teacher. She made sure they learned and did all the right things. But I don't know how much physical love she gave them. When you have a large family, even when there is love, it's hard to share equally. There are always some who feel deprived. After Joe and Kathleen, I don't think there was that much love left for the other kids. I think the parents gave most of their love to the older two. Those two got their main investment of hope. When those two went, I think the scene changed."

"My mother was either at some Paris fashion house or else on her knees in some church," John Kennedy told Bill Walton. "She was never there when we really needed her. . . . My mother never really held me and hugged me. Never! Never!"

"Most important," Rose Kennedy said, "was to bring up the oldest one the way you want them all to go. If the oldest one comes in and says 'good night' to his parents or says his prayers in the morning, the younger ones think that's the thing to do and they will do it. I also think it's much more effective to tell an older one to correct his sister—when our girl was using too much lipstick . . . because I think she thought I was old-fashioned, but she would really value his advice. Fortunately the older ones cooperated very effectively. When our oldest boy was alive, I think he seemed to feel that he was the leader and he had the responsibility. When we lost him, then it evolved upon Jack, who took it upon himself."

"I know she's been made into a saint and a legend," said one of the family friends, "but the truth is she's not very bright. And when I first knew her, she was not with it at all. I had been at their Hyannis house for years, eating their meals with them. And then one day I heard Mrs. Kennedy asking Eunice about me. 'Who *is* that man?'

"I know she influenced their manners and habits when they were kids, but later on she was nothing in their lives."

The same friend said that Jack had told him, in a bitter moment, that living at home as a boy was like living in an institution, and had mentioned "all the toothbrushes lined up in a row."

On the other hand, when he was asked, years later, how he prepared for the presidency, Kennedy said, "There's no *way* you can prepare for the presidency. The only things I ever learned from anybody that might have helped were some of the early things I learned from my mother. . . .

"You have to remember my father was away a lot of the time. He was in Hollywood four years. My mother was the glue. She's not as forceful as my father but she was the glue. She was deeply religious, highly devout. She wasn't interested in politics so much but she was interested in things like the Pilgrims' landing at Plymouth Rock, things like that. I wouldn't say she was interested in public affairs. And I wouldn't say my interest in history came from her. I just think I have an inquiring mind."

"Rose was a tough broad," said a friend and neighbor.

Mrs. Kennedy was a short woman with dark chestnut hair and gray-green eyes. She had the healthy outdoor tan of a woman who liked salt air and sunshine. She always stayed as slim as the day she was married.

She was a papal countess with "an iron faith" who drove herself to early Mass every morning—and the only gentile member of a Jewish golf club in Palm Beach. Always on the list of the world's best-dressed women, she sent her clothes to the local thrift shop for consignment sale, advising her chauffeur, "Be sure to get a receipt."

She set the family rules and taught them how to cope, and

pinned memos on her dress so that she would not forget all the things she had to do.

But her youngest daughter Jean (Smith) later complained: "I was shuffled off to boarding school at the age of eight. That's why I'm still trying to get my head screwed on straight. She's mad about Teddy, of course. He and I were the babies, kind of the last gasp, so we don't remember the close family life the older children had."

"Teddy was our surprise baby," his mother said, "and he's brought more joy into our lives than we ever thought possible. He has so much joy in him."

Teddy was "a small, fat boy," recalled Eunice, "overweight at eight, terribly good-natured, laughing constantly, and an incessant tease."

Ted recalled, "The day I walked home from kindergarten instead of waiting to be picked up, I was spanked with a coat hanger and my mother administered it. Justice was always immediate; no one ever said, 'Wait 'til your father gets home.'

"Mother was a strict disciplinarian. Lunch was at one, prompt. If you were late, you missed the course. Every Thursday we went to the public library to get books. We had tennis lessons, swimming lessons, our teeth straightened, all of us for seven years. We were computerized at an early age, but fortunately by a very compassionate computer."

Jean remarked, "Everybody's place in the family was different. Bobby first ate with us in the nursery, then graduated to the big table. She worried about him because there were four girls ahead of him, so much competition from the older brothers, and he was accident-prone—always falling out of trees, getting tar in his eyes. She would say, 'Pat, you warn him [Bobby] that older people won't vote for anyone with hair like that, including me!'

"She built herself a little house on the beach at Hyannis where she could nap. A storm blew it away, and she rebuilt it; that got swept to sea, too."

Rose Kennedy carried a ruler to paddle her children with occasionally "because when they're young, that's all they understand." Walking with one of her children, she might suddenly stop and say, "Look at that fence and give me three adjectives to describe it." She kept them busy and moving. Neighbors complained that she praised her children so constantly "that it got to be rather tiresome after a while." Marquis Childs told Jack Kennedy that she made him sound like a young Jesus.

"She was the first one who emphasized the family motto of 'Finish first.' I was twenty-four before I knew I didn't have to win something every day," Eunice said.

"People think they were born with that Kennedy smile," Rose Kennedy explained. "They all had their teeth straightened. That was hard work, getting them to the dentist."

But when her husband was home more and her children were grown, Rose was something of a shadow. In a houseful of people, she would quietly retire to her room for privacy. No matter what the weather, she would go alone for a walk, wearing her favorite black coat and old-fashioned babushka. When she needed surgery, she had it done without telling the family.

"In all the forty-six years we have been married, I have never heard her complain. Never. Not even once," her husband said.

Not even when he brought Gloria Swanson—or his other actresses—to stay at her home, often while she was there. When she went off to Paris for a fashion show, neighbors noted that her Rolls-Royce might be taking her to the airport at the same time that his Rolls-Royce would be bringing him home with another mistress—"so perfectly timed that they would have had to have passed each other on the road."

Once during a walk with Rose Kennedy, a woman neighbor introduced the question of when and where a wife should show "iciness" toward her husband. Mrs. Kennedy seemed uncomprehending until her friend said, "Well, you know, everybody does it in marriage. Haven't you shown iciness toward your husband?"

After a long pause, Mrs. Kennedy said, "Yes, I have. And I made him pay for that iciness—I made him give me everything I wanted. Clothes. Jewels. Everything. You have to know how to use that iciness."

There is some question about whether or not Rose Kennedy

knew about Cardinal O'Connell's visit to Gloria Swanson. Swanson later insisted that the cardinal had told her that Joe Kennedy had tried to dissolve his marriage with Rose so he could marry Swanson. The Church had refused. He then had asked Church permission to live apart from his wife, so he could stay with Swanson. The Church had told him this was impossible.

"I am here to tell you to stop seeing Joseph Kennedy," the cardinal said. "Each time you see him you become an occasion of sin for him."

Gloria Swanson suggested that he tell this to Joseph Kennedy.

*　　*　　*

John Kennedy made his first break from the Kennedy mold when he went to Princeton instead of Harvard. He went there to be with his friend Lemoyne Billings and away from the Harvard shadow of his hero brother. His own description of that time was short:

"Princeton? I didn't do much at Princeton. No, I didn't read much. It was mostly physical. Then I had jaundice." The jaundice kept him out of school, putting him in the class behind Billings, and so he decided to yield to his father's pressure and he went to Harvard in the fall of 1936. "Freshman year was mostly sports, football and swimming," he remembered.

Football was one of the keys to the Kennedy character, and all four brothers played it at Harvard—just as their father had. Coach Lloyd Jordan called them all "hard-nosed," capable of "magnificent second effort. They never quit. The harder you played against them, the harder they played against you. And they never got mad or complained to the referee."

"Jack wanted to be known in school as a jock," his classmate Blair Clark said, "even though he was really too light for football."

Kennedy told the story of working out on the Harvard freshman football team for six weeks, then asking to be put into the game. The coach stared at him. "Who the hell are you?"

"I knew Jack in college," Franklin Roosevelt, Jr., recalled.

"His brother Joe, who really had everything, was a year behind me, and Jack was a year behind him. Jack was then a nice, gay guy, warmer, nicer then, so much less self-centered."

John Kenneth Galbraith, who taught at Harvard and knew both boys, described Joe as "every faculty's favorite," and Jack as "gregarious, irreverent . . . far from diligent. One did not cultivate such students." He remembered that Jack led the Snake Dance of the Big Apple during his sophomore year, and how incensed Joe was because he had earned his money to buy a car while Jack had bought one on the installment plan without even consulting his father.

The father wrote to the Harvard dean, "Jack has a very brilliant mind for the things in which he is interested, but is careless and lacks application in those in which he is not interested. This is, of course, a bad fault." The father then mentioned something he had begun to see in his son, "the beginning of an awakening ambition."

"I guess it was during my sophomore year that I really found myself," John recalled. "I don't know what to attribute it to. No, not professors. I guess I was just getting older. It was during my junior year that I went to England for six months, which meant taking six courses as a senior and hard work. I had to work like hell."

Blair Clark said, "I remember we were walking along the beach in Hyannis, and we had a real shouting match about the Wagner Labor Act because he felt it was leaning much too far towards labor. I was saying, 'Come on, Jack, that's what your father thinks. You're just spouting what your father says.' Jack was *fils papa,* as the French say, his father's son. It was the same when we argued earlier about the Spanish Civil War. He was for Franco."

His close friend Charles Spalding had a memory of a more liberal Kennedy. "I remember we were on a picnic with bonfires. He talked at length about Roosevelt's programs, the necessity for them, and his impatience with people who stood in the way of those things."

When Jack and his roommate passed a bookshop featuring *I'm for Roosevelt,* by Joseph Kennedy, his roommate asked, "Any relation?" Jack had never told him before.

"Personalities were always more interesting to us than facts," John Kennedy said of that time. "I can hardly remember a mealtime when the conversation was not dominated by what Franklin D. Roosevelt was doing," his brother Bob added.

Joseph Kennedy and Roosevelt had much in common. Both knew how to mobilize and manage people of talent: Both were skilled actors with considerable charm, lovers of the outrageous, brilliant improvisers, egotistical, and ruthless. Neither was an intellectual. Kennedy was more explosive, intense, candid; Roosevelt was more urbane, confident, foxy. Neither fully trusted the other. When Roosevelt appointed Kennedy head of the Securities and Exchange Commission, he reportedly told a friend, "It takes a thief to catch a thief."

Both wanted power and had an instinct for it.

"I wanted power," Kennedy confided towards the end of his life. "I thought money would give me power, so I made money, only to discover that it was politics—not money—that really gave a man power. So I went into politics."

At a Harvard reunion, attended by Joseph Kennedy, one skit showed Kennedy in a top hat on the phone saying, "Get me Franklin at the White House," then adding, "Frank, this is Joe. It's nine o'clock and you can start the country."

He could call President Roosevelt—in Arthur Krock's presence—and tell him, "Listen, boy, if we do that, we'll land in the shithouse." Another time he told him, "You will either go down as the greatest president in history, or the greatest horse's ass." Then, when James Roosevelt reported to his father that Joe Kennedy wanted to be the first Irishman to be ambassador to the Court of St. James, "he laughed so hard, he almost toppled from his wheelchair." When Kennedy came to see him, FDR asked him to please drop his pants.

A puzzled Joe Kennedy slowly obliged.

Roosevelt examined him critically. "You are just about the most bowlegged man I have ever seen," he said. "Don't you know that the ambassador to the Court of St. James has to go through an induction ceremony in which he wears knee breeches and silk stockings? When photos of our new ambassador appear all over the world, we'll be a laughingstock."

Secretary of State Cordell Hull gaped at the new Ambassador

Kennedy when he explained to FDR why a candidate for the US Supreme Court had not confessed to his membership in the Ku Klux Klan saying, "If Marlene Dietrich asked you to go to bed with her, would you tell her you weren't much good in bed?"

Ambassador Kennedy soon became known as "Jolly Joe, the nine-child envoy," and a London music hall routine substituted him for George Washington as the "father of his country." Kennedy called austere, aloof Prime Minister Neville Chamberlain "Neville," and "Chamberlain's Adam's apple would work up and down convulsively three or four times before he could emit a forced 'Joe.' "

The Ambassador enlisted both his older sons as special observers in Europe. Jack later tried to minimize the influence of his father at that time. "Don't forget, I went to Spain, I went to England, I traveled all over Europe on my own. *He* wasn't with me. I went all over the place gathering information on my own. Obviously things were made easy for me. But I did these things because *I* wanted to find out what was happening."

After Britain went to war over Poland, Ambassador Kennedy told all who would listen, "This is not our war." He stayed on as a highly unpopular ambassador, even though he claimed that a bomb had fallen just three hundred yards from the Kennedy home, and that he had been in 244 air raids, but only twice in a bomb shelter. Later he told Roosevelt, "I hate all these goddamned Englishmen from Churchill on down."

Jack Kennedy strongly disagreed with his father, but said nothing.

"You're something of Irish and something of Harvard," poet Robert Frost told John Kennedy years later. "Let me advise you, be more Irish than Harvard."

Kennedy was only somewhat Harvard and even less Irish. The Irish was there in the wit and the wink and in some of his defiance and pride. The Harvard was there in his respect for brains and knowledge. But basically, in temperament, he was an English Whig.

Jack Kennedy truly admired the English. He had read broadly in English history and believed strongly in the Whig philosophy:

that in an imperfect world with imperfect people nothing would ever be completely right and nobody completely loyal; that life was a comedy to those who think, a tragedy to those who feel. He had made close friends among the British while in wartime England, particularly David Ormsby-Gore, of whom he envied everything from the play of his mind to the cut of his clothes. Ormsby-Gore recalled, "Jack's favorite book was Cecil's biography of Melbourne, and, of course, Cecil was my uncle, and so that was another bond between us. Then Jack's sister, 'Kick,' later married my best friend. So we were all like a family almost."

Years later, at the request of President Kennedy, Ormsby-Gore was appointed British Ambassador to the United States; later he became Lord Harlech.

In the growth of John Fitzgerald Kennedy, if his father was the force, his brother the spur, his mother the glue, then Raymond Asquith was his model.

Charles Spalding never forget how often Jack Kennedy talked about Raymond Asquith, quoted him, described him, discussed him. "I remember him saying over and over that there was nobody in our time who was more gifted," Ormsby-Gore said. "Whether Jack realized it or not, I think he paralleled himself after Asquith all the way, I really do."

Raymond Asquith, the son of a prime minister, was a remarkably gifted young man "of cool and grace" who was killed "in that stupid trench in World War I." In his book *Pilgrim's Way*, John Buchan wrote of young Asquith: "There are some men whose brilliance in boyhood and early manhood dazzles their contemporaries and becomes a legend. . . . He had a fine, straight figure, and bore himself with a kind of easy stateliness. His manner was curiously self-possessed and urbane, but there was always in it something of a pleasant aloofness, as of one who was happy in society, but did not give it more than a fraction of himself. He had the air of having seen enough of the outer world to judge it with detachment."

Kennedy must have seen many parallels in their lives: their dislike of emotion "not because he felt lightly, but because he felt deeply"; the profound respect for their fathers; their distaste for "cheap-jack argument"; their conservative temperament; their intolerance of mediocrity; their love of humor and wit and poetry and beautiful things.

* * *

"I wrote *Why England Slept* as a thesis because the subject interested me when I was over there," Jack Kennedy said of his book about Britain's unpreparedness for war. "I wouldn't say that my father got me interested in it. No, the book didn't contain anything that differed with my father's opinions at the time except perhaps the final part. There was all that resentment in America about Munich, and I didn't think that was justified on our part in view of the fact that we weren't ready to do anything. If we weren't prepared to get involved, what right did we have to criticize or be resentful? No, my father never saw it then. Arthur Krock was staying with a friend of ours who lived a few houses away, and I took it over and showed it to him. My professor didn't think it would make a book, but Krock did. I worked on it from April to June, so I couldn't have revised it very much. I needed a foreword, and a friend of mine suggested sending it to Henry Luce, and we did. He [Luce] took the manuscript out with him to Philadelphia to the Republican convention, and a week or two later told me that he would write the foreword. Several publishers turned it down, including Harper's. No one seemed to think it had a chance and it wouldn't have except for luck. It came out at the same time as the breakthrough in England. That's what made it."

Harvey Klemmer, who wrote speeches for the Ambassador, had been assigned to rewrite John Kennedy's college thesis into a book. "It was terribly written and disorganized, the sentences ungrammatical, and even the spelling was bad. I had to rewrite the whole thing, including the final sum-up paragraph."

After seeing the final book, Professor Harold Laski of the London School of Economics wrote Ambassador Kennedy. "You're doing the boy no favor by having anything he does puffed up artificially."

The elder Kennedy was then, however, more concerned with his own political future. The headline in the *Boston Post*, February 12, 1940:

KENNEDY MAY BE A CANDIDATE
Strong Move to Have Him Run for President

A *Washington Post* article said that Kennedy had "an excellent chance to be the first Catholic president." A May 1940 public-opinion poll put Kennedy fifth among Democratic presidential possibilities if Roosevelt didn't run for a third term.

Roosevelt thought Kennedy's candidacy "absurd." He told how Kennedy had faulted him for attacking fascism in his speeches, because we would have to "come to some sort of fascism here."

"Joe Kennedy, if he were in power, would give us a fascist form of government," Roosevelt told Secretary of Interior Ickes. "He would organize a small, powerful committee under himself as chairman, and this committee would run the country without much reference to Congress."

Congressman Lyndon Johnson was in President Roosevelt's office when a call came from Kennedy. "Ah, Joe, it's good to hear your voice," said the President, and invited him to come to the White House that night for a family dinner. "I'm dying to talk to you," he said, making a theatrical gesture of cutting somebody's throat.

Joe Kennedy told Clare Boothe Luce later why he had changed his mind and strongly endorsed FDR for re-election. "I simply made a deal with Roosevelt. We agreed that if I endorsed him for president in 1940, he would support my son Joe for governor of Massachusetts in 1942."

The Ambassador told his friend Kay Halle that he expected Joe to be President of the United States. "He also added then that, if it wasn't Joe, it would be Jack, and if it wasn't Jack, it would be Bobby, and if it wasn't Bobby, it would be Teddy."

Eric Sevareid recalled a Kennedy comment that President Roosevelt once had given Jack's father a clear indication that he would support him, Joe Senior, for the presidency in 1944.

The elder Kennedy soon destroyed his political future in a *Boston Globe* interview in which he said, "Democracy is finished in England," and added, "It may be here." He also provided a footnote that "Mrs. Roosevelt bothered us . . . to take care of little nobodies who hadn't any influence. She was always sending me a note to have some little Susie Glotz to tea at the embassy."

Mrs. Roosevelt would not forget that remark.

Called to Hyde Park to explain his interview, Kennedy was even more explosive with the President, and offered his resignation. When Mrs. Roosevelt came into the room, the President asked Kennedy to step outside. His wife said she had rarely ever seen him so angry, his face drained, his voice almost tremulously restrained.

"I never want to see that son of a bitch again as long as I live," FDR told her. "Take his resignation and get him out of here."

*   *   *

After Harvard, Jack Kennedy thought seriously about applying to Yale Law School, then switched to the business school at Stanford, where Eunice was studying. Harry Mulheim, a fellow student, remembered a party: "As the evening wore on, we listened mostly to Kennedy. He didn't force himself upon us. The talk just seemed to move easily to him, and he responded. Even when you didn't care much about the conversation, Jack Kennedy was compelling. He was quick to explain, to ask, and to consider. His sentences flowed spontaneously. Gags were naturally interspersed with straight material. Illustrations and examples were brought in without effort from several locations and several centuries. I had never heard one of my contemporaries *allude* to so many things."

Twenty-two years later, Mulheim attended a dinner at Newport in honor of the President. "I was surprised at his eyes," Mulheim said. "They had been prominent bulging eyes in a skinny face. Now they were set deep back in a massive head and almost hidden under the thick brows."

Harry introduced himself as "one of the eleven million Americans who knew you before you were elected and now expect you to remember them."

"Where were *you*?" the President asked.

"I rode with you in the green Buick convertible one night out at Stanford."

His face lit up in warm memory. "Ah, yes," he said, lingering, as if all the young careless years were rushing back, "the green Buick convertible."

Then came Pearl Harbor.

Jack Kennedy had no romantic conception of war. He saw it as an event of shattering waste and horror. "The poignancy of young men dying haunted him," Jacqueline recalled. He couldn't even stand the sight of a dead bird. "Get it out of here," he would say. He saw all killing as senseless, all death as disagreeable.

Yet, he enlisted in September 1941, when his country was in crisis. Assigned to naval intelligence in Washington, he was transferred to sea duty. According to his intimate friend Inga Arvad, he was angry. "Some son of a bitch has transferred me to sea duty and I'm gonna find out who it is." Another version was a Kennedy conversation with his Boston buddy Ted Reardon.

"You know what they tried to do? They tried to ship me to Panama. So then I called the old man and told him what I wanted, that I wanted to see action. And the next day, just like that, the very next day, I had orders sending me off to this PT outfit in the Pacific."

"I worked hard at it because I liked PTs," he said afterward. "I think I liked PTs because they were small. I don't think I gave much thought to world conditions and things during the war. Some, of course, but not much."

If there was some question of his command judgment when a Japanese destroyer cut his PT boat in half, there was no question of his courage.

"The PT boats were a joke!" recalled Robert Donovan, who wrote an authoritative book on the subject. "They had no radio, they had no radar, they had no lights. Everyone knew they were a joke. The truth of it was they probably sank more American tonnage than foreign tonnage. I talked to everyone in his crew and those men would do anything for Kennedy. There is no question that Kennedy was brave, that he saved that crewman's life. As for that Japanese destroyer, they had no idea where they were or when they might be coming through.

"After they had been sliced up by the Japanese destroyer and were hanging on to part of the ship, Jack told his men, 'I know I'm the skipper of this PT crew and I can still give you orders, but most of you men are older than I am. I have nothing to lose, but some of you have wives and children, and I'm not going to order you to try to swim to that shore. You'll have to make your own decision on that.' "

He towed ashore one of the wounded and bolstered up another by saying, "For a boy from Boston, you're not making a very good showing."

When word came to Massachusetts about Jack Kennedy's being missing in action, Jim Smith, a parochial school student in Fall River, recalled how he and his classmates fell on their knees to pray for him.

"I met Jack in Palm Beach after he came back from the Pacific," Charles Spalding reminisced. "He got off the plane in the evening. Before he even went home, he wanted to go right away to a place we both used to go before the war—some restaurant whose name I've forgotten but it had a roof that pulled back.

"I can still see him sitting there in that restaurant, the war running through his head, and certainly through a lot of his body —he was pretty well banged up. He didn't say a thing. He just sat there, looking and thinking. And you could just tell what was going through his head—the terrific discrepancy between people at home dressed in white jackets with bow ties, looking like asses, and passing under a silly roof that pulls back, and then thinking of the nonsense of people being killed, somebody having his leg blown off. You could see the anguish in his face as he was trying to put it together. We stayed there an hour and I don't think he said one word, not one word."

"I was in school in Miami when he came down there as a PT boat instructor," Ted Kennedy recalled, "and he used to smuggle me aboard a PT boat and take me for rides. We used to chew tobacco and spit and have a good time. Then I was in Boston later when he was at the Chelsea Naval Hospital and I spent a lot of time with him then, too. We did have a special relationship. After all, he was my godfather."

Jack's bad back had worsened considerably after the PT boat collision in the Pacific and now required surgery. To correct the disc problem, they put a metal plate in his spine. It was not a successful operation. The pain stayed with him for the rest of his life requiring constant hot baths, back braces, massage, and crutches.

While in the hospital, they gave him the Navy and Marine Medal.

So strong was the sibling rivalry that young Joe Kennedy reportedly cried when his brother Jack won the first medal in the family for courage in combat. Joe already had proven his own heroism, completing a tour of duty as a bomber pilot in Europe. Now he volunteered for an unusually hazardous mission. He was the pilot of a drone bomber filled with explosives that was supposed to be guided electronically against some heavily fortified rocket-launching sites in Pas de Calais in July 1944. The plane blew up before the twenty-nine-year-old Joe could escape. Elliott Roosevelt, the President's son, was one of the escorting pilots and was temporarily blinded by the explosion. Only after the war was it revealed that the launching sites had been abandoned three months before the attack.

A navy priest came that week to tell Joseph Kennedy the tragic news. Kennedy called his children together, told them what he had heard, then said, "I want you all to be particularly good to your mother." He then went to his bedroom, locked the door, and was never afterwards the same.

On the day after Joe Kennedy's death, Jack told his brothers and sisters, "Let's go for a sail, that's what Joe would have wanted us to do."

"Jack is not the kind of man who can stand still and look out of a window and do nothing," Eunice said. "He's a bustler. And he believes in immediate action. When all of us talked about how nice it would be to have a book written about Joe, it was Jack who disappeared every evening from five to seven-thirty and wrote letters and made calls, and collected information, and wrote the book while the rest of us were still playing games." The book was privately published in 1945.

Jack referred to Joe's intolerance "for the slower pace of lesser men." He described Joe's occasional hot temper and "a somewhat sardonic smile which made him appear as though he were kidding you, whether he was or not." For Jack Kennedy, such a smile "could cut and prod more sharply than words."

"I do not think I can ever remember seeing him sit back in a chair and relax," said Jack, who was twenty-seven when his brother died. "I suppose I knew Joe as well as anyone, and yet I sometimes wonder whether we really knew him. He always had a slight detachment around him, a wall of reserve, which few people succeeded in penetrating." Still, he added, "I don't know anyone with whom I would rather have spent an evening." Many would one day say the same things of him.

"You know, I've tried many, many times to read that book," his father said. "And once I even got to about page twenty-five. But I couldn't go on. I just couldn't bring myself to do it." His eyes were full of tears.

The Ambassador's bitterness over his son's death stayed with him always. When he saw Roosevelt's vice-presidential nominee, Harry Truman, during the 1944 campaign, he asked, "Harry, what are you doing campaigning for that crippled son of a bitch who killed my son Joe?"

Walking along the beach at Hyannis in the summer of 1959, John Kennedy talked about his young years.

"I don't know what I would have done if my brother had lived. I never gave much thought to politics then. I don't even remember writing letters to the editor of any newspaper. I suppose if he had not been killed, I would have gone to law school. All these things are a matter of events. It's always difficult for the younger ones and it would have been difficult for me that way just as I make it difficult for Bobby and we both make it difficult for Teddy. And if Teddy doesn't do something, why then he's just high tit on us and so he will try to do something. I suppose that's what contributes to the drive in each of us. It's partly due to being in a large family.

"I didn't have many views about things until after the war. That's when I wrote a paper (in 1945), mostly for my own benefit more than anything else, of what I thought should be done about peace. I covered the UN in San Francisco, and the British elections. My father and I began to disagree on most foreign policy matters. I can't say what made me drift away from his ideas, except logic.

"No, I don't think I ever react emotionally to a problem, but that doesn't mean I'm not emotional. It simply means I reason problems out and apply logic to them. We are all the products of our conditioning. I don't know why it is. I probably have as many emotions as the next person. I have emotional feelings about my family. You can see the way we feel about each other. My brothers and sisters and I see a lot more of each other than many people who are supposed to be emotional. I am not like some people who don't see other members of their families for long periods of time and then well up. I don't do that. This causes people to say Kennedy is a cold fish. I'm not a cold fish. If they want to say Kennedy is a cold fish, OK."

He always hated to be touched, "and yet it was a craving, I think," said Charles Spalding.

He maintained his outward coolness, his complete control, his ability to talk with detachment about things that stirred others deeply. He was suspicious of people who were zealous. The more excited they appeared to be, the more suspicious he was of their motives. Even his laugh, and it was a pleasant laugh, was almost always restrained, almost never boisterous. He mostly showed amusement by the crinkles and twinkles of his eyes.

Yet, the passion was there, banked deep. If he was much moved about something, he often left the room rather than show it.

It was true that nobody knew him whole. He revealed only small pieces of himself to different people, always keeping for himself his own core of mystery. He collected assorted people on various levels for separate needs. Even his most intimate friends only saw separate sides of him. And his father saw his son mainly in his own projected image.

For all the sour gall in him, Joseph Kennedy had the stubbornness of a man who never surrendered. When Boston society refused to accept them, he moved his family to New York. When his own presidential hopes were squashed, he transferred them to his son Joe. Now, when Joe was killed, he turned to Jack. This was all part of the force in him that lived in the phrase: *Someday he would show these bastards!*

Jack Kennedy sensed all this from the time his brother died.

He told his PT shipmate Red Fay early in 1945, "I can feel Pappy's eyes on the back of my neck when the war is over. I'll be back there trying to parlay a lost PT boat and a bad back into political advantage. I tell you Dad is ready right now."

"He didn't want to run for Congress," Joseph Kennedy remembered. "He felt he didn't have the ability but I told him he had to. . . ."

"It was like being drafted," Jack Kennedy told Hearst columnist Bob Considine. "My father wanted his eldest son in politics. 'Wanted' isn't the right word. He *demanded* it. You know my father."

Jack Kennedy was in San Francisco covering the founding of the United Nations for International News Service in 1945 when he queried his friend Spalding about a possible political career. He was then twenty-eight.

"Charlie, what do you think?"

"I was enthusiastic," Spalding recalled. "I told him, 'I think you can go all the way.' "

"Do you?" Kennedy asked him. "Do you *really*?"

There was a party at the Connecticut home of Time-Life publisher Henry Luce, and congressional candidate John Kennedy was there. After talking to him, Harris Wofford, a civil rights lawyer, decided that the young man was a lightweight, more interested in girls than in politics. Clare Boothe Luce quickly disabused Wofford. "If old Joe has his way," she whispered, "Jack will be the President of the United States."

For a long time, I was Joseph Kennedy's son, then I was Joe's brother, then Kathleen's brother, then Eunice's brother. Someday I hope to be able to stand on my own feet.

—JOHN KENNEDY

The Playboy Congressman

Singer Morton Downey was at the 12:10 Sunday "walking Mass" at St. Patrick's Cathedral in New York when he saw a "tall, skinny-as-a-rail, almost yellow young man." Downey was one of the very few who could put his arm around Jack Kennedy, without Kennedy's shrinking away. He had known him as a boy. Downey took the privilege of an old family friend to bawl out Kennedy for going out with Broadway showgirls. "You know, you damn fool, if you ever want to get any place in politics, you'd better cut out this nonsense with these long-stemmed beauties from Billy Rose's night club."

Kennedy laughed. "Oh Jesus," he said, "but I'm in love with *this* girl."

Now Downey laughed. "You've been in love with every girl you've ever met since I've known you!"

There's a picture of John Kennedy and this young woman sitting at a table in the Stork Club in New York City soon after he returned from the South Pacific in 1944. Her name was Florence Pritchett. There are many who say she was the love of Kennedy's life.

Her sister said, "She was terribly good-looking. Five-seven. Brown eyes, brown hair. Lots of girls were prettier, but she had so much personality." In her next to last year in high school, Florence went to see John Robert Powers and got a job as a Powers model.

She married "the bubble-gum king," converted to Catholicism, divorced him three years later, and became fashion editor of the *New York Journal-American*, a radio panelist, and a sparkling part of the social scene.

"She was great," Eunice Shriver said. "Very bright, great fun, and *au courant* with the news that was going on. She loved life. She had a good time. She knew everything. She wasn't an athletic type but she was a great dancer and loved to talk. She laughed all the time."

Charlie Spalding said that she was the only person who could always be guaranteed to make Jack laugh. Betty Spalding added that, for Jack, "over a long period of time, it was probably the closest relationship with a woman I know of."

In Jack's 1947 appointment book, for June 28, there is a note in her handwriting: "Flo Pritchett's birthday: SEND DIAMONDS."

She was twenty-seven then. A year later she married again, a much older man, millionaire Earl Edward Smith, Eisenhower's ambassador to Cuba. Kennedy made more than a dozen trips to Cuba to see them. The Smiths also spent much time in Palm Beach, where their home conveniently adjoined the Kennedy house, and Kennedy saw considerably more of her.

His reputation as a womanizer started early. In London before the war, Jack Kennedy was "silent, sulky, and talked mostly about girls." In the navy, he was known as "Shafty."

The women in his life later fell into a pattern: Hollywood starlets, divorcées, models—all of them bright, beautiful, and amusing, but all of them "safe" girls whom he would not and could not marry. So many of these women seemed to know and like each other. One of Flo's good friends was Olive Field Cawley, "a magnificent-looking girl, really beautiful." She had been the flame of Jack's Harvard years. His other "serious" girl was Frances Ann Cannon, daughter of the prominent Cannon Mills family, "tremendously attractive, a *great* girl who happened to be Protestant." She later married John Hersey, the novelist who wrote the PT boat story about John Kennedy that helped make Kennedy famous. Kennedy went to the wedding.

Even when he was running for Congress, he always managed time for women. Edward McLaughlin, who later became lieutenant governor of Massachusetts, recalled how Jack left in the middle of a parade in Boston to race for the train because he had a date in New York.

*   *   *

Kennedy did not look like a Don Juan when he talked to the Hyannis Rotary Club. Wearing a slackly hung suit and a shirt that gaped at the collar, Jack looked like "a little boy dressed up in his father's clothes." His voice was scratchy, tense, and high-pitched. But when he stumbled over a word, he flashed a quick self-deprecating smile that "could light up the room."

Campaigning for Congress, Jack was not a natural politician. "He hated the shaking of hands," said Thomas O'Neill, who succeeded him in Congress. "He just *hated* it."

Among the seventeen candidates, he alone was the millionaire's son from Harvard. In introducing the others, the speaker noted how each of them had come up the hard way. When it was his turn, Kennedy responded, "I do seem to be the only one here tonight who did *not* come up the hard way. I hope you will not hold it against me."

Kennedy kidded Boston politician John Powers that the house Powers was born in was nicer than his. "Yeah," Powers replied, "you came up the hard way. One morning they didn't bring you your breakfast in bed."

On Jack Kennedy's victory night, his eighty-three-year-old grandfather, "Honey Fitz," climbed up on a table, did a merry jig, then sang "Sweet Adeline." Many said he was the only man in town who could sing "Sweet Adeline" sober, and get away with it.

*   *   *

His first challenge was credibility.

When thirty-one-year-old Kennedy went to a President Truman rally in 1948, the Secret Service man refused to believe he was really a congressman and called in somebody to identify him. "Yeah, that's Congressman Kennedy."

Once, in Medford, Mass., a high school halfback yelled at him, "Hey kid, come on over and snag some passes." He caught some, tossed some, ran down a few punts, breathing heavily. The high school coach asked the halfback how the new kid was doing.

"He needs a lot of work, coach. What year is he in?"

The chuckling coach identified the new kid as the United States Representative from the Eleventh Massachusetts district.

That first year in Congress, in 1947, he was even mistaken for a House page and asked to run errands.

All this time, Jack was living with his younger sister Eunice in Georgetown. "Their house was a mess," Bill Walton recalled. "Eunice was not a housekeeper, and she was a terrible cook. One thing she liked was mashed potatoes and she always made a lot of mashed potatoes. But it was a noisy, friendly house, always a lot of people there, and very helter-skelter.

"Bob and Ethel lived close by too, and we really did play a lot of touch football then, on weekends."

*   *   *

During that time in Georgetown they got word that their sister Kathleen was killed in a plane crash in England. A friend who came to call remembered: "There was a grim, tragic restlessness about the atmosphere with the gramophone playing, but no emotional collapse," he said. "There was a disciplinary fortitude about them, an inborn courage."

Kathleen, or "Kick," was his favorite sister, gregarious, fun-loving, affectionate. "She was younger than Jack but more put together, more natural," Spalding said. "She was amusing, thoughtful, sensible, forthright and unpretentious." "Kathleen was Rose with a more released spirit," Arthur Krock said. When she worked for the Washington *Times-Herald*, and it was a cold winter day, she would put her mink coat into a brown bag before coming into the office because she didn't want to flaunt it.

The father, not the mother, went to see the body. An embassy official advised him against it because the body had been smashed by the crash. In gratitude, the senior Kennedy pressed a box into the hand of the young embassy official—a set of diamond-and-onyx cufflinks and studs from Van Cleef and Arpels.

In Washington, the new congressman was getting acclimated. "Toppy" and "Torby" were his best friends in the House. They were all brand-new congressmen. "Torby" was Torbert MacDonald, his Harvard roommate for three years, and "Toppy" was Frank Thompson of New Jersey, whom he called "Topper" because he always had another story to top the last one.

Torby had courted Kick, but decided against marrying her because he did not want to become "a corporate son-in-law." Torby, too, was one of the few to fault the elder Kennedy for "riding Jack," and once told the Ambassador to "shove it up your ass."

They were a droll, relaxed trio and saw a lot of each other. A chronic complaint of Toppy and Torby was that Jack never had any money in his pocket. "God knows how many taxi fares and lunches he stuck me for," Thompson recalled. The two got back at him by going to Harvey's Restaurant, where Jack had an account, ordering drinks and a steak dinner, and tossing a coin to see who would sign Jack's name to the check. Referring to their "wilder bachelor peregrinations," Thompson added, "I can only say that he had great taste then, as always."

He was a skinny, tousle-haired young man, but three hundred Washington correspondents voted him "the handsomest member of the House." "I could walk with Jack into a room full of a hundred women," Thompson said, "and at least eighty-five of them would be willing to sacrifice their honor and everything else if they could get into a pad with him." And he loved it.

State Department official Lucius Battle recalled his magnetic appeal. "I was freshly married and we were at this cocktail party and there was this Congressman Kennedy, whom we had never met before, and my wife was absolutely enthralled by him and I had to drag her away from him."

"He was young, rich, handsome, sexy," recalled reporter Nancy Dickerson, who dated him then, "and that's plenty for starters. But the big thing about him was that he was overpowering—you couldn't help but be swept over by him. But sex to Jack Kennedy was like another cup of coffee, or maybe dessert. You heard that one about Jack saying he had to have sex every day or else he got a headache."

"Dad told all the boys to get laid as often as possible," Jack told Clare Boothe Luce. "I can't get to sleep unless I've had a lay."

His father had established the pattern.

"I was at some posh restaurant in Washington," said Washington socialite Kay Halle, "and the waiter brought me a note inviting me to join friends at another table. It was Joe and his two sons Jack and Bobby. Jack was a congressman then. When I joined them, the gist of the conversation from the boys was the fact that their father was going to be in Washington for a few days and needed female companionship. They wondered whom I would suggest, and they were absolutely serious!"

The father worked the situation more delicately with his daughter and daughters-in-law in Washington. He asked them to arrange a dinner for eight, on different nights of the week. On the basis of the best food, wine, ambience, conversation, AND the quality of the extra women they provided for him, he would decide on the winner, and give her a thousand dollars.

Nancy Dickerson told of getting such a call from Ethel Kennedy to be the extra woman. "I'm sure glad I got to you before Eunice did," Ethel told her.

The family also knew and laughed about their father's favorite golf caddy at Antibes. She was a twenty-one-year-old dark-eyed blonde, Françoise. She described the elder Kennedy's game as having "an excellent swing," his shots short but very straight. Since he spoke no French and she spoke no English, they communicated in other ways. In French, she explained, "Mr. Kennedy is very generous."

Despite his social pastimes, the elder Kennedy religiously sat in the fourth row on the left facing the altar in the local Catholic church every Sunday.

Jack's father had had his own lurid Hollywood record with actresses. There was the famous story about Joe Kennedy's disappearing at a Hollywood party with some starlet into the bedroom for no more than five minutes. "Tell me," asked a family friend, "what is there about a man who really thinks he can get his rocks off in a few minutes?"

"By God, your old man was a helluva lot handsomer than you'll ever be," a mutual Hollywood friend told Jack Kennedy. Joan Fontaine told Jack how his father had propositioned her in her home but then said, "I can't marry you." Jack listened and smiled. "Let's see, how old would he have been then? Sixty-five. Hope I'm the same way when I'm his age."

Inga Arvad's son insists that his mother told him she had gone to bed with both Jack Kennedy and his father. What the son did not know was that his mother had been the mistress of Joseph Senior *before* and *after* she had been with Jack Kennedy. Arvad had been the former Miss Denmark and an intimate of Nazi leaders before she became a Washington newspaperwoman. The elder Kennedy had no qualms about flirting with one of Jack's women and telling her, "Why don't you get yourself a live one?"

It seemed as if Jack Kennedy spent a good part of his life proving that he was "a live one." Psychiatrists referred to it as the "Don Juan syndrome." Jack ruefully confessed to a friend that he had specifically sought out an actress with whom his father had supposedly slept. After a night with her, Jack asked her for a comparative report and was chagrined when she insisted she had never slept with his father.

Judy Garland claimed Jack Kennedy "was like a psychiatrist to me, my confidant." Jean Simmons never forgave her press agent for persuading her not to spend a weekend with Kennedy. Sonja Henie was anxious and ready for such a date, but friends talked Kennedy out of it. "She'll break your back."

It was not that Jack Kennedy was a remarkable lover. The women who should know claimed he was "a lousy lay, a bam-bam, thank you ma'am" who preferred being serviced and considered sex "a dessert" and "good clean fun." "I think he would lay anything that had wheels. Traveling with him was like traveling with a bull," said one of his fellow congressmen. George Smathers, who shared a room with him at the Fairfax Hotel, rated Jack Kennedy "a lousy lover—just in terms of the time he spent with women."

"A man can do justice to a cheeseburger in fifteen minutes," observed *New York Times* columnist Russell Baker, speaking generally of the sex patterns of Washington politicians, "and even have time to spare for a slice of pie, but a man who can have a woman, in the door and out of the door, at that clip is not a lover, except of himself."

One woman said, "I was fascinated by him at the time, but our lovemaking was so disastrous that for years later I was convinced I was frigid. He was terrible in bed, which I assumed was my fault. It wasn't until I had a loving relationship with someone else that I realized how awful my affair with Jack had been."

Actress Olivia de Havilland insisted that she was one of those who said no. "I can still remember his voice. It was a determined voice, I'll tell you that." Another actress, Gene Tierney, who said "Yes," was then separated from her husband, Oleg Cassini—who later became Jacqueline's dress designer. "He had the most beautiful eyes," she said. "And he knew the strength of the phrase, 'What do *you* think?' He made you feel very secure."

Charles Spalding recalled, "We were coming out of the River Club and there was this young woman getting out of a cab. Neither of us knew her, but Jack just went up to her and started talking. And the next thing I knew, they were both on a train going to California. He was like that. Extraordinary."

Jack often quoted a prayer he heard: "Oh Lord, make me good, but not yet, oh Lord, not just yet."

Perhaps as an explanation for his frenetic womanizing, he confided to columnist Joseph Alsop—his face serious and brooding—"I've got this slow-motion cancer, which they say gets you when you're about forty."

Massachusetts Governor Paul Dever once told a campaign crowd, "I hear it being said that my young friend Jack Kennedy isn't working down there in Washington, that he's too fond of girls. Well, let me tell you, ladies and gentleman, I've never heard it said of Jack Kennedy that he's too fond of boys."

*　　*　　*

The world had changed for John Kennedy.

"When I knew him as a young man in England," Ormsby-Gore said, "he was intelligent but not very intellectual and not very serious. I didn't think he was very 'clever' as a young man because he was not very serious. He was bored by the bureaucracy of the day-to-day work. If you had asked me then if he had much of a political future, I would have said no."

But toward the end of his second term, Kennedy's closest friends in the House suddenly noticed that he now had a new question about himself: "What's going to happen to me politically?"

Columnist Joseph Alsop presumed that doctors had told him he was no longer going to die young, that his father had lectured him about his future. His friends noted that he seemed more serious, that he no longer mimicked his peers. As a member of the House of Representatives, he said, "We were only worms." He told Rep. Hale Boggs that he was bored with the House and wanted to run for the Senate. "You don't know the House well enough to be bored by it. You haven't been here long enough," Boggs replied, then added, "All those who can't make it in the House go to the Senate."

Kennedy cornered Boggs with a question: "Do you think I've got a chance?"

Boggs said he didn't know.

"Well, I don't really think I've got a chance," said Kennedy.

"Well, how can you run, how can you campaign all day long, you know, on crutches?" After the surgery on his back, the pain varied only in intensity. Only his close family friends knew that Jack still used crutches whenever possible—but always out of public view.

It was the Ambassador who finally persuaded his son to run against the formidable Senator Henry Cabot Lodge in 1952. John Kennedy was then thirty-five. "When you've beaten him, you've beaten the best. Why try for something less?"

* * *

Both parents were present, as well as all his brothers and sisters. "The father was boss in every way," recalled a campaign aide. "It was a buffet lunch. He dominated everything, told everyone where to sit. They were just children in that house. The father wanted a complete report on everything I had found out. He thought Jack could beat Lodge easily. We started talking about sex appeal, making observations about both Lodge and Jack. I pointed out that Lodge really had it, too. The old man pooh-poohed Jack's sex appeal, saying that only *old* ladies liked him. Jack got as embarrassed as hell. There was talk about who would work in the campaign, and in what capacity. Jack delegated the task of making all the money to the old man. He said, 'We concede you that role.' "

Campaign assistant Tony Gallucio earlier had asked Kennedy what his old man was doing in the campaign. Jack rubbed his thumb with his four fingers, meaning "money."

When the *Boston Post* threatened to support Lodge, the elder Kennedy extended a $500,000 loan. Kennedy told writer Fletcher Knebel, a Harvard classmate, "You know we had to buy that fucking paper, or I'd have been licked."

"It takes three things to win in politics," his father told him. "The first is money, the second is money, and the third is money."

"And since it was his money," Dave Powers said, "he wanted to know how it was spent. 'My God, you've spent ten thousand dollars,' he would say, 'and you haven't come up with a goddamn vote.' "

His father put Bobby in overall charge of the campaign. Nobody worked harder than Bobby. He was the first to arrive at headquarters every morning, the last to leave at night. When a workman refused to put up a Kennedy sign on a drawbridge from a forty-foot ladder, Bobby did it. "And I'm saying to myself, if he falls and gets killed, what will I tell the Ambassador," Dave Powers recalled. "And I'm thinking that if I had that fella's money, I'd be sitting in a rocking chair in Cape Cod."

"We organized women," Bobby explained. "They'd leave

leaflets on seats when they got off a bus, and toss them through the doors of taxicabs so that the next passenger would have something to read—nine hundred thousand copies of our folder —were distributed by hand, nine hundred thousand! I mean, they were delivered by hand to every house on a block, or every apartment in a building, in 1952. We had a tremendous telephone campaign. We tried to telephone every voter in Massachusetts at least twice in that campaign."

An imaginative newspaperman called it *How to Get Jack Kennedy Elected to Anything*. "It really wasn't that much," insisted its author, campaign organizer Larry O'Brien, "just a few mimeographed pages." But it was full of specifics, particularly on how to contact each voter at least three times before he votes: first with a copy of the Kennedy tabloid, then a phone call, finally a personal contact just before going to the polls.

"It's a Sunday morning," Dave Powers said, "and it's the first day I've been off since the campaign started. I hear a horn outside the house and I look down and there's a big station wagon. And Bobby's yelling, 'Come on, Dave!' Well, I come down. It's Bobby and he's got Ethel and Eunice and Pat and Jean and Kenny O'Donnell and some other people. Bobby said there was a Republican neighborhood called Western and they weren't very well organized there and he wanted to make sure we delivered the brochures there that day. That was Bobby."

Robert Kennedy became curt, pushy, a buffer for all the pressures and complaints. "They don't have to like me," Bobby said quietly to Powers. "I only want them to like Jack."

"Every politician was mad at Bobby," Jack Kennedy said afterwards, "but what friend who was really worthwhile have we lost?"

Bobby's best-known speech in the campaign was: "My brother Jack couldn't be here. My mother couldn't be here. My sister Eunice couldn't be here. My sister Patricia couldn't be here. My sister Jean couldn't be here. But if my brother Jack could be here, he'd tell you that Lodge has a very bad voting record. Thank you."

Ted Kennedy, then twenty years old, made one of his first political speeches, to forty black leaders at the Boston Club.

Otherwise, he was mostly a listener and a watcher. People would have to remember, "Oh, yes, there's another brother."

And then there were the tea parties. "It was those damn tea parties that beat me," Lodge reportedly said. Both Rose Kennedy and her husband claimed credit for originating the idea. "I was the one who thought of it," Mrs. Kennedy said. "They wouldn't invite me to their tea parties, so I invited them to mine."

Admission was by engraved invitation only. The Kennedy women developed a system so that they could greet each guest by name—and there were up to six hundred guests.

"I let out more gowns this week than in the whole year before," said a Boston tailor. "I wish he'd run forever."

In those days, Mrs. Kennedy wore a hat "that looked like she had a coal scuttle inverted over her head." The guests were thrilled, especially when each of them later received a handwritten note from the Kennedys thanking them for the honor of their presence, inviting them to call again. Such was the success of those parties that the Kennedy women soon scheduled thirty-eight of them in thirty-eight Massachusetts cities.

"The main difference between our campaign and others was that we did work," Bobby said. "The teas were important, don't get me wrong, but you'd think they were half the campaign. They did not play that big a part."

"Those Kennedy girls worked like peons," said Dave Powers. "When they campaigned in Framingham, they knocked on every door in town. If someone was out when they knocked on the door, they'd go back the next morning."

Campaign aide John Powers saw a greater political potential in Rose Kennedy and asked her husband if he could use her more. "Christ, Johnny, she's a grandmother," Joseph Kennedy said. Then he thought about it, "Well, take it slow with her."

Powers described how she would dress up for one crowd, strip off her diamond rings and her bracelets for another, even put a wraparound skirt over a beautiful, expensive gown for other audiences.

She reserved her mink stole and dazzling jewelry for the matrons of Chestnut Hill. To them, she said, "I've just come back from Paris and let me tell you about the latest fashions I saw."

"She came in my car with my wife and myself," John Powers said. "We took her all over, wherever there were groups and meetings, into empty garages and stores. She gave a hell of a speech, twelve or thirteen stops a night, starting about October first and going steady through the campaign, whenever she was in Boston. She was at it for an entire month—more than that, in fact—six or eight weeks before the election. Every night including Sunday."

She spoke to Catholic Holy Name Societies, appeared on television, and talked to different ethnic groups, often in their own language. With Italian women, she shared recipes and discussed her nine children.

"She'd tell those people that she knew her son better than anyone, and she knew what kind of senator he'd be. There would be a lot of Gold Star mothers in her audiences, and mothers who were in anguish about the Korean War; and she'd tell them that she knew what it was to lose a son in a war. She was tremendous."

The only time Joseph Kennedy spoke in public for his son was as a substitute for Jack at a Knights of Columbus dinner in Cambridge. He said the reason he was "breaking the precedent" in making a public appearance was that the people of Cambridge had been so good to his boys—elected his eldest son a delegate to the Democratic National Convention, helped send Jack to Congress, and so on.

Joe Healy said, "Ambassador Kennedy's voice broke as he spoke. . . ."

John Kennedy's father became a campaign issue that would crop up again and again as long as he ran for office—like McCarthyism.

Senator Joseph McCarthy of Wisconsin was a Kennedy family friend. He had courted Eunice with the father's approval. He had hired Bobby as a counsel on his Senate committee. And he had played shortstop on the Kennedy family's "Barefoot Boys" softball team at Hyannis, although he retired after making four errors.

McCarthy was an American phenomenon. An almost unknown senator, he waved a piece of paper in front of an audience claiming it was a list of 205 Communists in the State Department, and suddenly he became an international headline. He never revealed that list of names, but his charges became more sensational. He seemed to touch a national nerve of expectancy and fear. He even accused the highly respected General George Marshall of being a traitor. So great was his power that few dared to challenge him. In his Senate committee hearings on TV, he felt strong enough to challenge American army policies. "Senator McCarthy today achieved what General Burgoyne and General Cornwallis never achieved—the surrender of the American Army," wrote the *London Times.* Even the enormously popular President Eisenhower refused to confront him.

At the hundredth anniversary of the Harvard Spee Club, a speaker said he was happy that the Spee Club had not produced a Joe McCarthy or an Alger Hiss. John Kennedy, in a voice high with anger, said, "How dare you couple the name of a great American patriot with that of a traitor?" And he stormed out of the room.

Republicans tried to bring in McCarthy to speak against Kennedy in the Senate race, but he refused. "Joe Kennedy directly asked me to persuade Joe McCarthy to stay out of Boston," wrote columnist Westbrook Pegler. Particularly in Massachusetts, McCarthy was also a hero. "Joe McCarthy is the only man I know who could beat Archbishop Cushing in a two-man election fight in South Boston." South Boston was the birthplace of the archbishop.

McCarthy was at a party at the Peter Lawfords' in New York and most of the Kennedys were there, as well as John Cavanaugh, president of Notre Dame. Father Cavanaugh, an old family friend, was about to leave when Senator McCarthy approached him and asked, "Well, Father, what do you think of the work I'm doing with the Communist conspiracy?"

The room hushed.

Cavanaugh looked at McCarthy for a long time before he answered, "Well, Joe, about the only way I can answer you is this way: If you came to confession, and I knew it was you, I would not give you absolution."

The quiet became intense. Then Cavanaugh turned and left.

The room could have exploded, but didn't. Bobby Kennedy said nothing. John Kennedy exercised his charm to relieve some of the tension. Nobody said anything to McCarthy. He had the look of a man who had been suddenly destroyed. Finally, he said, lamely, "Well, I guess it's time for me to go."

Kennedy's enthusiasm for McCarthy already had lessened.

"He had a great way of rolling his eyes, his favorite expression indicating disapproval of something. It always cracked everybody up," Bill Walton said. "When he was a senator I remember him coming into the room to tell me that his father had just read him a speech that Joe McCarthy was going to make. Without making any other comment—he just rolled his eyes."

Robert Kennedy, however, was unwavering in his loyalty to McCarthy. "OK, Joe's *methods* may be a little rough," Bobby Kennedy told some reporters on a Potomac boat ride. "But, after all, his goal is to expose Communists in government, and that's a worthy goal. So why are you reporters so critical of his methods?"

While writing the final report summing up the work of the Permanent Subcommittee on Investigations, Bobby Kennedy told Ed Welsh, "At least we can say that Senator Joe is one of the greatest senators we've ever had."

Welsh, who represented committee member Senator Symington, did not think so, and said, "Well, if you can find that in the transcript, we'll put it in."

They couldn't.

"One of the things that I was determined Jack should do was to make a statement about McCarthy," said "Pat" Gardner Jackson, former New Dealer and reporter on the *Boston Globe,* who was then working on the Kennedy campaign. "I prepared a newspaper ad that quoted ninety-nine men on the faculty of Notre Dame who issued a statement: 'Communism and McCarthy: both wrong.' Jack agreed to sign it, if John McCormack would co-sign it. McCormack agreed. So I took it up to Jack's apartment the next morning. Jack had on his coat and went dashing out just as I arrived. Sitting at a card table in the center of the living room were Joe Kennedy and three speechwriters, including Jim Landis." Landis was former head of the Securities and Exchange Commission and personal lawyer for Joseph Kennedy.

"Well, I read them the ad, at Jack's request, and I had not gone two sentences when Joe Kennedy jumped to his feet with such force that he tilted the card table over against the others; and he stood there shouting at me, one thing after another. 'You're trying to ruin Jack,' he said; and over and over again he said something about 'you and your sheeny friends.'

"Nobody has ever talked to me in that way, shouted at me that way, in my life. Then he left. The next morning I went to Jack's apartment in the morning as usual, let myself in, and he heard me. He came into the room and said, 'I hear you really had it yesterday, didn't you?'

"We talked about his father, and Jack said something I've never forgotten. This is on the plus side, and I've always remembered it. I'd asked him what made his father act this way about his children. And Jack said, 'My father's one motive that you can understand, Pat, is love of family.' And then he paused and added, 'Although sometimes I think it's really pride,' and he said it very quietly."

Whether Joseph Kennedy's anti-Semitism was a deep-seated bigotry or simply the slurring patois of his background, it was true that prejudiced epithets came easily to the Ambassador's lips. Nevertheless, he could turn to his son's aide, Ted Sorensen, and say fervently, "I think I'm going to become Jewish. The damn Catholics aren't supporting us the way they should. The damn Protestants never will. The Jews are the only friends we have."

Republicans accentuated the negative. They played up the discovery of Nazi documents in which were found expressions of the Ambassador's sympathy to the Nazis on the Jewish question. The army CIC (Counter-Intelligence Corps) had found records in Nazi files containing reports from the German ambassador in London quoting the elder Kennedy as saying before the war, "Don't worry about what you read in American newspapers. Most of them are owned by Jewish storekeepers." Joseph Kennedy countered by recalling his own plan at the time to transfer thousands of German Jews to Africa and the Americas.

Answering the attack on his father, John Kennedy told an audience of Boston Jews, "Remember, I'm running for the Senate, not my father."

"Jack's aide called me when he was running against Lodge," said Franklin Roosevelt, Jr. "They were in serious trouble in the Jewish districts because of the rumors that the old man was anti-Semitic. But more than that, Lodge had a real record with the Jewish voters. I went in, and they told me that inward after ward I swung the Jewish vote over big to Jack, and it was just about the margin of victory. He probably would have won anyway, I'm sure, but it helped. Jack never even dropped me a note about that."

"The thing that always bothered Arthur Schlesinger, Sr., was whether Jack had deep feelings about individual rights," said Kennedy speechwriter Ralph Coghlan. "He didn't. There was no deep, inner commitment to the rights of the individual. He felt none of this, this early. Jack thought things out and thought well, but he didn't feel."

Coghlan added: "I never detected in him any deep emotional forces. He at least *borders* on the intellectual. He *reads* about the poor, but, well, I think of him as a man who could love mankind in a mass but couldn't have much feeling for an individual."

At rare times, his emotions did show.

"I happened to be standing right next to him at the dedication of the Kennedy Home for Retarded Children in Brighton when the archbishop unveiled a big portrait of his brother Joe in uniform," Joe Healy recalled. "I know—I could see—that he was very affected by the whole thing, and I could see a faint trace of tears in his eyes."

A Cambridge tailor named Benny Jacobson, a family friend of the Kennedys, said of Jack: "He had a great heart. He helped boys who were financially embarrassed, but did it in a quiet way so there wouldn't be any embarrassment."

Kennedy's victory was a narrow plurality of some 70,000 votes. Rose Kennedy saw her son's victory over Senator Lodge as a personal victory. Not only had the elder Lodge beaten her father in a Senate election, but the Lodges also represented the Boston Brahmin society that had never accepted the Kennedys socially. "At last the Kennedys have evened the score," she said.

To one of the cheering crowds Kennedy sang his grandfather's old campaign song, "Sweet Adeline." "He sang it all," said campaign aide John Droney. "He had a terrible voice—he had no tone—and then Bobby sang. I think Bobby was worse."

"About a dozen of us went to Hyannis for the weekend right after the campaign," Larry O'Brien recalled. "First night there, we're having cocktails and the old man says, 'Bobby, what are you going to be doing? What are you going to do now?' And Bobby answers, 'Gee Dad, I don't know. I hadn't really thought about it.' 'You know, you've got to get moving,' the old man said. 'You know, Bobby, you've got to remember *you* weren't elected.' "

His long-time friend, John Sharon, once told him, "You'll probably marry the first woman who says no to you."

"He looked at me in a funny way," Sharon said.

4

The Luckiest Girl in the World

Jacqueline Lee Bouvier had been brought up in a world of blue blood and old money, a society strained pure where children rode their own horses, spoke French at the dinner table, and learned to sit still and disappear silently. She was bred in a credo that "fools' names and fools' faces are always seen in public places," and nobody expected her name in print except on the occasions of debut, engagement, marriage, and death.

Young women were expected to be only one thing, exquisite. Miss Porter's School taught poise, proper manners, and how to pour tea. Part of the pattern was a handshake so fragile that fingers seemed to melt, a voice so ethereal that people strained to listen. In her yearbook, Jacqueline listed her life ambition: *not* to be a housewife.

"A regal brunette who has classic features and the daintiness of Dresden porcelain. She has poise, is soft-spoken and intelligent, everything the leading debutante should be. Her background is strictly Old Guard. . . ."

That's what dapper Igor Cassini wrote in his widely syndicated Cholly Knickerbocker column when he dubbed eighteen-year-old Jacqueline Bouvier the Debutante of the Year at the Clambake Club in August 1947.

Jacqueline had long lashes, a beautifully shaped nose, sharply defined features, luxurious brown hair, and enormous, liquid, almond-shaped, dark eyes. Unkind critics claimed her head was too big for her body, her eyes set too wide apart, her teeth too small, her arms too bony, her calves too thin, her legs too bowed, and her feet too large (size ten). Photographer Cecil Beaton talked about her "huge, baseball player's shoulders and haunches, big boyish hands."

Yet the final result was a haunting kind of beauty, an aura of mystery, a projected elegance. Years later, when she walked into a party, people parted like the Red Sea. Her smile had such a dazzle that it converted excitement into electricity.

"You could never tell what she was thinking," said a friend. Another, not so friendly, noted that her collarbone protruded when she wore a low-cut gown and her fingertips were yellowed from cigarettes. That former friend also noted that "Jackie slept a lot, nine or ten hours a night, and then even wanted afternoon naps." "And she was utterly unpredictable," added another former friend, "charming one day, sullen the next. But one thing I will say for her, phonies did not survive in her presence."

Even in her young years, friends remembered, she was "never gawky or fluttery. Didn't spill out or giggle too much. Never revealed herself." Jonathan Isham, who dated her then, recalled that "she was rather aloof or reserved, seemed to talk a lot about animals, had the reputation of being rather frigid."

Her mother said of her that she was "very intense and felt strongly about things. She had enormous individuality and sensitivity and a marvelous self-control that perhaps concealed inner tensions."

"I think it's a job of work for *anyone* to feel comfortable with Jackie," said Jim Symington, son of the senator. "She always seems a little breakable so you don't get too close." Norman Mailer saw in her "something remote, not willed or chilly, not directed at anyone in particular, but distant, detached, moody, distracted, but not at all stuffy; perhaps a touch of that artful madness which suggests future drama."

Men first saw her as somebody to protect. Asked to describe her in a single word, John Kennedy quickly said "fey." A dictionary definition of that is "otherworldly." At a party, she named her secret fantasy, "I'd like to be a bird." George Balanchine said, "She looked like a pussycat." She took solitary walks for hours on lonely beaches, and once wrote a poem for her father:

> I love walking on the angry shore
> To watch the angry sea
> Where summer people were before,
> But now there's only me.

"I think I'm more of a private person," she said of herself. "I don't really like to call attention to anything."

But she could also be merry, arch, satirical. She could gambol in the snow like a kitten, impulsively jump into a pool in Yucatan with her clothes on, play outdoor tennis on a freezing winter day.

Her sense of humor was often "Alice in Wonderland," really wild, outrageous, and biting, the kind of wit that could start a fire. Those who knew her best soon sensed she was a blend of silk and steel. The wise Alice Roosevelt Longworth said that Jacqueline reminded her of a woman on a Minoan frieze in ancient Crete, then added, with her usual mischief, "I mean the woman holding the horns of a bull."

"This is a very strong dame," said her artist-writer confidant, Bill Walton.

She knew her mind and wasn't afraid of it. Her stubbornness was very strong. Once she decided to do something, she seldom swerved, and did it well. "Jackie and I would have lots of fights together," said her younger stepsister, Nina Straight, "but you always knew where she stood. She was forthright, direct, and honest, and very, very tough. She always knew what she wanted. I wouldn't want to stay in her way of something she really wanted."

Nina was still a teen-ager when she emerged from her bathtub at Hammersmith Farm to find herself being stared at by someone who had unexpectedly opened the bathroom door. Instead of a hurried apologetic departure, the man simply stood there, looked her over, and said, smiling, "In a few years, you'll be ready for my bed."

The surprise visitor was John Kennedy, then courting Jacqueline.

In an autobiographical novel called *Arabella*, Nina describes Savannah (a thinly disguised Jacqueline) as being "wicked in her determination never to fall in line . . . she learned at an early age that you don't have to get in line to be at the head of the line. . . . her motto was 'fight the good fight.' "

Describing her stepsister, Nina Straight added, "She has guts, taste, and style."

In her novel, Nina pulls out of her personal history the incident of two flat-chested young women trying to outmaneuver a saleswoman from poking her head into their dressing room to determine if they really need a brassiere. And there is also an hilarious scene in which the more knowing Savannah—still wearing white kid gloves, high heels, and an enormous hat—plops into an empty bathtub to demonstrate the art of the douche.

Five years younger than Jacqueline, Nina served as maid of honor at her wedding. When the elder Kennedy first saw Nina, he immediately tagged her as the future bride of his son Teddy —but Nina declined.

In the complicated world of divorces, Nina was the beautiful daughter of the former wife of Jacqueline's stepfather. In the same household there was also a stepbrother, a half-brother, and a half-sister. Nina was the granddaughter of the blind and famous Senator Thomas Gore of Oklahoma. Part of her heritage was Cherokee Indian.

Jacqueline developed her own independent mind early. If everyone at the dining table was speaking French, she might perversely speak German. When her mother refused to let her take her own horse to Miss Porter's School, she persuaded her grandfather to foot the bill by writing a poem for him.

Jacqueline sometimes referred to "my dear sweet mother," but there seemed to be little love between them.

"That was Jackie's way of getting back at me for divorcing her father," Janet Auchincloss said.

Publicly, Jacqueline said, "I hope to do as well for my children as my mother did for me." Privately, Jacqueline admitted that the primary love her mother passed on to her was a love of horses and eighteenth-century furniture.

Janet Lee Auchincloss liked to describe herself as one of the Lees of Maryland. Actually, her grandparents were Irish immigrants who fled the famine. Her father, who made his money in real estate, gave his daughters the best: New York City's Spence School, a debut at Sherry's, Sweet Briar, Barnard. Friends described her as a trim, petite brunette, "highly ambitious, smart, aggressive as hell, a daredevil rider who believed in self-reliance. Janet stands by to help but doesn't offer advice until it's sought. She never dominates."

If she was not a kissing-hugging mother, or a dominating one, her concern was still there. She put Jacqueline on a pony when she was a year old and, six years later, watched her win two national championships. One of the stories she told most often was of Jacqueline's getting lost when she was four years old, then calmly finding a policeman to give him her phone number.

"I wouldn't dream of telling Jacqueline what to do," said her mother. "I never have."

She did, however, urge her daughters to marry men with money, as she had. Until then, she kept them on a tight rein with a small allowance.

To Jacqueline, her stepfather, Hugh D. Auchincloss, was a sweet, bland man whom she called "Hughdie" or "Unk." He was an easy man to mock. When Jacqueline asked her mother, "What movie star does your husband remind you of?" she answered, "Say my husband reminds me of Harpo Marx because he's so garrulous. Except that he's a little better than Harpo because he can say, 'Yes, dear.'" To a similar query about his wife, Auchincloss replied, "I'd definitely say my wife is no star of the silent screen."

Asked how many rooms there were in the mansion at Hammersmith Farm in Newport, Rhode Island—where he and four generations of his family were born—Auchincloss answered, "I honestly don't know."

Hammersmith was a twenty-eight-room, rambling stone gabled house set high on a hill with a commanding view of Narragansett Bay. The seventy acres included a carriage house, a playhouse, a greenhouse, and a farmhouse that was used as a naval hospital during the War of 1812 and called "the Castle." There were also two stables for sixteen horses, and an animal cemetery.

The whole place had a sense of space and wind. The dining room bay window let in the southwest sea breeze called "the sailor's delight."

Of the ten family bedrooms, Jacqueline's was on the third floor, ". . . the best room in the house . . . sunny yellow with a hand-painted flower frieze, cane and whitewood furniture carved into garlands." Her mother remembered how Jacqueline stood in front of her mirror and carefully sketched herself.

The house had a dozen full baths, sixteen house servants, and thirty-two gardeners. The man who designed the gardens was Frederick Law Olmstead, the designer of New York City's Central Park.

Hammersmith was surrounded by other so-called summer cottages—the French chateaus, Rhine castles, and sixteenth-century Italian palaces of the Vanderbilts, Astors, Morgans, and Belmonts.

The other Auchincloss home, "Merrywood," in McLean, Virginia, had a similar ambience. Novelist Gore Vidal, who shared a stepfather with Jacqueline, described it:

"It was a peaceful golden life, a bit Henry Jamesian, a world of deliberate quietude removed from the twentieth-century tension. It was a life that gave total security, but not much preparation for the real world." Both houses "looked like an Irene Dunne movie," complete with Italian fireplaces, moose heads, bronze chandeliers, diamond-patterned rugs, and Fontainebleau chairs covered in mustard velvet. "In one way or another," Vidal said, "we have all tried to recreate Merrywood's heavenly ambience in our own households."

Before Hammersmith and Merrywood, however, there had

been for Jacqueline the different world of East Hampton and New York, and her own father.

John Vernou Bouvier III was the love of Jacqueline's life. "Drippingly handsome," he looked amazingly like Clark Gable. A sun lamp intensified his dark Latin look, and columnists called him "Jack the Sheik," or "Black Jack," or "The Black Orchid." Arthur Krock described him as "one of the most famously attractive men who ever lived." He was a tall, broadshouldered man with a pencil-line mustache, and his eyes were dark blue.

A privately published fantasy of Bouvier genealogy traced the family to French aristocracy, but the family were mostly tradesmen from Pont-Saint Esprit on the Rhone River in southern France. The first Bouvier came to the United States in 1815 and he was a carpenter in Philadelphia. But the Bouviers soon became men of money and position, steeped in high society.

John Bouvier III looked like breeding, wealth, and power. His was the world of custom-made cars, thoroughbred horses, and a Park Avenue duplex with a private gym. His was the reputation of a glorious rake who cut a great swath among society's eligible females, and many of the ineligibles. He was thirty-seven when he met Janet Lee, who was fifteen years younger. A favorite Jacqueline story for her close friends concerned her parents' honeymoon on the S.S. *Aquitania*. Her father saw Woolworth heiress Doris Duke aboard ship and took time out for a quick affair. Jacqueline also sometimes flashed a picture of her father, mother, and a woman friend, with her father endearingly holding the hand of the woman friend. Jacqueline's one-time fiancé, John Husted, remembered how Jacqueline laughed when she showed him the picture.

Jacqueline was born on July 28, 1929, and, soon after, her father lost most of his money on Wall Street. His marriage ended some nine years later. "Women are all the victors in my generation," he said.

After the divorce, Jacqueline became a much more private person. Despite the lush life of Hammersmith Farm and Merrywood and the newly acquired siblings from Auchincloss's previous marriages, Jacqueline was often alone in her room reading, sketching, dreaming, creating her own quiet Camelot of romantic princes and princesses. Making predictions at a birthday party, she said she would one day be the queen of the circus and marry the man on the flying trapeze.

She idolized her father. "He was a most devastating figure," Jacqueline said. "At school, all my friends adored him and used to line up to be taken to dinner when he came to see me."

Intimates said there was something almost illicit about the way he courted his daughter, but she loved it. He took her to the best shops, told her all the town gossip, taught her all the latest slang, turned the ordinary act of walking a dog into an exciting adventure. He also gave her advice about men: Don't throw yourself at a man. Hold back. That tantalizes. That excites.

At school, because of her coolness, she was called "Jacqueline Borgia." "I smoked since I was fifteen, but not on the school grounds."

"I was three years ahead of her at Miss Porter's; her mother and my mother were friends," recalled tall, blonde Letitia Baldrige, who later became her social secretary. "Most of the girls who came there didn't have to be taught manners; they had manners before they came. When the girls were lounging around and an older woman walked in, the girls stood up. Girls didn't have to be told anything; they copied their peers."

Jacqueline started at Vassar, then spent a year in France, mostly at the Sorbonne. She loved the freedom she found there.

She wrote her half-brother that she really led two lives, one "in a lovely quiet gray rainy world" of the Sorbonne, and the other "putting on a fur coat and going to the middle of town and being swanky at the Ritz Bar! I really like the first part best!" She also added that "I have to write Mummy a ream each week or she gets hysterical and thinks I'm dead or married to an Italian."

Later, she confided, "Most of the boys I knew were beetle-browed intellectuals who'd discuss very serious things with me." She insisted that there was "nothing romantic at all," and described herself then as a "chubby little thing eating pastries and studying with inky fingers half the night."

Letitia Baldrige, who was also in Paris then, remembers it a little differently. "She had lots of French boyfriends. She was very gushing and exuberant." Then, as later, she was a person who "knows her own mind and isn't afraid of it."

When she returned home in 1950, Jacqueline transferred to the co-educational George Washington University in Washington, D.C. She was then twenty-one.

Janet Auchincloss saw an announcement of the Prix de Paris contest sponsored by *Vogue* magazine. "I think I was under a dryer in a beauty parlor." To compete, one had to submit four papers on fashion, a personal description, the plan for an entire *Vogue* issue, and five hundred words on "People I Wish I Had Known." "I thought Jackie was just right for it so I mailed the clipping to her." Jacqueline wrote about playwright Oscar Wilde, ballet impresario Sergei Diaghilev, and French poet Charles Baudelaire. First prize was a job on *Vogue* in Paris, and she won.

"After all that, however, I didn't want her to go," said her mother. "She already had fallen in love with Paris and I was afraid, if she returned there, she would become an expatriate. I hoped I could persuade her to turn the prize down."

"I guess I was too scared to go," Jacqueline admitted. "I felt then that if I went back I'd live there forever. I loved Paris so much. That's such a formative year when you get out of college, don't you think?"

Consolation prize was a summer trip to Europe in 1951 for Jacqueline and sister Lee, without a chaperon.

Aboard ship, the two sisters climbed over the fence to sneak into first class and dance with the ship's officers. Ashore, they drove a Hillman Minx from London through France to Spain and Italy, collecting an assortment of snapshots with a great many young men. In Venice, Lee studied voice and wrote home that "Jackie has really gotten terribly interested in art and has found this teacher who has a lot of experience and she takes sketching lessons from him every day."

In Italy, the two sisters made a pilgrimage to the great art critic, Bernard Berenson. He gave them some non-artistic advice: "American girls should marry American boys. They wear better."

The sisters shared the same giggling sense of humor and the same taste in men and society, but Lee was more outgoing, more pointedly interested in romance while Jacqueline was more concerned with the scene.

After the fun and games of summer romances in foreign countries, American young men did not seem so exciting. One of the most persistent with Jacqueline was John Husted, Jr., a Yale man and a New York stockbroker with a Social Register background. They even had a formal engagement announcement. "But I was only making $17,000 a year," he said, "and her mother disapproved of our marriage." They separated with style. He came to see Jacqueline at Merrywood and they both had a couple of drinks, and then went upstairs to serenade her stepsister Nina.

"I didn't want to marry any of the men I grew up with," Jacqueline said. "I didn't know what I wanted. I was floundering."

Her mother, who had never held a job, persuaded her daughter to get one. "Unk" asked his friend Arthur Krock to help. "I always wanted to be some kind of writer," she said.

Krock called his friend, Frank Waldrop, editor of the *Washington Times-Herald*. Years before, Krock had similarly called Waldrop for a job for Kathleen Kennedy.

"She was very pleasant, very bright and charming," Waldrop said, recalling the interview with Jacqueline, "but when I asked her what she could do, it seemed as if she could do nothing much at all."

Waldrop hired Jacqueline as a "gofer" girl to get the coffee and substitute as a receptionist. When the Inquiring Photographer quit, she persuaded Waldrop to let her try it. She knew almost nothing about cameras. "Joe [Heilberger] stretched himself out on the floor to measure off six feet," she said, "and then he told me to take all my pictures from that distance."

She earned $42.50 a week.

Heilberger remembered her as "a lot of fun when you got to know her. She'd kid around like any other girl." When she asked the helpful photographers what they wanted for Christmas and they suggested it be in a bottle, she promised to oblige. She wrapped the bottle beautifully in a lovely box listing all their names. When they unwrapped it, they found a quart of milk.

In the real world of the Great Adventure, Jacqueline found it "sheer agony to stop perfect strangers to ask them questions." She almost got fired when she asked people what newspaper they liked best and actually printed some of those who preferred the opposition newspaper.

Her fellow photographers "liked Jackie," but generally regarded her "as a boy, not much interested in sex."

"Jackie, you know, is ultra-fastidious," said her stepbrother, Gore Vidal. "Therefore she never particularly concerned herself with sex. She finds it untidy." Other close friends noted that her reaction to her first sexual experience was, "Oh! Is that all there is to it?"

Godfrey McHugh has a different memory of her. He was then an Air Force major, working in the White House. Born in France and fluent in the language, McHugh was both handsome and debonair. They met when she interviewed him for her column.

"We had fun together," he said. "It was very easy to be with her. She was a very warm, enthusiastic, light-headed girl who enjoyed music, museums, and beauty. She liked to dance, liked to eat in chic places, and liked to talk French. Her French? Very high school primitive, but she did certain French phrases very well."

McHugh later became Air Force aide to John F. Kennedy.

Bill Walton, then a *New Republic* editor, remembered her as an adoring young woman sitting at their feet while he and *Times-Herald* writer John White talked about art and books and culture. "I think she thought we were the smartest men she ever met. And she was absolutely ravishing."

Again, in the intertwined relationships, White had dated Kathleen Kennedy when she had worked at the *Times-Herald*, and the two of them had double-dated with John Kennedy and Inga Arvad, almost ten years before.

"I knew Jackie when I first came to Washington," said Charles Bartlett, who was then a correspondent for the *Chattanooga Times*. "She was in a large group of young people who were sort of floating around. I used to take her out before I got married. She was enormously attractive, great fun, very artistic, really very lovely and unspoiled. I don't know why, but I thought she'd be good for Jack. They were both at my brother's wedding on Long Island in 1949 and I tried to introduce them then, but Jackie was talking to Gene Tunney, and Jack then disappeared."

When Jacqueline found a man she liked, she became "a bewitching lighthouse beacon of charm," a friend said. "And when the beam is on you, the light is lovely because Jackie doesn't look around the room to see who's there. She zeroes in on you with those wide-set eyes and listens to you with a shining, breathless intensity."

"Then she turns to talk to someone else," said her cousin, novelist Louis Auchincloss, "and it's as though you've dropped off the planet."

For Jack Kennedy, the light was lovely, and always on.

Jacqueline recalled how insistent Bartlett was about her meeting John Kennedy. "He got to be quite a bore about it," she said, smiling. That was the spring of 1951, and she was then still a student at George Washington University. She was twenty-two; Jack was thirty-four.

"She took to Jack right away," recalled Bartlett. "I leaned over the asparagus and asked her for a date," Kennedy reminisced. Jacqueline smiled at that. "There was no asparagus."

*   *   *

John Kennedy had come a long way from the time in 1939 when he had posed for sculptress Irena Wiley as one of the angels surrounding the statue of Saint Thérèse of Lisieux. That panel is now in the Vatican.

He was not an angel when he met Jacqueline. He had a reputation as a playboy congressman.

She may have read an interview with him on what kind of wife he wanted. "Something nice," he said. "Intelligent, but not too brainy."

Jacqueline knew Jack's reputation with women, and was not daunted. Her father, after all, had a similar history. In many ways, Kennedy may have reminded her of her father: the same ability to generate excitement, the same good looks, the same sense of humor.

Jack was twelve years older than she was, but that didn't bother her either. An Asian adage observes that the ideal wife should be half her husband's age plus seven years, and that made her perfect for him. Besides, her father had been almost exactly Jack's age when he married her mother.

Still, when Jacqueline was riding in her pony cart, Jack was confronting Hitler's storm troopers in prewar Berlin.

When she was a young girl in dancing class, his PT boat was sliced in half by a Japanese destroyer.

When she was a debutante, he was told he was going to die soon.

But if he was not Galahad, neither was she Rebecca of Sunnybrook Farm. What bothered her most was that she differed so much from the woman he seemed to prefer—seductive, sensual, full-bodied. She was so highly conscious that her figure was flat.

However, she felt that deep within him was a pool of privacy, which she herself had. She told a friend that she and Jack were both like icebergs with the greater part of their lives invisible. She felt they both sensed this in each other, and that this was a bond between them. Another bond was their wit—his perhaps more gentle, hers more biting.

During the Senate campaign, he occasionally called Jacqueline from a phone booth. "I could hear all this clinking of coins." She then held up a postcard from Bermuda showing a passion flower, which read, "Wish you were here. Cheers. Jack." She smiled ruefully and said, "And that was my entire courtship correspondence from Jack."

During the campaign, Kennedy asked Phil Fine, who was working hard for him, "Why don't you get married?"

"Why don't you?" Phil answered.

Kennedy replied that he was too busy campaigning to think of that, but added, "I'll tell you what. Whichever one of us gets married first, the other throws him a cocktail party."

"Two months later I announced my engagement," recalled Fine, "and to my amazement he remembered, came back, and we had a cocktail party."

He was a senator now and his father had painted the brightest picture of political promise but stressed his need for a wife and family. Jacqueline had all the assets, plus his father's enthusiastic approval. One thing worried him—the twelve-year age difference. When he discovered that Dave Powers was twelve years older than his wife, he asked, "And you two get along fine, don't you?"

"Jack asked me what I thought about Jackie," said Sen. George Smathers, "and I told him I thought he could do better. Then one day I was dancing with her at a party and she was mad as hell at me because he had told her what I had said. When I bawled him out, he just laughed and said, 'You know how it is. I wanted to make myself look good.' Then he told me that his father told him it was time to get married, and his father preferred Jackie."

Jacqueline's editor at the *Times-Herald*, Frank Waldrop, was another of her father figures. He knew what was happening and tried to warn her about Kennedy. He knew Kennedy for what he was then—a playboy congressman and a womanizer—and he didn't want Jacqueline to get hurt.

Waldrop told Jacqueline what he knew about Jack and the other women, but Jacqueline still felt that she would be "the luckiest girl in the world" if he would marry her.

When she was in England writing about Queen Elizabeth's coronation, Jack Kennedy sent her a telegram: ARTICLES EXCELLENT, BUT YOU ARE MISSED.

What awed her about him was the reach of his knowledge. "If I were drawing him," she said later, "I would draw a tiny body and an enormous head." She was flattered when he asked her to translate some French articles and books on Indochina. She catered to his taste. She preferred French films, but happily went with him, on short notice, to some adventure movie. He described her as a romantic "in the old-fashioned sense of the word." He was not. There were never flowers or candy. That was not his style.

She had long ago rationalized his womanizing reputation. Men were just like that. His father was like that. In her essay for *Vogue*, she had quoted Oscar Wilde: "The only difference between a saint and a sinner is that every saint has a past and every sinner has a future." She had also quoted Baudelaire, "A sweetheart is a bottle of wine; a woman is a wine bottle."

Her Inquiring Photographer columns were now asking whether the Irish were deficient in the art of love, whether husbands and wives should breakfast alone, whether wives should be struck regularly like gongs, and why a contented bachelor should get married.

She judged him well. "He looks young," she told her friends, "but he's never been a boy." She thought him restless and unpredictable, but exciting. And she sensed the main danger: how easily he was bored. If she preferred Debussy, his favorite music was "Bill Bailey, Won't You Please Come Home?" But they both liked Cole Porter, George Gershwin, "Limehouse Blues," and "all those real jazzy records." If she loved ballet, he considered them "faggy dances" and was more fascinated by football. She enjoyed Jack Kerouac, Proust, and Skira art books, but his preference was for seventeenth-century English history, the period of Cromwell. He smiled at the anomaly of an Irishman being caught by English history and said, "but that's the way it is." His favorite period of American history was several decades before the Civil War. But he also liked James Bond thrillers. Her favorite magazines were *Paris-Match*, *Connaissance des Arts*, and *Réalités*, while he devoured the news magazines, *The Economist*, all newspapers, and some comic strips.

They both enjoyed dancing, gossip, small parties.

This was no whirlwind courtship. "I'm not the heavy lover type," he explained. There were few signs of open affection. No kissing, no hugging, no hand-holding.

"Both of us knew it was serious, I think," she said. "But we didn't talk about it then."

Her sister Lee married a young man rumored to be the illegitimate son of the Duke of Kent. Jacqueline was the maid of honor. When Jacqueline was in England wondering about her own future, Jack finally proposed in a trans-Atlantic phone call. However, he had an unusual request: would she postpone the engagement announcement until the *Saturday Evening Post* published their article on him. The article was about the Senate's "gay, young bachelor."

Commenting afterwards on the engagement, a Washington

society editor noted coolly that it was a good catch and match for each of them, even though each desired the other for different reasons: She had the status in society and he had the money and power. The editor also commented that he never acted as if he were really in love with Jacqueline. The editor also said that Jack went off on a vacation without her right after their engagement announcement. "No man in love does that. If you're in love with somebody, you want to be with them."

On Jacqueline's first visit to Hyannis Port, *Life* magazine was waiting. She had expected to go on her first sail alone with Jack, but the *Life* photographer was sailing with them. The story would be called, "*Life* Goes Courting with a US Senator." Celebrity-seeking had shifted a bit from Hollywood, in the search for something fresh. The young photogenic Kennedys were perfect people for *Life*. They represented the rich and the beautiful, and the American people had a hunger for dreams and fantasies.

She knew he was ambitious, knew she would have to be in the spotlight, but didn't know how much, or how soon. She didn't want to pose for a photographer while she swung at a softball. She didn't like to compete. She didn't actually fight the publicity and glare, but quickly tired of it.

Jacqueline didn't have any of the resilience that the Kennedys would have liked, and she didn't want to do what they were trying to do. She didn't want to jump in a sailboat or exhaust herself playing tennis. She wanted to take an easel and go out and paint, or read books. She didn't want to move in a convoy; she wanted to move by herself. And the things she wanted to talk about weren't necessarily family conversations.

The Kennedy girls joked that Jacqueline pronounced her name "Jack-lean" to rhyme with "queen." They also laughed that they would bring peanut butter sandwiches on an afternoon sail and she would bring paté and quiche and wine. In one of his greatest understatements, Jack said of her then that she was "sensitive by contrast to my sisters who are direct and energetic."

A great many Kennedys felt that sitting down was bad for you; therefore you had to keep moving.

A guest at Hyannis told of taking part in fourteen athletic

events in one day, some of which were the trampoline, jogging along the beach, swimming, two separate sets of tennis, sailing (and letting himself be dragged behind a sailboat), golf, water-skiing (twice), touch football (twice), baseball. He also included eating a sandwich with sand in it. All this, he said, put him "something like only three events behind Ethel."

The Kennedy slogan for guests, he said, should be: "It's not how you play the game that counts; it's whether you survive."

Never before had Jacqueline been caught up in such frenetic physical activity. She later called the Kennedy women "the rah-rah girls." But the whole family had this same quickening feeling, this same boisterousness. They never seemed to relax. If they were waiting for a car and they had four or five minutes, one of them would say, "All right, we'll have ball practice."

Football was not Jackie's game. In her Vassar days, when a date took her to a Yale game, she asked, "Why are they kicking the ball?" At Hyannis Port, when they pulled her into a touch football game, she looked at Ted Sorensen with desperation and asked, "Tell me one thing: Which way do I run?"

Later, she had a thoughtful line about it: "If you can't cope with emergencies by the time you're twenty-five, you'll never be able to adapt yourself to situations."

She sensed the family feeling at first meeting: If any Kennedy brought a guest, "the rest of the family would look for a reason to like you."

But when she came down from her room wearing strawberry-colored linen shorts, a sleeveless yellow shirt, bright blue Capezio slippers with embroidered pearls, and a belt painted with bats and the words BATS IN YOUR BELFRY, she did not expect her fiancé to greet her in a voice loud enough for all to hear: "And where the hell do you think *you're* going?"

"You had to be strong not to be captured and absorbed by the Kennedys," said David Ormsby-Gore, "and Jackie was."

When they first met, Jacqueline thought Rose Kennedy was "scatterbrained." Later, she would say of her, "God, what a thoroughbred!" But never was there ever any real affection between them.

On the other hand, her mutual affection with Joe Kennedy

was quick and lasting. She was vacationing with the Auchin-closes at Hobe Sound, and dropped in on the Kennedy home at nearby Palm Beach. Only the father was there. The two seemed determined to charm each other, and they did. They went swimming, made each other laugh, talked about everything from Cardinal Spellman to Gloria Swanson. When she left, she had an ally and an admirer. "I'm more like Mr. Kennedy Senior," she claimed, "than any other members of his family."

Jacqueline was generally quiet during the cacophony of dinner conversation.

"A penny for your thoughts," Jack once asked her, and the dinner talk silenced to listen.

"If I told them to you, they wouldn't be mine, would they, Jack?"

A week before they were married, she asked him what he considered his best and worst qualities. His best quality, he said, was curiosity; his worst was irritability. By irritability, he meant impatience with the boring, the mediocre, and the commonplace.

"The wheels go round and round constantly in her head," her sister-in-law Ethel wisely observed. "You can't pigeonhole her. You have a hard time getting to the bottom of *that* barrel, which is great for Jack who is so inquisitive."

"I'm not going to be what *they* want me to be," Jacqueline confided. "I won't cut my hair. I won't go out and talk. I won't have twenty-five kids."

Still unsure of herself, she went with his sisters to hear Kennedy speak at Quincy and Fall River. She admitted to a reporter that she didn't know much about Massachusetts, "but I'm going to learn." She had come from a family of lifelong Republicans, "but I guess I'm a Democrat now." She had never voted before, "but I'm going to vote for Jack."

"What was Jacqueline's main interest during their campaigning?" Joe Healy was asked, after a short political trip with her.

With a perfectly straight face, not facetiously, Healy answered, "Chinese checkers."

*   *   *

Jack, with his sisters Rosemary,
Kathleen, and Eunice—1925

Tall, thin, and sickly, teenage Jack was never the athlete he had hoped to be.

The Kennedy clan in Hyannis Port, 1931. Left to right: *Bobby, Jack, Eunice, Jean, Joseph, Sr., Rose with Pat in front of her, Kathleen, Joe, Jr., and Rosemary*

The Ambassador to Great Britain and his family (MARCUS ADAMS)

Kathleen, seen here with Joe, Jr., and Jack in 1939, died tragically in a plane crash in 1948.

Jack and Joe Jr. Joe died in a bombing mission in 1944. (PICTORIAL PARADE)

Jack as PT-109 commander during World War II (UPI PHOTO)

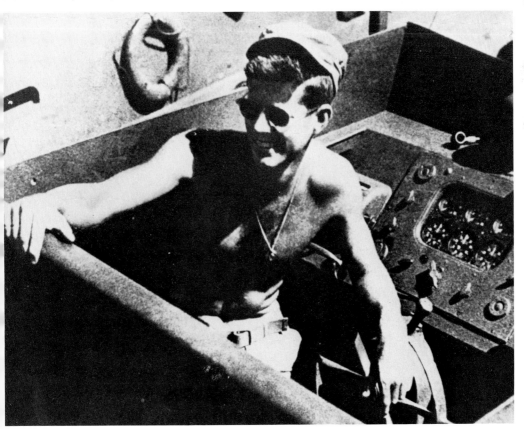

Jack, Bobby, and Ted in front of the family home in Hyannis Port, circa 1946

At the second family home in Palm Beach, Florida. Left to right: *Ted, Jean, Pat, Jack, Bobby* (kneeling), *and friend*

Jack's grandfather, Honey Fitz, and his father congratulate him on his victory in the congressional primary in June 1946.

Joseph, Sr., was the force behind the campaign for the senate in 1952.

Rose Kennedy campaigning for her son in 1952

What next?

The two men quickly liked each other. Jacqueline listened to her father and Jack talk about politics, sports, girls, "what all red-blooded men talk about," and delighted at their magnetic charm, their laconic wit, their ready laughter.

Bouvier later wrote his nephew about "this young kid who needs a haircut," and Jack joked about his future father-in-law who kept a massive electric box in his apartment that was supposed to melt off excess weight.

Their mutual appreciation was real.

The Auchinclosses had a genealogy that connected them with the kings of Europe. The New York Social Register had forty-seven separate listings of Auchinclosses. Many were not happy about the Kennedy connection.

"He had his feet on the dashboard, and he was really loose and singing. It was about 3 AM," said Ed Barube, who was driving Kennedy to Hammersmith Farm. But then Kennedy suddenly quieted. "Let's cut it down," he said. "I'm not in too solid with the family and they might throw me out."

Kennedy always called his mother-in-law "Mrs. Auchincloss." At the same time, Jacqueline delightedly insisted, "Mummy is terrified of Jack because she can't push him around at all."

Big hats, white gloves, pearls. The two mothers were sitting in a car at Bailey's Beach in Newport, discussing wedding plans, while Jack and Jacqueline were swimming. Jacqueline came out first; Jack dawdled.

"I remember she stood on the walk and called to her son in the water. 'Jack . . . J-a-ack!'—and it was just like the little ones who won't come out and pretend not to hear their mothers calling—'J-a-a-ck!' But he wouldn't come out of the water," said Jacqueline.

After a long interval, Jack reluctantly said, "Yes, mother."

Jack's mother was horrified when she saw that he was wearing a pair of bedroom slippers on the beach.

He was barely better dressed when they applied for their wedding license—summer shorts and a sport shirt. But when a newspaper photographer materialized, Jack quickly borrowed a jacket and tie from the city clerk and combed his hair. Jacqueline insisted that she was "awfully nervous on this side of the camera," but an envious reporter said of her, "She could be in a barn, leaning on a pitchfork, and she'd still look like Miss America."

Being at the other end of an interview also bothered Jacqueline. "I'm frightened to death," she told an interviewer, adding, "I hope you don't make me sound silly."

She didn't have an engagement ring yet "but Jack is fixing all that."

She didn't yet know where they planned to live "but Jack is fixing that, too."

And what kind of wedding did they want?

"We want a simple and very small wedding—just family, we think. Jack and I want it that way."

The *Boston Herald* editorial was headlined: EXIT PRINCE CHARMING. And it began: "Yesterday was a difficult day for American women. . . ."

Their engagement party at Hyannis had been a family scavenger hunt with Kennedys "borrowing" everything from a bus to a policeman's hat, but their wedding was "just like a coronation."

"Speak for Jack," the elder Kennedy told George Smathers at the wedding party the night before.

"I told him that they wouldn't understand my southern accent," Smathers said, "but he answered, 'Well, eliminate all those sloppy words. Get on with it.' He was *so* competitive. Old Joe was a cold, tough guy. We all had a great deal of respect for him, and some considerable fear, so I said, 'Yessir, yessir.' I don't remember exactly what I said, but I guess it was appropriate."

"It was an awkward affair," Spalding recalled, "and it didn't quite take off until everybody drank a little more."

Red Fay advised the bridegroom to make sure that he offered the first toast to the bride. "And when the glasses are drained, no one should drink out of them again. They should be thrown into the fireplace."

"Gentlemen," said Jack solemnly, "I want you all to rise and drink a toast to my lovely bride." The men all stood up and drained their glasses.

"Into the fireplace," said Jack, throwing his glass. "We will not drink out of those glasses again."

The eighteen men threw their glasses into the fireplace. Their host, Hugh Auchincloss, suddenly seemed pale and shaken, but asked the waiter to replace the glasses.

Kennedy was up again. "Maybe this isn't the accepted custom but I want to again express my love for this girl I'm going to marry. A toast to the bride."

Again, the drinks were drunk and the expensive crystal glasses thrown into the fireplace.

The next set of replacement glasses were ordinary kitchen glass.

Red Fay then recited a take-off on "Casey at the Bat," with Jack as Casey and Newport instead of Mudville. "Fay, how you continue to get away with that corn you pass out at parties is beyond me," Jack told him afterwards. "You're greeted as though you are a combination of Tennyson and Georgie Jessel."

"It's all in the delivery," Fay answered modestly.

"Jack was enjoying himself," said Spalding, "and yet I had the strange feeling that Jack was watching everything with an extra eye, as if the eye was outside of himself, in a corner of the room, surveying the scene with a kind of detachment. It was a very eerie thing to see this, and feel it, but there it was. I remember I cut myself and Jack was immediately at my side, looking at the cut, suggesting I should go to the hospital. It was one of his qualities that bound people to him. Concerned. Sensitive. But the point is, he could be part of what was going on, and yet that extra eye saw me. I know it sounds strange. But I felt he always had that extra eye."

*　　*　　*

Janet Auchincloss had refused to permit her former husband to attend that party, just as she had refused to let him stay at her home. She had not forgiven Bouvier's comment about her husband's brokerage firm: "Take a loss with Auchincloss." Nor had she forgotten the remarks made by guests comparing the handsome Bouvier with the bland, bald Auchincloss at Lee's wedding six months before. Except for Jacqueline's insistence, she wouldn't have invited him to come to the wedding.

On the wedding day, Michel Bouvier went to the Viking Hotel to bring his uncle to the church on time. "Black Jack" Bouvier was too drunk to come. The hotel had its instructions from someone to provide him with uninterrupted liquor service. Hughdie Auchincloss, who had been briefed earlier, was fully prepared to step in and give the bride away.

Jacqueline later wrote her father a loving letter of forgiveness, saying she knew how pressured he had felt and that, as far as she was concerned, she still really felt that *he* was the one who walked down the aisle with her. Bouvier showed that letter to many friends, saying, "Only a rare and noble spirit could have written that."

After the church service, a *Boston Globe* reporter remarked on Bouvier's absence. "You need glasses, girl," said Joseph Kennedy. "Of course he took her down the aisle." But the reporter had seen Bouvier at the rehearsal the day before and recognized him as the man who once tried to pick her up on a beach in Nassau.

When it came to control, this bride and groom were a match. Jacqueline was distressed about her father; Jack was in such pain with his back that he had difficulty kneeling. Nobody looking at them would ever have known.

Meanwhile, the Auchinclosses watched in horror while their hoped-for quiet, private wedding ballooned into a national event. On September 12, 1953, the *New York Times* reported that nearly three thousand people broke through police lines outside St. Mary's Roman Catholic Church in Newport, Rhode Island, and "nearly crushed the bride, Miss Jacqueline Lee Bouvier." Cars backed up for a half-mile at the reception at Hammersmith Farm, and the bride and groom spent more than two hours shaking the hands of their twelve hundred guests.

Jacqueline looked lovely in her gown of cream taffeta faille, wearing only two pieces of jewelry—besides her ring—a diamond bracelet from her husband and a diamond pin from her father-in-law.

The guest list included everybody from Sen. Joseph Mc-

Carthy (who couldn't come) to Patsy Mulkern (who did). "As a kid I loved a ham sandwich, and still do," said Patsy Mulkern, "and I think Joe Kennedy knows that we fellows from the wrong side of the tracks in Boston still prefer ham to chicken, and he has plenty of it." Joe Kennedy also provided two truckloads of champagne and two trucks to take away the presents, as well as a five-tier wedding cake from Azarius Piourde of Fall River, Massachusetts. Piourde called it "the biggest, finest, most important cake of my career."

Archbishop Richard Cushing performed the ceremony and the pope sent a special blessing. Almost unnoticed was the fact that Mrs. Alfred Gwynne Vanderbilt's jewels were stolen.

"Don't do what you did at Bobby's wedding," Eddie Dunn told Jack Kennedy. For one of the few times in his life, Jack had drunk too much and had passed out.

Joe Kane, a Kennedy cousin, had his own comment: "Jack married a nice girl, but he's no bargain to live with."

The young couple posed for the usual pictures but refused some "baloney" pictures such as posing with clinking glasses. They then danced on the terrace overlooking Narragansett Bay to the tune of "No Other Love."

"Well," his friend and neighbor Larry Newman told Jack at the reception, "this is the greatest thing for you that I can think of. Now that you've got a really charming, wonderful girl, and Mort [Downey] and I won't have to worry about those long-stemmed Billy Rose beauties, it's all downhill from now on."

"What do you mean?" asked Kennedy.

"Well," said Newman, "the next stop is the White House."

There was a long pause of quiet before Kennedy replied, "I think you're right."

As they walked out of the house onto the lawn, enjoying the lovely view of the Newport harbor, Kennedy stopped and stared and said, "That'd be a helluva place to sail in with the presidential yacht."

His Eminence Richard Cardinal Cushing revealed, years later, that something else was on John Kennedy's mind on that wedding day. Kennedy had asked him to take care of Jackie and any children if he should die early.

There are three things which are real:
God, human folly and laughter.
The first two are beyond our comprehension,
So we must do what we can with the third.

—Inscription on silver mug
John Kennedy gave to
Dave Powers

Scenes from a Marriage

He would find love
He would never find peace
For he must go seeking
The golden fleece.

It was part of a poem Jacqueline had written for Jack soon after they were married. She was right about the peace and the fleece, but there was some question about the love.

He had been so private for so long that it was not easy to give of himself. He had friends on many levels, and shared part of himself with each of them for a while. But he had no friend or family member in whom he could confide completely. Only parts and pieces, and at special times. But always, deep within him, was this reserve, this mystery.

"She was another girl crazy about her husband when she got married," Spalding said of Jacqueline Kennedy.

She found the enormous, natural energy of the family almost overwhelming. She always felt herself on the fringe. Even her sister-in-law Jean, one of the quiet Kennedys, admitted, "Jackie and I are very good friends, but I think her interests are . . . ah . . . different from mine. I think all the touch football stuff has been slightly exaggerated, but what else is there to do in the country before the sun goes down?"

On a weekend Jack would join his brothers to play against the five Kennedy women. When he once found himself on the bottom of a pile of players, Bobby stood over him and crowed, "See, a lot of guts, but no brains."

Jacqueline finally and gratefully quit football forever after she broke her ankle.

Her main solace again was her father-in-law. In that whole family, he alone became her anchor, her rock. "They would talk about everything, their most personal problems," said Bill Walton. "She relied on him completely, trusted him, and soon adored him."

She was one of the few who would stand up to him, and he liked it. "Being late with Big Joe can be fatal if he's in one of his Emperor Augustus moods, and Jacqueline was fifteen minutes late to lunch at Hyannis," Spalding said. "So when she came in, he started to give her the needle, but she gave it right back. Old Joe was always full of slang and so she told him, 'You ought to write a series of grandfather stories for children, like, "The Duck and the Moxie" and "The Donkey Who Couldn't Fight His Way Out of a Telephone Booth." '

"When she said this, the old man was silent for a moment, and so was everybody else at the table, and then he broke into an explosion of laughter."

The Georgetown section in Washington is an old-fashioned neighborhood of early nineteenth-century houses with trees, bright flowers, small shops, and quiet chic. Jack and Jacqueline found a house to rent: dining room and kitchen on the first floor, living room and terrace on the second floor, two bedrooms on the top. Bobby and Ethel lived four blocks away and Ethel lent her sister-in-law some drapes and slipcovers. Jack Kennedy would pick up the newspaper at Morgan's Pharmacy where he would meet his neighbors. At the dry-cleaning store he knew the owner well enough to lend him his car or go for a beer.

"Jackie never did any manual labor," Evelyn Lincoln said. "She didn't know how to clean a house. Not that the Kennedys did either, but they would know how if they had to."

To a reporter, though, Jacqueline insisted, "Housekeeping is a joy to me. When it all runs smoothly, when the food is good and the flowers look fresh, I have much satisfaction. I like gardening," she added, "but I'm not very good at it. I care terribly about food, but I'm not much of a cook." Then she described the preparation of her first dinner:

"Jack's secretary called and said he was leaving the office so I started everything. I'd heard those silly stories about the bride burning things and I just knew everything was going right when suddenly, I don't know what went wrong, you couldn't see the place for smoke. And when I tried to pull the chops out of the oven, the door seemed to collapse. The pan slid out and the fat splattered. One of the chops fell on the floor but I put it on the plate anyway. The chocolate sauce was burning and exploding. What a smell!!!! I couldn't get the spoon out of the chocolate. It was like a rock. And the coffee had all boiled away."

She had burned her arm, and it had turned purple. "It looks horrible, doesn't it?" she asked, then laughed. "I'm always so grateful when we happen to have an invitation to dinner on the cook's night out."

They entertained twice in their first six months of marriage. A dinner for twelve included her mother. "That was really terrifying," she said. "I think I could entertain a king or queen with less apprehension than my mother, when there are other guests present."

When the family cook was there, Jack ate well. "One night I dined with Jack at his home in Georgetown," a friend said. "God, I can't imagine what his cholesterol count might be. There must be no passage to his veins at all. There was easily an eighth of a pound of butter on his steak, an equal amount on the few stalks of asparagus. And the potatoes were drowned in it. Instead of milk, Jack drank two glasses of heavy cream, and for dessert we had pecan pie with whipped cream. And still he loses weight."

Jackie went to the Senate Office Building basement where

Senate wives rolled bandages for the Red Cross. "They'd talk about their children and grandchildren," Jacqueline recalled, "and I would talk about my little half-brother."

When she asked the Senate wives what they had been doing since the convention, she expected some references to "that madhouse." "But it was as if they were on television all the time," Jacqueline remembered, because their almost standard answer was, "I've been writing letters to all those good people who were so helpful to my husband."

At parties, she always found herself the youngest. She made sure her husband got his hot lunch delivered, returned batches of books to the Library of Congress for him, memorized some of his favorite poems, consulted him on "whether to get a new washing machine or get the old one fixed." When Dean Acheson criticized her husband in print, she promptly defended him in a sharp reply. Pleading that the argument not be personal, Acheson replied, "Jacquie, think of all the trouble which came to the unhappy Trojans because Athene got her feelings hurt about the golden apple."

She kept telling friends that Jack was her rock, "and I lean on him in everything." And she kept telling interviewers, "I'm an old-fashioned wife and I'll do anything my husband asks me to do." In her answers, she was a creature of her time, telling the press what she felt a proper campaign wife should say— perhaps even partly believing some of it. She was, after all, a young wife who truly wanted to marry this older man, this exciting man, and was willing to be guided by him. But, deep within her, she had her own independence, her own stubborn strength, her own core of mystery, her own magic—all of which would grow and show later. What she did not want to be was "a vegetable wife," which she described as "a humdrum woman."

She wanted her own home so "we can get our wedding presents out of storage." She loved it when he came home early and found something he liked in a book and read it aloud to her. But, more often, he worked late, or was away campaigning. "When Jackie was lonely, she'd come over to our house and maybe I'd take her to a movie," remembered Bill Walton, who lived nearby with his children.

Her friends were few, and mostly men. "Jackie and my wife Tony were saying that they didn't particularly like women," Ben Bradlee said, "and that's why they didn't have any girl friends." Besides Tony, her women friends included Martha Bartlett and Betty Spalding. They knew how difficult and how lonely her early marriage was. "It's not the right time of life for us," she said. "We should be enjoying traveling, having fun. . . . I was alone almost every weekend. It was all wrong."

"In their strangulated way, they loved each other," Betty Spalding said, "but neither was able to relate to the other, and there was never any affection between them at any time. He was always quite diffident toward her."

She added, "Jack and I had a warm brother-sister relationship. He would ask me personal questions about women and marriage. Jack had a total lack of ability to relate emotionally to anyone. I think that was one of the things that was so difficult for Jack when he finally married Jackie. Both of them were blocked emotionally. She had the same emotional blocks and panics that Jack had. And their relationship was extremely stormy at the beginning."

Betty Spalding knew them both well enough to make this observation. She and her husband were among Jack and Jacqueline's most intimate friends. Betty also had been one of Kick's closest friends, and perhaps Jack sensed in her a reminder of his sister.

Jack liked to tell friends that he was the straight line and Jackie was the ups and downs that intersected the straight line. As Betty Spalding put it, the two were imprisoned in a million habits long before they met, habits of which they were not even aware. Jack flirted with any pretty girl at a party, as he always had—even if his wife was there. For a man who was normally very kind and considerate of people, he was obviously not very conscious of how much he hurt his wife. Despite her rationalization, Jacqueline was not Janet Auchincloss, who would suffer a husband's infidelity on her honeymoon, and she was not Rose Kennedy, who would go on an ocean crossing with her husband's mistress. Still, the day would come when Jacqueline would accept her husband's mistress as her press secretary.

She knew even then, when he came home late, that he wasn't always working. Washington was a small town, and there were gossips willing to pass on ugly reports of orgies with senators at a nearby hotel.

"If I were doing it over, I'd still push Jack hard, because she was an enormous asset to him," said Charles Bartlett, who had introduced them. "He was very pleased with the whole setup. I never had any indication of any kind that he had any regrets about getting married. But I don't know how much of an asset he really was to her. He was a lousy husband. He inherited his old man's brains but he also inherited his love for women. That doesn't really go to make a very happy marriage. So, if I was doing it over, I don't know how hard I would push *her*."

*   *   *

A strong factor in his marriage and in his lifestyle was his constant pain.

"Jack had an actor's control," Spalding noted. "It was the kind of control that Joe Montana had playing for the Forty-niners. Montana said, 'It's the damnedest thing. The game's pretty rough and you're fighting for your life out there, but you're always watching yourself.'

"That's the way I always felt about Jack, as if he was always watching himself in the scene."

Kennedy called courage "the most admirable of human virtues," and liked to equate it with "grace under pressure," the phrase Ernest Hemingway had borrowed from Scottish playwright James M. Barrie. Proving his own courage once again perhaps gave him the quiet, inner confidence that he could do anything he wanted to do—no matter what the odds.

Kay Halle was with Jack at a party when he fell. She heard his spine hit the floor and saw his face pale. Nobody else had seen the accident because it happened in a corner of the room. Barney Crile, Kay's brother-in-law and a noted surgeon, once told her that anyone hitting their spine in a fall must get up evenly. "Why don't you just lie there a minute," she told Jack.

"No, no," he said.

"Then take my two hands and I'll pull you up evenly."

She pulled him up slowly and he righted himself, his face regaining its color, and she could feel him dominating his pain with the power of his will. He then kept on talking as if nothing had happened.

Part of his problem was that his left leg was three quarters of an inch shorter than his right. He wore shoes with a lift on the left foot, and a lower heel on the right. But the chief source of pain was still the disintegrated spinal disc. Throughout their courtship, Jacqueline remembered, he had been on crutches as often as not.

"You know," he said, "during my experience out in the Pacific, I really wasn't afraid to die. And I wasn't afraid of dying when I was in the hospital. In fact, I almost welcomed it. Because I didn't want to live the rest of my life the way I was living. The pain was so bad. I could stand the pain, but couldn't bear the thought of living the rest of my life with that kind of pain."

Surgeons recommended fusing some spinal discs, but warned that his Addison's disease multiplied the danger. "I'd rather die than spend the rest of my life on those damn things!" Within seven months, beginning in October 1954, there were two critical operations, and he almost died both times. "It was the first time I really prayed," said Jacqueline.

She was with him constantly, assisting him in and out of bed, putting on his socks and slippers, helping him eat, reading to him, telling him stories, playing checkers and Monopoly with him, and trying to make him laugh. She brought balloons for him to shoot at with a popgun, and called people to come who might amuse him. "Jack is feeling lousy . . . come on down."

To distract Jack, Jacqueline was part of a plot to have Grace Kelly pose as a night nurse. "When Jack opened his eyes, he thought he was dreaming. He was hardly strong enough to shake hands with her. He couldn't even talk." "I was terribly embarrassed when they pushed me into the room," the actress recalled. "He couldn't have been sweeter."

Adlai Stevenson phoned, a warm, sympathetic, almost fatherly call. Stevenson told Jack that he had had more than his share of trial and trauma, but that he was still a young man with a great future. "You and I have been given more than our good share of life," he added. Jacqueline later wrote Stevenson a glowing letter of thanks, telling him how much of a tonic that call was, how "it had transformed Jack."

The surgery involved the removal of the metal plate and a bone graft. "He had a hole in his back big enough for me to put my fist in it up to my wrist," said Dave Powers. George Smathers also saw that hole, and told his fellow senators that Jack would never be well enough to come back to the Senate. "How is it now?" Jack asked Spalding, as they walked along the beach. "Is it open?" he asked almost angrily. "Is any stuff running out of it?"

"At least half the days that he spent on this earth were days of intense physical pain," Bobby said of his brother. "I never heard him complain. I never heard him say anything that would indicate that he felt God had dealt with him unjustly. Those who knew him well would know he was suffering only because his face was a little whiter and the lines were a little deeper, his words a little sharper. Those who did not know him well detected nothing."

"The marvel was that he could make jokes about his own pain," Spalding said. "He'd turn everything into a funny remark, sometimes at the expense of the doctor or the nurse or himself or the hospital or science or anything.

"He laughed without much noise, but he really laughed. It was not a guffaw; it was more of a chuckle, but it was a full laugh. It wasn't strangled or anything, but he was obviously laughing. His expression would burst, but not his voice. And he laughed with his eyes. He always went on to add something to whatever started the laugh in the first place. That's how he got out of it. Until the pain tired him, and he'd go to sleep."

Jacqueline and Teddy brought him to Palm Beach. She seldom left his bedside, sleeping in a small room next to his. "They aren't worth a damn," he said of his pills. Since he slept so little, Jacqueline encouraged him to write his book about history's congressional leaders who put conscience over politics. Ted Sorensen supplied considerable research and Jacqueline even drafted her Georgetown University history teacher to help. When Jack was too tired to read, she read to him.

"Politics is a jungle," he wrote in his notes for *Profiles in Courage*. ". . . torn between doing the right thing and staying in office—between the local interest and the national interest—between the private good and the politician and the general good."

When David Ormsby-Gore visited him, Kennedy remarked that he was not sure he was cut out to be a politician, because he saw the strength of opposing arguments too well.

His father disagreed, and his father was always there. He was there when his son was near death after surgery. Throughout these many months, the intimacy between Jacqueline and her father-in-law intensified.

Thursday was the cook's night off and the Ambassador usually made his favorite lamb stew. He and Jacqueline not only shared personal feelings, but private jokes and even some outlandish games such as throwing lamb bones at the departing housekeeper, trying to hit her as she left the room.

"Next to my husband and my own father," Jacqueline said, "I love him more than anybody—more than anybody in the world."

*   *   *

"It all started during Christmas [1954] in Florida," Jacqueline recalled. He knew that she liked to paint "so for Christmas he bought me a real luxury painting set and an easel you'd never think of getting for yourself. When I came down Christmas Day, there was Jack at the easel. I guess it's like men giving their sons electric trains. That painting was a godsend for him. That first day he worked right through from morning until eleven that night. He really sticks to something when he gets started."

"I was at Harvard when he came back to the hospital in 1955, and we both did a lot of painting then," Ted Kennedy said. "We'd start out in the morning and pick out something to paint —we'd both paint the same thing. Then by suppertime, we'd have a daiquiri and get a visiting friend to decide which of our paintings was the best. He was immobilized a lot of that time, but when he could get outdoors this was the one thing he could do. I can remember there were about twenty of his paintings in a closet and they were all thrown out. There are still a few good ones around—Ethel has a couple. And he later did some good sketches of his house."

"He loves to paint on a weekend," Jacqueline said. "You should see this room. We put canvas and papers on the floor. He wears a surgeon's uniform I got for him. There's paint everywhere. It's really messy. I told him Churchill has a man who cleans his brushes with turpentine. So I do that."

Jack asked Bill Walton to teach him how to paint properly.

"I'll teach you how if you make me a promise that you will never have an exhibition of your paintings."

"He did a lot of terrible paintings," Walton remembered, "but he was enjoying himself. The three of us were in a boat on the Cape one day, and Kay Graham was with us while I was doing some sketch of a scene on the shore, and Kay said, 'Aren't you terribly nervous with the President of the United States looking over your shoulder while you're sketching?'

" 'He's my friend, and he doesn't know anything about painting and he wants to watch to see how I do it,' I said. When I finished," Walton continued, "Jackie snatched the sketch away and framed it and gave it to him as a present."

"*I* should be giving it," Walton told her.

"No," she said. "I'm giving it. It's my frame and it's my gift."

Walton afterwards laughed. "But that's the way they *both* were!"

For his wife's birthday present, Jack confided, "I'm drawing it."

"Jack painted those," Jacqueline said, pointing out a quay in Granada and a harbor in Cannes. She explained that he had never been to Granada but had been inspired by a magazine photograph.

He asked her to photograph some houses on their street, which he would use as models. He painted intensely for a short time, finally quit when he realized "he had no gift." But in this time of pain and painting, Jack and Jacqueline found themselves closer than ever. What they shared then was what they liked best in each other—their intelligence, their wit, their saucy irreverence towards the world.

"She's poetic, whimsical, provocative, independent, and yet very feminine," her brother-in-law Robert said. "Jackie has always kept her own identity and been different. That's important in a woman. What husband wants to come home at night and talk to another version of himself? Jack knows she'll never greet him with, 'What's new in Laos?' "

"But when Jack and Jackie and I were together, there was nothing shy or quiet about Jackie," Walton said. "She was involved with all our conversations, and actively. She was very talkative. She had opinions on everything. Jackie was always a lot more private than Jack because Jack had his privacy broken up by politics."

Kennedy always steered dinner conversation to politics, and politics bored Jacqueline into nearly total silence. She had tried. She took courses in American History at Georgetown University's School of Foreign Service in the spring of 1954, but they helped little. "The more I hear Jack talk about such intricate and vast problems, the more I feel like a complete moron. If he'd only change to European history, I'd have a chance."

Then she tried to rationalize it. "The men do talk most of the time, but that's the way it should be. The women add something from time to time. You don't ring a bell and say, 'Now we're going to talk about books.' "

She once decided to dazzle her husband at dinner with a probing, provocative question. She discussed the problem with her brother-in-law Robert, who advised, "Ask him whether it isn't true that confirming Albert Beeson to membership on the National Labor Relations Board has the effect of wrecking the Bonwit Teller clause of the National Labor Relations Act."

When she asked the question, her husband almost choked with laughter. He did not think it so funny when a prominent Democrat asked Jacqueline where the Democratic Party should hold its 1960 convention.

With a straight face, she answered, "Acapulco."

They both loved books. A friend visiting them on a Christmas vacation in Montego Bay, Jamaica, recalled how Jack borrowed a book after lunch and returned it at dinner, discussing it in great detail. "I read about twelve hundred words a minute but he must have read it at eighteen hundred words a minute. And he knew everything in it. It was remarkable."

"Knowing Jack devours all those words in a minute throws me into a state of depression," Jacqueline said. "He will know everything, and I will be illiterate."

In defense, she and her sister-in-law Jean took a speed-reading course. Jean recalled, "I was only halfway down the test page when she'd finished." At the end of it, Jacqueline was told that she read almost as fast as her husband.

Jack Kennedy once explained why he was able to concentrate and remember: "I'll pick up an article, and I'll read it, then I'll force myself to lie down for about a half hour and go through the total article in my mind, bringing to memory as much as I possibly can, analyzing the article, and then attacking it and tearing it down."

Even if he wasn't the fantasy perfect husband she thought she had married, he was still her husband. "And she had an elephant's memory when somebody cut Jack," according to Ethel. When her husband complained about some politician, she promptly put that person on her enemy list. It bewildered her when Jack spoke agreeably about the same man. "Why are you saying nice things about that rat? I've been hating him for three weeks now."

"You can't take things personally," her husband answered, adding that there were no friends or enemies in politics because one never knew when political winds would change. "He'll be nice enough next week when he wants me to do something for him."

"She breathes all the political gases that flow around us," Kennedy told a friend, "but she never seems to inhale them."

"Asking Jackie to get interested in politics was like asking Rocky Graziano to play the piano," Spalding said. "She just didn't have any desire in the world to do it. She was smart enough, but it was out of her field. She didn't have the taste or stomach for it. Her nature was literary and artistic. Let's face it, he loved politics and she hated it."

All her life she had been taught that politics was bad manners. Roosevelt was a dirty word to be hissed at, and politicians were "a bunch of baboons."

To add to her bitter suspicion of politics, there was the society item intimating that one of the reasons Jack had picked her for his bride was because he was politically weak in the French-speaking part of Massachusetts.

Adlai Stevenson was working on a speech and motioned to her. "Jackie, come over here. I want to try a line out on you." She went and listened and gave a weak "ha-ha."

"What kind of laugh is that for a politician's wife?" Jack Kennedy said to her quietly after she returned.

"And then he turned to me," Jim Rowe said, and added, "Jackie is superb in her personal life, but do you think she'll ever amount to anything in her political life?"

"Jackie popped up quickly," Rowe continued, "and I've always loved her for it—'Jack is superb in his political life, but do you think he'll ever amount to anything in his personal life?' "

The first to notice this attitude, and comment on it, were reporters' wives. They watched her at parties, often sitting by herself, her husband generally ignoring her. As she sat there, with grace and poise, it seemed that the most important thing to her was her privacy.

Sometimes her reaction was physical. When talk turned to politics at a party given by columnist Roscoe Drummond, "she almost literally took a chair, turned it towards a corner, and sat there for the entire evening without bothering to talk to anybody."

Life had changed for them in these few years after their marriage, she told a friend. Everything had been so much more informal at the beginning. They had gone to more movies, seen more young people. "Now it's more formal. Now we see much older people who are the ages of my mother's friends, or else political jackals who drive me up the wall." There were now the constant phone calls for him. "The damn phone rings so much we can't even get through dinner together."

Or Senator Kennedy might casually tell her one morning to expect forty people for lunch.

"I told him I felt like we were running a boarding house, and he didn't understand."

She became more quickly critical of "those terrible politicians" and admitted, "Politics was sort of my enemy as far as seeing Jack was concerned."

"I can understand the way she felt about those politicians," Letitia Baldrige said. "They sprawled all over her furniture, broke her Sèvres ashtrays, dropped their cigarette butts in her vases, and, most of all, took up her husband's time."

"My theories for a successful marriage? I was afraid you'd ask that," she told an interviewer grimly in 1955. "I can't say I have any yet."

Nevertheless, she had made her impact on him. When he was first sworn into the Senate, his secretary said, "He looked like he had just got out of bed and he was so fidgety, so ill at ease." Jack always looked rumpled then and might even wear unmatched socks. After their marriage his suits fit perfectly, were conservatively cut and perfectly pressed, and were predominantly single-breasted and blue pin-striped. "It was so odd to me the way he grew in stages," his secretary continued. "From a fumbling person who couldn't tie his own tie, and it was always too long, to an *immaculate* dresser. Jackie was so immaculate and maybe it rubbed off on him."

He became so conscious of correct clothes that he once told his friend Spalding, "Your suit doesn't make a statement." When he realized what he had said, they both laughed.

It was his father's personal plea to Senate Majority Leader Lyndon Johnson that helped put him on the Senate Foreign Relations Committee. Every member of the Senate Foreign Relations Committee was supposed to head a consultative committee and, since Kennedy was the most junior member, he got the subcommittee nobody else wanted—Africa. But he did his homework well. Marguerite Higgins of the *New York Herald-Tribune* once listened to his facts and figures on how many colonies in Africa were going to become independent countries, the level of literacy and per capita income, and how much aid they needed to prevent a Russian takeover. Higgins had a question: "Has your subcommittee on Africa ever met?"

The young Senator hesitated before he finally answered, "No."

Foreign Relations Committee Chairman J. William Fulbright, in trying to collect a committee quorum, told his assistant, "Call up that Jack Kennedy. All he does is sit there at the end of the table—if you ever get him here. And when he *does* sit down there, he sits there autographing pictures of himself."

Republican senators Hugh Scott and Kenneth Keating prepared a well-circulated letter chiding Kennedy's absenteeism. When Kennedy became a Harvard Overseer (on his second try), he was photographed in a formal cutaway, and Scott and Keating wrote: "We miss you, Jack, but of course we're here wearing plain everyday clothes." They offered to send him minutes of the many meetings he missed, and added, "Don't hurry back . . . we want you to know that the work of the Senate goes on."

The Senate began to bore him. He didn't like the interminable casual conversations that went on among senators: "shooting bull without responsibility"; he wasn't very good on the Senate floor because he never took time to learn the parliamentary rules; he didn't have the patience needed to push an idea into law by compromising positions and converting others. It was a chore. His attendance record was bad.

The personality trait Kennedy most struggled against, and unsuccessfully, was his impatience. He was unwilling to hear what he already knew. His signals included a nervous finger rubbing his forehead, and a quick word of interruption. He was not one for painstaking persuasion.

As for his overall record as senator, Ted Sorensen wrote, "His contribution as a freshman senator was too modest to be included in what I have termed the Kennedy legacy."

His prime time of growth was still to come.

The six were relaxing in the garden after dinner in Ben Bradlee's Georgetown house some months before the 1956 Democratic Nominating Convention. The guests were Sen. and Mrs. John Kennedy and Mr. and Mrs. Kenneth Crawford. Crawford was a distinguished foreign correspondent who was then the Washington bureau chief of *Newsweek*, and Bradlee's boss. In the midst of a quiet conversation, William McCormick Blair arrived. Tall, debonair Bill Blair was the best friend and closest adviser of Adlai Stevenson. No one was more aware of Stevenson's views. Before the end of the evening, Blair was making an impassioned pitch for Kennedy to make a serious try for the vice-presidency by stirring up widespread support. Kennedy listened hard and said little, but Jacqueline turned to Ken Crawford and said, in her soft voice, "Why is Bill trying to persuade Jack to run for vice-president when Jack *really* wants to be president?"

A Moment of Magic

With the growing certainty of Adlai Stevenson's renomination for president in 1956, the question of the vice-presidency took on a fresh urgency.

Kennedy saw an item in the Periscope column of *Newsweek* magazine mentioning him as a much-talked-about vice-presidential possibility. "He called me," said Periscope editor Debs Myers. "He asked me who were all these people discussing him for the vice-presidency, and I laughed and told him the truth, 'Me!'"

"I don't know where it all started," Kennedy said afterwards. "I remember I was up in Rhode Island visiting my mother-in-law and Governor Roberts talked to me about it. He's an old friend. Then Abe [Governor Abraham Ribicoff of Connecticut] openly proposed me for the vice-presidency at the governors' conference that year."

In a letter to Kennedy, Ribicoff reported that he had asked Connecticut boss John Bailey to urge Stevenson to pick Kennedy. Stevenson's divorce had been a serious issue in his 1952 defeat, and Bailey argued that a Catholic running mate might not only counteract that issue but also give great heart to minority groups. Bailey had been blunt: "I want a Catholic on the ticket."

Ted Sorensen quickly prepared a sixteen-page summary of argument and analysis, packed with statistics. Its essence was the Democratic need to recapture the thirty percent of normally Democratic Catholic voters who had shifted to Eisenhower in the previous election. Those Catholic votes represented the margin of victory over Stevenson. Sorensen passed the memo on to Connecticut State Chairman John Bailey for circulation and it became known as the Bailey Memorandum.

Adlai Stevenson remembered: "Now I had never talked to John Kennedy about the vice-presidency, but his father came to see me several times—he had contributed to my campaign— and we talked about Jack in a general way. I had a personal fondness for Jack and I admired him, and I told his father that. Then, of course, Jack's sister Eunice and her husband, Sarge Shriver, are good friends of mine. There was also our concern for the Catholic vote, which we had lost in 1952. Yes, we had thought seriously about Jack as a vice-presidential candidate."

Kennedy was driving Sorensen home from the office in Washington and they were discussing a letter from Arthur Schlesinger, Jr., who was pushing the Kennedy candidacy in the Stevenson camp. He had written, "Things look good." To this comment Kennedy said, "You know, I'm getting a little interested in the vice-presidency."

"That's against our agreement," Sorensen said, smiling. "You weren't supposed to get interested in it, so that if you didn't get it you wouldn't be disappointed. Now you will."

Kennedy fingered his heavy mop of hair, thought a minute, and said, "Yes I will, a little bit—from the end of the convention session on Friday to the time I head for Europe on Saturday."

In July, Jack received a telegram from his brother-in-law in Chicago, Robert Sargent Shriver, Jr., quoting the *Chicago Sun-Times* article in which Stevenson had said he liked Kennedy and Humphrey as vice-presidential candidates. The *Sun-Times* then editorialized that it preferred Kennedy, reminding readers that Franklin Delano Roosevelt was a year younger than Kennedy when he was nominated for vice-president in 1920.

On the Sunday before the convention opened, Kennedy suggested Sorensen call some friends to his hotel suite to discuss the vice-presidency. "You call them," said the senator with a smile. "You are responsible for the whole thing."

"No," Sorensen replied. "I'm responsible only if you lose. If you win, you will be known as the greatest political strategist in convention history."

"I went to see Jack Kennedy during convention week," said Adlai Stevenson's close friend Bill Blair. "I wanted to find out just how serious he was about the vice-presidency. And he told me he was very serious because he felt that the only way a Catholic could ever become president in our lifetime was if a Catholic could get on the national ticket in a low period of Democratic fortunes, when they were strongly concerned about the Catholic vote. And he felt that this was the year when Democrats were in real trouble and needed such help."

In a meeting of big-city political bosses, most of them Catholic, their argument against Kennedy was that a Catholic candidate would stir up too much controversy. Ribicoff found it ironic. "I didn't think that the time would ever come when a Jew would have to stand up in a room full of Catholics to urge the acceptability of a Catholic."

*   *   *

The room was filled with Roosevelts: Mrs. Franklin D. Roosevelt, two of her sons, James and Elliott, and Elliott's wife. They were all in the bedroom of a suite at the Blackstone Hotel and the phones never stopped ringing. Several grandchildren came in for their convention tickets, and Mrs. Roosevelt told them, "Just sit on the beds—I'm busy."

"When Jack and I arrived," said Abba Schwartz, a friend of

both the Roosevelts and the Kennedys, "there was also a young lady typing in the corner. Mrs. Roosevelt was rushed. She hadn't planned to be very active in this convention, but she was. This was eleven-thirty in the morning and she had to go on television at twelve."

If her timetable was tight, she kept it quietly on schedule. She had agreed to see the young senator at the behest of Schwartz. She had accepted the meeting reluctantly because she not only had qualms about the senator but a strong dislike for his father. She would not forget or forgive his father's intensely bitter fight with her husband before the war. Her young friend Abba had appealed to her openmindedness and generous spirit, so she greeted Kennedy with her usual grace; perhaps the look in her eyes was more quizzical than usual. In this meeting of the great lady and the young man, the tension was palpable.

"The room was so noisy," Kennedy recalled. "It was like eighteen people in a telephone booth—and it was such a short interview, and it was hardly a place of a basis for judgment."

"No, the room wasn't too noisy," said James Roosevelt, later a strong Kennedy supporter. "There were a few other people, but it really wasn't noisy, no. I introduced Jack to my mother and then I went over and sat on the bed and I wasn't really listening. But it was a very short interview.

"After it was over, mother told us what she had said. She had asked Jack if he didn't now feel that he should have taken a stronger position against McCarthyism and would he do so now. Something like that. And she wasn't satisfied with what he said; that's all."

On the first night of the 1956 convention, August 15, Kennedy went to the platform to take a bow after his narration of a film on the history of the Democratic Party, called *The Pursuit of Happiness.* The ovation was surprisingly loud and long.

CBS-TV considered the film too long and cut away from it to cover other things at the convention. Charles Collingwood recalled kidding Kennedy when he saw him later: "Well, you didn't make CBS," he told him.

Kennedy and Collingwood had been neighbors and friends in Georgetown for years, but Kennedy gave him a hateful look. "I know," he said, "you bastards."

"I was shocked into silence," Collingwood said. "I just didn't know it meant that much to him."

Newton Minow shared a cab with his law partner, Stevenson, and made a more fervent appeal for Kennedy as the vice-presidential nominee. Stevenson then went into a heated attack on Joseph Kennedy, Sr.

"How can you blame the kid for his father?" Minow protested.

For a moment, Stevenson was silent, then said more quietly, "He's too young."

Stevenson then asked Kennedy to make the nominating speech. Sorensen queried Stevenson aide Willard Wirtz on whether this meant that Kennedy was therefore eliminated from consideration as a vice-presidential nominee.

Wirtz, a Humphrey man, answered, "Yes."

Tom Winship of the *Boston Globe* was next to Kennedy when he looked over the copy of the nominating speech. "I remember the way he clenched his fists," Winship said, "and whispered to himself, 'Go!' Then he pushed himself towards the podium and gave his speech."

A woman reporter near the podium vividly recalled Kennedy looking "terribly thin, terribly tired, and terribly handsome."

Kennedy described Eisenhower and Nixon as "one who takes the high road and one who takes the low road"—and the crowd came alive. A photographer took a picture of an excited Jacqueline Kennedy standing on her seat in the convention box, furiously waving a Stevenson banner. Aside from that convention appearance, she kept close to her sister-in-law Eunice's apartment on Lake Shore Drive, alone much of the time. After three years of marriage, she was then seven months pregnant with her first child.

She did attend a breakfast with her husband at the Palmer House for the New England delegates, and also went to Perle Mesta's champagne party for campaign women at the Blackstone Hotel. As "the hostess with the mostest," Mesta may not have remembered Jacqueline as the Inquiring Photographer who had interviewed her four years before, but she was free with her comments. "I wasn't prepared for Jack Kennedy to be wearing brown loafers with his tuxedo." She also called Mrs. Kennedy "a beatnik," pointing out that she didn't even wear stockings. Privately, Jacqueline said that Mesta's extravagant party was "too obvious" and that Perle Mesta acted "like a distiller's wife."

A reporter described Jacqueline as looking wide-eyed, like a little girl at a grown-up party, and quoted her as saying: "It's all too confusing. I don't know if John is going to be nominated for vice-president or not. I'm very proud of him, no matter what."

"Jacqueline was standing by herself. She was a very pretty girl; she didn't seem ill at ease, exactly. But she was out of things, not really a part of what was going on." Jacqueline later confided that she was "unsure and too shy."

In the Stevenson camp, meanwhile, a young aide, John Sharon, had proposed an exciting idea to stir the dull convention: break tradition and let the delegates pick the vice-presidential nominee. Sharon's most crucial convert was George Ball, Stevenson's old friend, a distinguished international lawyer. Ball pushed the idea hard. Stevenson finally agreed and made the melodramatic request at the convention.

"We were absolutely stunned at that statement," said Ken O'Donnell. "Bobby Kennedy and I bummed a ride back to the hotel and I said, 'Now what the hell are we gonna do about it?' Bobby and I didn't know two people in the place. Neither of us had ever been to a convention in our lives. . . ."

"I remember Jack Kennedy coming in," said Newton Minow, "and telling Stevenson, 'It's a fixed convention. You've set it against me.' "

Soon afterwards, former Democratic National Chairman Steve Mitchell saw Kennedy "looking real down and discouraged and he asked me what I thought. I said I thought he had a helluva good chance but he better start scrambling. He just looked at me unbelievingly and said how could I say he had any kind of chance at all when he had no organization, no obvious support except from New England, and all the big states like New York and Pennsylvania had their own candidates. I told him he better stop talking statistics and get on a horse and ride because he had a lot of support he didn't know anything about, *'especially from the South,'* I emphasized. His whole face lit up after that and he asked me to help him and I told him why I couldn't, and then off he went, but he now had a lot of fresh hope in his face."

Kennedy and Charles Bartlett were in the elevator at the Hilton. There was only one other man in the elevator, and he was wearing dark glasses. It was Carmine DeSapio, Tammany boss of the New York delegation, with ninety-eight votes. Kennedy didn't recognize him, but Bartlett did. When the door opened and they all exited, Bartlett whispered, "Jack, that's DeSapio."

"Think I ought to talk to him?" Jack asked.

"Sure, why not, what have you got to lose?"

Kennedy walked quickly over to him and introduced himself, saying, "Mr. DeSapio, my name is Senator Jack Kennedy and I would like to talk to you about getting your support for my nomination."

"He was like a shy, aged little boy approaching some powerful man," Bartlett said. "I'll never forget it."

Bobby called their father on the French Riviera, informing him that Jack was making the race. The Ambassador had turned negative on that idea months before. "I told him it was a terrible mistake. I knew Stevenson didn't have a chance. I felt that if Jack ran with him, it would be a terrible mistake because it was hopeless." He had written Jack earlier noting that their friend Ambassador Clare Boothe Luce agreed with him because "a defeat would be a devastating blow to your prestige." Now, in his phone call with Bobby, the father's language was loud and blue, calling Jack an idiot for ruining his career. "Whew!" said Bobby. "Is he mad!"

"I was with Dad on the Riviera when Bobby called," Ted Kennedy said. "I know Dad was mad at first, but then he spent the next eighteen hours on the phone calling everybody he knew at the convention to help Jack."

"When I got to Jack's hotel room," said Jack's brother-in-law, Sargent Shriver, "there were Jack and Bobby and Eunice and Jean and Teddy and it looked like a family conference up at the Cape instead of a political meeting, except there were Ted Sorensen and Bailey and a few others. There was Bobby with a yellow pad in his hand, writing down the states and the delegates, and Jack would say, 'I think I can get four or five of those delegates,' or something like that. It was all pretty amateurish."

"And, finally, John Bailey jumped up," recalled young Representative Ed Boland of Massachusetts, "and Bailey said, 'This isn't the way to do this thing.' And then Bailey started to assign state delegations to specific people for them to contact before the balloting started the next day."

"I know I didn't change clothes all night," John Bailey said. "I don't suppose many of the others did."

"The only time I remember being involved was the night before the race," Jacqueline Kennedy recalled. "I don't remember Jack there exactly but I remember a lot of commotion and Bobby saying that we must try to get all the votes we could for the next day. I remember him asking me if I knew anyone in Nevada or some other states. I can remember being there a lot that night. I think when something like that starts and gets a momentum, then you want it, yes. . . ."

Someone who did know someone in the Nevada delegation was Kennedy's brother-in-law, actor Peter Lawford. Lawford's friend Wilbur Clark, the Las Vegas operator of the Desert Inn, was chairman of the Nevada delegation. Lawford and his pregnant wife Pat were sleeping in their Santa Monica home when a Kennedy called them at three in the morning. Lawford called Clark. That afternoon, Kennedy got thirteen of Nevada's fourteen votes.

Kennedy then went to see Governor Earl Long of Louisiana. Long greeted his young visitor still wearing his long, one-piece winter underwear that came down to his ankles. While Senator Kennedy told the governor why he felt he should be the vice-presidential nominee, "the last of the red hot poppas"—as Long described himself—carefully took out his false teeth, rubbed them reflectively, examined their polish, and replaced them. But by the time Kennedy had finished, Long had decided to support him.

"I talked to Lyndon too," Kennedy continued. "But he gave me a kind of noncommittal answer. Maybe Hubert thought Lyndon was for him and maybe Symington thought the same thing and maybe Gore thought that, too, and maybe Lyndon wanted them all to think just that. We never knew how that one would turn out."

After making his rounds of some delegations, Kennedy returned to the hotel "pretty discouraged." "It looked like Kefauver easily," he said. "He had Ohio and Pennsylvania. [Mayor] Wagner was in it and had New York, New Jersey, and Delaware . . . but then I heard the Illinois delegates were going to give me majority support. I really started sweating then."

It was a kind of madness, the candidates racing from one caucus to another. At one point Kennedy came barging around a corner and almost collided with Kefauver, who was doing a two-minute spot for TV. They solemnly shook hands, wished each other good luck, and Kennedy raced on to another caucus.

Convention tradition stands strict: Candidates will keep out of the convention hall during the balloting. Teetotaler Gore watched it on TV at a bar across the street, Humphrey planted himself in Speaker Rayburn's room behind the platform, and Kefauver and Kennedy stayed in small rooms at the Stockyard Inn, about five hundred feet from the amphitheater.

Staying with Kennedy in Room 104 were Tom Winship, a *Boston Globe* newspaperman, and Ted Sorensen.

"Everything was all taken care of that we could think of," said Sorensen, "so we took off our shoes, stretched out on the beds, turned on the television, and there it was, the culmination of everything."

And it was all so fairyland unreal. Kennedy, lying on his bed in undershorts, had a pillow supporting his shoulders, his left hand behind his head; and he lay there watching, his bare toes twitching, his face serious. The tub was running.

"What had been merely interesting to me," he said, "now became important."

"Bobby Kennedy was supposed to be a floor manager for Jack at that convention, but that's a lot of crap," Ken O'Donnell said. "There was no floor manager; there was just nobody in control. Everybody was out on his own, talking to anybody and everybody he could, and there was a helluva lot of overlapping."

In the Kennedy box, the Kennedy sisters were all chattering

nervously. The visibly pregnant Jacqueline Kennedy sat serenely among them. Whenever anybody looked at her, she was smiling. There was no hint of glamour girl about her then. *Chicago Sun-Times* reporter Rita Fitzpatrick recalled, "She looked like a dainty teen-ager, dressed in a teen-age-like dress, with very short hair. She was very shy of the press and talked in a tiny girl-like voice." She was then twenty-seven.

She told a reporter that her husband was "much more serious than I thought he was before I married him."

Asked what she thought of her husband's being the vice-presidential nominee, she answered, "I don't know whether I'll like it or not." Fitzpatrick's feeling was that Jacqueline would not like it.

Reporter Nancy Dickerson walked by and Jackie saw her and asked, "Oh Nancy, what do you think is going to happen?"

While the band was playing "The Star-Spangled Banner," a tall young man tentatively approached the equally tall, older man whose life had been sweetened and soured by political history. He was the Hon. James Aloysius Farley, once a candidate for President of the United States. The young man, Arthur Hadley, was press secretary for former Governor Averell Harriman of New York. Hadley politely passed on to Farley Harriman's invitation to meet immediately.

"Young man," said Farley in his booming voice, "I have made it a faithful practice of my lifetime, and I commend it to you, never to be in motion during the playing of our national anthem."

"Mr. Farley," Hadley said, "Mr. Harriman would like to discuss with you how to stop Kefauver from getting the vice-presidential nomination and how to give it to Senator Kennedy."

"Young man," Farley said, "I have just broken the practice of a lifetime. Lead the way!"

Somebody had taken down the totalizer board, which kept electronic score of the balloting. Delegates were now forced to keep score on backs of envelopes, stray paper, anything they could find—and everybody's score seemed different.

At the end of that first ballot the five thousand onlookers and the more than four thousand delegates and alternates inside the largest roofed convention hall in the world felt the first unexpected shock waves of a dramatic fight. Discounting the usual sprinkling of favorite sons, the sudden support of the South for Kennedy made him the surprise challenger.

The organist played "Linger Awhile" and officials retired to double-check that first-ballot count. It added up to 483½ for Kefauver, 304 for Kennedy, 178 for Gore, and 134½ for Humphrey.

The first big break for Kennedy on the second ballot came when Arkansas switched twenty-six votes from Tennessee Senator Gore to Kennedy. Just before that, Kennedy said, "Estes is going to win." Now he leaned back on his bed, obviously surprised. "I'll be!" he said, and nervously slapped his leg. Then he turned to Sorensen. "Ted, I wish we had a comparison of this roll call with the last." Ted smiled. "We do."

Delaware switched its ten votes to Kennedy. "I spoke to their caucus this morning," Kennedy said. "I think I got those then."

Ted suggested that maybe he'd better "go down to the hall and find out what the procedure is in case anything happens." Kennedy agreed: "I think maybe you better."

"That guy was cool," Shriver said. "He has this wonderful quality of self-containment. I was on the convention floor and I got the word from DeSapio that New York would switch ninety of its ninety-eight votes to him on the second ballot and that Texas was also going to switch to him, and I didn't need much arithmetic to add up the fact that this would put Jack over six hundred on the second ballot and that no candidate had ever lost before with six hundred votes. I ran up to Jack's room and there he was, stretched out on the bed, wiggling his toes, watching TV, and I told him about the expected switching of New York and Texas and six hundred votes and nobody had ever lost before with that many votes and he better get dressed and think of something to say."

Kennedy looked at Shriver and Sorensen and said, "Not yet."

Kennedy lay stretched out on his bed. "I'm bushed," he said. "Two hours' sleep in the last two nights." Ted announced that Jacqueline was on the phone, and Jack went into another room to take the call. He was still in his shorts when some TV men arrived, and he said, "Please, don't take any pictures." Then he turned up the TV louder and made a few comments, "If we don't make it after this one, it'll be a close one, I think. . . . Figure Humphrey will go to Kefauver before too long."

"We were watching the TV," Sorensen said, "and somebody came running in to say that Kefauver was out looking for Humphrey, and so Jack suggested that I better hunt for Humphrey, too, and suggest that he and Kennedy get together. Well, I went to several places and I couldn't find him, and finally I got into an elevator and there was Gene McCarthy [then congressman, later Senator Eugene McCarthy of Minnesota] and I told him what Kennedy had said. All he answered was that we should forget it because they had only Protestants and farmers in his state. Later McCarthy told people that Kennedy had sent a boy to see him."

"Now suppose you were Hubert Humphrey, running hard for Vice-President of the United States," Gene McCarthy said, "and you had this little room in back of the stands, watching the balloting on TV, watching the chances go down the drain, and feeling real lousy about it, and in comes this young man with the announcement that Senator Kennedy would like Senator Humphrey to come across to the Stockyard Inn to see him, almost as though you were being offered an audience with Kennedy. And suppose, minutes later, Estes Kefauver himself comes running up those two flights of stairs and says, 'Hubert, can you help me?' Now suppose you were Hubert Humphrey, which one would you help?"

"Hubert, you've just got to help me," Kefauver was pleading, "You've GOT to help me."

"Everyone was crying," one witness said, "grown men all crying. I'll never forget the water gushing in that room."

*   *   *

Torby MacDonald, Jack's Harvard roommate, was the one who raced into Kennedy's hotel suite and enthusiastically yelled, "Sam Rayburn just swung Texas."

One of the elder Kennedy's calls from the Riviera was to

James Landis. Landis and his partner, Abba Schwartz, paid a visit to Sam Rayburn. Rayburn had been overheard saying to Stevenson, "Well, if we have to have a Catholic, I hope we don't have to take that little piss-ant Kennedy." But Rayburn was even more bitter about Estes Kefauver, whom he regarded as a renegade southerner. After their conversation, Schwartz reported, "The meeting ended to our satisfaction."

It was a dramatic announcement, and Lyndon Johnson milked it.

"Texas proudly casts its fifty-six votes for the fighting sailor who wears the scars of battle. . . ."

In the Kefauver camp, somebody commented weakly to the press, "Texas is an awful big state, isn't it?"

In the Kennedy camp, Jack heard the Texas news and let loose a big grin.

"Oh, there's Jean on TV," he said. His sister and his wife and more of the Kennedy clan were sitting in a box directly behind Nancy Kefauver.

Bobby returned intermittently to yell at his sisters, "Things are going just great."

"Luckily, I had arranged for a couple [of] cops to stand in front of Jack's hotel room," Shriver said, "because the press had figured out what I had figured out and what everybody else had figured out, and they had started rushing over. Jack's room had a back porch running to Charlie Potter's suite down the hall. He runs the Inn. Anyway, I ran down and barged in on him and told him about the reporters and asked him if we could move into his suite. So he and his friends moved downstairs. I went back and told Jack, and he raced down that porch in his underwear and somebody else brought his clothes."

"Ted and I had been putting some words down on paper," Shriver recalled, "and we showed them to him and he looked at it and said, 'Yeah, that sounds all right, but what do I say if I lose?' Hell, New York and Texas had switched to him, nobody in that room thought he could possibly lose—it just never entered our heads. And there he was saying a thing like that."

A switch of several states would ensure Kennedy's nomination. Speaker Sam Rayburn returned to the podium and was deciding which state to recognize.

Soaping himself in the bathtub, Jack Kennedy kept busy thinking up words to accept the vice-presidential nomination. But as he put on his medium-blue suit, a soft-collared white shirt, and a red-dotted light gray tie, his brother-in-law Sarge Shriver rushed in with the bad news, putting a comforting arm around his shoulder, telling him that the trend had turned against him.

TV soon confirmed the fact.

"The moment was crucial," recalled Kefauver supporter Colonel William Roberts. "If Rayburn would recognize Tennessee, then Oklahoma, the tide would turn. I called the floor, told them to get runners down to Rayburn's platform, and yell, 'Tennessee is going for Kennedy. . . . Tennessee is going for Kennedy . . .' because I knew Rayburn never liked Kefauver. It worked. Clarence Cannon on the platform heard the runners and told Rayburn, 'Tennessee, Tennessee. . . .' And Rayburn recognized Tennessee, and there it was, that was the beginning. That's politics."

"Rayburn had just returned to the podium and wasn't looking for trouble," said Kefauver campaign worker Bill Haddad. "Tennessee had gone for Gore on the first ballot and I think Rayburn recognized Tennessee because he expected Tennessee to stay with Gore. I'll never forget that look on Rayburn's face as long as I live, after Tennessee went to Kefauver. He was so shocked, he really lost his composure for a moment."

"Tennessee couldn't switch to Kennedy—no matter what happened—as long as I was in the race," said Tennessee Senator Estes Kefauver. "The State Democratic Convention had decided that it had to stick to a favorite son. Gore had his chance, and if Gore withdrew, it would have to be me."

Kefauver supporter Dixon Donnelly explained why Gore withdrew. A Tennessee millionaire named Bullard had threatened to pour a million dollars into the upcoming Senate campaign to unseat Gore if he didn't release the delegation to Kefauver, and a newspaper publisher named Evans took Gore by the lapels, worked him over in rough language, saying, in effect:

We helped make you and we'll break you if you don't switch to Kefauver.

Whatever it was, it was pivotal. It broke the back of a bandwagon and created a new one. Kennedy supporters were stunned:

"Let's remember one thing: We had North Carolina and some other states ready to switch to Kennedy, and who does Rayburn recognize one, two, three, but Tennessee, Oklahoma, and Missouri, all of them switching to Kefauver. That's what killed us."

The editor of the *Stevenson Bandwagon* stood close to Stevenson and watched him carefully as the TV scoreboard announced Kefauver the winner.

Stevenson uttered an uncharacteristic word: "Shit."

"Something I'll never forget," said Mrs. Dixon Donnelly, a dedicated Kefauver worker, "was Nancy Kefauver and the beautiful Jackie Kennedy in their boxes during the voting. There was no one around Nancy, and Jackie was surrounded by people. Then Estes won and suddenly there was no one with Jackie. She was left by herself at the end. She was pregnant and she just stood there and she was a very sad and forlorn figure."

"When Kefauver got it," Sorensen said, "the Senator looked at me and said, 'Let's go.'"

"We all raced down the back stairs," recalled Sarge Shriver, who was also there, "and we got into the amphitheater through a back door, without any cops. In fact, the cops stopped us at the platform, and somebody recognized us and told the cops to let us through. While we were running, Jack and I talked over what he should say. We got up there on the platform, sat down, and somebody told Rayburn we were there and then he recognized Jack and introduced him."

TV coverage of conventions was still something fresh and surprising in 1956, and a hundred million Americans were watching. They saw this freshman senator on the podium before a packed national political convention, listening to the roar, picking at some invisible dust on his boyish, handsome face, nervously dry-washing his hands, waving to yelling friends nearby, his smile tentative but warmly appealing, his eyes slightly wet and glistening.

He spoke without notes, and his words were short, gallant, and touching. For the TV audience, it was a moment of magic they would not forget. Nor would they forget Jacqueline standing alongside her husband on the podium. Looking at her, one would not have known there was any despair in her pride. Her husband had lost but he was not beaten. Defeat was not in her face.

"After it was all over, we went over to his room, and it was pretty crowded, all of the family and a lot of Jack's buddies," Senator Smathers said.

"What impressed me was that Jack really showed more emotion than I'd really seen him display up to that point, and Jackie even shed some tears. I was just shocked that Jackie had taken it so seriously, felt so deeply about it. After all, the whole thing was only a twelve-hour operation. But then Congressman Ben Smith was crying and a lot of people were sniffling and crying. I guess a lot of hearts were set on it.

"Jack didn't say much. One great thing about Jack—he was a man of few words, really. He made a few remarks about some supposed friends who let him down, but then he stood up on the corner of the bed and I kept wondering if he was going to fall and hurt himself. But he told everybody, 'Look, it's all over. We did great considering what time we had. I want to thank everybody.' And then he made some joke about my speech being cut off. But I knew he was hurt, deeply hurt. The thing is, he came so close. These Kennedys, once they're in something, they don't like to lose. But it was great the way he could joke about it."

O'Donnell tried to console him, saying how lucky he was because Stevenson was "going to run a lousy campaign and probably lose."

Bobby told his depressed brother, "You're better off than you ever were in your life, and you made a great fight, and they're not going to win, and you're going to be the candidate the next time."

Kennedy bristled. "This morning all of you were telling me

to get into this thing and now you're telling me I should feel happy because I lost it."

To his close friends, Kennedy said, "I feel like the Indian who had a lot of arrows stuck in him and, when he was asked how he felt, said, 'It only hurts when I laugh.'"

One of his first telephone calls was to his father on the French Riviera. "We did our best, Dad," he said. "I had fun and I didn't make a fool of myself."

The elder Kennedy was at Val-sur-mer with his guest, Clare Boothe Luce, US ambassador to Italy. Mrs. Luce remarked on how proud Kennedy must be of his son's close race for the vice-presidential nomination.

"Yes, I was," Kennedy said, "but it would have pleased me a lot more if he had run on the Republican ticket."

What his father didn't say then, but said later was, "If I had been there, I would have won that nomination for Jack. How? I would have had a recess after the first ballot, and that would have given us enough time to organize and win."

Flying back to Boston, Bobby Kennedy was bitter. He said they should have won. "Somebody pulled something fishy."

But Jack Kennedy told his secretary there would be another time. The next morning he was on his way to Paris and the Riviera.

I've been here a long time and I've seen a lot of politicians come and go, and a lot of Presidents too. So I didn't pay much attention to Kennedy at first. I wondered how much depth was there or whether it was mostly veneer. And I think I concluded then that there wasn't that much depth. There was nothing in his senatorial career that made him stand out. It was only later that I realized he was something special.

—CLARK CLIFFORD, *Kennedy advisor*

The Man Who Would Be President

Jacqueline had been at her husband's bedside all those months when he needed her, and now she needed him. After an earlier miscarriage, she was now in the final months of another pregnancy—and wanted him close. But he had planned a trip to France with friends, right after the 1956 convention, and he was determined to go. Smathers insists that Jacqueline told him, "Jack's worked so hard and he's nervous about this thing and I think you all ought to go off and have a good time." But another friend similarly insisted that "Jackie was so bitter about him leaving her that she said she didn't care about the baby." His secretary recalled that he had slept at the Drake that night in Chicago after the convention and his wife again slept alone at her sister-in-law's apartment.

Jack and his friends stopped off in Paris at the George V for a night on the town, then went to Cannes on the Riviera to rent a fifty-foot sailboat and head for Italy. A *Washington Star* reporter later interviewed the skipper and cook, who reported the presence aboard of several young women.

Jacqueline went to Hammersmith Farm, her mother's home in Newport, and a week later miscarried a baby girl. Her brother-in-law Robert hurried to her side while the *Washington Post* headlined a front-page story: SENATOR KENNEDY ON MEDITERRANEAN TRIP UNAWARE HIS WIFE HAS LOST BABY. When Kennedy telephoned from Genoa, Smathers told him, "You better haul your ass back to your wife if you ever want to run for president." Kennedy returned two days later.

Within days of his return, Kennedy was away again. This time he was campaigning for Adlai Stevenson in twenty-six states.

*　　*　　*

After his defeat by Eisenhower, Stevenson had said that John Kennedy would be "the one person people will remember from the convention." It was true. The time had passed when a Chicago reporter carried a picture of Kennedy to search him out in a crowd because she didn't know what he looked like. Now, when Kennedy and a friend walked out of a Manhattan men's shop, people turned their heads to look. "Do you realize how prominent you are now, that all these people recognize you?" his friend commented.

"Yes," Kennedy said. "I am well aware of it."

He said it simply, without conceit, as a point of fact.

As they passed the newsstands, the two men could not help noticing John Kennedy's picture on the cover of so many magazines.

"Gee, Jack, you must be getting *sick* of all that stuff—all these—magazines, what do they write about? Aren't they all writing about the same thing?"

Jack Kennedy turned to Rowland Evans, Jr. "Yes, I *am* getting a little sick of it. What do you want me to do about it? Tell the magazine writers not to write about me and send them back to their offices empty-handed? Of course not." Then he paused and smiled, "Besides, these stories about me do have one effect. They help take the 'v' out of the 'v.p.' "

What he meant was that there was still too much press mention of him as a vice-presidential possibility in 1960. "I wish you'd take those goddamn words out of your typewriter because I'm never going to take second place," he told Associated Press reporter Jack Bell.

The vice-presidential discussion was one of the few ways to trigger his anger. At first, he had tried to pass it off with humor. "Let's not talk so much about vice. I'm against vice in all forms." Then he was simply serious. "I am not going to accept the vice-presidential nomination. . . . I don't recall a single case where a vice-presidential candidate contributed an electoral vote. . . . My guess is that, if I don't get the nomination this time, I would be through as far as the White House is concerned. It's all a matter of events, not of time. No, I won't keep trying. I wouldn't try at another date. Look, I've been on this bicycle for ten years. If I'm not going to make it this time, I'm not going to be another Kefauver, always grasping for something I can't have. To hell with that."

To others, Jack was even more intense about the presidency. His whole face contorted and he almost banged his fist and leaned his face close to a reporter and said, "I must get it NOW! NOW!"

"Why has Jack got this overwhelming compulsiveness that it must be now?" *New Republic* editor Helen Fuller asked. "If somebody else gets it, eight years is a long time to keep his face fresh . . . eight more years of decision votes, which will increase his enemies as well as his friends. There is also the personal thing. His marriage to Jackie is on the thin edge. Right now Jackie has got the White House bug. She feels it will compensate for a lot of other things, maybe for everything else. Getting the V.P. would still hold them together, but what would happen to Jack if he got neither? He might disintegrate. His marriage might bust up, too. Tie up a busted marriage with the Catholic issue and you're politically dead."

Friends noted a growing change in him. The highly opinionated young man who "couldn't see how anything he said wasn't absolutely right" now became a quiet, respectful listener. He became more discreet, more serious, more careful, more "obviously on the make."

A great many senators were jealous of Kennedy because he could always get on page one or on TV with his ideas, "while another senator with the same idea would be lucky to get near the classified ads."

Even his father felt the unending publicity was too much.

"Dad, all they're writing about is what I've done up to now. There'll be more to write of what I intend to do." Then John Kennedy quoted baseball manager John McGraw: "Every ball game you win in April is one you won't need in September."

The elder Kennedy never stopped fighting for control. At a Drew Pearson party, he recruited family friend and Washington social hostess Kay Halle, to help him change his son's mind on some Senate legislation. When his son arrived, Joseph Kennedy approached him with Halle and said, "Jack, I know you're going to vote on this bill this week, and I think you're wrong. I'd like to discuss it and we can get Kay's independent judgment on it."

Jack Kennedy gave his father a long look and answered quietly, "Dad, you've been marvelous to me, but I don't want you to interfere with my politics."

The Ambassador turned to Kay. "See? That's why I gave each of my kids a million dollars—so that they can spit in my face."

"Jack often votes against my views," the father later complained, specifying foreign aid and the oil depletion allowance. "We disagree on things all the time." Yet, he understood why. He once told Sen. George Aiken the advice he had given his son for political success: "Be against everything that your old man has stood for—in business, government, and philosophy."

But it always bothered him. "You know I must be nuts," he told liberal Supreme Court Justice William Douglas. "I can't understand how the two men I admire most in public life, my son and your own self, stand for ideas that I so bitterly oppose."

When his college classmate Torby MacDonald, then a congressman, complained about being known as a Kennedy protégé, Jack told him, "I had to live under my father's name for thirty years. I outgrew it and I guess you can outgrow me."

"I think he just decided it was time to have a fight with his father," Spalding mused. "The issue didn't matter. I don't even know what it was. But I know it happened. I think he just said of his father, 'He's never going to stop. I'll never get out from under. I'll just have to carry this thing around until I draw the line.' And then one day he just drew the line.

"It was as if Jack went down in the pit with his father and went to war with him. I know they didn't talk to each other for almost a year."

*   *   *

Following the Senate censure of Senator Joseph Raymond McCarthy, the Wisconsin senator faded fast. He drank heavily. "I was at his house once," recalled a *Newsweek* reporter, "and I saw him take a quarter-pound stick of butter, bite off half of it, and swallow it. I asked him what the hell he was doing and he answered, 'Oh this helps me hold my liquor better.' "

On the day McCarthy died, Bobby Kennedy called in his staff and told them he wanted to close the office for an hour out of respect for McCarthy's death. "I want to do this," he said softly, his head bowed, his eyes wet.

"It was the only time I had ever seen tears in his eyes," said his personal secretary.

Bobby went to the McCarthy funeral, but John Kennedy didn't. The two brothers later saw McCarthy's widow. Bobby embraced her, but John stood apart, "maybe because I was there," recalled Laura Bergquist of *Look*, "but I don't think he would have done it anyway."

*   *   *

John and Jacqueline's marriage was not helped by Jacqueline's lonely miscarriage, his frequent absences, and the continued stories of other women. She had spent much time decorating the nursery in a house they had bought on Hickory Hill in nearby Virginia. After her miscarriage, she could not bear to go back to that house, so they sold it to Bobby. When they were married, he had told her that he wanted five children, at least. She had four in seven years, but only two had lived.

Some said of him then that he had stopped chasing women and started chasing the presidency. But there were still too many rumors of too many women.

"We had a nice little place on the river when we were both senators, and we'd go there sometimes with a couple of girls," Smathers said.

"Once he had me called back to the Senate so that he could chase around. So I left, and was driving towards Washington, when it dawned on me that I couldn't be wanted back there because the Senate was in recess. I knew then that old Jack had pulled a fast one on me. So I turned around and drove back and entered the place, just like I'd left it. What do you suppose I found when I walked in? There was the old rascal chasing both of the girls around, having himself a fine old time."

"I don't think there are many men who are faithful to their wives," Jacqueline told a friend grimly.

She enjoyed a chance meeting with her former editor, Frank Waldrop. Waldrop gently ribbed Jack, in her presence, about a blonde reporter with whom Jack once had cavorted. Waldrop noted that Kennedy was plainly taken aback and he saw a small smile of triumph on Jacqueline's face, as if she had finally scored a point for her side.

When they went to Hyannis for a weekend and she was late for the plane, he was irritated, but joked to reporters, "This is the first of many, I guess, as you married men must know." When they were driving from Baltimore to Washington in a convertible, they gave Nancy Dickerson a lift. He assigned his wife to the back seat. "Don't bother about her," he told Dickerson, "she always gets carsick."

In times of despair about being swallowed up by politics, Jacqueline confided, "I'll get pregnant and stay pregnant. It's the only way out." Table talk at home always turned to politics, and once she told her brother-in-law Bobby, with frustrated anger, "Did you ever hear such a racket?" She also had a comment on politics, which she used often: "How dreary!"

A reporter once heard Kennedy berate his wife at a party because she wasn't being nice enough to some important people. "The trouble with you, Jackie," he said, "is that you don't care enough about what people think of you."

"The trouble with you, Jack," she said, "is that you care too much about what people think of you."

Another argument, overheard:

"You're too old for me," she said bitterly.

"Well, you're too young for me."

Those were the days when her frequent moodiness seemed to deepen into depression and intensified her habit of biting her fingernails. She said her natural tendency was to "brood too much." She would even walk past old friends without seeming to see them, as if she had pulled down an invisible shade over her mind.

"The four of us were talking about lesbianism," Ben Bradlee said. "Jackie asked him what he would prefer: If she left him for a man or a woman. And he threw up his hands and laughed and said, 'Typical Jackie question.' "

"She is not a happy person," Paul Mathias of *Paris-Match* said of her then. Mathias, one of her favorite reporters, described her as complicated, often erratic and out of control.

Valleyhead is a private psychiatric clinic in Carlisle, Massachusetts, specializing in electroshock therapy. A substitute anesthetist reportedly told his wife, who told others, that Mrs. Jacqueline Kennedy was a patient there. Clinic office manager Mrs. Joseph Delfino said she was not there at the time "but I remember people talking about it. Poor Mrs. Kennedy."

Joe Kennedy told Igor Cassini that he had persuaded Jacqueline not to leave her husband. He felt that a divorce would have been political suicide for his son. The whisper that helped defeat divorced Adlai Stevenson was "a man who can't run his own family can't be trusted to run the country."

"Joe Kennedy told me he had offered Jackie a million dollars not to divorce Jack," Cassini revealed.

The mood of the marriage changed for the better. They bought a house, their first permanent home, at 3307 N Street in Georgetown. She became pregnant again and gave birth to Caroline Bouvier Kennedy in November 1957. They had been married four years. They had a cook, a governess, a daily maid, a valet, and a visiting gardener.

"I am the housekeeper," Jacqueline said. "I work out all the menus, see that they're ready for ten—or no one, as the case may be." Her husband described her as "very efficient."

The person who was most impressed was her sister-in-law Ethel. Ethel described Jacqueline's house as "such heaven and so supremely well organized. I always get depressed getting back to my madhouse."

Jacqueline, however, complained that she had the living room painted and Jack didn't even know the difference. "He has no feeling about any possessions."

"Lots of men in politics wouldn't want to be married to a woman who was equally interested in politics—like me," said Joan Braden, the wife of a prominent California publisher. "A lot of men would rather have a woman who is home at five o'clock and has the dinner ready. That's what Jackie wanted to do for Jack: make a life for him that was separate from his political life.

"I think that Jackie was exactly the kind of woman he needed then for a wife. It would have been too much if she were trying to be terribly sexy, trying to interest all the men. There was that certain untouchable aura about her, but it was more shyness than aloofness."

"Jack was very proud of Jackie, the way she fixed up and decorated the house they bought in Georgetown," Bill Walton said. "It was a cozy, lovely house. Of course they had servants, but she was the one who got it organized. Jack was so pleased that he could actually get his laundry done and everything else taken care of. Most of the Kennedys were pretty tight about money and I remember Jackie telling me how much she paid for two rugs. 'For God's sake, don't tell Jack or he'll blow his top,' she told me. 'I've hidden the cost of those two rugs in different items so he won't know.' "

She knew her man. When she bought two antique French chairs, he had asked how much she had paid for them. When she told him, he was obviously irritated. "But you've got plenty of chairs," he said.

"The Kennedys had this extraordinary energy, but they didn't have much taste for excellence. That's what Jackie brought to him," said Ormsby-Gore. "She brought taste in furniture and food and clothes and music and art and style. He had none of that before Jackie."

*   *   *

Kennedy still had much to learn, even about national political campaigning.

"For God's sake, Jack, quit pulling up your socks all the time and start waving at the crowd, the people," Congressman Hale Boggs told him as they toured the French Quarter in Monroe, Louisiana. "Next time, get yourself a pair of garters or something." Boggs also observed the way Kennedy got rid of tension by playing with his fingers, and buttoning and unbuttoning his coat.

Bobby Kennedy was also learning. Always busy taking notes in a black notebook while traveling on the Stevenson plane, he later said, "I used to thank God at every stop that Stevenson hadn't picked my brother as his vice-presidential nominee because I knew that this whole Stevenson campaign was nothing but a great disaster area. He had to lose. I was learning what not to do in a presidential campaign for Jack in 1960."

"I cried when you didn't win," a teen-age girl wrote Kennedy after his vice-presidential defeat at the 1956 convention. "Just wait until I'm a little older, I will vote for you to be President."

Kennedy himself had told Dave Powers soon after that convention: "If we work our asses off from now on, we'll pick up all the marbles next time."

But first, he had to run for re-election to the Senate in 1958.

To prove his political magic as a presidential candidate, Kennedy wanted to win big, by the biggest plurality ever. As Powers put it, "He wanted *all* the votes." But it was difficult to create excitement for an unopposed candidate fighting a balloon, a man named Vincent Celeste. Or, as a Kennedy loyalist said, "Why should I go out and ring doorbells for a guy who's going to win by four hundred thousand?"

At a Gridiron dinner, Kennedy again joked about his father's influence, reading from a supposed telegram: DEAR JACK—DON'T BUY A SINGLE VOTE MORE THAN NECESSARY. I'LL BE DAMNED IF I'M GOING TO PAY FOR A LANDSLIDE.

John Kennedy and his father had had their differences, their conflicts, their long periods of bitter silence—but they needed each other. For all his strong, and often successful, attempts at independence, the son relied on his father's judgment, money, and influence. As for the father, this son was another window for his pride.

The father was always there, always watchful. The room was full of top advertising executives the Ambassador had hired for his son's campaign. They were watching a Kennedy speech on TV when the Ambassador asked, "What do you think?" The answers were sycophantic: They all thought the young man was superb, that he did just fine. "The hell he did," replied the Ambassador. "He was lousy, and the show was lousy, and you know it!"

The Ambassador next itemized his complaints. His son was earnest enough, but too stiff and a little pompous. He felt his son should be more informal, more direct, and he wanted these executives to get busy helping him.

"Nobody could be more charming than Papa Joe," Kenny O'Donnell said. "If he wanted to put it on, he could be the most gracious host, mixing the drinks, engaging in small talk. Nothing was too good for us. But then he told us, 'Get off your ass and go to work.' He never let his kids rest on their laurels or their money. 'That was yesterday,' he would tell them. 'What are you going to do today?' "

*　　*　　*

"The secret was women, telephones, and kids," insisted Larry O'Brien, discussing the 1958 Senate campaign.

When the elder Kennedy saw O'Brien's campaign schedule for his son, he told Jack, "It can't be done. This can kill you." Jack answered softly, "Dad, why don't we try it for a week." That whole week, the father trailed after his son, watching from the balconies in the audience.

The Kennedys were everywhere.

The sisters wore earrings inscribed VOTE FOR KENNEDY, and flared, bright-colored skirts with a superimposed photograph of the United States Capitol embroidered with their brother's name.

The theme Eunice hit most often in her speeches was, "Jack

Kennedy is responsible for firing the first shot against Communism in this country." Patricia ("Patticake") concentrated her talks on the Kennedy home life in Hyannis Port. Pat was probably the most attractive Kennedy, tall and chestnut-haired, but what impressed her audience most was that she was married to movie actor Peter Lawford.

Jacqueline made a one-line speech for him at an Israel bond rally in Boston, and a full speech in French to the Cercle Français in Worcester. "It was not as frightening as it would have been in English because in French you think you're pretending."

Jack was ever watchful of her.

"What are you trying to do, ruin my political career? Take it off!" he told his wife when she put on a particularly stylish hat.

But the greatest political asset was a videotape of the Kennedy concession speech in the vice-presidential race. "It was almost the centerpiece of our campaign publicity," said Mike Feldman, "because it always attracted crowds. Always."

En route to the polls on election day, Kennedy saw an old woman crossing the street. He got out of the car and went over to the woman to help her. "I hope," he said, "you'll vote for this nice young man, John F. Kennedy, who is running for the Senate."

"Young man," she said, "I have every intention to."

He said "Thank you," and left.

Dave Powers afterward told him, "You know, if she hadn't voted for you, you would only have won by 874,607."

His victory was the biggest plurality ever in Massachusetts.

The election night victory crowd in Boston wanted speeches. "More . . . more!" they shouted. The three brothers stood up to the deafening applause and Jack Kennedy answered for all of them: "No speech tonight," he said. "The Kennedy brothers are going to sing, 'Heart of My Heart.' " Nobody knew how badly they sang because everybody was laughing and cheering.

The Path to
Power

The credit belongs to the man who is actually in the arena, whose face is marred by dust and sweat and blood, who knows the great enthusiasms, the great devotions, and spends himself in a worthy cause; who at best, if he wins, knows the thrills of high achievement, and, if he fails, at least fails daring greatly, so that his place shall never be with those cold and timid souls who know neither victory nor defeat.

—THEODORE ROOSEVELT

The Primaries: The Tide Turns

"When he first told me he wanted to run for president," Charles Bartlett said, "I told him not to do it, that he was too young, that he didn't know enough, that he wasn't ready, that he had so much more to grow, that he ought to wait eight years."

"You're probably right, Charlie," Kennedy replied, "but by 1969 nobody will know me because there will be so many more fresh political faces."

Even his father urged him to wait: "They'll have to come to you." Later, his father reflected, "I remember asking him once if he realized what he was letting himself in for with all the crises waiting for him. And he said, 'Dad, for two thousand years every generation has thought that its problems were insurmountable. And yet these problems were solved, and solved by human beings. So why shouldn't I try?' "

Bartlett and Red Fay both remembered "the old man" telling them that Jack was running for the presidency too soon, that his timing was all wrong—the economy under Eisenhower was too good and there wasn't any threat of war. Besides, he was too young and would have to fight the Catholic issue. "He won't have a chance," the father told the two men. "I hate to see him and Bobby work themselves to death and lose."

"Then Jack walked in," said Bartlett, "and the Ambassador switched gears flip-flop. He was ebullient, enthusiastic, told Jack he would sweep the election."

Hearing about this afterwards, Jack laughed. "The great thing about Dad is that he's always for you. As soon as I do anything, there's Dad saying, 'Smartest move you ever made . . .' My father would be for me if I was running for the head of the Communist Party."

Supreme Court Justice William Douglas had encouraged Kennedy to run for the Senate in 1952. But he had been disappointed in Kennedy's Senate record, called it "second or third rate," and felt he was "too much of a playboy . . . didn't seem to be interested in much of anything." But after Kennedy's re-election in 1958, Douglas noted a sharp change in him. "He stepped out more and more as a thinker, [with] a new seriousness of purpose, a leader with the world as his oyster." He soon understood why. The elder Kennedy came to visit and told Douglas, "Well, this afternoon, we crossed the river. Jack has decided to make a go for it."

John Kennedy's personal lawyer, Clark Clifford, got his first inkling of future Kennedy ambitions when Ambassador Kennedy excitedly called him about suing columnist Drew Pearson and ABC for $50 million. Pearson had intimated that John Kennedy was not the real author of his Pulitzer Prize-winning book, *Profiles in Courage.* Clifford told Kennedy to collect his notes and present them to ABC and Pearson. Both publicly retracted their charge.

At a lunch, former Harvard classmate Blair Clark smilingly reminded Kennedy that he had spent six hours one weekend rewriting two chapters of Jack's previous book, *Why England Slept.* Kennedy was incensed. "What do you mean? You never did a goddamn thing on it. You never saw it!"

When Clifford asked Kennedy why they were making so

much of the Pearson charge, he answered, "I will tell you in confidence. I am going to be a candidate for the Democratic nomination for president of the United States."

Kennedy directed his staff on the kind of campaign he wanted. "I want you to run this like I'm a candidate for president—without saying I am."

To ease any friction in their symbiosis, the father and son kept their political action on parallel, but separate, paths. They talked mainly by phone, on a direct line. At infrequent meetings, the son could, and would, overrule the father whenever he felt it necessary. The father reluctantly accepted the new relationship. Nobody worked harder or more quietly behind the scenes. "The Ambassador was never present, but his presence was never absent" was the way Ted Sorensen described it.

"When Kennedy was in the House," Congressman Richard Bolling said, "I thought he was a third-rater. I don't mean second-rater, either. I mean third-rater. Well, a change has taken place, and I don't understand what it is. It escapes me. It's a matter of character. You can be a good president on domestic issues on the basis of intelligence. You can be right on the domestic issues if you have the right convictions. But on foreign policy, it is a matter of character. To handle foreign policy it's not only what you have in your head *but what you are.* That's what worries me about Kennedy. A big change has come over Kennedy which I can't explain. He's hardworking now, which certainly he wasn't in the House. He knows how to pick the brains of others, in which case I think the credit should go to the man who does the picking. It takes brains and talent to pick a good staff and get intelligent work out of that staff.

"He handled himself beautifully this time on the labor bill, and it took guts. And he stood his ground in conference with the House."

The labor reform bill looked like a political banana peel on which Kennedy seemed destined to slip and fall. Designed mainly to protect union members from racketeering and corruption, it also had provisions that responsible labor leaders denounced as destructive of labor's traditional rights. Kennedy was acting as chairman of the Senate-House Conference to produce a satisfactory bill. It was going to be enormously difficult to get any bill attacking labor movement abuses through the Congress without having it completely destroyed in the process.

The *Washington Post* called the result "a legislative miracle." Senator Paul Douglas, who was not a Kennedy partisan, remarked, "That performance convinced me he's got what it takes. He's tough and he's mature. It takes a rugged, full-grown man to make Congress do what he wants it to do, not what *it* wants to do."

A witness remarked of Kennedy that he could fall into a well and come up dry with two watches running—one on daylight and one on standard time.

Peter Lisagor, the highly respected Washington correspondent for the *Chicago Sun-Times*, had been skeptical of Kennedy. Lisagor had heard him talk to some Neiman fellows at Harvard, talking freely, perhaps too freely. Lisagor had heard him say of labor leaders George Meany and Walter Reuther, "I wouldn't give them the time of day, but in politics you simply have to." After Kennedy left, one of the listeners commented, "Can you imagine that young fellow thinking that he could be President of the United States anytime soon?"

Months later, Lisagor told Kennedy that Adlai Stevenson was an inevitable Democratic choice to run again in 1960. "Why, that's impossible," declared Kennedy. "Adlai Stevenson is a bitter, deeply disillusioned, deeply hurt man."

Lisagor remembered being almost facetious when he added, "Well, you're probably a possibility."

Kennedy quietly admitted he had been thinking about it.

"I came to the Senate at thirty-five, and what do you do?" Kennedy confided later. "I don't want to stay in the Senate the rest of my life; a man wants to move ahead. It's only natural. And in the years I've spent here, I have realized more and more that the real source of power is the Executive Branch, the White House. Congress retains a restraining influence, but the White House is the real source of power. I work on a labor bill for two years, and nothing happens, but the president makes a fifteen-minute speech and the bill is passed."

There were others who liked Kennedy as a friend, but simply couldn't see him as a president. One of them was Franklin D. Roosevelt, Jr.

"Jack invited me to dinner at his house the other night," reported Franklin D. Roosevelt, Jr., in 1959. "I know why. Jim Landis had already had lunch with me, to ask if I could and would talk to Mother about somehow changing her attitude on Jack.

"You remember that Mother was asked if she thought that any Catholic was qualified to be president, and she said, 'No.' Now you know Mother, she's stubborn.

"Incidentally, I came away from that dinner with Jack with a real dual impression of him. I said to my wife, 'How can a guy this politically immature seriously expect to be president?' The only thing Jack could talk about at that dinner was himself and his political problems. I'd never met somebody so completely obsessed in himself as Jack is now. And the trouble with Jack is that he's always had it smooth, he's never been clobbered. I mean clobbered hard. Of course, he had that operation, and he must have done some serious thinking at that time, but that was a piece of surgery, not a lasting deep hurt. Maybe if he had one smashing political defeat, it might sober him, mature him. He needs something to flatten out that overaggressive ego, and maybe this campaign will do it."

Sometime before that, Kennedy had gone to see Arthur Goldberg. "I think I'm going to get the nomination," he said. "I know you're very attached to Stevenson and I don't want a commitment from you, but I want to ask something from you which I asked way back in 1948—if you could save me from the pitfalls in regards to labor issues."

"After that," Goldberg said, "we became good friends."

*   *   *

The date was April 1959 and Kennedy and Lyndon Johnson were flying back to Washington in a small plane. Kennedy had invited Senator Johnson to speak in Boston at Faneuil Hall, and now the two talked politics incessantly. Then, suddenly, both men ran out of words and there was silence, enough silence so that reporter Sarah McClendon, the only other passenger, could interject, "You know, you two would make a great ticket."

Now the silence was profound. "You could tell what they were thinking," McClendon said later. "They were thinking, 'Which one would be on top?' It was funny."

At noon on January 2, 1960, John Fitzgerald Kennedy walked into the Senate Caucus Room, shuffled his papers, pushed his hair back nervously, barely managed a slight smile, and said, "I am announcing today my candidacy for the presidency of the United States."

Walter Cronkite later asked him why he wanted to be president. He paused, hesitated, stumbled, then finally used the phrase "sense of history." Months later, he would have a sharper answer. He wanted to be president, he said, because "it is the center of action." But it was also the power and the challenge. One of his favorite campaign anecdotes concerned an Irishman looking at a wall that seemed too high to climb. He then threw his hat over the wall so that he would have to climb over to get it. Kennedy had just thrown his hat over the wall.

He attended the annual fund-raising Circus Dance at Hyannis Port, during which one of his neighbors danced close to him and asked, "Jack, do you really *want* to be president?"

"I not only goddamn want to be president," he told her, "but I goddamn *will* be president."

Gone was the day when he ducked out of sight because he was embarrassed by the accompanying police sirens as he sped to the Harvard-Yale game. No longer would he ever expect to be both a public figure and a private citizen.

For his campaign manager, he wanted Bobby. "He's easily the best man for the job. He's the hardest worker I've ever seen. He's the best organizer. He went to work right after the convention. He took no time off. He's fantastic."

The headquarters looked like a confetti factory. The names of the states were posted along the walls with piles of newspaper clippings in front of each state. Two of the women sorting things were without shoes or stockings. The phones seemed to be always ringing and there was no race to answer them. It did not quite look like the birthplace of a presidential campaign.

The man in charge looked like Frank Sinatra in Jack Kennedy's clothes. He was Kennedy's brother-in-law Steve Smith, barely thirty, hard-boiled, terse, "a very classy guy." A critical assistant called him "a Machiavellian bastard." He was a tense chain-smoker who dug his fingernails hard into his hands. What sports did he play in school? "I played attack," he said. Smith handled the money, "hired the harem," kept card files on thirty thousand Democrats who might be helpful, scheduled trips, and knocked heads together. Bobby Kennedy once introduced him as "a beloved figure who is replacing me on the American scene —ruthless, mean Stephen Smith."

"When Steve first arrived, he couldn't even spell VOTE," commented a staff member. "But he could spell MONEY, and he cut waste wherever he went." Unlike the rest of the Kennedys, Steve Smith was very good at handling money. "Thank God!" his wife, Jean, said.

Minimizing his role, Smith noted that Casey Stengel looked great managing the Yankees, "and I looked good managing the Kennedys. But anyone would look good with the Yankees or the Kennedys."

In many ways, Smith was more like Kennedy than Jack's own brothers were. He and Smith liked gossip and wit, hated backslappers or wordy people. Both were listeners rather than confiders. What intrigued many was that Smith even started speaking with a slight Boston accent and reverted to his original Brooklynese only when he was angry. He was much more than a Kennedy clansman. "Smith reminds me of Kennedy before the mold hardened," reported a family intimate.

John Kennedy trusted Smith so completely that he announced, "Anyone can talk to him and feel he's talking to the candidate himself."

Smith not only went through his brother-in-law's closet to search his clothes for forgotten campaign contributions, but he would also often stand in the back of an auditorium during a Kennedy speech, note whether it was too loud or soft, too fast or slow, then race to the lectern to signal the candidate on this and rush to the rear again to lead the applause.

"What's your political philosophy?" somebody asked.

"My political philosophy," he answered, "is John F. Kennedy."

*   *   *

Kennedy's youth was a persistent issue.

"Senator, are you certain that you are quite ready for the country?" asked former President Harry Truman. "Are you certain the country is ready for you?" He then added, "May I urge you to be patient?"

Lyndon Johnson said the country needed someone "with a touch of gray in his hair." President Eisenhower repeatedly referred to Kennedy as "that boy."

A reporter asked: "Do you think a forty-two-year-old can meet the demands made on the president?"

"I don't know about a forty-two-year-old," Kennedy retorted, "but I think a forty-three-year-old can."

A grandmotherly lady with a sweet face stopped him on the street: "You're too soon, my boy, too soon."

"No," he answered, "this is the time. Right now. This is the time for me."

But he did trim his boyish forelock and welcomed a certain thickening around his chin that made him look slightly older, and he even became more concerned about whether a tweed coat or a blue coat made him seem more mature.

If some felt his age seemed wrong, the time was right. A great mass of Americans were ready for a change. Kennedy had said that Dwight David Eisenhower could have run for re-election after he was dead, and still have won. Eisenhower's popularity was immense, and he had represented a safe, secure time. Now that he was retiring, a great many Americans saw that time as eight gray years, boring years of drift and falling behind, years the locusts had eaten. Now they wanted a younger hero, a fresh excitement, a new shot.

Kennedy had worked hard for his shot.

"I worked like a bastard ever since 1956," he reiterated. "Take Utah, I've been there five times, [made] six trips to Indiana, and always in the end the hard work pays off—a key Mayor in Indiana you've made speeches for shifts to you, another man you've worked for comes out for you. Sooner or later you make a breakthrough. I worked for the tickets all over the country in almost every state . . . that's the basic reason for what you call a miracle."

He knew he had to make the full fight. "If I were a Protestant and the governor of a large state, I could sit back and let the nomination come to me." He thought Johnson was the most qualified candidate, but that a southerner couldn't be elected. He felt he could beat Humphrey in the primaries and that Symington was a dark horse. But the man who worried him most was the twice-previous candidate, Adlai Stevenson.

"I still think that maybe this excitement of politics is a kind of fountain of youth. Political fountain of youth," said Adlai Stevenson. "I like Jack. He's very bright, he has a full knowledge of contemporary affairs and problems—everything from housing to foreign affairs. He's very hardworking, energetic, does his homework. Whether he has a basic philosophy, I don't know. How deep he is, I don't know. It's a hard thing to measure in a man. He has this instinctive feel for politics that these Irish pols have, the Honey Fitzgerald instinct, and it's there and you should never underrate it.

"Whether he's gone in front too far too fast, I don't know. I wouldn't have done it that way. I think I would have tried to first create a working record in the Senate and go to more selected places, taken the issues to fewer and larger groups instead of going to all the highways and byways. But then he had to create a larger image of himself—if he wanted to be president. He had to create a real base of political strength around the country, so that his candidacy would not simply rise and fall because he was a Catholic.

"It's a brave thing he did, but I can't help the feeling that now it's perhaps just a little overdone, that the mop of hair and the pretty wife may turn out to be liabilities more than assets. He does lack a sense of maturity that people feel. On the other hand, this is now a young people's world, and maybe that's what people want now, maybe that's what will get elected."

*　　*　　*

Dinner party discussion was political as always. Editor Bill Atwood felt that the Democrats would pick Stevenson in 1960, and Stevenson would choose Kennedy for his running mate.

"I wouldn't take it," Kennedy said.

"Let Adlai get beaten alone," Jacqueline broke in. "If you don't believe Jack, I'll cut my wrists and write an oath in blood that he'll refuse to run with Stevenson."

Kennedy had confided his ambitions to his wife but still regarded her as a political minus. The trouble with Jackie, he said several times, was that she had too much status and not enough quo—the Pucci slacks, Italian hairdo, and French dressmaker. And the fox hunting. She seemed too glamorous, too chic, too Society. Many even felt she gave the impression of seeming slightly aloof or arrogant. "The American people just aren't ready for someone like you," he once told her, and added, "I guess we'll just have to run you through subliminally in one of those quick flash TV spots so no one will notice." She burst into tears and ran from the room.

Not that she really minded. She hated the idea of shouldering crowds, shaking hands, making speeches. How delighted she was not to be involved. "Thank God I get out of those dreadful chicken dinners. Sitting at head tables where I can't have a cigarette and listening to some gassy old windbag drive me up the wall."

When a reporter asked, "What is marriage?" her answer was both ritual and rueful. Once again, she was playing the part of the loyal campaign wife, telling the people what they wanted to hear—and what she partly believed.

"You do what your husband wants you to do. My life revolves around my husband. His life is my life. It is up to me to make his home a haven, a refuge, to arrange it so that he can see as much of me and his child as possible—but never let the arrangements ruffle him, never let him see that it is work. . . . I want to take such good care of my husband that, whatever he is doing, he can do better because he has me. And not be pulled away from it. How awful that would be. His work is so important. And so exciting."

She maintained up-to-date family albums. These were always personal, never political. He laughed when he read one of her captions on a picture of the two of them watching television. It read: "This is the last time Caroline goes on 'Meet the Press.' "

Caroline was omnipresent, usually chasing one of her two kittens (Tom Kitten and Mittens), a gift from a neighbor. Jacqueline took Caroline regularly to the nearby playground at Volta Place, and occasionally put her in a basket seat on her bicycle for a ride along the Chesapeake and Ohio Canal. She kiddingly claimed that Caroline's first word was "airplane."

Jacqueline told of Jack being in the tub when Caroline walked in carrying a copy of *Newsweek* with his picture on the cover, handed it to him, and said "Daddy." She was eighteen months old then. "And he was kind of ruefully pleased that she still knew what he looked like."

Her own life, while he was away so much? "Very lonely."

But she was prepared, she said, "to join Jack at a moment's notice, whenever he wants me."

During a Hyannis weekend, the Kennedys invited Arthur Schlesinger, Jr., and his wife to dinner. "Jacqueline was reading *Remembrance of Things Past* when I arrived," noted Schlesinger. "In the course of the evening I realized that underneath the veil of lovely inconsequence, she concealed tremendous awareness, an all-seeing eye, and a ruthless judgment."

For photographer Jacques Lowe, the impressive fact about Jacqueline Kennedy was her naturalness and her poise, "the poise of a person who knows what she wants, what she likes, and who she is." He also recalled how unfazed she was when she came downstairs in their Hyannis home one morning during the campaign for breakfast and found a hundred people milling through the house having a Minorities Committee meeting, speaking a dozen languages. "Mrs. Kennedy just smiled and went into the kitchen to see about her breakfast."

Kennedy had decided on a preliminary sweep of some midwestern states in the fall of 1959 before the primaries began, and had decided that his wife's presence was necessary—even if only for decoration.

Her feelings about campaigning were still unchanged, still negative, "but it was the only way I could see Jack those days." But she felt, too, that she had to renew an attempt to interest herself in it. As she explained to Ben Bradlee, "What if I didn't like it, and Jack lost?"

She learned fast. At first, on a campaign trip, she packed "simply everything." This quickly evolved into three dresses, for morning, afternoon, and evening, and one hat for church. The evening dress usually had sleeves. "It's chilly in those halls." Her jewelry was a string of pearls. She also took a traveling iron and a sewing kit.

"When I saw his schedule of the trip, I told him it was silly zigzagging back and forth, and he agreed. He told me to talk it over with Bob Wallace. I did, and things were changed. That's the first time Jack told me to go ahead and do anything like that."

Her husband was up at seven, usually went to breakfast with some businessmen, and she was also soon geared to go. They usually both attended morning meetings and also a lunch (unless there was a separate luncheon for local ladies). There was often a college in the afternoon ("Jack hates to skip a college."). Or there might be a factory. There was usually some rest before the evening speech. The day ended about eleven, usually with her husband and staff in a private political conference to sum up the day and plan the next.

"I married a whirlwind. He's indestructible. People who try to keep up with him drop like flies, including me. It sounds endless and it is. The first two days were the hardest—but then I got into the rhythm of it."

She learned how to live out of one small suitcase, smile at strangers, push herself onto a platform. After a day in western Wisconsin, near the Minnesota border, she returned to the empty family plane. While she mixed drinks, she recalled what happened:

"Jack woke me up and Steve [Smith] came in and, while he and Steve were talking about the news stories and things like that, I packed my bag and got dressed. Neither of us is very talkative so early in the morning, especially me. I don't think we said much in the car going out to the airfield. But I remember something in the car going to the airport in Ashford. I saw a crow and I told Jack we must see another crow and I told him the jingle I learned as a little girl: 'one crow sorrow, two crows joy, three crows a girl, four a boy.' And you should have seen Jack looking for crows until he found more. He would have liked to find four crows. I guess every man wants a boy. But that was a tender thing, I thought." She sat there quietly for a moment, and simply smiled.

"Jack is very considerate of me on these trips. When he thinks I'm too tired, he'll suggest I skip things like that boat trip in Duluth or the talks at the end of the Cleveland ox roast. I went back to the hotel, took a hot bath, and got into bed. On the plane, I try to curl up and relax when I can.

"It's not easy, this traveling, but we are together and he tells me how much it helps him just for me to be there. And I try to be natural with people. I think if you aren't then they sense it immediately.

"Jack says I help him by just being with him, but I try to help in other ways, too. I give him reactions from people I talk to when they say anything interesting. I thought of some lines from a poem I thought he ought to use and he told me to get the rest of it."

She once counted some of her husband's scholarly references in a single speech: Byron, Tennyson, Shakespeare, De Gaulle and Macaulay. "He's no cracker-barrel speaker," she admitted, "but he's not Olympian. He loves people.

"I used to worry myself sick when Jack said to me that he didn't know what he was going to say in his next speech, but now, even though he still says it sometimes, it doesn't bother me because he has picked up so much more self-confidence in himself and his speechmaking that he can get up without any speech and I absolutely know he'll be all right without fumbling for thoughts or anything because he has so much in his head and he has real presence. I think it's a compliment that I listen to his speeches the way I do because he always has some fresh things to say at the beginning of each speech, things that nobody knows he was going to say. Even in the things he's said before, the sections of speeches, he always changes them somehow so that each time it's just a little bit different."

She sipped her drink slowly, as if she were thinking about what she had said.

"We didn't talk much when we flew. Jack looked out at the farms and said you could really tell they were family farms, set all apart, all by themselves, and he made a note of it for his next speech at Rice. And he asked Ted Sorensen if he had any jokes. He was always looking for jokes.

"Ted is such a little boy in so many ways. The way he almost puffs himself up when he talks to Jack. He hero-worships him, of course. I think it was only last year that Ted started calling him Jack, and I think he first asked if he could. But there's been such a real change in him. He used to be so terribly, terribly serious all the time, but now he relaxes a little more, smiles a little more, but he's still very serious. But he's so very nice and so very intelligent.

"The places blur after a while, they really do. I do remember people, not faces, in a receiving line. The thing you get from these people is a sense of shyness and anxiety and shining expectancy.

"These women who come up to see me at a meeting, they're as shy as I am. Sometimes we just stand there smiling at each other and just don't say anything—anything at all for a while. They find it so hard to talk about things outside of the weather. But now, more and more often, they ask me about my baby, whether it looks like me or Jack, or else they tell me they saw the baby's picture and that it does look like me or Jack, or that I do look like my picture or that I don't look like my picture. It's so much nicer when we go somewhere where we've already been, and we meet people again whom we met before, so we can relax more with each other."

She stopped, again smiling slightly. "It's so boring when we keep going to places where everybody loves Jack, but on a trip like this we're going into Humphrey territory and it makes things more fun, more challenging."

She finished her drink and went for another and when she returned, she smiled and said, "There is a time when you're so tired, you don't even talk. . . ."

She reflected on that.

"How can anybody call Jack cold? He's warm, he's attentive, he has such a sense of humor and he's so considerate of people."

She told of the woman at Rice who wanted him to pose for a picture for her husband's old-fashioned camera, "and Jack went, even though we were late."

*   *   *

"I know some people do think of me as a cold fish," Jack Kennedy said later in the quiet privacy of his plane. "But I think I get along fine with people on a personal, intimate basis, people who come to hear me, people on these campaigns. As far as backslapping with the politicians, I think I'd rather go somewhere with my familiars or sit alone somewhere and read a book. I think it's more a matter of personal reserve than a coldness, although it may seem like a coldness to some people."

Nobody could be more self-critical than Jack Kennedy.

"My speech was dead," he said after one talk in Superior, Wisconsin. "I should have lifted it somehow." Then he added, "I think I'm primarily rational rather than emotional. I need more emotion in my speeches. But at least I've got a control over the subject matter and a confidence so that I can speak more and more off the cuff, and I know how much better that is than the prepared speech. Maybe when I get enough control and even more confidence, then I'll be able to make my speeches less declamatory and more emotional. We need more jokes, too, I know, and I'm always looking for them. Since we've broken up our ideas into sections, I now know these sections pretty well and so I can pretty easily piece them together into a speech aimed at the problems of a specific area. We've got enough pieces to last us through Indiana, and we keep adding to them all the time.

"Of course, when the campaign really starts, we'll have to get a lot more fresh material so the news guys can have fresh story leads to file. And I'll have to be more careful about the off-the-cuff stuff so that I get the essence of the press release in the speech, so that reporters don't get crossed up on filing stories about speeches that aren't said. I guess we keep learning all the time."

In the campaign against the hard-driving Hubert Humphrey, Kennedy was plainly worried about the repeated questions on his Catholicism.

"It's a hard thing to decide," he worried, "whether to keep the issue quiet and hope it dies down or whether to bring it out in the open and hope it clears the air. I know it's something that can't be swept under the carpet, but still, it's a tough decision on what to do. Right now, I just don't know. If people would come out in the open with specifics, then I could answer them point by point. But how can you answer a whispering campaign?"

He thought for a minute, then added, "The price of politics is high, but think of all those people living normal average lives who never touch the excitement of it."

＊   ＊   ＊

This particular trip was over. At first quick glance their plane had the feel of home: the soft sofas and softer music from the hi-fi, his wife resting in a far corner, the man of the house stretched out on the sofa, his shoes off, reading the Sunday papers. Suddenly the living room lurched, and a young woman came in to whisper something to Kennedy. He put his paper down and turned to his wife. "He's trying to find a hole over Hyannis. If he can't, then we'll land in Boston, rent a car, and drive home. OK?"

"OK," Jacqueline said, her voice and face resigned.

In the time interval before the primaries in the spring, Jacqueline was again more a mother than a wife. She saw her campaigning husband less and less frequently. She was also pregnant. She smilingly remembered that her husband had introduced her to a mother of thirteen in Wisconsin and said, "Shake hands with this lady, Jackie. Maybe it will rub off on you."

With the start of the primaries, Kennedy again wanted his wife to go along to some of them, and, again, she was ready.

She packed his suitcase, laid out his clothes, rescued his lost coats, saw that he ate, and supplied him with occasional quotes for his speeches, including one from Tennyson's "Ulysses" and another from George Bernard Shaw. She didn't even think he had heard the Shaw quote, but two nights later out it came in a speech.

Her shyness never disappeared, although her stiffness did. "Jackie isn't pushy or bubbly," said O'Donnell, "but she is friendly and interested in people."

She still had her moments of panic.

As she was heading up to the dais at a luncheon, she spotted Ed Morgan, a newsman and an old friend. Her voice seemed filled with a small sense of panic. "Ed, what am I supposed to talk about to those ladies on the dais?"

"I know how she felt, as if she was being dragged into something, like a zoo," Charles Spalding said. "After Jack had talked to a crowd, and it was her turn, she would say, 'Oh *God*, do I *have* to?"

A reporter from the South, schooled in simple courtesy, was surprised when Jack brought his wife into a restaurant to introduce her to some voters—and none of the men stood up. If it cut her, she did not show it. She was learning. She went into a supermarket and persuaded a reluctant manager to permit her to use the store's microphone to solicit votes. "Just keep on with your shopping while I tell you about my husband, John F. Kennedy." She talked briefly about his service in the navy and in Congress, then closed with, "He cares deeply about the welfare of this country. Please vote for him."

Helen Keyes, the daughter of the Kennedy family dentist, who was traveling with her that day, said, "While she was talking, you could have heard a pin drop." The shopping wives stopped, listened, and empathized. She also stood, hesitant and quavering, to speak for her husband when he lost his voice, and was delighted that so many men on a reception line wanted to shake her hand.

Senator Kennedy left his auto caravan in Wisconsin to hurry back to Washington for an important Senate vote on civil rights legislation. Jacqueline had the job of filling in for him at arranged meetings in the small towns of western Wisconsin.

His instructions were clear: Discuss no issues.

She talked instead about the man she had married, how he

had served his country in war, how hard he had worked in Congress, and how much he cared about the future of the country. In a school gymnasium in Fairchild, she pointed to the kindergarten children and told them how lonesome they made her feel for her own child. She was very nervous at first, but the audience was sympathetic. "Isn't she gorgeous" was one of the frequent comments. "Jackie was terrific," said her brother-in-law Robert.

Her staff was surprised when she asked a dairy farmer to show her through his barn. They were even more surprised when she asked knowledgeable questions about his Guernsey cows. Her stepfather had had a small dairy farm in Rhode Island. There she had learned how to milk a cow, and she had had a calf to display at the 4-H cattle show. "I had a little bull calf and my sister had a little heifer, but my bull calf wasn't good enough to keep." She also fed the chickens, but didn't like them "because they were so mean to each other."

"I think it would have appeared a little false if I tried to give the impression that I knew a lot about farming," she said apologetically afterwards. "I didn't want to pose as an expert."

Her husband was still not an expert speaker. He was serious, sincere, and slightly dull. But as an answer man after the speech, he was sharp, sparkling, and sure of himself.

It was his father's political poll that convinced him to enter the Wisconsin primary, "Otherwise people would say this was just a chicken outfit, that we were choosing all the easy ones and ducking the tough ones." With the Wisconsin victory not sweeping enough, it was again his father's poll that persuaded them of the necessity to fight it out in West Virginia.

Just before the West Virginia primary, Spalding was standing next to the elder Kennedy at his Palm Beach pool, watching Jack swim.

"I just can't understand that fellow," said the father of his son. "I don't know where he comes from. He's not like me at all. Bobby's like me. But Jack. I couldn't do what he's done. . . ."

Later he reminisced. "Since 1952, when Jack went to the Senate, I've never campaigned for him, never made any speeches."

West Virginia was a beauty contest. Its selected delegates

were not bound at the convention. Nevertheless, it was still decisive. Besides, Humphrey had issued an open challenge on this one.

Washington correspondents predicted disaster for Kennedy in West Virginia because of the religious issue. Against Bobby's advice, the candidate met the religious issue head-on, told voters that the 1960 nomination should not be decided against him "the day I was born." The initial public reaction was bad. "We got nothing but buckets of water, real ice water. I never saw anything like it," Kennedy said.

The Kennedy women moved in with their kaffeeklatches. The Kennedy father moved in with his money. The Kennedy amateurs took over the telephones, calling almost every voter in the state. Twenty-eight-year-old Teddy became the man at the factory gates at dawn, shaking hands. "In the pitch dark, it's sort of like a holdup."

"I asked Jackie to come down to West Virginia and help me out," Bill Walton recalled. "She was six months pregnant, and I knew that, but I needed her. A lot of people were asking for her. They wanted to see the candidate's wife. I kept the Kennedy daughters out of my area because they were good at teas but they weren't very good at ringing doorbells or simply talking to people.

"Well, Jackie did come and Jack came with her. She didn't make any speeches. She simply appeared with him and was very gracious and it all worked out very well.

"So many people say that the Kennedys threw money around and bought West Virginia. But if there was money around, I never saw it. I never got a single dime from anybody. They paid expenses, but that's all. There were people in my counties broadly intimating that they would like to get some money, but I didn't have any money to give them and nobody gave me any money to give them. When Jack came out to visit my area and they wanted to give a party for him, they told me that they expected me to pay for the party. When I told Jack about it, he was indignant. 'No way,' he said. 'They're giving me a party and they want me to pay for it? Don't you do it!'

"But we finally did have the party and I did pay for it. It cost a couple hundred bucks, that's all. That's why I say, if there was money around, I never saw it."

The brothers were also busy. Thirty-four-year-old Bobby, who had started out as a shy, awkward speaker, picked up so much self-confidence that he was soon making almost as many speeches as the candidate.

*   *   *

Poverty in West Virginia coal-mining communities was stark, pervasive, and dated back several generations. Tar-paper shacks—the Kennedys had never seen such places or people. They had never been down in a coal mine. It appalled them. Until then, poverty had been an intellectual concept to be discussed in rational, pragmatic terms. From that time on, Kennedy talked of poverty with a passion that had not been there before. It was now an emotional memory that lingered with him. It was part of his growth.

"I won't forget it. I can't forget it." And he didn't. After his election, he diverted a large number of government projects into the state. His new understanding also changed a campaign style. There was no talk of Boston tea parties in West Virginia. At political rallies, they had hot dogs and cokes because so many of the people who came were hungry. More than anywhere else, Kennedy learned there that the ballot box was the bread box.

Jacqueline not only visited the miners in their shacks, but lingered behind to talk to their wives. Driving along a stretch of railroad track, she asked the driver to stop so she could talk to a gang of railroad workers eating their lunch. It wasn't just a polite stop either, the driver insisted—she talked with them for half an hour.

Jacqueline discussed how she felt in a letter to a friend. "In all the places we campaigned—& sometimes I was so tired I practically didn't know what state we were in—those are the people who touched me most—The poverty hit me more than it did in India—Maybe because I just didn't realize it existed in the U.S.—little children on rotting porches with pregnant mothers—young mothers—but all their teeth gone from bad diet. . . ."

"The West Virginia pros were cold as ice water about Kennedy," noted his campaign aide Ralph Dungan, "but the voters were hot for this man. He was just dynamite. When a guy's got it, it's a beautiful thing to watch. He could take a thing right out of the side of your mouth, absorb it, and use it a few minutes later on a crowd with all the force of his personality. Many people might consider it superficial and insincere, but I never did. He was an operator, sure, but he was a political paragon. Basically, he knew what the hell he was doing. . . ."

"In photographing Kennedy for a TV commercial, they threw him in with a bunch of coal miners, without a script, without instructions—just recording the conversation. It was strictly off-the-cuff, fly-by-night," insisted his brother-in-law Steve Smith. "Jack never even saw the result. He was too busy."

The primary moved to a worried end. Kennedy cohorts were concerned about the many telephone calls Lyndon Johnson was making to key people in the state, trying to persuade them to vote for Humphrey. It was not that Johnson was hot for Humphrey but simply that he felt Humphrey would be easier to beat later on. Bobby made a speech defending his family's patriotism and religion, and even referred to his brother Joe's death for the first time. He had to cut it short because he was too emotionally overcome to continue. When he heard about it, Jack said, "Bobby must be tired." In his wallet, Kennedy carried a cartoon showing a harassed office worker standing on his chair, thumbing his nose at the desk, saying, "I quit!"

"That's the way I feel sometimes," Kennedy said quietly.

But the night before the primary, he told West Virginia voters how he felt about being a Catholic and an American. He talked so simply and movingly that Ralph Dungan—who knew what he was going to say—"was out of my chair cheering the way he said it."

"On the morning of primary voting day, Jack flew to Washington to spend the day with Jackie, and to appear with her at a Democratic Women's Luncheon," said Ken O'Donnell, who had been with Kennedy since his early political beginnings. "When Bobby and I drove back into Charleston after watching the *Caroline* take off, we felt that our presidential campaign was all over. Jack had won the primary in Indiana a week before and was running, and winning by a big vote, that same day in Nebraska. He was scheduled to run in the primaries in Maryland and Oregon. 'If we lose here today,' Bobby said, 'we might as well stay home and watch the convention on television. Damn that Hubert Humphrey!' "

Ethel was standing alone in the dusk in West Virginia on election night when someone walked over to her and took her hand in his. It was Hubert Humphrey. "When this is all in and our temperatures are down some, I hope we can get together with our families." And then he left. She stood there touched by the tender gesture of a good man.

The Kennedy workers filled the West Virginia hotel lobby, waiting with yellow pads and pencils for the vote count. Few there felt that Kennedy could win. They told each other bravely that they planned to keep going, even if they lost. Most of them sensed that a West Virginia loss on the Catholic issue meant the game was over.

Kennedy was in his Georgetown home wearing a blue blazer, gray slacks, and slippers, and his mood was mixed with hope, doubt, and fatalism. If he was not dressed for a victory, he had a bottle of champagne ready. "We'll crack that open, one way or another," he said.

Too restless to wait for a phone that didn't ring, Kennedy and some friends went to the movies. "We can't just sit here and wait," he said. Back from the movies, he saw a message to call West Virginia headquarters, and raced to the phone.

As he talked to Bobby, his hands were shaking, and a grin split his face. Bobby's message was, "Get your ass down here. You're winning by a landslide." When he put down the phone, he let out a war whoop. He was in. Somebody popped the champagne, while he called his brother-in-law Steve Smith to get their plane ready. Then he called his father in Massachusetts. "What do you think, Dad? Looks pretty good. OK, Dad. Thanks a lot, Dad."

Years later, Cardinal Cushing of Boston and Hubert Humphrey were reminiscing over drinks before dinner. "Ah, you think Kennedy won that campaign in West Virginia, don't you?" asked the cardinal. "Well, I'll tell you who won it! Joe Kennedy

and me! Sitting right here! We sat here and decided what magazines were gonna get the money, and what newspapers and what
West Virginia preachers."

But even Humphrey backer Joe Rauh acknowledged, "You
can't buy the kind of victory Kennedy racked up."

A change of clothes. A race to the airport. A last-minute call
to make sure the voting trend had not reversed. On the plane he
was bubbling, while the airline attendant massaged his head and
gave him some tomato soup.

*　　*　　*

Everybody was loud, and a little drunk. It was the victory
celebration, and Jack Kennedy was up front making a speech.
Jacqueline was in the back of the hall. Then somebody in the
crowd yelled, "How does Jackie feel about it?"

"Well, let's ask her," Jack said.

"Jackie, Jackie, where are you?" yelled the crowd.

Jacqueline was standing next to Rowland Evans, Jr., whom
she had known when she was still a Bouvier. Evans watched her
trying to shrink herself into invisibility as she asked him, almost plaintively, "Do I have to go up there? I don't have to,
do I?"

"You sure do," he said.

He watched her as she slowly forced herself up towards the
podium. He could see how difficult it was for her, how much
she disliked it—and how well she did it.

After that, "Jack ignored Jackie," Ben Bradlee said, "and she
seemed miserable at being left out of things." She and Bradlee's
wife, Tony, stood alone in the doorway, as Kennedy made his
victory statement on television.

"Her reaction was simply to pull some invisible shade down
across her face and cut out spiritually. She was physically present, but intellectually gone. We were to see that expression a
hundred times in the years to come."

Then she quietly disappeared, went out to the car and sat by
herself until he was ready to fly back to Washington.

*　　*　　*

Speaker of the House Sam Rayburn had told the press, "Me and Lyndon, we only want to be in LA to pick up the pieces. That Catholic boy is only going so far."

Now Kennedy told a reporter, "You can tell him that this Catholic boy doesn't think there will be any pieces left when they arrive in LA." Then he told Ben Bradlee, "How the hell can they stop me now?"

If the end brings me out all right, what is said against me won't amount to anything. If the end brings me out wrong, ten angels swearing I was right won't make any difference.

—ABRAHAM LINCOLN

Winning the Nomination

"I think I've got it, but I can't make a single mistake." While Kennedy said it and believed it, one of his partisans observed, "He couldn't lose if he came out against the Pope." By the end of May 1960, Kennedy had swept seven primaries. He had badly beaten Hubert Humphrey and several favorite sons, but Lyndon Johnson, Stuart Symington, and Adlai Stevenson still were waiting in the wings.

Candidate Kennedy never stopped speculating, pushing, smoothing. "The Kennedy organization doesn't run," wrote columnist Rowland Evans, Jr., "it purrs. It has the smooth rhythm of a delicate watch." *New York Times* reporter James Reston called it the most professional campaign he had ever seen.

Nothing amused Ted Sorensen more. "Mistakes were made, stop-gap decisions or substitutes had to make do. Often we fumbled our way through. But we were able to keep laughing because we were able to keep winning."

"So many people talk about the well-oiled Kennedy machine," added Bill Walton. "Shriver gave me three counties to take care of and all he told me was, 'We'll send you plenty of material later on after you get started.' And the only other thing he gave me was the telephone number of a woman in Chicago who knew the area. That was it, the sum total of my political instructions. The well-oiled political machine!"

"When we divided up the country at Bobby's house, my job was to cover the western states," Ted Kennedy said. "But all they gave me was a two-page memorandum with about ten different names on it, plus a speech my brother made in Montana in 1957. The rest was up to me. Lucky I learned how to fly a plane when I went to law school."

Kennedy himself, however, seemed to breathe politics.

"Tell me a delegate, and I'll tell you who he's for," Kennedy would say to members of his staff. "Give me a state, and I'll give you the delegate breakdown."

"It was an amazing tour de force, and I've never seen anything like it," remembered Mike Feldman, one of Kennedy's key aides. "He went through every section of the country, almost every state—their strengths, weaknesses, where the votes were, who were the key political figures, what had to be done—and he did it fluently, all from memory. I've been with a lot of presidential candidates since then, but I've never seen anything like that." Before the primaries were over, he would even know most of the delegates by their first names.

After Kennedy won one of the last primaries in Oregon, he arranged a secret meeting with Adlai Stevenson to get his support. Afterwards he asked Stevenson aide Bill Blair, "Why won't he be satisfied with secretary of state?" The answer was that a presidential candidate, once caught, seldom surrenders.

Just before the opening of the 1960 Democratic National Convention in Los Angeles, there was a Kennedy party in Santa Monica given by his sister Pat and her husband, Peter Lawford. Arriving late, Bill Blair found himself seated between Nat King Cole and Judy Garland. Blair had just come from a Stevenson rally. Wanting to be polite, he went up to the

Ambassador, whom he knew well, and said, "Good evening, Mr. Kennedy."

"And he looked at me with that *furious* look," said Blair, "and he replied, 'Your man must be out of his mind!'"

Blair reminded the Ambassador that he had wanted Stevenson to endorse Jack Kennedy, but that Stevenson felt he couldn't commit himself.

"He took his fist and waved it in my face and said, 'You've got twenty-four hours! . . .'" Out in the hall, Jack asked Blair if Stevenson could be persuaded to nominate and support him.

"Well, you know we've talked about this before," Blair answered. "I've done my best. I came out a week early and told him he doesn't have a prayer—that you've got it locked up. But he says he's made these commitments to Symington, Johnson, and others that he wouldn't support anyone else. He really hopes to be nominated. Anyone who's been beat twice would like another crack at it. He really hopes the convention will be deadlocked. It's that simple."

Jack was quiet for a moment, thoughtful. "Well, look, I understand."

Those who heard the father on the phone knew his toughness. "I saw him and heard him," Smathers said. "He worked his tail off. He had an enormous influence with all kinds of people all over the United States." Kennedy family friend Frank Morrissey insisted that "it was the Ambassador who made sure that the votes of the various delegations in the big states like New York, Pennsylvania, Illinois, and New Jersey all went for Jack."

California was pivotal because it was the first big state early in the convention roll call. Having the second largest group of delegates, it could start a bandwagon.

Joseph Kennedy had been conducting his own California campaign for his son, headed by a former Stevenson man, the highly professional, poker-faced Hy Raskin. Raskin set up a dinner for the elder Kennedy with California Governor Edmund (Pat) Brown.

"Pat Brown was a Roman Catholic and he wanted a Catholic elected president. Kennedy romanced him and he liked and respected Kennedy. But then Johnson started romancing Pat like crazy," Fred Dutton, Brown's administrative assistant, recalled. "Johnson said, 'I need a Roman Catholic for vice-president,' offered it to Pat, and Pat began to weaken.

"The deeper we got into the campaign swing, Pat started thinking of himself as a presidential candidate. Old Man Kennedy was up at Lake Tahoe and he'd call every week or so to talk to Pat. Bobby called me practically every day, too.

"One day the Ambassador and Hy Raskin came to have dinner with the governor in Sacramento at the mansion. It was an old wooden place that had been built in 1890. It had been Lincoln Steffens's childhood home. Anyway, the Ambassador was very courteous and gentlemanly—he couldn't have been more gracious. Pat was talking about the possibility of being a favorite son, a presidential possibility, and talked about Johnson's offer as the running mate. Pat's a lovely human being, but he could never ask for anything directly, so finally I said, 'Mr. Ambassador, if we're able to bring this California delegation around to Kennedy, what will be done for California? And for the governor?' "

"Mr. Kennedy just looked at me and said, 'Young man, there are no deals in this campaign. We're not running that kind of campaign. We haven't promised anything to anybody anywhere, and we're not going to start now.' "

Almost on the eve of the convention, friend and neighbor Larry Newman got a call from John Kennedy. "If you've got any money, go all the way with me. Put all your dough down. We've got the votes and we're gonna win it." There was a long pause and Kennedy said, "Now you see why I didn't speak to the Sigma Delta Chi?"

Larry remembered. Four years before, two weeks after the 1956 convention, Kennedy had talked to Newman:

"You know, everything I do from now on is going to be towards getting delegates. Everything is going to be directed toward that end and nothing else. Now, whatever you can do for me. . . ." Newman worked hard for Kennedy on assorted political jobs, then one day called Kennedy, inviting him to talk to the Sigma Delta Chi convention.

"How many delegates are going to be there?" Kennedy asked.

Newman explained that this was the national society of the country's most important newsmen and editors, and he named Walter Cronkite and Eric Sevareid, among others.

Kennedy persisted, "But how many *delegates*?"

"Well, none that I can think of," Newman reluctantly admitted.

Kennedy then specified exactly how few days he had left before the Democratic National Convention. "The rest of those people really don't count," he said. "The only thing that counts are delegates."

Now was the payoff time.

He knew how to bind people to him. Clark Clifford was his personal lawyer, but also the campaign manager for his rival, Stuart Symington. Yet, in the heat of the campaign, Kennedy called in Clifford with a personal legal problem. Clifford would not reveal the problem, but it might well have concerned Barbara Marie Kopczynska, a successful artist known professionally as Alice Darr. She had claimed that she had been engaged to Jack in 1951, but that his father had disapproved because of her Polish-Jewish background. Years later, FBI Director J. Edgar Hoover wrote Robert Kennedy that FBI files revealed a $500,000 settlement to Miss Darr. In any event, Clifford did say that what Kennedy had told him was politically explosive and could have destroyed his candidacy. "But never once did Kennedy say to me, 'Now I'm speaking to you as my lawyer.' I think it was one of the most dramatic compliments I've ever been paid. It bound me irrevocably to him. From then on, all he had to do was just call my name and I'd be there."

But there were some people he could not persuade. His good friend Senator George Smathers had refused to stay out of the Florida primary. "What kind of bastard are you?" Kennedy asked him. "You're spoiling my plans." But then Kennedy relaxed and showed him a poll he had taken in Florida. "In every area, I just beat the ass off him," Smathers said. Kennedy stayed out of that primary.

*   *   *

A reporter at a Los Angeles press conference had a question for the presidential candidate: Did he feel, objectively, that a Protestant could be elected president?

Amid general laughter, Kennedy kept his face expressionless. "If he is prepared to answer questions about the separation of church and state, I see no reason to discriminate against him."

The 420 reporters gave him a standing ovation.

He had assessed the scene many times before. He felt the great urgency of making it on the first ballot. If he didn't, some of his committed delegates might disperse. He felt Johnson's southern roots were too strong a handicap, but his lingering worry was still Adlai Stevenson, the two-time candidate whose emotional pull on the convention was powerful and incalculable—despite his lack of declaration. Given the unpredictability of any convention, it was still possible that Stuart Symington might emerge as the compromise candidate.

Bobby counted the delegates several times a day, and the count was close to victory, but still not set. Every political observer had his own convention scenario, including former Secretary of State Dean Acheson. Acheson felt that Kennedy had to win on a very early ballot "if he wins at all." And added, "Tom Corcoran tells me that the only person with whom, according to Joe Kennedy, John would run under the circumstances mentioned, is Lyndon. If, therefore, Kennedy threw his strength to Johnson, Adlai might be stopped, and the Johnson-Kennedy ticket might be nominated."

Noting that the polls preferred a Stevenson-Kennedy ticket to a Johnson-Kennedy ticket, Acheson wrote Truman, "The polls gave you no chance in 1948. I say, 'To hell with the polls!' Lyndon is the ablest man in national public life today. He has thousands of faults. But when we really take our hair down, he is a giant among pygmies."

Comparing Johnson and Kennedy, Humphrey said, was like comparing a heavyweight boxer to a ballet dancer. "The difference in the masculine force of the two men is like night and day." A reporter's wife explained, "One is a man, the other is a boy."

Kennedy and Johnson were not friends. Their primary interests were totally different. But they respected each other's strengths. Reporter Sam Zagoria was at an earlier Senate meeting when somebody asked Kennedy who might be the best president. "No question but that's Senator Johnson, but he can't become president." Then he added, "I'm the next best." Johnson told friends that Kennedy was not a man of warmth, "but he was a man of justice, and that for such a man he could act as a good soldier."

Johnson couldn't inspire people but Kennedy could, and did, and he exploited it. "Johnson talked in monologues, in a steady stream, dominated the conversation, and sometimes when he didn't he went to sleep," remarked a friend.

Kennedy was an omnivorous reader. Not Johnson. "Oh, Lyndon doesn't read," remarked his wife. "He hasn't cracked a book since he graduated from San Marcos Teachers College." When he later became president, Johnson would read memos and the most necessary documents on a problem. Johnson wanted five-page reports summarized on a single page, or better, into a single paragraph. Kennedy insisted, "I don't care how long it is—just cover the subject." Not only could he read fast, but he remembered. "On page eighteen, you say this, and on page twenty-three, you say this. . . ."

"Kennedy would read all around the subject," said Mike Feldman. "It wasn't simply yes or no with him. He was far more philosophical and global. He wanted to know, 'How does this fit into everything else?'"

Intimacy was another area in which the two men differed. Johnson treated his staff as if they were his children; Kennedy treated them as associates and assistants.

"Kennedy was incapable of any kind of intimacy," a staff man insisted. "The one thing Jack didn't want was an intimate relationship. Except maybe with Bobby. Maybe."

When Kennedy arrived anywhere during the campaign, he went to his room with his own small group, and nobody else was invited. Johnson's world was a continuous warm web, everybody invited everywhere. "What are you doing? Come on over." Secretaries came to family dinners. There was no upstairs, downstairs. De Gaulle once said that "Kennedy was a mask on the face of America, while Lyndon Johnson *was* America."

"I don't think Kennedy had vices," said Mike Feldman, who worked for both Kennedy and Johnson. "I think he only had virtues. I think Lyndon Johnson had great virtues and great vices."

One of Johnson's vices was his conceit—he felt no need to campaign against "this skinny senator from New England that nobody ever heard of." He expected this skinny senator to destroy himself on the religious issue. Then the convention delegates would come and seek him out, the national call would come for "The Great Compromiser."

"Jack was out kissing babies while I was out passing bills," Johnson told a crowd. "Someone had to tend the store. There I was looking for the burglar coming in the front door, and little did I know that the fox was coming through the fence in back. When I woke up, the chickens were gone."

What Johnson hoped was that Stevenson would stop Kennedy on the first ballot and the embittered Kennedy delegates would then favor Johnson over Stevenson. Some of Stevenson's more enthusiastic supporters provided their candidate with statistics to show excellent chances of nomination. Newt Minow, however, took him into the bathroom and said, "You can listen to what you hear from those people or to me—and Illinois is caucusing in fifteen minutes and it's almost one hundred percent for Kennedy."

"Really?" Stevenson asked.

"Really," Minow answered.

"What do you suggest?"

"I suggest you do not go out of here a defeated guy trying to get nominated a third time. I suggest you come out for Kennedy, be identified with his nomination, and unite the party."

"I know you're right but what can I do with people like Mrs. Roosevelt—kick 'em in the ass?"

Illinois caucused and gave Stevenson 2 votes, and Kennedy 59.5. Boss Richard Daley had asked Stevenson earlier that spring if he was a candidate, and Stevenson had said no. Now Stevenson called Daley. "Dick, I'm now going to run."

"Wonderful," Daley said, "and I hope you get some delegates. But you haven't got me. I'm going to vote for Kennedy."

The day the convention opened on July 11, Bill Blair got a phone call from Bobby about Stevenson nominating Kennedy, "I'm calling now, the last time."

"Well I'm afraid," Blair said, "that—"

Before he could finish, Bobby had slammed down the phone.

The Symington campaign collapsed quickly.

"We'd get a delegate we were pretty sure would be ours," said James Symington, Senator Symington's son, "and then we'd find him in tears, and he couldn't tell us why. It was because of some kind of pressure the Kennedy forces had applied to get him to switch to them. The Kennedys knew much more about all the delegates than we did. They knew all about their families, knew all the pressure points—and used them. They were fighting and they were honed. I guess we were just country boys in that department."

Kennedy earlier had asked Clark Clifford for his political support. Clifford told him he couldn't do it because he and Symington had been friends for thirty years and he was committed to his candidacy.

"Many politicians I know would have said, 'That shouldn't bother you; it's the question of the better man.' Or they would have walked out angrily. But Kennedy said, 'I understand fully and completely. Of course you must be for Stuart, be for him all the way. He's a good man. I've worked with him for years.' Then he said, 'You know, if I ever had a friend, and had him for thirty years, and then told him I was going to run for an important position, and if he hadn't been *for* me, I wouldn't think he was much of a friend.' "

Kennedy met Stuart Symington in the Biltmore Hotel corridor and told him, "You are my first available choice for vice-president." Ten days before, he had been equally specific with Clark Clifford about Symington. Symington called a family conference. His two sons were vehemently against it: "You don't want to hold someone's coat. You want to stay in the Senate where you can be your own man." Then Clifford spoke: "I suppose you would agree with me that the nominee of your party can ask no more important question than, 'Will you be my running mate?' Can you say no?"

Symington agreed that he could not say no.

＊　　　＊　　　＊

A prominent Washington lawyer, Joseph Rauh, had been one of Kennedy's contacts with the liberals. Some weeks before the convention Rauh had asked Kennedy about the vice-presidency "because this means a great deal to me." Kennedy had told him, "It will be Hubert Humphrey or another midwestern liberal."

"Well, I guess that relieves my fears about Johnson," Rauh said.

"There's no need for fears," Kennedy said.

But the question stayed alive.

Ben Bradlee called his wife just before the convention. She was coming to join him in Chicago, and she was traveling with Kennedy. Bradlee gave her a list of questions to ask Kennedy on the plane. She handed Kennedy the questions. To save his voice, he wrote the answers on the same piece of paper. The first question was "how about Lyndon Johnson for vice-president?"

"He'll never take it," Kennedy wrote.

Senator Smathers had queried Johnson a week earlier on whether he could consider running as the vice-presidential nominee with Kennedy, and Johnson answered simply that he wouldn't trade a vote for a gavel. He had not forgotten the judgment of his fellow Texan, John Nance Garner, vice-president to Franklin D. Roosevelt, that "the vice-presidency isn't worth a pitcher of warm spit."

＊　　　＊　　　＊

John Kennedy's respect and support of Lyndon Johnson had an early base. In the fall of 1955, Joseph Kennedy wrote Johnson that "both Jack and I are ready to support you in 1956." The elder Kennedy noted that if Johnson refused to run, he and Jack would probably have to support Adlai Stevenson. The Ambassador then mentioned his son's support for Johnson when he went after the Senate minority leadership in 1953, and his son Jack's gratitude for Johnson's guidance in both the House and early days in the Senate. He added that Jack was his own man in all actions and didn't need any pushing from "Big Joe," that he was damn tired of reading "how I tell him everything to do," and that Jack was "impossible to handle by me or anyone else," once he set his mind to something. The Ambassador also admitted that he and his son had had their battles, but that his son was in front of him in most political situations, and rarely wavered in his loyalty. "His decision in supporting you in 1956 was his own."

But this was 1960, and the two men were now presidential rivals.

They agreed to debate before a joint caucus of Texas and Massachusetts.

Kennedy's father counseled him not to do it, said Jack "would be a damned fool if he goes near him." His daughter Jean said, "I know, Daddy, but he's *challenged* him to a debate."

Johnson was exuberant when Kennedy accepted. He felt he could overwhelm these delegates, show them the contrast between a powerful, articulate person like himself and this very young, very junior senator.

Johnson spoke first, attacking Kennedy's youth first, then his money. "The forces of evil will have no mercy for innocence, no gallantry for inexperience." Then he added, "I haven't had anything given to me. Whatever I have and whatever I hope to get will be because of whatever energy and talent I have."

Towards the end of his speech, Johnson became more personal, almost vicious, in his attack on Kennedy and his father. A Texan said afterwards, "Lyndon has lost his fast ball, his curve ball, and now he's going to use his mud ball."

A reporter noted that, as he sat there on the stage, John Kennedy's leg was shaking, his trouser leg twitching. He saw it as nervousness due to the fact that Kennedy's acceptance of the debate was a last-minute decision and he was probably unprepared.

Bobby Kennedy later told how Jack turned to him just before he went on the stage, and whispered, "What shall I say?"

When it came his turn, Kennedy demolished Johnson with deft, thrusting humor. "So I come here today, full of admiration for Senator Johnson, full of affection for him, strongly in support of him—for Senate majority leader."

When Kennedy sat down he and his brother exchanged a kind of sly look, and he almost grinned. His leg no longer twitched.

*   *   *

CBS television producer Ernest Leiser saw Lyndon Johnson come out of his suite a day after the convention opened, staggering drunk, yelling about Kennedy, calling him a woman-chasing son of a bitch and everything else he could think of, until his wife came out and pulled him back into the suite.

Phil Graham was the highly energized, brilliant editor and publisher of the *Washington Post*, a strong Johnson supporter. The presidential nominations were to begin in four hours and Kennedy told Graham that "he might be twenty votes short." He then asked Graham "if I thought he could get any Johnson votes from a vice-presidency offer?"

Graham later reported to Johnson's campaign manager, Jim Rowe, "You know, Jack is talking about Lyndon as vice-president."

"Oh, horseshit, Phil," Rowe said, "he's offered that goddamn thing to at least thirty people out here. Don't bother us with this nonsense. Tell Kennedy he can play those games with somebody else."

Rowe passed on the conversation to Johnson, who simply said, "Oh bullshit!"

But that night at dinner, Johnson asked Rowe, "I don't see how we can beat this fellow, do you?"

"No, I don't," Rowe said.

*   *   *

Dave Powers had found Kennedy a hideaway apartment before the convention opened, the top floor of a three-story pink and white stucco building at 522 North Rossmore Avenue in Los Angeles, only a ten-minute drive from Convention Hall. The penthouse apartment even had a private elevator. It belonged to actor Jack Haley, the Tin Man in *The Wizard of Oz*.

Powers then installed four telephone lines with unlisted numbers.

Powers prepared the usual Kennedy breakfast—freshly squeezed orange juice, two four-and-a-half-minute boiled eggs, four strips of broiled bacon (except on Friday), toast, and coffee.

"Let's hope the breakfast tastes as good tomorrow morning," Kennedy quipped, thinking of the nomination the next day.

*   *   *

Out of sight on twelve manicured acres eleven miles from Los Angeles was the posh villa of Joseph Kennedy's intimate friend Marion Davies. There the older Kennedy worked the phone furiously. "If Jack had known about some of the telephone calls made on his behalf to Tammany-type bosses, Jack's hair would have turned white," said Kennedy staff man Ken O'Donnell. The elder Kennedy had contributed heavily to the coffers of political bosses all over the country, and it was now payoff time.

On this Wednesday, the third day of the convention, there would be the nominations, demonstrations, and a first ballot.

As the time neared, Bobby told his staff, "I want the cold facts. There's no point in fooling ourselves. I want to hear the votes we are guaranteed to get on the first ballot." Their private count showed them twenty-one votes short of a majority. "We can't miss a trick in the next twelve hours. If we don't win tonight, we're dead."

Cold facts were not things Stevenson wanted to know. John Sharon, Bill Haddad, and other advance men had done their work of preparation so well that it seemed the convention was storming for Stevenson. Placards were everywhere, the galleries packed with their people by virtue of tickets begged, borrowed, and stolen. A Stevenson volunteer posed as a guard and let in even more. When Stevenson appeared on the floor as a member of the Illinois delegation, the galleries "went mad." Taken to the rostrum, on the opening day, he could have roused the convention to pandemonium. Instead he dampened it with a flat remark that the convention nominee would be "the last man to survive." "I could have murdered him," said his staunch supporter Agnes Meyer. "He wanted it but didn't have the stomach to fight for it."

There still seemed to be a stray hope for Stevenson. An afternoon Los Angeles newspaper headlined KENNEDY BANDWAGON FALTERS. Reports indicated that Kennedy still did not have the needed votes for a first-ballot victory.

In his hideaway apartment, Kennedy was sipping a soft drink, his tally sheet in his lap. The first ballot was going almost exactly according to his figures.

"It's your last chance!" Sarge Shriver was yelling at Jim Symington.

They were calling the roll of Missouri's delegation. Missouri could have turned the tide. If they voted for Kennedy, then, Sarge was intimating, Symington might be the vice-presidential nominee.

In the California delegation, delegate Pat Lawford, wearing a "Kennedy for President" hat, waved a noisemaker and yelled, "Isn't it wild?"

When the balloting reached Wisconsin, the bandwagon total was 748. The needed majority was 761.

Wyoming was next with fifteen votes.

"My brother Bobby had it down in terms of numbers so accurately that he knew Wyoming was going to be the final key element in getting the 761-vote majority for the nomination," said Ted Kennedy. "We had ten and a half of Wyoming's fifteen votes. Bobby told me to make a deal with the delegation chairman to give us the full fifteen if it would make the margin of difference in getting the nomination."

Wyoming's chairman was incredulous. "We're just starting this vote now," he said. "More than fifteen hundred delegates! And you're saying that those few votes are going to make the difference?"

"All we're saying is that if it comes to that, will you agree to give us the votes?" Teddy asked.

The chairman smiled. "Sure, I'll make that deal."

"Then the time came," Teddy said, "just as Bobby predicted, and those Wyoming extra votes would make my brother the nominee. And when the mike came to the chairman, he couldn't believe it. He was choking but he got the words out: 'Wyoming casts all fifteen votes for the next President of the United States, John Kennedy!' "

*   *   *

Kennedy's secretary, Evelyn Lincoln, had been told to listen carefully for Kennedy's first words after his nomination was confirmed. When Wyoming put him over the top, "We all jumped up in unison and shouted 'Hooray!' " Mrs. Lincoln recalled. "And then he said, 'That's fine. Let's go!'

"After that, he said, 'Get Dad immediately and then get Jackie.' "

He also called Bobby, grinned, and said, "You son of a bitch, what happened to our two votes from Montana?"

Evelyn Lincoln was one of the first to call him "Mr. President"—before the final vote.

"Thank you, Mrs. Lincoln," he said with a small smile.

*   *   *

Judith Campbell, who claimed she made herself available to Kennedy throughout the campaign, insisted that he had told her, "There will be some changes in my life if I don't get the nomination."

"I got the impression," she said, "that it was Jackie who was planning to leave him if he didn't get the nomination."

To reporters in Hyannis Port the following morning, Jacqueline said that she was "absolutely rigid and mute with excitement. I'm nervous. How could I help it?" Somebody from the house said that Jack was coming on television, and Jacqueline said to the reporters, "I have to see it," and closed the door.

That night, Evelyn Lincoln, Torby MacDonald, and a few friends were waiting for him at his North Rossmore apartment in Los Angeles. Evelyn was at the piano playing "When Irish Eyes Are Smiling" as the candidate entered.

"I'll have that beer now, Dave," Kennedy said, and the group filled their glasses and toasted the new presidential nominee.

Then Dave Powers gave him a couple of eggs fried in butter, with some toast, jelly, and milk, and he read some of the victory telegrams. One of them, from Lyndon Baines Johnson, read, LBJ NOW MEANS LETS BACK JACK. The time was two in the morning when Kennedy called Johnson. But Johnson was asleep and an aide wouldn't waken him.

Kennedy then asked Mrs. Lincoln to send this note:

Dear Lyndon,

If it is agreeable with you, I would like to talk to you in your room tomorrow morning at ten. [Signed] Jack

What he wanted was to heal wounds. A bitter Johnson would make a difficult Senate majority leader. A vice-presidential offer might smooth and appease, even though Johnson would hardly be interested. If he were, if he accepted it, he would bring with him more votes than Symington or Humphrey—he would bring Texas and most of the South. It might be the margin of victory.

*   *   *

"Why don't we go up and talk to Kennedy and just see what he thinks about this?" columnist Joe Alsop said earlier to *Washington Post* publisher Phil Graham.

"You go, Joe, because I don't know him that well," said Graham.

"No," Joe said, "I will only go if you will go."

Finally they both went.

What they told Kennedy was that they hoped that he would not only offer the vice-presidential nomination to Johnson for the record, but make him take it.

"I intend to," Kennedy said firmly.

Speaker of the House Sam Rayburn had been vehemently against Johnson for vice-president. Why did he change his mind? Rayburn discussed the issue with Rep. Hale Boggs of Louisiana.

"What do you think of it?" he asked Boggs.

"Well," Boggs said, "do you want Nixon to be President of the United States?"

Rayburn made a colorful reply.

"Well, unless you approve of Lyndon taking the nomination, that's what's going to happen." As a clincher, Boggs added, "How can any man turn down being vice-president? You wouldn't turn it down."

"Well, that's right," Rayburn said quietly. "He's got to do it."

The point was made, the discussion finished, the decision reached.

"Get the President down here so he can decide it *immediately*."

John Kennedy was at Chasen's Restaurant that night, dining with some old friends. He saw Ben and Tony Bradlee at a nearby table and went over to join them. He ordered a coke and talked about the day's events with more detachment than excitement. Reporter Hobart Rowen was also at the table, still unbelieving that this young man was actually the presidential nominee.

Dinner was interrupted by a man with a message. Could Kennedy come outside to the parking lot to discuss it?

The man was Kennedy's congressional successor, Thomas ("Tip") O'Neill. The message: "If Jack Kennedy is interested in Lyndon Johnson's being the vice-presidential nominee, you have him call me and by golly I'll insist on it." The message was from House Speaker Sam Rayburn.

"Of course I want him," Kennedy said. "The only thing is I would never want to offer it and have him turn me down. I would be terrifically embarrassed. He's a natural. If I could ever get him on the ticket, no way could we lose. We'd carry Texas. Certainly I want him. You tell Sam I'll call him tonight."

Rayburn's comment to O'Neill afterwards: "Tom, I guess we played a part in history that will never get into the history books."

Nobody sleeps much at a political convention. At 2:30 AM, a Johnson backer woke Sargent Shriver. Harris Wofford, in the nearby twin bed, heard Shriver say, "Lyndon will? All right, I'll get word to Jack first thing in the morning."

At 4:30 AM, John Kennedy called Evelyn Lincoln. "Was my message delivered to Lyndon? Would you read it to me?" He was quiet for a moment, then said, "Thank you."

By 7:30 AM, Shriver and Wofford were in Kennedy's suite with their message. Bobby arrived and the two brothers adjourned to the bedroom. Bobby sat glumly on the bed and Dave Powers heard him say:

"Are you sure you want to do this?"

Jack answered, "Yes." Bobby put in a call to Johnson's suite —John Kennedy was coming down to see him.

As Kennedy left, Mrs. Lincoln asked him, "Do you think he will accept?"

"No, I don't," he replied. He decided to walk down the two flights of stairs, so he would not be noticed. But the reporters were waiting for him.

*   *   *

"There were no nights and no days and no time." Lyndon Johnson's aide Bill Moyers recalled. "I stayed in that suite through the whole of that convention. I didn't even go to the convention hall with him.

"I remember very distinctly that on the morning after the nomination, I walked into their darkened bedroom to get them up. The phone rang and Mrs. Johnson picked it up. She said, 'Just a minute,' shook Mr. Johnson awake and said, 'Lyndon, it's Senator Kennedy. He wants to talk to you again.' Johnson sat up in bed and said, 'Yes, yes, yes, yes, sure, come down about ten-thirty.' And he handed the phone back to Ladybird, who put it on the cradle. Then Ladybird said, 'I wonder what he wants?'

"And I knew at that moment, intuitively, that he was going to take the nomination," Moyers added. "There is no such thing as stasis in politics. Nothing stays the same, and he knew that. He had a new option and he would take it."

After listening to Kennedy's offer, Johnson asked, "Have you talked to anybody?"

Kennedy mentioned some of the political leaders: David Lawrence, Carmine DeSapio, among others. "Yeah," said Johnson, "but have you talked to Walter Reuther? Have you talked to Soapy Williams [governor of Michigan]?" Kennedy said he had not. "Well, you better talk to them because I don't think they're going to be for me." Kennedy said he would and left, reiterating his preference for Johnson.

After Kennedy departed, Phil Graham came to see Johnson.

Graham was strongly for it: "By God, you ought to be vice-president. You don't want to be a southern senator all your life."

Ladybird was there. "We sat on a bed, the three of us, about as composed as three Mexican jumping beans," Graham said. "Ladybird tried to leave. Johnson and I lunged after her, saying she was needed on this one." Graham told Johnson he had to take it, had to stick with it.

"Ladybird was somewhere between negative and neutral," Graham said. She talked about their friends and their ranch and their business and their life, and she felt no need for any change.

"I just don't believe you should do that," his wife said. "It's just not something that you'd want to do," but then added, "It's your career, not mine, and you have to make the choice if you haven't already made it."

Why did he want it? Did he feel he had reached the end of his political string, that a Senate majority leader with a Democratic president would no longer have the same force? Did he think he could still run Congress from the vice-presidency? Sen. Clinton Anderson had advised him, "You're young. You'll be elected someday yourself. Don't take a chance on getting messed up now." And Governor Price Daniel of Texas had warned, "We can't carry this boy [Kennedy]."

Did he feel that, as a southerner, he had no other chance, that this was as close as he would ever come to the presidency, "that power is where power goes?"

"I was up in his room when Jack came back," said Robert Kennedy, and Jack told his brother, "You just won't believe it."

"What?"

"He wants it!"

"Oh my God!"

"Now what shall we do?" John Kennedy asked.

Later Kennedy described the scene with Johnson: "I didn't offer the vice-presidency to him. I just held it out like this," he said, taking something out of his pocket and holding it close to his body, "and he grabbed it."

Bobby was glum but Kenny O'Donnell was furious. "Do you realize this is a disaster?" he said to Bobby. "Nixon will love this. Now Nixon can say Kennedy is just another phony politician who will do anything to get elected. I want to talk to your brother myself on this one."

The two went upstairs to the Kennedy suite and found it

filled with northern Democratic leaders delighted about John-son. Kennedy was telling them, "I believe he's available but he wants a little time to think it over."

When Jack saw the livid O'Donnell, he took him into the bathroom and closed the door. O'Donnell exploded:

"This is the worst mistake you ever made. You came out here to this convention like a knight on a white charger, this clean-cut young Ivy League college guy who's promising to get rid of old hack machine politicians. And now in your first move after you get the nomination you go against all the people who supported you."

Kennedy became so pale and upset, it took him a little time to recover. "I'm forty-three years old," he then said, "I'm not going to die in office. So the vice-presidency doesn't mean any-thing. If we win, it will be by a small margin and I won't be able to live with Lyndon Johnson as the leader of a small majority in the Senate. Did it occur to you that if Lyndon becomes vice-president, I'll have Mike Mansfield as the leader in the Senate, somebody I can trust and depend on?"

O'Donnell cooled.

Kennedy then called for Clark Clifford. "I went to this pri-vate room he had tucked away on another floor," Clifford re-called. "He was greatly agitated, and said, 'This is one of the most difficult things I've ever had to do. I have to retract the offer [to Symington] that I made last night.' He then told me that no one in his whole family liked Johnson and there had been a family ruckus about it, and it was a painful choice but he had no alternative. It would be a very tight election and he needed Johnson's southern support. Of course, the Symingtons were a little upset when I told them, but Mrs. Symington re-ferred to the Johnson convention slogan, 'All the Way with LBJ.' Now she said, it would have to be 'Halfway with LBJ.' "

*　　　*　　　*

Kennedy sat with his leg over a chair, tapping his teeth, never saying a word.

A variety of southern leaders repeated that Kennedy needed Johnson on the ticket to win. But Governor Mennen Williams of Michigan spoke up loud and clear: "I personally will lead the opposition to the nomination of Johnson on the convention floor." Governor Ribicoff walked in between the twin beds to face everybody and say that Johnson was the strongest man in the party and the Democrats must put their best men in the field. It went on like that until somebody said, "Look, he offered it to Johnson; it's now up to Lyndon."

Kennedy still didn't say a word. He just sat there, still tapping his teeth.

Then came the labor leaders.

Most of them saw the Johnson selection as a betrayal. As Arthur Schlesinger, Jr., put it, "It seemed to confirm the campaign stereotypes of the Kennedys as power-hungry and ruthless."

Labor leader Alex Rose was almost violent, his language raw. As United Auto Workers' leader Walter Reuther and others assembled for discussion, Rose called David Dubinsky of the International Ladies Garment Workers Union in New York.

"David, so you know what they've done to us out here? Know who he's picked for vice-president? Johnson! You think that's *all right?* David! You crazy?"

Then Rose turned to the others and said incredulously, "Dave thinks he's a good guy. He says it's all right with him."

"Well, it may be all right with him," Reuther muttered, "but it's not all right with us."

*   *   *

The two brothers debated the Johnson selection all Thursday morning and half the afternoon. Bobby Kennedy called it "the most indecisive time we ever had. We changed our mind eight times during the course of it. Finally we decided by about two o'clock to get him [Johnson] out." Realizing that Johnson might now be reluctant to give up the vice-presidential nomination, Jack Kennedy suggested, "Maybe he doesn't want to have a fight either. Maybe he'd rather be chairman of the Democratic National Committee."

In the Johnsons' suite, Bill Moyers went to open the door, and it was Bobby Kennedy. Johnson was on the phone in the next room. Moyers and Bobby stood together a minute and talked. They had never met before.

"You're awfully young to be doing this, aren't you?" Bobby asked.

"Look who's talking," Moyers answered.

Bobby laughed, but it was a short laugh and his face soon grew grim again. He had a serious message for Johnson.

He saw Rayburn first and blurted out the suggestion that Johnson might want to avoid a floor fight and settle for the chairmanship of the Democratic National Committee. Rayburn stared at this abrupt young man and almost spat out the word, "Shit!"

Bobby Kennedy then went into the other room to talk to Johnson, "just the two of us. He [Johnson] was seated on the couch and I was seated on his right. I remember the whole conversation."

That was two-thirty Thursday afternoon.

"There's going to be a lot of opposition," Bobby told him, and the President didn't think that he wanted to go through that kind of an unpleasant fight, but the President wanted him to play an important role and he could run the party and he could get a lot of his own people in and then if he wanted to be President later, he could have the machinery whenever he could run.

"But he just shook, and tears came into his eyes, and he said, 'I want to be vice-president, and if the President will have me, I'll join him in making a fight for it.' "

They called Jack Kennedy.

"We've got Bobby here and he seems to think that you don't want Lyndon for the vice-presidency."

"Well, Bobby does not *know*; he's not up to things yet—not on top of what we've already decided. Let me talk to him."

Bobby listened to his brother say, "I just got a call from Clark Clifford saying this is disastrous. We've got to take him. I'm going to make an announcement."

"Well, all right," Bobby said.

Then John Kennedy again talked to Johnson.

"Do you really want me?" Johnson asked.

"Yes, I do," Jack Kennedy told him.

"Well, if you really want me, I'll do it."

"All right," Johnson said to his friends in the suite. "Let's go out and accept."

* * *

Henry and Clare Boothe Luce had dinner with Lyndon Johnson just before the 1960 convention. He seemed so certain that he would get nominated. Mrs. Luce asked, "Lyndon, what are you going to do if you don't get it? Will you get on his ticket?"

"Well, you should have heard him," Mrs. Luce went on. "He had a terrible foul mouth, you know. He and I knew each other so well. He said, 'Clare, honey, no way will I ever join that son of a bitch.'

"Well, the next time I see him, it's the inauguration," she continued. "There was a terrible snowstorm, you remember, and they put us on some dreary bus and took us around to the inaugural ball, and who do I end up sitting next to but Vice-President Lyndon Johnson. And I said, 'Lyndon, come clean. Come clean.' And he said, 'Clare, honey, Bird's been wanting me something fierce to slow down and my health ain't been good lately, and, well, I thought this job might suit me a spell.'

" 'Come clean, Lyndon.'

"And he leaned close and said, 'Clare, I looked it up: One out of every four presidents has died in office. I'm a gamblin' man, darlin', and this is the only chance I got.' "

* * *

Spalding went to see Joseph Kennedy the night before Jack's acceptance speech and expected to find him exultant, but instead found him packing. His plane was leaving within the hour.

"You can't leave now," Spalding said. "Why don't you stick around for the speech. This means more to you than anybody."

"No, there's work to be done and I've got to get out of here."

Sometime afterwards, the father admitted, "If *asked*, I would have stayed."

* * *

Los Angeles was calling New York, the former Ambassador Joseph Kennedy calling magazine publisher Henry Luce. The convention had just nominated John Kennedy. Could they meet at Luce's Waldorf apartment the next night? Luce asked him what he wanted to eat. Joe Kennedy's answer: "Lobster!"

They were all going to watch Kennedy's acceptance speech, scheduled for ten o'clock. Luce's son was there. Joe Kennedy had given him a job as his special assistant on the Hoover Commission, the young Luce's first job after college. After dinner, at nine, Luce decided to get down to cases.

"Well, now, Joe, I suppose you are interested in the attitudes *Time* and *Life*, and I, might take about Jack's candidacy." Luce divided the matter into domestic and foreign affairs. "As to domestic affairs, of course Jack will have to be left of center."

"How can you say that?" Joe exploded. "How can you think that any son of mine would ever be a so-and-so liberal?"

Luce had refused to translate the "so-and-so" except to say that it was not suitable for tape recording.

Luce explained that any Democratic presidential candidate had to be a little left of center to win the northern liberal vote, and it was okay with him because he understood and expected it.

"Now on the foreign matter. If he shows any signs of weakness, in general, towards the anti-Communist cause, or to put it more positively, any weakness in defending and advancing the cause of the free world, why then we'll certainly be against him."

"Well," Joe replied, now relaxed, "There's no chance of that. You know that!" Then he added, "I just want you to know that I, or we, are very grateful for all that you've done for Jack."

Luce later declared for Nixon, but this defection still did not disturb his relationship with the Kennedys. He still had his power and they still needed it. "I like Luce," John Kennedy admitted. "He reminds me of my father."

*   *   *

With the convention's approval of Johnson as his running mate, Kennedy made his acceptance speech Friday afternoon at the outdoor Los Angeles Coliseum before eighty thousand people:

"We stand on the edge of a New Frontier," he said in his acceptance speech, "the frontier of the 1960s, a frontier of unknown opportunities and paths, a frontier of unfulfilled hopes and threats.

"The New Frontier of which I speak is not a set of promises: It is a set of challenges. It sums up not what I intend to *offer* the American people, but what I intend to ask of them. It appeals to their pride, not to their pocketbooks. It holds out the promise of more sacrifice instead of more security. Beyond that frontier are uncharted areas of science and space, unsolved problems of peace and war, unconquered pockets of ignorance and prejudice, unanswered questions of poverty and surplus.

"It would be easy to shrink from that frontier, to look to the safe mediocrity of the past, . . . but I believe the time demands invention, innovation, imagination, decision. I am asking each of you to be new pioneers of that New Frontier."

"It was magnificent," commented one listener, "but what did it mean?" For most people, it was simply the excitement of hope.

*   *   *

Three hundred reporters and TV people had come to Hyannis Port from all over the world to make their first full appraisal of a shy young woman, the wife of the new nominee, who was pregnant with her second child. Her friend and neighbor, Larry Newman, had arranged the press conference at Kennedy's request.

"I told Jackie what the format was going to be and then she told *me* what the format was going to be. Mine was that she was going to come out, make a statement, have a short question and answer period, and then get off. But she said, 'Well, I'll tell you what you do. All you do is get me through the door, get me to where you want me to do the formal part of the photographing and my little speech. And then I'll handle it from there.' "

This was not the little fey woman with the whispery voice; this was a strong-minded person who had made up her mind what she wanted to do, and how.

Newman went on. "She walked through that door a pure amateur and in six seconds turned into Ethel Barrymore. Oh God, it was the greatest acting job I've ever seen! She made an incredible little speech and then said, 'Instead of having a question and answer period, I'd prefer that we just all go inside and I'll just walk around and you can all talk to me personally, and ask me anything you want.' "

Plans for the White House?

"After all, we're only the nominee; we haven't been elected. That would be presumptuous of me."

Social life?

"An official minimum so that a man who makes a million decisions a day can go to bed at night."

Her husband's pace?

She wasn't worried about her husband going too fast "because he's equipped for all the excitement and turmoil. He enjoys the strife and pace of campaigning. Jack never relaxes, even at home. But there's a certain joyousness in his tension. He never gets snappish or irritable."

But wasn't he too young?

"Of course Jack looks young. He's the tall, thin type. He'll always look younger than he is. Is that bad?"

To French reporters, she talked in French; to Spanish reporters, in Spanish. She had everybody at ease, everybody in the palm of her hand, and she seemed in no hurry to leave. She was there for an hour and a half, talking about Jack and showing them the family pictures on the wall. Her self-possession was complete.

*　　*　　*

The nominee was coming home to Hyannis, and of course his wife would be at the airport to meet him.

Mrs. Kennedy was still in bed when the Boston politician Frank Morrissey went into her room to tell her that her husband was signaling for a landing and they'd better hurry.

"He was out of there in twenty seconds, she threw him out so fast," Larry Newman said.

"Then I went upstairs. She was still in bed in her nightgown and she said, 'I'm not going.' "

"Well, you're gonna go," Newman insisted.

"Oh no, I'm not!"

"Well, why not?"

"Well," she said, "I'll go out to the airport, and as soon as I get there, some Democratic lady will give me some old, tired, red roses and I'll be standing there with these old, tired, red roses with a lot of people around me. And then the airplane will land and he will get out. Then everybody'll take off and leave me standing in the middle of the airport, all by myself!"

"Jackie, I'll make you a promise and a bet," Larry Newman said. "You get dressed and get in the car and everything you say is gonna happen, except one thing. They'll all be chasing him along the fence as he shakes hands with the crowd, and politicians will be all around him. But you and I will be standing together in the middle of the airport along with your tired, red roses.

"All right then," she promised, "I'll go."

It happened just as she said it would, except Newman was there with her at the end, as they stood alone together in the middle of the airfield.

He had such a curious mind. He was so open to discussion that you could talk to him about almost anything without him getting angry. I felt, if I was deeply interested in a specific issue, and talked to him long enough, that I might even change his mind about it. At least he made me *feel* I could do that.

What this man could do that was so extraordinary was to reach out to people—anybody—and give them the feeling, 'I'm for you!' He made you feel you were a real *person*, you were someone who counted. He made you feel important. If he thought you had something, he listened. If he didn't, he could kick the crap out of you with a few words.

—LAURA BERGQUIST, *Look* reporter

All in the Family:
The Kennedy Campaign

Clark Clifford's phone rang early one morning a week after the Democratic National Convention. It was Kennedy, the new presidential nominee. "He asked if I would come over and have breakfast with him. He wanted to talk over the campaign of '48.

" 'I'm not interested in '52 and I'm not interested in '56. We lost those.

" 'I'd like to go back to one that we won!'

"We sat there, I know, from nine o'clock in the morning—he had people waiting for him for lunch—talking out the whole '48 campaign. That done, Kennedy said it was 'most useful,' then said, 'I'm going to win this election. And I don't want to wake up the morning after being elected president, look at my father, my brother Bobby, my staff, and say, "Now what do I do?" I want a book of information right here in hand so we will know exactly what to do.' "

Clifford worked all summer to produce a book of eighty pages.

*   *   *

The Cambridge group was a low-key, low-profile think tank for Jack Kennedy. He would get an idea he wanted elaborated, and Ted Sorensen would pass it to the precise mind of Archibald Cox, and Cox would assign experts to expand it. Some of the experts included John Kenneth Galbraith, an economist who felt we used too much production for private consumer goods; Paul Samuelson, an economist who would win a Nobel Prize; Walt Whitman Rostow, who had worked in foreign affairs for several presidents and created the phrase, "Let's get this country moving again"; Henry Kissinger, who had worked for Rockefeller; Lt. Gen. James Gavin, a combat commander who believed in a nuclear test ban; civil rights lawyer Harris Wofford, a contact to the civil rights movement; and historian Arthur Schlesinger, Jr.

These men all became linchpins of the Kennedy administration. All helped create the Kennedy excitement of hope.

With Jack at the hub, his staff members were like spokes of a wheel. The inner circle was like an extended family, each partner respected for his talent, and all of them tied tightly together by a personal bond of affection and a hard-minded view of assignment based on specific strength. Always, though, he was the center.

Larry Newman's house across the street in Hyannis Port became the headquarters for the Kennedy staff. Jack would call and say, "Would it really upset you if I talked to one of the members of my staff?" If they had had a few drinks or a few jugs of wine, that call was enough to sober up the man he wanted.

*   *   *

His hands never seemed still. His fingers were always drumming something. He was always straightening his tie, pulling up his socks, or massaging his ankles. Any handy pencil became another thing to tap, twirl, point, or doodle with. He was often reaching for a butterscotch candy. People couldn't help noticing how often he combed his hair.

The press also reported the way he rubbed the knuckle of his fourth finger left hand, jiggled his right knee up and down, and flicked his right thigh with his right hand; used a white manicurist's pencil to make his fingernails whiter; sometimes smoked an Upmann cigar after dinner; preferred his father's drink, a daiquiri; and seldom read any fiction except James Bond and comic strips.

Remarkably, he seemed able to nap almost anytime, anywhere, and he held conferences while he was taking a bath. His anger seldom burst, and his laughter seldom roared. Irritation quickly returned to unruffled calm. Once when a packed crowd barred his way to a speaker's platform, he walked across the hoods of three cars.

On a campaign tour, he walked with long strides. Relaxed at home, he was a sloucher who liked to surrender to a chair with dangling legs and arms. However he sat, wherever he was, he had the great gift of being able to view himself with detached amusement.

He was, after all, a complex man of contradictions, a political man who believed in poetry, pursued excellence, and wanted power. A man of many sides, many depths, too many for any single confidant.

*   *   *

Bobby was not only the campaign manager, he was his brother's buffer, protector, adviser, and one of the few who could and would say no, no, no.

Bobby Kennedy hero-worshipped his brother, quoted him, copied him—even to the hand thrust in his pocket while his other hand jabbed the air with an extended index finger.

Campaigning for his own election, many years later, Bobby always carried a frayed, oversized tweed coat that had belonged to his brother. Once he dove into an angry sea to reclaim an old jacket, simply because it also had been his brother's.

The eight-year gap in their ages was only a minor difference between them. More important was what they loved and hated.

Bobby burned with a fiercer flame "throwing sharper lights and deeper shadows." He was grittier, more vulnerable, more difficult to know. "I was the seventh of nine children," he liked to say, "and when you come from that far down, you have to struggle to survive."

Bobby was the one who went up the Amazon River in Brazil, as far as he could go by boat, switched to an Indian canoe, and then took off into the vast waste without a compass. "Bobby was an all-out—whatever he was doing, he was doing it in an all-out way," observed Supreme Court Justice William Douglas, who took him along on several trips. "If he was climbing a peak or hiking a trail, there was nothing else to do in the world but to do that."

When the two men were together in Russia, "his tendency was to get into arguments with Communists, trying to convince them they were wrong," Douglas recalled. "I said, 'Bobby, that's whistling in the wind. You never can argue with those fellows, so why don't we just forget it and spend an evening doing something else rather than wasting it trying to convert some guy who will never be converted?' "

His wife explained, "With Bobby, it's always the white hats and the black hats, the good guys versus the bad guys."

"I make up my mind very quickly and go ahead and get it done," his father remarked. "Bobby is the same way. Bobby is very decisive." Bobby was like him, too, in not caring what other people thought of him, the father insisted. "If you're with him, okay; if you're not, then the hell with you."

He had a mean streak, could be glacial in his coldness and furious if his demands were not met. "He was tough, God, he was tough," noted one of his admirers. "Bobby? From what I saw, he was just a hard-boiled, nasty little son of a bitch," recalled a critic.

He was an activist, often snappish with his abrupt, jabbing questions. His slogan was not simply "Get it done!" but "Get it done *fast!*" A Nixon supporter warned Robert Kennedy before the convention, "If your brother gets the nomination, he's going to know he's been in a fight. Dick Nixon's a very tough apple, and he very much wants to win."

After a short pause and a show of teeth, Bobby Kennedy answered tensely, "We want to win, too."

A reporter saw Bobby turn on a young man who worked for him and who had made some mistake. "I've seldom *seen* a human being treat another human being like that," Jim Deakin recalled. "He just demolished this guy in cold fury in front of everybody. It was really brutal. He just tore this guy to pieces."

Bobby would not hesitate to say, "I think that's the most ridiculous idea I've heard all day," or, "That's a stupid question." He had fires burning in him all the time.

Bobby grew slowly on Jacqueline. She soon learned how complex he was: the mixture of shyness and aggressiveness, the concern he had if somebody hurt himself in a game at his house, the way his hands shook under a table "knotted up with one another," when he answered questions from a group of Supreme Court law clerks. She remembered the tender way he held the hand of a dying woman in a nursing home during her final moments, how long and patiently he talked with a retarded girl in an institution, and the warm, wonderful way he romped with his own children, carried them piggy-back, took them hunting for frogs.

She learned of his intellectual insecurity as well as his intellectual curiosity. "Bobby is immensely ambitious," she confided then, "and will never feel that he has succeeded in life until he has been elected to something, even mayor of Hyannis Port. Being appointed to office isn't enough."

"Jack and Jackie and Ethel and Bobby were not the greatest foursome in the world," a friend related. "Bobby had never learned to entertain his brother, and Jackie and Ethel were just too different."

Some reporters felt that Jackie was snooty, Teddy's wife, Joan, was dull, Mama Rose too distant, and the Kennedy sisters too aggressive, but that Ethel was friendly, generous, outgoing, thoughtful, and not "highfalutin." She not only remembered their names but the names of their wives and kids. Reporters touring with the Robert Kennedys on a fourteen-day overseas trip bought her a motor scooter and a crash helmet. They gave it to her at lunch in a restaurant at the Piazza Fontanella

Borghese in Rome. Ethel promptly revved up the motor inside the restaurant. "A charming idea, really," an English lady was overheard to say at an adjoining table, "but wouldn't it be easier to ride outside?" She had orbited the piazza, grazed a zooming Fiat, and bruised her leg before it was obvious that she didn't know how to stop. Newsmen corralled her, grabbed the machine, and held it until she got off. It made a marvelous Washington story for many months.

Bobby's secretary remembered when Ethel and Bobby first came to Washington "looking like a couple of young high school graduates filled with impulsive freedom." The two of them would drop in on her unexpectedly and say, "We're going to the movies, come with us." It was usually a western, she recalled. "Bobby loved westerns."

To Ethel, religion was exciting, something deep, meaningful, and happy. She refused to argue about it or intellectualize it. She simply strongly believed there was something more than this world, something beyond our range of comprehension. She prayed directly to her different saints, read the Bible to her children at night, and did not take it kindly if she saw someone smiling during grace before dinner. "Hey, put that fork down!" Yet there was nothing pompous about her faith. The dowager duchess of Devonshire was a dinner guest when Ethel said grace, adding, "And, please God, ask Bobby to get me a bigger dining-room table!" She did not hesitate to confront Chief Justice Earl Warren on the school prayer issue at a party: "There is no way to ban God from public schools. God is everywhere." When the Robert Kennedys gave each of their children religious pictures to hang on their bedroom walls, Jack and Jacqueline confided that they wouldn't be caught dead with those pictures in their house.

Queried about the advisability of big families on this overpopulated planet, Ethel Kennedy paused and answered, "But what would we do without Teddy?"

A mathematically-minded reporter noted that Ethel Kennedy was pregnant forty-three percent of her married life. Somewhere early in her production of eleven children, her mother-in-law indicated she should not hurry too much with the next, indicating a certain jealousy if Ethel had more children "in less time than I had." "There's magic about children," said Ethel, the bride who couldn't make an omelet. With a staff of eleven to care for her house and parties, Ethel diapered her own babies, bought them clothes and books, and drove them to school. "When I drive, everyone in the car has to have three news items to report. . . . I get a kick out of listening to them talk to each other."

Jacqueline occasionally went to her husband's committee hearings when he was a senator—if there was something special —but Ethel seldom missed one of Bobby's meetings. "I like to see Bobby in action," she said. She arrived in the morning, attended the hearing, drove home for lunch with the children, returned for the afternoon session, then went home to tell her friends how brilliantly Bobby had performed. "I don't think a politician's wife should *not* get involved in politics," she added. "She always thinks I'm right and they're wrong," Bobby added, smiling.

Ethel became more Kennedy than the Kennedys, more Irish, more Catholic, more athletic. "I like competition, but I like to win better." As a girl, she called her sailboat *Sink or Swim*. When she lost a tough tennis game, she once knelt on the court and banged her head against the surface in frustration. "She'd drive a tennis ball down my throat," said Fred Dutton, a White House staff man.

For Ethel Kennedy, Bobby was the best sailor, the best skier, the best husband, the best father, the best lover. In a birthday album for him, she included a photo of herself in a cap and gown alongside a Catholic dignitary with the heading, "The Tremendous Lover." The caption read, "I never would have thought it of the attorney general until I heard her confession."

Jacqueline, who didn't like Bobby at first, later said of him, "Sometimes I wish Bobby were an amoeba so we could breed him on himself." In a specially bound copy of Bobby's book, *The Enemy Within*, she inscribed, "To Bobby, who made the impossible possible and changed our lives. The brother, within, who made the difficult easy." Observers insist that Bobby and Jacqueline later became so close that Ethel had reason to be jealous.

When Jacqueline had her miscarriage in 1956, when her husband was vacationing on the Riviera, Bobby was the first at her bedside. Trying to explain her husband's absence, her voice faltered as she said, "We couldn't get Jack in time."

Jack Kennedy claimed that he didn't see any contradictions in Bobby, but Jacqueline insisted, "Oh, yes there are!"

Comparing the brothers, Kennedy friend Charles Spalding felt "it wasn't that Bobby was more passionate than Jack. It was simply that Bobby's emotions were closer to the surface, and Jack's were buried. Jack had greater control."

Then, too, it was the question of their different roles in the campaign. Bobby had the dirty job of being the point man on controversy, knocking heads together, tying up the loose ends. "Jack always had a Bobby in a campaign," Dave Powers remarked, "but Bobby didn't have a Bobby."

"He had his role in the campaign and I had my role," said Bobby of Jack, "and we would meet and discuss, when there was a crisis that came up. But he never involved himself in what I was doing—the running of the campaign—and I was not directly associated with what he was doing—running around the country—except with schedules or something.

"We had to have our own areas. I had to be apart from what he was doing so I wasn't working directly for him and getting orders from him as to what I should do that day. That wouldn't be possible."

*   *   *

Ted Kennedy was twenty-seven years old when Jack made him coordinator for eleven western states plus Alaska and Hawaii. His job was to make speeches, find leadership, and build organizations for his brother.

Reporters generally agreed that Jack was the brightest and most gentlemanly, Bobby the most passionate, and Ted the most friendly.

Jack Kennedy came in, saw Johnson campaign manager Jim Rowe at a table, waved at him.

Bobby came in, saw Jim Rowe, and sort of lifted his eyebrows in recognition.

Teddy came in, walked over to Jim Rowe, and shook his hand.

"I was really on my own," said Ted Kennedy. "I'd check in with a state chairman, get some names, set up meetings, breakfast in one town, lunch in another, dinner somewhere else, on the go pretty much in my little plane. Hard work and not much fun." Byron White (later Supreme Court Justice White) joined him in Colorado and the two worked the state for five days. "We had a free day before I went to join Jack and brief him on the West, and Byron noted twelve inches of new snow in the state and suggested skiing." By the time Ted joined Jack, he had a good sunburn. "And the first thing my brother said was, 'You been skiing in Colorado all these weeks?'"

Ted was a technician rather than a theorist. Like his brothers, he did not seem capable or willing to plumb the depths of his own feelings. "I don't have any complexes, if that's what you mean," he told a reporter. A Republican congressman who felt he knew him well said, "He is intelligent, in the sense that he is shrewd, incisive, sensitive, and retentive. But not in the sense of depth." Other politicians who watched him also noted that "his instincts are awful damn good."

Ted moved his wife Joan to a rented home in San Francisco, but only managed to be with her thirteen nights in the next three and a half months. "I've had to get used to being alone," she said.

Until she met Ted, Joan's knowledge of politics was almost nil. Her parents were both Republicans and never discussed politics. In this, she was like her sister-in-law Jacqueline. When Joan was told that she was expected to help during the 1960 campaign, she felt overwhelmed and unprepared. She was pregnant, and she didn't even have the proper campaigning clothes. The equally pregnant Jacqueline loaned her some. "I think that for a girl to lend her clothes to another girl," said Joan, "is one of the greatest signs of friendliness there is."

"Jackie and I decided long ago we just don't have the stamina of the Kennedy girls." Joan told how the Kennedy sisters teased her about being a recluse at Hyannis "because Teddy and I ate alone one Sunday night instead of joining the group."

They bought a house at Hyannis about a mile away from the Kennedy compound. "It's close enough to go down to the big house for movies, and yet far enough away not to be in the midst of the family. Ted loves his family, but there are times when we enjoy being alone."

Joan most admired Ethel among the Kennedy women. Eight years her senior, Ethel had introduced her to Ted. She wanted to have as many babies as Ethel had (at that point, Ethel had eight). In the next eight years, however, Joan had three miscarriages and one child. In this, too, she was like her sister-in-law Jacqueline. Unlike Ethel, Joan was very unsure of herself, not at all competitive, and most unathletic.

Ethel was chagrined at how quickly Joan learned political tactics. The two shared a dais in Denver and Joan asked, "Ethel, what do you say when you get up to speak?"

"Like a fool, I told her," Ethel later complained. "So when she got up, she recited my speech verbatim. What a memory that girl has. Gosh, kid, WOW! I can't think while sitting down, much less on my feet. It was nightmare material."

"Whatever you want to do," Joan told her husband, "I'll do it with you." They were together on one western swing during that 1960 campaign. "We went around by car, with me bumping in the back with my fat little figure." Her baby was due in a few months and she didn't want to go, "but it was the only chance I had to see him. He came home so seldom, it was like being courted again.

"I never put anything back in my closet that needs pressing or cleaning and I keep a cosmetic bag always packed and ready. I lead an absolutely last-minute life."

Kennedy women went where they were sent. "I'll do anything Bobby wants me to do," Ethel repeated often. She completely disarmed an unfriendly audience of Republican women in Aberdeen, South Dakota, telling them what her husband had told her, "Whatever you do, don't speak!"

In introducing one of his sisters, Patricia Lawford, Jack told a crowd, "Somebody asked her last week if I was her kid brother, so she knew it was time this campaign came to an end."

Typical of the Kennedy family frenzy during the campaign

was Eunice's throwing a glass of water in the face of a Nixon supporter and later calling campaign headquarters to ask, "Where was I yesterday?"

*   *   *

A reporter asked a favor. He was trying to romance a beautiful girl and this girl's prime interest in life seemed to be Jack Kennedy. Would Kennedy come and say hello? Kennedy happily did so and the reporter beamed. Later he said that Nixon would never have done it.

Contrasting Kennedy and Nixon, another reporter recalled their reaction to a similar incident: When a Nixon campaign plane took a sudden, steep drop, Nixon people anxiously requested that the newsmen not report the incident. When something similar happened to the Kennedy campaign plane, Kennedy himself told the reporters, jokingly, "If we'd really gone down, I just want you fellows to know that your names would have been in very small type."

Campaigning reporters did have complaints: clothes ripped by the crowds, waiting in lines to shave in the cramped washrooms, missing laundry, missing typewriters, missing coats, never enough telephones for long-distance calls, the tight nerves when a plane searched to land at a small airport somewhere in the mountains in a dense fog, the candidate making too many speeches with the same stories and the same jokes.

Kennedy staff men pointed out that reporters filed only two or three stories a day with some "add leads" while Kennedy was making ten speeches a day. On the ground, the reporters traveled mostly in air-conditioned buses, but Kennedy was usually balancing his bad back on top of a jouncing convertible in all weather and enduring the endless handshaking.

They shared adjoining urinals at a gas station, the young reporter and the presidential candidate. The young reporter noted that Kennedy's right hand was bloodied. They had just been touring the Pennsylvania coal-mining country.

Kennedy said, smiling, "Those fuckers. When they shake hands, they *really* shake hands."

It was the first time the young reporter, Chuck Roberts, ever heard a presidential candidate use a four-letter word.

Kennedy never used the "Irish switch"—vigorously shaking one person's hand while talking enthusiastically to someone else. His grandfather, Honey Fitz, improved on that by pumping one hand while speaking to a second person and gazing fondly on another. Kennedy always looked directly at the person whose hand he shook. Many politicians used the standard ploy of grabbing a person's hand at the base of the thumb so he couldn't squeeze back. When you're shaking hundreds of hands, this can be most important. Kennedy didn't do this. His handshake was straightforward but he did sometimes alternate hands.

Handshaking is friendly until your hands bleed.

Confetti looks festive until you're forced to spit out mouthfuls hurled directly into your face.

Applause is wonderful until you can hardly hear yourself speak.

A crush of screaming women is flattering until they tear your clothes.

A campaign is a drama of fixed time into which an impossible schedule gets squeezed. With the pressures of political appearance requests from all over the country, the guidelines can come only from the candidate.

Logistics break down. Plans on paper look neat; time schedules seem simple. But what do you do when there aren't enough cars or enough police? How do you handle too many people, surging crowds who keep everything bumper to bumper? What do you say to your wife when she worries aloud—"It feels like the sides of the car are bending"?

Reporters could growl, sneer, sleep, but he had to smile, smile, smile, and wave, wave, wave. Their answer was that the brass ring was his, not theirs; that he didn't have to do it; nobody ordered him to do it; nobody even asked him to do it. The choice was his. And the price was right.

*   *   *

"Kennedy causes turmoil in women and he causes turmoil in young people, too, and we should *have* a candidate who does cause turmoil," said newspaper editor Zel Rice.

A reporter described some of this turmoil:

"Newcomers to the Kennedy entourage receive a mysterious

piece of advice: 'Watch out for the jumpers.' The mystery clears the moment the motorcade gets under way. As Kennedy's car passes by, the women lining the parade route begin jumping up and down. It makes no difference—the jumpers may be young schoolgirls, mothers with infants, middle-aged matrons, even prim old ladies. In addition to the standard category of 'jumpers' there are the 'double leapers,' women who jump together while holding hands. Then there are the 'clutchers,' women who cross their arms and hug themselves and scream, 'He looked at me! He looked at *me!*' Finally, there are the 'runners'—women, sometimes with infants, who break through the police lines and run after Kennedy's car."

"We actually counted empty shoes along the route of the motorcade, abandoned by women who had literally leaped out of them when they saw the waving, smiling Kennedy," a reporter said.

Perhaps it was all summed up by that woman in a Missouri crowd who yelled to her friend as Kennedy pushed his way through: "Touch him for me. . . . TOUCH HIM FOR ME!"

Writer Joe McCarthy was with Kennedy on a plane filled with stewardesses returning from a special training course. "While talking to him," Joe said, "I noticed about twenty stewardesses sitting or kneeling on nearby seats, all of them watching Kennedy intently. None of them spoke or appeared to be listening to Kennedy. They sat and stared at him for more than an hour without moving or making a sound. Now and then Kennedy glanced at the pretty girls, smiled, and went on talking to me calmly, as if we were alone."

On his campaign plane, Kennedy had his own stewardess, Janet des Rosiers, who once worked for his father.

She was an attractive brunette of French ancestry who specialized in super-service. Her prime concern was John Kennedy. She would take his dictation as fast as he could speak, swiftly provide his favorite food, massage his head, comb his hair, sew on his buttons, and rub his back as he lay stretched on the bed in his private compartment. And she always came on the run when he called, "Miss Janet!" Reporters who stayed with Kennedy for most of the campaign liked to speculate that Miss Janet's services for the candidate were even more varied. For a short time, she even served on his White House staff.

A grateful Kennedy later provided Miss Janet with some oil wells in Louisiana, where she decided to retire.

A diplomat's wife tried to understand Kennedy's sexual appeal. "You know, I don't understand those women who think Jack Kennedy is the great sexual Don Juan. He's like a little boy. . . ."

It was something, though, to walk with Kennedy into a room full of women, watching him work on them, grabbing one reporter's wife's hands, staring into her eyes, telling her, "Why don't you come with us on more of our trips?" Or whispering confidentially to another, "I've been to *so* many banquets. . . ." An observer described it as "animal charm," and confessed that his own wife thought Kennedy was "the Second Coming." A congressman complained that his wife worked harder for Kennedy than she ever did for him.

He still managed some unstructured fun. "I hitched a ride on the Kennedy campaign plane going from Texas to Oregon," said Blair Clark, who was then doing a nightly radio show around the country. "The plane stopped at Las Vegas at noon, and there was no goddamn reason for stopping there except fun and games. I remember Jack took two of us to Frank Sinatra's suite at the Sands. We had a couple of drinks and the two of us left because we sensed that Jack and Frank and a couple of the girls were going to have a party. One of the girls was Judith Campbell, although I have absolutely no memory of that charmer. The plane didn't leave until the next morning."

Campaigning with him in Pennsylvania, Charles Spalding recalled another charmer, a previous passion during Kennedy's navy days in Washington, the former Miss Denmark, "Inga-Binga" Arvad. Spalding remembered that Inga lived nearby with her husband, Hollywood actor Tim McCoy. "Why don't we go see her?" he suggested.

Kennedy almost recoiled. "Inga? Why she must be *forty* years old!"

Kennedy kept a two-page picture spread from *Life* magazine, which he described as "one of the great moments of my life." It showed him in swim trunks on a California beach, surrounded by swarming women. Particularly impressive was a gorgeous blonde in a bikini, glued onto his arm, staring at him as if there were stars and bedrooms in her eyes.

Kennedy explained the greatness of the moment to Larry Newman: *"They're* chasing and *I'm* running!"

John Powers thought he was a man's man as well: "You've heard the line 'He's the kind of man that every elderly woman wants to mother and every young woman wants to marry,' " Powers added. "Well, he's also the kind of man that another man would like to go on a lion hunt with."

*   *   *

"He's the best natural politician since Roosevelt, and maybe better than Roosevelt," concluded Jim Rowe, who had worked for many presidents.

Reporter Peter Lisagor asked Kennedy, "Do you like these crowds and this sort of thing?"

Kennedy's face became intense, "I hate it."

When precinct worker Shirley Green asked him whether he was too young to deal with world leaders, he took a full five minutes to talk to her as if she were the most important audience in the world, while his staff was pulling at him to go elsewhere.

He once explained that the only way to reach people was to find the human being in them, and do it quickly. It was the same, he said, with an individual or a crowd.

He was most at ease with a college audience. At Wisconsin State College, he quoted John Quincy Adams, George Bernard Shaw, Aristotle, Professor Sidney Hook, Walter Lippmann, Thomas Jefferson (twice), President Eisenhower, Abraham Lincoln, and Daniel Webster. He knew that many students were not old enough to vote for him, but his defense was, "Where else can you get an audience at ten in the morning or three in the afternoon? And, don't forget, these students have parents."

One of the students was Melody Miller, studying to be a gym teacher. "We not only kept scrapbooks of Kennedy's every move," she said, "but we could look at a picture of Jackie and tell you where she wore that dress before." Melody switched from gym to government, and later went to work for Senator Ted Kennedy.

Some of the school signs read, "WHEN I GROW UP, I'M GONNA VOTE FOR YOU," "ELECT HIM FOR US NOW AND WE'LL PUT HIM BACK IN 1964," and "IF I ONLY HAD A VOTE, YOU'D HAVE IT." One he liked was "LET'S PUT A NEW JOHN IN THE WHITE HOUSE."

A sign that really made him laugh was one held up by two pretty girls, saying, "NOBODY CAN LICK OUR JACK."

* * *

A poem by an anonymous Kennedy staff member:

> The well-financed stable of writers
> Whose numbers the press do stun,
> You might never dream, if you saw them,
> But they are Ted Sorensen.

Ted was still in his twenties when Senator Kennedy interviewed him in 1953. There were two five-minute interviews. In the first one, Kennedy asked the questions. In the second, Sorensen queried Kennedy about his relationship with Senator McCarthy, the influence of his father, and his views of the Catholic Church.

The next day, Sorensen went to work for Kennedy.

Ted was "an extra lobe of Kennedy's mind," "more like Jack than Jack himself." They were "in each other's skin more than any other superior and subordinate I've ever seen." "When Jack is wounded, Ted bleeds." Equally uncanny was the exact way Ted Sorensen imitated Jack over the phone—if Kennedy requested. When someone wanted to know exactly how Kennedy felt about something, they came to Ted, not to Bobby. Sorensen's comment was quick: "I can say what the Senator thinks because, after all this time, I ought to know."

Sorensen unconsciously copied his gestures, his language, the rhythm of his speech; knew what phrases he preferred, and the points he would stress. Rarely would Sorensen put something into a speech that Kennedy flatly disliked. McGeorge

Bundy remembered one time when Kennedy found such a phrase and said, "Now Ted will never take it out so I'm gonna take it out."

Ted Sorensen did not have the status of FDR's Louis Howe, who could tell Roosevelt to "go to hell." But Sorensen was overheard to tell Kennedy at a Nebraska airport, "Presidential candidates don't chew gum."

Kennedy called Sorensen "my intellectual blood bank." He was more than that. He was a kind of conscience on social issues, from civil rights to human rights.

"The point of confusion for me in the Kennedy picture," said a strong Washington liberal who didn't much like Kennedy, "is how he has managed to keep Ted Sorensen with him. You have to judge a man by the people he keeps closest to him, and Ted himself is one hundred percent a Norris liberal, a pure type like his father was, with real brains, heart, dedication."

Sorensen's father had been an insurgent Republican and a campaign manager for George Norris, and later attorney general of Nebraska.

"Remember, Senator George Norris was a conservative before he became an independent liberal," Sorensen insisted. "As for Kennedy, I'm a Norris liberal, and so is he."

"Ted is indispensable to me," Kennedy said. "I want to keep Ted with me wherever I go in this campaign. You need somebody whom you can trust implicitly."

* * *

The press consensus was that Kennedy didn't like public speaking, and wasn't very good at it. He talked too fast, without suitable pauses or emphasis. When reading a speech, he often got only part value from his better lines and his clipped New England twang tended to become monotonous. He also seemed to look away from the camera too much and chopped the air when making a point. His set speeches often sounded like a harangue. His ad-lib speeches were better except they sometimes sounded "like a phonograph record being played too fast," skipping a groove now and then as his swift thoughts jumped from one theme to another.

He asked a friend for judgment on one of his speeches.

His friend was honest. "It was a bomb."

"Well, hell, you can't make a great speech every day. I'm doing too many speeches."

Advance men searched out local issues to put into speeches. "We were going nuts trying to find out how to feed this guy," commented one. Kennedy seldom used their material until they found a formula, compressed their local findings into a single page of notes, using thematic sentences with a punch line for each point to give it structure. Or else they would brief him while he was shaving, bathing, dressing, or eating breakfast.

What he now said often in his speeches was that our values were wrong, not our capabilities, that American idealism was the product of the advertising man, not the by-product of national purpose. Private interests, he said, had priority over public interests, and American idealism had lost its power to move Americans.

He promised he would change all that.

His delivery lacked warmth, he seldom smiled, his tone was undramatic, his gestures were awkward. His speech had a peculiar cadence, his voice falling when it should have been rising for maximum effect. Still, there was a magnetism in him and in his words. He told the crowds that some people felt that the more a politician promised, the better he was. But he wasn't going to promise the moon, he said; he wasn't going to make promises he couldn't keep. Again and again, he told the people that America was caught dead center in a dynamic age and he would "get this country moving again." The repeated power of that phrase, "get this country moving again," seemed to touch a national nerve.

He had difficulty talking to farmers, just as he had difficulty understanding their problems. "Where I grew up, we were taken out on a bus to see a cow," he told economist John Kenneth Galbraith. Then he added, "I don't want to hear about agricultural problems from anyone but you, Ken. And I don't want to hear about it too much from you either."

To the farmers, he said, "We have not had manure on our shoes up to now, but we're catching up fast." His Boston accent once backfired on him. He was an hour late for a farm rally in Sioux City, Iowa. In his best Harvard accent, he asked the farmers: "So I ahsk what's wrong with the American fahmah today?" While he paused for effect, a farmer yelled, "He's stahving!" Kennedy almost collapsed with laughter as the audience joined in.

There were times when his eloquence was moving, such as when he spoke in the pelting rain at the National Plowing Contest in South Dakota: "Ours is a great country, but we can make it a greater country. It is powerful, but we must make it more powerful. I ask your help. I promise you no sure solutions, no easy life. The years ahead for all of us will be as difficult as any in our history. There are new frontiers for America to conquer in education, in science, in national purpose—not frontiers on a map, but frontiers of the mind, the will, the spirit of man. . . ."

As he said this, the rain stopped, the sun came out on the crowd in startling brilliance—as if he had arranged it—and the normally undemonstrative farmers gave him thunderous applause.

At times like this, Kennedy "almost seemed to seize the audience physically." Introducing Kennedy to a California audience, Stevenson summed it up well: "You remember that in classical times, when Cicero had finished speaking, the people said, 'How well he spoke'—but when Demosthenes had finished speaking, the people said, '*Let us march!*' "

It took him a long time to develop a speaking style of his own. He learned to speak quickly, glibly, amusingly, but oratory was something else. If he had a model, it was Winston Churchill. If there was a particular speech that impressed him most, it was Churchill's speech to the joint session of Congress seventeen days after Pearl Harbor discussing his "blood right to speak . . . in our common cause." Churchill added, "I cannot help reflecting that if my father had been the American and my mother British, instead of the other way round, I might have gotten here on my own."

"Jack and I were in a hotel room, listening to this thing, wrapped in it," said his friend Spalding, remembering the Churchill speech. "He just hovered over that radio. In the elevator afterwards, we were still going through the speech and he was imitating it, asking me, 'What do you think of this gesture, Charlie?' It was just as though he had gone to a Wagnerian opera, and he was trying to recapture it with all its implications. He did it in such a strangely classy way . . . like a beautiful ice skater or dancer . . . with such graceful moves. . . .''

Fred Dutton, later a White House staff man recalled, "I was in Kennedy's Georgetown house in the spring of '60. There was some kind of front hall and a room next to it and that's where Kennedy was. He was all by himself, smoking a cigar, having a brandy, and listening to Winston Churchill speeches on records. He kept us waiting about fifteen minutes until he heard what he wanted to hear. I guess he was listening for the cadence and the style as well as the language.''

Kennedy would have been intrigued by the fact that Churchill learned much of his own oratorical style from his mother's lover, the great American orator Congressman Bourke Cockran.

Kennedy had a theatrical sense of how to start a speech, almost as if he could smell the audience mood. He was a better editor than writer and could take a speech draft, strike out what he didn't want, and know exactly what he did want. He was not apt to change his mind easily but would listen to technical criticism. If it worked, he remembered it. He learned to use a lower pitch, which gave his voice more drama. His father provided a Boston University voice teacher, a life-long Republican, who taught him timing and breathing, which helped to make his speech less nasal and harsh, and gave it more cadence. He learned not to rush his sentences, to avoid overworking his favorite phrase, "I must say, . . ." and to wait for applause and laughs.

The press generally agreed that his audiences liked him. They liked the warmth of his face, his refreshing directness, and —the phrase they used most—"his sincerity."

In his short talks from the back of a truck, he started to improvise more and more. An aide suggested he was doing fine without his notes and perhaps didn't need them anymore. Without them he felt insecure, he answered—he needed them to fall back on.

There were some things he could not do on a public stage. When a microphone stopped working during a Pennsylvania rally, Governor David Lawrence whispered, "Jack, get up there . . . get up there and start talking . . . hold the crowd."

"I can't do that," Kennedy answered tensely. "I can't *do* that!"

Nor was he always verbally masterful.

"When I heard Kennedy at a meeting one day, it was like trying to nail custard to a wall," said Bill Mauldin, Pulitzer prize–winning author and cartoonist.

In every age there comes a time when leadership suddenly comes forth to meet the needs of the hour. And so there is no man who does not find his time, and there is no hour that does not have its leader.
—THE TALMUD

11

The Kennedy/Nixon Debates

Concerned about her previous miscarriage, Jacqueline, who was five months pregnant, kept close to home, sunning on the chaise at Hyannis, listening to "Mack the Knife," and taking two-and-a-half-year-old Caroline for horseback riding lessons.

Columnist Dorothy Kilgallen intimated that perhaps Jacqueline wasn't really pregnant but was using it as an excuse not to campaign. Mrs. Kennedy quipped, "Do you think I should stuff a pillow under my dress to convince her?"

When Joan Braden became National Women's Chairman for Jack Kennedy in 1960, Bobby asked her to tell him her top priority: "Bring Jackie into the campaign," she answered.

Bobby was highly dubious, but he called his sister-in-law. He still seemed amazed when he told Braden, "She'd be delighted to do anything you want her to do."

"By chance, I was the same number of months pregnant as she was," Braden remembered. "The difference was that this was my seventh child and I had never had any problems; but she had lost a couple of children and had to be more careful. If she hadn't had her tragic experience with pregnancies, she would have done more."

Jacqueline was less than candid when she wrote that she "loved every minute of it." She privately confided that she disliked campaigning as intensely as ever, particularly personal appearances and a TV program called "Caucus for Kennedy."

Something she seemed to enjoy was a column she started, "Campaign Wife." In it, she wrote about all kinds of things, such as "the lonely autumn days" in Hyannis Port after Labor Day.

"Nearly all the houses have boarded windows, boats have been taken out of the water, and only sea gulls cry above the deserted pier where Caroline and I go to throw them bread. The thirteen cousins she played with this summer are gone. . . . Jack telephones late each night. . . ."

In another column, her frustrations crept in.

"The worst part was not being in Los Angeles for the nomination," she wrote, "but my obstetrician firmly disagreed. Since then I have resigned myself and have kept up with my husband by reading several newspapers every day."

Part of still another column read:

"This week was one long moving day for me. I closed our house in Hyannis Port, and we all trooped back to Washington and have been unpacking ever since. Our cat and dog don't seem to get along half as well in the cramped quarters of our Georgetown house! And many of Caroline's friends, with whom she used to play in the park every morning, have now graduated to nursery school.

"Though my child won't even begin nursery school until next year, I worry already about where to send her, all the way through high school and sound out friends with older children about which school in our area is best for which type of child. Many of them are happy with their children's schooling—but more are not. Several days ago I read that the Prince George's County School Board in Maryland had bought trailers to be used as classrooms to reduce double sessions in elementary schools. . . . It emphasized the urgent need all over the country for additional classrooms. . . . My husband has been deeply concerned with these problems . . . and has recently supported in the Senate a successful effort to pass legislation providing federal aid for school construction and for teachers' salaries."

"Caroline was very excited about having her picture taken for TV," she later wrote, "but when it went on and on and she had fed her baby three or four times and smelled the flowers ten times, she got a little fidgety."

Jacqueline used her fluency in languages to make radio tapes in Italian, Spanish, and Polish, and to broadcast in French to a group of Haitians living in Boston. She invited leading women into her home for discussions, and organized a TV listening party for her husband's first debate with Nixon. "Of course I thought he was marvelous," she said afterwards. In organizing Women's Committee for New Frontiers for panel discussions on leading issues, she quoted her husband as saying, "One woman is worth ten men in a campaign." Commenting on how well her husband got along without her while he was campaigning, she admitted, "Every time I see him, he looks better than before. It's really bad for one's ego."

Jacqueline also sponsored a campaign program, "Calling for Kennedy," to get women's opinions on campaign issues. She collected advice from two hundred women precinct workers:

"Tell Senator Kennedy to speak more slowly on television."

"I've been telling Jack to speak more slowly," she replied, "but he's so earnest about it, he can't slow down."

Another suggested that the senator should be more "homey" like Nixon in appealing to home and mother and against sin.

"I know what you mean," Mrs. Kennedy answered, "but it's a little late to change him now."

"I would like to have Senator Kennedy keep saying, 'Mr. Nixon, you are not telling the truth.' "

Mrs. Kennedy almost smiled and all she could answer was, "Well. . . ."

"People say I don't know anything about politics," she told a reporter. "And, in a way, it's true. But you learn an enormous amount just being around politicians. . . ."

A political leader smiled at this. "She didn't know me from

a load of hay," he said ruefully. "She seemed like a fish out of water."

*   *   *

A loud drunk was making ugly comments to his wife about Kennedy at the Voisin restaurant in New York City. Kennedy and his companions were seated at an adjoining table, and his friends raised their voices trying to drown out the drunk. It didn't work, and one of them started to call for the head waiter. Kennedy caught his arm. "No, don't bother. Think how the fellow's wife must be feeling."

*   *   *

It was a small dinner party at the Averell Harrimans' and Joan Braden watched Senator Kennedy turn over one of the plates to see the maker's name.

"I have no idea what possessed me," Braden said, "but I was sitting right next to him and I suddenly heard myself telling him about a doctor I had met who had told me that Senator Kennedy had Addison's disease. I didn't say who it was. Jack didn't get angry. But the next day he called me to ask who the doctor was. At first, I didn't want to tell him, but then I thought it important for him to quash the rumor, so I did tell him. I don't know what happened."

Jack Kennedy later contacted prominent liberal Joseph Rauh. "Your friends on the *New York Post* are going to print the story tomorrow that I have an incurable disease, and this will hurt me badly in the campaign. I think you ought to tell them that it isn't fair, and that I am not using any suppressant drugs, and that I really am wholly healthy and able to take this job."

Rauh passed on the message.

*   *   *

He was still a senator, living in Georgetown and driving his own convertible. En route to his office, he saw civil rights lawyer Harris Wofford waiting for a taxi, and he stopped to pick him up.

"Now in five minutes tick off the ten things a president

2 1 0

ought to do to clean up this goddamn civil rights mess," Kennedy said, tapping the car window with his restless fingers.

He had been challenged by the Mississippi Republican state chairman to come to Mississippi and state his views on integration and segregation. His southern friends begged him to back out. They reminded him that Mississippi's Governor James P. Coleman already had blessed his civil rights stand as "sober and temperate," adding his judgment of Jack Kennedy: "He's no hell-raiser or barn-burner." How wise was it to muddy such politically clear waters when they seriously needed the South? What Kennedy wondered was how one could keep this support and still win the black vote. He soon found part of the answer.

To an overflow crowd in the Roof Room of the Heidelberg Hotel in Jackson, Mississippi, Kennedy boyishly tugged at his ear, tweaked his nose, ran a finger around the inside of his shirt collar. He began:

"You who have been gracious enough to invite me here realize that we do not see eye to eye on all national issues. I have no hesitancy in telling the Republican chairman the same thing I said in my own city of Boston, that I accept the Supreme Court decision as the supreme law of the land. I know that we do not all agree on that issue, but I think most of us do agree on the necessity to uphold law and order in every part of the land." Kennedy paused, then quickly added: "And now I challenge the Republican chairman to tell us where *he* stands on Eisenhower and Nixon!" The crowd came to its feet, alive, roaring, stomping its approval.

"I never thought I'd see anybody in central Mississippi speak up for integration and get a standing ovation," a local congressman said in wonder.

"You know what?" added a slightly tipsy young Democrat. "All those Baptists and Methodists are going to vote for you, my Catholic friend. And I'm proud to say I'm one of them, too."

Kennedy's southern support came from everywhere. A reporter with him in South Carolina noted that their publisher-host was both anti-black and anti-Semitic. He wondered aloud why the publisher supported Jack Kennedy as strongly as he did, since Kennedy was neither of those things.

"Well," said the publisher, "we know Papa Joe. And Papa Joe will keep him in line."

But the undercurrent against his father never stopped. "I'm not against the pope, I'm against the pop."

"You know the old man is hurting you," a reporter once told Kennedy. "Can't you keep him out of the picture?"

"What do you want me to do?" Kennedy answered. "My father is working for his son. Do you want me to tell my father to stop working for his son?"

The influence of his father?

Kennedy tried to minimize it with humor. At an Alfred E. Smith Foundation dinner, during the campaign, he remarked: "I had announced earlier this year that, if successful, I would not consider campaign contributions as substitute for experience in appointing ambassadors. Ever since I made that statement, I have not received one single cent from my father."

To the owner of the famed "21" restaurant, Jack Kennedy said, "My grandfather had a saloon and my father was in the liquor business, and I don't usually get such a warm reception from people to whom my father sold something."

With all this, Jack saw his father whole and knew how large he loomed as a political liability. London *Sunday Times* correspondent Henry Brandon told Kennedy he wanted to see his father, and Kennedy replied, "Henry, if you do, you'll never speak to me again."

When Bill Walton was approached by someone who wanted to contribute $100,000 if he could become an ambassador, Walton called "the old man." The senior Kennedy's reply was quick: "Any man who is dumb enough to ask you to do that is too dumb to be an ambassador."

"I was surprised how liberal the father was on many issues," Walton said. "For example, he suggested all kinds of reforms that the Securities and Exchange Commission ought to make. Of course, he had headed the SEC under Roosevelt. But he also felt that a newspaper should not own either the TV station or radio station in the same town, that they all ought to be independent. He felt the same way about television being a monopoly. Maybe it was partly because the Kennedys had so much trouble buying TV time in many places."

"Why don't you ask about my mother?" Bobby Kennedy angrily challenged a reporter querying again about his father. "She's campaigned for Jack in a lot of states and Dad never has."

What nobody could control was the candid quality of Rose Kennedy's remarks. She felt Nixon was doing well "without the advantage of a powerful family." She loved everybody "in little Wyoming." When her son Jack was a boy, "he didn't work as hard . . . he was more like me." What irritated her most was press comment on Kennedy campaign spending:

"It's *our* money, and we're free to spend it any way we please. It's part of this campaign business. If you have money, you spend it to win. And the more you can afford, the more you'll spend."

"Once we were down in Palm Beach," Spalding said, "and his mother said, 'Jack, I wish you could stay.' And he said, 'Well, you got me started in this.' "

Kennedy staffers indicated that the Ambassador was tolerated as an adviser, but seldom heeded. Occasionally, at a staff meeting, Jack Kennedy would say, "Dad thinks this. . . ."

His father had a direct line to his son's Senate office and it rang often. "No, Dad, I'll never do that," his son was heard to say.

"Sometimes he'll call up and say you ought to see so-and-so in New York or you ought to get in touch with somebody in Nevada," Kennedy recalled.

"Dad is a financial genius, all right," his son said often, "but in politics, he is something else. His political judgment can be very wrong—I now know more about politics than he does, a lot more. He can't run my campaign sitting out in Cape Cod, and he doesn't. He's really had less to do with my campaign than any of the other members of my family."

"If Jack ever feels he has anything to ask me," his father said, "he knows where he can find me, and I'll tell him what I think. But I feel very strongly about older people keeping their noses out of the businesses of their children."

"He was never as involved in the making of the President as was reported," said Ken O'Donnell, who did not much like the elder Kennedy, "but it is also very likely true that without him Jack wouldn't have made it."

He did so much that his son never knew about. A New York public relations man practically guaranteed a *Life* magazine cover for an enormous fee. The Ambassador paid and the cover appeared—perhaps by coincidence. Jack Kennedy's labor adviser, Arthur Goldberg, needed an operation and the senior Kennedy tried to persuade him to come to Boston's Leahy Clinic under the care of Kennedy doctors. Goldberg refused but the Ambassador persisted. Goldberg finally agreed to let a Kennedy doctor examine him for a second opinion. Jack's only involvement was to send Goldberg another copy of *Profiles in Courage* —he had sent him three others at different times. "Richard Nixon sent me a bottle of Chivas Regal," Goldberg said, smiling.

Joseph Kennedy also told his son, "You do what you think is right and we'll take care of the politicians." Generally, he kept out of political sight. "No interviews," he said, "it only hurts Jack." His wife explained, "He thinks it's easier for his son if he doesn't appear on the scene."

When his father made a rare appearance at Kennedy's campaign office, "we tried to get him the hell out," Kennedy assistant Ralph Dungan said.

The father helped in other ways. Jack wanted Harris Wofford as a civil liberties adviser, but he was then on the faculty of the University of Notre Dame and they refused to release him. The Ambassador called Notre Dame President John Cavanaugh and used some vivid language. Wofford arrived. Such were his contacts in the Church that when a butler announced, "The cardinal is on the telephone," he replied, "Which one?"

"Don't underestimate Mr. Kennedy," Sargent Shriver said. "He didn't make a quarter billion dollars by being dumb."

The senior Kennedy once brought a big contribution from one of his friends. His son considered the original source and then returned it as too hot to keep. Jack also canceled a strategy session of the family and top aides called by his father. At another Palm Beach staff conference, the father made his usual acerbic comments. His son quickly added, "Well, we've heard the Ambassador's views, now let's get on with our business."

After a spirited Labor Day speech, Jack telephoned his friend Charles Bartlett. "The old man just called me from Palm Beach and said if I keep talking the way I did today, they're going to bury me six feet under. You know, I'm not going to talk to Dad anymore about this campaign. The one thing he doesn't understand is that if the Democrats are to get elected, they've got to excite a lot of people to believe that if they win the election, then life is going to be a helluva lot better, and if they don't excite the people then they're not going to get in."

Joseph Kennedy usually kept his lingering doubts to himself, but occasionally opened up. When New Hampshire editor William Loeb visited him, the former Ambassador pointed to a portrait of his son Joe. "*That* is the boy who should have been president. That's the one, and he would have made a wonderful president." Then he pointed to a picture of Jack, "This one would have been a college professor."

When Bob Considine told Jack Kennedy that his father burst into tears when he talked about Joe, Jr., Kennedy responded, "Dad always does that. I'll tell you about Joe. He was the star among the kids. He was taller than the rest of us, stronger, better looking. He was the best athlete of the bunch, could jump higher, run faster, hit harder. He brought home the best report cards.

"Joe would have been the politician of the family, not me. Joe would have won the congressional seat from our district in 1946. Joe would have beaten Henry Cabot Lodge for his Senate seat in 1952. Joe would have beaten Estes Kefauver last summer for the vice-presidential nomination, where I just missed. It would have been a Stevenson-Kennedy ticket."

He paused and grinned.

"And Eisenhower would have knocked their brains out. Right now, Joe would be picking up the broken pieces of his political career."

He paused again.

"I guess I owe a lot to Estes."

There was no question of the father's political bent. He admired Herbert Hoover almost more than anyone. They had served together on the Hoover Commission for government reorganization. When Hoover sent him an autographed picture with the inscription, "To Joe Kennedy, our greatest member,"

Joe Kennedy wept. Rose Kennedy quoted her husband as saying that former President Hoover was one of the few people in the world who really enlightened him.

When conservative Republican Senator Robert Taft died, Joe Kennedy announced from his verandah that it was "the greatest tragedy to befall the American people in the loss of a statesman since the assassination of Abraham Lincoln."

As for his support of Senator Joseph McCarthy, it never deviated.

"When we grew a little older, we realized he wasn't perfect," Robert Kennedy would say of his father, "that he made mistakes, but by that time, we realized everyone did. I remember listening to him talk with an important figure in business, the theater, or politics, and always observing that he was the dominant figure—that he knew more—that he expressed it better. . . . If he was more clever or wiser than others, he would be unusual. But then, perhaps everyone's father is cleverer and wiser than anyone else."

Part of the father's drive was that he would not consider failure. Gloria Swanson recalled the looming disaster of a film production and how he sounded like "a wounded animal whimpering in a trap . . . little high-pitched sounds escaped from his rigid body." Then his voice became quiet and controlled and he said, "I've never had a failure in my life."

*   *   *

Jacqueline confided to a friend the pressures the Catholic Church was putting on her to be a good campaign wife. "I think she was a little more than sore," the friend related, "because she told me, 'I might quit after all this is over. The Church, I mean.' "

"I remember once," Bill Walton said, "when Cardinal Spellman had done something or said something with which Jack and Jackie and his father all violently disagreed. Jack said, 'I'm going to quit the Church,' and Jackie said, 'I'm going to quit the Church,' and his father said, 'No, neither of you can quit the Church, but I can, and I'm *really* going to quit the Church.' "

Kennedy and Charles Spalding were talking about it one day and Jack asked. "How do you come out on religion?"

"Well," Spalding said, "I can't get an answer."

"That's where I am," Kennedy said.

He also mentioned Churchill's reply, when asked if he considered himself a pillar of the Church. "No," he said, "more like one of the flying buttresses. I support it from the outside."

"I wish we could start a new religion that would bring all people together," Kennedy told Kay Halle.

"I think it's so unfair of people to be against Jack because he is a Catholic," Jacqueline told columnist Arthur Krock at a Washington party. "He's such a poor Catholic. Now if it were Bobby, I could understand it."

Jack was "skeptical" about religion and the Church.

"But he went," Spalding said. "He always went."

"There are an awful lot of pressing things going on around me," Kennedy had said, "and I just accept the fact that I'm a Catholic and live by their rules." He mentioned sometimes that Einstein had said that one of the indications of God was the incredible order of the universe. But he also added that it was something that he never expected to solve "and I can't see that anybody else has."

"What kind of Catholic are you?" somebody asked.

"I go to church on Sunday," Kennedy said simply, and stopped there.

"He was a very old-fashioned Catholic," said John Cogley, a former editor of *Commonweal* magazine. "Fish every Friday, Mass on Sunday, that kind of thing, a very Boston kind of Catholicism."

"He was just as good a Catholic as I am," the late Cardinal Cushing added, "and he had ideas similar to mine. I don't like to parade my religion. I try to live as I'm supposed to live. He was the same."

"He'd be on his knees every night," Dave Powers recalled. "Nobody saw him more often than I did, except Jackie, so I know. Now sometimes when I go to bed, I'll say my prayers in bed, lying down. But he was always on his knees, every night that I saw him."

What Kennedy never forgot was the tone in the voice of Adlai Stevenson's sister after Kennedy's defeat for the vice-presidential nomination. "Oh, those poor little Catholics. . . ."

Kennedy reacted to the Al Smith–Catholic issue in typical Kennedy fashion. At the Alfred E. Smith Memorial Dinner in New York, he said: "I think it is good to recall what really happened to a great governor when he became a presidential nominee. Despite his successful record as a governor, despite his plainspoken views, that campaign was a debacle. His views were distorted. He carried fewer states than any candidate in his party's history. He lost states that had been solid for his party for half a century and, to top it off, he lost his own state, which he had served so well as governor. I think you all know his name, and his religion—Alfred (at this point Kennedy paused) Alfred M. Landon, Protestant!"

As the audience howled its appreciation, Kennedy added, "In spite of that, I see no reason to suggest to Governor Rockefeller that the Republicans should not nominate a Protestant in 1960."

On the issue of papal infallibility, Kennedy later quipped: "The last time I saw Cardinal Spellman I brought up this question . . . and asked the cardinal for his views. He said, 'All I know is that he calls me Spillman.' "

His first loyalty was to his country, not his religion, Kennedy repeated. He pointed out that in every instance where Catholic political power bore down on a controversial issue, he voted the other way. He sponsored federal aid for school construction that omitted aid to parochial schools. He opposed sending an ambassador to the Vatican. He supported the nomination of James Conant as ambassador to West Germany, when the Church had attacked Conant for speaking out against parochial schools.

He told reporters that he felt a Catholic president could more easily withstand Catholic political pressure than a non-Catholic. He felt attacks on his religion would not be too politically dangerous because they would be attributed to bigots. Besides, he said, a great number of those who opposed him because he was a Catholic were Republicans who wouldn't vote for a Democratic candidate anyway.

"Let's not con ourselves," his father insisted. "The only issue is whether a Catholic can be elected president."

"I'm getting tired of these people who think I want to replace the gold at Fort Knox with a supply of holy water," Kennedy told O'Donnell.

When the Vatican implied some criticism of Kennedy's campaign efforts to prove himself free of papal influence, Kennedy said ruefully to a pair of reporters: "Now I understand why Henry VIII set up his own church."

The question of a confrontation on the issue came with an invitation to address a convocation of Protestant ministers in Houston. Before that, he had tried to bury the issue, but it wouldn't bury. He remembered a remark from Gen. James Gavin: "If you want a decision, go to the point of danger." His father remained adamant against accepting the invitation.

"You have to understand my father," said Jack Kennedy to a reporter. "He'll throw an idea up into the air, and see how it looks, what the reaction to it is. I discussed the religious issue with my father, but I didn't get his permission or anything before I made that speech—the relationship doesn't work that way."

Speaker of the House Sam Rayburn was similarly unhappy with the confrontation. Watching the speech on TV with Ken O'Donnell, he said, "You know, Mr. O'Donnell, this is the biggest mistake he's made in this campaign."

O'Donnell could not disagree.

There were few speeches in which Kennedy did not improvise. This was one of the few he read word for word.

"I believe in an America where the separation of church and state is absolute—where no Catholic prelate would tell the president, should he be a Catholic, how to act, and no Protestant minister would tell his parishioners for whom to vote."

He urged the clergymen to "judge me on the basis of my record of fourteen years in Congress. . . . I do not speak for my church on public matters—and the Church does not speak for me.

"Whatever issue may come before me as president, if I should be elected—on birth control, divorce, censorship, gambling, or any other subject—I will make my decision in accordance with these views, in accordance with what my conscience tells me to be in the national interest, and without regard to outside religious pressure or dictates. And no power or threat of punishment could cause me to decide otherwise."

As Rayburn watched Kennedy quickly demolish the ministers in the question and answer period on TV, he excitedly clapped his hands. He had considered it stupid for the Democrats to nominate a Catholic, but now he said, "That boy's really got it! He's gonna make it, that boy! He's eating them blood-raw! This young feller will be a great president!" Then he turned to O'Donnell, looking happier and younger, "Get me a bourbon, sonny!"

*   *   *

Eleanor Roosevelt was not the kind of woman who forgot a kindness. During the campaign, one of her granddaughters fell off a horse and was killed. Candidate Kennedy was due to arrive in Hyde Park that day. Mrs. Roosevelt and Kennedy had had their differences, often publicly aired, and it would have been easy and proper for her to cancel this appointment. But she knew his tight schedule and decided to see him.

"That young man behaved with such sensitivity and compassion throughout that whole day," she said afterwards, "he gave me more comfort than almost anyone around me, my family or anybody else. The manner in which he treated me during the day of his visit won me—as did the many things he believed in and what he wanted to do."

Her son John, however, a strong Republican, called Kennedy "a whiz kid who makes snap judgments and should not be entrusted with the leadership of the nation."

His mother disagreed.

"He has matured. He has the qualities of a scholar, and a sense of history. He will make a very good president, if elected."

"I don't think anyone in our politics since Franklin had the same vital relationship with crowds," Mrs. Roosevelt told Arthur Schlesinger, Jr. "Franklin would sometimes begin a campaign weary and apathetic, but in the course of the campaign he would draw strength and vitality from the audiences, and would end in better shape than he started. I feel that Senator Kennedy is much the same—that his intelligence and courage elicit emotions from his crowds which flow back to him, and sustain and strengthen him."

Jacqueline Kennedy found it difficult to forgive Eleanor Roosevelt, whom she called "pigheaded, mean, and spiteful," for her earlier negative remarks about Jack. She found it difficult to think kindly about any of her husband's critics but she admired the way he "learned to roll with the punches . . . was more bemused than upset." "Whenever I was upset by something in the papers, he always told me to be more tolerant, like a horse flicking away flies in the summer."

A reporter was alone with Jacqueline Kennedy in a small room watching the tape playback of "Face the Nation." On the program, the reporter had asked some probing questions about Kennedy's subtle use of the religious issue.

When it was over, the reporter, Peter Lisagor of the *Chicago Sun-Times*, said to Mrs. Kennedy. "You seem a little angry with me. Am I right? And why?"

She had coolly ignored him in the room, even refusing to acknowledge his nod.

"Oh well, I was," she said. "It was because I thought you were asking mean, nasty questions. But Jack says that you were doing your job and that you're really a nice fellow. If I seem to be angry, why I'm sorry. I'm just getting a little tense. The thing is building up now, and I'm a little tense. I'm sorry."

         ★   ★   ★

Nixon and Kennedy had come to Congress together, worked together on a number of issues, and now they were in offices 361 and 362, facing each other across the third-floor corridor in the northeast corner of the marble Senate Office Building. The plaque on one door read, "Mr. Kennedy, Massachusetts"; and the other, "The Vice-President."

A cartoon of Nixon and Kennedy showed them peeking out of their office doors each to see if the other were there. Nixon autographed it for Kennedy: "To Jack Kennedy, my good friend, who I wish the best in almost everything."

"Nixon is a nice fellow in private, and a very able man," Jack Kennedy told a foreign correspondent. "I worked with him on the Hill for a long time, but he seems to have a split personality; and he is very bad in public, and nobody likes him."

As freshmen congressmen, the two had shared a debating platform in April 1947, in western Pennsylvania. Kennedy then considered Nixon dull, coy, and too conservative. "Against Nixon," he said, "I might even get a few votes from the Ku Klux Klan." Then he added, "When you compare Nixon and Goldwater, Goldwater seems like Abraham Lincoln."

Nixon had equal contempt for Kennedy. Nixon had been a champion debater in college and he saw Kennedy as a young man still groping for a speaking style. He expected to demolish him.

Kennedy, on the other hand, thought Nixon "a damn fool to agree to debate me on an equal-time TV basis. Just imagine if Eisenhower had had to do this against Stevenson in 1952 and 1956. He would have looked silly." Kennedy also felt that the press had regarded him generally as a naïve, inexperienced young man. Now he would have his chance to show the whole nation "his true colors."

Two days before each debate, Kennedy's assistant, Mike Feldman, took a stack of briefing papers to him, wherever he was. On the day of debate, Feldman, with Sorensen and another staff man, Dick Goodwin, spent up to four hours with him rehearsing probable points, and answering anticipated questions. Before bedtime, Kennedy flipped through a file of 3 x 5 cards filled with facts and statistics. The available topical index of all of Nixon's policies and views ran to a thousand pages of single-spaced information. The Kennedy briefing team played the hunch that Nixon would use the same arguments in the television debates that he had used in his speeches around the country.

The hunch paid off.

For Kennedy, there were no queries his team had not anticipated. Kennedy was "the cool candidate on the cool tube" whose blood pressure soared to normal in a crisis.

A Nixon aide naïvely asked Robert Kennedy his opinion of Nixon's makeup. Bobby noted Nixon's paleness, his sunken cheeks and shadowed eyes, and replied, "Terrific! Terrific! I wouldn't change a thing!"

Watching them on TV monitors, columnist Doris Fleeson commented, "Why, Nixon has lost the thing. He sat there spraddled out almost as if his fly were open."

As the two debated, the consensus was that Nixon failed to offer an inspiring view of the future, seemed to "talk down" to his audience. Kennedy, they said, showed assurance and confidence with a challenge to "move forward."

"Nixon was best on radio," observed *New York Herald Tribune* reporter Earl Mazo, "simply because his deep resonant voice carried more conviction, command, and determination than Kennedy's higher-pitched voice and his Boston-Harvard accent. But on television, Kennedy looked sharper, more in control, more firm—his was the image of the man who could stand up to Khrushchev."

CBS commentator Eric Sevareid was caustic about both candidates, calling them "tidy, buttoned-down men . . . completely packaged products." Both, he said, were "sharp, opportunistic, devoid of strong convictions and deep passions, with no commitment except to personal advancement . . . I always sensed that they would end up running the big companies in town but I'm damned if I ever thought one of them would end up running the country."

"They're both hardworking, both intelligent," said Abe Fortas, a Johnson adviser who became a Supreme Court justice, "and I think neither has a core. I think there is nothing that either man wouldn't compromise on to get the job."

"Here are two tight-lipped, image-conscious, rigid, nervous, totally humorless young men," wrote British M.P. Richard Crossman in his diary. "Oh dear, oh dear! Compare them with Mr. Khrushchev or Colonel Nasser, or Mr. Ben-Gurion, or Mao Tse-tung. Oh dear, oh dear! That's the ally we rely on."

Jack Kennedy needed no makeup for his tanned face except a dab of powder for the shine on his nose. Sorensen, however, suggested sharpening the lighting so that he could "stand out in appearance as dramatically as you did in the first debate." He also advocated camera close-ups to give a personal feeling and eliminate any show of handling the manuscript. The Nixon people decided to cool the studio more so Nixon wouldn't sweat so much in front of the camera.

With his usual enthusiasm, Kennedy's father told him, after the first debate, "It's all over." His wife added, "You looked wonderful, Jack." When he talked to Jacqueline, Jack "could not suppress his delight." He felt he had wiped out the issues of youth and inexperience, that "Nixon's build-up as a debater was too big."

On behalf of her husband, Jacqueline telephoned Arthur Schlesinger, Jr., and John Kenneth Galbraith and asked them to help prepare him for the next debates. Galbraith observed Kennedy in the elevator, en route to the TV studio, as being "a bit tense." Galbraith recalled saying to himself, "Kennedy, you're the only thing that stands between Nixon and the White House." Jack Kennedy himself then said, "When I first began this campaign, I just wanted to beat Nixon. Now I want to save the country from him."

When the debates were over, liberal independent columnist I.F. Stone didn't feel there was much choice. "Kennedy is beginning more and more to resemble the late John Foster Dulles." Comedian Mort Sahl offered another opinion on the election: "Neither candidate is going to win."

In her weekly column for the Democratic party, Jacqueline Kennedy stuck the needle into Nixon's need for makeup to cover his heavy beard. "I was proud of him [Jack] for *not wearing any makeup*, simply presenting himself as he is . . ."

She also commended her husband's "absolute calm" before the debates, his "great control under stress . . . more than I ever could." When it was over, she added, "He relaxes and is happy to talk about it with me."

*   *   *

The small parlor of Jacqueline's Georgetown house often had reporters filling the blonde settees and easy chairs while Jacqueline sat on the bench in front of the fireplace. She looked around puzzled. "Jack gets seventy-five people into this little place."

Did she expect the White House to change her?

"I wouldn't put on a mask and pretend to be anything I wasn't."

Was she up to White House entertaining?

"I have been married to one of the busiest men in the country for seven years. I ran three houses for him."

Reporters found her refreshingly frank.

Was she a great sailing enthusiast like her husband?

"They just shoved me into a boat long enough to take the picture."

What about their new adventures into art?

Her paintings had a measure of finish, she said, but her husband's painting was "definitely primitive."

Did she like cats more than dogs?

She got a cat because her husband was allergic to dogs.

Was she really helping her husband in his legislative duties?

"I'm trying to help with this bill to relax the McCarran Immigration Act. I feel strongly about it. A bill that restrictive might not have let in the Bouviers or the Kennedys from Ireland, or the McCarrans!"

She responded to more questions:

Would he put a woman in his Cabinet?

"He certainly could pick a good woman if he's looking for one. But he's not picking his Cabinet until after November 8th."

If he won, what would be her White House role?

"I would do whatever he wanted. . . . I certainly would not express any views that were not my husband's. I get all my views from him—not because I can't make up my mind on my own, but because he would not be where he is unless he were one of the most able men in his party, so I think he's right."

In the days to come she would change her mind about some of this.

Creating much more of a political stir than any of her seminars or conference calls was a national flap over the cost of her clothes. The headline question: WHOSE CLOTHES COST MORE? MRS. KENNEDY'S OR MRS. NIXON'S?

"I'm sure I spend less than Mrs. Nixon," insisted Mrs. Kennedy. "She gets hers at Elizabeth Arden, and nothing there costs less than $200 or $300." In the past year, she said, she had bought only one Paris dress, and she bought that from her sister. Her mother-in-law went to Paris for the fashion shows every year "and always brings back one outfit for each of the girls in our family."

She confided she had a little dressmaker in Washington, "the only one who can fit into my crazy schedule. I don't have much chance to plod around the stores but anybody in public life must be equipped with clothes in advance." So she picked out styles she liked from magazines.

"I hate a full closet," she continued. "I've gotten ruthless about what looks best on me."

"Every time I had to shoot her, I'd look through her wardrobe and there'd be like ten dresses," claimed Jacques Lowe, who photographed Jacqueline Kennedy more than anyone. "She buys very few things, but they're just right, and she keeps them a long time."

Some reporters expanded their criticism to include Jacqueline's hairdo, which they described as a "floor mop."

"I'm surprised at them," Mrs. Kennedy said. "I try to keep it neat and well-groomed."

She then asked the reporter, "Do you think it looks offensive? All the talk about what I wear and how I fix my hair has amused and puzzled me. What does my hairdo have to do with my husband's ability to be president? They're beginning to snipe at me about that as often as they attack Jack on Catholicism. I think it's dreadfully unfair."

For a half hour she had been answering questions from nine women reporters, and a single male. Her unpolished nails were bitten to the quick, and she was staring at them. She was telling a reporter that her husband would be "absolutely magnificent" as president, and then added, almost inaudibly, "And I hope I won't fail him in any way."

To a woman reporter, she said, "I think a wife's happiness comes if her husband is happy."

It was the male reporter who asked: "Mrs. Kennedy, we have all heard about the tremendously enthusiastic response of the women and girls in the crowds to your husband. Does that response make you jealous?"

"Of course not," she said emphatically. "Women are very idealistic and they respond to an idealistic person like my husband. I am delighted that they responded to him so enthusiastically."

The reporter followed through. "As the girl who married Senator Kennedy, you can understand the attraction he has for women?"

"Well," she answered slowly, "if *you* want to put it that way."

"Can we say that you approach the White House confidently, Mrs. Kennedy?" another reporter asked.

"I would rather not say that," she answered politely. Then she added even more quietly, "In my life there have been a lot of adjustments. . . . I have entertained for large and small groups on long and short notice."

Had she told three-year-old Caroline about her newly expected baby?

"I have followed Dr. Benjamin Spock's advice not to tell her too soon because children that age get tired of waiting." She thought of a happy footnote and smiled. "Dr. Spock has just come out for my husband, and I am for Dr. Spock."

Had her husband changed much since he was a presidential candidate?

"I don't think Jack has changed much, I really don't. He still thinks nothing of answering his door at home when he's wearing his shorts."

*   *   *

Somebody mentioned it would be just like Jackie Kennedy to have her baby on election eve. Quick with the quip, straight-faced, she came back: "Oh, I hope not. I'd have to get up the next day to go and vote."

When asked what she would do in the event her baby was born on Inauguration Day, Jacqueline asked, "When's Inauguration Day?" Everybody laughed. She seemed startled by their laughter.

*   *   *

The Kennedys believed that every part of the campaign fund bottle should have its own top. When his own bottle was empty,

Bill Walton went to Kennedy campaign treasurer Steve Smith. "I'd been spending my own money during the campaign and I didn't have any left at all. Nobody had offered me any money and I hadn't asked for any money.

" 'Why didn't you *tell* somebody you needed money?' said Smith, and he took a thousand-dollar bill out of his pocket.' "

"But that's the only money I got from the Kennedys during the whole campaign," Walton emphasized, "outside of rent and things like that. Oh, yes, I did get a thousand dollars from a New York lawyer in the campaign who said, 'I know the Kennedys and I know what's going on and I'm sure you need money.' And indeed I did."

A friend asked Smith what it meant to be part of the Kennedy family.

"It means there is a hell of a lot of excitement and you become part of all that is happening. . . . You are extremely lucky if you come out, I suppose, with some ego. You're struggling, you're struggling, and wondering whether you're up to it. . . . But there is great pleasure and the excellent and real friendships with all three brothers. . . . Everything in life is on balance, I guess, and on balance it's been interesting and satisfying, and a real pleasure."

Would he be in politics at all if he had not married a Kennedy? His answer was crisp and quick: "I doubt it." Then came the twinkle and he added, "If I never married into this family, I would have been perfectly happy spending my life on the Riviera."

*   *   *

"They're going to kill him. I know they're going to kill him."

Coretta King was talking about her husband, Martin Luther King, who had been sentenced by a Georgia judge to four months of hard labor for driving with an out-of-state license. She was calling Harris Wofford in Chicago in October 1960.

"The trouble with your beautiful passionate Kennedys is that they never show their passion," Wofford told Sargent Shriver. "They don't understand symbolic action."

Shriver raced to the airport and caught his brother-in-law just as he was leaving. After telling him about King, he added quietly, "Why don't you telephone Mrs. King and give her your sympathy?"

Kennedy listened thoughtfully. "That's a good idea. Why not? Do you have her number? Get her on the phone."

Wofford remembered Bobby's reaction after he heard of the call. With tight fists and cold blue eyes, he said to Wofford, "Do you know that three southern governors told us that if Jack Kennedy supported Jimmy Hoffa, Nikita Khrushchev, or Martin Luther King, they would throw their states to Nixon? Do you know that this election may be razor close and you have probably lost it for us?"

Bobby had a long flight home to think more about it.

"It just burned me up . . . to think of that bastard sentencing a citizen to four months of hard labor for a minor traffic offense and screwing up my brother's campaign and making our country look ridiculous before the world. . . ." He called the judge from a phone booth. "I made it clear to him that it was not a political call, that I am a lawyer who believes in the right of all defendants to make bond. I said that if he was a decent American, he would let King out of jail by sundown." The judge did.

"You are now an Honorary Brother," a black leader told Bobby.

Ten days before the election, Martin Luther King, Sr., announced, "I had expected to vote against Senator Kennedy because of his religion. But now he can be my president, Catholic or whatever he is. It took courage to call my daughter-in-law at a time like this. He has the moral courage to stand up for what he knows is right. I've got all my votes and I've got a suitcase and I'm going to take them up there and dump them in his lap."

King's comment was printed in a blue-colored pamphlet called *The Blue Bomb*, the single most explosive piece of the literature for the black vote. Its words echoed from the pulpits of Negro churches all over the country. It had the emotional impact of a hallelujah. It brought out the black vote in unprecedented numbers, greater than for any previous election. In the razor-thin election result, this surely was a vital margin.

"The finest strategies are usually the results of accidents," Jack Kennedy afterwards admitted to John Kenneth Galbraith.

Kennedy had a postscript on the Martin Luther King, Sr.,

statement: "He was going to vote against me because I was a Catholic, but since I called his daughter-in-law, he voted for me. That was a helluva bigoted statement, wasn't it? Imagine Martin Luther King having a bigot for a father?"

Then Kennedy grinned. "Well, we all have fathers, don't we?"

*　　*　　*

Towards the end of the campaign, the pressures mounted. Her doctor was telling Jacqueline Kennedy to do less and less and everyone was asking her to do more and more. "I'm scared about this baby," she confided to Joan Braden.

There was a television program and a Boston rally. Could she come?

No.

"He's not going to get elected on the basis of her being there," Braden said. "Nothing is worth losing her baby."

Then came the last two days of the campaign in New York. The state was pivotal. Her husband insisted that her presence was crucial. Her doctor warned her not to do it.

"If he lost," Jacqueline told Braden, "I'd never forgive myself for not being there to help."

"My Spanish is poor," Mrs. Kennedy told an Hispanic audience in New York, "but my knowledge of your history, culture, and problems is better." She ended her speech with, "Viva Kennedy!" She made similar speeches in Italian and French. Her husband once followed up by saying, "I assure you that my wife can also speak English."

A reporter admiringly described her impact as that of "a Florentine madonna dropped into a Jack Levine painting." Analysts later noted that these minorities in New York had voted in much larger numbers than expected.

She didn't go to everything. Her husband, representing her before an audience of dress manufacturers, told them, "I know you'd rather have my wife here." But everything was so tiring and she was pregnant. After the New York ticker-tape parade, she put on an old raincoat and went to a gallery with Bill Walton to quiet her mind with abstract art. "I've looked at your paintings," she told Walton, "now come and look at mine."

"We rented a lot of rooms in the Waldorf," Walton said, "and Jack would have his room where he dressed and Jackie would have her little room where she dressed. We'd have people waiting in a lot of different rooms. Jack would go from one room to another room for five minutes at a time. I remember we even had Arthur Goldberg waiting in a bathroom. Anyway, I was with Jackie when Jack came in, threw a big fat wad of money onto the bed and told us who gave it to him.

" 'I want you to take care of this because I can't,' he said. 'I'm going onto the dais and I can't make a speech with that bulge in my pocket.'

" 'Well, I'm going up with you too,' I said, 'and so I can't have that bulge on me either.'

" 'And Jackie looked at us both and said, Well, *I* can't carry it.'

"So we put it under the mattress in her room, and we all went into the main dining room and onto the platform. Right after the speech we all hurried back to look under the mattress to make sure it was still there. We never had counted the money to see how much there was."

At the campaign lunch, with her husband sitting six seats away, she said wistfully, "This is the closest I've come to lunching with my husband in four months. I haven't seen him since Labor Day . . ."

Later she recalled, "I really didn't see Jack for more than a few moments alone, but at least I was part of things again."

*   *   *

Mr. and Mrs. Kennedy posed for a picture in color—in white tie and tails and fancy dress—for the cover of the *New York Daily News* Sunday magazine. Kennedy worried that such formal glamour might be bad politics. Ed Plaut reassured him, suggesting that ordinary people like to think their leaders live more extraordinary lives. "You may be right," Kennedy said quietly.

*   *   *

It was a Sunday, and Kennedy and Powers were walking down the middle aisle of a church in Anchorage, Alaska. Powers reminded him of the three wishes you could make anytime you went into a new church. As Kennedy genuflected and looked towards the altar, Powers heard him whisper, "New York, Pennsylvania, and Texas."

His wishes were granted.

It had happened often. A call from Kennedy for Dave Powers to accompany him on a speaking engagement. Powers called his wife to say he wasn't coming home for dinner.

"Where are you?" she asked.

"Des Moines, Iowa."

En route home, Kennedy showed Powers the afternoon paper, and a headline about Mike Todd's being killed in a plane crash. "You know, Dave," Kennedy said, "the plane Mike Todd crashed in is the same kind of plane we're flying in."

"Next thing I know, he's snoring," said Powers, "and I spend the night watching the propellers go round."

*   *   *

Rose Kennedy's ninety-five-year-old mother lived on Lighthouse Lane, a back road between the Kennedy compound in Hyannis and the church. Jack Kennedy would sit on the back stoop with her and listen to her tell stories about Honey Fitz and the Boston "pols."

After Sunday Mass at St. Francis Xavier Church, he had the car stop off at his grandmother's house while he went in to say hello. Jacqueline and the others sat in the car while he and his grandmother had a leisurely chat, sitting on the stoop as always.

The old lady seemed a little flustered by the crowd of newsmen, and asked, "What shall I do?"

"Just look at me, Grandma," Kennedy said, gently holding her hand.

"How many photographers are there?" she said, squinting behind thick glasses.

"Quite a few," Kennedy said. "Some still taking pictures, and some taking movies."

She patted his arm and, smiling sweetly, said, "You're the next president."

You were one helluva candidate.
                              —MURRAY KEMPTON

12

You Can Call Him Mr. President Now

On the night before the election, the Kennedy campaign plane was three hours late.

"We landed at Bridgeport [Connecticut] after midnight," said Ken O'Donnell, "and drove from there in a motorcade along Route 8 in the Naugatuck River valley to Waterbury. All along the road for more than twenty-seven miles there were crowds of cheering people waving torches and red lights, most of them wearing coats over their pajamas and nightgowns. At the firehouses in every town the fire engines were lined up beside the road with their lights flashing, bells ringing, and sirens wailing. So it was almost three o'clock in the morning when we reached Waterbury. There was a roaring crowd of more than forty thousand people in the city square outside of the Roger Smith Hotel, where Kennedy was to spend the night."

"It was virtually impossible to get through the crowd into

the lobby," Evelyn Lincoln added. "When we did get into the lobby, we couldn't get to the elevator. When we finally reached the floor where our rooms were located, the corridors were just as crowded as the lobby."

"Jack came out on the balcony of the hotel and made a speech," O'Donnell continued, "closing with the reminder that it was three o'clock and time for everybody to get to sleep. The crowd refused to let him go.

"He introduced Governor Ribicoff, who said a few words. The crowd demanded Kennedy again, and he had to talk to them once more. After he finally went inside the hotel and got into bed at four o'clock, the square remained filled with cheering people until daylight."

There's a bronze plaque in the Roger Smith Hotel, which reads: "From this balcony, at 3 AM, November 6, 1960, John Fitzgerald Kennedy, campaigning for the presidency of the United States, addressed a gathering of 50,000 people who had waited for six hours to hear him speak."

Thomas Carroll had slipped away from his bar at the Shamrock Café to hear his hero. Behind the bar was an oversized photo of John F. Kennedy along with a string of green cardboard letters spelling, "Erin Go Bragh."

*   *   *

"On the morning of election day we woke him up at seven-thirty, so he would be ready to meet Jackie when she came from Cape Cod to vote with him in Boston," O'Donnell said. "He was nervously leading Jackie through the cheering crowd that had gathered at the voting place, because she was then in her eighth month of pregnancy, and he held his arm in front of her to protect her from being jostled. After they voted, the Kennedys went to the airport in East Boston and flew to the Cape on the *Caroline*.

"Jack was completely exhausted. During the last hectic week he had never gotten four hours of sleep on any night. 'Well, it's all over,' he said. 'I wish I had spent forty-eight hours more in California.'" (He lost California by a mere 35,623 votes, out of a total of more than six and a half million.)

*   *   *

The grandchildren had been sent to the Ambassador's house for the night. At Bobby Kennedy's house, women were manning the banks of telephones, each one responsible for several states. Everyone was dressed casually in slacks and sport shirts.

First word came from Connecticut: a big victory. "Fantastic!" Kennedy said, and lit up a big black cigar. Eunice gleefully started singing, "When Irish Eyes Are Smiling."

The mood soon changed. Long past midnight, it was still too close to call. Someone murmured, "Their bigots beat our bigots." Ted was deeply depressed because they were losing ten of his thirteen states including California. Lemoyne Billings was sobbing. "He's lost another state," explained Jack. "His record is still minus one hundred percent. He's lost every county and every state of which he was supposed to be in charge."

Illinois, a critical state, remained undecided. Chicago political boss Richard Daley called with encouragement. "With a little bit of luck and the help of a few close friends, you're going to carry Illinois."

Everything, though, was still up in the air at 3:30 AM, and Kennedy announced that he was going to bed.

"How can you go to bed now?" Powers asked.

"Because it's too late to change another vote," Jack answered. "But next time, we'll go to bed early."

Shortly afterwards, Evelyn Lincoln decided that she, too, would go to bed. As she walked past John Kennedy's house, she saw him sitting in his big easy chair in the living room, reading, the light streaming over his shoulder. "At that moment, I *knew* he was going to be president."

"I woke at four o'clock when Jack came in," recalled Jacqueline, who had gone to bed at 11 PM. Her husband told her then that the election was still doubtful, but that the tide seemed to be turning against him.

He was wrong. It was not a tide—it was an ebb and flow. When he woke at eight and stuck his head out of the window, Bill Haddad saw him, waved, and gave him a thumbs-up sign.

Nixon had not yet conceded but the Secret Service men had arrived.

It was this close. Kennedy received 34,321,349 votes, only 112,803 more than Nixon—the smallest popular vote margin in the century. A shift of less than one percent in eleven states would have switched their electoral votes.

Jacqueline had breakfasted earlier with her daughter while the other Kennedys were playing touch football on the lawn. Soon after Jacqueline went for a walk alone on the windy beach, the nurse told Caroline, "Your daddy's upstairs. You can call him 'Mr. President' now."

*   *   *

When Kennedy came through the door of his brother's house later that morning, still wearing the same casual clothes he had worn the night before, everybody who was there stood up. He paused for a moment while everyone congratulated him, then sat down. He barked no orders. He merely started discussing the election and his future responsibilities.

When the first photographer arrived, Jack Kennedy ducked into the kitchen to stuff his shirttail in his trousers to prepare for his first formal picture as president-elect. "I've photographed him doing that a hundred times," the photographer said, putting down his camera as he watched him tuck in his shirttail. "But now he's president and somehow I don't think it's right."

Richard Nixon had not yet conceded and Jacqueline still asked, "Is it really that certain?" A reporter described her as being filled with "a childlike enthusiasm."

The Kennedy home in Hyannis soon resembled chaos: people, politicians, press, arriving and departing, filling up the lawn. "Hello, Mr. President," said one of his neighbors. "How do you like the title?"

"I like it very much," he said quietly.

"I am promising you one thousand days of exciting presidential leadership," he told a crowd, then smiled. "So now my wife and I prepare for a new administration and a new baby."

Was she awed or frightened, a reporter asked Jacqueline. "It has been rather unreal," she said slowly. She was worried about her husband. "You can't race a car endlessly without taking it into the shop." She wanted to get him away for a month's rest "or else he won't be able to be as good a president." She was concerned about her children. She planned to be with them even more now because "I don't want them to be brought up by nurses and Secret Service men. Also they probably won't see as much of their father as ordinary children."

She was more plaintively pointed with one of her friends. "I've hardly seen Jack in the last five years. Now that he's president, I suppose we won't see him at all."

What if he had lost? "If he had lost, he'd have been around the world three times now and written three books," she said, "but it wouldn't be the same."

In the early afternoon, the family grouped for a photograph. Jacqueline was changing her clothes, and was the last to arrive. When she entered the room, Jack got up to escort her in and "everybody broke into applause."

*   *   *

The night after the election, reporter Peter Lisagor of the *Chicago Sun-Times* was having terrible pains in his back. Kennedy heard about it and told Lisagor that his plane would fly him to New York the next morning to see his doctor. "We'll get you a couple of shots which I get regularly for my back, and you'll be able to stand the next few days. Then I'll have the doctor who comes up here take care of yours too at the same time." Lisagor, thereafter, bristled when anybody called Kennedy "cold."

Kennedy knew how debilitating his own back trouble was, and would be. His Addison's disease had to be carefully controlled. Still, as a student of history, he was fully aware that American presidents had a cloudy record of disease, dementia, and disability, ranging from President Pierce's cirrhosis of the liver to President Roosevelt's polio. There was also no secret about President Wilson's stroke, or President Cleveland's operation for cancer of the jaw aboard a ship in the East River. If they could cope, he would, too.

*   *   *

The victory was so thin. A single vote in each precinct would have changed the result. Would Nixon contest the election because of the close vote count?

"Jim Landis was my law partner," said Abba Schwartz, "and he was also Joe Kennedy's personal lawyer. It was Jim who called former President Herbert Hoover to say that it would tear the country apart if Nixon demanded a recount on the election."

Hoover then arranged a meeting in Palm Beach between Nixon and Kennedy. The critical moment was Nixon's initial greeting when Kennedy arrived at Nixon's stucco villa.

"How are you, Mr. President," Nixon said, acknowledging in his own way that he would not contest the election result. He later explained that doing so would have taken some eighteen months and would have caused a constitutional crisis.

Author Victor Lasky, who knew Nixon well, noted that there was a natural envy of poor boy Nixon towards rich boy Kennedy—but that there was no hatred. When Lasky sent Nixon a copy of his Kennedy book, Nixon called him. "Victor, I never knew before what bastards the Kennedys were."

Each one of the thirty-one hundred counties was colored by its politics and prejudices. Nixon clearly had run better than Eisenhower in some of them because of Kennedy's Catholicism —southern Missouri, southern Indiana, southern Ohio, central Pennsylvania, the spine of California—the map was clear. On a national average, Kennedy still ran eleven points better than Stevenson had four years before.

There was a lingering question: Was he elected in spite of being a Catholic, as political scientist V. O. Key, Jr., insisted? Or was it the strong support of Catholic voters that gave him the margin to squeak through?

There could be no precise answer.

*   *   *

The lieutenant governor had had too much to drink that day. But he was absolutely determined to make the welcoming speech when Lyndon Johnson arrived at Otis Air Force Base. The humidity seemed about 110 percent, but the lieutenant governor kept talking and talking while Johnson and his wife just stood there. The army public-relations man then tried to get the microphone away from the lieutenant governor and there was a battle for it, the lieutenant governor insisting that "the Vice-President is going to be properly recognized by the Commonwealth of Massachusetts." Finally the microphone was killed and the reception was over.

Kennedy got the tape and had a private press party at his house on a Sunday afternoon. As he played it, the reporters were rolling on the ground with laughter, "and Jack was absolutely hysterical, actually holding his stomach and saying, 'Oh my God.' "

But when the tape was over and there was silence, Kennedy announced, "Now we've all had our laugh and I think we ought to destroy the evidence." He then burned the tape in front of the reporters. There were no other copies of it. The lieutenant governor had had a good record and Kennedy knew that this tape could ruin him.

"They [the Johnsons] came to stay with us in Hyannis," recalled Jacqueline. "It's a rather small house we have there, and we wanted them to be comfortable; so we gave them our bedroom. But we didn't want them to know it was our bedroom, because we thought they might feel they were putting us to trouble. There was a lot of moving things out of closets so there'd be no trace of anybody's toothbrush anywhere.

"I remember that evening how impressed I was with Mrs. Johnson. She and my sister and I were sitting in one part of the room, and Jack and Vice-President-elect Johnson and some men were in the other part of the room. Mrs. Johnson had a little spiral pad, and when she'd hear a name mentioned, she'd jot it down. Sometimes if Mr. Johnson wanted her, he'd say, 'Bird, do you know so-and-so's number?' And she'd always have it down. Yet she would sit talking with us, looking so calm. I was very impressed by that."

Kennedy, however, had told some friends, "Come back in an hour, because I want him out of here in an hour. An hour's just about as much as I can stand of Lyndon. I like him, but he might be here all night."

The friends came and took Lyndon with them until four in the morning, drinking. Two hours later he was back, "and you'd never know he'd had a drink the night before. It was amazing. He had an early appointment with the President," Larry Newman recalled.

*   *   *

The home of Larry and Sancy Newman is a large, handsome historic house that sits on a corner at Scudder Avenue in Hyannis Port, almost directly facing the John Kennedy house. Their house was the headquarters for some key Kennedy staff.

One afternoon the President-elect was sitting in the Newman home listening to some of his assembled staff discussing how they should isolate the President from many things that should not concern him. He was drinking a Heineken, obviously perturbed that they would discuss such matters in front of him. His face was flushed when he put down his beer and said, "Listen you sons of bitches, I want you to remember one thing. You know there's a guy right behind each of you who's working for me. And there's a guy behind *him* who's working for me. So there's not a goddamn thing any one of you guys can do to keep things away from me. So if you try to pull any bullshit, the next thing you know, you'll be out."

You could feel the freeze in the room, but then he suddenly said, "How about another beer?"

He didn't need another beer. He still hadn't finished the one in front of him, but he had made his point and now he wanted to warm the chill.

*   *   *

There was nothing "quaint" about Hyannis Port—no tearoom, no bar, no fishermen, no "Welcome" sign for tourists. The day's high excitement occurred after dinner, when most of the village collected at the post office for the evening mail delivery. It was a peaceful place, well off the main highway, and nobody came there unless invited. That's the way it was for ninety years, when suddenly, one summer, appeared a thousand cars filled with sightseers who wanted to know where the President lived. Tour boats plied the harbor and overhead were the airborne sightseers.

Joe Kennedy had been thirty-seven when he brought his family here in 1926 to move into a waterfront house with fourteen rooms, a great front porch that circled the house, and nine baths. They would need them all. By 1926, the Kennedys had seven of their nine children.

What came to be called "The Kennedy Compound" (so christened by neighbor Larry Newman) was a small group of adjoining shingled houses, weathered, silvery-gray, on Irving Avenue. The low-slung houses on tree-lined Irving, surrounded by hedges, well-kept lawns, and pink ramblers, had a neighborly look. Some had odd shapes, bay windows, cupolas, and porches that went around corners.

His father's house swept to the sea. His brother Bob's house flanked the father's, and his own rented house sat behind Bob's, adjoining Scudder Avenue. It was only a three-bedroom home, hardly big enough for a presidential entourage.

Jacqueline had furnished it with wicker chairs and yellow cushions, cozy chintz couches, and the casualness of early American pine. Scattered around the house was her mother-in-law's colorful old glass. The whole feeling was easy and comfortable.

Some Hyannis neighbors—and the Kennedys knew who they were—hated the Kennedys, hated the Irish, and deeply resented the mass influx of tourists that the Kennedy presidency brought in.

One of the local social leaders, very stiff and upper crust, asked him, "Jack, what do we call you, now that you're President?"

"Well, 'Maggie,' it will be the same as it always was. I'll call you Maggie and you call me 'Jack.'"

Nobody *ever* had called her 'Maggie.'

Newman told Kennedy that 58 percent of Hyannis voted for him.

"You mean I carried Hyannis Port?"

"Sure."

"Well, did you vote for me?"

"Hell yes, I voted for you in the primary!"

"You mean you registered Democrat on Cape Cod?"

"Sure."

"You've got a lot more guts than most of these bastards."

* * *

"Welcome Home, President Jack!" was on a banner borne by a dozen young ladies, students from Cape Cod Secretarial School.

For a little while it was all very casual.

A visitor at the Kennedy door was greeted by three-year-old Caroline, who said, "I suppose you've come to see my Daddy. Well, he isn't dressed yet."

Then the crowds came.

Jacqueline wanted a high stockade fence, and he didn't. "Oh hell, I want to meet the people," he said. People, after all, were votes. Then, even he finally admitted, "Jackie's got a point." She was now in the final month of her pregnancy and she wanted some privacy and quiet and family life, as much as she could get of it.

She was particularly pointed about the politicians. "They have a way of working their way in," she said, "and I don't particularly like to deal with them."

* * *

The newly elected President had ten weeks before inauguration. Ten weeks of transition, ten weeks of selection and reflection, ten weeks of preparing for a job for which there is no proper preparation.

The day after the election, Kennedy called Clark Clifford. "You have the book ready?"

"I do," Clifford said.

"I'll send the Secret Service by to pick it up."

The eighty-page book on which Clifford had worked all summer became the Kennedy bible for all the necessary procedures, projects, and appointments during the presidential transition.

Kennedy enjoyed playing political games. He asked his friends Ben Bradlee and Bill Walton: "OK, I'll give each of you guys one appointment, one job to fill. What will it be?"

Walton said he should replace J. Edgar Hoover, who had

headed the FBI for thirty-six years. Bradlee suggested replacing Allen Dulles at the CIA. The next morning Kennedy made his first two appointments: Hoover and Dulles.

The rationale was that he had been elected by such a thin margin that he didn't want to make political waves with the conservatives. "Father was a good friend of his," said Bob Kennedy of J. Edgar Hoover, "and they used to see each other and keep in touch." Someone later recalled a file Hoover had on Lt. John Kennedy and a former girl friend, a suspected Nazi spy (who was never charged).

There was one other announced appointment at the time: his father's friend and attorney, James Landis, former head of the Securities and Exchange Commission, to make a survey of regulatory agencies.

*   *   *

"This is one part of the job I had hoped would be fun," Kennedy told Sorensen, as he considered his key appointments, "but these are the decisions that could make or break us." And then he added, "I spent four years getting to know the type of person that could help me win this fight. Now I have only a few weeks to get the people who will help me be a good president."

He insisted he wanted the best people he could get, regardless of party, but there was always room in government for some old PT-boat buddies, some Harvard friends, and even the former landlord of his Georgetown house.

Kennedy also brought into the New Frontier fifteen Rhodes scholars, plus a large number of Yale men; both talent searchers, Sargent Shriver and Adam Yarmolinsky, were graduates of Yale. So many appointees were also from Harvard that the word was, "Pretty soon Harvard won't have anything left but Radcliffe." Besides "initiative, intelligence, and imagination," the premium was on toughness and loyalty. The kind of people they did not want, said Shriver, were "too ideological, too earnest, too emotional, too talkative, too dull." On the fifth floor of a building a block from the White House, brothers Bill and Fred Haddad had some two hundred names on charts "all over the wall" that Shriver had given them to check out. "The big thing we were looking for," Bill Haddad said, "were people young enough to be excited about what Kennedy wanted to do."

"I had unwittingly joined a new youth movement," explained George Ball, a brilliant lawyer who became Undersecretary of State for Economic Affairs. His was a distinguished record of government service, here and abroad, that stretched back to the Roosevelt years. During the transition, Ball was in charge of preparing position papers, recommending appointments in the international area. Examining one of Ball's suggestions, Kennedy said, "Fuck *him!* I couldn't get him approved for anything." In his more diplomatic language, Ball transmitted the decision to the others, saying, "The President disapproved of that selection."

When Lyndon Johnson told Speaker Sam Rayburn how smart the Kennedy people were, Rayburn answered, "Well, Lyndon, you might be right, and they may be every bit as intelligent as you say, but I'd feel a whole lot better about them if just one of them had run for sheriff once."

Jack and Bobby talked excitedly about how they planned to reform the State Department, replacing tired bureaucrats with young people. Their father interrupted, told them he once had heard Franklin D. Roosevelt saying the same thing with the same heat. "He talked about razing the whole thing and starting from scratch. He didn't do a damn thing about it, and neither will you."

*　　*　　*

At the end of the presidential campaign, Ted Sorensen's last four words on a memo were "weariness, rush or tension."

But here was Sorensen, in this transition interim before inauguration, listening to the former director of the budget explain the intricacies of a national budget. It was a weighty discussion on how to search out vast sums that can be so easily hidden, and the way billions of dollars are so delicately balanced. Sorensen sat there, listening, absorbing, trying to remember how important it all was and thinking, "Gee, this is fun . . ."

*　　*　　*

The Bouvier sisters, Jacqueline
and Lee

"Black Jack" Bouvier and his adoring
daughter, Jacqueline

The Courtship—Hyannis Port, 1953

(HY PESKIN/FPG)

(HY PESKIN/FPG)

Wedding Day, September 12, 1953

John Kennedy's political star was on the rise at the 1956 Democratic convention.

Nobody was closer to Jack than Bobby. Jack chose Bobby for his campaign manager in 1960.

(UPI PHOTO)

Though Ted was only twenty-seven, Jack named him campaign coordinator for thirteen western states.

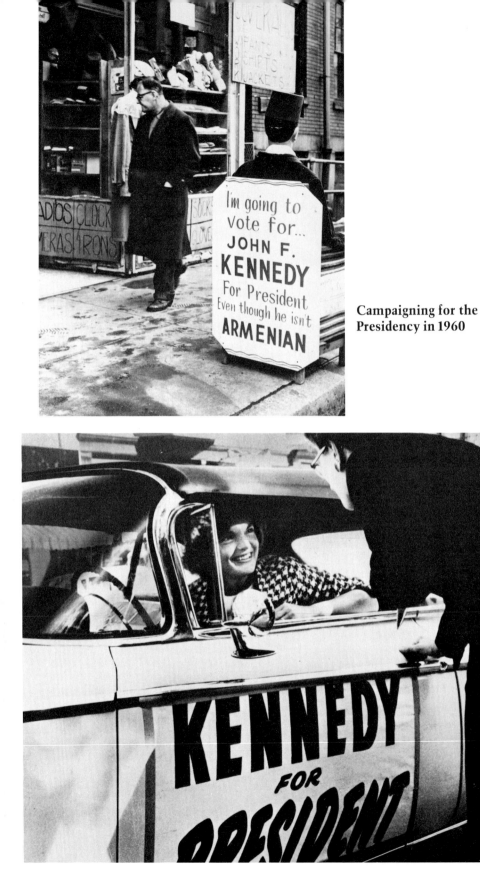

Campaigning for the Presidency in 1960

The Kennedy-Nixon debates
[UPI PHOTO]

Inauguration Day, January 20, 1961:
"Ask not what your country can do
for you, ask what you can do for your
country."

Pivot man of the Irish Mafia was Kenneth O'Donnell, who controlled entree to the President. O'Donnell, thin, wiry, looking something like a ferret, was not a charming fellow. Nor was he an "issues" man, and he himself said, "The President doesn't consider me an intellectual." He had been a superb captain of the football team at Harvard. On the White House staff, some called him "the executioner." He was tough, fast, blunt, almost taciturn, always fully aware of who was on which side, and where to put the pressure. His main concern was "them or us." But even most of his enemies admitted that "you always knew where you stood with him . . . there was no bullshit, no fooling around, and his word was good."

When O'Donnell called Brig. Gen. Ted Clifton to report for duty to the President as his military aide, Clifton patiently explained that the chief of staff had other candidates for that job. O'Donnell impatiently answered, "Well, just put it this way. If you're not over here tomorrow, we'll probably have a new chief of staff."

"The people closest to Kennedy in the White House were his Irish cronies from the old days," Pierre Salinger said. "He came all the way up with them and he felt comfortable with them. He could tell them absolutely everything, and nothing would ever get out. With the rest of us, he was close, but then, somewhere, there was always a wall."

* * *

Kennedy knew the political importance of the women's vote "because there are more of you, because you live longer and have all the money." And he appreciated the judgment of intelligent women. When Nancy Dickerson was trying to say something at dinner amid much noise, Kennedy demanded, "Be quiet and let her talk!"

But when it came to political appointments, John Kennedy was his father's son. He could not see women in positions of political and administrative responsibility.

* * *

Jacqueline had some personal questions for Larry Newman.

What happened when Newman's second baby was born?, she asked.

"It was another baby. We loved it. There wasn't any difference between the children."

"Oh, there *is* a difference," she insisted. "There will be. You've got to be very careful not to play one against the other. You have to give them both the same things."

"It's no problem," Newman insisted. "You'll be just as much in love with the second one as you are with the first one. I know that. You'll be a great mother."

She seemed comforted.

They had a small family Thanksgiving dinner in Washington with friends Walton and Bradlee as their only guests.

"Jackie never looked more beautiful," Walton remembered. "She was full of bounce, getting up and down from the table to help serve dinner."

She was not happy when her husband left for a Palm Beach holiday without her, but her Caesarian was scheduled in another two weeks and she had to stay close to home. In his defense, he needed all the rest he could get.

Two hours after he left, Mrs. Kennedy began hemorrhaging. She called her doctor, who sent an ambulance. The ambulance attendant remembered her smiling and looking "like a baby doll" in her pink nightgown, white cardigan sweater, and red overcoat.

But, inside the ambulance, her smile was gone and she asked, "Will I lose my baby?"

The doctor reassured her.

Her husband soon got the news.

After leaving the pilot, the stewardess came out white-faced, hesitating, then reluctantly went into Kennedy's compartment to tell him that his wife was hemorrhaging. As soon as the plane landed, it taxied within twenty feet of the administration building and Kennedy rushed out to make a phone call. Chuck Roberts of *Newsweek* remembered, "He came out as grim as I've ever seen him and yelled to Harold, the pilot, 'Which plane is faster?' Harold pointed to the back-up press plane, where a pack of reporters had just unloaded. 'OK,' said Kennedy, 'let's go!' and charged up the ramp of the press plane, followed by a rush of confused reporters."

Still on the press plane was a slightly inebriated airlines publicity man who had acted as host and shepherd for the reporters, happily satisfied that his day's work was done, celebrating with another drink. Before he could collect his senses, reporters were filing back into their seats with their gear, and the plane was airborne, back to Washington. "What's happening?" he wailed.

Observing Kennedy's concern, a woman reporter was not sympathetic. "Why was he going to Palm Beach in the first place when his wife is back home pregnant? If it had been me ready to have a baby and my husband went away to have a good time, I'd be sore as hell!"

Midway home, Kennedy got the word on the plane. "It's a boy!" and his wife was fine. The father wanted to know the exact time of delivery (12:22 AM) and the baby's weight (six pounds, three ounces). The entire planeload of reporters burst into cheers. Kennedy told Salinger to pass out cigars to the reporters "out of your regular supply."

The President-elect was back in Washington before dawn, bounding up the steps of Georgetown Hospital for a short visit with his wife and a quick look at his son in the incubator. To reporters, he was all smiles and his answer to everything was "fine."

"Do you want your son to become president?" he was asked.

"I hadn't thought about it," he said, smiling. "I just want him to be all right."

Vice-President-elect Johnson sent a telegram: NAME THAT BOY LYNDON JOHNSON AND A HEIFER CALF WILL BE HIS. But the child's name was John Fitzgerald Kennedy, Jr.

The father had brought a pair of live ducks home for three-year-old Caroline, a present she had especially requested. He had the problem of breaking the news of the baby to her. The two took a walk around the block and reporters queried if he had told her. The press secretary informed them, "He couldn't figure out how to do it." He finally told her "that her mother had gone away to bring her back a baby brother for her birthday" and she was "very happy" and wanted to see him. The hospital waived its rules so that she could do just that. Asked whom he looked like, his mother said, "I don't think he looks like anybody."

John Fitzgerald Kennedy, Jr., opened his eyes only when a photographer took his picture. Besides his father's christening gown, he wore a ruffled white lace bonnet that had once belonged to his mother. Apart from a single, subdued cry, he was relaxed and drowsy as the Georgetown pastor of Holy Trinity Church conducted the eleven-minute baptismal ritual—breathing gently three times on the baby's face, commanding the spirit of evil to leave, then placing a few grains of sacred salt on the baby's tongue as a token of wisdom, touching the baby's nostrils "so that you may perceive the fragrance of God's sweetness," anointing his breast and the space between his shoulders with holy oil in a sign of the cross, and wetting the baby's head with water from a golden dish while saying, "I baptize you in the name of the Father and the Son and the Holy Ghost.

"John Fitzgerald Kennedy, Jr., go in peace and may the Lord be with you. Amen."

The mother in the wheelchair held her baby and asked her husband, "Isn't he sweet, Jack? Look at those pretty eyes."

"In this lovely family atmosphere, I thought we were going to have a fist fight," Bartlett recalled, "because, at this point, Jack wanted to make Bill Fulbright secretary of state and Bobby was indignant at the idea. He had known Fulbright on the McClellan Committee and was vehement about him. I was saying nice things about Fulbright, too, and I thought Bobby was going to slug me. It all started at the chapel and ended up in Jackie's room at the hospital. It was a hot fight."

"I mentioned that I had been at a party where I had heard Fulbright make some racist remarks," Walton added. " 'See?' said Bobby, 'that's what I told you. We can't possibly have anyone who's a racist as secretary of state.' "

Kennedy later went to columnist Walter Lippmann's Georgetown house to discuss Fulbright. Former Secretary of State Dean Acheson was against Fulbright "because he likes to call for brave, bold new ideas and he doesn't have a great many brave, bold new ideas." But Walter Lippmann was strongly for

Fulbright, and Kennedy admitted, "he's probably the best man for the job."

Just then, the telephone rang. Helen Lippmann recognized Robert Kennedy's voice. After taking the call, the President-elect turned to Lippmann and said, "I don't think we're going to be able to go with Fulbright. There's too much opposition at home and abroad on the segregation issue."

Lippmann had known Kennedy since his early years, felt he was "talented, but a bit ruthless and too much in a hurry." But he then told his readers that Kennedy had "outgrown many of the mistakes and vacillations of his youth," and that he now admired "his instinct for the crucial quick point."

"I may be getting old, and I may be getting senile," commented Arthur Krock, who had voted for Nixon. "But at least I don't fall in love with young boys, like Walter Lippmann."

Kennedy proposed Dean Rusk as secretary of state, a man he had never met. Lippmann had known Rusk as the head of the Rockefeller Foundation and assistant secretary of state for the Far East under Acheson, and considered him an unimaginative bureaucrat. "You're hardly likely to get from him the kind of original advice a president needs. How about McGeorge Bundy?" Lippmann shot back.

"I hadn't thought of that," Kennedy answered, surprised. "He's rather young, isn't he?"

"Yes," Lippmann retorted, "but you're a very young president."

There is nothing more temporary than political power. In 1956, Jack Kennedy was paying court to Adlai Stevenson, hoping to be picked as the vice-presidential nominee. In 1960, Adlai Stevenson was paying court to Jack Kennedy, hoping to be picked as secretary of state. Neither succeeded.

Kennedy understood Stevenson's last desperate reach for power at the convention. Under different circumstances, his sympathy might have been greater. Had the two men been more direct with each other, had Stevenson nominated Kennedy, he might well have become secretary of state. Kennedy himself once had said that if he were being considered for a Cabinet office he would be interested only in secretary of state or defense. Stevenson's enemies included Philadelphia political boss Bill Green. After a meeting with Green, Stevenson said, "Open the window and let some fresh air in—and get the odor of corruption out."

Green never forgave that remark and urged Kennedy not to appoint Stevenson to any Cabinet post. But Kennedy was more concerned with his own personal relationship with Stevenson. Robert Kennedy told many people that his brother didn't want to spend any time with Stevenson. Adlai Stevenson was an astute, beguiling man of pungent wit and charm—but not with Kennedy. With Kennedy, he was stiff, solemn, often pedantic. Kennedy was the one with the cutting quip. When Stevenson arrived in a Rolls-Royce and seemed to be having trouble getting out of the car, Kennedy told him, "You're the only man I ever met who couldn't get out of the door of a Rolls-Royce."

When Walter Lippmann later recommended Stevenson as the ambassador to the United Nations, Kennedy quickly agreed.

Kennedy called Stevenson to his Georgetown home and offered him the UN post; Stevenson was most reluctant. Outside, he told the press, "I want to make it clear that I was invited down here. I didn't come here [uninvited]."

That same morning, Stevenson went to see Lippmann for his counsel.

He also went to see Hubert Humphrey.

"Adlai, you have an obligation to take it," Humphrey told him.

"Why?"

"Well, didn't you campaign for this fellow? This was a very close election. Your campaigning alone might have been responsible for his election."

"But this isn't the job I want."

"It doesn't make a damn bit of difference. You can't turn him down. You have an obligation. You went around telling everybody to vote for him. Now he has asked you to get on his team, and I think you've got to do it. Frankly, I wouldn't think much of you if you didn't." Stevenson reluctantly agreed to accept.

Dean Rusk was a rather reserved man. "Kennedy and I could

not communicate," he said, about their first meeting. But Kennedy had been impressed with his quiet competence even though he was not "his type of guy." Kennedy called Robert McNamara "Bob" almost immediately, but he always called Rusk "Mr. Secretary."

"Kennedy told me he took Rusk because he was a good errand boy," Justice William Douglas later said. Kennedy also told him that the whole weight of the State Department was on the side of the status quo, "not rocking the boat, not doing anything." Like many presidents, Kennedy planned to be his own secretary of state. Domestic problems troubled him, but foreign affairs fascinated him.

*　　*　　*

Mrs. Eisenhower was waiting in the White House with a wheelchair, in case Mrs. Kennedy wanted it.

"I had come straight from the hospital," Jacqueline recalled. "I had walked about my room and a little bit down the hall, since I had John. I really shouldn't have gone. But what could you do?"

Mrs. Eisenhower took her on a comprehensive tour of everything on all three floors, explaining that thirty rooms were set aside as living quarters for the family.

J.B. West, White House chief usher, noticed the pain in Mrs. Kennedy's face as she said good-bye to Mrs. Eisenhower and walked slowly over to her three-year-old station wagon. Two months later, Mrs. Kennedy asked West why he had not made available the wheelchair her doctor had ordered. He said it was waiting for her request.

West recalled, "To my surprise, she giggled. 'I was too scared of Mrs. Eisenhower to ask,' she said."

But after the two-hour marching tour, the new President's wife returned to her Georgetown house, "crying hysterically." She described the White House as cold and dreary, the worst place in the world. "It looks like it's been furnished by discount stores." She compared the ground floor with "a dentist's office bomb shelter," described the East Room as "a roller-skating rink," and said the curtains were "seasick green" and the ash-

2 5 1

trays "looked as if they came from a railroad pullman car." She couldn't bear the thought of moving in. "I hate it, I hate it, I hate it." That afternoon, she flew to Palm Beach. "And there I collapsed. I had to stay in bed five days." She complained to a friend that Mrs. Eisenhower hadn't even offered her a cup of tea.

She was still in bed in the Kennedy Palm Beach home when Rose Kennedy asked Jacqueline's secretary, "Do you know if Jackie is getting out of bed today? You might remind her that we're having some important guests for lunch. It would be nice if she would join us."

The secretary relayed the message and Jacqueline responded by mimicking the singsong speech of her mother-in-law, repeating her words, "You might remind her we're having important guests for lunch."

Jacqueline did not appear.

If Jacqueline had small regard for Mrs. Eisenhower, John Kennedy had less regard for her husband. He had no illusions about his political appeal. "Eisenhower could beat any of us if he could run again." But he still considered him a weak, cold president. Weak, because he seemed to have done so little homework in so many key areas; cold, because "he's had so many friends in the armed forces through the years and yet all he does now is play golf with his rich businessmen friends. You never see him with any other friends."

Schlesinger told Kennedy of a poll of important presidents by his fellow historians. They ranked Eisenhower number 21, "right near Chester Arthur." The Democratic joke: Eisenhower couldn't read because his lips were chapped.

When President Eisenhower invited the President-elect to the White House to discuss nine major issues, Kennedy asked Clifford and Sharon to prepare briefing papers. Kennedy absorbed the material so fully that Eisenhower was impressed enough to note in his diary: "Certainly his attitude was that of a serious seeker for information."

Kennedy's reaction to Eisenhower was more negative. "He calls me 'Kennedy.' How do you like that?" Within months, Jack openly referred to Eisenhower as "that lying son of a bitch."

★　　★　　★

The President-elect wanted Bobby in his inner circle, but where? Put on the White House staff, he would be regarded, in effect, as vice-president. "I'm the chief," John Kennedy told O'Donnell. "Ain't no other chief. And if anything happened, everyone's gonna say, 'Bobby said. . . .'" After one of Bobby's press statements, Kennedy asked O'Donnell, "Will you tell your roommate that *I* am President of the United States."

"If I was going to do anything, I wasn't going to work directly for him," Bobby said. "I mean, that would be impossible. I had to do something on my own or have my own area of responsibility. And it would be impossible with the two of us sitting around an office looking at each other all day."

That left the Cabinet. Since Bobby had never been inside a courtroom in his life, prominent lawyers felt it would take "the guts of a burglar" to make him attorney general.

"Look, there's so much in that secretary of defense job that can get a president in trouble," Brig. Gen. Ted Clifton warned Bobby. "There are so many internal fights on the horizon. Don't take that job. It's not fair to your brother, not fair to the country."

"But my brother can get into serious trouble by not having someone he can trust around there."

"If you insist, then take the job of deputy secretary of defense. You can sit there and watch what's happening and get a good education and have someone else be the responsible man."

Bobby thanked him and said he would think about it.

"We'll make Bobby attorney general so he can throw all the people Dad doesn't like in jail," Eunice had said at the previous Kennedy Christmas party. "That means we'll have to build more jails."

It was the Kennedy father who pushed first, and hardest, to make Bobby the attorney general. After all, he had predicted the appointment in a magazine article several years before.

Jack Kennedy told friends that his father was "absolutely determined" about this, had said, "Damn the torpedoes, full speed ahead." The President-elect had a "very serious reservation" about the appointment, noting how many people regarded it as political suicide. There was strong public insistence that an attorney general should be a practicing attorney with broad experience in the courts. Some even felt he should be a man nominated and approved by the United States Supreme Court.

"He asked me what I wanted to do," Bobby recalled. "He asked me if I wanted to be attorney general. I said I didn't want to be attorney general. In the first place, I thought nepotism was a problem. Secondly, I had been chasing bad men for three years and I didn't want to spend the rest of my life doing that. In the meantime, I'd gone to see J. Edgar Hoover, Bill Rogers, and Bill Douglas. Hoover said it was a good job, thought it was worthwhile. Bill Rogers was not enthusiastic about it."

Supreme Court Justice William Douglas recalled: "Bobby came to see me." He had quite a decision to make: whether to continue to sit in the shadow of his brother. Would he hurt or help his brother? Would he make a good attorney general? Would it hurt or help him in *his* future?

"We talked about it at great length," Douglas said. "And I told him that, from Jack's point of view, it was perfect. Because he would be attorney for the President, his brother, and there was nothing to worry about. The only thing he *should* worry about: What's best for Bobby Kennedy?"

Jack Kennedy called in Clark Clifford.

"I have one thing to tell you. My father wants me to appoint my brother Bobby as attorney general. But I'm just really not completely comfortable with it. Bobby's bright, but I'm just not comfortable about it because Bobby hasn't practiced law."

"I agree with you," Clifford said.

"Tell you what I want you to do," Kennedy said. "I want you to go to New York and have a meeting with my father and see if you can persuade him that we ought to put Bobby someplace else."

Clifford set up a lunch in New York with the senior Kennedy. The former ambassador "couldn't have been nicer." Then Clifford said, "Now I want to talk to you about Bobby." He then set forth his objections as the elder Kennedy listened politely and then said, "Thank you very much. I appreciate that. Now we'll turn to some other subject because Bobby is going to be attorney general."

Here was Kennedy, clearly uncomfortable about his brother

as attorney general, and yet he accepted his father's recommen-
dation. Why? He had fought him before, refused him on other
things. Why would he go along with his father, when even
Bobby didn't want the job? Plainly, this was not just a father's
suggestion; this was the full force of the father, an insistent
decision on which he could not be denied.

To minimize the flak, Kennedy organized a press party on
the family yacht, primarily to present Bobby in a softer light.
Chuck Roberts of *Newsweek* agreed that "Bobby could not have
been more charming." Teddy was there, too, "but he was sort of
the cabin boy. He just got the drinks for us."

Despite all this, Bobby had made up his own mind. "I don't
want to be *appointed.* I want to run for office and let the people
decide if I should have a job. I called my brother and said I'd
finally decided that I wasn't going to do it. My brother asked me
to come over and have breakfast the next morning. Which I did.
We talked for about forty minutes. He said that all those people
who'd been selected were people he didn't particularly know
well, and it would make a difference if he could have someone
[with whom] to talk over some of these problems. So he thought
it was important that I become attorney general. So I said I
thought I should think about it. He said, 'Well, let's go out and
announce it.'

"But it was my father. I would never have been attorney
general if it hadn't been for him."

When Ben Bradlee asked Kennedy how he proposed to announce his brother's appointment as attorney general, Kennedy
said, "Well, I think I'll open the front door of the Georgetown
house some morning about 2 AM, look up and down the street,
and if there's no one there, I'll whisper, 'It's Bobby.'"

When the moment finally came, and the brothers started out
the door to face the press, he said, "Damn it, Bobby, comb your
hair." Then: "Don't smile too much, or they'll think we're
happy about the appointment."

Bobby warned his brother, "They'll go for our balls if you
announce the appointment."

"You hold your balls," Jack said, "and I'll announce it."

Much of the press responded negatively to the appointment.

The *Chicago Tribune* quoted President Woodrow Wilson's letter refusing to appoint his brother as postmaster in Nashville, Tennessee: "It would be a very serious mistake both for you and for me."

But both brothers treated the newspaper reports with humor. "I've been made attorney general," Bobby told his staff, "because I went to the right schools, because I have an understanding of the issues, and because my brother is in the White House. Not necessarily in that order of importance."

* * *

Political analyst Richard Neustadt watched with fascination as Kennedy flipped through his memorandum on the Economic Council while he talked on the phone with Walter Heller about being chairman of that council, then—still talking—picked up the morning *New York Herald Tribune,* looked at the front page and editorials, dropped it and picked up the *New York Times,* examined its front page and editorials, and picked up the memorandum again, read parts of it aloud to Heller, let it drop to the floor, and then hung up, having completed a complicated conversation as well as an examination of the morning papers.

McGeorge Bundy also typified the tense, eager, young staff people. "Jack and I were at school together," Bundy said, "and we got to know each other better in Boston and London." Bundy was a Harvard dean, brilliant, energetic, dynamic, who "could grasp an idea and produce an answer as fast as a computer."

"You can't beat brains," Kennedy said of him. To Bundy and other staff members, John Kennedy was not simply their tuning fork; he was their tune.

The Kennedy type was tough, terse, yes-or-no. The man he most prized in this category was his Defense Secretary Robert McNamara, former president of Ford Motor Company.

Kennedy described McNamara's acceptance of his job as defense secretary. "I'll accept the job under these conditions," he told the President, handing him a piece of paper for his signature at a place marked "approved and signed." One of the conditions was that he would not be required to go to cocktail parties.

"What did you do?" Roswell Gilpatric asked the President. Gilpatric became McNamara's deputy.

"Well, I read it, laughed, stuffed it in my pocket and later threw it away."

"McNamara had concise and impressive views on any subject that arose" said George Ball. "These he reinforced with footnotes and statistics." The President found his performance "scintillating," just as he also found McNamara a man of humanity and imagination, capable of strong commitment to unpopular causes. There was no lack of respect and no feuding. "We were all too busy and we had no time to waste in petty maneuvers," said McNamara.

Kennedy described how General Curtis Le May came to a Palm Beach conference to discuss the military budget and complained bitterly about an important item that had been eliminated.

"General, that's not right," said Defense Secretary Bob McNamara, "the money is there."

"No," blustered Le May, "that money is not there."

McNamara then quietly told him to look on a certain page of the budget book, a certain sub-section of a certain paragraph.

Le May turned the pages and there was the money.

"Le May looked like a man who'd been hit in the face with a bucket of warm shit," said Lyndon Johnson.

Later, Kennedy told Johnson, "Now you see why the founding fathers put the military in the hands of the civilians."

*　　*　　*

"The Kennedy staff was *viciously* loyal," noted admiring observer Ed Welsh. "They treated Kennedy as an extraordinary product." Political veteran Jim Rowe was less complimentary of the staff. "I've seen nobody as arrogant in Washington since we grew up."

"Our loyalty to Kennedy transcended everything," Mike Feldman, an integral part of the White House staff, insisted. "Presidential assistants are of course always loyal to their bosses. But our feelings were so unique it made these other staff people look like a bunch of Judases. John Kennedy was the one man I'd follow blindly on anything. Blind faith. I don't know many staff people of many presidents who could say that."

Feldman told of bearing the brunt of Joseph Kennedy's rage

during the campaign because of his stand on the higher minimum wage. The candidate listened quietly, then asked Feldman if he still felt he was right. Feldman said yes.

"Then that's the way we'll do it," Kennedy said.

"And he said that to me in front of his father," Feldman said. "That's high support. After that, what wouldn't I do for this guy?

"I've never met anybody with as powerful a personality, that kind of magnetism, that special ability to attract people to him and his ideas, and do it with all kinds of people."

"I don't think Kennedy had the brilliance of mind in the traditional sense of knowing everything. He didn't have a great grasp of our policies and really didn't know all the basic materials and nor did he care about it. But he always had in mind the way things worked. And even if he didn't know something, he had the ability to ask questions, that probing, curious mind that sifted the facts and figures—and never forgot them. You'd give him a fact and he'd remember it forever, and fit it in someplace. He had an intellectual curiosity about people—following a person's line of thought to see where it came out. He wanted to know the facts no matter what the direction. And then you know he had the ability to judge, to get the long view of a problem. When he came to a conclusion, that was it. It filled you with confidence.

"But the key factor was the relationship he established with everybody who was close to him, and the ability to meld different personalities. He raised such excitement in us. He had such an array of talent, such great sensitivity, a quick grasp of everything, a wry wit, a flashing mind. Scintillating! That's the word for him—scintillating!

"I think every member of his staff would have died in place of him."

But before the end, there was the beginning, his inauguration as the thirty-fifth President of the United States.

IV

A Year of Crisis

Every president must endure the gaps between what he would like and what is possible. If I do the right kind of job, I don't know if I'm going to be here four years from now.

—PRESIDENT JOHN KENNEDY

Oh God, Thy sea is so great and my boat is so small. . . .

—*Words on plaque given to Polaris submarine commanders—on the President's desk*

The Pay Is Good and I Can Walk to Work

The world of the new President was a quiet one. The Korean War had ended some six years before and the Eisenhower years had been years of peace. No immediate crises loomed. Nikita Khrushchev, who had replaced Stalin in Soviet Russia, even seemed inclined to allow some thaw to filter through the cold war. The United States had passed through economic recession but was now almost on an even keel again. Its young people seemed more tethered than turbulent. The only looming issue of danger was "the goddamn civil rights mess"—as Jack Kennedy called it.

Washington was no longer a relaxed company town with a strong southern flavor, but neither was it Versailles on the Potomac. Some still considered it "a trifle boorish."

Out of his book of quotes, Kennedy picked one from Benjamin Franklin. Assessing the painting of the signers of the Constitution, Franklin was asked whether the sun was rising or setting.

"I think the sun is rising."

"The difference between the outgoing Eisenhower and the incoming Kennedy," an observer commented, "was the difference between a slow march and a jig. Washington is crackling, rocking, jumping. It is a kite zigging in the breeze." A much-quoted Kennedy line was, "Some men see things as they are and say, 'Why?' I dream things that never were and say, 'Why not?' "

The incoming Kennedy people were described as "the richest, prettiest, most interesting young people in the country," a youth movement with "the savor of springtime in the air." The torch had been passed.

Many felt that the air of expectation in Washington was comparable only to that of 1933, when President Franklin D. Roosevelt brought in the new faces of his New Deal. While Kennedy did not have the sheer charismatic vitality of Roosevelt, or the quick instincts of Truman, or the team ability of Eisenhower, he had some parts of all of these. What he did have most of all was a curiosity about absolutely everything, together with a willingness to understand "what the hell they were about." For a man without much obvious passion, he could arouse an enormous passion in others. He had a special ability to handle the fluent phrases of the English language, combining poetry with power to evoke a tremendous vibrancy. He made people feel good about themselves, telling them that they belonged in government, belonged to the world, belonged to the New Frontier.

"He was only six months older than I was," said Arthur Schlesinger, Jr., "but he was the most spectacular, extraordinary man in my whole generation. He was an unfettered man. And I was caught by his charm, his concern for the country, his vision of the future, his irony, his humor, his rational view of issues. His personal charm was enormous."

"The first time I saw him in the White House," Boston friend Edward McLaughlin said, "we talked back and forth, and suddenly he starts looking around and says, 'Is anybody here?' Then he looks at me and asks, 'Then what the hell is this "Mr. President" bullshit?' "

"You're the President of the United States," McLaughlin replied. "I can't call you anything else."

Kennedy looked at his friend a long time, then simply shook his head and continued.

When Mrs. Franklin D. Roosevelt came to lunch at the White House, Kennedy held the door open for her. "You go first now, Mr. President," she said firmly. He hesitated, gave her a quiet look, and did as he was told.

Did the Kennedy family relationship change when he became President?

"Heavens no!" Joan Kennedy said. "Jack still dishes it out and takes it like the others."

*   *   *

The night was bitter cold and the President suddenly noticed the Secret Service man standing outside the Oval Office in the garden. He opened the French doors and asked the Secret Service man to "come in and get warm." The man refused, insisting it was his duty to patrol outside.

Ten minutes later President Kennedy was back again, this time with his fleece-lined coat. "I want you to put this on. You're not warm enough, I can tell." To oblige him, the man put on the coat.

Within another ten minutes, the President was back again, this time with two cups of hot chocolate. He was coatless but he sat down outside on the icy steps and insisted the Secret Service man join him "and we drank hot chocolate together."

Telling the story, many years later, the Secret Service man wept unashamedly and said, "That's the kind of president I've been serving."

*   *   *

One of Kennedy's early concerns was his vice-president. Kennedy called in his staff shortly after the inauguration and told them: "A few months ago you were clerks on Capitol Hill while he was the most important man there. Johnson's not going to enjoy having to deal with you, and you should always take that into consideration.

"I understand that a lot of you guys have been bad-mouthing

the Vice-President. Now I'm going to tell you this: If I ever catch anybody demeaning the Vice-President, I'm going to fire him. I just want you guys to know how I feel about it."

To his chief of protocol, Angier Biddle Duke, Kennedy said: "I want you to take care of the Vice-President and Mrs. Johnson. I want you to watch over them and see that they're not ignored, not only when you see them, but at all the occasions."

"What do you mean?" Duke asked.

"Because I'm going to forget," Kennedy said. "The staff is going to forget. We're all going to forget. We've got too much to do around here. And I want you to remember."

What made Kennedy most mindful of all this was something Prime Minister Macmillan had told him, that Eisenhower almost never let Vice-President Nixon into the White House. Not only did the Kennedys invite the Johnsons to everything, but the Johnsons went upstairs to Kennedy family quarters before a state dinner so that the four could walk down together with the Color Guard to greet the guests.

Kennedy's personal toleration for Johnson's company was limited. Jim Rowe noticed Kennedy and Johnson sitting together at the opening game of a baseball season, Johnson talking constantly. The next year, there they were again at the baseball opener, but Rowe looked at them and smiled. They were no longer sitting together. Dave Powers was sitting between them.

Jack still probably liked Lyndon more than Lyndon liked him, but Kennedy never took himself as seriously as Johnson did.

Lyndon Johnson made an early bid for power. "All vice-presidents are political eunuchs," Johnson once told Henry Luce, "and I am not, by God, about to let Kennedy cut my balls off." His staff drew up an executive order for the President's signature, which would have conferred greatly expanded powers on the Vice-President. Kennedy was more amused than angered.

He knew that Johnson was hurt because he had been a major-general in the Senate and he had now reversed roles with a former lieutenant. He knew that Lyndon had a terrible inferiority complex about the Kennedy crowd, whom he referred to as "those people," or "the smart-asses," or "the Georgetown Jelly

Beans." Some of the Kennedy people in turn called Johnson "a great guided missile," and referred to Kennedy in Johnson's presence as "the majority leader's leader," and then asked Johnson if he had his orders for the day. They would let him sit in the President's outer office, munching his chocolates and nuts while he waited, sometimes interminably, to see the President, always feeling left out of the swirling activity.

Among the Kennedy group there was some contempt mixed with fear. Contempt came because they saw Johnson as a "southern pol," a crude kind of man who enjoyed letting out an explosive fart. Their fear came from his former position of well-established political strength, which they had not long before regarded as "the enemy," and which they felt he might exercise to stir up a cabal of southerners against Kennedy legislation.

"Kennedy took extraordinary pains to keep the Vice-President informed," said Walt Rostow, who was then on the National Security Council. "For example, Kennedy re-scheduled a major item on the agenda in a foreign policy meeting because Johnson's plane was late, circling in bad weather over Washington. He also saw a good deal of Johnson alone. In a relationship inherently awkward, no modern president dealt with his vice-president in as serious and substantive a way as Kennedy with Johnson."

When Kennedy solicited opinions at a meeting, Johnson seldom spoke. "I recall only three occasions in 1961 when he expressed opinions of substance in a large meeting," Rostow said. "One was evidently observing a man under sustained self-discipline and restraint."

"I don't know what to do with Lyndon," Kennedy told Arthur Krock. "I've got to keep him happy somehow." He called it "one hell of a job." Another time, he added, "All Lyndon wants to be is loved. He never will be, probably. He wants to be remembered as 'one of the boys.' He never will be."

For Lyndon Johnson, the vice-presidency was a very cruel post, a torment. He was quick to see gunfire "where no guns were loaded." There were many who said he drank more heavily then. He was so unlike the Kennedy crowd that he didn't even know where Martha's Vineyard was. When three administration people were fogged in there, he called Bundy to ask what the "whole goddamn administration is doing on some female island in the fog?"

Years later, Johnson claimed that the Kennedy staff had been "poisonous" to him. It was clear to the Kennedy inner circle that Johnson felt ambivalent about them: On the one hand, he tried desperately to gain their affection and respect; on the other, he knew that he could never succeed.

*   *   *

"Mr. President, it's close to seven-thirty."

He was almost instantly out of bed, a robe over his night-shirt, moving into an unused room, stretching out on a fresh bed to devour four newspapers in fifteen minutes. Then into the bathroom, a shave, a hot tub, and ready for breakfast.

Caroline would come in for her morning hugs and kisses, crawl into his bed, watch him dress. His valet already had laid out his clothes from a choice of eighteen suits and eight pairs of shoes. If his back hurt badly enough, his valet helped him dress.

When he arrived with his folder, the two Secret Service men were waiting for him at the elevator door to walk with him to the Oval Office. One of his jokes at the time was, "The pay is good and I can walk to work." Clark Clifford advised the President that he shouldn't live in the White House. "I know that one of the hardest things for Jack at the beginning was to work in the house he lived in." Another friend suggested that he walk around the driveway twice in the morning so he could pretend he was walking to work.

It was eight-thirty when the President arrived at the Oval Office to begin his day.

Evelyn Lincoln would get there at eight o'clock in the morning, and he would start dictating before he'd even get through the door. "I'd have to run even before he sat down," Evelyn Lincoln said. "He'd come to my desk a lot and say, 'Well, you can answer this and this, but here's one I want to answer my-self.'

"Everybody says it's a glamourous job, and it is," Lincoln added, "but you're busy all the time and you work every day until eight, Saturdays until four, go to conferences if you have to take notes, and you work very, very hard. I never went out to lunch. But it was a wonderful experience and I want to tell you there were fifty thousand people behind me waiting to grab my job if I ever stepped out. That's why I had lunch sent in."

Evelyn Lincoln, a slight, soft-spoken woman, preferred plain stockings, black leather high-heeled pumps, a black velvet mini-skirt, and the ends of her bouffant hairdo curled up in wispy bangs and a jaunty flip. She had started with him as a volunteer typist and she couldn't get over it. "He was concerned about my welfare, not about his. He kept asking, 'Is the seat all right? Is the desk all right? How about the light?' " Ten years later, when she was his personal secretary, he still asked her often, "How are you getting along?"

Kennedy's swim was a daily ritual: Every afternoon at one-thirty it was a half-hour swim in the nude, into his robe, back through the exercise room, the Flower room, through the ground-floor corridor, up in an elevator, into bed, usually a hamburger lunch on a tray, and then some private time with his wife. There was another swim after the day's work, before dinner. Each time, Kennedy changed clothes. That meant he wore three suits a day every day he lived in the White House.

Those first days in the White House, John Kennedy was like a kid in a candy store with five dollars. He loved it: the honors, the trappings, the power, the perks, the gadgets. Press a button for the helicopter, *Air Force One* always ready to go anywhere, instant telephone contact with anyone. He echoed the feeling of President Theodore Roosevelt, who had said, "I love the White House. I greatly enjoy the exercise of power."

Kennedy joked about how he could wave his hand or move his little finger, and twenty people would jump. "I can't remember what it was like *not* to be president." In those early days the President roamed all over, poking his head into doors, asking secretaries how they were getting along. When he wanted somebody, he went to find them.

"It's hard to get exercise when you have a job like this," Kennedy said, stopping to talk, making decisions on his feet, leaning over someone's desk to sign an executive order, leafing through a memorandum while standing up.

"This is precisely what I want done," he told one staff member. On the telephone, he was insistent, "I want an answer by this afternoon. . . ."

The presidential extra Kennedy enjoyed most was the White House switchboard. The switchboard seemed like a miracle. The President might pull a name out of the past with only the vaguest idea of the man's whereabouts and, seemingly within minutes, he was on the line.

On a so-called average day of controlled confusion, there might be as many as seventy visitors, fifteen telephone conferences, a television appearance, and a variety of unscheduled events and visitors. Once he found a group of thirty-seven foreign students singing songs in the outer room, not expecting to see him, each with a gift for him. He took them into his office.

From the time he began work and asked his secretary, "What have you got?" to 7:56 PM when he left to head upstairs, he had a total of some forty-nine minutes all to himself in the Oval Office, most of them spent dictating memos and letters.

A typical Kennedy impulsive touch was to take the reading copy of his inaugural address, sign it at Evelyn Lincoln's desk and tell her, with a twinkle, "I read the other day that one of the former presidents was offered $75,000 for his inaugural address. Here, keep this $75,000 for me."

"He did everything around here but shinny up the Washington Monument," James Reston wrote of a typical day.

If it was 7:30 PM, their usual bedtime, and their father was still at the office, Caroline, and later John, would come down to their father's office to say good night. They would be in their pajamas, ready for a romp. Their father would get on the floor with them, and they would be all over him, jumping up and down, pounding him, all of them laughing. He would laugh with them and relax in a way that he did with no one else. Then the children would go upstairs to bed and he would go back to being President of the United States.

After dinner, if there was work to do, as there almost always was, he sat there with his folders. When he was done, the family was already in bed. He straightened his back by putting the palm of his hand hard against it. Then he turned out all the lights, except a small one in the hall. That was in case someone came to wake him in the middle of the night with a crisis.

He had no illusions about the White House being his home. He liked to tell the story of President Coolidge's overhearing a foreign visitor outside the White House gates asking, "I wonder who lives there?"

"Nobody," President Coolidge answered. "They just come and go."

There were always minor complaints.

"There are servants everywhere you turn around. You go to the bathroom and there are servants standing in the bathroom."

There was also the time the President lent his second-best dinner jacket to a friend. The friend returned it with a small hole, which Kennedy did not notice at the time. When he finally did see it, he said, "I break my ass to get into the White House, and the damn place has moths."

"Well, Pierre, going to another ball or party?" the President asked Salinger, who was in a tux and black tie.

"Yes, Mr. President," Salinger said, "but I didn't have a black tie so I took the liberty of going up to your room and taking one of your black ties."

"You mean to say you went upstairs and took one of my ties without asking me?"

"Yes, sir, I did," Salinger said.

Kennedy's face then broke into a smile. "Well, go out and have a good time."

"It was some time after the inauguration and I was in the bathroom in the White House," Bill Walton recalled. "Jack was in the tub. The door was slightly open and we were just talking. He wanted to know all the gossip. He just loved gossip. 'What's new in New York? Who's doing what to whom?' Suddenly he said, 'Wait a minute.' He got up out of the tub, still wet and, naked, went outside the door and grabbed Jackie and brought her back. She had been listening. 'Oh, you two little boys, chattering about all this gossip.' He bawled her out in a nice, funny way for eavesdropping: 'I don't open your mail. You don't open mine. You're not supposed to listen to these things. These are private conversations.'

"After she left, he said to me, 'Eternal vigilance is the price of freedom.' "

*   *   *

For the First Lady, the contrast in private lives was sharp.

"We had such a wonderful house in Georgetown," Jacqueline Kennedy said. "You'd come in at night and find the fire going, and people talking, and you didn't stay up late. My fears were that we wouldn't have this anymore in the White House. But that's been the most wonderful side of it. You can talk when he comes home at night. It's better than during the campaign—you don't just dump your bags and go off again. That's been wonderful for the children. Sometimes they even have lunch with him —if you'd told me that would happen, I'd never have believed it. But I should have realized because, after all, the one thing that happens to a president is that his ties with the outside world are cut. And the people you really have are each other. Sometimes I think you become sort of a—there should be a nicer word than 'freak.' I should think that if people weren't happily married, the White House would really finish it."

She wanted home to be his release; she wanted him to concentrate on her and their children.

Alice Roosevelt Longworth, daughter of President Theodore Roosevelt, visited the Kennedys at the White House. She observed the casual way the children were running around on the second floor and said, "This is just the way it was when I lived here."

Caroline and John had stayed in Palm Beach with their grandparents until February. They arrived on a Saturday to a welcoming snowman the White House gardener had made to greet them. Caroline soon made it a ritual to walk her father downstairs to work every morning.

She called him "silly Daddy" and he called her "Buttons." She had a way of parking herself in his lap during breakfast meetings with his staff. He always let her stay. Or, she might imperiously walk into a meeting to announce, loud and clear, "Mommy wants you!"

The First Lady was concerned about keeping their children

out of the public eye as much as possible, away from photographers. "Someday," Mrs. Kennedy said, "she is going to have to go to school and, if she is in the papers all the time, that will affect her classmates and they will treat her differently."

She organized a class of a dozen children of friends and White House aides—including a black child. They met for two hours in the morning, three times a week in the third-floor solarium. Mothers alternated as helpers. Tony Bradlee reported how appalled Jacqueline was when she realized she had to help the little boys in the bathroom.

All the children brought their own lunch. They also had a playhouse under one of the trees on the south lawn near one of former President Eisenhower's putting greens. The President would often walk through the open French doors of the Oval Office to watch the children playing. Whenever he clapped his hands, Caroline would come running towards him. Ted Sorensen was with him one day in the Rose Garden when he saw Caroline racing for her swing. She saw him and jumped into his arms and he swung her around in a sweeping arc, and then off she raced again toward the swing while he went back to work.

It was her mother's idea to get her a pony. The President demurred, but she had insisted, "This is what I think is appropriate. This is why Caroline should do it." The pony was quickly named "Macaroni" and a U.S. Navy band even introduced a number called "My Pony Macaroni," complete with trumpeted whinnies and percussive hoofbeats. The President then asked Mrs. Lincoln to buy some small sculptured horses that he could give his daughter one at a time. Mrs. Lincoln finally got a note from the First Lady: "Please, Mrs. Lincoln, don't buy any more horses." In an interview, she observed, "I think the people must be as sick of hearing about us and Macaroni as I am."

She was wrong. Anything about the Kennedy children was news. Anything.

"She wasn't the hugging-kissing mother that Ethel is," Joan Braden said. "Or that I am. But the love is there." Ethel had her own comment, after seeing how Caroline behaved. "I've revised the way I'm going to bring up my own children."

Jacqueline worried much that their children would be spoiled. At any sign of brattishness, she told a friend, "Someone, her father or me or the nurse, will draw a line. To check her in time is the biggest favor we can do her." Asked about her philosophy for rearing children, the First Lady answered, "Love and discipline." Yet there was a permissiveness. Caroline knew she could turn on the garden faucet and race away without reprimand. She could also jump onto a guest's lap on impulse and her mother would apologize, "I know I should stop her from jumping in your lap, but I just can't."

"I was reading Carlyle, and he said you should do the duty that lies nearest you. And the thing that lies nearest me is the children." She paused, seeming to choke up. "You feel torn to pieces, pulled so many ways at once."

"Most men don't care about children as much as women do, but he did," she later said of her husband. "He was the kind of man who should have had a brood of children."

The father needed no urging to be with his children. With them, his love was full, without reservation.

Once Caroline walked into his office and said, "Good morning, Mr. President," and he answered gravely, "Good morning, Mr. Ambassador."

On another occasion, he asked Caroline how her baby brother was doing. "He's coming along fine," she announced, with the authority of a big sister.

"How much does he weigh?" the President asked solemnly.

"Seventy."

He hardly had seen his three-year-old daughter during the campaign, but in the White House he fully discovered her and doted on her. He took pride in the small poems he taught her, which she memorized. He made up all kinds of little stories for her, and he reveled in the poise she had in walking up to any stranger, smiling, and saying, "Hi!" Before she was three, she drew a birthday card for her father. Their relationship was tender and deep. When she skinned her knee and was close to tears, he told her gently, "Kennedys don't cry."

When Caroline did a finger painting in class, Jacqueline had it framed and told her husband that Bill Walton had done it and she had bought it for $600. "Good Lord, what kick is Walton on now?" he commented. His wife finally confessed that Caroline had painted it. The President smiled. "Pretty good color."

"Caroline's very bright, smarter than you were at that age," Joseph Kennedy said to his son Jack.

"Yes, she is," the President said, "but look who *she has* for a father!"

His son, John, was a different story. Jack Kennedy was upset by his sister-in-law's comment to the press that his back was so bothersome that "he can barely pick up his own son." The quick White House reply: "The President's back is improving but his son is getting heavier."

"Jack keeps urging me to pick John up and throw him in the air because he loves it so, and because he can't do it because of his back," Bradlee said. "He doesn't know it yet, but he's going to carry me before I carry him."

Charles Spalding recalled, "I'd come to see him in the morning sometimes and he'd be in the bathtub with John and some of John's toy ducks, and I said, 'What a picture this would make: the President in the bath with his ducks!' "

*   *   *

Jacqueline told Joan Braden, "You know, Joanie, now that Jack is President, it's difficult because I don't like to ask people for dinner and have them think they *have* to come." Joan Braden explained that people were absolutely delighted to come to dinner at the White House.

The Bradens came to dinner the night after the inauguration, with the Leonard Bernsteins. "We sat in the small Oval Room and had a fire and it was relaxing and fun. We talked a little about what had happened in California and then went into the small dining room for dinner. Jackie started in and the President said, 'Jackie, the President *always* goes first.' And we all burst out laughing. Then, of course, he stood back and Jackie went first."

"So there we were, just the six of us in the upstairs dining room," said Bernstein, the composer-conductor. The others were his wife, Felicia, Tom and Joan Braden, and the John Kennedys. Tom Braden was a liberal California newspaper publisher.

"It's a marvelous little room. You dine on Abraham Lincoln's china with Madison's spoons, and it's just very moving. We had a perfectly marvelous dinner. After dinner, we were all in great high spirits, and we were sitting around the drawing room just chatting about everything. Some of us were sitting on the floor. At least I was. It was that informal. It became the sort of place that you were happy to be in. You felt there it was all so familiar and familial at the same time."

The phone rang and the President answered it and talked for a while and then handed the phone to Bernstein. "You talk to her. I can't talk to her anymore," he said. It was the President's sister, Eunice, whom Bernstein had never met. She was saying, "Oh come on, what are you doing now?" It was a twenty-minute conversation.

"I think Jackie may have resented Eunice a bit because Eunice was such a confidante of Jack's, and she wanted to be the only one," Braden said. "Almost every time I was there, Eunice called."

Leonard Bernstein took time out to view a performance of a special concert on TV in Caroline's bedroom. As the conductor watched the performance, entranced, Caroline and her nurse watched him. Finally, the enthusiastic conductor turned to Caroline for her reaction to the music. She looked at him with her clear face and said, "I have my own horse."

The composer quickly returned to the other guests.

"Yes, he was a wonderful dancer, bad back and all," said Braden of Jack Kennedy. "I remember we once did the Twist. I was terrible but he was great."

It was 2 AM before the party broke up.

"It was just so delicious an evening," Bernstein said. "That happens very rarely, where everybody is so happy sitting right there that you don't ever want it to end. We weren't doing anything except talking and laughing, and I couldn't tell you *one* thing we talked about the whole night."

*   *   *

The President had a private concern. Kennedy remarked on how difficult it was to make new friends after you got to the White House. What he plainly meant was that once you were president you inevitably always had the feeling that everybody wanted something from you.

"All he had in Washington really was me and Ben Bradlee and Charlie Bartlett," Bill Walton said. "There was Lemoyne Billings but he was a dud, and Chuck Spalding was in Greenwich. And Ben was with *Newsweek* and his antennae were always out for a story. Charlie was a newspaperman, too, but more of a friend. As for me, my children were grown and I was single and had no axe to grind. I was the most easily available, I guess. And when Jackie was away, he needed ears to listen to him and an old friend to relax with."

Walton recalled: "Eunice invited me to a dinner party for some foreign dignitaries and I said I'd come. But then I got a call from Evelyn Lincoln, and she said the President wanted me to join him for dinner that same night. I told her I couldn't because of Eunice's invitation, but Evelyn said, 'He still wants you tonight for dinner.' So I called Eunice and told her I was sorry and couldn't come because of the President. She got vehement. 'You can't let me down like this. I'm counting on you.' And she went on and on like that. All I could say was, 'I'm sorry, Eunie, but I can't turn down the President. . . . '

"That night I had dinner with the President, just the two of us, and I told him about Eunice and he said, 'Oh, I'm sorry she turned on you like that.' "

The President later called his sister and said, "Eunie, you can have anyone you want for dinner. I can't." Eunice then burst into tears because she realized how lonely her brother was.

Both the Bradlees and the Bartletts came to expect the unexpected call from the presidential secretary. As Bradlee put it, "If he invited us both the same night, then who would he invite the next night? He didn't have that many old friends." What was interesting, too, was that his intimate friends were not intimate with each other. The call usually came at six in the evening, asking either couple if they were free to have dinner with the President that night. This was particularly true when his wife was away. He never liked to be alone. As they arrived, his opening questions were always the same: "What's new? What's going on?"

Charlie Bartlett told about another party on another night: "You'd arrive about seven-forty-five and go up to the Oval Room," Bartlett said. "The President would have finished his exercises and his swim. You'd feel fine as you sat in the Oval Room with a drink. The President, who always wore his blue suit, would sit in the rocking chair by the fire."

There had been quite a bit of wine drunk that night and finally the question was raised, "Where is the bathroom?"

"You've lived here before," the President said to Franklin D. Roosevelt, Jr. "Where's the plumbing?"

FDR's son simply smiled. "I don't think I ever used the plumbing downstairs in this house."

The party finally trooped upstairs searching for bathrooms, and stayed upstairs for a while. Roosevelt, Jr., told how his uncle Teddy's six children all slept in the Lincoln bed crosswise.

A presidential prerogative is the right to leave a dinner party at any time, even during dinner, without apology or explanation. Some guests complained that it was like electricity leaving the lamp. The President usually left a party by ten, but here it was past midnight and he showed no sign of retiring. A guest asked Mrs. Kennedy whether she felt it was time for them to go. "Don't worry about it," she said, "if he wants to stay up, let him stay up. He hasn't done this in ages."

What people did not understand about Kennedy was how his pain influenced his sense of time. So seldom was he fully free of all pain that he considered that interval euphoria.

"When you did see him in that euphoric state," Spalding remembered, "he was always the greatest, greatest company— so bright and so restless that he just set a pace that was abnormal. I can think of a lot of people who live at a terrific pace, and have the high-blood-pressure point of view towards life. That wasn't his. He just gave you a pleasant heightened sense of being. And he did that with everybody. I've never seen any company in which he wasn't the brightest and most entertaining. When you were with him, life just picked up. With him, it was always like that. It accounts for the remarkable attraction he had for people."

All through his presidency, to the time of his death, Kennedy almost always used his crutches when he was out of public sight. Even during his final visit to Hyannis Port, just before he went to Dallas, he walked around inside his house on crutches. He even used his crutches in the yard if there was no one else there. Only his closest friends and family knew. He would watch a family game of touch football from the sidelines—if the ball came near him, he might drop his crutch, hobble over to get the ball, then run to throw it.

The pain was constant, varying only in degree. Some swimming pool exercises took most of the weight off his painful back. Without those exercises, without novocaine shots, he wouldn't have been able to walk anywhere without his crutches.

"My daughter was then just a little thing," Larry Newman said, "and the President was very fond of her. But he couldn't reach down and pick her up. He would have to tell me, as he did, 'Larry, pick up your daughter and put her in my lap.'"

The suffering and the lifetime crippling by polio converted a carefree Roosevelt into a deeper-thinking, more compassionate man. Critical back operations and the never-ending pain that followed created a similar sensitivity in Kennedy.

Only a few knew this was so.

And she got no help from anyone, none, zero. She was fighting for her life, her individuality. To everyone else, she looked just fine, but the tension inside of her was tremendous.

—CHARLES SPALDING

14

An Elegant First Lady

Jackie had come to hear her husband's first address to Congress as President in January 1961. Applause greeted her arrival and a reporter noted she hesitated "like a schoolgirl," uncertain the applause was for her, "then gave a little bow that was somehow appealing."

Discussing other First Ladies Jacqueline felt the greatest affinity for Bess Truman.

"Mrs. Truman brought a daughter to the White House at a most difficult age and managed to keep her from being spoiled so that she has made a happy marriage with lovely children of her own. Mrs. Truman kept her family close together in spite of White House demands and that is the hardest thing to do," observed Mrs. Kennedy. Bess Truman was also never cozy with the press, guarded her family privacy jealously, and refused to be pushed around.

Mrs. Jacqueline Bouvier Kennedy brought the first small children into the White House since the Theodore Roosevelts, fifty years before. In a further description of the First Lady, a reporter commented that she also "observes elegance as if it were a Cecil Beaton set, without being the least chi-chi herself. Maybe Jacqueline Bouvier Kennedy wouldn't have reached the White House entirely on her own—back of every successful woman you'll find a man—but I think it's becoming obvious that she has as strong a personality as her husband's, and that she will keep as firm a hand on the First Ladyship as he's expected to keep on the presidency."

Brother-in-law Steve Smith commented, "Jack always said how smart Jackie was and she really was. What they had going between them was this sense of humor. And she could cut him down, and did—there was no question about it. When she felt strongly about something, she let him know it and let everybody else know it." Two of her more damning and often used adjectives were "drab" and "dreary." Initially, though, she was overwhelmed by everything, and kind of lost, their friend Betty Spalding recalled.

"Please, Mr. West," Jacqueline told the White House chief usher, "the one thing I do not want to be called is 'First Lady.' It sounds like a saddle horse. Would you notify the telephone operators and everyone else that I'm to be known simply as 'Mrs. Kennedy,' and not as 'First Lady.' "

She had been surrounded by servants all her life. She knew how to judge them, what to expect of them, how to treat them. The morning after the inauguration, she was up early and wanted a full White House tour to meet the staff at its work. The chief usher persuaded her instead to let him bring the staff to her, in small groups. When he brought them, she was wearing jodhpurs, brown boots, and a shirt, her hair in some disarray. It was quite a change from the carefully prepared Mrs. Eisenhower.

Mamie Eisenhower had had a 9 AM staff conference at her bedside; Jacqueline Kennedy had no regular wake-up time. If there had been a late party, she might not get up until noon. Her conferences were impromptu and anywhere, but mostly she put ideas on a yellow legal pad, and often in great detail.

Her breakfast was standard and simple: orange juice, toast and honey, coffee with skimmed milk, served on a tray in bed.

After breakfast she usually took a solitary fast-stepping walk on the sixteen acres surrounding the White House. She always wore slacks, with a shirt or sweater. The chief usher never remembered her wearing a dress in the White House "unless she had company."

For lunch, Jackie happily settled for her favorite grilled cheese sandwiches. She never kept regular hours on any disciplined schedule. She succeeded, more than most First Ladies, in being as free a spirit as possible inside "the prison" of the White House. The only inviolate hours in her schedule were those set aside to be with her children and the private time with her husband.

She pushed her son's carriage around the circular driveway and under the trees, and read regularly for an hour to Caroline before dinner. She and Caroline never talked baby talk. "Let's go out and kiss the wind," she would say to her. They went for long walks, picked flowers together, looked at books of paintings, spent summer weekends on the Hyannis beach, went wading at Big Hunting Creek. "She works like hell with that child," Bill Walton said. "She spends more time with that child than most mothers I know."

Her private time with her husband was every afternoon, after lunch, while the children were napping. She had installed a stereo in the passageway between her room and his, and the music usually played during their private time. It was another signal for the staff to stay away. No matter what her afternoon duties were, Mrs. Kennedy left them to be with her husband. If there were visitors, others had to entertain them. Otherwise her husband's valet would be searching for her to say, "The President says that if you don't hurry, he'll fall asleep."

Her husband had had his afternoon swim, gone directly to bed in the four-poster where Truman had slept, had his lunch in bed off a tray, and waited for her. During their time together, the doors were closed and they accepted no phone calls, no interruptions. No staff person went upstairs for any reason. This was a daily ritual.

Jacqueline then usually had her own nap in her own bed. Her maid afterwards changed the bed, "because Mrs. Kennedy likes fresh sheets."

Although they had their own separate bedrooms, valet George Thomas, who had the morning job of waking the President, would often find his bed empty. It was then Thomas's job to tiptoe into Mrs. Kennedy's bedroom and gently wake the President without waking his wife.

*   *   *

Evelyn Lincoln recalled, "I remember him saying to me one day soon after the inauguration, 'You know, we've got to have something for Jackie to do. She's a very private person. She likes being by herself. She prefers reading books. What do you *do* with her?'

"Then he got the idea of having her redecorate the White House. It was his idea. He went to his wife and said, 'You've got great taste, Jackie, and the job for you is to get your experts together and make the White House a living example of the best in America.' "

*   *   *

"The White House is the sacred cow of the American people and woe to any President who touches it," warned Clark Clifford.

"The White House is the property of the nation," President Theodore Roosevelt had said, "and so far as is compatible with living therein, it should be kept as it originally was." But Roosevelt had declared the White House a national museum only after he had virtually gutted and redecorated it. Before that, Dolley Madison added a green bathtub. The Jefferson furniture collection was destroyed when the British burned the White House. Jackson hauled a fourteen-hundred-pound cheese into his quarters for a final reception before he retired from office, smelling up the place for months. Mrs. Lincoln sold much of the furniture after her husband's assassination because she was deep in debt. Chester Arthur, sniffing that the White House "looked like a badly kept barracks," auctioned off twenty-four wagonloads of furniture, and hired Louis Comfort Tiffany to redecorate the place to look like a gambling parlor.

What would Mrs. Kennedy do? Would she "turn the White House into a living museum" as her social secretary had announced? Would she cover the downstairs White House walls with abstract art? Would she decorate it with French art and French antiques?

Jacqueline Kennedy said, "It seemed to me such a shame when we came here to find hardly anything of the past in the house, hardly anything before 1902."

What Mrs. Kennedy decided to do was to have the White House reflect the whole history of the presidency.

"Everything must have a reason for being there," Mrs. Kennedy said of the White House, which she had previously described as "early Statler." And she added, "It would be sacrilege merely to redecorate—a word I hate."

"I felt like a moth banging on the windowpane when I first moved into this place," Jacqueline said. "It was terrible. You couldn't even open the windows in the rooms, because they hadn't been opened for years. The shades you pulled down at night were so enormous that they had pulleys and ropes. When we tried the fireplaces, they smoked because they hadn't ever been used. Sometimes I wondered, 'How are we going to live as a family in this enormous place?' I'm afraid it will always be a little impossible for the people who live there. It's an office building."

Of the 132 rooms in the White House, the presidential family was restricted to the two upper floors, which included five bedrooms. Guests such as Queen Elizabeth occupied the rooms at the end of the hall where Lincoln had had his bedroom.

Mrs. Kennedy made an early decision that it was too dreary to eat downstairs, in the blue dining room "with five butlers hovering around," and too awkward to eat off trays upstairs "and you had to wait an hour for a pat of butter from the downstairs kitchen, or else go down the elevator yourself."

Her first order was for an upstairs dining room. It took only two weeks for the White House staff of thirty-five carpenters, electricians, plumbers, and upholsterers to create a kitchen out of Margaret Truman's dressing room, a pantry out of a bathroom, and a food storage area from a closet. Mrs. Kennedy used her delicate, round-backed French chairs she'd had in Georgetown.

She then continued with the family rooms, which the tourists never see. Mamie Eisenhower's favorite pink became a bluish green in the bedroom, with the pale blue and green curtains of hand-screened French fabric Mrs. Kennedy had had in her Georgetown home. She also hung some French drawings.

The White House second floor had a long dark corridor with bedrooms on each side, and a light yellow oval-shaped room for tea and drinks. On the west side of the corridor was Jacqueline's room. Dinner guests used the President's bathroom. It was not a house for spacious living.

Chief Usher J. Bernard West provided photographs of the rooms, and her memos to him were sharp: "This is Jack's bedroom adjoining mine. Furniture arrangement is fine for him—all furniture is okay too—you just have to think of a pretty color wall—chintz and rug." In another room she found a handsome four-poster bed and several fine Oriental rugs. "Good idea, move this to Jack's room," she wrote on a torn sliver of paper. "Perhaps one of these rugs, preferably the red one . . . he would love it—then we would not have to spend $$$—just move furniture."

She noticed that there were no bookcases in the President's bedroom. "Doesn't any President *ever* read? No bookcases anywhere. You would see on the plans where they could go—along the walls."

The President's bedroom had the antique four-poster bed with a blue and white canopy. His heating pad was always on the night table shelf in case his back became too painful. At the foot of his bed was a table with books and magazines, and his rocking chair was nearby. The walls were off-white and the one painting in the room was called *Flag Day*.

Mrs. Kennedy's bedroom was white with accents of light blue in the silk curtains, bedspread, chair coverings, and picture mats. She had a small couch, a round table, a fireplace, and a number of pictures on the wall, including a pastel drawing of Caroline. Her dressing room had a chaise, a mirrored door, a white rug, and many paintings and family photographs.

"Mr. West," she wrote, "would you look into the possibility

of really darkening the White House floor. It would make it stop looking like a roller-skating rink."

West knew exactly how to react to the new First Lady. "I assumed that Mrs. Kennedy's wish, murmured with a 'Do you think . . .' or 'Could you please, . . .' had as much command as Mrs. Eisenhower's 'I want this done immediately.'

"She was thirty years younger than any of the First Ladies I had served and, I was to discover, had the most complex personality of them all. In public, she was elegant, aloof, dignified, and regal. In private, she was casual, impish, and irreverent. She had a will of iron, with more determination than anyone I have ever met. Yet she was so soft-spoken, so deft and subtle, that she would impose that will upon people without their ever knowing it.

"Her wit, teasing, exaggerating, poking fun at everything, including herself—was a surprise and a daily delight. She was imaginative, inventive, intelligent—and sometimes silly. Yet there were subjects that did not amuse her one bit.

"Relaxed and uninhibited, she was always popping up anywhere, wearing slacks, sitting on the floor, kicking off her shoes, her hair flying in every direction. We all had fun along with her."

A dressing-room closet between the bedrooms of the two children was made into a room for their nurse. "She won't need much," Mrs. Kennedy whispered merrily of Maude Shaw. "Just find a wicker wastebasket for her banana peels and a little table for her false teeth at night."

"This is a beautiful room," Mrs. Kennedy said of the second-story Oval Room. Beyond the windows was Harry Truman's famous balcony and a spectacular view of the Washington Monument and Jefferson Memorial. "I love it most. There is this magnificent view. It means something to the man who stands there and sees it—after all he's done to get there." The Oval Room soon became her redecorated prize, refurnished in exquisite Louis XVI style, "but in my bedroom, I had all my Georgetown things and I worked at Daddy's Empire desk."

She also provided a secret hiding place for her daughter by removing an old-fashioned radiator from a window enclosure in her bedroom.

Of all the White House rooms, the one that delighted her most was the Lincoln bedroom, with its yellow walls, tufted settees, marble-top tables, and monstrous Victorian bed with a nine-foot-high rosewood headboard carved in tortuous curlicues.

"Lincoln's bedroom!" she wrote in her notes. "The only room in the whole place I like! Can't change it—wouldn't want to, even though it isn't really Lincoln's bedroom. But it has his things in it. And you see that great bed, it looks like a cathedral. To touch something I knew he had touched was a real link with him. The kind of peace I felt in that room was what you feel when going into a church. I used to sit in the Lincoln Room, and I could really feel his strength. I'd sort of be talking to him."

"Jackie had a terrific overall grasp, the idea of what should be, and a great sense of what was right for the state rooms," said Mrs. Charles Wrightsman, a member of the Fine Arts Committee. "She never stopped working for one second. Nothing was too much trouble. It was a miracle what she did in three years."

"She had total mastery of detail—endless, endless detail—and she was highly organized, yet rarely held herself to a schedule," West added.

Throughout most government offices in Washington, there is a standard use of green and brown. The Oval Office was no exception: green walls, green draperies, green rug, brown furniture, and beige curtains. The single exception was a cerise-colored sofa on the southeast wall. There was also a massive desk with eight telephones.

All this would change.

First, the desk was replaced. It was the kind of history the new President loved. His wife had found this desk covered with green baize in the White House basement. It had been used as a base for television cameras. Once it had been part of the timbers of the H.M.S. *Resolute,* one of the five British ships sent out in 1852 to find a missing explorer who had been searching for the Northwest Passage. Americans found the ship, abandoned and drifting off the coast of Baffinland, refitted it, and presented it to Queen Victoria. In appreciation—when the *Resolute* was finally scrapped twenty years later—the British had a desk carved from its timbers for President Rutherford B. Hayes.

Now President Kennedy sat behind this same desk in the Oval Office.

Kennedy wanted white walls. He also wanted a white fabric to cover the two red sofas flanking the marble fireplace. He asked his wife to find naval battle scenes to decorate his walls. On his desk, he had already placed the preserved coconut on which he had scratched the message for help after his PT boat was sliced in half. Between bookends were a world almanac, the Bible, and a book by Mao Tse-tung, among others. There was also a crystal ashtray for his several cigars, and a formidable leather-sheathed dagger.

A television set was to the left of the desk, and near it, on the wall, a picture of his wife and daughter.

The President himself chose each memento that he wanted to display in the Oval Office. One that meant much to him was the tattered jack, the blue flag with white stars that flew on the bow of a ship that belonged to Commodore John Barry, one of the naval heroes of the American Revolution. Then there were models of some of the great sailing ships: the *Constitution*, the *Wasp*, the *Saratoga*. Opposite his chair in the Cabinet Room he put a model of one of the new aircraft carriers, the *America*.

Jacqueline came into his office to look at some pictures that had been chosen for its walls.

"Mrs. Lincoln, will you have them remove these curtains at the window? They keep the scenery out, and the view is so beautiful."

The curtains were quickly removed.

Jacqueline Kennedy was not a gardener but she loved flowers. She recruited her friend Bunny (Mrs. Paul) Mellon to redesign the President's Rose Garden. Mrs. Mellon was not only a woman of taste but a noted horticulturalist. Her father-in-law once had been secretary of the treasury and her husband was president of the National Gallery of Art. She was one of Jacqueline's few intimate women friends. She arrived with her garden supervisor, her maid, and her decorator, Mrs. Helen Parrish. Her objective: "Let's gay up the White House quickly." Part of her contribution was the use of Flemish floral arrangements, using harmonizing varieties of delicate blossoms in each vase.

Jacqueline had her own sense of history. Some close to her said that she was furious to discover her trivial notes about household matters were thrown away. She insisted that her every written scrap be preserved for posterity.

Mrs. Kennedy brought in a dramatic, bubbly little French decorator named Stephane Boudin and told him, "I want it done the way Versailles does it."

Gifts soon poured in from everywhere: a side chair George Washington used in his Philadelphia house, Hepplewhite secretaries, Duncan Phyfe settees, a painting of Boston harbor, a scene at Valley Forge. To help her select and search, she had a distinguished committee of twelve—seven women and five men, including artists and art museum directors.

It looked like a national treasure hunt. All over the country, antique experts were searching for pieces that were American originals, part of our history.

Antique dealers quickly classed the First Lady as "a terrible tightwad," because she always asked, "It won't be too much, will it? We don't have very much money."

Yet, when she found an old home being demolished in Alexandria that had a mural of a Revolutionary War battle, she had it moved, inch by inch, to the wall of the White House Oval Room. A Swiss visitor later noted that her husband's factory produced an identical wallpaper, "one of our best sellers." Jacqueline Kennedy moaned, "Oh no. . . ."

The White House had two basements used for storage and she made her own check for treasures. "I had a backache every day for three months, but it was a new mystery story every day."

The President was fascinated with the incoming gifts and discoveries, and he scribbled suggestions he found in catalogues. Kay Halle recalled his early knowledge of antiques when he was a senator, how he crawled under one of her tables to check if it was an original.

"You can tell by the boards—the underside of the table— what age it is, whether it's of the period or a reproduction," he told her.

When he stood up, he was glowing, "It's a beautiful table," he said, but added that he favored heavy Chippendale.

Shortly after the inauguration, he took Kenneth Galbraith on a White House tour. "Ken, look at this. It's not even authentic. It's not even a good reproduction. I hope to make this house the repository of the best of the decorative arts in America."

*　　*　　*

"She changed the White House from a plastic to a crystal bowl," Letitia Baldrige said. Critics stopped calling the First Lady a "decorative bird in a gilded cage."

Yet, despite all the excitement in her transformation of the White House, despite its new elegance and her enormous satisfaction, the White House still never meant home to Jacqueline Kennedy. The phrase she used most often to her closest friends was, "It's like a prison."

The poking cameras waiting outside the gates, the inability to go to the theater as often as she wished, the ever-present Secret Service men. It seemed a great event when she and her secretary went to the nearby Sans Souci restaurant one evening and stayed until 11 PM.

Her husband felt the same way. When the President and his friend Charles Bartlett went to Sunday morning Mass, they took a short walk on the Ellipse, drove over to look at the Aeronautics Building at the Smithsonian, walked along the reflecting pool near the Lincoln Memorial, and considered it a small adventure. That same evening Jacqueline joined him and they walked out the southwest gate, around the fence that bounded the south lawn, along the north fence on Pennsylvania Avenue, and finally into the northwest gate.

Noting their exhilaration afterwards, one might have thought they had been down the Grand Canyon rapids on a rubber raft.

*　　*　　*

Betty Beale wrote an open letter to the First Lady—who she might be—just before the 1960 election. Betty Beale's society column was a Washington must.

What Beale knew, and said, was that the White House was a national showcase. During the Eisenhower days, White House guests went to dinner, two by two, and sat at an enormous U-shaped table that seated 106. At the head of the U, with no one opposite, the Eisenhowers sat side by side, like a king and queen. A guest talked first with the person on his right, and then with the one on his left. You could not talk to anyone across the table, because floral decorations were so high.

Dinner finished, the women went to the Red Room for their coffee—with or without liqueurs—and the men went to the Green Room for cigars and brandy. Then they joined one another again, two by two, to go to the East Room for a concert. Eisenhower preferred the music of Fred Waring's Pennsylvanians.

By general agreement, White House dinners were considered *dull.*

Now, wrote Beale, something should be done to change the tone and the mood and the showcase. Beale itemized a long list of specific suggestions.

Soon after the election, Beale got a note from Jacqueline Kennedy: "You wait; I'll have done them all in a year."

Gone was the U-shaped table. Instead, guests found tables for eight with ranking guests interspersed among them, the President and his wife sitting at separate tables and circulating.

Gone was the seven-course dinner, now cut to four. In President Grant's day, there had been twenty-nine courses.

Gone were the view-blocking floral arrangements. Instead, each table had a low bouquet of vivid red and purple anemones and tulips "looking more like a country house, instead of a florist's." When the crabapples and cherry trees were in bloom, branches of the blossoms were brought indoors.

Gone was the separation of the sexes after dinner. The Trumans had served spiked punch and the Eisenhowers provided liquor, but only to diplomats. The Kennedys kept an open bar, and you were offered a drink when you came in.

Gone was the interminable reception line, which sometimes took as long as an hour or two during the Eisenhower years to get a three-second handshake from the President and his wife. Now the President and his wife mingled freely, each going off to different parts of the room.

There was the army's "Strolling Strings," playing gay, danceable music. There were skits from plays, poetry readings, ballet, great musical artists. Conversation was animated, laughter came loud and often, and the museum-like atmosphere of the White House was now transformed to that of an informal Georgetown home.

Elegance was the word. The right wine, the right crystal, the right china. The Women's National Press Club's cookbook called the White House "the best French restaurant in town."

Perhaps because of his social position, McGeorge Bundy, head of the National Security Council, was one of the few White House staffers invited to the intimate Kennedy parties. "Jackie and I had a very friendly, cheerful but slightly distant relationship," Bundy said. "I made the mistake of saying that redecorating the White House was of the lowest priority."

The social course of the New Frontier was set.

It had created a mild brouhaha when word leaked out that the White House wanted to lure away the chef of the French Embassy in London. When Mrs. Kennedy couldn't get him, she turned to her father-in-law for help. Joseph Kennedy corralled René Verdon, a former chef of New York's Carlyle Hotel restaurant. Verdon arrived with his Italian assistant and their white chef's hats, all prepared to make trout with wine and meringue shells filled with raspberries. Instead, the President preferred fish chowder and chocolate ice cream. "He told me you had to be from New England to make fish chowder," said the chef, "and I believe him." Verdon also wanted all menus to be in French, compromised on making them bilingual for a while, and only reluctantly agreed finally to keep them in English.

The First Lady's own interest in the kitchen was minimal. Queried on her plans to redesign the kitchen, she answered, "I couldn't care less about the kitchen! Just make it white and ask René what he wants in there."

When there was a press murmur of protest about foreign cooks in a White House kitchen, Joseph Kennedy suggested: "Tell them the President feels that there are so many Irishmen in the White House, the French and Italians ought to be given a chance, too."

"She was wary of the press because she knew how they attacked every First Lady," her social secretary, Letitia Baldrige, said. "They mocked Mrs. Truman, intimated that Mrs. Eisenhower was an alcoholic, later called Mrs. Nixon 'Plain Jane' and 'Plastic Pat.' "

Mrs. Kennedy once returned from Hyannis with a German shepherd puppy, a gift from her father-in-law. A reporter on *Air Force One* wrote a note asking what she planned to feed it.

"Reporters," she answered.

She bristled when photographers requested permission to photograph her children. Even her husband was reluctant to intercede, explaining, "My wife is a strong-minded woman."

But she could be most sympathetic to some individual reporters. On a receiving line for women reporters at a luncheon, she whispered to one of them, "I put him away." The woman smiled. She had interviewed Mrs. Kennedy earlier and had gotten hysterical when one of Caroline's kittens jumped on her shoulder; she had a phobia against cats.

Of course she appreciated the press and public support of her White House restoration efforts. "I have worked harder on this project than I have on anything." She received nine thousand letters a week, and she understood. "After all, it is their house." But she did not appreciate that the press and public interest in her was "total." She felt there should be a dividing line between the public and private part of her life, and a respect for it. That's why, she said, she didn't hold press conferences—she didn't want to answer any personal questions.

Jacqueline knew her public-relations problems, but had no intention of changing. She gave the President's press secretary, Pierre Salinger, a photograph of herself for Christmas, signed, "To Pierre, from the greatest cross he has to bear." An aide commented, "Jackie's not Eleanor Roosevelt, so that's that."

Reporter Frances Lewine, who traveled some ten thousand miles with the First Lady, freely admitted, "I have no idea of what Mrs. Kennedy is really like."

And Dave Powers said, "Just when you think you understand her, you're in trouble."

*   *   *

Jacqueline Kennedy's first international exposure as First Lady was the Kennedy trip to Canada early in 1961. Men removed their hats as she passed by, women cheered her name, and the prime minister talked of the crowd's "divided attention, a special glow and warmth for Mrs. Kennedy."

She did not enjoy overhearing a conversation between the Canadian Air Marshal and the President's Air Force aide, Godfrey McHugh. The Canadian was commenting on the way the President stopped and stared at an attractive woman passing by.

"I say, the President has a good eye for girls."

"Well, he likes to look at beauty," McHugh answered.

On the presidential plane home, Mrs. Kennedy berated McHugh. "I'm astonished. Don't you respect the President of the United States? To make such a comment. To say that the President of the United States has an eye for pretty girls is not nice!"

McHugh did not try to argue.

The President and his wife were so private about their relationship that it only heightened outside speculation, even among their closest friends and staff.

"I never had any impression of any great love between them," an intimate reported. His secretary, Evelyn Lincoln, felt "she didn't make much effort to please him. Neither one did. But she was a very odd woman. You couldn't get close to her." Her personal secretary, Mary Gallagher, described her as "a terrible-tempered petty tyrant whose personal maid was required to change her sheets for an afternoon nap and iron her stockings." The secretary added, "I sometimes thought it would be nice if Jackie would eat breakfast with him or at least come downstairs to see him off."

A friend called her a free soul in a glass cage.

"Jacqueline can't win, really. If she clams up completely, refuses to talk to the press, and hides from photographers, people will wonder what's wrong. 'Is she ill, is she fighting with Jack, or is she just snobbish?'

"If she bares her innermost thoughts to interviewers, people all over the country will criticize her for being a publicity hound —and if there's anything in the world that she isn't, that's it. She is not as American as apple pie, she is as American as caviar."

Nobody considered her the country's mother; she was the country's bride. She looked like a princess and Americans loved princesses. Deputy Defense Secretary Roswell Gilpatric who knew her well, as he knew Princess Grace, claimed that Grace acquired her sense of royalty only after she married the Prince of Monaco, but that Jacqueline always had it.

Secretary of Commerce Luther Hodges explained the Jacqueline charm: "She looks right at you while you're talking and makes you feel as if you're the most important person she has ever met."

She soon started enjoying her role. At first she had ridiculed the name of "First Lady," but she gradually realized the full impact of the phrase. "I *am* the First Lady." She dispensed with the entire traditional social season in 1961 because "the inauguration was quite enough." When her social secretary insisted that she greet a certain group, she responded, "I don't *have* to do anything. . . . People told me ninety-nine things I had to do as First Lady and I haven't done one of them."

Some said she began believing all the things written about her. Her mother-in-law was now referred to by White House telephone operators as "Mrs. Joseph."

"I am *the* Mrs. Kennedy," Jacqueline proudly announced to the chief usher one day.

*   *   *

The days were gone when First Lady Eleanor Roosevelt could ride her horse in Washington's Rock Creek Park.

"Glen Ora is my salvation," Jacqueline insisted. "I'd die if I didn't have some place to get away from the terrible pressures around here."

Glen Ora was mostly for Jacqueline. Forty miles west of Washington, in the horse and hunt country near Middleburg, Virginia, the 600-acre estate included stables and pastures, and its fields and fences were part of the Orange County hunting course. The Kennedys had leased it "for weekends," the President said, and added thoughtfully, "but not every weekend." What Jack Kennedy liked best about Glen Ora on a weekend was that he could relax and read.

The main house had six bedrooms and five baths, terraced gardens, French furnishings and French decor, and a guesthouse. There was even a farmer's house on the grounds for the Secret Service. Mrs. Kennedy had her White House decorator, Helen Parrish completely redecorate Glen Ora. When the returning landlord later objected, they had to restore everything to the way it had been originally.

When her Secret Service men stayed too close, even popping up from behind bushes on her long solitary walks, she told them, "You keep doing that and you'll drive the First Lady into an asylum."

She loved wearing old clothes. "When she's in the country," a friend said, "you get the feeling that she hasn't looked in a mirror for five hours. There's no vanity."

If she had a private passion, it was fox hunting. It was to her not only a sport, but an art; not only the chase, but the ambience. She bought her husband a hunting outfit, and some Secret Service men soon started riding lessons, but the President decided it was not for him. It was for her. It made her feel "clean and anonymous," she told a friend, and she felt she could lose herself in the excitement of the chase.

What impressed reporter Helen Thomas was that the First Lady sometimes used a government helicopter to go on a fox hunt.

The 761 Middleburgers near Glen Ora try to keep their place "a mind-your-own-business town." "I was across the street at the B&A grocery the other day," said Maj. Norris Royston, the village funeral director, "and Mrs. Kennedy waited ten minutes to get waited on. She wants to be treated like anyone else, and she is."

The drugstore clerk later reported an overheard conversation at his counter between Mrs. Kennedy and her daughter. The two sat on stools at the far end of the counter and ordered hamburgers.

"You'll have a nice glass of milk, won't you Caroline?"

"No, Mommy, I want a coke."

"Milk is better for you."

"Please, Mommy, a coke."

They compromised on a glass of chocolate milk.

"For the first three months I saw so little of the children it almost broke my heart," Mrs. Kennedy said. "And you could *see* it in Caroline. This sad little face. But luckily, I worked very hard and got it all organized."

Middleburgers saw Mrs. Kennedy walking down the street licking an ice cream cone, sitting on a packing case in the saddlery shop checking riding gloves, dining at the Red Fox Tavern with a woman friend, going through the seventy-nine-cent nylons at the store counter. When she came for the morning papers, she told the girl at the store, "I'd better take five today. We have company at the house."

*   *   *

Kay Halle brought him a book with inscriptions from the most important Americans in arts and letters whom she had invited to the inauguration as guests of the President. One from Ernest Hemingway commented, "We thought how beautiful Mrs. Kennedy looked." The President read it aloud and asked, "*Didn't* she look beautiful?" Then he added, "Kay, you have no idea what a help Jackie is to me, and what she has meant to me."

The newly elected President offered his friend John Sharon a job on the White House staff. Sharon refused.

"Why?" Kennedy asked.

"Because I wouldn't survive," Sharon said.

"What do you mean?"

"That Irish Mafia of yours is too tight a circle."

Kennedy's eyes twinkled. "That's why I want you there—to protect me against them."

15

The Men Behind the President

"He clearly wanted to establish a place in history," Robert McNamara said. "We had these Hickory Hill seminars about once a month that were held in different houses, not just Bobby's. One was held in mine. But there was one in the White House and I couldn't go, but my wife went. She said it was absolutely marvelous, but nobody could get a word in edgewise because the President insisted on dominating the conversation. He kept asking Arthur Schlesinger's father why he felt this president was strong and that president was weak and what were the qualities that went with a great president. Of course he was thinking about his own place in history and wanted to make sure he was moving in the right way."

Unlike Lyndon Johnson, to whom the presidency itself was a prize he had yearned for since boyhood, Kennedy saw the prize as the power. At a state committee meeting in Massachusetts he once had said, "I gotta deal with these bastards, too. I'm not a power until I *am* the power."

He had no illusions that just because a man had an inborn quality of leadership he could lead well. What determined whether power was good or evil was the way it was exercised, he said. He liked it when some called him the candidate of intelligence and imagination. As a young reporter, he noted that he was an observer; as a politician, he was an activist. One thing was now certain: The presidency was pulling out of him the utmost of his potential.

"Kennedy?" asked Bundy. "He was a political leader, and it's a splendid thing to be."

Tom Wicker of the *New York Times*, who was highly skeptical of Kennedy at first, later decided that he had "the kind of mind that could entertain visions," deal with "the maneuvers of the moment," and see "the futility of most things, the uncertain glory of most ends."

What kind of world did he have in mind, what was his vision of the future? James Reston asked Kennedy.

After a pause, the President answered, "I haven't had time to think about that yet."

Kennedy preferred facts, unadorned and objective. Some felt that his claim to presidential authority was that he knew more facts than anyone else. His policy was to avoid abstractions, keep clear of political theory and social criticism, and use ideas only as tools.

He remembered what former President Truman had said: "Neither Genghis Khan nor Alexander the Great nor Napoleon nor Louis XIV of France had as much power as the President."

Besides the power, there were the problems. "The thing that surprised me most," Kennedy said shortly after he took office, "was to find that things were just as bad as we'd been saying they were."

*   *   *

Decision making for Kennedy was seldom swift. He preferred sampling minds as diverse as a low-level man in the CIA, the secretary of state, and a newspaper reporter. He might call White House aide Fred Dutton and say, "McNamara and Harriman are urging me to do this. What do you think about it?" Or if somebody proposed something interesting, he would ask for a memo and pass it around to selected people for comment and discussion. Only then would he make up his own mind.

Kennedy didn't invent the technique of creative tension—giving the same assignment to different people at the same time. President Franklin Roosevelt was a master of it. When a reporter pointed out to President Kennedy that several people were working separately on the same Latin American policy project, he stared towards the ceiling, and said, with the merest hint of apology, "I simply cannot afford to have just one set of advisers."

The one adviser he leaned on most was his Special Counsel, Ted Sorensen. Ted Sorensen could serve Kennedy better than anyone. Their minds worked together like a synapse.

Except for his closest kin, nobody knew Kennedy better than Sorensen. Not his social side, or his Irish side, or his private core, but the mind of the man. Ted Sorensen knew all of Jack Kennedy's moods and methods and dreams. He knew the workings of his thoughts, the words he would use, the groove of his opinions. He knew his gestures, his humor, and the depth of his funk. If ever a man became another man—in the best sense—Ted Sorensen became a clone of Kennedy.

Those who did not know the inner Sorensen thought him brash, brusque, and rude. Those who knew him a little better realized that his seeming arrogance was really the result of a brilliant, analytical mind intolerant of chit-chat. Those who knew him best found a keen wit beneath the cool surface, and a total commitment to Kennedy.

Young as Ted was (only thirty), Kennedy wanted to make Sorensen director of the National Security Council. Ken O'Donnell was against it because Sorensen had once been a conscientious objector.

"Barry Goldwater would tear your guts out with it, the guy who said 'invade Cuba' wouldn't go himself."

"I never thought of that," Kennedy said. "You're absolutely right."

The President later talked to Sorensen about a possible promotion to a Cabinet appointment in the second term, but Sorensen was happy to be where he was. "To be at the center of influence in world events," Sorensen later explained, "was the fulfillment of a lifetime's dream." But the price was high: ulcers and divorce.

They became so close that Sorensen was in several overlapping concentric circles of White House power: the political circle with O'Brien, O'Donnell, Salinger, and Bobby; the legal circle with Mike Feldman and Lee White; and the inner circle with Bundy and David Bell.

No matter what the issue—if it was important—Sorensen was involved, or involved himself.

"We agreed on some figure for parity in our agriculture program," White House staff man Mike Feldman said. "I was at Ted's house when Ted got a call. 'That was the President,' Ted said. 'We ought to go for ninety percent of parity. Gee, you know that's right.'

"I can't remember a single case where we disagreed with the President."

For all their mental empathy and instant understanding, there was no social bond between Sorensen and Kennedy. The President never invited Sorensen to an intimate party or dinner on the upper family floors of the White House. The only informal party Sorensen ever attended with him was a New Year's Eve party for the Kennedys given at the home of Kennedy family friend Charles Wrightsman—and Sorensen left early.

"I was not very social," Sorensen said. "I was just a country boy from Nebraska, and just divorced, and, besides, I was working too hard."

"Hell, most of us were too tired anyway," echoed White House aide Ralph Dungan. Appointments Secretary Ken O'Donnell put it more bluntly, "I never put my name on a list for parties because I knew that the President liked it better that I didn't."

If the President put a social wall between him and his staff, his office door was always open to them. "Anybody who wanted to see him on something important could see him," Bundy recalled. They checked the situation through the peephole in Evelyn Lincoln's private door to the Oval Office. "The best time was at the end of his working day," Bundy related, "sometime about seven, just before he went upstairs. You could see if he was busy or not, and if he wasn't busy, you just walked in. But it better be important. The thing was that he was very open and very straight and very willing to have you talk straight with him. 'Come on in, I want to read you a cable,' he would say if he saw me outside. I guess I was in his office three or four times a day, and we were on the phone a lot, too. Whoever he was with, he was with them completely. I don't mean he always told you what was on his mind. But you'd never have the feeling that you were questioning a decision that he was still in the process of making.

"And it wasn't always business. We'd talk about all kinds of things, and he'd often use me for a sounding board. He'd throw personal questions at me, too. 'Was it wise to let Jackie go to a horse show in her beautiful riding clothes?' "

Bundy went on, "Feldman and I dropped in on him in the Oval Office when he was having one of his pretty girls rubbing some goo on his hair, some perfect prescription that somebody had recommended for healthy hair. I said I didn't think this kind of thing was sufficiently dignified for the Oval Office. He looked around at Mike and me, both of us without much hair, and said, 'Well, I'm not sure you two *plan* your hair very well.'

"He was just terrible about his hair," added Bundy. "He had that damn comb in his pocket and went through that hair at least fifty times a day. I don't know what he would have done if he lost his hair."

*   *   *

"At the beginning we people around the President all looked at each other very suspiciously," military adviser General Maxwell Taylor recalled. "We didn't know each other. But we ended up being a very close, warm team."

"It was the cockiest crowd I'd ever seen in the White House," Clark Clifford claimed.

The staff people who tried to improve their own relative importance didn't last long. Neither did those intent on always presenting their own point of view first. The ones who stayed on were those who were really interested in trying to do it the President's way.

"I don't recall his saying 'Thank you' five times,' " McGeorge Bundy said. "Oh, he'd say it about you to somebody else. It wasn't that he was ungenerous, but you don't get to be President without being concerned about Number One."

"You could tell when things were annoying him," recalled his secretary, Evelyn Lincoln. "He'd tap his fingers of his right hand if he was talking to someone. If he was having a meeting and he was sitting on his rocker, he would be swinging his right foot if things weren't going well. And if he was really annoyed, his left eye would get a little askew and sort of droop a little, as if there was an irritation behind it. Then I would know something was really wrong. My job was to move in anytime I saw any sign of this. I could tell him there was a phone call for him so he could break away for a while. I had to anticipate what he was going to do in order to relieve his feelings. It's a little bit of an art."

His voice would go up two or three levels when he was really angry, and he would say, "Jeezus Christ!" But that was seldom apparently. "Even when he was in a flaring temper, it was usually all over in five minutes," Ralph Dungan said. "He'd more likely be a heavy critic of his own behavior and I'd sometimes hear him cuss himself out, calling himself a 'goddamn dummy.' "

Another time, equally angry, he called State Department Press Secretary Robert Manning to complain about an announcement. Manning thought about what the President had said, fortified himself with another drink, then called Kennedy back and told him, "I think you're overreacting."

The President was silent for a moment and Manning expected an explosion; instead the President said, "I guess I am."

President Eisenhower tended to be somewhat aloof and blunt, his staff often standing at attention, as they did when he was a general. Kennedy brought to the Oval Office a greater informality, where everyone was asked to sit back and chat. He never seemed hurried. He was more cheerfully outgoing. Few went away from him with bitterness. He had the ability to color even short relationships with great intimacy. Partly this was the result of his candor, partly his wit. He tried to put himself in the other person's place. He tried to imagine what arguments he would want to push if he were this other person proposing something to the President.

He was a man devoid of hatred. He could say, as he did to Blair Clark during the campaign, about CBS President Frank Stanton, "Wait till I'm President—I'll cut Stanton's balls off." But it was a rage that disappeared quickly.

He disliked qualities rather than people. He never complained about the "terrible loneliness" of the office or its "awesome burdens." "In many ways," he said, "I see and hear more than anyone else." He had the knack of ventilating his problems in great detail without revealing his own position or without making his visitors conscious that he was holding back.

"Reserve is a characteristic of most presidents," claimed Bob Donovan, who has written books about several of them. "I think even Truman kept a lot to himself. I don't think anybody got in with Johnson. I think it's just a characteristic of the job."

The reserve, though, was only part of it. The greater part was his zest for life. "He lived at such a pace," said his wife, "because he wished to know it all."

"You could never relax with Jack, because he never relaxed," Nancy Dickerson said. "I remember Charlie Bartlett saying, 'You could kick him, you could rob him, but you must never bore him.' The President wanted to be amused, entertained, informed."

"He wouldn't listen to a dirty joke, especially if it was an ethnic joke," Larry Newman emphasized. "And especially if there was a mimicked accent involved. He would simply say, 'I don't want to hear it,' and walk away."

But he could spend hours composing a three-page cable of ribald and relevant quotes on love and marriage from Shakespeare's *Hamlet* to send to Ambassador William McCormack Blair in Denmark on his wedding day. Blair considered the cable a hoax until Evelyn Lincoln confirmed that she had never before heard the President laugh so long and so hard as he did then.

Best of all, he could on occasion turn his humor on himself.

"Oh God, yes, he could laugh at himself," Newman said,

"but not very often. And he didn't like it if other people laughed."

Dave Powers could say things to the President that nobody else dared. For a moment the President might seem irritated, even angry, but then the sheer shock of something outrageous made him laugh and laugh.

The President once mentioned the name of a friend he planned to appoint. Powers said, "Are you crazy? He couldn't get *arrested!*" Kennedy laughed for almost fifteen minutes.

Nobody relaxed the President more than Dave Powers did.

Nobody cared for him more.

How much had he given to the church collection that day, Kennedy asked Dave Powers.

"Ten dollars, Mr. President."

"Are you sure? This guy told the newspapermen I put in a hundred-dollar bill."

"Anytime you can put in a ten and get credit for a hundred, you're lucky," Powers said.

Kennedy had a reaching mind, but he knew some of his own limitations. He never considered himself an intellectual. "I'm forced to deal with a lot of things that I don't know enough about. I just have to do the best I can within the limitations of time."

Often he didn't want facts, he wanted opinions. But nothing irritated him more than verbosity.

"I handled the independent agencies and I went in to see him with one chairman who was very bright and all business, but he talked in these long, rounded sentences," said Fred Dutton. "You could see Kennedy's eyes glaze over. After a few of these meetings, Kennedy told me, 'One of your chief responsibilities is to see that I don't have to talk to that man again!' "

"When he sent Henry Kissinger to Germany on a mission and Henry returned to tell the President that he needed 'conceptual schemes,' a certain chill came over Kennedy's eyes," Bundy recalled. "Henry didn't stay with us long after that."

If he wanted both sides of a question, he asked for them, and expected them. Sometimes, though, he simply wanted conclusions.

His love of books was real, and so was his feeling for poetry and pungent phrasing. "If more politicians knew poetry and more poets knew politics," Kennedy said, "the world would be a little better place to live in."

"I feel better when there are books around," Kennedy told Larry Newman, whose walls are covered with books. "That's really where my education comes from. Most things I learned, I read, good and bad. The rest I learned the hard way, campaigning."

"He was not a profound reader," Joseph Alsop added. "He didn't read at all the range of books that I read, but he read a great deal. He would swallow books." Kennedy later confided that one of the mistakes of his first year "was letting it be known that I read as much as I do."

Eisenhower preferred oral briefings, Kennedy wanted them in writing. "I'm not a listener, I'm a looker."

"I'd get the President thirty-five or forty pages on hunger, say," recalled White House aide Fred Dutton, "and he'd come back in a day, day and a half, with notes all over the margins. It was incredible—his ability to consume paper, to read it, make intelligent comments."

Dutton added, "He was hard to work for because he didn't lead you to anything. You had to be a self-starter. Before Cabinet meetings I'd ask him what he wanted discussed. 'You think of something,' he said. He hated meetings. He was bored by them. And so we'd have them with decreasing frequency. If you were working for him, it was up to you to get the ball in the air. If he didn't like it, he'd say, 'What a goddamn idea *that* is!'"

He was the classic pragmatist. He valued ideas only if they promised results. "Kennedy was a 'now' guy," Bundy said forcefully.

"Here's the way it's going to look in three years," George Ball told him. "All right," he would say, "but what do we do tomorrow?"

*   *   *

Some insisted that Kennedy's relationship with the press "was the greatest con game in the world."

"I know he hated the press," *New York Times* writer Harrison Salisbury said. Then Salisbury added thoughtfully. "I don't think there's any other way for a president to be."

"I don't tell anything to the press, on any basis," Kennedy said, "that I don't expect to see in print. When you're president, you are president twenty-four hours a day. Unless you are in the john at midnight, you're on record, always."

Despite this conviction, he was sometimes mildly annoyed to find so many of his remarks to his friend Ben Bradlee, of *Newsweek*, appearing in the *Newsweek* Periscope. He was once truly angry at the leak of some important story only to ultimately discover that he himself was the culprit, that the ship of state leaked from the top.

"How do you think I handle the press?" Kennedy asked Larry Newman.

"Gee, I think you handle it like no other president, probably since FDR."

"Do you think I do better than FDR?"

"Yes, you haven't called anybody a son of a bitch in *public* yet."

"It was almost as if one of our own had made it," said *New York Times* correspondent Jack Raymond. Some of the press were as devoted to him as his own staff. "I'd hate to go back and read the copy I wrote then," one reporter added. "I believed all the things the President said then. I've learned a lot since." A young woman reporter called him "a fun president." The President was so candid with so many newspapermen that one said, "You can't go to the men's room for fear of getting scooped." He was very protective about some journalists. He told his aide Ted Clifton that Hearst reporter Marianne Means wanted to be a columnist "so give her some stories. Give her all the help you can."

He pleased reporters because he didn't give conventional answers to questions. Most of his answers were rational and thoughtful, and even self-critical. "I played it too cute," he said, when asked about congressional rejection of his plan to set up a Cabinet post for urban affairs. He had simultaneously let it be known that he planned to appoint a black, Robert Weaver, to head the department. "It was so obvious it made them mad."

"Kennedy made the presidency elegant and vocal and powerful," summed up Robert Donovan, Washington editor of the *New York Herald Tribune.*

"Kennedy didn't need a press secretary," said Pierre Salinger. "He was his own best public-relations man."

"The President spent a helluva lot of time with newspaper people in his first year," Bundy said. "Some *New York Times* editor called me for an interview and I told him I was too busy, and I got the message, 'Please tell Mr. Bundy that I spent two hours with the President. Does Mr. Bundy really think he is busier than the President?' "

Kennedy's love affair with the press quickly became a love-hate relationship.

A poll showed that forty out of forty-three top Washington correspondents believed the Kennedy administration was more accessible than any previous administration; but that forty also believed the Kennedy administration's efforts to manage news were more intense than those of any previous administration's.

A reporter compared it to "a reigning monarch's court."

Like all presidents, Kennedy classified reporters as "friend-lies" or "unfriendlies" and judged them by the ferocity of their uncritical love. "As long as you glorify them in every respect, it's fine," an observer said. "But the Kennedys can be very vindictive."

Those favoring the Kennedys found their entree easier, their White House press job a lot more pleasant. Those patently against the Kennedys encountered the ruthlessness, and worked hard. What was obvious to them was that the Kennedys did not tolerate divergent opinions. Unlike the openness to discussion —even opposition—Kennedy displayed to his staff, the President left little doubt with the press as to how he felt on specific issues: "This is the way it's going to be."

The press quickly understood. Those who went along, got along.

"I always had the feeling when I was writing about President Kennedy that he was standing right there behind me," columnist Rowland Evans said, "watching the words come and waiting to bore in. No question about it, friendship with a president can be a burden on a reporter's professionalism."

On the other hand, such friendship was also a plus. When Evans wrote a column mentioning that Senator Fulbright was becoming disenchanted with foreign aid, Evans got an early Sunday morning call from the President asking him how he thought Fulbright would deal with foreign aid, and how Evans would deal with it. Evans contrasted this approach with the later heavy hand of President Johnson, whose press secretary called with the cold warning, "Rowly, why don't you get wise and play ball with us? Things have changed, you know. You don't have a pipeline into the White House anymore."

Pierre Salinger once asked the President if he had read the most recent issue of *Time*.

"Yes, it's the worst thing I've ever seen," the President said. "It's just too much. It makes me mad. It isn't so! It isn't accurate."

"I couldn't agree with you more," Salinger said. "I just don't understand how they can say I'm *that* fat!"

The President stared at him. "I'm not talking about what they were saying about *you*. It's what they're saying about *me*!"

Knowing the power of *Time*, Kennedy was keenly sensitive about everything they printed about him. He was once angry enough to invite *Time* publisher Henry Luce to the White House and ask, "Now just what would *you* do?"

* * *

"How am I doin'?" Kennedy asked a friendly reporter.

"Great."

"You have to kiss a lot of people's asses."

"I know. I know. But you wanted the job."

At the bottom of a highly critical column, Kennedy scribbled, "Well, any time they would like to take over this job, they can have it."

"I'm reading more and enjoying it less," he told reporters.

The second Kennedy bible was the *New York Times*, devoured each day from start to finish. What bothered him more than any assaults on his programs was any attack on his integrity, compassion, or truthfulness.

As candid as he was, he had his own presidential quota of lies. In his first press conference, he denied there had been any quid pro quo in the return of American pilots interned in Soviet Russia. In reality, we had made a hard-nosed deal to return the Russian spy, Colonel Abel.

His press people also had a subtle way of planting questions at press conferences. After lunch and drinks, a reporter would be told, "You know, I think if you ask the President this question today, you might get an interesting answer."

President Kennedy was the first president to make an art of the televised press conference. He was always in control, never caught short by an unexpected question, and his quick wit seldom showed to better advantage. He enjoyed them, so did the press, and so did the American people. It was more than presidential show business; it was a dramatic way to transmit the Kennedy excitement to the people.

"When I suggested putting the presidential press conferences on live television, there was vigorous opposition in the White House," Press Secretary Salinger said. "Their argument was that, if you're on live and you say something stupid, it goes around the world pretty fast. My argument was, if you're *not* on live and you say something stupid, it goes around the world pretty fast anyway. The President agreed with me. But he did tell me, 'I don't want to be on television too much. Don't overexpose me.' "

His staff culled questions from everywhere, and put each on a separate card. They met for a two-hour breakfast on the day of the conference, and the President flipped through their cards, saying, "I think I can handle this one," or, "Get me more on this."

James Reston noted wonderingly, "How Kennedy knew the precise drop in milk consumption in 1960, the percentage rise in textile imports from 1957 to 1960, and the number of speeches cleared by the Defense Department is not quite clear, but anyway, he did. He either overwhelmed you with decimal points or disarmed you with a smile and a wisecrack."

Such was the personal rapport of the reporters with the President that they seemed inhibited, too many of their questions resembling blooper balls lobbed up for smashing. Peter Lisagor felt "we became spear carriers in a great televised opera. We were props in a show. I always felt we should have joined Actors Equity. Those of us who had a chance to ask questions should have charged that much for speaking lines. It was like making love in Carnegie Hall." What Lisagor wanted to see, and seldom did, was that "the Irish temper behind the cool Harvard facade had been excited."

Kennedy was his own most severe critic when he watched himself on TV. He remembered President Eisenhower's problem with syntax, his seeming inability to finish a sentence. He knew the importance of a smooth quote with a subject and predicate.

When Fred Friendly of CBS suggested a TV program of the three living presidents, Kennedy bristled. "Do you mean to say you want me to appear with the hero of World War II? Forget it. I'll look like a kid." Eisenhower's reaction was similarly blistering. "Do you mean to say you want me to appear on the same program with the computer mind who remembers everything? Forget it. He'll make me look like a dumb old asshole."

But he was particularly pleased with his TV interviews. "I always said, when we don't have to go through you bastards," he told Bradlee, "we can really get our story to the American people."

* * *

Kennedy had transmitted not only his story to the American people, but his excitement of hope. He was no longer the happy-go-lucky congressman with mismatched socks, the uncaring senator who was on his boat during the debate on medical care for the aged. Within a few short years, he had grown into a man with a more furrowed face, a bit heavier around the jowls, wearing a serious suit, and ambitious for greatness.

Ambition was the spur of his growth. He knew his history. He knew that "Americans build their triumphal arches out of brick so they have missiles handy when their heroes have failed,"—as cracker-barrel American philosopher "Mr. Dooley" had said. Perhaps he was still "not profound either in his analyses or his judgment"—as his Under Secretary of State George

Ball had said—but Ball gave him high marks for being intellectually alert and quick to understand any given problem.

From that point on, he grew in giant leaps. As his friend columnist Charles Bartlett then wrote, "Life under the Kennedy administration is more likely to be varied than dull."

He knew how to act with women, how to absolutely ingratiate himself. He was courteous, he was solicitous, he was considerate, he was warm, he was friendly, and it all came across as genuine. It was his secret charm.

—CONGRESSWOMAN LINDY BOGGS

16

The Other Women

There was an easier morality in Washington during the Kennedy years. Perhaps it was part of the excitement. "The Kennedy administration will be known for its screwing, the way the Eisenhower administration was known for its golf," a White House aide predicted. When he heard this remark, the President reportedly replied, "You mean nineteen holes in one day?"

"If Jack Kennedy screwed all the women he was supposed to have screwed, he wouldn't have had time for much else," Ben Bradlee observed.

But a woman reporter who covered Kennedy—"in more ways than one," some said snidely—was reflectively bitter about him. "He had his father's attitude toward women—there was only one place for women and that was horizontal."

Some psychologists close to politics insist that the sex drive is similar to the power drive. They cite a survey that "most women would rather go to bed with the President of the United States, whoever he might be, than with Robert Redford."

"Power is the ultimate aphrodisiac," said Henry Kissinger. Politicians generally agree. "If you examine it, the whole concept of politics is sexual," Boston politician John Powers said. "The guy balls up the crowd, turns 'em on, revs them up. That's what it's all about."

"And imagine how much more sexy it is when you couple power with grace," a Kennedy aide observed.

The power and grace of President Kennedy were such that he had the great luxury of absolute selection. A regular ritual at Palm Beach was a slow walk down Worth Avenue with an aide pointing out particularly beautiful women. Many of them later found their way to the President, usually at the home of a neighbor or friend. Reporters saw them either going in at night or coming out in the morning.

Such activity was always predicated on the fact that Jacqueline was not with him on that particular trip. Reporters conceded that he would have had to be superhuman to withstand all the women throwing themselves at him. Feminist Gloria Steinem called him the first sexually viable president. "I think he was discreet to an extent," an intimate said, "and yet I think he wanted people to know he was better with women than his father was." Nor was he overly concerned about being caught. "They can't touch me while I'm alive," he said, "and after I'm dead, who cares?"

He was irritated when press coverage got to be press surveillance. He vetoed the suggestion that a reporter go with the Secret Service wherever the President went. "Does the AP pay you to stay here and wait to see what time I get in at night?" he angrily asked a reporter waiting for him in his New York hotel.

Once he even tried to get away from the Secret Service through a side door. The Secret Service then closed off the side door of the hotel. When the President returned at 3 AM, he was forced to come in through the main door where the Secret Service was waiting. "OK, you got me," he said, and he didn't try it again.

"The President will do what he damn well pleases."

The press accepted that, and so did his intimates. But the consensus was that it was a fault of character to continue his womanizing inside the White House. George Smathers insisted he found the President and a highly disarranged, pretty young woman in the Cabinet Room. Another intimate revealed that the President had asked him to try to make it with Letitia Baldrige, Jacqueline's social secretary, and report to him how she was in bed. "Look," said the friend, "if you want to find out how it is with Tish, you make it with her yourself."

When the President decided that his wife needed a press secretary, he sent her Pamela Turnure.

Pam Turnure had met John Kennedy at the wedding of her friend, Nina Auchincloss, Jacqueline's stepsister. He was then almost forty, a senator, and she was barely twenty, a small, fine-boned brunette with a pale complexion and blue-green eyes that looked directly at you when she spoke. She came from a conservative family in the Virginia hunt country and graduated from Mt. Vernon Seminary. At that time she was a receptionist in the Belgian Embassy. She was reported to have been an intimate friend of Aly Khan.

Pam went to work for Senator Kennedy as a receptionist. During her three years with Kennedy, her landlady related, the senator was a frequent visitor at Pam's upstairs apartment.

"We were up late one night and heard someone outside throwing pebbles at Pam's window, about 1 AM," Mrs. Leonard Kater recalled. "We looked out and saw Senator Kennedy standing in our garden yelling, 'If you don't come down, I'll climb up your balcony.' So she let him in.

"My husband and I were so intrigued by the whole thing that we set up a tape recorder in the kitchen cabinet, and another in the basement, to pick up the sounds from the bedroom. The next time Kennedy came over, we turned on the tapes and listened.

"I can assure you that he was not a very loquacious lover."

The landlady ultimately paraded in front of 1600 Pennsylvania Avenue with the sign, "Do you want an adulterer in the White House?" She passed out copies of a photograph of Kennedy trying to hide his face as he reportedly left their house early in the morning. Sometime after that, Kennedy and an intimate were talking about courage when he pulled out a print of that picture and said, "Now, *that* takes guts!"

One thing remarkable about the Kennedy women was the

way they befriended each other, liked each other. It was true of many of the women he had known before he was married, and of many of the young actresses, and now it was true of Pam Turnure and Mary Meyer. Mary was Tony Bradlee's sister. She was then divorced and Pam Turnure moved in with her for the summer. Within a year, Mary Meyer also became the President's mistress.

"The only indication I ever had that Jackie knew about all of Jack's women was when she asked me if I knew he was having an affair with Pamela Turnure," Betty Spalding said. "I said I didn't know, and even if I did, I wouldn't tell her."

"Jackie told me that I was one of the few friends who didn't bring women to Jack," confided another intimate.

A reporter who knew Turnure well recalled a White House party when Jacqueline was away. "I remembered the President suddenly disappeared from the party, and, soon afterwards, I saw Pam discreetly heading for the elevator to go to the upstairs family rooms."

Pam Turnure somewhat resembled Jacqueline. A Kennedy intimate described her as "nice, gentle, with an understated prettiness and an unflappable poise, but she didn't seem a very passionate person. I'm susceptible to pretty women myself, but she didn't smite me. She's just not the kind of girl I'd have thought would appeal to the President."

What titillated some reporters was that Turnure soon copied Jacqueline Kennedy's clothes, coiffure, and even her speaking voice.

"I was surprised," Jacqueline's secretary, Mary Gallagher, said, "when Pam Turnure, who was only twenty-three, and had no newspaper experience, was named press secretary to the First Lady. The President simply told Pierre Salinger, 'Put in Pam and tell her what to do.' "

"What in the world do I need a press secretary for?" Jacqueline asked J. B. West, the White House usher.

Jacqueline wrote Pamela her reaction, for the public: "I'm so *glad* you are doing it, the more I think of it—for this very reason that you haven't had previous press experience—but you have sense and good taste enough not to panic, and to say the right thing."

314

More privately, Jacqueline added specific instructions. She wanted "minimum information given with maximum politeness."

An intimate confided that the President privately enjoyed having his mistress work for his wife, "like living life on a high wire."

Turnure also served as still another personal presidential contact. He would call her when he wanted to know who was sitting next to whom at what White House dinner, or how long the fireworks would last at the celebration for the King of Afghanistan. He didn't want them to last that long, and did she know that she needed special permission for them from the District of Columbia? He had one other question: Were the fireworks made in Japan or the United States?

When Jacqueline kept Pamela busy, the President had other women to massage his hair. He still had Fiddle and Faddle. They were both barely twenty when they applied for jobs, both wearing identical dresses, both attractive, and both were hired. The blonde, Fiddle, worked for Evelyn Lincoln, and the brunette, Faddle, worked for Salinger. Fiddle got her nickname at college and Faddle got hers by being friendly with Fiddle. White House reporters soon noted that both women were available to the President at all hours, that one of them always accompanied the President on his trips.

Fiddle and Faddle lived in Georgetown, and moved often, possibly because their parties often lasted until three in the morning. Guests were usually from the top level of the New Frontier. The favorite dance of the group was something called "The Limbo." Besides being full of the latest gossip, Fiddle and Faddle were full of fun, and sparkling. Fiddle was perhaps a little more breathless and vague. But it was easy to see how well they must have pleased the President.

During a presidential interval at Palm Beach, a reporter had a late dinner date with Fiddle when she was called to the phone in the middle of the meal. "It's the President," she explained when she returned. "He wants me. Right now." She shrugged her shoulders apologetically. "I've got to go." The reporter understood. One of Fiddle's other specialties was to sign the President's name for requested autographs. She once suggested to the President that she might take steno and typing and he laughed. "Why? Are you starting to get ambitious?"

Like his airline stewardess–secretary, Fiddle also was eventually sent to work at the American Embassy in Paris.

Faddle, who had gone to Berlin with the President, remembered, more than anything else, how vulnerable he was. "He was always asking everybody, 'Did I do the right thing?' " She also described how he would often wander around the halls "corralling some of us to come and talk to him. And if we disagreed on something, we could stand up to him and he wouldn't resent it." Faddle also recalled Mrs. Kennedy poking her head into their office and asking, "Anyone for tennis?" Faddle went with her.

Jacqueline knew about her husband's Fiddle and Faddle. When she took a French photographer on a tour of the White House, she opened one of the doors and told the photographer in French, "And this is a young lady who is supposed to be sleeping with my husband."

It was not a Washington secret.

One Washington dowager hostess, who had seen many administrations come and go, smiled and remarked that she knew that the President was "quite naughty." Others were more pointed, "I remember going to a party and the hostess said to me, 'How could you be friends with that . . . that *alley cat!* ' "

The President was concerned about his unexpected women guests in the White House when his wife was away. The Secret Service was sworn to silence, but the servants were not. He had his attorney prepare a statement pledging that no employee would write about his or her experiences in the White House, and had them all sign the pledge. Word slipped out to the press and caused a furor. In defense, the President asked his chief usher to take the blame for initiating the idea.

*   *   *

Years after their marriage, Jack Kennedy reportedly told Jacqueline that he had decided that very night of their first meeting that he would one day marry her when the time was right for him to get married.

"How BIG of you," she snapped.

She was a wife who refused to live by the values of his father's household. He was not her household king whose word could never be questioned. She was ready, instead, to deflate him whenever she felt it was necessary.

"When I start to ask him silly little insignificant questions about whether I should wear a short or long dress, he just snaps his fingers and says, 'That's your province.' And I say, 'Yes, but you're the great decision maker. Why should everybody but me get the benefit of your decisions?' " She was also heard to tell him, "Where is this great Irish wit you're supposed to have, this celebrated wit? You don't show much of it when you come home."

He retaliated by openly flirting with every pretty guest they had at a dinner party. "I remember a White House dinner party where Jackie put a woman on each side of Jack," Nancy Dickerson said, "and each of these women was supposed to be having an affair with him." Of course he might have seated them there himself. The President often inspected the seating arrangements for dinner, and once specifically placed a man and a woman facing each other who were known to be having an affair. He placed them directly next to him as if to show that adultery was not his private province, and he approved.

"Jackie was a woman full of love and full of hurt," noted Lindy Boggs, who succeeded her husband as a Louisiana congresswoman. "When she really loved something, she gave herself completely. But I don't think he could love *anyone* too deeply. They were two private people, two cocoons married to each other, trying to reach into each other. I think she felt that since he was so much older than she was, that it was up to him to reach more than she did. But he couldn't."

"The marriage? I think Jack and Jackie were both ambivalent about each other," reported another confidante. "I think they were both attracted by the image and mystery of what they thought the other represented. And then, when they were married, they found themselves disenchanted by the same things that had caught them."

Smathers recalled how Jacqueline caustically broke into

their conversation "and needled him something fierce," saying, "Oh, I'll bet you and Jack sit around and talk about those good old days when you fellas used to run around. Well, I guess you fellas would rather be somewhere else tonight."

Social Secretary Tish Baldrige laughed at the idea that Jacqueline was basically a shy person: "She was only shy with people she didn't like." "Her candor was remarkable," confided another intimate. "She talked about everything. She even told me how many times a week she and Jack had sex." As for the fact that she had more men friends than women, "I'm sure it stems from the fact that she never got along well with her mother," Betty Spalding observed. "But she was not flirtatious at all, and there was absolutely nothing sensual or seductive about her. She was too guarded."

She seldom asked him what kind of day he'd had. "He told me," Salinger said, " 'You know, I don't want to go home and have dinner and talk about Laos.' " David Ormsby-Gore remembered, "When he did try to bring up a political question at dinner, she always tried to change the subject, and you could tell how irritated he was."

Some felt the fault was hers, that she should have made it a point to immerse herself in politics, learn as much as she could about it, surprise him with her knowledge to show how much she wanted to share this major interest in his life. She was surely intelligent enough. Others felt it was like touch football to her. She knew she could never be good enough to compete. She had been born and bred into the idea that politics was a dirty business. She didn't like most of the politicians she met. She found them uncouth, uncultured, messy, and rude. She even called Ken O'Donnell "a wolfhound." She never invited any political people to her small dinner parties, except for Arthur Schlesinger, Jr., and McGeorge Bundy. She felt she could never know politics as deeply as her husband did, and so might as well stay out of it entirely. After all, her mother didn't read the *Wall Street Journal* because her stepfather was a stockbroker.

A woman once asked Kennedy if he ever discussed politics with his wife, and he shot back at her, "What are you, one of those feminists?"

The strain of the marriage seemed obvious to close friends

and some journalists. Reporter Fred Sparks overheard a Kennedy family row from a nearby table at New York's posh La Caravelle restaurant. Jacqueline asked for the check, saying, "I'm going to walk out on you. Every Kennedy thinks only of *the family!* Has anybody ever thought about *my* happiness?"

When somebody said, "It must be wonderful being the President's wife," she answered, "So I'm his wife. So what?"

The question was unanswerable. Was Jacqueline's problem in marriage her particular husband? Or was it something that would have happened to her no matter whom she had married? Would any marriage have been difficult for her?

*   *   *

"Jack was even more isolated than I," Jacqueline said, "so I tried to have a few friends over for dinner as often as possible. I would check with Mrs. Lincoln in the afternoon and ask her to find out whom he wanted that evening—and then have her call them." Susan Mary Alsop remembered that "it was a time when I always felt that I had to have my hair done all the time, just in case I'd be asked to the White House."

A friend described them, saying "two ravishing people appear in the doorway who couldn't be more charming if they tried, who make you feel utterly welcome."

"At one of their small parties, Jackie put on some Noel Coward-Gertrude Lawrence music, and announced that 'Bunny,' her nickname for her husband, did a marvelous imitation of Coward," a guest recalled. "We all tried to get Jack to perform, but he wouldn't do it." Jacqueline's own imitations were also superb, particularly the one she did of her sister-in-law Ethel making an effusive greeting of, "Hiya, Keed! . . ."

The First Lady was very much in charge of her dinner parties.

"She was full of beans," Jim Symington, a Washington lawyer and family friend, said. "She liked to keep things moving and popping, and she had a way of adding some unique flair to all her parties. The first big dinner party we ever went to at the White House, Jackie came over to me and said, 'Now get your guitar and sing us some songs.' All I could say was, 'Aw, come on, Jackie.'

" 'Oh, you're chicken,' she said to me. And she was right."

Symington mused about that, and added, "I don't think Jackie was chicken about anything."

The First Lady knew how to mix her compliments with criticisms. She told housekeeper Anne Lincoln that the food was "fantastic" after a dinner party, but that the brie cheese was like "hard rubber" and should have been left out of the refrigerator all day to get soft, and that the wine shouldn't have been served until after the fish course, and that the name of the dessert was misspelled on the menu.

"The thing about Jackie was that she had a solid core of steel," said Roswell Gilpatric, the tall, debonair deputy defense secretary who dated her for a long time after her husband's death. "I went to a lot of their parties, and she often invited me without my wife. She was much more interested in talking to men than to women. I once took her down to my farm outside of Washington, just for the day. You could tell how constrained she was, how much she wanted to break loose and yet how concerned she was about her image, how determined she was not to embarrass her husband.

"She was always asking me all kinds of questions about the Pentagon, about the flow of power. She had heard her husband mention all kinds of names of people at the Pentagon and she wanted to know what kind of power they had, whether they were motivated mostly by ambition or by their loyalty to the President. She was deeply concerned with how much they could be trusted. She was not interested too much in the maneuvering techniques of Pentagon politics, but she was interested in translating everything in terms of people. She was very, very astute."

When the historical quality of Lafayette Square—fronting the White House—was being threatened with destruction by a congressional committee, the President assigned Bill Walton to fight it.

"The whole thing seemed to be going down the drain," Walton recalled, "when Jackie stepped in and told us, 'You white-livered characters need some help and I'm going to get involved. The wreckers haven't started yet and, until they do, it can be saved.'" Walton added, "Without her, and her Fine Arts Committee, we never would have saved the square."

She was also very jealous of her prerogative as the leading Kennedy woman. She seldom invited her sisters-in-law to any of her intimate parties. Nor did they ever drop by for lunch. There was simply a minimal relationship. The same was true of her mother and her mother-in-law. Only Joseph Kennedy, Sr., was always welcome at any time. "When the President's father came to visit," recalled Chief Usher West, "she fairly danced down the halls, arm in arm with him, laughing uproariously at his teasing, her face animated and happy."

Her husband had said that he got his brains from his mother, but Jacqueline passionately disagreed. To a small group of old friends, she later referred to her mother-in-law as "a dimwit, without a brain in her head," and then discussed at great length, and in a most emotional way, all the great qualities of the father.

An air force aide went to the airport to pick up the Kennedy patriarch, who had come in to see his son and talk with Bundy about the defense budget.

"He started ranting right away," the aide recalled.

"I don't know what the President is doing," declared the father. "Damn it, I taught Jack better than that! Oh, we're going to go broke with this nonsense. *I* told him that I thought it was ridiculous."

Then he grinned. "The election is over. I can disagree with him anytime I want to now."

The father was a never-ending target for the press. Earlier that year, Fletcher Knebel wrote lyrics to the tune of "All of Me" for the annual Gridiron Club dinner. Part of it went:

> All of us,
> Why not take all of us,
> Fabulous,
> You can't live without us.
> My son Jack
> Heads the procession
> Then comes Bob,
> Groomed for succession.
>
> We're the most
> We stretch from coast to coast

Kennedys
Just go on forever,
I've got the dough
You might as well know
With one—
You get all of us.

Kennedy and Evan Thomas once discussed their fathers. Norman Thomas had been a perennial Socialist candidate for President.

"Look, you have a famous and controversial father," Kennedy said. "Do you agree with him on everything?"

"No," Thomas answered.

"Does he dictate what you do?"

"No."

"But you love him, don't you?"

"Yes, I do."

"Well, so do I," Kennedy said, referring to his own father.

"What nobody should every forget," George Smathers said, "was that Jack had a tremendous respect for his father, just a *tremendous* respect. He was really quite in awe of his father all the time; he had the greatest admiration for him of anyone, and I mean *anyone!*"

Earlier that year, just before he delivered his State of the Union message to a joint session of Congress, Kennedy had called his father in Palm Beach to make sure he would be watching him on TV.

The President liked to talk about his father's toughness. "He held up standards for us." He intimated that his father could do no wrong, "but I don't have to do anything that my father wants me to do." His father, he said, knew more about the problems of the past, but he was the President who had to resolve the problems of his generation. "Now I'm in charge."

This is such a tragedy . . . the most excruciating period of my life . . . I haven't slept. . . .

—JOHN F. KENNEDY

Unless you are prepared to use our planes to knock out Cuban planes, then you shouldn't have started the thing in the first place . . . once we decided we could not support it with American forces, it was bound to fail. It was as simple as that, really. . . . There is a time when you can't advise by innuendos and suggestions. You have to look him in the eye and say, "I think it's a lousy idea, Mr. President. The chances of our succeeding are about one in ten." Nobody said that.

—GEN. MAXWELL TAYLOR

17

The Bay of Pigs: An Early Challenge

"America under a Kennedy administration is going to be an exciting place. Europe will need monkey glands to keep up," wrote the *London Spectator*. "The American people have chosen adventure," added the *London Daily Telegraph*. Only Fidel Castro predicted a sour future: "Four years of a rich illiterate."

Castro had reason for concern. During the 1960 campaign, Kennedy had attacked Eisenhower for permitting communism to flourish "eight jet minutes from the coast of Florida." The *New York Times* had headlined a story: KENNEDY ASKS AID FOR CUBAN REBELS TO DEFEAT CASTRO

Kennedy did not know then that Eisenhower had a plan in progress to put some 700 Cubans ashore on their island for guerrilla action. "Before my inauguration," Kennedy said, "I asked him, 'Now, Mr. President, is there anything really urgent, or anything that can prove embarrassing to us, to the United States, during my administration, at this time that I should know about?' And he said, 'Well, there is a hit-and-run raid that has nothing to do with the United States, or the U.S. Forces, that's going to come out of Guatemala. But we have nothing to do with it.'

"That lying son of a bitch!" Kennedy exclaimed, but the vehemence came later.

It started as a CIA adventure, secret and dramatic, a guerrilla landing scheduled at the *Bahia de Cochinos*, the Bay of Pigs, almost midway along the southern side of Cuba, about 120 miles from Havana. The CIA organized and trained Cuban exiles, mostly in Florida, acquired its own private air force, then escalated the plan into a full-scale invasion, a private war. The final details were so private that Cuba's government-in-exile was not aware of them. Even the President of the United States did not know the full extent of the CIA plans and preparations.

In the spring of 1961, the Kennedy administration had something of the Midas touch. They could do anything they wanted and it would turn to gold. "Those were the days when we thought we were succeeding because of all the stories on how hard everybody was working," Bobby Kennedy said.

It seemed paradoxical to the few who knew. Here was a president announcing an Alliance for Progress, a vast, imaginative plan to pump huge sums into Latin America for peaceful revitalization, while, at the same time, he was planning a military attack on part of the area.

The man in charge of the Bay of Pigs was Richard Bissell of the CIA. "I'm your man-eating shark," he told Kennedy.

Bissell was six-feet-three, hard-nosed, witty, and elegant. Kennedy admired him inordinately. Many regarded Bissell as a brilliant natural leader, a walking computer with a gift of genius. He had helped detail the Marshall Plan for European recovery, and was a driving force behind the U-2 and satellites. Kennedy already had earmarked Bissell to replace Allen Dulles as head of the CIA. As Schlesinger put it, Kennedy was "transfixed" by him, "fascinated by the workings of this superbly clear, organized, and articulate intelligence."

Meeting with the CIA and the military was still a shock wave to Kennedy. "There he was, a lieutenant junior grade," Dave Powers said. "In walks the joint chiefs of staff with all their fruitcake of medals and braid, with generals carrying their briefcases and maps, and there's nothing more impressive. They all come to tell him that the plan is good and that it will work. How could you not believe them?"

"Bear in mind, they were strangers to each other," explained General Taylor, who later became Kennedy's military adviser. "The President barely knew his own secretary of state and secretary of defense. He didn't know any of the military or CIA. Here was this vast machinery of government and they didn't know how it ran, where you put in the gas, where you put in the oil, where you turn the throttle. And like all other administrations, they'd gone to great pains to throw out the old rascals so they could let the new rascals get in and bring a utopia of some sort."

The generals answered CIA questions about the training of troops, supplies, logistics. Instead of a night landing to get the Cubans into the nearby mountains, Bissell had expanded "toward making a Normandy landing out of this and the CIA didn't have the wherewithal to do that," said Chief of Staff Lemnitzer. "We kept emphasizing, emphasizing, emphasizing to everybody how important it was to knock out Castro's air force."

"What am I going to say to the President?" asked CIA deputy director, Gen. Charles Cabell, who had been a director of intelligence for the air force. "Am I going to say this is going to fail if we don't get those planes in? He immediately could ask me, 'Suppose I put them in. What is your guarantee?' "

The Bissell projection was that a successful landing would trigger a popular uprising resulting in the eventual overthrow of Castro. There is no record that Sen. Claiborne Pell's report on Cuba ever reached the decision-makers. Pell left Cuba that spring of 1961 convinced that no revolution there was possible because Castro's enemies had been jailed, or had fled, or were dead. Pell found no masses ready for revolt.

The President talked about the Bay of Pigs with his father. "Everytime he came back from a Palm Beach weekend, he had all kinds of new ideas. The old man wanted him to go in for an

air strike," Smathers said. He talked about it, too, with Charles
Spalding during a Glen Ora weekend. Spalding expressed the
hope that it would not turn out like the British invasion of
Suez.

"Well, everybody's gone over it," Kennedy said. "They're
pretty sure they can make it work."

The quiet, courtly Secretary of State Rusk reported the
Cuban plan to his deputy, Chester Bowles. "Will it make the
front page of the *New York Times?*" Bowles asked.

"I wouldn't think so," Rusk answered.

Among the lean, young, eager men around Kennedy, Bowles
seemed "a curiously heavy figure" who "preferred exploring
long-range ideas to expediting short-range experience." He was
not a man with whom Kennedy found it easy to work.

Bowles, Robert Kennedy, and Ted Sorensen—his special
counsel—were brought into the invasion plans during the days
of the final planning. Sorensen was critical. Kennedy dismissed
Sorensen's criticism, saying, "I know everybody is grabbing
their nuts on this." Chester Bowles told Bobby Kennedy, "Well,
I hope everybody knows that I was always against the Bay of
Pigs." Bobby turned on him angrily. "I just said it was a helluva
thing to say now that this decision had been made and as far as
this administration was concerned, he should keep his mouth
shut and remember that he was for the Bay of Pigs."

The man who felt it was morally wrong was United Nations
Ambassador Adlai Stevenson. He and the President had little
rapport. Even when they were together in a sailboat at Hyannis,
"these guys just talked straight past each other," State Department Assistant Secretary Harlan Cleveland reported. "They
weren't even communicating." When Stevenson telephoned the
President while Chuck Roberts of *Newsweek* was there, Kennedy listened for some moments and then held the phone away
from his ear for twenty seconds before listening again, and said
quietly, with contempt, to Roberts, "And *that's* Adlai Stevenson!" To another reporter, he confided that Stevenson was "all
right when he had a bunch of dowagers around him," but with
men he somehow "didn't know how to act" at times.

Yet Stevenson was one of the few men to disagree openly

and strongly about the Bay of Pigs invasion. "One man with courage makes a majority," was an oft-repeated Kennedy quote, and he then might well have applied it to Stevenson.

Kennedy had called Stevenson's integrity and credibility "one of our great national assets," and insisted he didn't want to jeopardize it. Yet Stevenson was not fully briefed on the Bay of Pigs. He did not know that the CIA planned an initial air strike of eight planes on three Cuban airfields with the false claim that the pilots were Cuban Air Force defectors. The CIA even supplied Stevenson with photos of these planes bearing forged markings. In an impassioned speech to the UN, Stevenson claimed they were genuine. When the pilots were not produced to the press after their landing in Florida, the CIA cover story unraveled and Stevenson, justly feeling that his image was tarnished, was "disgusted."

"Stevenson was on the telephone this morning from New York giving us hell," Kennedy told Senator Goldwater. "He threatened to stand up in the UN and tell the world we were behind this operation."

The *New York Times* had pieced together the Cuban invasion story when the President learned about it and personally called James Reston. He persuaded him not to print it because it would jeopardize national security. Kennedy later regretted the suppression "because if the story had appeared before the invasion, I might have had second thoughts about it—I might have called it off."

However, he had told his brother Bobby, "I would rather be an aggressor than a bum." Bobby told General Taylor that if his brother had not proceeded with the plan, Moscow would have judged him as a paper tiger, and "everybody would have said that it showed he had no courage."

Except for a handful of Kennedy's advisers, the overwhelming majority of his Cabinet and staff were enthusiastic about the invasion. State Department Latin American expert Adolf Berle expressed their overall enthusiasm at a final meeting when he said, "Let 'er rip!"

On Tuesday, April 11, 1961, Ethel Kennedy had a birthday party and Hugh Sidey of *Time* magazine was there. He noticed

Bobby Kennedy sitting alone in a corner, quiet and reflective, and went over to him.

"Have you got a man in Havana?" Kennedy asked rather abruptly.

Sidey said he wasn't sure.

"Well, you'd better get one there as soon as you can," Bobby said, "because things are going to happen there."

Robert Kennedy also approached Arthur Schlesinger, Jr., at the party. "I hear you don't think much of this business," he said. Schlesinger told him why. "You may be right and you may be wrong," Kennedy replied, "but the President has made up his mind. Don't push it further. Now is the time for everyone to help him all they can."

The President maintained his regular schedule on April 17th, including a two-hour meeting with the Committee on Mental Retardation. If he seemed quieter than usual, nothing else was visible on his face. He even went to Glen Ora that afternoon with his wife to watch some steeplechase races, then hit some golf balls with his brother-in-law Steve Smith. In discussing the invasion with Smith, he told him, "It just doesn't feel right."

The CIA had recruited some 1,400 Cubans in Miami, sent them to a secluded mountain camp in Guatemala for training, even built a complete air base there. The CIA bought some obsolete World War II B-26 bombers, and six old freighters for transport. An American destroyer would lead the flotilla into the Bay of Pigs, an American jet squadron would fly reconnaissance only, and an American aircraft carrier would wait in the area.

D-Day was April 17th. Red Beach in the Bay of Pigs, almost midway on Cuba's southern shore, was protected by coral reefs. The CIA failed to report them, and the reefs cracked open the hulls of many landing craft. Nearby Blue Beach was surrounded by swamps. Cuban planes destroyed two invasion vessels before they could unload, and also hit a freighter that had run aground. Fidel Castro personally directed defenses. He knew the area well —it was his favorite fishing place.

Despite Kennedy's orders, one of the first men to land on the beach was an American soldier. An American destroyer was near enough to the beaches to undergo shelling. In the final hours, six Americans flew combat missions without the President's knowledge, and four were shot down and killed.

The initial news was bad and soon got worse. The fourteen hundred men of the Cuban brigade were trapped on the beaches. Castro's forces were moving in fast. Bissell looked haggard, unshaven, almost stricken. The Cabinet Room had been turned into an emergency command post, men rushing in all day with urgent messages to the President and his brother. The room was littered with maps, newspapers, notes, tiny magnetic models of ships. Word from the beaches was that ammunition was critical. Harlan Cleveland was impressed with the President's reassuring manner, how much faster he recovered psychologically than anyone else in the room.

The annual Congressional Reception at the White House began at 10 PM, a formal party of white tie and tails with a marine band in red dress uniforms. As the President and his wife entered, the band played, "Mr. Wonderful," and he and his wife started the dancing. The way he smiled and mingled with the guests, no one could ever have imagined that this was a day of crisis. Later, though, as Senator Smathers danced with Jacqueline Kennedy, Bobby Kennedy interrupted, pulled him aside, and exclaimed, "The shit has hit the fan. The thing has turned sour in a way you wouldn't believe."

Shortly before midnight, the President left the party, along with the Vice-President, secretaries of defense and state and the joint chiefs to assemble in the Cabinet Room to listen to more disaster news from Bissell.

A supply ship with all the communication equipment had been destroyed by rockets, and Cuban planes were strafing the beaches.

Bissell called it a "moment of desperation" but claimed they still could avert tragedy if they sent in jet planes from the aircraft carrier *Essex.*

The President refused. He had warned them "over and over again" that he would commit no American forces to this operation. After hearing this, an admiring aide later commented: "You suddenly knew why these guys were born to command."

An admiral wanted to bring in a destroyer to support the men on the beaches, and the President again said we must not get involved. "Hell, Mr. President, but we *are* involved!"

As the news grew more desperate, the President finally agreed to a flight of six unmarked jets to act as cover for an anti-Castro B-26 attack from Nicaragua. The jets were ordered not to attack unless shot at. Rusk protested the deeper involvement, and now Kennedy answered, "We're already in it up to here," holding his hand at his nose.

"Stevenson called Kennedy a couple of times while I was there," Smathers said, "and Kennedy wouldn't talk to him. Finally, he had to. 'I had to tell that damn Adlai Stevenson that we weren't involved as much as we were,' Kennedy told me, 'and that we weren't going to do any more.' At that point, that's what kept us from doing anything more. Stevenson threatened to resign."

The meeting broke up shortly before 3 AM. The President had told a distraught Bissell to "keep your chin up." But in the Oval Office afterwards, Ken O'Donnell found Kennedy "as close to crying" as he had ever seen him. O'Donnell watched him go outside his office about 4 AM, his shoulders slumped, his hands jammed into his pockets. He was out there almost an hour, walking alone. O'Donnell remembered saying to himself, "That's the first time Jack Kennedy ever lost anything."

Later that day, as the defeat became stark, an anguished Robert Kennedy stared at the staff in the President's absence and exclaimed that they must not "sit and take it," that they must not be "paper tigers," that they must "do something." National Security Council member Walt Rostow took him aside and said quietly, "If you're in a fight and get knocked off your feet, the most dangerous thing is to come out swinging." This was a time "to pause and think," he said, and there was plenty of time to prove that they were not paper tigers.

"That's constructive," Bobby Kennedy answered. Rostow later wandered into the Oval Office to see the President looking at the headlines of the *Washington News* about the final collapse of the Cuban brigade—most of whom had surrendered. The President "let the paper crumble onto the floor without a word."

"I must have been out of my goddamn mind to listen to those people," Kennedy told Dave Powers as they were swimming in the pool. Walking on the White House lawn with Sorensen, he said, "How could I have been so far off base? All my life I've known better than to depend on experts. How could I have been so stupid to let them go ahead?"

Bobby Kennedy described the physical impact on his brother of all this, how his brother "kept shaking his head, rubbing his hands over his eyes . . . more upset this time than he was at any other time." He "felt very strongly that the Cuban operation had materially affected his standing as President and the standing of the United States in public opinion throughout the world. The United States couldn't be trusted."

Castro spoke on TV the next morning for four hours with utter contempt for the United States and the CIA. At his own press conference, Kennedy said, "Victory has a hundred fathers and defeat is an orphan." Then he added that the only thing that mattered was that he was the responsible officer of the government.

Defense Secretary McNamara afterwards told him that the responsibility should be shared. "We could have recommended against it and we didn't."

"Absolutely not," Kennedy insisted. "I'm the President. I could have decided otherwise. It's my responsibility."

Kennedy called in Gen. Maxwell Taylor that Saturday morning. Taylor felt he was in a command post of a headquarters about to be overrun by the enemy. "I've been in that situation and there's a glazed look to the eye, and hollow voices. It was obvious: They were in a state of shock."

"When I got to the White House I didn't know how sticky the flypaper would be," Taylor said.

The President sat in the rocking chair and told the general, "I'm in a situation here which I don't understand. You now see what the whole world knows, what a fiasco has taken place in Cuba. Yet, all my advisers were for this. I thought it was going to be successful—that there was very little risk involved. And now quite the contrary has been proved. What I want to do is not to find scapegoats. I take full responsibility. But I must find out what has happened. I want you to take charge and have an investigation made, and as soon as you can, lay out in front of me just what happened, and why."

"One of the freedoms of being a consultant was that I could be absolutely frank with him," Taylor said. "The Pentagon used to call a consultant 'that smart son of a bitch from out of town.' Well, that described me, I'm sorry to say."

*   *   *

The meeting in the Cabinet Room the next week had the mood of a funeral parlor. Never before had the President talked at such great length. It was almost a monologue. Everybody sat and listened, disturbed and introspective, as the President detailed all the planning of the Bay of Pigs, all the things that went wrong. He seemed to be talking more to himself than to anybody else. He didn't ask them to rally around. He didn't tell them to adopt any particular public line. He said he didn't want any backbiting or Monday-morning quarterbacking. He accepted full responsibility and he didn't want to hear anything more about it. His voice had dignity and strength, and this was as much as he was going to give them of himself. The easing of tension in the room was almost palpable.

When he was done, there were no questions. He walked out to the terrace, onto the grass. Within several minutes, Bobby joined him and walked with him awhile and then returned. The President continued walking by himself.

Kennedy then called in Clark Clifford, who once had told him, "The average high school junior in Kansas City, Missouri, equipped with hindsight, is smarter than any President of the United States."

Kennedy said to Clifford, "I made a very bad decision. The reason I made the bad decision was that my advice was wrong. My advice was wrong because it was based on incorrect facts. The incorrect facts were due to faulty intelligence. I want you to head a committee to find out what's wrong with the intelligence operation of this country."

Assistant Secretary of Defense Paul Nitze was next. "You'll take charge of developing a paper for my consideration on what our policy for Cuba will be from here on out," Kennedy told him. Nitze protested that this should be handled by the State Department, not the Defense Department. Kennedy glared. "I don't give a goddamn who heads it up. *I want you to do it!*"

He was surprisingly kind to Bissell. Bissell blamed the failure on "a lack of control in the air. If we had been able to dump five times the tonnage of bombs on Castro's airfields, we would have had a damn good chance." He admitted the contingency planning was "sloppy," but generally he was unregenerate.

"If this were the British government," Kennedy told Bissell, "I would resign and you, being a senior civil servant, would remain. But it isn't. In our government, you and Allen have to go, and I have to remain."

Bissell not only remained for a long interval but the President even awarded him the Medal of Freedom. Observers found it difficult to understand. Perhaps Kennedy felt he shared the guilt of failure because he had not immersed himself in the facts, because he had not authorized the follow-up force of air strikes, because he had not insisted on knowing what the options were in case of failure. How could he punish this daring, brilliant adventurer who represented the kind of man he himself wanted so much to be?

Monday-morning quarterbacking was always rampant. Richard Nixon told the President, "I would find proper legal cover and I would go in." Henry Kissinger told his Harvard students, "Well, as long as we're there, I don't think it would do us any good to lose." A well-circulated joke was, "Caroline Kennedy certainly is a nice kid, but that's the last time we shall let her plan a Cuban invasion."

"One little mistake . . . one little mistake . . ." Eunice Kennedy sadly repeated at parties. "I told Reston he was full of shit," Joseph Kennedy said. "All that criticism about what happened in Cuba, but no constructive ideas. We could use some ideas. They don't have any."

"And to think I really wanted this goddamn job," Kennedy told Stuart Symington after a breakfast meeting with him and Adlai Stevenson.

"Then he looked directly at me," said Symington," and

added, 'I wish you had gone into West Virginia!' " [Had Symington entered the West Virginia primary in 1960, the consensus
was that he might have won because Kennedy and Humphrey
would have split the liberal vote. Had Kennedy lost that primary, his presidential hopes might have been crippled.] Kennedy
was more bitter when he saw Goldwater. "So you want this
fucking job!"

Part of the early staff response to the Bay of Pigs was "emotional, almost savage."

What angered Kennedy was the Gallup Poll after the invasion disaster that gave the President an unprecedented 82 percent approval. "Take a look at that," he said. "The worse I do,
the more popular I get. If I had gone further, they would have
liked me more, even more."

Columnist Clayton Fritchey told Kennedy, "Mr. President,
it could have been worse."

"How?"

"It might have succeeded."

In his sum-up, General Taylor concluded, "There weren't
any heroes; they were all bums."

In the aftermath, a senator read into the record a letter from
an American mother who wondered how her son could have
been killed in the Bay of Pigs when there were not supposed to
have been any Americans involved. The senator quoted an eva-
sive reply the woman had received from the White House.

"How could you do that to me?" the President demanded in
a phone call to his air force aide, Godfrey McHugh, at 2 AM. "To
lie to her. Absolutely disgraceful. How could you do that to that
poor woman?" Then he hung up. McHugh didn't know what the
President was talking about. He hurried to his office long before
dawn and soon had the answers. As an aide, he had entree to the
President's bedroom without the need to knock. When he arrived that morning to wake the President with his report,
McHugh was surprised to find Mrs. Kennedy sharing his bed.
She hurriedly pulled the sheet over her head and the President
growled, "What the hell do you want?" McHugh hastily explained and the President responded, "All right, get the hell out.
I'll be out in a few minutes."

McHugh told the President that the woman's son had been an air force pilot drafted by the CIA for a bombing raid on the Bay of Pigs. When McHugh forwarded the mother's query to the air force, they denied he was in the air force. He then forwarded it to the CIA, which was noncommittal and urged an impersonal reply.

"Why the hell are you standing there?" the President asked after he had heard the report.

McHugh looked puzzled.

"You've got a lot of asses to chew," the President said.

The CIA commented afterwards. "We were a sick dog then. Anybody could kick us and we wouldn't bite back."

"I made a mistake in putting Bobby in the Justice Department," Kennedy said at the time. "Bobby should be in the CIA."

Particularly galling to Kennedy was that the Soviets had put their first cosmonaut into orbit less than a week before. He recalled that his father once had told him that more men die of jealousy than of cancer.

In the welter of fantastic rumors that followed, a Fort Lauderdale publisher insisted that the President had told him that Bobby had made the final decision not to use American power in the Bay of Pigs. An intimate of Marilyn Monroe's similarly insisted that she had told him Bobby ran the country for one day during the Bay of Pigs crisis "because Jack had been taking medication for his back and wasn't feeling well."

*   *   *

"I went down to the house at Glen Ora the weekend after the Bay of Pigs," Spalding recalled. "There were just the four of us and it was as painful as you'd expect. Not so upset about the technical things that had gone wrong but just that he felt so *badly* that it had gone wrong. He kept reproaching himself with all the advantages of hindsight. He just wanted somebody to talk to who was sympathetic, who wouldn't ask too many questions.

"He really was as low as I ever recall him. He just kept saying over and over to himself, 'How could I have done it?' He repeated it again and again. That's the only time, in all the time that I knew him, that he was really beside himself over a mistake. He was really hard hit."

He might have remembered President Truman's philosophy, "Never kick a fresh turd around on a hot day."

"Jackie was great—very subtle," Spalding continued. "She wouldn't come out and put a sympathetic arm around him, or anything like that. But she knew it was a hellish time for him, that after the spectacular beginning, he had suddenly been brought up short, sandbagged. How could he allow himself to be sandbagged? Suddenly all the excitement ceased to be fun.

"There was this big cornfield outside the house. He had this golf club and six or seven balls. Once in a while he'd just take a wild swing at a ball and knock it into the cornfield. We just walked and walked all over the place and he couldn't talk about anything else.

"It made it hard. You couldn't play cards. You couldn't listen to music. It was the only thing on his mind and we just had to let him talk himself out." There was something a friend had once told him—"You will learn how to turn your scars into stars."

"But that weekend [April 22nd 1961] began a big change. After that, he was totally different in his attitude towards everything. From then on it mainly became an arduous backbreaking job that will kill you, one way or another.

"Before the Bay of Pigs, everything was a glorious adventure, onward and upward. Afterwards it was a series of ups and downs, with terrible pitfalls, suspicion everywhere, [with him] cautious of everything, questioning always."

Another time Spalding commented: "I remember once when we were having dinner together at the White House and he walked down with me to the gate, to that big fence on Pennsylvania where I was getting a cab. He actually came out on the street with me, with the Secret Service men scrambling all over the place, and he said to me, 'Charlie, what's out there? What's out there?' and I said, 'There's people out there. People and places to go.' And he said, 'Tell me, am I missing something? What am I missing?'"

336

The Growth of
a President

"How safe is it to send a man into space now?" the President asked Ed Welsh, director of the space project, two weeks after the Bay of Pigs. Alan Shepard was primed to go on a ballistic shot, up into the stratosphere, and down again. A failure, so soon after the Bay of Pigs, would have been a political catastrophe. A staff consensus counseled caution.

"Well, Mr. President," Welsh said, "there's no more danger in this flight than in taking an airplane trip from here to Los Angeles and back, in bad weather."

"There *isn't?*"

"No, sir," Welsh said.

The Man Who Came with Jacqueline Kennedy

The American people understood the challenge illustrated by the story Kennedy had told during the campaign of throwing your cap over the wall so that you had to climb the wall to get it. Now he could proudly tell the world, "America has tossed its cap over the wall of space."

In a special, second State of the Union message on urgent national needs in May 1961, the President added, "I believe we should go to the moon before the decade is out."

The Soviets had embarrassed the U.S. with their Sputnik, the first man-made exploration into space four years earlier. Only a few months before, they had put their first man into orbit. American pride had been badly dented. A crowded Congress and an anxious America felt stirred to hear their President fling down the gauntlet.

"Landing a man on the moon and returning him safely to earth . . . no single space project in this period will be more impressive to mankind, or more important for the long-range exploration of space; and none will be so difficult or expensive to accomplish. . . . In a very real sense, it will not be one man going to the moon . . . it will be an entire nation. For all of us must work to put him there."

The real birth of the American space program took ten minutes.

Kennedy had assigned the space project to his Vice-President because Lyndon Johnson had headed the Space Committee in the Senate.

"What do you think ought to be done?" Kennedy asked Johnson at a meeting in early April in the Oval Office.

"I think that Ed Welsh knows more about it than I do," Johnson answered with uncharacteristic modesty. Welsh was a mild, middle-aged man with a firm voice and a decisive mind. Welsh made a short, impromptu presentation of the program's needs and estimated budget. The President then asked Budget Director David Bell if the funds were available.

"I'm sure," Bell said, "we can get whatever you need, Mr. President."

The meeting was over. The American space age had begun.

*   *   *

Welsh went to work without pencils, paper, staff, or salary. It took a week before he got some money from the President's emergency fund to pay for a part-time secretary. Before that, he dictated his memorandums over the phone for his wife to type. He was even evicted from his third-floor office in the Executive Office Building by a three-star general. Within weeks, however, his power was formidable. As executive director of the National Aeronautics and Space Council, he had the President's authority to coordinate all space projects, prepare policy, and draft legislation.

"Do you know there are only five people at General Motors who can sign a letter for any direct action at all?" Welsh said. "If I thought I should call and talk to somebody about something, I would, but I could clear anything myself without consultation."

Every Friday morning Welsh and a staff of eight prepared a two-page report updating the President on U.S. space progress and problems.

The President wanted to know:

1. Do we have a chance of beating the Soviets by putting a laboratory in space, or by a trip around the moon, or by a rocket to land on the moon, or by a rocket to go to the moon and back with a man? Is there any other space program that promises dramatic results in which we could win?
2. How much additional would it cost?
3. Are we working twenty-four hours a day on existing programs? If not, why not? If not, will you make recommendations to me as to how work can be speeded up?
4. In building large boosters, should we put our emphasis on nuclear, chemical, or liquid fuel, or a combination of these three?
5. Are we making maximum effort? Are we achieving necessary results?

"Manned exploration of the moon is not only an achievement with great propaganda value," Welsh replied, "but it is essential as an objective." We had the resources, he added, to have "a reasonable chance of attaining world leadership in space during this decade."

As the Shepard launching was ready to go, Kennedy saw his wife outside the Oval Office and rushed out to get her. "Come and watch this." He displayed all the excitement of a young boy on his first sail. Indeed, he saw the whole space project as a need "to set sail in this new sea." Eisenhower, on the other hand, denounced the space program as a $40 billion boondoggle.

Shepard had taken a monkey into space with him. When he arrived at the White House afterwards for a courtesy call, Caroline Kennedy had a question, "Where's the monkey?"

The American public was excited by the space launch, but its excitement was mitigated by the large lead of the Soviets. The Russians were then so far ahead that they had brushed aside

Kennedy's approach for East-West cooperation to "explore the stars." Kennedy was more convinced than ever that we must be the world leader in space no matter what the cost.

*   *   *

The President had, however, more immediate problems with the Russians, as well as with the French. He felt the time had come for frank discussion with Khrushchev and with De Gaulle. Their common range of concern included Berlin and nuclear disarmament.

To prepare himself on De Gaulle, Kennedy turned to his new friends, the Alphands.

Hervé Alphand, the dashing, attractive ambassador from France, joked easily with Jacqueline in French, and his vivacious wife, Nicole, seemed to have a particular attraction for the President. In their introductory meeting, the President said to Mme. Alphand, *"Comment allez-vous?"* then added in English, "I understand only one out of every five French words, but always De Gaulle."

The French ambassador later wrote in his diary about Jack Kennedy, "He likes a good time and women. This could be used against him; he is careless." Alphand did not record the many Washington rumors about the President and Mme. Alphand. Nor did the rumors disappear while Kennedy was President.

The President was "unceasingly excited, always having a new thought, or telephoning and asking questions on all subjects," Alphand noted. "His mind holds much, he reads ferociously, loves to talk to foreigners." In general he found Kennedy to be natural, direct, and "bursting with youth and happiness."

The four lunched often. Jacqueline told the Alphands that Jack wanted Hervé to telephone him directly whenever he felt it important, "even at midnight." Nicole also told her husband that the President had advised her that he wanted to see them as often as possible.

The Alphands frequently joined them at Palm Beach. Alphand remembered the President aboard the *Honey Fitz* wearing shorts and a back brace, joking about the French loan of the

Mona Lisa to the United States. Just before their trip to Paris, the President wanted to know all the detailed plans, including the menu and entertainment. He asked about Paris fashion and French theater, and obviously had been reading digests of French newspaper articles. He discussed an article by a French general who wrote that the United States would never defend Europe with atomic weapons. Kennedy called the article unjust and dishonest because a free and independent Europe was absolutely vital.

Other guests aboard ship included the Radziwills—Jacqueline's sister and her husband—and the Peter Lawfords. Alphand watched the President take a short swim in the rough ocean, then come in quickly when someone spotted sharks. He saw how Kennedy dressed with great difficulty because of his back. Later, Alphand wrote in his diary of seeing the President and Nicole on the beach, "the two of them laughing and obviously enjoying each other."

Lunch was crab salad, hot dogs, and coconut cake. Alphand recorded Jacqueline's remark that she hoped that when De Gaulle came to the United States, he would visit Hyannis and not Palm Beach—which, she said, she detested.

Jack Kennedy had no deep feeling for France, or any foreign country. What French feeling he had came from his wife, and the Paris of his youth.

Kennedy admired De Gaulle as a great man of history, but also for his way with words. When Harry Hopkins returned from his first trip to wartime England, FDR's first question about Churchill was, "Does he really write his own speeches?" Kennedy was similarly admiring of De Gaulle's literary style. His wife read aloud to him from De Gaulle's memoirs. He even kept with him, for a while, a letter from De Gaulle and showed it to his staff because he so much admired its elegant language.

But Kennedy had no illusions about the French leader. "Why is De Gaulle trying to screw us?" he asked National Security Council adviser Walt Rostow. Rostow's explanation was that De Gaulle couldn't make much of an issue on French enemies and so he attacked his friends. "De Gaulle needed an enemy," McGeorge Bundy added. "Maybe that's too strong, but he did

343

need a big guy to whom he could stand up." The friction, thought Bundy, would distract the French people from the country's domestic problems. Kennedy was determined not to provide a cause for conflict.

The President had told Gen. James Gavin, his ambassador to France, "If you can get along with De Gaulle, that's all I ask you to do."

General Gavin was not a man most presidents would have made ambassador to France. He had been an Eighty-second Airborne Division combat commander in World War II. The ambassadorship was a rich man's post and Gavin was not rich. But he had impressed Kennedy when they met during Kennedy's first campaign for Congress. An imposing man of words as well as of action, the tall, handsome Gavin was Kennedy's type. He recalled expressing doubts about the ambassadorship, "John looked me right in the eye and asked, 'Are you reluctant to help me?' And I said, 'No, I'll go.' "

Gavin became part of a personal Kennedy network of key ambassadors who reported to the State Department on routine matters but contacted the President directly on any issue they felt important. The State Department, for example, was bitterly anti–De Gaulle, and Kennedy was not.

The Kennedy trip to France in June 1961, less than two months after the Bay of Pigs, was a diplomatic deadlock but a personal triumph. During the airport arrival ceremonies, however, the State Department translator abysmally failed to translate the sparkle of the Kennedy wit. Kennedy's Air Force aide, who spoke fluent French, later advised the President of what had happened. "You can't crucify somebody for not being as witty as I might be," Kennedy replied, "but we won't use him again."

The Kennedys were quartered at the Quai d'Orsay, a vast palatial building fronting the Seine River, near the heart of Paris. On instructions, the French put them in separate bedrooms— his wife at one end of a huge hall on the third floor, with his room at the other end, and their staff quartered in between.

Kennedy found De Gaulle the man he expected: courteous, proud. At their first conference, De Gaulle supplied cigarettes for Kennedy, but Kennedy didn't smoke because he knew of De Gaulle's sensitive eyes. Kennedy brought a gift that De Gaulle appreciated, an original letter from the Washington-Lafayette correspondence.

The President had come prepared to treat France "the way we treat England," to consult them with equality and intimacy. De Gaulle emphasized his pride. "You know I never asked your country for nuclear information."

Kennedy told De Gaulle, as politely as possible, that only a superpower could afford a nuclear deterrent, and the American policy was to defend Europe with nuclear weapons, if necessary. With the same politeness, but with more chill, De Gaulle replied that, while Russia might have "ten times the killing power of France," the Soviet Union might be deterred from attacking France if it knew that French nuclear weapons could "tear off an arm" of Russia.

The two leaders did not resolve much, but they respected each other.

De Gaulle later wondered about Kennedy's ambitions, his youthfulness of experience, his willingness for change. He was worried that Kennedy could select Rusk as secretary of state, having seen him only once. He was also worried about Robert Kennedy's influence in the inner councils.

* * *

Paris was Jacqueline's triumph. Some said the cheers for her almost drowned out the 101-gun salute for her husband.

"*Jacqui. Jacqui. Jacqui . . . Vive Jacqueline!!!*"

"What do you expect," said an American reporter, "she's part French."

"About a month before we went to Paris," Press Secretary Salinger recalled, "the President called me in and said, 'You know what we ought to do? We ought to get French television to do a show with Jackie as the star—have Jackie take French television through the White House, and talk to them in French. And I'll do a little interview at the end in French and English. Then have it appear on French television just before we show up, and the people will know who we are a little better.'"

The show appeared on French television two nights before their arrival and was an enormous success. They reveled in her French heritage, her fluent use of their language, her dazzling beauty. Every action, every word, every change in costume was described in infinite detail on front pages throughout France. Cheering crowds massed everywhere she went. The mayor of Paris gave her a diamond watch. The press compared her visit to the reception for Queen Elizabeth.

"Queen Elizabeth hell," Dave Powers said to the President. "They couldn't get this kind of turnout with the Second Coming."

Her conquest was complete. She felt like a queen. She slept in the *Chambre de la Reine* in a bed whose most recent occupant had been Belgium's Queen Fabiola. She bathed in a silver mosaic tub in a mother-of-pearl bathroom used by Queen Elizabeth II. When she went anywhere, in a black bubbletop Citroën limousine, she had an escort of plumed horsemen clattering alongside. At the Elysée Palace, white-stockinged footmen lined the stairs.

Two of the two thousand guests at the Elysée Palace reception were her cousins, Michel and Kathleen Bouvier. They reported later that as they approached the reviewing line, De Gaulle "had us pegged for imposters, and turned towards us with outraged anger. Jackie immediately apprehended the disaster and somehow managed to leap across the floor, despite the tight fit of her stunning formal evening gown. She cut off the official bouncer in his tracks and embraced us both." Jacqueline then introduced them to De Gaulle, raising "her voice in a normal whisper to a sufficiently emphatic level."

Jacqueline not only acted like a queen, she looked like one.

A month before, she had sent Alexandre a lock of her hair and reserved his services for the duration of her visit. Known as the "hairdresser of queens," Alexandre came twice a day to brush and shape her hair, and transform her girlish casualness into a hairdo of elaborate and queenly sculpture. "A beautiful face needs foliage around it," he said, and swept two bouffant curves around her cheekbones, and added a tambourine of false hair adorned with a diamond rose at the back of her head. His inspiration for her, he said, came from Gothic madonnas as well as from one of Louis XIV's loveliest mistresses.

Also alerted was Europe's leading cosmetics expert, Nathalie, who changed many things, including Jacqueline's lipstick, which became "a tender red."

The First Lady had planned her wardrobe meticulously, and had made it all-American to quell any criticism at home. The single exception was a new gown by Parisian designer Hubert de Givenchy, with a bell-shaped skirt and fitted sleeveless top, embroidered all over with multicolored flowers. With it came a coat of matching white silk.

When her husband was impressed with her clothes, he usually made an OK sign with his hand. This time, he exclaimed, "Well, I'm dazzled!"

De Gaulle honored them, in the beautiful Hall of Mirrors at the Versailles Palace, with a six-course dinner served on gold-plated Sèvres china dating from 1850. De Gaulle and Jacqueline discussed the dynastic complexities of the Bourbons and Louis XVI. De Gaulle leaned over and told the President that Mrs. Kennedy knew more French history than most French women. Kennedy felt proud, later said it was as if Mme. De Gaulle had asked him about Henry Clay.

De Gaulle had met Mrs. Kennedy before at the French embassy in Washington when her husband was a junior senator. She had told him then, "You know, Monsieur le Président, my ancestors were French." With an almost imperceptible smile, he had answered, "Really, Madame, so were mine." But they had had such a good time together afterwards, that he was quoted as saying, "The one thing I would like to take back to France from America is Mrs. Kennedy."

Now, at the dinner in the Hall of Mirrors, observers noted that the French president concentrated so completely on Jacqueline that he ate little dinner. Capturing the mood, a French cartoonist depicted De Gaulle in a great canopied double bed with his wife, but dreaming about Mrs. Kennedy. Mme. De Gaulle is shown sitting upright in the bed as if she knows what her husband is dreaming. The simple caption was "Charles!"

The cartoon so delighted President Kennedy that he kept it framed on his desk.

That evening after the theater, the presidential limousine stopped outside the Palais de Versailles. "The *son et lumière* was on," said presidential aide Godfrey McHugh, who was with them, "all the lights and music and sound and it looked like fairyland. Jackie got out and so did the President, still wearing his top hat and white tie. And the three of us started walking— followed by Secret Service. Then we saw some more cars coming and Jackie wondered who it was. It was De Gaulle. He also stopped his car and joined us, walking in the night. De Gaulle was taken with Jackie. When she wanted to, she could focus tremendous attention on someone and do it beautifully. She was a master at it. She was laughing with him, telling him that these memories would last a lifetime. It started to sprinkle, a slight, misty rain, but nobody seemed to mind it. Then it came down a little harder and we all went back to our cars. The whole thing had lasted maybe fifteen minutes, an absolutely delightful interval."

More than anything else in Paris, Jacqueline told friends, she wanted to see André Malraux. He was not only a man of words but a man of action; romantic words, romantic action. She had read his noted novels *Man's Fate* and *Man's Hope,* and followed his dramatic career as a pilot in the Spanish Civil War and a leader in the French Resistance during World War II. He was now, of course, French minister of cultural affairs and the closest De Gaulle confidant.

Just before the Kennedy arrival, Malraux's two sons were killed in an automobile accident, but he still came to the State Dinner to be with the Kennedys. He made her laugh by telling her that her husband "spoke French with a bad Cuban accent. He apparently doesn't believe in French verbs." He escorted her on a tour of Impressionist paintings at the various museums. Her favorite: Manet's reclining nude, *Olympia.* He took her to the flower-filled Malmaison, the home of Empress Josephine Bonaparte, and commented that Josephine had been "extremely jealous" of Napoleon. "She was quite right and I don't blame her," Jacqueline answered. They lunched at a Madame Pompadour hideaway on lobster thermidor and *mousse aux fraises des bois*. Meeting men like Malraux brought out the best in Jacqueline. Leaders and heroes intrigued her enormously. Observers said she then became "an outrageous flirt."

Malraux, afterwards confiding his absolute admiration of her, felt she might make an excellent ambassador to France. "She is unique for the wife of an American president," Malraux told De Gaulle. "Yes, she's unique," De Gaulle replied. "I can see her in about ten years on the yacht of a Greek petrol millionaire."

A French newspaper headlined them: LES MAGNIFIQUES. Jacqueline now knew that she was no longer simply a pretty prop for her husband. Her impact was real.

"I am the man who came here with Jacqueline Kennedy," he told a Paris audience. It was the kind of quote that bounced all over the world.

"He was the President," Letitia Baldrige commented, "but she was our movie star."

The First Lady even agreed to a rare press conference. American women reporters resented the invitation, which read: "Mrs. John Kennedy will be very happy to receive you." French female reporters were also invited.

Mrs. Kennedy arrived late, chose not to greet her guests, and preferred to stand. The French reporters quickly grouped around her, and the American reporters largely retired from the field. Inez Robb announced afterwards that their press honeymoon with the First Lady was over. Robb described their treatment as a snub. "The press, having created a lovely legend, now finds it hard to be hoisted on a petard of its own creation. The American press swells with pride that the First Lady is glorious in public. But it finds it difficult to understand the wife of a politician who must stand for re-election who models herself, it is reported, on Queen Elizabeth II."

The French reporters, however, were delighted. Their questions came quickly:

What would you like to be if you were not the First Lady of the United States?

"I should like to be the wife of my husband."

Why wasn't she going to any fashion shows in Paris?

"I have more important things to do this trip."

How was it possible to bring up children in the White House with all the attention they were getting?

"They are properly disciplined, I can assure you. I hate spoiled children."

How did she manage to look so beautiful all the time? When did she rest?

"Well, I rest in the evening."

What did she think of President De Gaulle?

"I have long admired President De Gaulle. I have read every volume of his memoirs."

Describing her husband, Mrs. Kennedy said, "He reads and reads and reads. Never relaxes."

"Even when he is in his rocking chair?" asked a reporter.

"Even in the rocking chair," she answered.

She also added, "I don't like him to bring his problems home in the evening."

Jacqueline later also had her fun—persuading her staff to put on wigs and try to get past the guards. She also stole away for a few hours to make a sentimental journey to the old Left Bank haunts of her Sorbonne student days.

The Kennedys left France with De Gaulle's farewell words, "I have more confidence in your country now." As they left for Vienna, De Gaulle also warned Jacqueline to beware of Madame Khrushchev, who was *"plus maline que lui"* (more sly than he is). The First Lady had small need for concern.

* * *

President Kennedy, however, had greater need for concern. It had been only two months since the Kennedy humiliation at the Bay of Pigs. Arthur Goldberg had warned the President that he wasn't ready to talk to Khrushchev at Vienna because he hadn't been President long enough.

What Kennedy felt was the need of communication among leaders. World War I started because there wasn't enough communication "and this must not happen again." He believed he and Khrushchev had to know how far they could go with each other. All his life, he had felt he could charm and reason with anyone, and he was at his best exchanging views with those with whom he disagreed.

For a gift to the Soviet leader, the President brought a magnificent model of the U.S.S. *Constitution*. His father had given it to him for his forty-fourth birthday less than a week earlier. In return, Khrushchev presented him with a model of an early American whaling ship carved of whalebone.

Kennedy had done his homework on Khrushchev. Right after the inauguration, he had told his staff to read Khrushchev's speech of January 6. "You've got to understand it and so does everybody else around here. This is our clue to our future with the Soviet Union." In it, Khrushchev had said: "We will beat the United States with small wars of liberation. We will nibble them to exhaustion all over the globe, in South America, Africa, Southeast Asia."

Everybody was ready with advice. Harriman, who had talked with Khrushchev for ten hours, warned Kennedy that he was a tough, rough talker who would try to bully him. Harriman's advice was to laugh it off, have a good time. Walter Lippmann advised that Kennedy could get along with Khrushchev by being patient and self-confident. "He's a revolutionist," Lippmann said, "but he never can carry a revolution to the point where he thinks it's going to produce war with us." Ambassador Llewellyn Thompson recalled: "Kennedy picked my brains until there was nothing left." In the final analysis, though, Kennedy was on his own with the sixty-seven-year-old Russian leader.

Khrushchev later told some Westinghouse businessmen that he could deal with Eisenhower "because we're contemporaries," but that he found it difficult to take Kennedy seriously "because he's younger than my son."

Khrushchev was determined to dominate the five-hour talk, and he did. Former Ambassador to Russia George Kennan felt Kennedy should have challenged Khrushchev on many more points. Khrushchev blistered Kennedy on the Bay of Pigs fiasco, and warned him that Berlin was 110 miles inside his area, and added, "I'll step on your corns anytime I want." When Kennedy urged Khrushchev not to back wars of "national liberation,"

Khrushchev's passionate answer was that the spread of communism throughout the world was inevitable.

Discussing disarmament with Khrushchev, Kennedy had quoted an Asian maxim, "The journey of a thousand miles begins with one step."

"You seem to know the Chinese very well," Khrushchev said.

"We may both get to know them better."

As he listened, Kennedy felt that Khrushchev was determined to take Berlin. At one time, he asked Khrushchev what medal he was wearing. Khrushchev said it was the Peace Medal.

"I hope you get to keep it," Kennedy said.

Kennan felt that Khrushchev saw Kennedy as a "tongue-tied young man, not forceful, who doesn't have any ideas of his own." Lyndon Johnson later made a private assessment: "Khrushchev scared the poor little fellow dead."

Former Secretary of State Dean Acheson judged that Khrushchev found Kennedy a "weak, vacillating figure, a pushover, because he had not taken Cuba," and that the Soviet leader now felt that "all he had to do was show strength and he [Kennedy] would back down."

Kennedy was pacing the floor afterwards when Mrs. Lincoln asked him, "How did it go?"

"Not too well," he answered.

He felt shocked, humiliated. "Now I know there is *no* further need for talking."

Going through his papers on the plane from Vienna, Mrs. Lincoln found a little slip of paper on which he had scribbled,

> I know there is a God—and I see a storm coming;
> If He has a place for me, I believe I am ready.

Later, he would say of Khrushchev, "I guess he has his bad days too."

*   *   *

If the trip was a diplomatic failure for the President, it was an utter triumph for his wife. Wherever she went, crowds gathered.

"Jah-kee" was a solid smash in Vienna. The contrast between the tall, handsome Kennedy and the short, stocky Khrushchev in his gray suit with three medals was no sharper than between Mrs. Kennedy and Mrs. Khrushchev.

"We all felt sorry for Madame Khrushchev," Letitia Baldrige said, "because she looked like somebody's grandmother." She was, with five grandchildren, and she wore "sensible shoes." Her arrival at Pallavicini Palace drew scarcely a murmur from the large waiting crowd, but Mrs. Kennedy's coming caused an unbroken, five-minute chanting and cheering, "Jah-kee! Jah-kee!"

The state banquet was at Schönbrunn Palace, Vienna's Versailles. Fourteen hundred rooms and the immaculate formal gardens divided by geometric white pebbled walks were all ablaze with light. Also ablaze was Premier Khrushchev, whose interest in Mrs. Kennedy was concentrated. The 250 guests were quick to notice how he moved his chair even closer to her during dinner. They talked about horses and Ukrainian traditional dances. When he told her that the Soviet Ukraine had more teachers than the czarist Ukraine, she said, "Oh, Mr. Chairman, don't bore me with statistics." He laughed. When she talked about the dogs in space, he promised to send her one. He was also interested in the story that her husband had a gold bathtub in his Paris suite while she had a silver one in hers, and that her husband had said, "It may seem funny to us, but maybe it's a better use for gold than locking it up at Fort Knox."

Khrushchev thought her long pink-beaded white gown was "beautiful." When photographers asked him to pose shaking hands with the President, he pointed at Mrs. Kennedy and said, "I'd rather shake hands with her."

SMITTEN KHRUSHCHEV IS JACKIE'S HAPPY ESCORT headlined the *New York Herald Tribune.*

On the plane to London, she wrote a long personal letter to General De Gaulle thanking him for making their visit so memorable. She walked to the back of the plane, handed it to Godfrey McHugh, and asked him what he thought of it. McHugh's French was fluent.

"It's a lovely, lovely letter," he told her, "as sweet as can be.

But as a lady, as a woman, you can't use *'mon général.'* " He explained that *mon général* was strictly a man's form of address. The French were very strictly sexist about that.

She was furious, really angry. "Well, the State Department can write the goddamn thing!" she said, and strode away.

*   *   *

Their next stop was London, where the President was god-father for his niece, the daughter of Princess Radziwill, at West-minster Cathedral.

Thousands of people waited in the rain outside Buckingham Palace that night, when the Kennedys came for a glittering din-ner in the state dining room with Queen Elizabeth and Prince Philip. The crowd quickly indicated that they had come to see "Jackie."

She did not disappoint the fashion watchers. Her sleeveless blue gown had a boat neckline in front, and a plunging V-neck-line in back, and a loosely gathered bell-shaped skirt fitted at the waist with a bow. She wore long pendant diamond earrings, long white gloves, and carried a small silver handbag. Her hair-dresser, Alexandre, had piled her hair on top of her head with a diamond spray, fastened on a chignon, and placed pearls at the back of her neck.

She walked with a perfect carriage, in contrast to her hus-band who often couldn't stand straight because of his bad back.

But not all Britons were uncritically ecstatic. When she vis-ited the queen, cartoonist Vicky in the *Evening Standard* pic-tured her as the Statue of Liberty, one hand holding the torch of freedom, the other holding a copy of *Vogue.* The same paper, however, also editorialized, "Jacqueline Kennedy has given the American people from this day on one thing they have always lacked—majesty."

Clark Clifford tried to explain the Kennedy's worldwide im-pact: "She was the princess and he was the prince, that must be it. She was the beautiful princess on the balcony and he was the handsome knight in shining armor who comes riding by on a white charger, gathers up the princess in his arms, and off they ride into the sunset. That's why they transcended boundaries; that's why they appealed to the world."

354

ı   ★   ★   ★

Jacqueline Kennedy needed some time for herself. When her husband went home from London, Jacqueline stayed on with her sister for a holiday in Greece. The Greek government quickly made available a luxurious villa and a 125-foot yacht for a tour of the Cyclades Islands. She danced to Kalamatianos folk music with the artist colony on Hydra, wandered among the lemon trees of Poros, and went swimming and water-skiing (an enterprising Greek reporter in skin-diving gear was warned away with, "We are instructed to spear any large sea life moving toward the Kennedy party"). They visited Delos, where Apollo was born—the island was cut off from tourists for a day, so Mrs. Kennedy could enjoy the rubbled splendors in private. At Mykonos, a small island with 333 churches, the cobblestoned streets were given a rush coat of whitewash in her honor. Wherever she landed, the streets were strewn with flowers.

If Mrs. John Kennedy had become an American queen, the women's press in Washington were no longer going to pay her court. At their annual spoof, Helen Thomas impersonated the First Lady, singing a song called "Chez Moi," part of which went:

If I want to fly away without taking J F K
That's me, Jackie.

If I'm fond of French champagne, if I'd rather not campaign
That's me, Jackie.

If I want to give a ball—for just me and Charles De Gaulle
I have absolutely all the gall I need.

If I like to water-ski and I want my private sea
Don't look askance, With half the chance
You'd be like me, Jackie.

If I have a sultry voice, Why I sound that way by choice
That's me, Jackie.

If I want to be bizarre, And restore the DAR
That's me, Jackie.

If I use Mount Vernon's lawn
For amusing Ayub Khan

And we choose to dance 'til dawn
Then *c'est la vie.*

If I rewrite history
Name the White House Chez Jackie,
Am I to blame?
You'd do the same
If you were me, Jackie.

An encore lyric:

London says my smile is warm
Vienna went wild about my form
I've taken the whole wide world by storm
Monotonous!

Mrs. John Kennedy, in the audience, had a very small smile on her face.

*   *   *

The President smiled then even less.

Gore Vidal saw John Kennedy in the White House soon after his return from the meeting with Khrushchev. "He used to sit there in the Oval Office for hours in total silence. Nothing like that had happened to him before."

I don't know the qualifications of a good president. The presidency pulls out of a man everything he has within him, all his intelligence, all his energy, all his heart. I don't think anybody can say in advance whether this or that man will make a really good president. The test of the presidency is the test of the strain of the office.

—JOHN F. KENNEDY

Grace Under Pressure

Kennedy called Arthur Goldberg soon after his return in the middle of June. "You were quite right. I wasn't prepared. I wasn't long enough in the presidency. I didn't feel like a President."

"I got off one good line," Kennedy told Goldberg. "When Khrushchev was threatening to take Berlin, I said, 'If you do, it'll be a long, cold winter.' "

But Kennedy's official response was to ask Congress for more of everything for defense—more money, more troops, more weapons. He asked the Western allies to join in a "firm stand" on Berlin, and he called up the military reserves.

Khrushchev commented: "Kennedy is too young. He lacks the authority and prestige to settle this issue correctly and that is why he has induced these mobilization measures. But he doesn't want to fight. Only an idiot wants war.

"If Kennedy appealed to the people—if he voiced his real inner thoughts and stated that there was no use fighting over

Berlin, no use losing a drop of blood—the situation would be settled quickly. All this talk of our desire to seize West Berlin is an invention.

"Why? If Kennedy does the logical thing, the opposition will raise its voice and accuse him of youth, cowardice, and a lack of statesmanship. He is afraid of that. Kennedy is probably abler than Eisenhower. Kennedy is reasonable, but he is taking a very wrong stand now."

*   *   *

On August 14, 1961, about 10 AM, the East Germans began to build the Berlin Wall.

Kennedy asked a variety of people what they would do about the wall. "I think we should blow it up as fast as they put it up," Larry Newman told him.

"Why not knock down the wall?" the President asked Gen. Lyman Lemnitzer, chairman of the Joint Chiefs of Staff.

Because the Communists had built it six inches inside their line, breaking that wall would be like invading Russia.

Why was Russia doing all this? he asked.

To test him. Stick in the knife until it hits steel.

"We were not in a position in Berlin to say, 'Remove the wall or else,' because what's 'else'?" Walter Lippmann observed.

"I haven't made up my mind on how far *I'm* prepared to go," Kennedy told Newman. "We can't give what we haven't got," he added later. "We don't have East Germany and it's not something we can bargain over. The chances of settling this without war are not yet too good." He had warned Khrushchev, "We will not yield on Berlin because this symbolizes our entire position in Europe."

That weekend he kept close to Washington. He remembered that General Marshall was away from headquarters on Pearl Harbor Day. He saw the world entering a new danger zone and he kept repeating, "If we push the button, if *I* push the button, I may be killing two hundred million people."

Nine months after his inauguration, Kennedy asked the American people to "face the fact that the United States is neither omnipotent nor omniscient—that we are only six percent of the world's population—that we cannot impose our will upon the other ninety-four percent of mankind—that we cannot right every wrong or reverse each adversity—and that therefore there cannot be an American solution to every world problem."

"I was in the Oval Office with him until just before we were going to a dinner party with Senator Gore [of Tennessee] and his wife," Walton said. "He had a tray of tea on his desk and he was reading cables about the Berlin crisis. He threw them at me to read. He wasn't asking my judgment or anything. It was just his way of sharing things with friends. He finally gave me a cable and said, 'Put this one in your pocket. I want to look at it later.' And then the two of us went up to dinner with the Gores. After dinner, Jackie and Mrs. Gore went their way and Jack said to me, 'Show Gore that cable on Berlin I gave you.' I took it out of my pocket and gave it to Gore. It was a very important cable and highly classified and I'll never forget how impressed Gore was that I had it in my pocket, that I was privy to such secret stuff. And he has treated me with awe ever since."

Why did Kennedy do that? Was it simply his way of relaxing and amusing himself with a play of power? Did he want to inflate Walton and deflate Gore? Or, in the complex of his personality, was it a combination of many things? It did add a mystery to the presidency, and was this, perhaps what he wanted most of all?

The President called Gen. Lucius Clay in Berlin.

"How are things?" he asked.

"I think things are a helluva lot better here than in Washington," replied General Clay, "because there seem to be a lot of nervous guys in Washington."

"Well, you're not talking to one of them," Kennedy answered. "I'm not a damn bit nervous. You do whatever the hell you want to do!"

Clay later recalled: "I'm impressed all over again with the awful loneliness of the President." They had just had a meeting about a Berlin crisis, a projected convoy of armored trucks carrying fifteen hundred American soldiers traveling the one-hundred-four mile stretch of autobahn through the Russian sector into West Berlin. The Russians had intimated that they might stop such a convoy.

Clay remembered, "In that meeting President Kennedy was twisting a paper in his hands, and then after a while he asked to see me alone. We went into the next room and he said, 'General, I've heard all the advice pro and con. This is touch-and-go. We may lose the whole thing. What do you think I should do?' I said, 'I think you should let the tanks roll.' He smoothed out the paper and it was an order for the tanks to roll, and Kennedy had already signed it."

"That son of a bitch won't pay any attention to words," Kennedy said. "He has to see you move."

The 1st Battle Group of the 8th Infantry moved down the autobahn into West Berlin without incident. Kennedy had sent Vice-President Johnson to Berlin to greet them.

Khrushchev tested Kennedy again in September by breaking the moratorium on atomic testing. Kennedy's reaction was unprintable. He had talked about all nations "sharing a goal to tame the savageness of man and make gentle the life of the world." Pressure now multiplied on the President to resume testing. He waffled, hedged, hesitated, finally agreed but only if it remained under highly restrictive control. Nor did he stop negotiations for a test ban treaty. Adlai Stevenson expressed regret about his decision to resume testing.

"What choice did we have?" Kennedy answered. "They have spit in our eye three times. We couldn't possibly sit back and do nothing at all. We had to do this. The third test was a contemptuous response to our note. Anyway, the decision has been made. I'm not saying it was the right decision. Who the hell knows, but it is the decision which has been taken."

The President was growing into his power.

*   *   *

His greatest power problem was with the State Department.

Kennedy called the State Department "a bowl of jelly," and complained that it took them "four or five days to answer a simple yes or no." Sending them an instruction, he said, was "like dropping it in a dead-letter box." Of all the thousands in that department, he said, "I can hire fewer than one hundred thirty. Presidents come and go but those bastards stay there forever."

Before his inauguration, Kennedy had asked John Sharon for "a shit list" of the deadwood in the State Department. Sharon prepared a list of forty names, men who should be transferred or fired, and typed it on a piece of plain white paper, without any heading or authorship, "without any fingerprints even."

A month after the inauguration, Sharon visited Kennedy in the Oval Office. "John, how many of those forty do you think have been kicked out since I got that list?" asked the President.

"Well, it can't be too many," Sharon said. "I would guess about ten or twelve."

"Not one," Kennedy replied, banging his fist on the table. "Not a fucking one."

"What's wrong with that goddamn department of yours, Chip?" he asked Charles Bohlen.

"I told him that *he* was," Bohlen recalled. Bohlen told Kennedy that he had made Rusk's job almost impossible by appointing his two top assistants before appointing Rusk. Then he had had Bundy create a capsule State Department within the White House.

"Damn it! Bundy and I get more done in one day in the White House than they do in six months."

"I know we somewhat overstate the operational role of the White House staff," Bundy said. "We were *not* running the foreign policy, the President was in charge. But I don't think he ever sent a cable that wasn't sent through the secretary of state. Oh sure, Gavin would come in to him personally after his return from France, and Llewellyn Thompson would send him long cables from Russia, but the cables all came through the State Department. No bypassing. And Thompson would never say one thing to the President and another to the secretary of state."

Secretary of State Dean Rusk was the only Cabinet officer whom Kennedy did not call by his first name—and Rusk claimed he preferred it that way. He was a man of quiet humor, absolute loyalty, and strongly held principles, with a deep dedication to his work, a man of discipline and patience. A cool, courtly man, he was nicknamed "the Buddha." What was missing between the two men was a personal relationship.

*   *   *

Foreign policy had a softer side. Pakistan was hardly the most important country, but Mohammed Ayub Khan was the next state visitor, and Mrs. Kennedy was bursting with ideas for a glamourous gala. She planned a lawn party at nearby historic Mt. Vernon, the home of George Washington. It involved intricate logistics using army field kitchens to keep the different courses hot or cold, and army trucks to transport White House china, silver, and gold ballroom chairs. She wanted a bandstand built for the National Symphony Orchestra and persuaded Tiffany's to provide colorful tents. A fife and drum color guard was dressed in colonial uniforms with powdered wigs, tri-cornered hats, red coats, and knee breeches, and air force violinists were recruited to stroll through the grounds. Even the President provided suggestions. One of his memos read: "See that they have all the Lowenstoft bowls in the house filled with flowers—very low." After an inspection trip with White House Chief Usher West, Mrs. Kennedy said, "I suppose you're going to jump off the White House roof tomorrow?"

"No, not until the day after the dinner."

He made no reference to one of Mrs. Kennedy's cushions, embroidered with the message, "You don't have to be crazy to live here, but it helps."

The guests traveled aboard three canopied boats, each with its own guitar and violin music. Landing at Mt. Vernon after an hour's trip, the formally dressed guests arrived in an area lit by flaring torches, with a military honor guard presenting arms every few paces, just as the French did at Versailles. They ate baby veal, drank champagne, and listened to the National Symphony Orchestra play Gershwin.

Even those reporters who resented the First Lady felt forced to admit that the evening was memorable. It was especially so for a woman reporter who had had too much champagne and kept flipping the medals on the chest of Gen. Curtis LeMay, saying, "Oh look at the pretty medals." The general, with his hanging jowls, tried desperately to ignore her and look straight ahead.

Another reporter on the receiving line got a similar cold reception from Pakistan's President Khan. In Pakistan, journalists are considered inferior beings, and the six-foot four-inch Khan gave reporter Jim Deakin the frozen Sandhurst stare, looking directly over his head. Kennedy caught the stare and interjected himself forcefully, saying, "Mr. Deakin is a distinguished journalist for one of our most distinguished newspapers."

"That's what he could do, you know," Deakin said. "That was style. That was class."

But it was the First Lady's night. Early in her marriage, someone said of her, "She's a nice girl but sort of a pilot fish, don't you think?' "

Nobody would ever again call her a pilot fish.

*   *   *

When Princess Grace and Prince Rainier visited Washington, they were invited to lunch at the White House, since Monaco was too small a country to rate an official dinner. The princess, Bill Walton, Franklin D. Roosevelt, Jr. and the President sat at one end of the table while the First Lady sat next to the prince. "I want to be up there with *you*," Jacqueline told her husband. "What am I going to say to *him!*" The President's appreciation for Princess Grace was obviously mutual. A photographer caught a picture of the two of them in which her look was strictly sensual.

Most of the conversation at the table came, loud and merry, from Walton, Roosevelt, and the President. Princess Grace was particularly quiet and Walton later learned why. "She was so scared of coming to the luncheon that she had two double Bloody Marys and was bombed." On a stroll on the south lawn, the President said to the princess, "I see you're wearing a Givenchy dress."

"Yes, but how did you know?"

"I ought to. I've paid for enough of them."

"We always shuddered when he went to see his father for a weekend," George Ball said, "because we knew we were going to catch hell on the question of balance of payments when he came back. And we always did. I remember one long argument I had with him about it. 'George,' he said, 'I understand you and I agree with you, but how do I *ever* explain it to my father?' "

See the New Frontiersman Run

Most incoming presidents know little about economics. Kennedy was no exception. "The Depression had no effect on me," he admitted. "I have no memory of it at all, really, except what I read in history books." A White House aide, Ralph Dungan, amplified: "Jack Kennedy doesn't know from a *second* mortgage, much less a first."

When he had come into office, Kennedy had found an economy sinking into a recession with a stagnant gross national product. Unemployment reached 8.1 percent by February 1961. During the campaign, he had promised the American people a five percent growth in our economy.

"What shall we do?" Kennedy asked his economists. "What *can* we do?"

For economic advice, he relied a great deal on his father. His father's fiscal conservatism made it all the more remarkable that Kennedy accepted the liberal solution of a tax cut to help the poor by creating more jobs.

Preparing for a five-minute TV speech on the tax cut, Kennedy asked Walter Heller, chairman of his Council of Economic Advisers, to select some letters on the subject from the public from which he might quote. As Kennedy read the letter on top of the pile, he laughed so hard and so long that he was unable to record the TV speech. The first letter had begun, "You motherfucker. . . ." Because of the tax cut there was considerable laughter at the National Association of Manufacturers convention when the President mentioned that he and President William McKinley were the only two presidents ever to address that group, "so I suppose that President McKinley and I are the only two that are regarded as fiscally sound enough to be qualified."

Yet he did have a strong concern for public money. When reading a proposed budget of $342.1 million for some project, the President declared, "I want them to put in every zero. I want them to realize they're spending public money and not their own."

Aides passed on to the President anything they felt warranted his attention. One such cable came from an overseas American woman who wanted to know why the American forces planned a $200,000 addition to their officers' club near Paris. The President demanded immediate information; the project was canceled within hours.

*　　*　　*

While Kennedy was constantly learning about the economy, he was a natural master of publicity. His best assets were his directness, his candor, and his wit. For all this, TV was a superb medium. Friendly correspondents advised him on the effectiveness of Franklin Roosevelt's fireside chats on radio. But, Kennedy knew exactly how many fireside chats FDR had made, "only twenty-six." If Kennedy could not be a fireside-chat teacher with the Roosevelt warmth, he still, somehow, did transmit to the American people the fact that he wanted to help them, that he didn't like to see people suffer. The memory of West Virginia poverty always remained sharp with him. When Sen. Hugh Scott of Pennsylvania suggested that our army in

Europe buy its coal at home to help our depressed coal industry, he answered, "Sure, I'll put an order through right away."

Discussing the attitude towards America of Third World countries, Kennedy told Larry Newman, "If only they knew us better. If only they knew the American people, how they could go and knock on a guy's door and say, 'I'm hungry,' and be fed. They just don't *know* America. And you can't spend all your lifetime telling them."

Generally, though, he resented the liberal prod. "It's a funny business. Such groups are as intolerant, or more so, than the very persons they criticize. . . . Boy when those liberals start mixing into policy, it's murder." Then he smiled. "What breaks their ass is that seventy percent popularity index."

Kennedy never regarded himself as a liberal. He personally liked few liberals, generally felt uncomfortable in their presence, and seldom ever invited them to the White House. Still, he understood them, was sensitive about them, and felt that he needed them. Personally, he much preferred the company of Sen. Barry Goldwater, with whom he disagreed politically.

Whether he was a Tory Democrat—as Arthur Schlesinger, Jr., had said—or a pragmatic liberal or even "a spiritually rootless modern man of emotional thinness . . . with a dismaying pattern of retreat before pressure," as the London *Economist* saw him, few accused him of being hypocritical. Wily, yes; coldly calculating, surely, with a fierce will to succeed; but an honest man with a solid core of ability, native political skill, and great finesse.

With all of this, was he thinking more about personal politics than about the country? Did he really believe he could reach the goals he preached? How true was it that "Jack Kennedy was never carried away about anything in his life"?

And why did Congress pass so few of his bills in his first ninety days?

"When I was in Congress," he said, "I thought all the power was down at the other end of Pennsylvania [Avenue] at the White House. Now I'm down here and am amazed at all the power those bastards have!"

When a reporter had suggested writing a book about Kenne-

dy's first year in office, the President had said, "Who would
want to read a book about disasters?" Then he added, "It's been
a tough year, but then they will all be tough."

Kennedy never expected to get all he wanted, claimed White
House aide Harris Wofford, and he "learned to live cheerfully—
perhaps too cheerfully—with the continuing tension between
what we know and what we ought to be."

"At this point," McGeorge Bundy commented, "we are like
the Harlem Globetrotters, passing forward, behind, sideways,
and underneath; but nobody has made a basket yet."

Some of the press judgments were that the Kennedy program
was all gristle and no cake, that the Kennedy rocking chair was
a good symbol of the New Frontier because it moved without
getting anywhere. Even Sorensen admitted that his President
"generally resisted urgings of disappointed partisans who would
have him stir up the public against Congress."

Kennedy gave a quick excuse to Schlesinger: "There is no
sense in raising hell, and then not being successful. There is no
sense of putting the office of the President on the line on an
issue, and then being defeated." He quoted Jefferson: "Great
innovations should not be forced on slender majorities."

"See the New Frontiersman run," wrote Russell Baker.
"Running to the Capitol to save his program!" Cartoonist Bill
Mauldin showed him counting tokens of popular esteem like
Croesus counting gold, with Jacqueline saying, "You may have
to spend some of it."

His political sense was remarkable but, because of his style,
he could not translate it into congressional action. Congress
seemed to be waiting for clearer marching orders, a more fo-
cused direction. It was not his style to ask a member of Congress
for his vote on a bill. He could not deal with the standard political quid pro quo—you give me something and I'll give you
something. It was one thing for a candidate who didn't want to
be touched to handshake himself through a campaign; it was another for a president to go against his pragmatic-logical grain by
emotionally begging, pushing, and fighting for votes in congress.

Even his close friend Senator Smathers admitted, "He never
asked for my vote on anything."

"We passed a lot of legislation that we never got full credit for, but I'll admit they weren't the key bills," said his legislative aide Larry O'Brien. "The thing is, Jack never twisted arms. He didn't have it within himself to put his arm around a guy or get angry enough to put his nose against the other guy's nose.

"Lyndon Johnson not only cajoled them and twisted arms, but he wanted to fight personally for every vote," said O'Brien. Johnson once told him: "If you're up on the Hill bleeding, I want to bleed with you."

O'Brien continued: "I don't know if Kennedy ever fully recognized what he had going for him in Congress—the real affection of so many of those fellas."

Kennedy still didn't like to lose, O'Brien reported. "I remember we lost out on the minimum wage bill by just one vote and when I called him about it," O'Brien said, "he was so mad about it that he stabbed his pencil into the desk."

*   *   *

Kennedy felt it more within the presidential province of power to make decisions and create programs. One of Kennedy's campaign promises was to create a Peace Corps using the skills of dedicated Americans to help people abroad. When Robert Sargent Shriver made his first plea for this proposal to his brother-in-law early in the campaign, Kennedy liked it. It was Shriver's wife, Eunice, who said, "Wait a minute. Listen to this son of a bitch spend my money." Kennedy later insisted, "Nobody's given me any idea for a long time that I haven't had myself." Indeed, Gen. James Gavin had independently voiced a parallel plan shortly before the election.

But it was Shriver who made it happen. "I searched all my life for someone like my father," Eunice Kennedy said in a toast at her wedding, "and Sarge came closest."

The Kennedys called him "the Boy Scout"; the press named him "Mr. Clean," and his wife called him "Toughie." He was really an easygoing, bustling man, more liberal and idealistic than most of the Kennedys.

His family was old Maryland, dating back to the 1600s, with Shrivers fighting in the French and Indian Wars and in the American Revolution, as well as serving in the Confederate cavalry in the Civil War. A Shriver even signed the Bill of Rights. "We're nicer than the Kennedys," Shriver's mother said.

"Was it a liability or an asset to be the President's brother-in-law?" a reporter asked.

"It's a fact of life," Sargent Shriver replied sharply. "Why think about it at all?"

Still, he resented being called a "half-Kennedy."

Shriver was a Washington question mark, and he knew it. He knew the dimensions of his challenge. The President had spelled it out for him. "He told me that everyone in Washington seemed to think that the Peace Corps was going to be the biggest fiasco in history," Shriver said, "and it would be much easier to fire a relative than a friend."

The initial plan was to put the Peace Corps under the economic umbrella of the Agency for International Development and get a single congressional appropriation for it. Shriver felt strongly that the Peace Corps deserved its own identity with separate funding. He persuaded his wife to press his case with her brother and he got Lyndon Johnson to side with him.

Kennedy was indignant because it meant that he had to ask Congress for two appropriations instead of one. "OK hotshots," he told them, "you wanted to be on your own—you're on your own. Get the damn bill through Congress yourselves."

Shriver made a resolution: "By God, I'll never ask for anything from the White House as long as I live. I'll never ask a favor from the President—never."

For four months, Shriver lobbied intensively. And he kept his promise to stay away from the President. Occasionally, however, he casually told Bartlett, "If you happen to see my brother-in-law one of these days, I'd appreciate your asking him if he's aware of this situation. . . ."

"And then we ran the Peace Corps without ever asking permission or getting clearance for anything from the White House," Shriver recalled.

The President later called Shriver the most effective lobbyist in Washington, and added, "I don't think it is altogether fair to say I handed Sarge a lemon from which he made lemonade." Kennedy said he had given the Peace Corps "one of the most sensitive and difficult assignments which any administrative group in Washington has been given almost in this century."

The press, at first, called it the "Kennedy Kiddie Korps."

The young saw it as a magnetic idea and five thousand of them volunteered to go to forty-seven countries. They built health centers, schools, bridges, aqueducts, and roads. They grew lettuce in Brazil and taught the Twist in Nyasaland. A Peace Corps story that reached the President—and which he particularly enjoyed—concerned a young female Peace Corps volunteer who took on an extracurricular job after working hours. The village postmaster in the highlands of Eritrea was romancing a young woman in Addis Ababa who could read English but not the postmaster's Tigrinya language. The Peace Corps volunteer recalled and repeated a sentence the postmaster had dictated for her translation: "And so I have loved you, I am loving you, and I will love you until my perpendicular is horizontal and I die."

The volunteers were adopted as sons by Southeast Asian aborigines, treed by African buffaloes, serenaded by Filipino gigolos, frightened by playful natives tossing pythons; and they ate everything from cat meat to sheep intestines to fish heads. Six volunteers died, and 448 were either fired or quit, but the Peace Corps itself was considered an overwhelming success, a major jewel in the Kennedy diadem.

Kennedy was not quick on compliments. He expected his people to do their jobs without his acknowledgment.

The President and Dave Powers were at Hyannis one day, the two of them watching Sarge Shriver water-skiing.

"Sarge does everything well," the President told Powers.

"I wondered if he had ever told Sarge that," Powers thought afterwards.

"Do you know who financed the beginning of the Peace Corps?" asked Bill Haddad, who became Shriver's deputy. "We were financed by old man Kennedy's credit card. We had no government funds at all at the beginning and so we all stayed at the Mayflower Hotel and charged everything. That's exactly the way it was."

* * *

Joseph Patrick Kennedy seldom asked patronage favors from his political sons, but now he had one. He wanted his good friend Francis X. Morrissey made a federal judge.

When President Kennedy signed a bill creating seventy-three new federal judgeships, he listed the qualifications as "respected professional skill, incorruptible character, firm judicial temperament, the rare quality to know when to temper justice with mercy, and the intellectual capacity to protect and illuminate the Constitution."

Morrissey, in his biography submitted to the American Bar Association, listed among his qualifications his seven children, identified one as a godchild of Joseph Kennedy, another as a godchild of President Kennedy, and then told a Senate committee that his son Richard Cushing Morrissey was the first child ever baptized by a cardinal on live television.

Morrissey had been a Boston Welfare Department social worker hired by the elder Kennedy during Jack's Congressional campaign to keep a watchful eye on his three sons, arrange their reservations and accommodations, meet them at the airport, and report periodically to the elder Kennedy. A dumpy, florid-faced man of fifty-five, Morrissey was an uncomplicated person with a sense of humor who had never gone to law school. John Kennedy described him as "a tough, able man of common sense who was a very effective municipal court judge. He may not be one of the patrician Ivy League types, but he'll make a good federal judge."

Morrissey was found unqualified by the ABA, the Massachusetts Bar Association, and the Boston Bar Association.

In view of this Bar Association rejection, the President could not openly support his candicacy, although he told McGeorge Bundy to help the appointment "but do it quietly." In assessing Morrissey, Sen. Scott announced that the kindest thing you could say for Morrissey was that he was not a national disaster. The appointment was laid aside.

"What shall I tell Dad?" Robert Kennedy asked his older brother.

"Tell him he's not the President."

* * *

Camp David sat on a ridge eighteen hundred feet high in the Catoctin Mountains, a hundred wooded acres with a beautiful view of the valley. It was the closest available retreat for the President and he often had friends there. It had a heated swimming pool, tennis courts, bowling lanes, and a practice golf range with three tees. But the mattress was too soft, so the President slept on the floor. Some guests felt it had the look of a prison camp with marine guards everywhere. The fog was sometimes so thick that even the helicopters couldn't move in or out.

"We wouldn't get much notice," Spalding said. "Maybe he'd call us the night before. The Bartletts might be there and maybe some other people. He didn't like to be with the same people for forty-eight hours, if that long, and he didn't like the idea of other people coming in.

"We would just sit around and relax, walk in the country. There was a big pool for swimming. Maybe Jackie would ride a horse and we'd watch her. Or some of us would go trapshooting. Then we'd talk.

"We'd always talk about things in the news. You remember that Profumo scandal that rocked the British government? Well, he felt terribly sorry for Profumo, and sympathized with the way Profumo was caught. Jack also thought the girls involved were kind of cute.

"If Jackie got into it, she could be *funny*. Those were really the best moments. Then everybody would contribute.

"Jackie could really keep up with Jack."

*　　*　　*

Glen Ora, Palm Beach, and Camp David were all weekend places visited in the spring and winter, but in the summer the President headed mostly for Hyannis Port.

There was the local adage that if New York ate horseradish, Cape Cod got heartburn. It became much worse when Kennedy became President. The Hyannis area became a tourist mecca. The road from Hyannis to the port became a horror of pastel-tinted motels, miniature golf courses, gift shops, and "Leaning Towers of Pizza"—all with glaring neon lights.

Otis Air Force Base was twenty-two miles from the Kennedy

The First Family moves into the White House.

"The pay is good and I can walk to work."

Elegant evenings became the custom at the White House.

They were called America's favorite couple.

Jacqueline Kennedy with an admirer,
Nikita Krushchev (UPI PHOTO)

President Kennedy and admirer,
Princess Grace of Monaco
(UPI PHOTO)

Watching an American in space: "Let us explore the stars."

The President's cabinet at work.
Left, standing: *Robert Kennedy;* at
table, clockwise from left: *Assistant
Secretary of Defense Paul Nitze,
Deputy USIA Director Donald
Wilson, Special Counsel Theodore
Sorensen, Executive Secretary NSC
Bromley Smith, Special Assistant
McGeorge Bundy, Secretary of the
Treasury Douglas Dillon, Vice-
President Johnson, Ambassador
Llewellyn Thompson, William C.
Foster, CIA Director John McCone*
(hidden), *the President, Secretary
of State Dean Rusk, Secretary of
Defense Robert McNamara, Deputy
Secretary of Defense Roswell
Gilpatric, and Gen. Maxwell Taylor.*

*The strain of the office was now more
often seen on the President's face.*

The President listens as civil rights leaders air their grievances.

The President seen here discussing his options during the Cuban missile crisis with McGeorge Bundy, Gen. Maxwell Taylor, and Robert McNamara.

The President's top advisor throughout the missile crisis was his brother Bobby.

The final burden always rested on the President. (OLLIE ATKINS)

Few knew that the President used crutches to the end of his life.

Sailing trips at Hyannis Port relieved the tension of the presidency.

Jacqueline made a superb ambassador.

The President greets Jacqueline on her return from India.

Jacqueline receives a standing
ovation at a fundraiser for the
National Cultural Center—
November 1962.

Wit, charm, and a disarming smile
made the President the master of the
press conference.

The President addresses the citizens
of Berlin on June 26, 1963, declaring:
"Ich bin ein Berliner!"

Family Album

The President says goodbye to his father.

The Kennedys arrive at the Dallas airport—November 22, 1963.

The President's widow (UPI PHOTO)

The final tribute (UPI PHOTO)

compound, and there were always helicopters waiting for an *Air Force One* arrival. Even on the short helicopter ride to the compound, Kennedy kept busy reading documents or signing autographs. If he signed a picture for a personal friend, he always liked to do it in front of the person. "If it just came from the White House you would never know whether I signed it or not."

The presidential helicopter always landed on the flat stretch of land overlooking the sea in front of his father's house. The land adjoined the Coleman property and the elder Coleman always raced to the top floor to see the helicopter come in—even though he hated the Kennedys. He also periodically billed the President for damage done to his lawn furniture by the helicopter exhaust—and the President always paid, and promptly.

"I don't know why it is that all of us here are so committed to the sea," he told an audience of sailors, "except I think it's because, in addition to the fact that the sea changes, and the light changes, and the ships change, it's because we all came from the sea. We are tied to the ocean. And when we go back to the sea—whether it is to sail or to watch it—we are going back from whence we came."

Give him a small piece of ocean, a boat, and half-decent weather, and he was happy. In a spanking, whistling southwester he would take the tiller of the trim twenty-two-foot family sloop, and skim by the rock breakwater with full sails, cutting through the chop.

Kennedy loved to sail in almost any weather. A friend remembered a dark, chilly day when a group of them huddled together in the cold aboard ship, while the President sat in the stern, in a black sweater, the wind blowing his hair, blissfully happy.

The wind was nearly thirty knots, a blustery day at Hyannis Port, and the President and Mrs. Kennedy were rigging the sails for a race around the bay. Ethel and the John Glenn family came along too. It soon became obvious that the wind was so strong, the force on the tiller so great, that the President had some sudden concern about the strain on his back. John Glenn's son Dave was drafted as helmsman even though he had never sailed a boat that size before. The President showed him how to brace his feet to keep the tiller under control. Glenn, who had no qualms about going out into unknown space, worried about sailing in that roaring wind, but "I felt that if *he* could go out that day, it would probably be all right for us to venture out."

His sailing was part of his privacy. When a boatload of photographers came too close, he deliberately turned his back on them. That's when they began calling him, "Jack the Back."

His sailing was also part of his pride. Returning to harbor in a strong wind, he tried to bring the boat smartly against the jetty, when the top of the mast gave way and the rigging collapsed. He sheepishly accepted his brother's comment, "I always wondered how exactly we lost PT-109. After that performance, I suggest we have a new inquiry into it." However, Kennedy resented the stories in the press. "What are you bastards trying to do to me?" he asked Larry Newman. "What do you think the Republicans are going to do when the commander-in-chief can't even get a sailboat ashore?" Salinger told reporters that the story was "absolutely false" until a photographer quietly handed Salinger his pictures of the incident. Kennedy later called Newman. "I think you're right. I've been looking at it from a political point of view. I should have had more sense. The people *will* look on me as a human being."

If the sea was too heavy, he would still pack a lunch and go out on his father's fifty-two-foot cruiser, maybe tie up at a nearby island, and dive off the fantail. Once a catamaran scooted past the President and he hailed it, "Is there any chance of getting a ride?" The crew of the twenty-seven-foot *Pattycat* came aboard and the President and his friend navy Undersecretary Paul "Red" Fay scrambled aboard the cat and heeled over for a fifteen-minute ride with the barefoot President at the tiller, the cigar still in his mouth, exhilarated.

There were very few things that touched him more deeply.

One of his happiest times was aboard the USS *Joseph P. Kennedy, Jr.,* with family and friends, watching the America's Cup races with Australia in September 1962. "I can still see that long, lean, completely relaxed figure stretched out on deck," remembered the naval aide. "It was good to see him sit back, light one of his slender cigars, adjust his binoculars, and study the racing yachts—or push his sunglasses back on his forehead and laugh with those around him. I can see him, too, at times gazing over the sea, lost in thought, and idly chewing on the frame of his sunglasses."

The President was in the bow of the ship watching the races, surrounded by a slew of sailboats, when one of the boats started to cut across the bow of the destroyer. Kennedy realized suddenly that something had to give, so he turned and yelled at the captain behind him, "Shut this son of a bitch down!"

He was wearing the jacket with the seal of the United States on it and he was proud of being commander-in-chief, fully aware he was boss. The small boat eased by, the man in the wheelhouse saluted him, and Kennedy returned the salute.

"When the children began to get restless aboard," recalled his naval aide, "the President quieted them with a story. They sat enraptured at his feet, especially Caroline. When her father started a story, it was like a magic wand being waved over her. The storytelling sessions were the only times I ever saw her really still."

One of his favorite stories was about a white shark who ate people's socks. The President pretended to see a shark and said, "Franklin, give me your socks; he's hungry." Franklin D. Roosevelt, Jr., who was also a father, promptly took off his socks and threw them into the water. Caroline looked on, wide-eyed.

The President also taught Caroline some poetry:

> Where the bee sucks, there suck I;
> In a cowslip's bell I lie
> There I couch when owls do cry.

He found it particularly difficult this time to say good-bye to his children when he flew back to Washington. Commenting on this to his naval aide, he said, "John sees so little of his father. How can he ever know me?"

In this job there's always going to be a flare-up about something. And you just must somehow get it so it doesn't upset you. I think I was always fairly good at it. I can drop down this curtain in my mind.

—JACQUELINE KENNEDY

21

The Uncrowned Queen

"Jackie is an *immense* woman," Spalding said. "I mean, bigger than anybody knows. She had the kind of awareness that Jack obviously found attractive, but it also made her more vulnerable. She has a toughness, like a fighter who doesn't go down, but gets hurt. I think she probably suffered to beat the band but nobody ever saw the hurt. But she filled out the picture for Jack. If you look at pictures of the two of them and take her out of the picture and put somebody else in, then you'll see what I mean. Sometimes I wonder if he ever knew."

"This is a very strong dame," Bill Walton said. "She'll discuss topics with the President and beat him down. But she has no present interest in public causes or controversy for herself."

Strangely enough, one of her frequent quarrels with her multimillionaire husband concerned money.

Even the President's most intimate friends said how strange he was about money. He could call a State Department official and demand an item-by-item explanation of a traveling expense account, and yet had no qualms about flying his special mattress and golf cart to Florida every fall. When he was ready to return to Washington from his father's Palm Beach house, the RC-121-D with a nineteen-man crew was again sent down there to pick up the mattress and cart.

A friend questioned Kennedy. "I need them down there," the President answered.

The friend persisted. Why didn't he simply buy another mattress and another golf cart and keep them down there?

"It's a waste of money," the President replied.

What griped him most was the money his wife spent. "I don't understand it," she confided to a friend. "Jack will spend any amount of money to buy votes, but he balks at investing a thousand dollars in a beautiful painting. He seems more concerned these days with my budget than with the budget of the United States."

The President quoted Truman, who had said, "Tell you what, it's not the Congress spending money that worries me, the one who worries me is Bess."

"That Jackie, she's unbelievable," Kennedy told Smathers. "She thinks she can keep on spending it forever. I don't understand what the hell she's doing with all those things. How much does she need? God, she's driving me crazy, absolutely crazy, I tell you." Kennedy similarly complained to Bradlee: "Wouldn't you think it would cost us about what it cost us in Georgetown, considering all the things we get free here and had to pay for there? It costs a fantastic amount more."

Some of her expenses: "Givenchy clothes—$4,000; $900 for riding accessories; and $800 for a vacuum cleaner for her horses." One item read: "Department store—$40,000." "What the hell does this mean?" he asked. "Oh heck, I don't remember," Jackie whispered. "What do you mean, you don't remember?" Total personal expenses for the first White House year: $145,446.14.

"Do you realize I only make $100,000 a year as President? If we didn't have a private income, we'd be bankrupt," Jack Kennedy told his wife.

Ethel was once overheard saying to Jacqueline, "You've hurt

the family a lot with all this publicity about your almost ob-
scene spending."

The man in charge of finances at the Kennedy office on Park
Avenue sent Mary Gallagher, the First Lady's secretary, a cartoon showing a distraught housewife telling her husband, "I'll
bet Jack wouldn't yell at Jacqueline if she were overdrawn!"

*   *   *

"I am determined that my husband's administration—this
is a speech I find myself making in the middle of the night—
won't be plagued by fashion stories."

It was not to be because fashion suddenly became part of
political news.

Oleg Cassini held a press conference to announce, "I have
been chosen in competition with the most expert designers in
the nation to be the official dressmaker to Mrs. John F. Kennedy." Cassini was also the couturier for Mrs. Joseph Kennedy
and two of the Kennedy daughters (Mrs. Peter Lawford and Mrs.
Sargent Shriver), and for Princess Grace of Monaco.

"She has a strong style of her own, interested more in dignity
than in novelty," Cassini said of the First Lady. He added that
she did not believe a public figure can be photographed only
once in the same outfit. "If I had to choose one word for her, it
would be *impeccable.*" He called his assignment "the plum of
my career." He was selected, he said, for his "synthesis of Mrs.
Kennedy's elegance." When asked if the First Lady had put him
on a budget, he countered quickly, "This is not a good question."

The economic fact was that the American women's clothing
industry added up to $11 billion a year, with another $4 billion
for women's accessories, and the First Lady was "the most po-
tent force in international fashion today."

Did she plan to influence the nation's fashions?

"I have no *desire* to," she answered impatiently. "That's
about at the *bottom* of things I attach importance to."

Whatever her desire, "the Jackie look" soon swept the country, and even much of the world. A women's magazine editor
worried, "It's going to be perfectly ghastly, every young woman
is going to look like Jacqueline Kennedy."

When she bought a pillbox hat at Bergdorf Goodman and wore it on the back of her head, "Everybody wanted pillbox hats to wear on the back of the head." There was a big rush to copy the sleeveless, collarless sheath she wore as a summer dress. She liked tight pants, relaxed dresses, pure line or silhouette rather than frills and puffs, casual clothes with undefined waistlines, pumps with medium heels, black accessories in the winter, beige in the summer, and a mix of colors—purple slacks with an orange sweater, pink blouse with pale yellow slacks, black dress under a gay red coat. She defied tradition by being "fantastically chic."

Fashion writers tended to catalogue her dresses. She had a favored raspberry red, two-piece woolen dress they called her King Tut dress because she wore it to the opening of a King Tut exhibition. At a White House tea, a fashion writer almost held her breath when Mrs. William Paley arrived in a duplicate King Tut dress. The room hushed, expectantly awaiting Mrs. Kennedy's arrival. Would she or would she not wear her favorite dress? She had, indeed, planned to wear it, but decided on a black velvet suit at the last minute. The disappointed fashion writer, however, did note a new hairdo that included bangs, and the suspicion of a slight auburn rinse in her dark hair.

Mrs. Kennedy sent a plea to Oleg Cassini:

"PROTECT ME—as I seem so mercilessly exposed, and don't know how to cope with it. (I read tonight I dye my hair because it is mousey-gray!)"

"I think she has a great, great influence in breaking down a certain Puritanism there has always been in this country," added Eugenia Sheppard of the *New York Herald Tribune*. "A frame of mind that feels it is wrong to wear jewelry. It is wrong to wear fancy hairdos. It is wrong to live in elegance and graciousness. She broke down the whole feeling that it isn't right to wear brightly colored coats or low-heeled shoes, or the woman who used to say, 'I can't wear my skirts that short. It isn't nice.' She's broken all this down. And I think it's going to last."

"I should like to be known for something other than my gowns," Mrs. Kennedy said. At the same time, when she read that her sister Lee was more elegant, the First Lady promptly wrote a note to Letizia in Paris, who checked Paris fashions for her: "What I really appreciate most of all is your letting me know before Lee about the treasures. Please always do that—now that she knows you are my 'scout,' she is slipping in there before me. So this fall, do let me know about the prettiest things first."

Women liked her. A Gallup Poll noted that the majority of American women thought she was "intelligent . . . attractive . . . charming" and 7 percent admitted they thought seriously of having their hair done in the famed bouffant of the First Lady. Some 80 percent of women's magazines all over the world soon listed her as Woman of the Year.

As for the men, a returnee from McMurdo Station in the Antarctic reported, "They've got her picture all over the place down there—she's a Marilyn Monroe to the armed forces. They think she's a doll."

"The wife of a President is supposed to be a washrag hanging beside him," author-artist Ludwig Bemelmans volunteered, "and here is this glorious creature—and she has not made one mistake."

The critics, of course, as always, were everywhere.

"When I hear that the Kennedys brought culture to Washington, I want to vo-mit!" columnist Betty Beale said. "This city has had culture for two centuries."

The play at the National Theater was a musical spoof on the current White House, and the First Lady was not amused. She did not join in the applause for the first scene, which showed a Twist party at the White House. Nor did she join in the laughter when the actress playing the First Lady took off her wig and parked it on a bust of George Washington. Mrs. Kennedy had been criticized in the press for her Twist parties and mocked for wearing an occasional wig.

"What do you suppose they want me to be?" Mrs. Kennedy asked Joan Braden, "for I've always been exactly the same."

Her defenders included a Baptist minister in Colorado. "If you ask me, they're entitled to do as they darn please once in a while. And we're Republicans, too."

"They complain because the Kennedys go swimming with

too many clothes on, and now they're complaining because they don't wear enough," added another defender. "Maybe they don't act like other presidents but other presidents were older people."

"She does people good in getting their minds off Khrushchev for a while."

"If only I looked like Jackie," the new Miss America said.

She had been making sketches for as long as she could remember, later she did them for the *Washington Times-Herald*, and now she loved to do them for her family. She did one of her husband washing his socks in a hotel bathroom while campaigning for Stevenson in 1956. The style had something of the child-like and the sophisticated in the mood of Ludwig Bemelmans, Raoul Dufy, and Grandma Moses. A watercolor for her father-in-law showed dozens of Kennedys on a beach while overhead a plane carried a banner, "You can't take it with you. Dad's got it all." Another showed a line of pickets marching with signs that said, "Put Jackie and Joan back in American clothes." A Christmas present for Ethel Kennedy from Jacqueline featured Ethel sunning by her pool, dictating to a secretary while three sons galloped across the lawn trying to lasso their governess. In the background a newly hired maid arrived on one driveway while a second maid left by another.

One of Jack Kennedy's favorites was her watercolor entitled, "How the Kennedys Spend Wedding Anniversaries." In the first scene, she is visiting him at the hospital; in the second, he is visiting her.

There were times when she needed to run away from everybody and everything—her husband, her children, the aura of the White House. At such times, she liked New York. Even then, she was hardly alone. There was the ubiquitous pair of Secret Service men, a secretary, and, often her sister. The sisters analyzed everything together, from fashion to friends, used each other as sounding boards, and even had an abbreviated sign language so that they could almost communicate without words. Comparing the two, a columnist noted that Jacqueline looked "marvelously put together," while Lee "seemed blown out by a hurricane." "Lee was one of her best friends," confided an intimate, "but Lee was still a shark." Jacqueline had had a White House party for her sister and her husband, a cross section of "fun people," including the New York jet set and Aly Khan. The dancing continued until 3 AM. The First Lady put her sister in the queen's bedroom that night.

The press never stopped:

Was there any special reason why the President and Mrs. Kennedy would observe their eighth wedding anniversary 450 miles apart, he in the White House and she in Hyannis Port?

Was it his idea or hers to arrive at receptions from the elevator and simply mingle with the guests, rather than coming down the stairs to "Ruffles and Flourishes?"

Did her son John really come in while his mother had her breakfast in bed and share her toast and honey?

How true was it that the Secret Service now used Eisenhower's bubbletop limousine for her because she complained of the wind blowing her hair?

Her response to all this was what she called "The PBO"—polite brush-off. Mrs. Kennedy once went to the point of calling the White House Kennel Keeper, "Bryant, don't give Helen Thomas any information about the dogs. Not a damn thing!"

She applied the PBO to other people, too, including both her mother and her mother-in-law. She was seldom in the White House when either of them called or came. What concerned her husband much more was her PBO to political affairs.

She once asked her social secretary Letitia Baldrige to represent her at a Congressional Wives' Prayer Breakfast, saying, "I can't bear those silly women."

"God, how she mimics them," Baldrige commented, "making fun of their dowdiness and their slobbering devotion to their husbands' political careers." She thought all those events were "tacky."

A big scheduled event for the congressional wives was the Distinguished Ladies' Reception in honor of the First Lady. They persuaded Van Cliburn to play, decorated the head table with miniatures of antique furniture, and filled the hall with the First Lady's favorite flowers. That morning, she told her husband she was not going.

"His language was absolutely blue," recalled a staff member who was there. "Jesus Christ, you can't do this," the President said. But she was adamant and the President substituted for her. Neither the congressional wives nor the press were appeased. They pointed out that Mrs. Robert Kennedy and Mrs. Edward Kennedy, both even more pregnant than she was, had attended the luncheon. They also noted, more sharply, that the morning's paper featured a photograph of a radiantly healthy Mrs. Kennedy attending the Royal Ballet in New York.

Mrs. Kennedy had said of Mrs. Lyndon Johnson that she would run down the street naked if Lyndon wanted her to. Mrs. Kennedy was not Mrs. Johnson.

Despite her attitude towards many official functions, she still combined tradition with style. When she smashed a champagne bottle against the hull of a Polaris submarine and announced, "I christen thee Lafayette." Then in a softer voice, "*Je te baptise le Lafayette.*"

Propriety was part of her breeding. It took a long time for her to forgive Leonard Bernstein for kissing her in front of a TV camera when she went to see him backstage during a Lincoln Center performance. "It really bothered her," Joan Braden, who was with her, recalled. "She even wrote me a note asking me to promise to keep Lennie away from her husband, away from the White House." Bernstein couldn't understand, "But Jackie, you kissed everybody," he later told her. "Of course it got all patched up and they became great friends," Braden continued, "but that's the way she was—very, very conscious of who she was and what was proper.

"I remember how shy and careful Jackie was. 'Do you think I can smoke?' she asked me, when we were at the Center. I told her sure, we could, as long as we weren't on camera."

Jacqueline Kennedy seldom had protocol problems with guests but she once did have a confrontation with Sen. Stuart Symington. Symington found himself at a White House dinner seated next to the granddaughter of one of his former law partners. He made a laughing remark about his dinner partner, which Mrs. Kennedy overheard.

She remembered that remark when she seated him at another dinner party, an intimate gathering for eight. The President loudly remarked to his wife, "How come Stuart isn't sitting next to you? He should be sitting next to you."

After dinner, Symington confronted his hostess quietly. "Look, you and I have got to have a talk. If it's about that young granddaughter of my law partner at the last dinner, I just want to say that I was *honored* that you would put a young, pretty, attractive woman next to an old coot like me."

"She gave me a long look," said Symington, "then threw both arms around me and gave me a big, warm kiss. I loved her for that."

"There is a lot of the little girl that is part of her charm," fashion designer Oleg Cassini added. "I think there is a lost look there at times. If you look very carefully, you can see that the immensity of her problems appears sometimes in her face, and bewilders her."

"I was very fond of Jackie," Gen. Maxwell Taylor said, "but I felt sorry for her. When you get to be with this Kennedy gang —even if you married into the family, you were not really a Kennedy, not quite in the club. Except for Ethel, who was tougher than they were and could beat them at their own game. Jackie was not. She was rather retiring. On a boat trip, she'd be over by herself, nobody talking to her, and I'd go over to her and we'd talk about the world and literature and all kinds of things. But her interests were quite different from the rest of them. The atmosphere that surrounded the Kennedys was very wholesome, rugged, and outdoor. Jackie wasn't."

A vivid image for Chuck Roberts of *Newsweek* was a joyful, noisy Kennedy family party at Palm Beach with Jacqueline in a corner, all by herself.

Go to a party, said Joan Braden, and you often see Jackie standing there all alone. "The reason is that people are scared to talk to her. I'm sure many men would love to know her better, but there's a certain aura about her, always was, even before she was First Lady—that she's untouchable.

"I remember one night, at one of those small White House parties, she said to me, 'I don't understand it. Everyone flirts with you and Lee, but not with me. Is it because I'm the President's wife?'

" 'That's right,' I said."

It wasn't always that way. White House staff member Traphes Bryant said, "I remember one particular White House party. Mrs. K. was loaded on champagne and I looked through the ushers' window, which guests don't know is a one-way mirror, and saw her kick her shoes while dancing—she seemed to flirt with every guy she danced with—making eyes, throwing her head back lovey-dovey. All the men danced with her. I could see that some of the female guests were plenty jealous."

Her wistfulness was still the most striking thing about her that novelist Norman Mailer remembered. He had been discussing the unique beauty of Provincetown, which he called the Wild West of the East. "Oh, I'd love to see it," she told him, and then suddenly realized who she was and added, "I suppose now I'll never get to see it."

Her range of moods was extreme.

At a Hickory Hill seminar at Bobby Kennedy's house, she didn't simply sit and listen—she asked hard, searching questions and got deeply involved in the discussions. She was also a reader. "On her evenings at home, she reads, and reads some more," Truman Capote said. "I mean she reads more than anyone I've ever known—including me."

Capote had a further comment. "That girl reads everything that is written about her and she's totally aware of everything that is said about her on television, who said, and where. And she bounces people around like rubber balls. She will deliberately bury you, then six months later say with surprise, 'Darling, where have you been? I've missed you.' "

A reporter who had had an animated discussion with her the night before greeted her cheerily and received a frozen stare and dead silence. He tried to get an explanation from Hugh Sidey.

"You just got the treatment," Sidey said. "Jackie's a funny lady. I've known her since before she and Jack were married, but I never speak to her unless she speaks first. You just never know what kind of mood she's in."

She could be girlish when she wore a mask on Halloween and took her children in a station wagon to the homes of friends for trick or treat. She could be angry when her husband reluctantly agreed to accompany her to a horse show and then said, "Get me out of here!" At the same time, she was touched when she learned how much time and concern he took in selecting her Christmas present—a Renoir drawing. She was ecstatic when he asked her to create a gift for the King of Laos—a link chain made from the green stone of Arizona.

She felt a mother's joy when she heard John's squeal as eighty-six-year-old Chancellor Adenauer tossed him repeatedly into the air. Unthinkingly she had commented that John hadn't been thrown up in the air like that for a long time—and then she saw the hurt in her husband's face because his back didn't permit him that pleasure.

Their birthdays were only a few days apart, so the First Lady had a joint party for five-year-old Caroline and two-year-old John, Jr. Twenty-eight young friends sat at a charming table with linen napkins and tablecloth and china plates in an up-stairs private presidential suite: creamed chicken, ice cream, cake, and milk; each guest getting a hand puppet of a modern fantasy animal; a cartoon movie afterwards in the President's own movie theater. It was all very special.

*   *   *

A former prime minister referred to the Kennedys' "casual sort of grandeur about their evenings . . . something we have lost. . . ."

This casual grandeur was typified in a party for the shah of Iran. The table service was gold, but the President's toast was wry and light.

The informality continued when Jacqueline and the em-press, "looking like a Christmas tree with all her crown jewels," were making a short visit upstairs. The President told her that he and Lyndon Johnson were also heading upstairs. "But Jack," asked Jacqueline with a twinkle, "what are we going to do with the shah?" Her soft voice then became softer as she said, "The woman behind us would give *anything* to know what we're talking about!"

*   *   *

She could be puckish.

A startled, strolling Republican senator told a female reporter how the First Lady leaned out of her presidential limousine and mentioned a Kennedy education bill he opposed and added, "I thought you were going to be nice to us. If you're not, I won't let you take out Tish Baldrige anymore."

And she could be royal.

A critical observer noted how regally Jacqueline sat on a couch, how elegantly she took out a cigarette and waited for someone to light it for her. When the men seemed too mesmerized to act, she gave a resigned sigh and lit it herself.

"I never saw Jackie act coldly towards anyone except a Secret Service agent who was smitten with her and could not conceal his admiration," said Rita Dallas, who worked as a nurse to Joseph Kennedy.

She could be cutting. Of a tiny, slim interior decorator, she commented, "I did see him the other day. I almost stepped on him in the elevator."

An odd habit of hers was to pause in her speech as if she were trying to think of something—when she wasn't. She could always call on her "small talk with a Farmington accent." A not-so-good friend said she was better at "bestowing presents than presence." A reporter who had interviewed her a number of times described her as steely, "not quite like Marie Antoinette, but I personally did not feel at ease with her."

Hers was a whim of iron. She could tell a group of friends: "We're going to the museum." When one of them insisted he wanted to get a hamburger, she stamped her foot. She was used to being obeyed. She would rather go fox hunting than attend lunch with the National Council of Negro Women, and she did. She also told a South American diplomat that she was "too tired" to see him and then went water-skiing with John Glenn.

"That little-girl voice of hers had quite a way of attracting attention," Evelyn Lincoln commented, "but I've heard her little-girl voice disappear many times. If she didn't have a secretary with her at Palm Beach, she would dictate to me, and her voice would be very normal."

One of the intimate White House gatherings was for the

astronauts and their wives. When Jacqueline arrived, she found the atmosphere slightly strained. "You're all doing what I did for the first two years in this place," she told them. "You're whispering."

Whispers stopped when the Kennedy children arrived to say good night. The President was soon on his hands and knees with his son John, warning him, "I'm gonna get you." When he did, he tickled John into such uncontrolled delight that he wet his pants.

She was at her relaxed best at her informal parties for friends. Society columnist Betty Beale, who had known Jacqueline since she was a teen-ager, reported how the First Lady did the Twist with Defense Secretary Robert McNamara. "I didn't say anything was *bad* about it," Beale said, "but in those days in Washington, the idea of swishing your fanny in a dance was still a big deal that had to work its way up into the social strata." Beale was banished from future White House functions but the President quickly ruled otherwise. He also overruled his wife's "statue order," which forbade female reporters from mingling or talking with guests at parties.

A much messier story concerned another informal party where Bobby and Gore Vidal had a shoving match preliminary to a fight. "The story is that Gore put his hand on Jackie's ass or something," said Blair Clark, who was there, "but Gore's story is that he just brushed up against her. Bobby told him to get out of there and Billings came over and pushed Gore to prevent Bobby from hitting him." In a note to columnist William Buckley, Bobby wrote, "I thought I'd send some blood to the Viet Cong; now I think I'll send Gore Vidal."

Women reporters delighted in those stories. The First Lady, in turn, called them "harpies." She disliked one of them enough to refer to her as "that bitch"—she was wearing the same off-the-shoulder black velvet sheath dress at a reception—the reporter's dress, of course, being an off-the-rack imitation.

One thing was certain: The impetus for music and art in the White House came from her. She painted a scene to be made and sold as a Christmas card to help raise funds for a performing arts center in Washington. She persuaded her husband to appoint a special consultant on the arts, and got his agreement that a national cultural center be kept in one area instead of scattered around the city. She was the one who arranged for great performers of the world to use the White House as a show-case.

One such highlight was Igor Stravinsky, the great seventy-nine-year-old composer, whom the President had first heard when he was a Harvard freshman. Mrs. Stravinsky amused the President by telling him how the Paris audience in 1912 had disapproved of Stravinsky's first performance of his *Rite of Spring* by striking their canes on the backs of the seats. "Then they shouted that the music was horrible."

Mrs. Kennedy led the women into the newly redecorated Red Room after dinner while the President took the men into the Green Room. Stravinsky devotedly followed his wife into the Red Room until he was redirected.

Greeting some other guests, Stravinsky kissed them on the cheeks, in Russian fashion, when a voice was heard from the other side of the room: "What about me?" It was President Kennedy.

Mrs. Kennedy also persuaded Pablo Casals to perform at the White House. Pablo Casals was an old and proud man, the world's greatest cellist, and he had sworn never to give a perfor-mance in a country that recognized the dictator Generalissimo Franco. Republican Spain had been Casals' country and he had never forgiven Franco for destroying it.

But Casals had been caught and uplifted by the hope of Pres-ident Kennedy and here was this President asking him to play at a state dinner at the White House for the Governor Luiz Muñoz Marin of Puerto Rico—whom he also admired. His pre-vious White House concert had been in 1904, for President Theodore Roosevelt. Alice Roosevelt Longworth, who had heard him play then, was invited to hear him play there again.

Kennedy joked about the upcoming concert with Larry New-man. "Pablo Casals? I didn't know what the hell he played—somebody had to tell me." At the dinner, however, the presiden-tial remarks were more fitting. "We believe that an artist, to be true to himself and his work, must be a free man."

Good minds presented a challenge to Kennedy. "I'll have to think of some witty things to say to all those characters because there'll be a lot of hotshots there," Kennedy told Newman about his upcoming dinner for Nobel Prize winners. Schlesinger and Sorensen both worked on that speech, but the President added the final memorable fillip.

"Ladies and gentlemen: I want to welcome you to the White House. Mr. Lester Pearson informed me that a Canadian newspaperman said yesterday that this is the President's 'Easter egghead roll on the White House lawn.' I want to deny that! . . . I think this is the most extraordinary collection of talent, of human knowledge, that has ever been gathered together at the White House—with the possible exception of when Thomas Jefferson dined alone."

André Malraux's arrival warranted the royal Kennedy treatment. The First Lady made it a Washington gala, with Isaac Stern playing his violin, and her French chef outdoing himself with lobster, pheasant, and vintage French wines. The guest list included the great writers, artists, actors, and performers of our time. "All these people are used to earning their living using a pencil or a fiddle," commented playwright Tennessee Williams. "They are not used to talking. They were absolutely overwhelmed by being invited. If our mothers could see us now."

Jacqueline wore a pink strapless Dior and the President puffed on an Upmann cigar and told the guests: "I am very glad to welcome here some of our most distinguished artists. This is becoming a sort of eating place for artists. But they never ask *us* out!"

"Whenever a wife says anything in this town," the President remarked later, "everyone assumes she is saying what her husband really thinks. Imagine how I felt last night when I thought I heard Jackie telling Malraux that Adenauer was *'un peu gaga'*!"

The great success of the Malraux dinner spurred Kennedy family competitiveness. No two women were more un-alike in the Kennedy clan than Jacqueline and Ethel, and nothing illustrated this better than the dinners they gave for Malraux.

The wife of Assistant Attorney General Salvatore Andretta had observed, "We got the impression that, whatever Jackie did,

Ethel was quick as a flash to do the same thing. When the papers said Jackie was buying new china for the White House, Ethel selected a pattern of Lenox china with the seal of the Justice Department on it."

Jacqueline's dinner was absolute elegance, every detail, every dish, every flower. Ethel's party, later in the week, also a black-tie, long-dress affair, was outdoors. Ethel's guests always faced the same hurdles in the hall—a variety of animals. Malraux was no exception. He stumbled over two dogs, one a huge New-foundland that was easily mistaken for a rug.

It began raining in the middle of dinner, a heavy rain difficult to ignore. Astronaut John Glenn found the back legs of his chair sinking into the lawn and Ethel assigned someone to stand behind his chair to keep it upright. The more it rained, the more Ethel laughed about it. Malraux insisted he had "a perfectly grand time," and told the story for years afterwards.

Malraux's next book, *Voices of Silence*, was dedicated to Jacqueline.

The President rarely showed any public anger towards his wife. An observer vividly remembered, however, an incident in the Oval Office, at the time when Winston Churchill was being granted honorary American citizenship. All the guests were waiting for Mrs. Kennedy.

"When she finally came in," the observer recalled, "Jack was furious with her. He grabbed her by the wrist and said, 'God-damn it, can't you get here on time? Don't ever let that happen again.' It really was a tense episode."

On the other hand, the President was very proud of her when she spoke in Spanish before forty thousand people in the Orange Bowl. Bobby Kennedy had raised the ransom of $53 million in food and drugs for Cuba in return for the captured prisoners of the Bay of Pigs. At the Orange Bowl reception, the President told them, "I can assure you that this flag will return to this brigade in a free Havana."

More movingly, his wife spoke about their son. "He is still too young to realize what has happened here, but I will make it my business to tell him the story of your courage when he grows up. It is my wish and my hope that someday he may be a man at least half as brave as the members of Brigade 2506."

Family friend Jim Reed never forgot something else she said. "The three of us went for a swim at the Newport Beach Club. The place was crowded. Here was the President of the United States, but not a single person in that club either talked to him, looked at him, or even furtively smiled at him. They were all conservative Republicans determined to ignore him. As we were leaving, I commented on this and Jackie pointed to a long line of cars on the road to Hammersmith Farm filled with people waiting for a glimpse of the President. '*Those* are the people who are *important*,' she said."

*   *   *

"I saw a lot of her," said Blair Clark, who had known her for years and had known her husband since Harvard, "and I can tell you that she has a greater sensibility than people give her credit for. She could be cool sometimes, but not cold. And of course she liked gossip, but we also talked about much more substantive things. If she had been a snob, I would never have liked her. And I do like her. Very much."

"I had to persuade her to do that CBS-TV tour of the White House," Clark recalled. In an hour's television tour in February 1962, while almost one-third of the nation watched with wonder, she told the history of the house and what she had done to it. Her poise was so inbred that she could walk into any party, knowing nobody, and still maintain aplomb and presence. Faced with tons of TV equipment, nine looming cameras, and a tangle of several dozen technicians, she talked to host Charles Collingwood about yoga and asked if he could stand on his head. "Nehru tried to teach me," she said, "but I had to rest my feet against the wall."

"She never pushed us, although there were dinner guests coming," said Collingwood. "She didn't worry about her makeup or 'best' camera angles. When the director gave her instructions, she followed them exactly, just as though she had done nothing else all her life. If she was tired, she didn't complain and didn't show it. By the end of the day, *I* was tired, but she was fresh."

She also impressed Collingwood with her "shy manner, even

a sort of shy way of moving, very girlish and youthful yet quietly assured, though not arrogantly so. She speaks very precisely, enunciating carefully. She had a beautiful smile. She was perfectly groomed—with a simple, two-piece, plum-colored wool dress and a three-strand necklace."

CBS researchers had spent two months checking every piece of White House furniture, but Jacqueline Kennedy insisted, "I don't need any research. I don't need any script. I can do it right now."

Her retentive memory was even more remarkable than her husband's. When he needed a quote from Tennyson's "Ulysses," she recited it from childhood memory. "Beneath her wide-eyed manner she knows everything that's going on," said Arthur Schlesinger, Jr.

She herself supplied the show's opening, a letter to Congress from President Theodore Roosevelt that she had found in a book. Working without a script and wearing a "bosom mike," she wandered through the White House rooms, never once fluffing her lines. She seemed so relaxed and did it so well that the film shooting took only one day instead of the budgeted two.

"When General Grant became President Grant," she said in the East Room, "he put false elaborate timbers across the ceiling and furnished the room in a style crossing ancient Greece with what someone called 'Mississippi River Boat.'" As the camera zoomed in on Gilbert Stuart's portrait of George Washington, she said, "So many pictures of later presidents are by really inferior artists. I just think everything in the White House should be the best."

The President had a small part, was unhappy with it, and had it refilmed. It was also the first time he had called her "Jackie" on TV and he wondered whether he should have said "the First Lady." After watching the show in their small sitting room next to the Lincoln Room, the President was the first to congratulate his wife enthusiastically on her first American TV performance. "Terrific. Can we show it in 1964?" He later confided to friends how unhappy he was "not because Jackie had done so well but because he had so few good lines to say and she outshone him."

A TV critic called her "our uncrowned queen." One even gushed that she was "the most famous woman in history since Cleopatra." And another added, "She's already done more for modern woman than the suffragettes."

What pleased her husband most was how she had grown into her responsibilities.

*   *   *

At a rural housing project in La Morita, Mexico, the President stood on an unpainted platform under a spreading Saman tree and made a standard speech to polite applause. "There is one member of my party who does not need an interpreter," he continued.

Jacqueline had memorized a five-minute speech she had written at her husband's suggestion. A State Department interpreter had helped her polish it. "She was not very good in Spanish, but she was a very good student," the State Department man commented. "Her voice was delicious, an adorable voice, that sweet high-schoolish voice saying, 'El Presidente. . . .' " She spoke good Castilian without hesitation, keeping her hands behind her as she stood there. The two thousand farmers applauded almost every sentence and cheered and cheered at the end.

"She stole the show," observed Pierre Salinger.

Admiring Mrs. Kennedy's performance, a member of the group commented to a reporter, "That guy has everything."

Of course I screwed around when I was younger but you don't think I'd be crazy enough to do that now, do you?

—JOHN F. KENNEDY *to author, 1959*

A Marriage in Crisis

Two of the important things in the life of this President were his politics and his pain, and he shared neither with his wife—even though she was intelligent enough and strong enough to absorb them.

The President's instructions to his doctor, Janet Travell, were strict: "Don't go into my medical problems with Jackie. I don't want her to think she married an old man or a cripple."

Few photographers ever caught him using crutches. "He would hide his crutches and canes around the office," Evelyn Lincoln recalled. "It was hard for him to use them even in front of me. He used them mostly when he was alone. He was a proud man. But I used to buy those athletic rubber supporters for his back."

A female naval officer massaged his back two or three times a day. His minimum pain was equivalent to a toothache, but it could become excruciating. He had some quick-acting barbiturates that Dr. Travell prescribed. She had prescribed the same drug for John Kenneth Galbraith, who felt they caused "dullness and impaired judgment the next morning." When pain persisted, Kennedy sometimes sent a plane to New York to pick up Dr. Max Jacobson. Jacobson, later prosecuted for his use of drugs, injected amphetamines into a great many celebrity patients to increase their vim and vigor. Some said the drugs also heightened the sexual appetite.

If his back pain was in remission, and if his wife was away, the President would have his own private parties at the White House. "We saw Kennedy really tight only once," Ben Bradlee said. "The occasion was a small dinner in the family dining room upstairs, with only the President, Lee Radziwill, Bill Walton, and ourselves present. Jackie was out of town. The Twist had really hit Washington, and after dinner Lee put Chubby Checker's records on and gave all the men lessons. The champagne was flowing like the Potomac in flood, and the President himself was opening bottle after bottle in a manner that set the foam flying over the furniture, shouting, 'Look at Bill go!!' or, 'Look at Benjie go!' He practiced with the 'princess.' "

Princess Lee often came alone to her brother-in-law's intimate parties. "Lee was crazy about Jack," Jacqueline admitted. "No one was off limits to Jack," Smathers speculated, "not your wife, your mother, your sister. If he wanted a woman, he'd take her. I have no doubt he gave it a run with Lee."

Lee was the more mischievous, more feminine, more gregarious of the two sisters, and full of impulsive whims. She was also more interested in clothes than books. Between the two sisters there was intimacy, jealousy, love, and rivalry.

"He liked coming to my house, even after he was President, and I was very proud of that," Joseph Alsop said. "He and Jackie used to come six or seven times a year. We'd have a small, jolly party and I'd try to get those people I knew they especially wanted to see. I know enough of the world to realize that when you have the President in your house you can't think of anything at all except to give *him* pleasure. I always made sure that I never had the type of people who would grab at him and try to get something.

"And I always called him Mr. President, always, even in the

men's room. He'd not much liked it from people he'd known very well, but I noticed that the people who had the sense to do it came out in the wash rather well!"

* * *

How much of the Judith Campbell story was true?

It isn't every red-blooded American girl who can have simultaneous love affairs with both the President of the United States and a leader of the Mafia. Campbell claimed that Frank Sinatra introduced her to the President on February 7, 1960, in Dean Martin's hotel suite in Las Vegas. Sinatra, she said, also introduced her to Sam Giancana. "They both smoked Schimmelpenick cigars." She also reported that she had a gold cigar case made for each of them and sometimes went from the bed of one to the other's. Besides meeting the President some twenty times in the White House, Miss Campbell insisted she also lunched with him in the Oval Office and met him in New Hampshire, Los Angeles, New York, and Washington.

As footnotes, Miss Campbell mentioned that she was also a patient of the President's doctor, Max Jacobson, and that the President's youngest brother had tried to initiate an affair with her—which amused the President.

Seventy phone calls between her and the President were recorded in the White House log from the end of 1960 to mid-1962.

A Senate committee report on the CIA described her as "the President's friend."

Several recorded calls from Miss Campbell to the President came from the home of Salvatore "Sam" Giancana, also known as Sam Flood. Giancana was a Mafia leader recruited by the CIA to kill Castro.

FBI Director J. Edgar Hoover met with the attorney general and Ken O'Donnell on February 27, 1962, and detailed the President's relationship with Miss Campbell. The FBI concern was that Giancana would use his Campbell connection and his CIA relationship as a double blackmail against future prosecution.

Senator Church's Senate committee almost a decade later decided to subpoena Sam Giancana's testimony about his Mafia connection but Giancana was killed in his home in Oak Park, Illinois. The murder was not solved.

The Campbell affair ended in the spring of 1962, about the time that the President's affair with Mary Pinchot Meyer began.

"I really didn't know—and I swear I didn't know—that Jack was having an affair with my sister-in-law," Ben Bradlee said.

"I found out only afterwards. Someone in the family called to say that Mary had a diary she wanted burned after her death. Tony and I went over to her house and there was another friend of Mary's, a CIA agent. Mary had a studio right behind our house. The three of us searched for the diary and couldn't find it. When we found the diary, months later, there were several dozen references to Jack, and it was obvious that she had been having a love affair with him. We gave that diary to Mary's CIA friend to dispose of it."

Mary Pinchot Meyer had moved to Georgetown after her divorce from Cord Meyer, Jr., chief of the covert action staff of the CIA. She had known John Kennedy since college. She and Jacqueline were also good friends and would take long walks together along the tow path of the old Chesapeake & Ohio barge canal. In her diary Mary recorded that John Kennedy first asked her to go to bed with him in December 1961, but that their affair began early the following year. She reported visiting the White House several times a week when Jackie was out of town.

"I brought Mary to one of the White House parties, and she simply disappeared for a half hour," Blair Clark reported. And so did Jack. "Finally I went looking for her. She had been upstairs with Jack and then she had gone walking out in the snow. So there I was, 'the beard' for Mary Meyer.

"What did she look like? She was a very attractive, medium-blonde, half-serious girl with a mysterious hidden quality. Talented, cheerful, sexy, a super girl. Better than that, she was spectacular."

Mary told one of her confidantes that she once brought six marijuana joints to the President and they smoked three of them. He had laughed, saying, "We're having a White House conference on narcotics here in two weeks." He would not smoke any more, saying, "Suppose the Russians did something now."

Mary Meyer was mysteriously murdered, months after the President's death, and her murderer was never found.

Strangely enough, the Bradlees and the Kennedys were close friends, dining and sailing and partying together. The President would always ask Tony Bradlee, "How's your sister?" and Tony once petulantly asked her husband, "Why is Jack always asking about my sister? Why doesn't he ask more about me?"

Ben Bradlee often wondered if the President sometimes had seen him and his wife soon after he had had a rendezvous with Tony's sister, and whether this, too, was his way of adding excitement to his life.

None of these stories, although rumored, ever surfaced at the time. However, a strange story did emerge. A punster said it almost resembled a soap opera called "John's Other Wife."

In the Blauvelt family genealogy, published in 1956, on page 884: "Durie then married John F. Kennedy, son of Joseph P. Kennedy, onetime ambassador to England. There were no children. . . ."

The Kennedys and the Malcolms were neighbors in Palm Beach, and Durie Malcolm had been twice married and divorced. She and Jack Kennedy had dated in 1947 and a newspaper item noted, "She is beautiful and intelligent. A tiny obstacle is that the Kennedy clan frowns on divorce."

There was no record anywhere of a marriage. Sarah McClendon called Durie to ask the direct question and her breathless reply was "oh, no, no, no, no." John Kennedy called the story "too ridiculous to deny." A Blauvelt told a reporter that the genealogist was a careful man and "would not have put it in his book unless he was sure of the facts." Another Blauvelt insisted to the *New York Times* that he believed that there had been a payoff to the family to quiet the story.

Learning that *Look* magazine planned a story on the reported marriage, an unsmiling President warned one of its editors, "If you run that story, I may wind up buying *Look* magazine."

"That sounds like a threat," replied the unsmiling editor.

Kennedy also told his lawyer to warn the *New York Daily News* that they could publish that story "at their peril." However, he finally agreed to a *Newsweek* story. A marriage, if it had ever happened, would have had to take place in a brief interval between the woman's other marriages, and seemed highly unlikely. What intrigued both *Newsweek* reporters in interviewing Kennedy on the story was that "he never flatly denied it."

Family friends later admitted that the elder Kennedy, before his stroke, had heard the rumor and authorized his personal lawyer, James Landis, to investigate it. Landis discovered that Jack Kennedy and this woman were together in southern France when they unexpectedly met one of his mother's friends. "From the way Jack introduced Durie, the woman understood Durie was Jack's wife." But there were no other supporting facts.

The "other wife" stories might well have triggered Jacqueline Kennedy's trip to Italy to visit her sister. She took her daughter. Fifty Italian *paparazzi* swarmed into the narrow street below the Capitoline Hill in Rome as she entered the palace of Count Fernando "Dino" Pecci-Blunt. The handsome count was a Harvard graduate whom she and her husband knew well. An embassy spokesman vehemently denied there would be "a Twist party" at the palace that night.

The man she saw most was Gianni Agnelli, owner of Fiat, Italy's largest automobile manufacturer, who made his eighty-two-foot yacht available to her. Photographers trailed them to Ravello and Capri, where they visited small bistros and listened to serenading mandolin players. She was photographed on deck, barefoot, wearing green capri pants, and looking happy. The Washington rumors were that Mrs. Kennedy was getting "a bit of her own back" with Agnelli, because the President had been particularly attentive to Mrs. Agnelli.

One day a man would tell her, "Jackie, taking you out isn't like taking out a woman; it's like taking out a national monument."

She turned to him and giggled, "Yeah, but isn't it fun?"

The President was there at the Rhode Island naval station when his wife and daughter arrived from Italy. The Rhode Island governor gave them a sterling silver cocktail set and they took the helicopter across Narragansett Bay to her mother's home in Newport.

While his wife was in Italy, the President commented wistfully on his wife's frequent trips, "Ethel is *always* there."

The First Lady's popularity was strong enough then that she was not concerned about the negative publicity on her Italian trip. Years later, she said that the American public would forgive her anything "unless I run off with Eddie Fisher."

The President had small cause for complaint. To a close friend contemplating divorce, he said, "Why don't you try it the way I'm doing it?"

"I go home five nights a week," the friend replied. "You're in this Arabian Nights never-never land of the White House, and some nights you don't go home at all."

Kennedy called several nights later to confide to his friend, "You're right. If I had to go home three nights a week, I'd go up the wall."

Some of his resentment towards his wife cropped up when one of his biographers, James McGregor Burns, decided to run for Congress and asked for a Kennedy endorsement. Kennedy agreed and Burns wrote a script involving both the President and his wife. The President's response: "Please cut out any reference to my wife."

*　　*　　*

Among the women who intrigued President Kennedy most was Barbara Ward, Baroness Jackson of Lodsworth, a gloriously irreverent woman with a voice "compounded of grit and soft soap."

Lady Jackson first met Kennedy in 1945 when "he seemed so young—still hardly with the eggshell off his back." She knew then that this "cool" personality had little empathy for the trained, intelligent woman. Despite this, their relationship became close enough for her to act as his conscience and spur. "Of those outside government," noted Walt Rostow, "I believe only Jean Monnet ranked in the same class as Barbara Ward among those whose advice Kennedy was pleased to receive." As the brilliant editor of the *Economist,* she told him exactly what she thought on everything from economic assistance for India to a Volta River dam in Ghana. He called on her often to help him pinpoint emerging problems out of the "mush area" of American government. Their closeness came from the fact that they both wanted the same things for the human race.

*   *   *

The President's duplex penthouse suite at the Carlyle Hotel was a swinging bachelor's dream. It had some of the most spectacular views of New York City, giant picture windows, a white phone under his bed, and absolute privacy. The owner made it a point of personal service to call Kennedy's secretary to find out what book he was reading and what page he was on. When the President arrived, the book would be in his room, opened to that page.

His privacy was so complete that even the Washington pouch was not delivered to his room. When he was notified of its arrival, he came down to the lobby to get it. "Whatever happened in there, nobody ever knew," an aide said.

A few knew. A Hyannis couple told of being in the Carlyle elevator when in walked an old school chum of the President's, accompanied by a gorgeous blonde. The man explained, with some embarrassment, that this woman was an admirer of the President and wanted to meet him.

Reporters were always waiting in the hotel lobby. The Secret Service, however, discovered a series of tunnels beneath the hotel that connected to nearby midtown apartment houses and other hotels. This meant the President could attend small parties of intimate friends nearby without the press ever knowing about it.

"It was kind of a weird sight," Spalding admitted. "Jack and I and two Secret Service men walking in these huge tunnels underneath the city streets alongside those enormous pipes, each of us carrying a flashlight. One of the Secret Service men also had this underground map and every once in a while he would say, 'We turn this way, Mr. President. . . .' "

Kennedy held his own intimate party at the Carlyle suite after his celebrated Madison Square Garden birthday party, in May 1962, which featured Marilyn Monroe dressed in "skin and beads," singing a sexy, slithering, "Happy Birthday, Dear President Kennedy." Adlai Stevenson said of Monroe that night, "I do not think I have seen anyone so beautiful . . . my encounters, however, were only after breaking through the strong defenses established by Robert Kennedy, who was dodging around her like a moth around the flame." By the time Marilyn Monroe arrived at President Kennedy's private party, she was two hours late, and very nervous. The Madison Square Garden party had had all the loose excitement of a revival meeting and it had drained her.

"I could see her looking very fearful," recalled an intimate who was there, "and so I told her, 'You're doing better than you think.' Then I saw her eyes relax. If she was the last to arrive, she was the last to leave. I think Jack satisfied his curiosity about Marilyn Monroe that night."

"You know what she liked to do best? Laugh," Peter Lawford explained. "Marilyn had a natural kind of humor, the sort that just bubbles out of a person. She never fed you an old line; everything was fresh and quick, out of nowhere. And there wasn't a mean bone in her body."

The rumor about the President and Marilyn Monroe was an unfailing headline in the exposé magazines. Writer Joe McCarthy raised the question with Steve Smith. "Jack?" Smith said wonderingly. "But I thought it was Bobby."

"I remember a party at Pat Lawford's house in California," Joan Braden recalled. "I was sitting on the floor talking to Bobby when Marilyn Monroe came in. Pat kicked him and said, 'Bobby, this is Marilyn Monroe,' and Bobby kept right on talking to me. I whispered, 'Bobby *this* is *Marilyn Monroe*,' and it finally got through to him." What Marilyn did was to use her lipstick to write questions for Bobby, such as 'What does an attorney general do?' He answered the questions, then talked to her. A man there said to me of Marilyn, 'She's just never grown up and we have to take care of her.' I thought that was very funny."

"I remember walking with Bobby past a pretty girl," recalled an intimate, "and I said, 'What if she loved us? Would it be wrong to have a relationship with her?' Bobby's eyes twinkled, as if he had been thinking of it, too."

He had been the "straight brother," the "good boy," the happily married man knowing that his father and all his brothers had been womanizers. The time had come for the Puritan middle Kennedy son to break loose. The pattern of father and brothers was perhaps too much to ignore. The temptation of someone like Marilyn Monroe was perhaps too overwhelming. Robert Slatzer, an old friend of the actress, insisted that Monroe had shown him her diary detailing meetings with Robert Kennedy, that her final phone bill itemized a number of recorded calls to the Department of Justice, that she had told him, "Robert Kennedy promised to marry me. What do you think of that?"

Monroe's former husband, Joe DiMaggio, had heard about the affair. On Old Timer's Day at Yankee Stadium, Robert Kennedy extended his hand to DiMaggio but DiMaggio spurned it.

In her last days, living on drugs and hysteria, Monroe even threatened to hold a press conference to reveal her relationship with the attorney general, who no longer accepted her phone calls. A friend asked then if she had ever slept with the President, too. "I'll never tell," she replied. Shortly before she died in August 1962, she whispered to Peter Lawford, "Say good-bye to the President."

In a sworn deposition on the Monroe death, Robert Kennedy testified that he had gone to see her shortly before her death because she had been bothering his brother. He had taken a doctor with him and she had clawed at him when he held her so that the doctor could inject a tranquilizer. The final police report, condensing the 723 pages of original testimony to 53, made no reference to the Kennedy statement.

* * *

John Kennedy's forty-fifth birthday was a day like most other White House days:

A weekly meeting with Democratic congressional leaders about pending legislation.

A conference on the tumbling stock market with Secretary of the Treasury Douglas Dillon and other economic experts.

An unannounced visit to the Pentagon to talk to senior officials and officers, where he remarked on his rapid rise from a navy lieutenant commander to commander-in-chief of all American forces.

A meeting with Defense Secretary McNamara and other top military leaders.

A message to Congress for an election reform law, and a pact to the Senate calling for atomic cooperation with Belgium.

Announcement of a White House conference on narcotics.

A quiet family birthday party in Glen Ora.

It didn't matter much to him that he became the beneficiary of the second part of his father's multimillion-dollar trust fund. It might have amused him that the Board of Selectmen in Brookline, Massachusetts, put up a bronze plaque on his birthplace at 83 Beale Street. It might have worried him to get a CIA report about some new assassination threats. "If I am to die," he answered, "this is the week for it."

"You talk to McNamara, but mostly on defense matters," Bobby wrote the President in a memo. "You talk to Dillon but primarily on financial questions, Dave Bell on AID matters, etc. These men should be sitting down and thinking of some of the problems facing us in a broader context. . . ." In proposing that the President use the best minds in government in times other than deep crisis and emergencies, Bobby Kennedy put an asterisk after "best minds" and wrote in the margin "ME."

The Brothers: Jack and Bobby

"The two of them shared the presidency," Eunice Kennedy Shriver said of her brothers, Jack and Bobby. "They supplemented and complemented each other; not only worked well together but almost thought together. They sometimes seemed to communicate by a shrug of the shoulder, a shake of the head, a pause or a mumbled phrase; a shorthand of phrases. Jack explained it as a communication 'by osmosis. We're both cryptic.' "

Eunice, however, explained that the personal closeness of Jack and Bobby was exaggerated. "First, there was a difference in years [eight]. They had different tastes in men, different tastes in women. It was politics that brought them together. That's a business full of knives. Jack needed someone he could trust, someone who had loyalty to *him*."

"My motivations really could never be questioned," Bobby said. "There wouldn't be anything to be gained by me and I wasn't running for any office, so I didn't have any political future that I was attempting to work for."

With all the closeness of the brothers, somewhere deep was still the sibling rivalry. When *Time* magazine published a cover story on Bobby Kennedy, the President told correspondent Hugh Sidey, "A great story. Why don't you do one like that on me? You're always doing those good things for Bobby, but never me."

At a party on the presidential yacht, Bobby seemed slightly hesitant as to how to begin a toast to his brother. The President whispered a comment to a friend, "Bobby's all choked up. He can't deal with this occasion."

Bobby bristled when any reference was made to his relationship with his brother. When a State Department man referred to "your brother," Bobby snapped back, "You mean the President, don't you?"

His great value to his brother was that he could and did tell him to "go to hell" when they strongly disagreed. But once the President had made a decision, Bobby's support was then unshakable. Bobby was his brother's eyes, ears, and closest confidant; he was the first to arrive at a presidential news conference, and the last to leave.

Both Bobby's secretary and the President's secretary agree that "Bobby wasn't around the White House all that much." "Maybe a few times a week on a one-to-one basis," Mrs. Lincoln recalled. "And, of course, they were always on the phone together. But he just didn't come that much to the White House, except during the missile crisis, when he was there all the time."

Gen. Maxwell Taylor felt the President then was an impressive, appealing young man, but disorganized and unaware that his staff work wasn't good enough. He also felt that Kennedy was a loner with a natural suspicion of the people around him.

Taylor told Bobby: " 'You and I have the same objectives, I'm trying to help your brother and I know you are too. We must pass information. If you have anything on your mind you think I can help you with, pass it to me, and vice versa.' So we had a little conspiracy. I'd keep him informed on the President's military problems, and he'd tell me about the personnel problems. Here was the younger brother taking care of the older brother."

*　　*　　*

Word got out quickly. This new attorney general might drop in on anybody anytime. He was concerned, he asked questions, he really cared.

Morale zoomed.

They soon knew his moods. If somebody didn't do his job properly, the AG promptly let him know how *unhappy* he was. When he was angry, he was very controlled. In certain circumstances, he could be caustic. However, his loyalty to his staff was absolute. "Don't you pick on him," he told an outside critic, in reference to one of his staff. "This is my responsibility. If you have anything to say about that, say it to me."

They worked hard for him because, as his secretary, Angie Novello, said, "He treated you like you had a brain. He gave us jobs without spelling them out." He himself worked later than anyone, often until 9:30 PM. A random office photograph of Robert Kennedy always showed him with a telephone at his ear. Even in his limousine, he kept busy signing mail or reading.

"It's kind of a screwy job. You never know what you're going to do next."

When Bobby Kennedy first walked into his attorney general's office, he found a huge, elegant, wood-paneled room with a fireplace, big windows, and an oversize empty desk. On the bare desk was a bottle of aspirin and a note from his predecessor, William Rogers. The aspirin, wrote Rogers, was the most vital thing needed for this job.

One of the first things Bobby Kennedy said to his assistant was, "Let's take a look at what's happening in the department." The two then stalked the corridors, and Kennedy suddenly turned and opened a door, confronting another assistant facing a mass of papers.

"And what are you up to?" he asked.

The man explained the particulars of the case in which he was involved.

"Well, how long have you been at it?" Kennedy asked.

The man said he had started in February.

"Well, gee, it's May. Why should it take so long?"

The man explained, and they talked about it.

One of the things he poked fun at the most was his reputation for ruthlessness. "One day, Teddy called me from the hospital in Boston and said, 'You know, I think I'll hold a press conference and invite those New York reporters. I could really tell them about how ruthless you used to be to your younger brother.' "

He also joked about the family dynasty. Noting that the President, Vice-President, and Congress were then all out of Washington, he told an audience that he had just received a telegram from his brother Teddy: EVERYBODY'S GONE. I HAVE JUST SEIZED CONTROL.

A reporter who once caught him in an inaccuracy expected an outburst. Instead, Bobby laughed. "Well, I lie sometimes."

"Why do people hate me?" Robert Kennedy repeatedly asked.

He didn't have his brother's grace or tact. "I've felt that one should hold some part of one's self in reserve, never be too completely sure of being right," John Kenneth Galbraith said. "None of this suited Robert Kennedy's mood. His commitment was complete."

Robert Kennedy's world was black or white. He found it difficult to temper conviction with discretion. He was a man with fire in his belly. He wanted to climb the mountains, run the rapids, right the wrong. He had awesome energy, unshakable nerves, a bravura charm. Friends felt he almost had a joy in his hate. "Bobby had a vile temper when things weren't done as they should be," Evelyn Lincoln remembered. "The President would also explode, and sparks flashed, but just for a minute. Then it was all over. Not with Bobby. Bobby was vindictive."

Perhaps he was harder to like because he was harder to know. He guarded his inner self tightly and this sometimes gave an impression of coldness. Yet, when he heard about a reporter's alcoholism, he sent him to a clinic, picked up his bills, and found him another job. When his car killed a dog, "We went into every house, every single house, for ten miles, I suppose, until we finally found the owner," Spalding said. "Bobby then explained how the dog raced in front of the car, and asked if he could replace it or do anything else." Tell him an old lady in sneakers was outside his office and he would treat her like a queen. And his patience was unlimited when he taught a retarded child at Saranac Lake how to use a camera.

His courage was unquestioned. "Do what you are afraid to do," he wrote in his notebook, and underlined it. When the President's airedale, Charlie, jumped off the boat and seemed about to be sucked into the big ship's propellers, Bobby unhesitatingly jumped in and saved the dog. The President embraced his brother.

Ethel Kennedy claimed her husband wanted to be an astronaut. Alice Roosevelt Longworth insisted he should have been a revolutionary priest. Photographer Stanley Tretick told him, "You should be in the hills with Castro and Che." After a long pause, Bobby Kennedy replied, "I know."

"I don't think Jack needed causes," added Fred Dutton, "but Bobby did." On a world trip, Bobby used a bullhorn to confront thousands of students shouting anti-American slogans. Telling the President about it, Bobby urged, "So many of the young people of the world are against us. We've got to do something about it."

"All right," replied the President, "why don't you do it?"

Bobby then spurred a half dozen programs, bringing in large numbers of foreign students to discuss with their American peers all kinds of issues.

At a Gridiron dinner for Washington correspondents, Bobby Kennedy sang, "I'm his everything. . . ." And everybody laughed. But the President quietly told Larry Newman, "You know, there's only one President of the United States and that's *me*. I have no alter egos—including Bobby."

Hickory Hill, a big three-story white Georgian house (built in 1810) with a bright red door, sits on a six-acre hill in McLean, Virginia, about twenty minutes' drive from Washington. General McClellan used it during the Civil War as his headquarters.

Once Robert and Ethel acquired the place, it soon had a crescent-shaped driveway, a long sloping lawn, two swimming pools, a tennis court, a trampoline, a sauna, a cabana with a jukebox, and an obstacle course that most guests were encouraged to try that involved jumping off a roof, wriggling under sawhorses, climbing ropes, and diving over a bale of hay that landed you face first in the mud.

This is a house that had "the pandemonium of a hopped-up day camp combined somehow with a continuing campaign headquarters." Producer Leland Hayward came, saw, and said, "You know, this would make the damnedest musical comedy the Broadway stage has ever seen."

The society pages made most of the fact that people at Robert Kennedy's parties often got pushed into the pool.

"They made a big deal about it, but it was just a lot of fun," said Kennedy secretary Novello. "I always felt that Ethel was behind much of the pushing. Bobby went in once, and even I went in once, in my gorgeous chiffon. Wow, it was fun, a happy, wonderful evening. And after a few drinks, who remembers what happened?"

"I think Ethel must have fallen in three times," said one of the guests after a party. "The President was not there and I know he did *not* think it was funny. The rest of the country was appalled, amused, and maybe a little disapproving."

"There hasn't been anything as gay as this in my time," recorded columnist George Dixon, "and I date back to President Coolidge."

The social life of the New Frontier was frenetic enough—the rustle of *haute couture* mixed with an exuberant casualness was just as liable to wind up on the front page as on the society page. A careful reporter counted some six hundred noteworthy Washington parties that first Kennedy season.

Besides parties at Hickory Hill, there were the standard monthly seminars which included everyone from economist John Kenneth Galbraith to cartoonist Al Capp. These gatherings seldom had fewer than six or more than ten participants, and were always on a specific subject. Arthur Schlesinger, Jr., might talk about the Roosevelt years. USIA head Ed Murrow might open with, "How the hell can we expect to persuade foreigners if we can't get our own people to understand what we're doing, why we are doing it, and what is expected of them?" In a discussion on the Peace Corps, Ethel felt their work was brilliant, but they should not hand out "those things"—her reference to contraceptives.

★   ★   ★

"He had a fixation about businessmen," recalled Roswell Gilpatric of the Defense Department. "He didn't understand their motivations, the way they operated, the way they thought. Since I was a lawyer with a lot of business contacts, he was always calling me, asking me about them, trying to get me to explain them."

Kennedy didn't understand businessmen—he never really knew many. His father was hardly a typical businessman: He was a loner.

In April 1962, when the chairman of the board of U.S. Steel came to the President of the United States and asked for help, Kennedy was most sympathetic. U.S. Steel, after all, was an anchor of American industry. Besides, the President's own economic tendencies were conservative. What U.S. Steel wanted was government intervention for a reasonable wage settlement with the union to keep steel prices down. The President thought that a fair request. "So I helped them."

He brought the two sides together at the White House for "a little talk," Roger Blough, the head of U.S. Steel, and David McDonald, the head of the Steelworkers Union. Kennedy wanted them to hold down wage demands and steel prices. McDonald agreed to stay within the administration's 3 percent steel productivity guideline and offered to sign an agreement right then and there. According to McDonald, Blough "never made one commitment on prices, not one commitment. He talked around the mulberry bush."

"We got a splendid contract," Kennedy said.

"I want to thank you fellows for showing the kind of responsibility you have as Americans," President Kennedy told assembled steel union workers by telephone over a loudspeaker. "You're great pals of mine, great supporters of mine, all the time. But I think now you're doing something for your country, accepting this kind of agreement. . . ."

Their cheers were so intense that Kennedy was moved. "They're really great guys," he told Ken O'Donnell.

Then the President called Roger Blough to thank him, too, for showing responsibility in accepting the steel agreement. Blough's answer was cool, almost detached.

"Jeez, isn't it funny how different their reactions are," Kennedy said. "These cold bankers. I got *no* reaction from this guy. You'd think if the President of the United States called and thanked you. . . ."

McDonald returned home from the opening-day baseball game in Pittsburgh four days later to get a White House phone call. It was the President, "really, really angry," and he told McDonald, "Dave, you've been screwed and I've been screwed."

The elder Kennedy once had said, "When you deal with a businessman, you screw him first or he'll screw you."

Wearing his dark-rimmed glasses, Roger Blough had called on the President at the White House to hand him a four-page press release declaring that U.S. Steel was raising steel prices six dollars a ton. A furious Kennedy told O'Donnell, "You know what those sons of bitches just did? They raised prices. We had an agreement. The workers wouldn't take a raise and the owners wouldn't raise their prices. Now this son of a bitch comes in and hands me a press release and says, 'It's all done.' He hands this press release to the President of the United States."

Kennedy told Bradlee, "They kicked us right in the balls." The President suspected the steel industry had made a deal with Nixon not to raise prices until after the election—so that Nixon would not be hurt by it. "The question really is, are we supposed to sit here and take a cold, deliberate fucking? Is this the way the private-enterprise system is really supposed to work? When U.S. Steel says 'go,' the boys go? How could they all raise their prices almost to a penny within six hours of each other? They've fucked us, and we've got to try to fuck them."

Few on his staff had ever seen the President so angry for so long. "My father once told me that all businessmen were sons of bitches," he told them, "I never believed it until now."

The country's reaction was mixed. Business executives wore buttons saying "SOB. Sons of business." A cartoon showed two businessmen at their club, one of them saying, "My father always told me that all Presidents are sons of bitches." A Wall Street joke was, "When Eisenhower had a heart attack, the market broke. . . . If Kennedy would have a heart attack, the market would go up."

"Some time ago," Kennedy told reporters, "I asked each American to consider what he would do for his country, and I asked the steel companies. In the last twenty-four hours, we had their answer."

The President now hit the steel industry with the full power of government. "We were going to go for broke," Bobby said. "I told the FBI to march into their offices the next day and interview them all. All of them were subpoenaed for their personal records and company records. I had a grand jury waiting. I agree it was a tough way to operate, rather scary, but we couldn't afford to lose it."

The President liked fights, but he liked to win them. "There is no sense in raising hell and then not being successful."

To break the price rise, they had to persuade Inland Steel not to join the other steel companies. A group of White House advisers were in the Oval Office waiting for the critical call from Inland Steel, when another call came through. It was the governor of Delaware. A puzzled President listened, hung up, then asked his secretary, "Mrs. Lincoln, what the hell was that about?"

"That was the governor of Delaware saying that he was just installing the first telephone line to Washington, D.C., on a special circuit and he wanted the first call to be with the President."

Everybody laughed.

Inland Steel agreed to hold the price line but the President still wanted big steel companies to retract their price rise. He sent Clark Clifford to persuade them. Kennedy was no longer the sensitive, understanding President who refused to twist arms for a congressman's vote; he was now an angry President who felt betrayed.

Seventy-two hours later, the steel companies rescinded their price increases.

A tough President had won.

A front-page cartoon in the *New York Herald Tribune* showed Salinger after his return from Russia telling the President, "Mr. Khrushchev said he liked your style in the steel crisis." Later, at a party, Kennedy joked about it:

"I was talking to [Thomas F.] Patton [president of Republic Steel] this afternoon, and told him what a son of a bitch he was, and he was proving it. Patton said to me, 'Why is it that all the telephone calls of all the steel executives are being tapped?' I told him that I thought he was being unfair to the attorney general, and that I was sure that wasn't true. He asked me why the income-tax returns of all the steel executives all over the country were being perused. And I told him that, too, was totally unfair, and that the attorney general wouldn't do such a thing. And then I called the attorney general and asked him why he was tapping the telephones of all the steel executives. And the attorney general told me that was wholly untrue. But of course, Patton was right."

Bobby Kennedy interrupted, saying, "They were mean to my brother. They can't do that to my brother."

The President worried that Robert was overzealous in sending the FBI to wake reporters in the middle of the night to ask questions about a Bethlehem Steel stockholders' meeting. Bartlett called to say that Bobby also planned to indict a mutual friend on steel price-fixing. "What this administration needs more than anything," quipped the President after a pause, "is an attorney general we can fix."

There were many observers of the steel crisis who claimed that Kennedy had grown as a President. In that crisis he had grown out of anger; in civil rights, he would grow out of compassion.

*   *   *

Some Hickory Hill seminars concerned civil rights.

"We're in trouble with the Negroes," Bobby Kennedy told Harris Wofford. "We really don't know too much about the whole thing."

"What are Negroes really like?" Jack Kennedy once asked. "I've never spent any time with them."

He certainly knew no Negroes in Hyannis or Palm Beach, or at Choate or even Harvard. There were no blacks on his PT boat —the navy then kept its black sailors in the kitchen. The Kennedys didn't know any black people personally until they got into politics.

Kennedy told Bartlett about a group of leaders from the National Association for the Advancement of Colored People who had come to discuss a civil rights bill.

"They wanted a commitment," he said.

"Did you give it?"

"No," Kennedy gave a big laugh. "I showed them Lincoln's bedroom instead."

Roy Wilkins of the NAACP sensed this attitude. He talked about the arrogance of the White House staff, "not a black face among them. None of them brought to the table the anguish, the agony, the outrage that is so much a part of the black experience in America." Abe Fortas had an added view of Jack Kennedy's attitude: "He seemed quite oblivious to the impending social revolution. He didn't seem to realize that appointing some blacks to top federal government jobs really didn't do anything for the plight of the poor blacks in the ghettoes."

Kennedy had his own view. He felt he had come a long way when he invited his black White House aide Hobart Taylor to join him on his forthcoming trip to the South.

"No," Taylor replied, "I'd much rather you invited me and my family to come to Palm Beach."

Kennedy could not have made the passionate speech that Hubert Humphrey did at the 1948 Democratic National Convention in Philadelphia when he electrified the delegates on the national need for civil rights legislation to take blacks "out of the shadow of states' rights into the bright sunshine of human rights."

Civil rights was not something Jack Kennedy philosophized about. "We just didn't sit down, wring our hands, shake our heads, and have meetings about how awful it was about the Negro in Mississippi," said Bobby Kennedy. The most the President said about white rioters was, "Aren't they bastards?"

"Injustice, inequality, lack of opportunity, meanness, unfairness shocked him," said Bobby Kennedy about his brother, "and made him want to do something about it." But the President didn't believe in sending up civil rights legislation when he felt the Congress and the country weren't ready for it. "He didn't believe in just going through the motions on things," said his brother. The President wanted a legislative victory, not a moral one, added Sorensen.

"A civil rights bill? Jack just didn't have the muscle to push it through the House committee," O'Brien said. "Liberals didn't like it; southern Democrats didn't like it, and it's tough to get together a coalition to pass it when you've been elected on such a thin margin."

"What the Kennedys didn't realize is that we were not really in control," civil rights leader Andrew Young said. "A movement like ours is sort of like an ocean tide. You don't really stop it, but you might direct it constructively."

"At first Bobby was even less sympathetic to us than Jack," a black leader said. "He became more sympathetic because he was the kind of person who'd expose himself to things."

"I remember when we were driving through Harlem," said Defense Department deputy Adam Yarmolinsky, "and Bobby pointed to the rat-trap slums and said, 'If only I could do something about *this!*'"

Yarmolinsky, one of the Pentagon "whiz kids," a crisis-solver and a strong liberal, then thoughtfully added, "When I first knew Bobby, he was somebody I really didn't like. And I came to love him."

A new boil burst at the University of Mississippi in Oxford in September 1962, when the courts ruled that black James Meredith had a right to register as a student. The attorney general sent an aide to calm town leaders, and James Symington even shared their baked squirrel, using a lobster fork for the brains. His efforts earned a favorable article in the *Memphis Commercial Appeal* and a thank-you call from Senator Stennis. But it wasn't enough.

A young man happened to come to the Office of Legal Counsel to finish some work one Sunday. Deputy Attorney General Nicholas Katzenbach saw him and asked, "Will you go too?"

"Where?"

"To Oxford."

"When?"

"Now."

Before he got on the plane the young man called to tell his wife he wasn't coming home for dinner.

Mississippi Governor Ross Barnett insisted to Attorney General Robert Kennedy that the situation was peaceful and controlled. Kennedy listened quietly but exploded when he hung up. "They're lying." The President called Governor Barnett to warn him that law and order would be maintained, and that he was federalizing the National Guard.

First there were jeers, then acid-filled bottles, then gunfire. Students assaulted the building that housed Meredith. More troops arrived during the night. The President stayed in his office, rocked in his chair, paced the room, and kept going back to the phone.

The phone line from the attorney general's office to the University of Mississippi was kept open for twelve hours:

". . . Running out of tear gas. . . ."

"A guy is shot, we need a plane to get him out. . . ."

"Some of those guys outside have baseball bats with nails in them. . . ."

". . . We're improvising a jail downstairs. . . ."

". . . When is the airborne coming?"

The fighting stopped when the paratroopers arrived. When it was all over and everybody in the AG office collapsed, Angie Novello told her boss, "Boy, Bobby, when I'm reincarnated, I'm not going to work for *you*. I'm going to work for a janitor."

"And I'll be the janitor," he told her with a sad smile.

Framed on Robert Kennedy's bedroom wall:

> Seek to persuade the sea wave to break—
> You will persuade me no more easily.

On civil rights, Bobby Kennedy was now persuaded to break his waves. He had come a long way from the man who, a year before, had felt black protest marches were wrong because they took children out of school. Now he had in his office an Oxford souvenir, the beat-up helmet of one of his federal marshals. He now became the presidential prod on civil rights issues. "The attorney general has not yet spoken, but I can feel the hot breath of his disapproval on the back of my neck," said the President. The attorney general had tried to persuade the President that his first Supreme Court appointment should be a black person. This, he said, would mean more than a symbol. Instead the President picked his old friend, Byron "Whizzer" White, an all-American halfback and Rhodes scholar who had gone to Europe with him before the war.

Robert Kennedy also prodded Lyndon Johnson when he headed the President's Committee on Equal Employment Opportunity. An aide compared Bobby with the offspring of a parrot crossed with a tiger. "When he talks, people listen." Listening to one progress report, Bobby barked, "This is totally inadequate. Can't we do better than this?"

Dressed down like this in front of his own committee, the Vice-President was visibly affronted. More than ten years later, a week before he died, Johnson recounted the whole incident in dramatic detail to a friend. The fact was, Johnson had his own passion for civil rights. "He gets his bullets from a different direction," the President said.

*   *   *

"Stroke of a pen," the President muttered, "Who said 'stroke of a pen'? "

The phrase was a campaign reference in which Kennedy derided Eisenhower's inaction on civil rights and claimed that a presidential "stroke of the pen" could eliminate housing discrimination. It took Kennedy two years to lift the pen to make the stroke. Civil rights groups began an "Ink for Jack" campaign to send him bottles of ink for his pen stroke. Critics called his delay cowardice, claiming he was waiting for the moment to get maximum political mileage. "To have done it any earlier would have caused such antagonism and controversy that any gains would not have been worthwhile," Bobby Kennedy insisted. "An awful lot of people were anxious that we not do it before the election of '62, including some so-called quote liberal unquote congressmen from northern places like Michigan."

The President signed an executive order banning discrimination in housing—with some qualifications that pleased some southern senators. "If tokenism were our goal, the administration moved us adroitly towards it," Martin Luther King, Jr., commented.

King had not seen Kennedy much in the White House, but during one visit Kennedy had told him: "Nobody needs to convince me any longer that we have to solve the problem, not let it drift . . . but how do you go about it?" King later said of the President, "I think historians will have to record that he vacillated like Lincoln, but he uplifted the cause far above the political level."

Who is this Mrs. Kennedy that mother is always talking about? Is she queen of America?

—Son of a doctor on staff of All-India Institute of Medical Sciences

Ambassador Jacqueline

Jacqueline Kennedy's original travel plans to India and Pakistan "sounded informal and fun." "Jack says I'm young and ought to do things like this that I want to. Jack was so nice to let me come."

The short, private trip soon evolved into an expedition. The State Department and the U.S. Information Agency saw the trip as a goodwill gesture, a way of easing the growing friction between the United States and India after its seizure of the island of Goa. It became a semiofficial tour for the First Lady, lasting almost a month, in March 1962, with a press corps of a hundred.

"Jack spent the last day of his vacation screaming over the telephone on a poor connection telling Ambassador Galbraith to shorten Jackie's schedule, that it was worse than a political campaign. 'It's too much for her, I'm not going to let her do it.' "

"Jack's always so proud of me when I do something like this, but I can't stand being out in front."

One of the reasons Lee was going was that the two sisters were making a stopover in Rome to see Pope John, hoping to speed up the annulment dissolving her first marriage so that she and Stas would not be "living in sin." "You two better start practicing your curtsies so you can show His Holiness what fine Catholic girls you are," the President had told them.

"I was determined to curtsy three times on the way in, as you're supposed to do," Jacqueline said. "I did once, and then he rushed forward so I barely got in one more curtsy. I read in the papers I had an unusually long audience, but it didn't seem that long. It was all so simple and natural. He is so wise and understands both worlds—the world of men and the world of God. A person like that could affect your life and thoughts so much by telling you what to read and talking to you. When I think of the years I wasted when he was apostolic delegate in Washington and I didn't know him—I could weep."

Pope John XXIII asked about her maid Provie, sent her a special rosary, and later granted her a semi-private audience. Mrs. Kennedy presented Pope John with a book of her husband's speeches. They spoke in French. Some time later, the Church granted Lee her annulment.

Reporters wanted to know if Mrs. Kennedy had really brought along sixty-four pieces of luggage, a hairdresser, and a wig. "That's like asking a woman her age," answered Letitia Baldrige.

The First Lady later confided that she took only three half-filled trunks and one suitcase. "The only reason I took that much was because Lorraine Cooper [wife of Senator John Cooper, a former ambassador to India] said it might be so hot I'd have to change often." As for the wig, she admitted, "I did think of taking one, but I couldn't find one that looked natural. I did try one, but when I walked into the room, Jack said, 'My God, what have you done to yourself?' " And she had no hairdresser. "Provie put in the rollers. I can't do that, but I'm pretty good at combing it."

Jacqueline admitted they felt "scared to death." When they arrived in India she seemed "a bit stiff," shook a few hands, smiled but seldom said anything, and barely responded to the crowds. Prime Minister Nehru offered her an apartment in his home. Ambassador John Kenneth Galbraith saw this offer as a friendly sign because it was the same apartment used by Lady Mountbatten, wife of the last viceroy of India, with whom Nehru had had a celebrated love affair.

Nehru's daughter, Indira Gandhi, taught Jacqueline the *namaste*, the traditional Indian greeting with palms placed together. The first time Mrs. Kennedy did the namaste standing in an open car at Udaipur, the dense crowd went wild. "Jackie Ki Jai!" ("Hail Jackie!").

"I have promised her crowds several times larger than the largest so far attracted by her husband," Galbraith told reporters. A Rajasthan official verified, "Many more people have come to welcome Mrs. Kennedy than came to greet Queen Elizabeth."

"She is Durga, the goddess of power," said an old woman who had walked sixteen miles to see her.

"Nothing else happened in India while Mrs. Kennedy was there," said Prew Bhatia, editor of *The Times* of India. "She completely dominated the Indian scene."

"WEELKOMME TO MISUS KAANADYE," piped some well-schooled children.

Other children pelted her with rice in the ancient pink city of Jaipur; young women with jeweled rings in their noses sprinkled rosewater from a silver chalice around her feet and hung garlands of lotus blossoms around her neck—all symbols of good fortune. To ward off any remaining evil, a circle of women performed *arti*, an ancient ceremony, dabbing *tilak*, a tiny, reddish-brown dot, on her forehead.

Women sang a song to her. Translated, it said:

"These pearls, dived from the ocean deeps, are to adorn your beauteous head, dear Kennedy, we offer this with felicitations."

The venerable governor of Rajasthan then presented her with a gold-enameled necklace studded with diamonds and pearls. "Everybody loved her," said Indira Gandhi, and then, with the wonder of understatement, "Her appeal is different from that of an official diplomat."

"A camel makes an elephant feel like a jet plane," Jacqueline said after she and her sister took a sidesaddle ride on one, despite their straight-skirted dresses. Sitting in a heavily gilded two-seat howdah decorated with embossed roses, they also rode an eight-foot-high elephant named Bibi. The First Lady challenged one of the photographers to let the elephant pick him up with its trunk. The photographer politely refused.

"My wife took her *last* ride on an elephant," the President reported to the press, adding, "I know my Republican friends were glad to see my wife feeding an elephant in India. She gave him sugar and nuts, but, of course, the elephant wasn't satisfied." Getting more mileage out of his wife's trip, the President spoofed Sarah McClendon, the reporter who often asked embarrassing questions at press conferences. "I saw a picture of my wife watching a snake charmer. As soon as I learn Sarah McClendon's favorite tune, I'm going to play it."

The First Lady pointedly told Ambassador Galbraith that she did not regard this trip as a glorified fashion show. He then instructed the press secretary not to volunteer any fashion information to reporters, unless specifically asked. Earlier, reporters had queried Galbraith:

What did she wear when she went riding?

"What do you mean, what did she wear?"

Did she wear boots?

"I don't know. Sure, I guess she wore boots."

Did she wear a hat?

"Yes, I think it was a sort of a hunting hat."

Her day dresses were always brightly colored, fitted and sleeveless, and her evening dresses, much photographed for the papers, seemed to be increasingly spectacular. She wore pearls, diamond chandelier earrings, and a ruby-set diamond pin clipped under her modified topknot.

"In a nation known for its grinding poverty," wrote one newsman, "she has not hesitated to dress herself in high fashion. Moreover, the Indians love it."

At the Taj Mahal, the jewel-like building with its marble dome and scintillating slender minarets set in a formal garden lined with cypress trees, she was told that this was a memorial built by the Mogul emperor Shah Jehan for his favorite queen, who died giving birth to her fourteenth child. In the setting sun, Jacqueline Kennedy had studied its symmetry from different angles. Reporters asked for her reaction.

"But what can a person say, except 'wonderful?' "

What can anyone say about the Taj Mahal when there is a mass of reporters "hanging on your every word?" "Isn't it funny?" she told Joan Braden. "I always felt myself, but with so many reporters watching, listening, how can anyone not seem like someone you're not?"

When she slipped off her shoes and put on velvet slippers to visit the Gandhi memorial, a reporter from the *Chicago Daily News* checked her shoes and cabled home, "I can state with absolute authority that she wears 10A and not 10AA."

Nothing about her was too insignificant for the newsmen. They noted she drank her own supply of bottled water, brought from Washington, D.C., and had bread brought in from Beirut for the cream cheese sandwiches she liked for lunch. But they also observed that she willingly ate wild boar curry—the wild boar killed only hours before—as well as paprika and chili peppers baked until crisp. She also seemed to like *burfi*, an exotic Indian sweet made of condensed milk, and some small sugar candies wrapped in thinly pounded silver, the sugar making the silver more digestible.

She admired two gold statuettes studded with tiny precious stones, but balked at the price.

"Why not send the bill to your husband?" suggested Galbraith.

Mrs. Kennedy barely smiled.

Newsweek reported that the First Lady was perhaps spending too much time seeing princes and palaces instead of the poverty of the real India.

"That wasn't one of your better efforts, was it?" the President complained to Ben Bradlee. "She's really broken her ass on this trip, and you can always find some broken-down Englishmen or some NBC stringer to knock anything. I don't get all this crap about how she should've been rubbing her nose in the grinding poverty of India. When the French invite you to Paris, they don't show you the sewers. They take you to Versailles. When we have distinguished visitors, we take them to Mount Vernon. We don't take them to some abandoned coal mine in West Virginia. Ken Galbraith told me that Jackie took all the bitterness out of our relations with the Indians. If I had gone, we would have talked about Kashmir and Goa. But Jackie did a hell of a job."

"Before we left Washington, I said I wanted to spend one night in a village," Jacqueline revealed. "The date and the village had been decided upon, but somehow it got out of the schedule. You know, the Indians decided our trip, and I don't blame them. They could have shown me their deepest poverty, hoping I'd go home and say they needed more aid, but they were too thoughtful for that. They just wanted us to have magical memories of an enchanted visit."

Jacqueline insisted on seeing the erotic carvings of the Black Pagoda of Konarak, including —as Galbraith described it—"one accomplished woman making love to two violently tumescent men at the same time." Galbraith was concerned that a photographer might take a picture of her there.

"So, sheepishly, I went to her husband," Galbraith recalled. "Kennedy said only, 'Don't you think she's old enough?' "

Kennedy was increasingly critical of Galbraith's conduct of the tour. "There is to be no, repeat no, repetition of the following," he said in one cable, and in another, "No, I *don't* think . . ." To his staff, he complained, "That goddamn fool is keeping Jackie longer. I told Jackie. Damnit, I told Galbraith . . ." In an angry moment, he said, "If you gave Ken a good enema, you could bury him in a cigar box."

The First Lady and Prime Minister Nehru had quickly formed a close friendship. Nehru gave her a variety of gifts, a dozen books on Indian art, and two caged tiger cubs ("Can't we let them out?").

"He was terribly good to us," she said of him. "He spent an hour or so each day walking in the garden with Lee and me. We never talked about serious things—I guess because Jack has always told me the one thing a busy man doesn't want to talk about at the end of the day is whether the Geneva Conference will be successful, or anything like that."

Holi is the day all Indians throw colored chalk powder at one another, regardless of caste, to signify the triumph of good over evil. "They [the Secret Service men] didn't want me to play

Holi," recalled the First Lady, "because they said the powder was made from manure. I said I didn't care, and I did it anyway."

Nehru dipped a finger into the red powder and dabbed it delicately on her forehead. She did the same to him, and it matched the red rosebud he always wore in his buttonhole. She then reached into the green powder to put some on the Indian ambassador to the United States. When he stepped back, she tossed it onto the shoulders of his coat. And when he reached for some green powder to put on her, she laughed and slapped his hand, sprinkling the green powder on his natty suit. It was not very statesmanlike, but the Indian observers loved it.

At departure time, Nehru told her how much she had enriched "the psychological pull" between the Indian and American people. Mrs. Kennedy spoke of her own sadness at leaving India. "At the end of every day," she said, "I could not decide which day was best."

In a letter to the President, Ambassador Galbraith described Nehru as "deeply in love." "He has a picture of himself strolling arm in arm in the garden with Jacqueline displayed all by itself in the main entrance of his home. . . ."

*   *   *

Pakistan and India were such intense rivals that the Jacqueline Kennedy visit now became a matter of dramatic importance for Pakistani President Ayub Khan. Somehow he must outdo the tremendous Indian success.

None of this mattered to Jacqueline Kennedy. The trip so far had been exhilarating, but exhausting. It was particularly trying to her sister. They would sometimes ride together, but most often "I'd go ahead with the most interesting person and Lee would follow along five cars behind," Jacqueline remembered. "By the time I got there, I couldn't even find her." At Fatehpur Sikri, the First Lady watched Indians diving 170 feet into a 50-foot pool. Her sister arrived too late to see it, so Mrs. Kennedy asked the divers to do it again. When the day was done, the sisters "would always have such fun laughing about little things."

Pakistan was a Moslem man's world. It was highly unusual

for the President to greet the First Lady at the airport with the full honors due a head of state. This was the same Moslem leader who refused to greet a representative of King George VI because "he was only the king's brother."

"Have any sleep?" Khan asked Jacqueline Kennedy.

"A little."

This trip was a turning point for her, just as Paris had been. De Gaulle, Khrushchev, Nehru, and Khan found her fascinating and she discovered how much at ease she was with them. Crowds put her on a pedestal and they no longer frightened her. She could wave to them, warm to them. In the minefield of international diplomacy she had made no mistakes. She was now no longer a young woman who had married a famous man; she was now a famous woman married to a famous man. She was now a fit consort.

"I just pray I was all right," she told Joan Braden on the plane home. "I'm glad I went but I'd never take a trip like this again without Jack. There were moments, like the time in Lahore at the governor's house, when I sat at the window and looked at the fantastic lighted trees reflected in moonlit pools, and wondered what I was doing so far away alone, without Jack or the children to see them."

Her husband had little wish to visit that part of the world.

"He really disliked Nehru," Bobby claimed. "Nehru was really rude to us when we went to India in 1951. Jack and Pat and I went to see him, and he was terrible." Nehru had offered Jack Kennedy the *pièce de résistance*, the eye of a lamb served on a gold plate. Kennedy stared at it, then popped it into his mouth, and gulped it down. Now that he was President, Kennedy found Nehru just as difficult to talk to, just as stuffy and opinionated. "It's like trying to grab something in your hand, only to have it turn out to be just fog. . . ." When the President later made a short speech that sounded like a jumble of words, he apologized, "I've just spent three days with Nehru, and that's what happens after listening to him talk for that long."

As a private joke, Kennedy once took Prime Minister Jawaharlal Nehru past the great mansions of Newport's millionaires and told him, "I wanted you to see how the average American lives."

* * *

While Jacqueline was away, the President drafted his sister Eunice or his mother to act as White House hostesses at state functions.

Every Kennedy had a favorite sister. When Kathleen died, it was "Eunie" for Jack. "They had the same psychological makeup," her husband noted. "They were even subject to the same ailments."

"Eunice not only could make Jack laugh," Dave Powers remembered, "but she could also bawl him out for something he ought to be doing."

Once Eunice swam unconcernedly near a school of sharks, and the sharks scampered away. When she was out of danger, Jack yelled at her, "See, Eunie, even the sharks are afraid of you!"

A ticking time bomb, Eunice was a restless woman strung together with high tension wires who spoke in a staccato stream, paced the floor, and thumped the table. "I've never known a woman who tried so hard to beat the hell out of a man on a tennis court," confided her husband. "If Eunice had balls, she would have been President," insisted her father.

Reporting to her father on her brother Jack's early speeches, she said, "He's pretty good, Daddy, but I could do it better." She was not only a good speaker, but an impressive one. Long, leggy, with a wiry grace, she had a striking face with bold bone structure, a mop of tawny hair, and soft blue eyes. She was also a superb mimic, particularly of the British.

When Eunice married Shriver, one of the wedding ushers met them accidentally at the airport on their way to their honeymoon in Portugal. Young Ted Kennedy was there, too. Their friend said wasn't it nice of Ted to meet them there, and Eunice said, "Oh, Ted is coming with us." "But not on your honeymoon trip?" "Why of course," Eunice replied. "Ted wanted to do it with us a long time ago. It was all arranged and decided."

She was as religious as her mother, and as outspoken as her father. As one of her friends put it: "If you phone her at seven in the morning, thinking you can get her, you can't—she's at early Mass. Talk to her about women's lib and motherhood, she will tell you, 'Women's lib has been good in [combatting] job discrimination and things like that, but it's resulted in a downgrading of the whole concept of motherhood.' "

She reluctantly admitted that her father was probably a male chauvinist because "he had all kinds of political plans for his sons but nothing for his daughters." Eunice was the only one among her sisters to seek secular higher education after finishing convent school. She graduated from Stanford University with a degree in sociology, and then worked with the retarded in Chicago and Harlem. "If my [retarded] sister Rosemary had never been born, I would still be doing what I am." Her husband agreed. "She really loves the people who have the least. In any room she'll seek out the loneliest person."

When his wife was away, and John Kennedy wanted somebody from his family to talk to and laugh with, he never called Bobby, he called Eunice.

*   *   *

Rose Kennedy at seventy seemed to be in her prime, and happily substituted as White House hostess when her daughter-in-law was away. She still told her President son to keep his hands out of his pockets and to wear a striped tie on TV "because it's chic." She still kept up a flow of notes to her children, reminding them of religious holidays and that "apples are a good buy this season: Be sure to stock up on them."

She also kept an eagle eye on the White House staff when they came down with the President to her Palm Beach home. After one visit, she complained to the chief usher that the staff had left "a lot of dirty dishes, pots and pans, and linens strewn around the kitchen. I should appreciate it if you would tell the staff to leave everything clean in the future, as we have had trouble with rodents."

"Rose was amazing," Defense Secretary Robert McNamara recalled. "I remember the first time I saw her at a White House party. She was on the reception line just ahead of me, waiting her turn to shake hands with her son. And she introduced herself to me, 'I'm the President's mother.' "

Discussing her son's presidency and what it meant to her,

Rose Kennedy confided, "My husband was never one to social-
ize, you know. He was always working. . . . When he took time
off, Mr. Kennedy usually preferred sitting around to visit with
his old faithful companions. But once in a while, particularly
when he was the Ambassador, we would have marvelous times
. . . all my life I've adored parties and balls. . . .

"You reach a certain time of your life when you think it's all
over and the only things you have to look forward to are creak-
ing bones and an aching back, but for me life is just beginning,
and it's all new and shining. I can hardly believe it."

Adlai Stevenson made her smile by calling her "the head of
the most successful employment agency in America."

She was in the presidential helicopter, en route to meet Emperor Haile Selassie of Ethiopia, when she pointedly informed
the air force aide: "I'm trying to bring up these children properly, and I can't get it through Jack's mind that a woman walks
out first. I am a lady and I know what ladies should do and I
want to walk out of this helicopter first!"

McHugh passed on this message to the President.

"Well, I don't want that," he said. "I love my mother, but as
President of the United States, I will walk off first. I'm charging
you with seeing to it that she doesn't get off first."

As the helicopter landed and the door opened, McHugh so
positioned himself behind the President that Mrs. Kennedy
could not get past him. The President walked out very fast with
McHugh very close behind him, and then came the President's
mother, running to catch up. To the waiting crowd, she said,
"I'm Rose Kennedy, mother of the President."

"And now I'll tell you something you may find interesting,"
she told a reporter. "I have just come home from Paris, and
skirts are longer and tighter there!" She also reported the bikinis
on the Riviera were shorter. "Put that in about the bikinis, because everyone thinks I'm so saintlike!"

She sometimes arrived for a visit unexpectedly. The President took George Burns and Carol Channing to see the eight-
foot bed in the Lincoln room. He opened the door and quickly
closed it. "Sorry, the tour is off. Mother is in there."

To a Philadelphia TV audience, Rose Kennedy confided, "I

used to say that a lot of women have been the mothers of one President, but there's never been a woman who's been the mother of two or three Presidents, so I've told my other sons to get busy."

I have never kept it a secret from my family that I don't think much of people who have it in them to be first and who finish second. If you've got a second choice, then you haven't got a first choice. I also have a theory that if, after you've done the best you can, you still don't come in first, put it out of your mind. Forget it.
—JOSEPH P. KENNEDY

25

The Patriarch

Joseph Kennedy had created an incredible godfather myth—four sons without a rebel in the crowd.

He was seventy-three and the color had faded from his reddish hair but his handshake was still firm. He had the same toothy grin of his children as well as the carriage of a retired army officer.

"And to this day, not one of the boys has beaten me at anything," he said, smiling broadly. Then he added, "But I think they may have thought that I retired from tennis a bit too early." He had last played tennis with them in 1935, when Joe, Jr., was nineteen and Jack was eighteen. "But I beat Bobby and Teddy at golf the last time I played them, and that was last spring."

Asked how he felt about being the father of the first Catholic President of the United States, Joseph Kennedy said, "That's nothing. If Kathleen and her husband were living, I would be the father of the duchess of Devonshire and the father-in-law of one of the titular heads of all the Masons of the world."

"You know, when he visits me, he still borrows my socks, if I have some clean ones," Joseph Kennedy said of the President.

He thought of something and got grim. "I've gone to his bedside to watch him die. But he fought back. Jack is a fighter. He'll do the right thing."

The phone rang and he picked it up and listened and said, "Yes, Doctor." When he finally hung up, his voice trembled again. "That's the terrible thing about growing old—your friends go, old friends. You can't replace them."

That conversation was just two weeks before he had his own stroke in December 1961. Dave Powers never forgot the last words he ever heard Ambassador Kennedy speak. Jack and Jacqueline had spent the night in Palm Beach after their trip to Latin America, and they were on their way to Washington. Still dressed for golf, Ambassador Kennedy had gone to the airport to see them off. In his good-bye to Dave Powers, the Ambassador said, "Take good care of him, Dave."

The Kennedy patriarch had taken his four-year-old granddaughter to the airport to say good-bye to her father. Later there were other grandchildren to romp with, and then off to the Palm Beach golf course. At the sixth hole, he sat down suddenly on the grass and told his niece that he was not well. She took him home. Just before going to his bedroom, he sternly warned Jacqueline and his niece, "Don't call any doctors." Soon afterwards, they found him unconscious on his bed and hurried him to the hospital with a motorcycle escort. He had had an intracranial thrombosis, a blood clot in an artery of the brain, so deep that it was inoperable. The chaplain there gave him the last rites of the Catholic Church.

Jacqueline called Washington. Pierre Salinger remembered how stunned the President looked when he put down the phone. "Dad's gotten sick."

The hospital waiting room for the Kennedy clan had a bronze plaque. It read, "In memory of Joseph P. Kennedy, Jr., donated by Mr. and Mrs. Joseph P. Kennedy, Sr." Children and relatives took turns in a round-the-clock vigil, listening to the distant Christmas carols of fifty girls from the Rosarian Academy Glee Club at a hospital Christmas party.

For two days, there was no flicker of recognition from the father. Three reporters were always with the President at the hospital, representing the pool of reporters. They watched his silent pacing. Was there anything he could say, asked one of the reporters.

The President shrugged his shoulders, put up his hands almost beseechingly. "Hell, there's no way to write that. . . ."

The reporter persisted. "Well, is there *anything* you can say about it, Mr. President?"

The President groped in silence and obvious despair and then said, "We're just hoping and waiting." At the Kennedy Palm Beach home, the secretary of state arrived with an entourage to prepare the President for his scheduled conference with Britain's Prime Minister Harold Macmillan in Bermuda.

Just as they arrived, Kennedy got word that his father was having moments of wakefulness. With barely a nod to Rusk and the others, Kennedy and Jacqueline and Pierre Salinger hurried off in his white Lincoln Continental. When they emerged from the hospital room an hour later, the President was visibly more relaxed, his face brighter, and Jacqueline was beaming. Trailing behind, Salinger told the press that the elder Kennedy had "shown recognition" when his son bent over him.

After he recovered, Joseph Kennedy could examine his financial portfolio and understand it. He could smile and nod and say "no" very clearly. His eyes could light up. When he tried to say something, his children strained to understand. The father still dominated the dinner table simply by his presence, but the President was no longer fidgety when his father was around. Associates recalled how his father's presence once made the President tap his front tooth and stroke his jawbone more often than usual. Now the President showed the same kind of tender concern towards his father as he did towards his children. He would sit with him for long stretches, trying to understand his father's gibberish.

"If my Dad had only ten percent of his brain working," the President once said, "I'd still feel he had more sense than anyone else I know."

They would take him on a wheelchair ride, sail with him on

the presidential yacht, make him the center of attention at dinner, dip him into the pool on a dunking chair.

"It was strange to me how so many people still talked about the father's influence over Jack even though it was after the father's stroke and the father couldn't even talk at the time," Ormsby-Gore said.

When the stricken father first saw the Oval Office, with his son as President, the tears streamed down his cheeks. The President kept talking, pretending he did not see his father crying. Then he moved his father's wheelchair over to his own rocker near the windows.

"This is my rocker, Dad," he said, sitting opposite his father. "It looks as though we both need special chairs, doesn't it?"

Some months later, the elder Kennedy was taken to the famed Rusk Institute for Physical Rehabilitation in New York for further treatment. The family inspection team swept in. "Everything works, Dad," Bobby yelled, after flushing the toilet and checking the plumbing. Eunice never entered a room, she exploded into it, always in a rush, her hair tossed, her laugh gutsy. "Oh, Daddy, Daddy, you're a real whopper," she would say to him. Before she saw him, she always checked first with his doctor for a progress report. And, always, she would tell her father, "You can do anything you want to. Anything at all."

Jacqueline's warmth and tenderness were never more visible than when she was with her father-in-law. When she came, she brought a sense of quiet with her. She sat on a footstool in front of him, and said, "I'm praying for you every day, Grandpa, so you work hard while you're in here." She put her head in his lap and when he placed his hand on her cheek in a caress, she kissed his hand, then stood up to kiss his cheek. While his children ignored the paralyzed side of his body, she made a point of holding his useless hand and kissing the deformed side of his face.

Jacqueline read the newspaper to him, chatted about the children, told him funny stories about Jack. When he was ready to walk for the first time, she alone was there to watch him and brought him a beautiful, glistening, black walnut walking stick inscribed, "To Grandpa with love, Jackie." She praised his every step, and when he faltered she stood in front of him, held out her arms, and looked into his face. "Come on, Grandpa! You can do it, you *can* do it!"

He did it, walking the full length of the corridor.

"Oh, Grandpa, do you have any idea how proud I am of you? How very proud?"

Then she took out her handkerchief and wiped the tears from his eyes and hers.

The President shed his own tears months later when he watched his father grab a pole and pull himself to his feet without anyone's assistance. He rushed over to his father, embraced him tightly, kissed him, and said proudly, "Oh, Dad!"

When they took him to Palm Beach, the First Lady sat between the chauffeur and her father-in-law and started to put her arm around his shoulder, when he stopped her. With great effort, he turned slightly in his seat, stretched his left arm and put it around her shoulder to hug her and pat her cheek.

Jacqueline impulsively told her husband she wished his father lived with them at the White House. "You know how I feel about him," she said. "Just love him."

* * *

The three brothers went over to their father, picked him up in his wheelchair, and carried him into the dining room where the family had gathered. It was their father's seventy-fourth birthday. And suddenly he was surrounded, kissed, and nobody was more lovingly affectionate to him than his three sons.

Before the grandchildren entered their grandfather's room, Ethel Kennedy had a speech for them: "Everything we have, we owe to Grandpa," she told them. "Everything! So when you go in to see him, remember that everything you have, every toy, every pet, the house we live in, everything, we owe to Grandpa."

Ethel Kennedy usually wrote the skits for her father-in-law's birthday parties, and there were usually roles for everybody in the family, even the small children. They not only memorized their roles, but they rehearsed together.

When the play was over, they all lined up in front of him in family groups to sing "Happy Birthday." Joan and sometimes Rose Kennedy played the piano; Teddy sang "When Irish Eyes

Are Smiling," usually off-key; the father kept time with his foot or his hand; and then all of them sang the old Irish songs. When it was all done, including the cake and ice cream, each Kennedy kissed him separately and wished him happy birthday. The President was always last.

The President was at Hyannis Port another time when his father had a sudden seizure. He called for his own doctor and ordered him to stay with his father while he called the New York specialists. When he returned, his doctor was not there—he had gone to get some medical supplies.

The nurse recalled this incident as the only time she had ever seen the President "lose his cool."

"Oh, that's just great," the President said. "Just great. When I say I want the doctor in here with my Dad, that's damn well what I mean. So you go over there, tell him that I said he's to sit with my Dad all the time, and I mean all the time, until the other doctors get here."

Such was the power of the presidency that a whole covey of specialists arrived from various places by special planes that evening.

Discussing her disabled husband, Rose Kennedy commented: "I sometimes wonder what life is all about." She also told neighbors of her future plan, "When Mr. Kennedy dies, I'm going to sell this big house and get an apartment."

A reporter later tried to probe the Kennedy matriarch a little more deeply, and she responded, "Why should I bare my emotions?" Then she added, in mock protest, "I don't need the publicity."

Only occasionally would Rose Kennedy complain aloud about her husband's condition. "Why do these things have to happen?" She had said: "I think to lose a husband when you're young . . . is much more severe and heartbreaking than for a mother to lose her son."

In fact, her husband would outlive three of their sons.

Dear Mother,

It is the night before exams so I will write you Wednesday. Lots of love.

P.S. Can I be godfather to the baby?

> —JOHN F. KENNEDY *at the age of fourteen, on the birth of his brother Ted*

Teddy: The Godson

"I don't know why the House isn't good enough for Teddy," the President told Bartlett. "It was good enough for me." Bartlett had told him he planned to vote for Lodge, who was a personal friend. Kennedy replied that he understood, and added, "If the old man only left Teddy alone. . . ."

The President had told his father, before his stroke: "We ought to have one playboy in the family, and that's Ted. Don't force him into politics, Dad. Let him be the playboy." Ted agreed. If he could do what he wanted, he told friends, he would set sail for the Caribbean, hobo, idle, explore "and just plain live."

Ted Kennedy now insists, however, that he saw his brother shortly after the presidential election and "talked to him about what I might or might not do. He had talked a lot about arms control during the campaign, and I told him I was really interested in getting into arms control. He listened to me and then he said, 'Look, if you're interested in politics, pack your bags this afternoon and go back to Massachusetts and start getting around.' That's when I went back to work as an assistant district attorney."

Anyway, his father had made up his mind about Ted's future. Minimum age for a senator was thirty and Ted was only twenty-nine, and he would barely qualify. His only experience was as an unpaid city attorney in Boston. He idolized his brothers, but he explained, "The disadvantage of my position is being compared constantly with two brothers of such superior ability." When he went to see his brother John with a new idea, the President was apt to examine Teddy carefully behind his ears and say, "Hmmm, still wet, I see."

"Aw, Jack," Teddy would say.

Ted was what they called in Boston "a corner guy," a man who enjoyed standing around on the corner talking to people. He enjoyed it much more than his brothers did. His was "an Irish potato face, planes going at every angle, broad forehead, chin like a fist, chipmunk jowls. . . ." Jack Kennedy playfully captioned a picture of Ted with a bulging cheek, "Honey Fitz's grandchild stores nuts for the winter."

After he became senator, Ted Kennedy had that picture framed and proudly pointed it out to a visitor, once again smiling at the memory of it as he read aloud the caption.

His early reputation was "helpless, hapless Ted," and yet "he could talk a dog off the meat wagon." He was the kind of son who could not say no to his mother and yet not the kind who opened his wallet to show family pictures. Not a voluminous reader or a piercing intellect like his brother John, but, according to political pro James Farley, "Ted had more moxie."

"I don't think people would expect me to sit on my hands for the rest of my life because my brother is President and my other brother is attorney general," Ted said. "I wasn't brought up that way. Listen, this thing is up for grabs and the guy who gets it is the one who scrambles for it. And I think I can scramble a little harder than the next guy."

"The only argument I ever had with Jack that I could remember was about Teddy's decision to run for the Senate," Spalding said. "I thought it was a big mistake, that it laid the Kennedy family open to all the dynasty charges of too many Kennedys."

Furthermore, if his brother ran and lost, it would be a hard political slap against the President in his home state. Bobby was unhappy because he had thought of running for governor, and Teddy's candidacy would close this option.

The Kennedy patriarch was unwavering. "You boys have what you want now and everyone else helped you get it," he told John and Bobby. "It's Ted's turn now. Whatever he wants, I'm going to see that he gets it."

Or, as one of his sisters put it, "Teddy has to do *something!*"

The clincher was a poll by the Massachusetts state Democratic chairman that showed Ted would win both the nomination and the election, while Jack Kennedy's preferred candidate, his former roommate Ben Smith, would lose to incumbent Massachusetts Attorney General Edward McCormack, favored nephew of the Speaker of the House, John McCormack.

The Kennedys were great believers in polls. The President and his White House staff now gave Teddy the green light. As the President told Dave Powers, "Why, it's like giving up a Senate seat if Teddy doesn't run. . . ."

*   *   *

The fact was that the Kennedy coattail was a mile wide. Nobody knew it better than Ted; nobody used it more. "Ted Kennedy, whose brother, incidentally, is President of the United States"—that was the typical introduction. "Jack used to kid me about using his coattails," Ted Kennedy said, "but I noticed that everytime he spoke in Boston, he never wanted to be introduced as 'John F. Kennedy,' but as 'John *Fitzgerald* Kennedy.' So I used to kid him about always using our grandfather's coattails." Ted followed that up with a joke about two brothers who went fishing, with one brother catching all the fish. The other brother went out alone the next day, borrowing his successful brother's line, hook, and worms. He still didn't catch anything. A fish finally jumped out of the water and asked, "Where's your brother?" Ted then told the audience, "I hope none of you wonderful people is going to ask me, where is my brother?"

Ted made his oratorical debut in a speech before the Young Democrats of Palm Beach, Florida. Salinger called a reporter who was there. "You-know-who wants to know how his brother did."

"You can tell you-know-who that it was the lousiest speech I ever heard in my life—Teddy made absolutely no sense on any subject."

One night, at the beginning of the campaign, Ted called the President, a little discouraged. "What are you doing up there?" asked the President.

"Well, I got a speech on Africa which is putting them to sleep," replied Ted.

"How long is it?" asked the President.

"Goes about forty-five minutes."

"Oh, you've got to cut that," said the President.

"That's tough; what am I gonna cut?"

"Well," said the President, "If I can cut the State of the Union message to four thousand words, you can cut *that* speech."

Whatever happened now reflected on the President. His prestige now rode with his youngest brother. Ted had to make no mistakes. And he had to win big.

"The hot issue in Congress then was aid to education," Ted Kennedy recalled. "I knew my brother was trying to work out a compromise and the discussions were very delicate. And so when I went on 'Meet the Press,' the moderator, Larry Spivack, naturally asked me how I stood on that issue. Afterwards my brother called up Spivack and asked, 'How did Teddy do?'

" 'He did very well,' Spivack said, 'but I couldn't figure out his answer on education.'

"And my brother said, 'Perfect!' "

What were his qualifications for the Senate, a reporter asked.

"What were Jack's when he started?" Ted Kennedy countered.

"Teddy was a shrewd, tough operator," columnist Joe Alsop reported. He insisted to his audiences loud and clear and often that his brothers weren't running his campaign. "However, I would appreciate their votes at election time." But Teddy still met with his brothers at Hyannis for long sessions on weekends.

He also picked up his brother's 1952 slogan, "HE CAN DO MORE FOR MASSACHUSETTS."

"If his name was Edward Moore, his candidacy would be a joke," proclaimed his rival in the primary, Edward McCormack. "Nobody's laughing when your name is Edward Moore *Kennedy*."

Ted felt good at the gate of a factory when a worker told him, "Teddy, me boy, I hear that you have never worked a day in your life. Let me tell you, you haven't missed a thing."

The critical point of the campaign was the Kennedy-McCormack TV debate. The President sent Bobby and Ted Sorensen to spend the day preparing Ted on the issues. Teddy was not as cool as Jack nor as hot as Bobby. His father had drummed into him the dire need to control his temper—bite your lip but never make a personal attack.

He sat on a high stool, his face tense, as he heard McCormack say, ". . . You've never run for elective office. . . . We need men with consciences, not connections."

Teddy had his hair combed like his brother Bobby's, and now he contained his aggressiveness like his brother Jack. He responded quietly, "If we are to move forward, we shouldn't talk personalities or families—we should talk about the people's destiny in Massachusetts. . . ."

"Jack and I were in Florida on a boat," Smathers said, "when we had to rush back because he wanted to watch Ted's debate. I think he was more nervous about Ted's debate than he was about his own Nixon debates."

"They told me how he [John] couldn't sit still," Ted Kennedy said, "how he was pacing up and down, walking in and out of the room."

After the debate, Lyndon Johnson told the President, "You know, he's the best politician in the family." The President agreed. "He can hold an audience much better than any of us can—he has better political instincts."

"I'm not running as a Kennedy, but as a candidate of the Democratic Party," Ted kept insisting, while everybody smiled. "I have disagreed with the President before and I imagine I will disagree with him in the future."

The President seemed solemn when he said, "I will not take

part in the campaign except to vote. My brother is carrying his campaign on his own."

"This may be true," columnist Mary McGrory said, "but it's about as descriptive as saying that Marlene Dietrich is a grandmother and that the Prince of Wales is a schoolboy."

*　　*　　*

Campaigning came hard for Joan Kennedy. She was pregnant again. "I don't campaign for fun," she said later. "I do it for Ted." Jean Kennedy Smith defended her on this. "I don't think it's necessary for women to stomp all over the place for their husbands. After all, *they're* not the ones who are running!"

Joan felt her greatest kinship with Jacqueline. "I admire her more and more for going her own way where the Kennedys are concerned. The family can be overwhelming. For years I went along with everything they said because I didn't dare to do otherwise. I tried to be like the Kennedys, bouncy and running all over the place. But I could never be that."

*　　*　　*

The President and his wife were entertaining twenty-two guests at Hammersmith Farm on primary election day. The President was anxious to call Boston for the first returns, and ate dinner quickly. The President was always served first. As soon as he finished, his plate was removed. At the same time, the plates of all other guests were picked up, regardless of whether or not they had finished the course. At this point, guests talked less and ate faster. By the time guests had eaten their second spoonful of a delicious ice-cream dessert, the President stood up saying, "I guess everyone is through," and left the room.

"The reason he was so worried," Ted Kennedy remembered, "was because somebody had showed him a poll of Boston taxi drivers which had me being beat 128 to 70. That made him very edgy."

When the President returned, the woman next to him asked about the election. His face lit up. "Teddy is winning big. It looks like a landslide."

The President joked that Ted had wanted to make it on his own and even considered changing his name.

"To what?" someone asked.

Kennedy smiled. "To Roosevelt."

On Election Day Ted Kennedy won more votes in some areas than his brother had years earlier. "Not bad for a callow youth," said Steve Smith, his campaign manager. To the reporters' first question, Ted answered, "No, I haven't talked to the President." Comedians now had a new reference: King Kennedy III.

On the plane to Washington, the reporter was impressed with the way Ted Kennedy detailed the dire needs of unemployed shoe and textile workers in his state. "You know we've got to do *something!*"

Ted Kennedy's swearing-in ceremony was simple. His brothers were *not* there, but his mother and wife were, along with family friend Benny Jacobson. His sisters arrived with their husbands for the office reception and they all ate chicken sandwiches on brown bread. Responding to a question on what help he expected from the administration, Teddy answered smoothly, "I hope they would extend me the same kind of assistance they would give to any senator."

What he said in an insistent aside to a friend was, "What no one can understand is that I don't EVER want to be President."

He probably meant it then.

*   *   *

"When Teddy became a senator, he didn't even know where the men's room was." As the youngest member of the U.S. Senate, he was properly quiet and respectful, sitting in the back row of the far section on the Democratic side, wearing a blue suit and a serious tie. With the double-edged impact of his name, he had the delicate, difficult job of keeping the Kennedy aura but stepping out of the Kennedy spotlight.

Ted used the desk that godfather John had used in the House and Senate, a modest-sized English antique desk that had belonged to their father. All around his office walls were photographs of the Kennedy brothers sailing, laughing, campaigning, playing football. There was also a painting of a destroyer plunging through heavy seas, the U.S.S. *Joseph P. Kennedy, Jr.* On the wall of his office was a message framed in gold: "This office represents the people and products of Massachusetts. Signed, Edward M. Kennedy."

His office, Room 432 in the Old Senate Office Building, had a small, cramped reception area with five straight-backed chairs, and a staff of ten secretaries in adjoining offices. It may have been one of the most cluttered offices on Capitol Hill but also one of the busiest. Some seventy-five visitors a day and three thousand letters a week, many of which began, "Would you please tell your brother, the President. . . ."

"That first year in Washington, both Ted and I were feeling our way, trying to make good impressions," his wife revealed. "We avoided the White House like the plague. I think we only went to dinner there once or twice—and then, in the small family dining room upstairs. Which is sad, considering that it is the only year we spent in Washington while Jack was President."

Kennedy aides assumed that the brothers had had an early understanding on minimizing their appearances together. "I think he must have called his brothers together and said, 'This is the way we do it. . . .' "

"There was no such family conference," Senator Ted Kennedy said. "Keeping our distance in public was a natural thing. After all, I didn't want to have people think he was calling the shots on my votes. In the first place, he didn't have to—we both believed in the same principles, thought alike on the big issues. We parted company on some votes that I thought might hurt Massachusetts. It's true that Joan and I only went to a few official functions together. But my brother and I liked each other too much to stay away from each other. We really enjoyed each other—we always did have a special relationship. I've got that letter on the wall over there, when he wanted to be my godfather.

"Anyway, what I did was to stop by on the way home from the Senate and go into the Oval Office by the back door at the end of his working day. Then we'd have a daiquiri, take a swim together, then just sit around and talk about everything. Sure I'd make him laugh. We'd gossip about the Senate. I remember him laughing about a story I told him about Senator Robertson's story at a prayer breakfast. Robertson told about the pharaoh's daughter coming back with the baby Moses and saying, 'Look what I found in the bulrushes . . .' Then Robertson added with a wink, 'That's what *she* said!'

"I remember during the summer, when Jackie and the kids were away, the two of us would go upstairs and have dinner alone and sometimes spend the whole evening just talking and laughing. Sometimes, on a weekend, we'd all go off to Camp David—without the press knowing about it. Or on a Sunday, we'd fly over the Civil War battlefield sites. He was fascinated by the Civil War."

There were also the family parties at the White House. Ben Bradlee described one of them when their father was there. Bradlee remembered "Jack roaring with laughter at some of Ted's stories."

The evening was movingly gay, because the old man's gallantry showed in his eyes and his crooked smile. Bobby and Teddy sang a little two-part harmony for him, calculatedly bad and off-key. For an encore, Teddy did his imitation of Honey Fitz, bearing down on the false-tooth lisp, and everyone applauded, especially Old Joe. "Only he applauds with his eyes."

Joe Kennedy's handshake was strong, even though he used his left hand. Jacqueline supported him as they went in to dinner, kicking his right leg forward between steps since he couldn't move it himself. Niece Ann Gargan walked slightly to the rear of him, giving further support. As he ate, and drooled out of the right side of his mouth, Jacqueline quickly wiped his lips, keeping up a running one-sided conversation reminding him how he and Judge Morrissey had helped persuade Jack to marry her. Jack commented on the high quality of the crabs his father had brought from Florida. "I must say, there's one thing about Dad," the President said. "When you go with him, you go first class." Ben Bradlee noted that the President asked his wife, Tony, to crack his crabs for him, probably because his back was bothering him. The President joshed his father about the Churchill citizenship ceremony that day, which his father had glimpsed. "All your old friends showed up, didn't they Dad?" Most of the men there had been longtime enemies of his father.

When it was time for his father to go to bed, they all came up to shake his hand or kiss his head.

Other family reunion times were the occasional weekends at Hyannis.

Ted was riding his tandem bicycle once with his wife, his child in the handlebar basket, when he suddenly saw his father watching. To make his father laugh, Ted wiggled his handlebars, threw his hands in the air, and stretched his legs out straight. His father laughed and laughed.

Ted had his prime time at the Women's Press Club, his first public Washington speech since his election.

His opening line brought down the house: "Well, now that we are *all* here at home. . . ." He assured his audience that there was no reason to think he was emphasizing his connection with his brother "just because I had a rocker installed in my Senate seat this afternoon. . . ." As for his influence at the White House, he had gone down to make some suggestions to the President about a major speech "but all I got from him was, 'Are you still using that greasy kid's stuff on your hair?' "

"Are you really independent?" a reporter in the audience asked.

"I'm independent," he answered. "I've been helping him [the President] for a number of years, and I think it's time he stood on his own feet."

"Some pipeline I have into the White House," he told Bradlee. "I tell him a thousand men are out of work in Fall River, and four hundred men are out of work in Fitchburg. And when the army gets that new rifle, there's another six hundred men out of work in Springfield. And so you know what he says to me? 'Tough shit!' "

Ted talked of his struggle to pull himself out of his brother's shadow. But the President had also told a Boston audience that "my last campaign, I suppose, may be coming up very shortly— but Teddy is around, and, therefore, these dinners can go on indefinitely."

After his election, John Kennedy had given Ted a gold cigarette case engraved enigmatically, "And the last shall be the first."

But one of the Republican jokes of the time was:

Question: If Jack, Bobby, and Teddy were on a sinking boat, who would be saved?

Answer: The country.

VI

The Times of
Trial

I have a curious and apprehensive feeling as I watch JFK that he is sort of an Indian snake charmer. He toots away on his pipe and our problems sway back and forth around him in a trancelike manner, never approaching, but never withdrawing; all are in a state of suspended life, including the pipe player, who lives only in his drama. . . . Someday one of these snakes will wake up; and no one will be able even to run. . . .

—DEAN ACHESON *in a letter to*
President Truman

27

The Missiles of October

One of the snakes woke up in October 1962. Our government suspected the Russians were sending missiles to Cuba.

Missiles in Cuba meant that our entire east coast was under nuclear threat. When he took office, John F. Kennedy had said, "Before my term is ended, we shall have to test anew whether a nation organized and governed such as ours can endure. The outcome is by no means certain." Before the nuclear age, any President in crisis could go to sleep knowing he would wake up in a living Washington. This was no longer true.

*   *   *

A publisher at a White House luncheon bluntly told the President that our cold war policies weren't cold enough, that we had to make clearer that we could annihilate Russia, that "too many people think you are riding Caroline's tricycle."

"I'm just as tough as you are," the President replied, "but

the difference between you and me is that I was elected President of this country and you were not. And I have the responsibility of the lives of a hundred and eighty million Americans, which you have not."

The President's back had been bothering him and he went to bed early on October 14, 1962. In another part of Washington, the secretary of state was enjoying himself at a party when he received an unexpected visitor—the head of State Department research and intelligence. On his return home, Secretary Rusk's face was pale. He quickly called McGeorge Bundy, White House coordinator of security affairs, to inform him that we now had confirmed photographic evidence of the missiles. Bundy decided against waking the President. "Let him get a night's sleep. He'll have enough trouble in the morning."

Analysts later presumed why Khrushchev had made this move. Khrushchev would have understood if Kennedy had left Castro alone or destroyed him in the Bay of Pigs invasion nineteen months before. But when he saw a young President rash enough to strike at Cuba but not bold enough to finish the job, Khrushchev decided he was dealing with an inexperienced leader who could be intimidated and blackmailed. That's when he gambled with the missiles.

At six-thirty the next morning, Bundy walked into the President's bedroom and woke him with the bad news: The Russians were coming. Enlarged photographs had been double-checked and cross-checked by CIA and military analysts. The President reacted with short, hard, Anglo-Saxon words. Sitting in his tub, the President listened to Bundy's background briefing on the crisis, and continued listening as he ate his breakfast and dressed. Dave Powers arrived with his morning schedule and thought, "God, he looks like someone has just told him the house is on fire." As Powers left, Kennedy asked him, "Dave, will you make sure that Adlai Stevenson comes to the mansion upstairs after dinner?" His initial decision was to maintain absolute secrecy and keep to his prepared schedule so that nobody would suspect anything. He asked Bundy to return to his office later that morning with more details. Bundy recalled the President's first comment: "I'm going to call Bobby as soon as I get to the office."

That morning the astronauts arrived at the White House for their handshake, small talk, and PT boat pins. When they left, six men walked into the Oval Office with their proposals that might end the world. The joint chiefs of staff had prepared their "horse blanket," their attempt to cover all options. In one column, they put down all possible events. In another, all agencies involved in order of priority. In twenty-five pages they detailed the range of options that might determine the world's fate. "My God," murmured the President, "this is just what I need."

"When they give me these decisions to think about, I'm interested in the little things, the details," Kennedy had said earlier. "I want to know from A to B to C up until where it comes to me, where I have to make the decision. I don't necessarily agree with 'the buck stops here.' I think that what Truman really meant was 'OK, I want all the input. But when they don't give it to me, I've got to dig into their minds to find out how they came up with certain things.' "

The President depended on no one—not even the secretary of defense—for definitive information. He had many sources. One of them was called PIC (President's Intelligence Checklist). Prepared by military aide Ted Clifton, it culled a variety of intelligence sources, including covert material that bypassed the CIA. Clifton digested each item in any given news story. If the President wanted to know more about a particular item, he checked it and soon received an amplified four-page report. For a time the President was its only reader.

* * *

Heads of state did not like to be kept waiting and the President had a lunch date with the Crown Prince of Libya. Bobby hurried along with him to the dining room, conscious of a poem by Robert Graves that he carried in his wallet:

> Bullfight critics, row on row
> Crowd the enormous plaza full
> But there's only one man who knows
> And he's the man who fights the bull.

Never before and never again would these two brothers be as close as they would be in the next thirteen days. During that period, the President not only learned more about how to use people, but how to test them. He knew that his presence in a room changed the chemistry of those present, changed their words. "The prince often gets to hear what he wants to hear," Admiral Hyman Rickover reflected. "Everybody in high places stands in a room full of mirrors and sees himself multiplied by servile reflections." Within the "shadow of the President," some waited to hear what he said, then agreed with him. Others felt intimidated and did not say what was on their minds. Bobby was one of the rare few who said exactly what he thought to the President.

There was a panel discussion that afternoon in the Cabinet Room on some proposed reforms in the food and drug law concerning the effect of drugs on a fetus. The President seemed solemn, indulged in none of his usual banter, but listened attentively and asked some hard questions.

He sent a plane to California to pick up CIA Director John McCone, who was attending his stepson's funeral. The President decided, in matters connected with the crisis, to use Bobby as his deputy to keep him abreast of minute-to-minute developments. He also told Bobby to maintain his private discussions with the Russians.

It seemed an unlikely liaison. A man named Georgi Bolshakov, supposedly a Russian Embassy public-relations man, was actually a direct contact for Khrushchev with the President's brother. The practical Russians simply moved in where the power was. The two had met every two weeks for some time, discussing everything from Berlin to nuclear weapons. Through Bolshakov, Bobby had persuaded the Russians to get their tanks out of Berlin within twenty-four hours to defuse an earlier crisis. Now, however, their meetings took on a fresh urgency. Bolshakov insisted that there were no missiles in Cuba. After reporting all this to Moscow, Bolshakov received a reply to the President "so insulting" that Bobby refused to accept it. "That really was the end of our relationship." Bolshakov was recalled.

The President himself saw Russian Foreign Minister Andrei Gromyko in Washington. The stone-faced, unflappable Gromyko, after two hours, again denied the missiles' existence. Facedown on the President's desk were the missile pictures, but it was not yet determined whether they were defensive or offensive. At a meeting of the executive committee of the National Security Council, the President exploded, "Goddamn it, is that an offensive or a defensive weapon? We will not tolerate offensive weapons in Cuba."

As they swam together in the White House pool that day, the President told Powers, "I had the strongest desire to go over to Gromyko and say, 'What the hell is this?' If I had the conclusive pictures, I'd have difficulty keeping from ramming them down his throat."

After the meeting, he talked with some of his staff, including his brother. He discussed the miscalculations of the Germans, Russians, Australians, French, and British in World War I, how they stumbled into war "through stupidity, individual idiosyncracies, misunderstandings, and personal complexes of inferiority and grandeur." Bobby remembered, "He did not want anyone to be able to write, at a later date, and say the U.S. had not done all it could to preserve the peace."

"You make a thousand decisions," noted President Kennedy. "You're lucky if six hundred turn out right and only four hundred are wrong." He told his advisers that he didn't want their advice to begin with the phrase "from a military point of view." His view had to be the broad view.

"You could see his mind working," General Taylor recalled. "A compression in time and space of crisis decision making. What made him more furious than anything else was not the fact of the missiles but that senior Soviet officials had lied to him. What we couldn't understand was why in the world they'd put themselves out on such a limb without any idea of how to scramble back? Our question was whether there was a surprise behind the surprise?"

The President emphasized that Khrushchev was unpredictable and said, "Let's not push this guy into a situation from which he cannot get out." Schlesinger added, "Kennedy refused to show emotion, not because he felt too little, but because he felt too much."

*   *   *

Her name was Phyllis Mills and she worked in the White House. On the way home a car crashed into her automobile. "I'm in the hospital wondering whether I'll ever walk again, and I get a note from the President, giving me some courage. I hardly knew him but he had heard about my accident. And the reason it meant something so special was that it was right in the middle of the missile crisis. Yet he took time out to write this note to me."

*   *   *

Ted Kennedy called Sorensen that week. He didn't know what was happening but he had heard rumors. He was planning to make a speech on Cuba and wanted to clear the idea with Sorensen. "Get another topic," Sorensen said.

*   *   *

The Alsops were having a party for the newly appointed ambassador to France, Charles "Chip" Bohlen, and the President was coming. They gave their usual small dinner party for ten, a mixture of "old Kennedy pals like the Bartletts" and people like famous philosopher-historian Isaiah Berlin. The President and his wife arrived on time, but seemed somber.

"It was October and rather chilly, but he and Chip went out into the garden and it seemed as if Chip was arguing with him," Joseph Alsop remembered. "He was asking Chip not to leave for France just then, but Chip pointed out that if he changed his plans it would immediately arouse suspicions among the Russians. He was dead right, of course, but it must have been very hard to resist the President. When they said good-bye in the hall, Chip said, 'Unless you see some reason I'm wrong, sir, I really ought to go. . . .'

"I think it was one of the finest things Chip ever did. Of course, I didn't know any of all this at the time, didn't know about it until long afterwards."

The President and Bohlen talked for some twenty-five minutes. Susan Mary Alsop was concerned about the lamb "becoming uneatable." The President apologized for delaying dinner. "The President sat at the head of the table and he damn near threw a ruin on the evening because he was in such a deep brown study," Alsop said. "He was beyond any effort of any of us to get through to him."

In the course of the meal, Susan Alsop noticed a strange thing. She heard the President asking Bohlen and Berlin what the Russians had done in the past when they were backed into a corner. She heard him ask the same question, slightly rephrased, a second time. "I was sitting next to him and I think I was the only one to notice this and I realized how unusual it was because he never ever repeated himself on any question. And that night in bed, I told Joe, 'Darling, there's something going on. I may be crazy, but I think something is going on.'

" 'I think you're crazy,' he said. 'It was a delightful party even though the President delayed the dinner. Damn him, he really did ruin the lamb.' "

* * *

Maintaining his announced schedule, the President went to Connecticut on October 17th. Bobby was waiting for him at Andrews Air Force Base when he returned. His news was gloomy. There were still no conclusive pictures that the missiles were offensive. A U-2 pilot had gone back for more photographs.

With the weight of the world on their shoulders, the two brothers spent an hour with their father. He had slept the night before in the Lincoln bed. The two brothers tried to cheer him up, telling him funny stories, remembering a hundred family anecdotes, never once mentioning Cuba. Then they kissed him good-night.

* * *

The latest photographs were conclusive. The Russian missiles were offensive.

"Well, you know all the shit is going to hit the fan when you tell him that," CIA Deputy Director Ray Cline said. Cline made some calls using double-talk over the phone. Cline's daughter, who had been eavesdropping, asked, "Dad, I can't tell whether those missiles are in Cuba or China. Which is it?"

Bobby Kennedy took no one's word. He went to the basement of the White House to check the photograph evaluation for himself. His comment to Bundy: "Shit, shit, shit!"

The President's first reaction was similarly angry. "The son of a bitch lies to you, rubs it in your face, and you have to take it," he said of Khrushchev. His quieter reflection was something he himself had written: "Never corner an opponent, and always assist him to save face. Put yourself in his shoes—so as to see things through his eyes. Avoid self-righteousness like the devil —nothing is so self-blinding." Then he stood there looking at the famous magnolia tree planted by President Andrew Jackson at the end of the rose garden. "I guess this is the week I earn my salary."

His question, he said that week, was like Lincoln's: whether he could control events or whether events would control him.

An air strike or a blockade? How surgical is an air strike? If the strike missed a single missile, could that missile wipe out Washington? What about an invasion? How much force would that take: how many ships, how many divisions, how many planes, how many casualties? How many would die? And the blockade—could we do it without a declaration of war? Was it a violation of international law? How would the world see it? How would the Russians react if we stopped one of their ships at sea? Would war now with Russia mean the end of the world?

*   *   *

Too many limousines at the White House would have attracted too much attention, so some went to the Treasury Building, which had a secret passage through the White House bomb shelter into the White House basement. No senior official canceled normal appointments, so some meetings were held close to midnight. One Executive Committee meeting with Defense Secretary McNamara and CIA Director John McCone was held in George Ball's conference room on the seventh floor of the State Department while Secretary of State Rusk was giving a prearranged dinner for Gromyko on the eighth floor.

"Slow Track" was the code name for the blockade; "Fast Track" for the bombing. Former Secretary of State Dean Acheson, who was brought in for consultation, was adamant. A blockade was not tough enough—we must not be found weak, we must clean out the missile bases with an air strike, the sooner the better. Nor was he concerned with international law. In a situation like this, he said, we must make our own international law.

"I can't see letting my brother be a Tojo and make an unannounced Pearl Harbor attack on a little country," Robert Kennedy answered. "He just can't do that. You can't make a secret attack. I can't let my brother do something which would blacken his reputation as a moral and honorable man." He added that "we were fighting for something more than just survival," and that "all our heritage and our ideals would be repugnant to such a sneak military attack."

Robert Kennedy spoke with such "intense but quiet passion" that he converted Treasury Secretary Douglas Dillon to his point of view. Dillon called that "a real turning point in history." Acheson felt it "a silly way" to analyze the problem. "To talk about it as a Pearl Harbor in reverse seemed to me high school thought that was unworthy of people charged with the government of a great country."

Senator J. William Fulbright, head of the Senate Foreign Relations Committee, who had declared himself against the Bay of Pigs invasion, this time also preferred direct action instead of the blockade. So did the joint chiefs of staff. When the President asked them what the Russian response might be, Air Force Chief General LeMay assured him there would be no reaction. Even British Ambassador Ormsby-Gore agreed that Khrushchev would *never* go into a nuclear confrontation over Cuba and Castro because he didn't care strongly enough about them.

The dissenting voice of UN Ambassador Adlai Stevenson was strong and firm. He suggested a settlement in which we took our missiles out of Turkey and evacuated our military base in Guantanamo, Cuba. The President answered that such an action might tell the world "we had been frightened into abandoning our position." Stevenson stubbornly held his ground.

"Kennedy was the coolest man in the room," Vice-President Johnson recalled, "and he had his thumb on the nuclear button."

*   *   *

"If it weren't for the children, it would be so easy to press the button!" Kennedy told Powers as they stood at the shallow end of the pool. "Not just John and Caroline, and not just the children in America, but children all over the world who will suffer and die for the decision I have to make."

*   *   *

"I got a call from the White House saying that President Kennedy would like me to come down to Washington to see him," recalled Clare Boothe Luce. She was then writing an article for *Life*.

"We chatted a while and then he turned to me and asked, 'Clare, what's on your mind?'

" 'A great man is one sentence,' " I replied, "and that sentence is characterized by having an active verb in it which describes a unique action. You shouldn't even need to know a man's name, because the action describes him.'

"He listened for a minute, then said, 'I don't follow you, Clare.'

" 'Well,' I said, 'you and I are both Americans and Catholics, so I'll give you a sentence that we both are familiar with: "He died on the cross to save us," or "He set out to discover an old world and discovered a new one," or "He preserved the Union and freed the slaves," or "He lifted us out of a great depression and helped to win a World War." I don't have to tell you who any of these men are. So if you ask me again, What was I thinking? it's this—I wonder what sentence will be written after your name when you leave the White House. It certainly won't be 'He got the agricultural bill passed.' The President suddenly read my thoughts. 'Oh,' he said, 'you're talking about Cuba.'

"I had to admit I was, and I felt compelled to tell him the sentence that could only apply to him: 'He broke the power of the Soviet Union in the Western Hemisphere'; or the reverse—

'he didn't.' 'So you think it will come to force?' the President asked. I told him I couldn't answer that but I would stand by my one sentence. As we walked out through the sitting room that overlooks the Lincoln Memorial and the Washington Monument, he said, 'You know, Clare, you've spoiled this room for me, because every time I look out of the window I'll never forget that one sentence.' "

* * *

He slipped out of Washington quietly. He was never, of course, completely alone. There was always a military aide, the Secret Service, always the warrant officer with the black nuclear control box.

Almost nobody in Hyannis Port knew he had come. He had come without his wife and his children, although they now loomed larger than ever before in his mind. He had come to walk the narrow stretch of lonely beach far from phones, far from people. He had come to think his unthinkable thoughts and make his decision.

From a distance, he looked like any other beach-walker in deck shoes and seagoing pants. Only when you came closer did you see the presidential seal on his leather jacket.

He had come here alone, always unexpectedly, at least a half dozen times, almost always to make some critical decision.

The crisis was less than a week old. His advisers were still divided on the question of blockade or air strike.

The helicopters arrived at Hyannis Port the next day, discreetly landing at a golf course not far from the Kennedy compound. The top military men in the country had come to tell their commander-in-chief what they thought he should do. Their consensus was for an air strike and an invasion.

Joseph Kennedy pointed to the President's flag and indicated to his nurse that he wanted to see his son. The President was in a meeting with the military and replied, "Tell him I'll be right there." The father, not happy with the answer, pounded his fist on the chair. The nurse again interrupted the meeting. "Mr. President, your father wants you now!"

The President, who had been in the midst of a heated discussion with the secretary of defense, now suddenly stopped and chuckling, said, "When Dad wants something, he wants it."

After embracing his father, he asked, "What's on your mind, Dad?"

He listened patiently to a long garble of indistinguishable syllables as if he understood everything. "Thanks, Dad, I'll take care of it. I'll do it your way. Right now I better get back to the boys." As the President left, his head sagged, his shoulders slumped. Just before he entered the meeting again, he straightened sharply and walked in briskly.

Neighbor Larry Newman, a noted war correspondent, reported to the President that there seemed to be no public awareness of the crisis in Cuba. With the President's permission, he had flown over the main boulevard in Havana in a four-engine RC-21D, a radar reconnaissance plane and he saw no crowds.

Nor did congressional leaders seem to feel any urgency. The mid-term congressional election was two weeks away and the President continued his campaigning schedule so as not to arouse concern. He was in Chicago when he got an urgent call from Bobby telling him to return to Washington because his crisis advisers were still divided. "I am depending on you to pull them together," the President replied. Still, he cut his campaigning short, pretending he had a cold and fever.

"Mr. President, you don't have a cold, do you?" his press secretary asked.

"No, I don't."

"Well, what's going on?"

"You'll find out soon enough," Kennedy told Salinger, "and when you do, grab your balls."

The real fever was waiting for him.

When the President arrived in Washington, he went straight to the White House pool for a swim. Bobby was waiting when he came out, and he quickly briefed his brother on who wanted what before the meeting.

"It's going to be a blockade," the President said firmly. The die was cast. The orders were given.

"You never want to make decisions that you don't have to make," Kennedy said. "You must not try to swallow a hedgehog, quills and all, but the time does come when a President must say, 'This is the way I want it done!' " He had made *his* decision. He had resisted tremendous pressure from others.

If you could put the growth of this man on a graph, that decision marked a giant leap.

*   *   *

Joan Braden and her young daughter came to dinner at the White House. "Jackie put on some Cole Porter and Gershwin and the three of us just relaxed, talking. You'd never know the weight of the crisis on him. He joked with the girls that they couldn't put their pumpkin on the balcony because people would think it was Castro. I remember Susan cried because she wanted to sleep in the President's bed. And he did a marvelous thing: He carried her into his own bed. He was sleeping in his office that night. And when I left, he walked all the way down with me to the White House door, down the elevator—he always did that," Braden said.

Mrs. Kennedy later called in the White House chief usher to tell him to cancel their big dinner for the maharajah of Jaipur, and do it as quietly as possible. "It's all very secret," she said.

She kept her calm, played her usual tennis, and entertained her visiting sister. Her more immediate concern was that her son had a high fever. She hardly saw her husband most of the time. She knew that many of his staff were sleeping on cots in their offices.

"I remember there was a little squib on page 38 or something in the *New York Times*," Spalding said. "It said that 'at four o'clock in the afternoon, the President had called up Mrs. Kennedy and they went and walked out in the rose garden.' He was sharing with her the possible horror of what might happen.

"If it was earlier in their marriage, I don't think he would have called her then. But things were beginning to break up in his head."

Kennedy once had written that "great crises create great men," but now he knew better than anyone that things seldom work out as they are planned, that the President is often a prisoner of moving history.

465

On Sunday, October 21st, the American people still did not know the details of what was happening—only that there was "an air of crisis in the capital tonight."

*   *   *

Former Secretary of State Dean Acheson held small brief for Kennedy, considered him "out of his depth" in the presidency, "not in any sense a great man. . . ." But Acheson willingly represented the President in briefing European leaders. "Could I ask whether you're here to consult with me on a matter," De Gaulle asked, "or to tell me of an action you are about to take." When Acheson explained, De Gaulle replied, "You can tell your President that he is doing exactly what I would do. Speaking for France, we will support you. Now can I see the pictures?" Chancellor Adenauer in Germany asked Acheson to explain Kennedy's overall policy. Acheson's reply was "faith moves mountains."

The President and Dave Powers were kneeling in the back pew of St. Matthew's Church in Washington when Powers again reminded Kennedy that he was entitled to three wishes when he prayed in a new church.

"I have only one wish."

Intelligence sources informed the President that Soviet merchant ships and submarines were on their way to Cuba. The American blockade waited for them in a picket line five hundred miles off the island.

"It looks really mean, doesn't it?" the President worried aloud. "I am not going to push the Russians an inch beyond what is necessary," he told his brother Bobby. "What if we go through all this effort and find that there's only baby food on board?" Bobby recalled thinking at the time, "How many times I had heard the military take positions which, if wrong, had the advantage that no one would be around at the end to know." Bobby also pointed out that if any of a half dozen Kennedy advisers had been President, the world then would have been "very likely plunged into a catastrophic war."

Bobby described his brother at the time of the crisis: "His hand went up to his face and covered his mouth. He opened and closed his fist. His face seemed drawn, his eyes pained, almost gray. We stared at each other across the table."

* * *

At 6:15, George Ball began briefing forty-six ambassadors of foreign countries at the State Department. In the President's study, Kennedy's secretary arrived with a hairbrush for a final smoothing of his hair.

As the President explained the crisis in full for the first time on TV at 7 PM on Monday night, October 22nd, he seemed "the calmest man in the whole United States of America." He told of the presence of the nuclear missiles in Cuba capable of striking Washington, D.C., and called it "a deliberately provocative and unjustified change in the status quo, which cannot be accepted by this country if our courage and our commitments are ever to be trusted again by either friend or foe." Any nuclear missile launched from Cuba, he said, would require "a full retaliatory response upon the Soviet Union." He announced his blockade of all ships bound for Cuba. All ships that contained missiles would be turned back.

As his mother listened, she covered her face and cried, "My son, my poor son, so much to bear and there is no way now for his father to help him."

The country reacted with the usual mix of pragmatism and panic. Listening to his speech with some ambassadors in the State Department, George Ball exploded into nervous laughter when the TV commercial afterwards asked, "How much security does your family have?"

The main conversation at the Vietnamese embassy party was the imminence of a Soviet atomic attack on Washington. One official expected it that night. A reporter asked her husband whether they should head for the air-raid shelter nearest their home, at the Library of Congress. They decided not to because they couldn't take their dog with them.

After he finished his speech, Kennedy told Mrs. Lincoln, "Well, that's it, unless the son of a bitch fouls it up."

Robert tried to reassure him. "I just don't think there was any choice. If you hadn't acted, you would have been impeached." The President thought about that and agreed. "That's what I think—I would have been impeached."

Just before making his speech, the President told Sorensen, "If they want this job, they can have it—it's no great joy to me."

"Sometimes he'd find me, wherever I was, and call me up in the middle of the night, just to relieve his tension, I guess," Spalding continued. "He would talk about anything from Voltaire to girls, always warm and funny. Just to be encouraging, I told him, 'It's OK; it's gonna work.' "

By the start of the second week, our photographs showed bulldozers clearing new missile sites and improving launch pads. Nineteen American navy ships were now in an arc awaiting twenty-five approaching Soviet ships. Navy orders were to stop the first ship with a cargo hold deep enough to carry a missile.

As the radar screens watched, the first blip entered the quarantine zone, then turned around and went back. Should we pursue it, examine its cargo? The President said no. Soon half the other Soviet ships also turned around, while the other half remained in place. The analysis afterwards was, "Doomsday did not happen then only because we were lucky."

For the President, the critical question now was the missile sites. Four were considered almost operational—the nuclear missiles had not yet been installed.

Powers followed the President upstairs to the family quarters. The President already had Caroline in his lap, reading her a story before her afternoon nap.

"I had the strangest feeling," said Powers, "that perhaps he was thinking, 'This is the last time I'll ever read to her.' "

*   *   *

The President's secretary observed him carefully that week: "His actions were never jerky. He never banged the desk, waved his arms, or raised his voice in a shrill shout," said Evelyn Lincoln. "Instead he would sit crouched at his desk, push his hair to one side, stand up, turn around and stare out the window, sit down, pick up the telephone and place a call, then hang up the receiver and wait for the operator to get his party."

The State Department teletype from the American Embassy in Moscow at 6 PM Friday, October 26, transmitted a letter from Khrushchev. It was a plea to stop the drift to war, insisting that the missiles were defensive and not offensive, that the Russian ships bound for Cuba carried no weapons. The chairman of the Soviet Council of Ministers then said, "We and you ought not now to pull on the ends of a rope in which you have tied the knot of war, because the more we pull, the tighter the knot will be tied. And a moment may come when the knot will be tied so tight that even he who tied it will not have the strength to untie it; and then it will be necessary to cut the knot . . . and thereby doom the world to the catastrophe of thermonuclear war. . . ."

Khrushchev then proposed that President Kennedy promise not to invade Cuba and then there would be no further need to keep Soviet military specialists in Cuba.

The next day, another Khrushchev letter arrived, this one tougher: The Russians would remove their missiles from Cuba only if we removed our missiles from Turkey. Kennedy advisers generally agreed that such a deal would undermine the faith of the North Atlantic alliance in the pledged word of the United States. What infuriated President Kennedy was that he had asked for the dismantling of those Turkish missiles two months before, and his orders had never been carried out. Once again the Executive Committee of the National Security Council talked of air strikes and invasion.

*　　*　　*

A naval aide who walked unexpectedly into the Oval Office at the peak of the crisis saw the President staring out of the window, his hand slowly caressing the model of an old sailing man-of-war he kept on the table.

Most of the generals were in sports clothes that warm Saturday afternoon, watching the final quarter of the football game between Army and George Washington University, when they were alerted to come to the White House for an important meeting that afternoon.

"The noose was tightening on all of us," remembered Robert Kennedy. Suddenly Bobby got a startling idea—so simple and so inspired that the President agreed immediately: Forget Khrushchev's bellicose second letter and answer his first one. Bundy compared it to the Victorian maiden who construed the tiniest gesture as a marriage proposal, which she could eagerly accept.

"I never thought much of Bobby at first," George Ball said. "I thought he behaved in a small-boy, arrogant way, everything black and white. I thought he was a man of very uncomplicated mind and I didn't like him very much. But then I went through the missile crisis with him, on an hourly basis, and there you saw the real depth and quality of the man."

"Thank God for Bobby," said the President.

Robert Kennedy went back to his office later that afternoon to await Russian Ambassador Dobrynin. The Russian ambassador was ebullient and Kennedy was somber. Looking at Kennedy, Dobrynin reflected "one could see from his eyes that he had not slept for days."

Robert Kennedy told of the Pentagon pressure on his brother for an invasion, assured Dobrynin that the President did not want war but that the situation could get out of control. "The President is not sure that the military will not overthrow him and seize power." Then Robert Kennedy delivered his doomsday scenario: Agree to remove your missiles from Cuba, unilaterally and unconditionally, within twenty-four hours or we will bomb them.

Robert Kennedy then returned to the White House to join his brother for dinner.

Dinner was carrots, potatoes, squash, and chicken. "Just like in Charlestown," Dave Powers told the President, "you leave the chicken breast on top of the thing." Powers had a big glass of white wine and the President a tall glass of milk. Jacqueline and the children were away, and the servants had been sent home.

"Bobby came in then," Powers said, "and, God, all the news was bad." Bobby had some of the chicken and a Heineken and told about his meeting with Russian Ambassador Dobrynin. Bobby felt Dobrynin didn't know about the second Khrushchev letter. "He couldn't be that good an actor. He was happy." Bobby then said there was going to be another meeting in a half hour with the Executive Committee. The President sent Bobby to see if he could get some good news before the meeting.

"I continued eating nervously, see," Powers said, "and I heard, 'Dave, you're eating that chicken and drinking that wine like it's your last supper!' "

"And I said, 'Mr. President, after listening to you and Bobby, I'm not so sure it isn't.' "

The world received the news in a special radio bulletin from Moscow at nine o'clock on Sunday morning: Khrushchev had accepted the Kennedy terms on withdrawing the missiles.

"Isn't it great to be alive today?" Rusk asked Ball. "We were eyeball to eyeball and I think the other fellow just blinked." Ball recalled a Georgia O'Keefe painting of a rose blossoming through an ox skull.

When the President walked into his office that morning, "He looked ten feet tall" and "we all stood up," Sorensen remembered. When a staff man suggested a gloating victory report to the American people, Kennedy replied, "Khrushchev has eaten enough crow. Let's not rub it in." As to the national euphoria, he commented wryly, "That will wear off in about a week." What he really felt, he expressed to Dave Powers as they attended 10 AM Mass: "Dave, this morning we have extra reason to pray."

He was even more reflective that evening when his brother returned to the White House. He talked about Abraham Lincoln and his crisis, and his end. "This is the night I should go to the theater," he told Bobby.

"If you go," said his brother, "I want to go with you."

Powers was the last to leave the President. He saw him get on his knees to pray, tucked him in, and heard him say, as always, "Good night, pal."

Out in the dark of the street, Powers always looked back at the President's room. "Sometimes he kept the light on to read a little longer," Powers said. "Of course, I knew the Secret Service men were downstairs. But I knew that Jackie and the kids were away and the servants had gone home and so he was really all alone up there. And I felt bad."

If I had to live my life over again, I would have a different father, a different wife, and a different religion.

—JOHN KENNEDY *to John Sharon*

Goodnight Mrs. Kennedy, Wherever You Are

The presidency also had its light side.

For Jack Kennedy's forty-sixth birthday, on May 29, 1963, the staff had a surprise party for him at the White House mess. Pierre Salinger was master of ceremonies, and he handed Kennedy a speech to read. "We know you usually write your speeches, Mr. President. But here is one which was written by a ghostwriter, and we'd like you to read it." It was a take-off on Lincoln's Gettysburg Address, and began: "Two score and six years ago there was brought forth at Brookline, Massachusetts. . . ." They also presented him with a model space capsule with a card: "Hope you have a good trip." It was signed "Barry" [Goldwater].

In the middle of the proceedings a workman brought in a huge basket of dead grass. It was Jacqueline's joke because he was always after her to "see if you can do something about the grass." The card read, "From the White House Historical Society —genuine antique grass from the antique Rose Garden." It was a gay twenty minutes.

A group of doctors sent him a keg of forty-six-year-old cognac "for his health and pleasure." And he also received a birthday horoscope: "You are domestic, fond of children, affable, and considerate. You love your family and are very affectionate towards them. You have a sweet, even disposition but are aroused to bitterness if your trust is violated."

"That was true," his friend Jim Reed said. "Jack didn't have a mean streak in him."

The scene would have fit into a Hollywood movie. In fact, his wartime buddy, Red Fay, did sing "Hurray for Hollywood," for the umpteenth time, simply because it was such a Kennedy favorite. The presidential yacht, *Honey Fitz*, sailed down the Potomac with a happy birthday party of friends and family of the President, complete with noisemakers and music and birthday cake. Teddy mysteriously lost one leg of his trousers sometime during the evening. The President disappeared at the same time that David Niven's wife also mysteriously disappeared. George Smathers made a long, sentimental toast, and Bobby Kennedy yelled, "Where were you when we needed you, George?" There was a thunderstorm that drenched everybody but nobody particularly cared.

The President told Ben Bradlee during an interval, "Do you think you could get used to this kind of life? Pretty hard to take, isn't it?" A guest, having perhaps had too much to drink, put his shoe through a rare old engraving Jacqueline had bought for Jack's birthday. She somehow managed to say, "Oh that's all right, I can get it fixed."

The President told how his wife's stepfather had been approached for a political donation to his 1960 campaign. He promised not to give his usual donation to the Republicans and "eventually the old boy came up with a magnificent two hundred and fifty bucks." Kennedy also confided that he had approached his doctor for a shot for his back pain just for the birthday party and the doctor had said that such an injection would remove all feeling below the waist and he had said, "We can't have that, can we, Jacqueline?"

* * *

Friends observed that Mrs. Kennedy was not smiling much those days. She excused herself from a large number of official functions. She wasn't even there to greet a group from Miss Porter's School and another from the Museum of Modern Art. After almost ten years of marriage, and fewer than three years in the White House, her husband seemed to want her less, need her less, and there were the never-ending rumors about his other women. Every once in a while, she took a short trip on her own to New York.

On these trips, she would see what was new in the art galleries, buy an eighteenth-century flower bowl, a doll for Caroline, a pair of alligator shoes, go to the ballet with Adlai Stevenson, or to a small cocktail party that might include the Henry Fords and Col. Serge Obolensky, known as the best waltzer in America. Once she even took off for Palm Beach without informing anyone on the presidential staff.

And, while she was in Washington, she almost always extended her weekend at Glen Ora in Virginia to four days. There she could ride her horses and enjoy her children. Sometimes her husband joined them, and sometimes he didn't. An enterprising United Press reporter wrote an article specifically detailing how little time the First Lady actually spent in the White House. Comedian Jimmy Durante's familiar TV signature was, "And good night, Mrs. Calabash, wherever you are." A paraphrase swept Washington: "And good night, Mrs. Kennedy, wherever you are."

* * *

With or without his wife, the President seldom lacked company.

Congresswoman Lindy Boggs knows all about charm because she herself is one of the charmers of Congress. Her husband represented a Louisiana congressional district until he was killed in a plane crash, and Lindy was elected to replace him. Both she and her husband were good friends of the Kennedys.

Lindy Boggs remembered an afternoon when she was showing her mother and mother-in-law what Jackie had done in the White House. "I never would have thought of bothering the President, but he got word we were there and invited us into the Oval Office. And then what a to-do he made over these mothers! He showed them all over the office and told them stories about the different things in it. Then he told them what great people Hale and I were, and what we'd done, but he didn't put it on too thick so that it would still be believable. Then he rang for the photographer to take a picture and he kept ringing until they came in stumbling all over each other. And he himself carefully posed the mothers for the pictures.

"What adjective would I use to describe him? You mean, after I say 'adorable'?"

*   *   *

Reporters then did not report on everything they saw. Robert Pierpoint of CBS recalled one Palm Beach incident when the President and a young woman emerged from a cottage in the early morning and embraced before she stepped into a waiting limousine. The President apparently decided to prolong the farewell, and also entered the limousine, "and the woman disappeared into the President's arms and the inside car light went out again." Pierpoint and another reporter then saw one of the Kennedy sisters drive up in a convertible, cruise over to her brother's limousine, and call out, "Come on, Mildred!" The inside limousine lights went on again, Mildred gave the President another lingering kiss, and came out to join the President's sister.

Look magazine reporter Laura Bergquist was still flabbergasted. She told a friend, over a drink, "I can't believe this guy! He's the President of the United States and when I go up there for an interview, he's in his shorts, that's all. And they're shorts that don't even fit! And he's sitting around scratching himself in various places and the first thing he says to me is, 'Hi, Laura, getting much?' "

"I remember coming back from Cuba," Bergquist continued, "where I'd talked to Che Guevara. He wanted me to tell him about Che. I told him that in many ways, they were very similar. They were both pragmatic, both intelligent, both bright and witty. I thought if they were not on such opposite sides of the fence that they might even like each other. And do you know what he said? He told me, 'I think you have the hots for Che.' Then he took off for his helicopter. That burned me. Here I'd come back from Cuba with all kinds of information that might have had some value for him, and he dismissed it all with that macho remark.

"After another trip I'd made to Cuba, he asked me to tell all about Fidel Castro and his first question was, 'Who's Fidel sleeping with?' Well, I didn't know who Fidel was sleeping with. It didn't matter to me, but it did matter to him. It burned me because I had so much to tell him about Castro, and he didn't ask me!"

More reflectively, Bergquist added quietly, "I think Jack was vulnerable. I think he always felt an insecurity about himself. Not simply because he felt he was part of the upward-mobile Irish, but because I think he recognized himself as an image that had been manufactured. And his question was: 'Who loves me and wants me for myself, and who loves me for what they think I am, and what I can do for them?'

"I always thought he was a loner, an outsider, a watcher of everybody, especially a watcher of himself. It was as if he was on the sidelines, looking at the whole picture, rather dispassionately."

A Kennedy neighbor commented curtly that she had been brought up in a world of ladies and gentlemen, and she was a lady and the Kennedys were no gentlemen. Her pointed reference was to their extramarital affairs. The Kennedys, of course, were complete gentlemen in regard to polite manners. When it came to sex, it was more a matter of life-style and family pattern. John Kennedy confided his fantasy of being a beachcomber "with enough money and a lot of broads." He was not Byron consuming himself, or a drug addict promising to quit. He enjoyed what he was doing. As he told Bradlee, "If you and I could only run wild, Benjy? . . ."

Trying to put the President's proclivities into perspective, another friend, Charles Spalding, described it this way: The importance of great men in history had nothing to do with their sex lives.

Kennedy and Bradlee and their wives were discussing women "who castrate their husbands for various reasons." In the course of it, Jacqueline blurted out, "Oh, Jack, you know you always say that Tony is your ideal."

"Yes, that's true," he replied, stared at Tony Bradlee, then quickly caught himself. "You're my ideal, Jackie."

The talk turned to men, the sex appeal of Secretary of Defense McNamara. The women were effusive, and the men seemed irritated. Jacqueline laughed. "Look at them. They look like dogs that have had a plate of food grabbed from under their noses."

The Secret Service was always electronically alerted to the specific whereabouts of "Lancer" (the President) and "Lace" (the First Lady), whom they also referred to as Number One and Number Two. A Secret Service man always informed the President exactly when his wife would arrive.

White House kennel keeper Traphes Bryant recalled "a beautiful, tall, blonde girl skinny-dipping in the pool" with the President and several other naked male and female swimmers. Bryant was privy to the scene because the blonde wanted to see the famous Soviet space dog Pushinka—which Khrushchev had sent to Mrs. Kennedy. Bryant described the President lounging naked alongside the pool, sipping a daiquiri, when the alarm went off, indicating that Mrs. Kennedy had returned unexpectedly from Virginia.

"It was easy to get rid of the bodies," said Bryant, "but gathering up the drinks was another matter. Only the President remained in the pool."

Bryant indicated that the President had a penchant for blondes, and Bryant heard the upstairs maid complain, "Why can't he make it easier for us? Why do we always have to be searching for blonde hairs and blonde bobby pins? Why can't he get himself a steady brunette?"

A vivid Bryant memory was seeing a naked blonde coming out of the elevator, her breasts swinging as she raced down the hall. "There was nothing to do but for me to get out fast and push the button for the basement."

The President occasionally had small White House parties where his guests cavorted without clothes, but an intimate admitted that even this had begun to bore him. At one such party, the naked President left the group "to settle in a chair and read Walter Lippmann."

Actress Shirley MacLaine summed up the Kennedy defense: "I would rather have a President who does it to a woman than a President who does it to a country."

Some Kennedy loyalists steadfastly denied the whole thing.

What pulled his marriage together at this time were the children. He would never have given them up. What he knew, too, was that his wife was strong enough to leave him. What he also knew was that he may have been the President, but the public saw her as the movie star. Letitia Baldrige commented, "She was getting more and more fabulous, her popularity almost as great as his."

*   *   *

A President's day has its quota of presentations. This one was for him: a brass plaque of American flags created by an artist named John Johns.

In the midst of it, Mrs. Kennedy arrived unexpectedly.

"She looked absolutely delightful," recalled Bill Walton, who had arranged the ceremony. "She had a purple kerchief on her head, wore a fresh cotton dress, and was very very pregnant."

"I'm sorry, Jack," she said. "I didn't know you had somebody here. It's a hummingbird feeder. I'm trying to figure out a place to put it outside so that you can see it all the time."

The plaque was promptly forgotten while everybody got involved in the proper placement of the bird feeder. Walton observed the pleasure in the President's face at his wife's thoughtfulness.

Artist John Johns afterwards noted to Walton how moved he was by the tenderness and the family feeling of the scene.

*   *   *

If the family scene was warming, the Washington mood was not. Some critics talked of a malaise in the administration at this time, a feeling that events were controlling men, an emphasis on national unity instead of the excitement of new ideas. A few felt that—after two years in the White House—the President was bored, even depressed.

A visitor, however, compared the Washington atmosphere to "a reigning monarch's court." As in any court, there was always show, drama, fun. The fun started that February 1963, with a letter Jack Kennedy read that President Theodore Roosevelt had written in 1908 suggesting that marine officers should hike fifty miles periodically to prove their fitness.

Pierre Salinger made the mistake of telling the press that anybody could walk fifty miles. To the delight of reporters, and the public, Kennedy pinpointed Pierre to make the hike. "I may be plucky," Salinger replied, "but I'm not stupid." His secretaries tried to goad him into the walk by saying they would walk, too. Salinger answered that his secretaries had better legs than he did. He then produced a letter from his doctors advising him not to make the hike.

Bobby Kennedy promptly took up the hike as a challenge to the New Frontier, and enlisted a few friends, including his assistant, Jim Symington. The group was to assemble at the Chain Bridge on the C & O Canal at 4 AM, and walk the fifty miles to Camp David. Symington came home from a party at 2 AM, took off his tuxedo, and put on some old clothes. "My wife, Sylvia, thought I was out of my mind. After all, it was February, cold as the dickens, maybe twelve degrees. But then I figured, what the heck! A rather sprightly Park Service fellow joined us as a lark. He fainted after five miles.

"So we marched off. Since I had been up all night, I wasn't in all that good shape. I fell into the drink once and I fell asleep twice while walking. One guy brought his immense dog, and he kept jumping on me, so I was fighting off the dog all the time, too.

"We all got about twenty-five miles, in different stages, then started fading. At the half point, Bobby sat down and took off his shoes, so we all did. Now that's a very important moment.

479

When you take off your shoes, you don't really want to put them back on again. I don't think any of us would have put them back on again if a helicopter hadn't landed and disgorged three photographers.

"Well, that wasn't enough to get *me* back into my shoes, and the rest of us thought, 'This game isn't worth the candle.' But Bobby put on his shoes and started off, all alone. He was going to walk the final twenty-five miles all by himself. He was going to prove to the world that he represented an administration that was lean and hard and tough, could take on all comers and beat the best. His grit and determination still stick in my mind. Like a chisel taking on a granite challenge and cutting right through. It was as if he was saying, 'Damn it, I'll show you!' "

Informed in his Oval Office that all the attorney general's companions had given up, the President said, "Oh, I know Bobby will make it even if he has to crawl."

"Anyway, we had a funny evening at Camp David that night, all of us nursing our wounds," Symington continued. "There were some navy medics there checking us out because most of us weren't in very good shape. But we really had a lot to laugh about. And we were all very proud of Bobby, proud and quite envious because he had done the whole darn thing."

The fifty-mile hike was just a small piece of show business, but the people loved it. Politics was cynical stuff to most Americans, but this was something they could laugh at; this was fun. This was something they never got from Eisenhower. It tied together the people and the President in greater intimacy.

*   *   *

Fun and wit relieved the pressure, and often the pain. A quote the President repeated was, "We are not collected in ice nor frozen in amber."

"You want to know something?" his friend Jim Reed asked. "Jack couldn't tell a joke—if it was somebody else's joke. But his instinctive wit was wonderful."

They were all small jokes, but they were mostly his. He didn't need writers to create them. When he began to gain too much weight and his wife counted his calories, the whipped cream was omitted from his dessert at a White House dinner. The President sent it back with a message, "Am I different?"

And the American people laughed with him. Cigar sales soared and hat sales fell. Photographed carrying a felt hat, the President explained to reporters, "I've got to carry one for a while. They tell me I'm killing the industry."

Once Barbra Streisand entertained the press at the Annual White House Correspondents' dinner. A White House aide had cautioned all the entertainers not to detain the President as he came through the line—just shake his hand and let him go.

But Barbra didn't. She curtsied to him, then shoved a program at him and asked for his autograph. Kennedy looked at her, thought of something, grinned, and signed.

Merv Griffin asked what the President had written.

Barbra smiled. Kennedy had written, "Fuck you. The President."

What he never tired of were the perks of being President, particularly the presidential flourishes from the Air Force band when he alighted from the plane at Hyannis. There was always a spirit in his stride when he walked across the grass to get into the helicopter to take him home. His father was always waiting as he stepped out of the plane and the President would say, "Let's go find Mother."

Hyannis Port went through a metamorphosis, not simply reflected in the hordes of tourists outside the Kennedy compound and the streams of sightseeing boats in the harbor, but also in the Kennedy family activity. The President took the children—sometimes as many as eighteen—for their ritual ride to the nearby candy store in his golf cart, and he still attended a birthday party for neighbor Larry Newman, but he no longer lived alongside Bobby and his parents. At the urging of the Secret Service, he had moved a mile away to the more easily protected Squaw Island. His rented sixteen-room house sat on a high bluff with a splendid view of Nantucket Sound, a tennis court, steam room, heated pool and a private beach—and it was separated from the mainland by a 500-yard causeway. His brother Ted lived across the road from him. Neither he nor Ted was expected every night at the elder Kennedy family dinners. "Once a week is great," Jacqueline had said. "Not every night."

"His loyalty to his family was absolute," said Ormsby-Gore. "He wouldn't say a bad word about any Kennedy—except possibly Peter Lawford, who was never quite part of the family."

At family dinners, the President was now the prime presence. His father was an old man who had to be fed and could only say, "No, no, no." His mother and Ethel and the children still went to 7:30 AM Mass every day of the summer, but his mother announced that she was going to change her image. With his father's illness, his mother had emerged as a force and a celebrity. "People think that all I do is go to church because that's where the photographers know where to find me. I'm going to Europe again, and I'm going to be seen coming out of a nightclub, or I'm going to be in a bikini on the Riviera next time. So don't be surprised. I'm tired of that other image."

She also confided that Mrs. Khrushchev "asked me for my beauty secrets" in Vienna. "I like her," Mrs. Kennedy continued. "She was the kind of woman you'd ask in perfect confidence to baby-sit for you, if you wanted to go out some evening."

*   *   *

Jacqueline pressured her husband for a hideaway home of their own, away from their families, away from everyone. For almost a year, wearing a bandanna and dark glasses, she went hunting for possible sites. She found what she wanted in the heart of the Virginia hunt country, in the shadow of the Blue Ridge Mountains, near the sleepy crossroads village of Atoka.

She did the initial design herself: fifteen rooms on one floor, a master bedroom with a thirty-two-foot glass wall, and, beyond the house, stables, servants' quarters, a fall-out shelter, and a helicopter pad. After advice from Supreme Court Justice Arthur Goldberg, the President personally paid for the helicopter pad, instead of letting the government do it. Cost: $250,000. "The helicopter pad is the best yet," noted the President.

She had wanted very much to please him with the place, even calling it "Wexford" after the county in Ireland where his grandparents had lived. She brought in some French provincial furniture from their Georgetown home, ordered several pieces of Oriental lacquerware, and fixed up a cozy study for him.

He deprecatingly referred to it as "Snake Hill," and quoted his sister Eunice ("You can hardly travel on the road when it rains") and the plumber who observed, "They can have it. It's too lonesome out there for me." At a play in Washington, one line got a good laugh from the President: "I myself do not like the country," the actor declaimed. "It is my wife who likes horses and the hunt."

Wexford epitomized the differences in their taste. He liked the open sea and she loved the sweeping forest and mountains. To her, this place meant supreme privacy, the chance to ride her horse, unobserved, into happy exhaustion, a place of peace where her children could play outdoors. To him, it provided no beach to walk, no ship to sail, nothing he truly liked to do. Wexford excited her and bored him.

So strong were his feelings about it that they rented the place soon after it was completed. A Washington columnist observed, "It's just like renting your new mink jacket before you've even been seen in it." It would have amused Jack Kennedy to know that President-elect Ronald Reagan would one day rent Wexford. He would have also smiled to know that Hammersmith Farm would one day be owned by Camelot Gardens, Inc., which charged the public three dollars admission "to see how the rich lived." He once told Larry Newman that he hated Hammersmith. "I come here and all around me I see ponies and horses running around the backyard. What the hell is there for *me* to do? I get lost in those rooms."

The mystery was why the President had not complained about Wexford while the house was in the planning or the building stage. During the White House restoration, he had involved himself in everything from the size of the rugs to the color of the walls.

It was a sad-faced First Lady who asked her chief usher: "Mr. West, has a President ever sold a house while he was in office?"

Jacqueline's birthday on July 28, 1963, was quieter. She was thirty-four years old, and expecting her third child within three weeks. She worked on her family scrapbooks "in very good spirits," took her daughter to the Barnstable Fair, went with her husband on a three-hour cruise aboard the *Honey Fitz*, and watched Caroline outdo her father in a "cannon-ball dive." She had her own guests, her sister and British Ambassador David Ormsby-Gore. They all watched her blow out her birthday candles and make her private wish.

Kennedy remembered when he was in school and was sometimes asked to make lists of great, good, and bad presidents. "How the hell can you tell? Only the President himself can know what his real crush is, what his real alternatives are. If you don't know that, how can you judge performance?" The essence of great presidents, he said, consisted of "a thousand imponderables."

Ich bin ein Berliner

What he could not understand was why so many people wanted to see him fail. If he failed, he said, the country failed, maybe even civilization failed. If he failed badly, there might not even be another President. He had wanted all the votes when he ran for election, he now wanted all the love. Bitterness baffled him.

Cruel jokes hurt: The Kennedy rocking chair was a symbol of the New Frontier because "you get the feeling of moving without going anywhere." A Kennedy cocktail was "stocks on the rocks." The President really got the country moving again —"down another fourteen points." His father had asked Jack what he wanted as a career and he said he wanted to be President: "I know that," said his father, "but I mean when you grow up." A parody of his inaugural phrase: "Don't think about what you can do to help your country, think about what your country might do to you." And Caroline looking out of the White House window at a parading line of pickets and asking, "Mommy, what has Daddy done wrong now?" In Texas, they passed out cards, "I MISS IKE," and, in smaller type, "Hell, I even miss Harry."

All these represented what only a minority of the American people felt. A Gallup Poll taken earlier in 1963 rated the President's popularity at 76 percent.

American popularity in Europe was more questionable. The Italian government was changing. Macmillan was in trouble in England, and Adenauer was not then very friendly. Germany was the European linchpin and the President sent Henry Kissinger as a special envoy to find out what was wrong with our German policy. "That will be easier," Kissinger said, "if you'll tell me one small thing: What *is* our German policy?"

Against the advice of experts, Kennedy decided to tour Europe that June. "When you go to Berlin," Bobby Kennedy told Air Force aide Godfrey McHugh, "there's a fella who I don't want the President to see at all. That's an order."

Presidential aides only take orders from the President. When McHugh reported the conversation to the President, his answer was, "Well, I want to see him."

He had briefed himself very well, as he always did. Besides the State Department background, he had read several books, including a short history of Germany and one on the Berlin blockade.

Kennedy collected all kinds of ideas about Germany. He listened to one friend who was suspicious of any friendship with a country whose cities we had decimated, even though we had helped rebuild its prosperity. His friend worried that the lingering German resentment might last several generations. Because of this, he said, we must never strengthen the Germans by advocating a united Germany.

Kennedy's own feeling was that the world's memory was short, and that people can be stirred to change—any people, any change. The United States's strongest enemies were fast becoming its best friends. He wanted his trip to cement that friendly feeling.

*   *   *

The White House seemed almost deserted. Mrs. Kennedy and the children had gone to the Cape, and the President was alone. It was a few days before his trip to Germany, and Hugh Sidey of *Time* had come to talk to him about it. "Berlin is decided," the President said. "It's now up to Khrushchev what we do on that." He planned to announce an increase in American forces in Germany, and there was no question they were there to stay. Suddenly he said to Sidey, "Come along. Let's go swimming."

"I don't have a suit, Mr. President," Sidey said.

"Oh, you don't need one in this pool."

Sidey noticed how he went down the steps very slowly. The fused discs had never properly healed. "I was surprised how stiff his back still was. He swam quite a bit, had a good strong stroke. Then he walked around in the warm water and paddled up and down. Then he got out and got on his crutches. I was surprised. I hadn't realized that he was still on crutches then."

The two men went up to the President's room and had lunch, and Sidey watched the President get hot packs on his back before he went to bed for a nap.

*   *   *

Thinking about his Berlin trip, Kennedy had an inspiration.

"Know what? We've got to go to Ireland."

O'Donnell thought he was kidding, and laughed. The trip itinerary called for Italy and Germany.

"I'm serious."

"I think you're crazy. The Italians and Germans are going to be delighted, but you don't need the Irish at this stage of the game. It's unnecessary. It looks like you just want a pleasure trip."

"Kenny, let me tell you something. *I* am the President of the United States, not you. And I want to go to Ireland. And I *am* going to Ireland. Now you arrange the trip; that's your job."

*   *   *

Europe was looking for a young hero to electrify it. Chancellor Adenauer was past eighty, and Macmillan, Khrushchev, and De Gaulle were also older men. "Out of these ancient regimes, there can no longer come the leadership we need," George

Washington had said of Europe. "We must provide our own now."

On the plane the President reminisced about the Germany he knew as a young man in 1939. He was then with his friend Byron White, whom he later appointed to the U.S. Supreme Court. They were traveling in a car with an English license plate. They were stopped by Nazis wearing armbands, holding rocks, and ready for a fight. White was also ready, until Kennedy suggested that the Nazis had mistaken them for Englishmen because of their car license. Kennedy never forgot the hate in those faces.

Now a new generation of Germans waited for him in Frankfurt, with excitement and great expectations. He told them what they wanted to hear: "The United States will risk its cities to defend yours because we need your freedom to protect ours." This point was made even more dramatically in Berlin, that isolated internal island surrounded by a sea of East German communism, where more than two million people were waiting to give him the most tumultuous reception of his life. The mood of Berlin was contagious combustion.

He went first to look at the ugly wall that divided the city. He was supposed to gaze over the wall through the gate onto Unter den Linden, once the celebrated avenue of the German capital. But the five arches of the Brandenburg Gate had been covered the night before with huge red banners, put up by the Communists to partially block his view of desolate East Berlin. Facing the podium on the wall where he stood was a Communist sign in English saying that they had fulfilled allied pledges to uproot the Nazis in East Berlin and called on him to do the same in West Berlin. Beyond the forbidden zone behind the wall, a small group of East Berliners saw him and cheered. As he stared at the gray, grim emptiness, "he looked like a young, angry lion."

The motorcade arrived late at Schöneberger Rathaus, West Berlin's city hall. The square was so packed with surging people that it seemed as if the whole city was there chanting, "KENNEDY . . . KENNEDY . . . KENNEDY. . . ." Placards were everywhere. "JOHN YOU OUR BEST FRIEND." There was even a reference to the pregnant Jacqueline: "WE HOPE TWINS."

Bobby had talked to his brother informally about saying something in German while he was in Berlin, and the President explored the idea with McGeorge Bundy.

"*Ich bin ein Berliner* was not my idea; it was his," Bundy insisted. "I just told him how to say it in German. He had no feeling for the German language. He had no feeling for any foreign language. That's because he had no sense of music, no *ear*. So there we were in the goddamn airplane, coming down on Berlin, while he repeated the phrase over and over again—I don't know how many times. But they knew what he said, and it worked. God, how it worked!"

As far as Kennedy could see there were thousands of faces so closely packed they seemed almost a single mass with a single voice chanting his name over and over again. These were a people in danger and he was their hero who would save them, protect them. Such was their emotion that some of the Kennedy staff on the platform were in tears.

The crowd's emotion caught Kennedy when he shouted, "Today in the world of freedom, the proudest boast is *Ich bin ein Berliner.*"

The response was unimaginable, almost an animal roar, as if every person there was venting the frustration of a lifetime in a single exciting, exhilarating moment. He had touched the exact nerve with the exact phrase.

He intensified the hysteria when he added "There are many people in the world who really don't understand, or say they don't, what is the great issue between the free world and the Communist world.

"Let them come to Berlin!

"There are some who say that communism is the wave of the future.

"Let them come to Berlin!

"And there are some who say in Europe and elsewhere that we can work with the Communists.

"Let them come to Berlin!

"And there are even a few who say that it is true that communism is an evil system, but it permits us to make economic progress.

"*Lass' sie nach Berlin kommen*. Let them come to Berlin!

"Freedom has many difficulties and democracy is not perfect but we have never had to put up a wall to keep our people in. . . ."

The roar was so intense and so prolonged that Kennedy felt he could have asked them to march to the Berlin Wall and tear it down and they would have done it. "We'll never have another day like this as long as we live," he told Sorensen.

Leaving Germany, Kennedy felt as if he had conquered a country. He would leave a note to his successor, he said, to be opened in time of discouragement. It would simply say, "Go to Germany."

Berlin boiled his blood, but Ireland delighted his soul.

He remembered the sentimental journey he'd made as a young congressman who had come to Kilkenny County searching for his roots. An aristocratic British lady tagged along. He had found a small, thatched cottage where his great-grandfather might have been born. He had talked to the people there for more than an hour, interrupted by pigs, chickens, and children who ran in and out of the place. The British lady was appalled at the poverty. "She had not understood at all the *magic* of the afternoon," said Kennedy.

Robert Frost once advised him to be more Irish than Harvard. He usually took along his favorite album of Irish records whenever he went abroad, but there was no need for them here. He needed no music to move him into magic. Children perched on their fathers' shoulders to see him, old women held up their rosary beads, and nuns danced in the streets. Eamon de Valera, the president of Ireland, the almost-blind man from Brooklyn, New York, was beaming as if his son had come home. De Valera and Joseph Kennedy, Sr., were "old and valued friends."

The Secret Service didn't want him to walk into the crowd, but Kennedy insisted. The crowd closed in and the Secret Service men strained to keep the President from being crushed. As far as anybody could see there were screaming people. "We got him in the car," his aide said, "and it scared him a little bit. It was a frightening thing but it didn't stop him from doing it again."

For three days, the whole country stopped. "The pubs were open at five o'clock in the morning," said a man in New Ross, "and most of the town was drunk by eight, for days on end. They were dancing there on the quay. When the town wasn't burned down that time, it never will be!"

New Ross in Wexford County was his ancestral home. Kennedy laughed at the report that the mayor of New Ross had told his citizens not to clean up the manure from their front steps for the President's arrival. "If he wants chrome," the mayor said, "he can find it on Madison Avenue." In Dublin, a newspaper reported afterwards that some 375 Irish women had confessed that they had intimate relations with President Kennedy during his three-day stay in Ireland.

"You're the only man I know who could defeat Valera in his own district," Powers told Kennedy.

John Fitzgerald Kennedy had scoured the White House for staff members of Irish descent and had brought along fifty of them. His entourage also included his sisters Eunice and Jean, labor leader George Meany, Jacqueline's sister Princess Lee Radziwill, Pamela Turnure, and Faddle—of Fiddle and Faddle—who had come along to take his dictation and massage his head. Dr. Jacobson was also there with his pain-killing shots, and so was Kennedy's chef, who brought both food and bottled water. One other item: the presidential scales, so he could watch his weight.

As he left, he told of a New Ross resident who came to Washington with his family, had himself photographed in front of the White House, and sent the photograph back with the message, "This is our summer home. Come and see us."

"I hope you *will* come and see us," the President added.

"Last night, somebody sang a song, the words of which I'm sure you know, of 'Come back to Erin, Mavourneen, Mavourneen, come back aroun' to the land of thy birth. Come with the Shamrock in the springtime, Mavourneen.' This is not the land of my birth, but it is the land for which I hold the greatest affection and I certainly will come back in the springtime."

A choir sang "Come Back to Erin" as he boarded the plane and "he had the sweetest and saddest look on his face."

"Those were the three happiest days of my life," he later told James Reed.

*　　*　　*

The President originally had planned the visit to Italy to see Pope John XXIII, whom he called "the pope of peace." He echoed that by saying he hoped to be known as the President of peace. But the great pope was dead. The new pope, Paul VI, was an old friend of the Kennedy family. Kennedy had consulted Cardinal Cushing about whether he should time his arrival for the pope's investiture and the Cardinal had advised against it because he would "upstage" the new pope.

Rome's crowds were thin when Kennedy came. Newspapers commented that people were exhausted from the papal coronation the week before. Not Naples. Naples went wild. Nine million Neapolitans cheered and chased the Kennedy caravan through the streets, climbing over cars, trying to get closer. Boulevards were littered with the sandals of women who simply stepped out of them and kept chasing, trying to see him, touch him.

He left for home exhausted, but exhilarated. He had some handmade sweaters for his wife and children and an antique silver goblet given him by the people of New Ross. Jacqueline sent it to the White House's floral room with a note of instructions: "This antique silver goblet is to be kept on the table to the left of the fireplace in the President's office. Would you have the Flower Room keep it filled? I would like it to have always three or four fat roses—red or white, the kind you find in a garden, not the florist-type ones. Or, when this becomes impossible, a couple of big red geraniums, or a red peony, dahlia, or, even in winter, just red carnations. The thing I want to avoid is a dainty bouquet which would look too feminine for a man's office, so I think it's best if we stick to one kind of flower only in the goblet. Thank you. JBK."

James Reed was their guest at Hyannis Port the weekend of the President's return and they saw a film of the tour that was earmarked for German-American groups around the country. Kennedy watched himself in Berlin making his *Ich bin ein Berliner* speech. At the end of it, automatically and enthusiastically, he applauded, almost as if he were applauding someone else.

Said the general: "The Diem government was strong, popular, and the war was going fine."

Said the State Department officer: "The Diem government is on the verge of collapse."

"Are you sure," asked President Kennedy, "that you two gentlemen are talking about the same government?"

—*Cabinet Room, September 1963*

Vietnam: The Looming Crisis

Gen. Douglas A. MacArthur was coming to the White House for lunch and the President was waiting, along with his brother Robert and Dave Powers. The President quoted from MacArthur's Distinguished Service Cross citation, "On a field where courage was the rule, his courage was a dominant feature. . . ."

The President then turned to Powers and said, "Dave, how would you like to have that said about you?" Before Powers could answer, Bobby did: "I would love to have that said about me."

The old man's hands were shaking from palsy, but his voice was as strong and eloquent as ever. The small audience at the special White House lunch was absolutely quiet and attentive. The old general was saying, as forcefully as he could, "Never ever, ever put American soldiers on the mainland of Asia."

MacArthur also told the President, "The chickens have come home to roost, and you have to live in the chicken house."

"Charlie, I saw MacArthur and he said, 'Never get involved in a land war in Asia,'" Kennedy later told Spalding, "And I must say, it makes sense to me."

"When you take over a job like this, you simply have to depend on the judgment of the men around you," the President confided to Cyrus Sulzberger of the *New York Times*. "And you don't know them at first. They have good records and excellent reputations, but their judgment may be lousy—generals and diplomats and others. And you can't tell at the start. Of course, after you have had a few months, you gain a hell of an advantage."

Was he scared about the immensity of the task and responsibility of the presidency at the beginning, asked Sulzberger.

"No, not scared. At the beginning, you are protected by the value of your own ignorance. But I can do the job much better now, and I could have done much better earlier if I'd had experience. Let me show you what I mean. After Cuba—the Bay of Pigs—we began to talk about maybe going into Laos. But all the generals and the other people disagreed about this, and you don't know whom to believe and whom to disbelieve. It is a very hard thing at first."

Laos was a tiny kingdom on the northwestern part of the Indochinese peninsula. The Americans and the Soviets were supplying and supporting different factions in their civil war. President Eisenhower had warned Kennedy before his inauguration, "You might have to go in there and fight it out." Kennedy had discussed his reluctance with Sorensen: "Whatever's going to happen in Laos, an American invasion, a Communist victory, or whatever, I wish it would happen before we take over and get blamed for it."

Kennedy remembered De Gaulle's advice: "You can listen to your advisers before you make up your own mind, but once you have made up your mind then do not listen to anyone."

He sent De Gaulle a message: "We'll respect neutrality and freedom in Laos and we're not going to put military troops in there. . . . If we do anything as stupid as that, we'll have a land war in Asia. . . ."

"Thank God the Bay of Pigs happened when it did," Kennedy

later told Sorensen. "Otherwise we'd be in Laos now—and that would be a hundred times worse."

*   *   *

When Kennedy was a congressman, just returned from Indo-china, in 1951, he said the U.S. must not ally itself "with a colonial regime that had no real support from the people. The single most powerful force in the world is man's desire to be free."

When he was running for the Senate in 1952, he put a pointer on a map of Vietnam and told a Massachusetts audience that it was "a white man's war against the natives."

When he was President of the United States ten years later, he cursed Eisenhower as "a lying son of a bitch" because he had told him that we wouldn't need any more people in Vietnam to handle the situation because most Vietnamese were pro-American.

Kennedy confided his feelings about Eisenhower to Larry Newman, and his friend said that President Truman had used the same phrase about Eisenhower. Truman had approved the first military assistance plan to Vietnam; Eisenhower had sent in the first military advisers and had pledged to South Vietnam that the U.S. would help them resist any aggression.

The Geneva agreements of 1954 had split Vietnam into two countries, North Vietnam and South Vietnam. The American commitment to South Vietnam was to help maintain a strong viable state and resist subversion or aggression through military means. North Vietnam leader Ho Chi Minh was seen as an agent of Red China and Russia, and part of a plan to sweep all of Indochina into Communist orbit.

Kennedy felt he had inherited a commitment. He had sent Gen. Maxwell Taylor on an inspection trip and had told him forcefully, "I don't want to send troops there." "The troops will march in," Kennedy told Schlesinger, "the bands will play, the crowds will cheer, then we will be told we will have to send more troops. It's like taking a drink. The effect wears off and you have to take another."

General Taylor warned that any deep involvement would

put American prestige on the line and could "increase tensions and risk escalation into a major war in Asia."

Trying to explain why his brother was determined to let the Vietnamese win the war for themselves, and therefore was sending only military advisers, Bobby said, "We wanted to avoid a Korea."

"Before he was inaugurated," recalled Deputy Defense Secretary Gilpatric, "we presented him with a list of possible crises he could expect to face in his first year and Vietnam wasn't even on the list. Vietnam came on all of us unexpectedly when those Buddhist monks burned themselves in protest.

"McNamara and I went over for the first time in April 1961, and we recommended some 2,000 Americans be sent there as instructors in all kinds of categories. Kennedy cut that down to 200. Then Rostow and Taylor went over and they wanted a whole corps of combat engineers sent in, and he cut that down, too. He wanted minimum involvement."

By 1963, Vietnam was in a state of chaos. The Buddhists rose against the Catholic-dominated Diem regime. Kennedy stepped up American aid and increased our "military advisers" to fifteen thousand. By September, he began having doubts. "In the first analysis it is their war," Kennedy said in a television interview. "They are the ones who have to win it or lose it." Significantly, he added, "I don't agree with those who say we should withdraw. That would be a mistake."

Prime Minister Ngo Dinh Diem of South Vietnam was a devout Catholic and a dictatorial mandarin. He also had no interest in becoming a popular democratic leader, and resented American insistence on fighting communism with reforms.

The presidential question was, "If we can't win with Diem, with whom can we win?" The prime Kennedy concern was expressed in a cable from McGeorge Bundy to our ambassador in Vietnam, Henry Cabot Lodge: ONCE A COUP UNDER RESPONSIBLE LEADERSHIP HAS BEGUN IT IS IN THE INTEREST OF THE U.S. GOVERNMENT THAT IT SHOULD SUCCEED.

Kennedy insisted that he did not know of the "blood oath" that Vietnamese generals had taken to kill Diem in the coup. The Diem death "upset him unbelievably," said an aide. "He was horrified." General Taylor recalled how the President rushed from the room "with a look of shock and dismay on his face which I had never seen before. I had not seen Kennedy so depressed since the Bay of Pigs."

"I think he thought Bobby screwed up Diem's assassination, that Bobby knew something before he did," White House aide Fred Dutton suggested. "I think it wouldn't have happened if the President had known. I know he really was very upset about it. Maybe partly because Diem was a Catholic. No, he wouldn't have been disturbed if Castro was killed."

"You go and represent me [at the funeral]," Kennedy told Godfrey McHugh, Pierre Salinger, and Ken O'Donnell.

"You know, Mr. President, we can't do that."

"Well, by God, that's what you're going to do. I'm not going to go. I can't face the situation."

Discussing his brother's responsibility for the Vietnam War, Bobby Kennedy thought a minute and said, "I don't know which would be best: to say that he didn't spend much time thinking about Vietnam; or, to say that he did and messed it up." Bobby then thrust his hand to the sky and said, "Which, brother, which?"

If he once had been a hawk at the time of the Bay of Pigs, a cold warrior, a captive of the "thinking generals," Jack Kennedy was now once again the moderate in late 1963. "He would not stand for long the sight of pine coffins coming back from a futile battle," columnist Mary McGrory said. He had not taken the hawk course in the Cuban crisis, bombing the missiles. He had not taken the hawk course on Laos, sending in troops.

Sorensen believes that he would not have sent combat divisions into South Vietnam, nor would he have sent bombing missions over North Vietnam. David Ormsby-Gore, who also talked to Kennedy about it, agreed. "The great feeling I had from him then was that he would not have gone into any mass involvement of troops." The President told Rep. Frank Thompson that he was committed to send in a maximum of twenty thousand troops, but then planned to phase out the operation. "He could not have been more firm or more specific."

"Would he have pulled out if he had lived? It's a hard thing to know," Undersecretary of State George Ball answered. "He kept asking me, 'What do we do next?' I have great doubt that he would have done anything different than Johnson did. It was a kind of creeping thing. It was hard, at any point, to say, 'This is enough and no further.' And he probably would have said, as Johnson did, 'I'm not going to be the first President to lose a war.' "

Ball added, "I told him then that, if we went down the course, we'd have three hundred thousand men in Vietnam in five years' time and we'd never see them again."

"George, I always thought you were one of the smartest guys in town," Kennedy told him, "but you're crazy as hell; it isn't going to happen."

"He just didn't seem to want to talk about it," Ball said.

Just before his death, Kennedy had told Director of Intelligence and Research Roger Hilsman, "The South Vietnamese couldn't make it, and if we used American troops, they couldn't make it."

"If I tried to pull out completely now from Vietnam, we would have another Joe McCarthy red scare on our hands," Kennedy told O'Donnell, "but I can do it after I'm re-elected. So we better make damn sure I'm re-elected. In 1965 I'll become one of the most unpopular presidents in history. I'll be damned everywhere as a Communist appeaser. But I don't care."

"We were all in the Cabinet Room a month before he died," McNamara recalled. "We were discussing his authorized withdrawal of a thousand troops from Vietnam by December. There was a lot of pro and con at the meeting, but the final decision was Kennedy's. His reason there was that our role in Vietnam should be limited to training and assisting Vietnam to carry on their war, but it was their country and their responsibility and their war. All we could do, and should do, he said, was to provide the hardware and a certain degree of training."

"Tell them that means the helicopter pilots too," the President said to McNamara.

Some 16,657 American troops had been sent to Vietnam. Sixty-nine of them had been killed.

Larry Newman saw the President and talked to him during

his last visit to Hyannis. Kennedy talked about a lot of things, including Vietnam. "This war in Vietnam—it's never off my mind, it haunts me day and night," he said. He told Newman that General MacArthur and General De Gaulle had used almost identical words warning him not to commit the United States to a land war in Asia.

"The first thing I do when I'm re-elected," he said. "I'm going to get the Americans out of Vietnam. Exactly how I'm going to do it, right now, I don't know, but that is my number one priority—get out of Southeast Asia. I should have listened to MacArthur. I should have listened to De Gaulle.

"We are not going to have men ground up in this fashion, this far away from home. I'm going to get those guys out because we're not going to find ourselves in a war it's impossible to win."

In the back of Kennedy's mind were his own speeches as a congressman during the French-Indochinese War, where he saw the French suffer a humiliating defeat in a colonial war.

"It is much easier to make speeches," Kennedy reflected, "than it is finally to make the judgments."

He was still growing.

The black bag belonged to twenty-four warrant officers. One of these officers carried that black bag and went wherever the President went. The black bag had no vacations. It was there twenty-four hours a day, every day. The warrant officers worked in three eight-hour shifts. In that black bag was the atomic signal system that could mean the end of the world.

Human Rights/Civil Rights

It was a rainy day and the President asked his special assistant for science, Jerome Wiesner of the Massachusetts Institute of Technology, whether the radioactivity was right there—in that rain. Yes, he was told, it was. He stood silent for several minutes, looking out the window of the White House at the rain.

Atomic fallout preyed on the President's mind. He took his helicopter to Germantown, Maryland, for a briefing on atomic energy. Instead of the ten allotted minutes with each division director, Kennedy doubled the time for his searching questions.

"You did not have the feeling that, because you were in the presence of the President of the United States, you had to be on your best behavior. You could interrupt," said Glen Seaborg, chairman of the Atomic Energy Commission. "He'd start out by saying, 'I've got X questions I want to ask,' and after asking them he'd go around the room and ask each person what he thought.

Then, on the basis of that, he'd formulate a consensus. Then he'd say, 'All right, what's wrong with that?' "

With time running short before his return to Washington appointments, his aides pressed him to skip his questioning of the director of Biology and Medicine.

"All right," said the President, "but I want to ask him one question—Why don't we hear anything about the fallout anymore?"

That was because the Russian-American moratorium had made the fallout minimal.

"Yeah," Kennedy said, "but what if it starts again?"

If testing was resumed at the previous level, the director said, "then civilized man will be in trouble."

"Now I begin to wonder if my son, John, will ever grow up," Kennedy said afterwards.

In thirteen years of nuclear testing, since 1949, the United States, Great Britain, and the Soviet Union had made 336 nuclear explosions in the atmosphere. In 1962, the United States and Great Britain had proposed a treaty to ban all nuclear tests, except those carried out underground. In the seesaw negotiations with the Soviet Union, the great hurdle was the number and nature of inspections.

"We are making nuclear tests," Nikita Khrushchev told *New York Times* reporter Cyrus Sulzberger. "But what the hell do we want with tests? You cannot put a bomb in soup, or make an overcoat out of it."

"The advantages Eisenhower had over Kennedy were that he was an older man," Khrushchev later recalled, "a hero of World War II, a man who commanded great respect in the U.S., and therefore, if he said the USA should not go to war, no one would dare accuse him of being afraid. President Kennedy is in a different position. Politically, he has a much broader outlook. When I talked with him in Vienna, I found him a worthy partner. He himself conducted the talks without depending on Rusk the way Eisenhower always depended on Dulles. At Geneva in 1955, Eisenhower always waited for Dulles to scribble something on a piece of paper, telling him what to do before he said anything. He took everything from Dulles and read it out. We were amazed. Kennedy formulates his own ideas. That is his superiority to Eisenhower. I had a feeling he understood things better. I am sure, if Kennedy himself were able to decide matters, he would not enter into any argument over Berlin and Germany. He is not a lawyer; he is a President."

"One of the ironic things is that Mr. Khrushchev and I occupy approximately the same political positions inside our governments," Kennedy later commented. "He would like to prevent a nuclear war but is under severe pressure from his hard-line crowd, which interprets every move in that direction as appeasement. I've got similar problems. The hard-liners in the Soviet Union and the United States feed on one another."

"The President was moving on pretty good ground with Khrushchev, and it would be original ground," Spalding observed. "He was getting over the paranoia that Kissinger talks about. He was closer than anybody. He had a chance. It takes somebody like that, somebody you can reach, and apparently he had reached Khrushchev."

"What was fascinating," noted Pierre Salinger, "and what nobody knew, was that Kennedy and Khrushchev were carrying on a wonderful dialogue in private letters—things they couldn't possibly say aloud. Some of that stuff is absolutely mind-blowing and will be kept secret until 1988. But the two men really got to know each other that way. There were some sixty letters between them and Khrushchev's first letter was thirty-two pages long. In the language they used, the references they made, it was like a peasant writing to an intellectual—but they were on the same wavelength. When I saw Khrushchev, I remember how impressed he was with the Kennedy he now knew. And I remember his saying, 'I'd never have believed that my daughter could have lunch at the White House.' But what really emerged from those letters was the success of the test ban treaty."

Kennedy's representative at the test ban negotiations was Averell Harriman, then seventy-one and undersecretary of state, a roving ambassador. Harriman had been a presidential troubleshooter since the Roosevelt administration. The President earlier had told Bill Walton, "If you want your friend Harriman to have a place in my administration, tell him to get an earphone."

Harriman was known as "the crocodile." "When the President is looking around the room at a time of decision, you can't wait. Mouth open, I bite."

"Khrushchev loved Harriman," Salinger added. "At one point, he suggested that Harriman come and work for him and he'd send over a guy to work for Kennedy."

Kennedy explained to Harriman that he didn't want daily summaries of the meetings, and he didn't want the facts filtered through Harriman's mind. He wanted everything blow-by-blow "so we can appraise it ourselves" and send specific instructions back to Harriman.

Kennedy's key adviser on the subject was his old friend, British Ambassador David Ormsby-Gore. Bobby Kennedy called him "almost part of the government" and "a motivating force." Then he added, "I think that he'd [the President] rather have his judgment than almost anybody else's."

"I was the unofficial minister of disarmament for the British government at the time," Ormsby-Gore said, "and I was full of the subject. I talked to him about it from 1954 on. I reminded him the Soviets had been invaded by the Germans and lost heavily in that war. And they never afterwards could or would trust anybody. But the Soviets didn't want nuclear war any more than we did, because they *knew* what the holocaust would be, just as we did. Jackie told me she took notes when Jack and I talked about this.

"Jack was not passionate about nuclear disarmament at first —he was logical and unemotional, just as he was about every other issue, national or international. He became emotional about it during the missile crisis. That's when he finally realized that the decision for a nuclear holocaust was his—and that final decision was just over the horizon. And he saw it in terms of children—his children and everybody else's children. And then that's where his passion came in, that's when his emotion came in."

"If you could think *only* of yourself," Kennedy had said, "it would be easy to say you'd press the button, and easy to press it, too. It may sound corny but I am not thinking so much of our world, but the world that Caroline will live in."

It haunted him. "What kind of world are we going to leave

behind to the children? What kind of world am *I* going to leave behind?"

"I know how strongly anti-Communist Jack was," Ormsby-Gore continued, "but he grew more flexible about the Russians because he realized that we all have to live in the same world. That's why he believed that some accommodation must be made on disarmament by both sides. That's why his American University speech was probably his most important speech."

In that speech on June 10, 1963, Kennedy reminded Americans that "enmities between nations, as between individuals, do not last forever." He offered friendship to the Russian people in admiration for their many achievements.

"And if we cannot now end our differences, at least we can help make the world safe for diversity. For in the final analysis, our most basic common link is that we all inhabit this planet, we all breathe the same air. We all cherish our children's future. And we are all mortal."

Reminding the world that a single nuclear weapon contained almost ten times the explosive force delivered by all Allied air forces in the Second World War, Kennedy made an impassioned plea for a nuclear test ban treaty. As a point of good faith, he declared that the United States would unilaterally stop its nuclear atmospheric tests.

Kennedy's American University speech hit Khrushchev with the force of shock. He told Harriman that it was the best speech by an American president since Franklin D. Roosevelt. It surely must have taken great courage on Kennedy's part to make such a speech, he said, and perhaps he had overestimated the cold warrior dominance in Washington, perhaps it was a time for a thaw.

Khrushchev not only ordered Soviet radio to broadcast the Kennedy speech in full—despite some derogatory references to the Soviet Union—but he also gave orders not to jam our Voice of America broadcasts. Russia said it was ready to re-open the stalled nuclear negotiations for a test ban treaty.

Khrushchev then predicted that history would judge Kennedy as "an outstanding statesman." In his memoirs, Khrushchev wrote, "I'll always remember the late President with deep respect because, in the final analysis, he showed himself to be sober-minded and determined to avoid war. He didn't let himself become frightened; nor did he become reckless."

The negotiations, which had been dragging for months, suddenly took on a new urgency, with Harriman's presence and the President personally riding herd to eliminate trivial issues. Both Macmillan and Khrushchev wanted major publicity at the signing, but Kennedy was cautious. The treaty would mean nothing until Congress approved it. He concentrated on key Republican senators, sent emissaries to Eisenhower and leading conservatives, and pressured for passage of the treaty as he had never pressured for anything else.

Thirty United States senators found themselves shouting at each other at a White House luncheon on the test ban treaty. As the arguments grew more heated, the President finally interrupted. In his typical, cool manner, he rose to his feet. "Well, I'm certainly glad to see that we've achieved agreement on the American side. Now let's see if we can get the Russians to agree."

The test ban treaty was approved overwhelmingly in the Senate, 80–19.

For once the pickets outside the White House were positive: "THANKS FOR THE A-TEST BAN!"

For the world, the moment was high with hope.

In the growth of this man, it was a peak point. This was not growth out of despair, as in the Bay of Pigs; or out of victory, as in the missile crisis; or out of anger, as in the steel price fight; or out of compassion, as in the civil rights issue. This was growth out of concern and wisdom and leadership. This was growth of a real depth and dimension.

*   *   *

In foreign affairs, the world was still filled with many more problems.

"It takes all our Presidents a good deal of time to learn about foreign affairs," said Dean Acheson years later. "Roosevelt took many years and never got a real grasp. Mr. Truman caught hold pretty quick, perhaps in eighteen months. Ike never learned much of anything. Jack Kennedy was just catching on in 1963."

"I know he saw the total bankruptcy of our China policy," George Ball said. "He was very tempted to support China's admission to the UN, but he said, 'Look, give me some time. This is a very thin mandate. Coming in with this small majority, I don't want to move and give the enemies too much.' "

"We are not wedded to a policy of hostility to Red China," Kennedy noted in his last press conference, and later added, "Let's face it. There's a subject for the second term."

His initial instinct always was to learn through his own investigations. When the Chinese invaded India, he asked Paul Nitze to go to India.

"When?" Nitze asked.

"There isn't any urgency. We don't suggest going until tomorrow morning."

He was willing to hear anybody's answer on anything, however blunt. When he found fault and error, however, "he could be hard as nails. He could cut people off right at the knee and I've seen him do it," White House aide Fred Dutton said.

"Bundy and I had approved of a statement by an ambassador critical of Diefenbaker in Canada, and Kennedy called us in," Ball recalled. "He was angry. 'Goddamn you! Mac here—he doesn't know a damn thing about politics and is never expected to know anything about politics—but *you've* been around a long time! Why in hell did you do it?' It took him about twenty minutes to cool off."

Still, he faulted himself as easily as he faulted others.

He told Carl Kaysen of the National Security Council that he was not doing very well in his negotiations on the Panama Canal with the Panamanian president.

Kaysen asked why.

"He says we've been screwing them all these years, and I agree."

Counter-insurgency had been the Kennedy answer to Third World revolutions, but, to the Kennedys, it was also high drama and adventure and meetings in a super-super secret room in the inner-inner Pentagon sanctum. Bobby Kennedy had persuaded the President to "use all our available assets to help Cuba overthrow the Communist regime." Sabotage the sugar mills. Pollute the motor oil. Poison pills for Castro's soup. Anything and everything—almost. The President had a framed copy of a George Washington letter on "the necessity of procuring good intelligence" and urging that "upon secrecy, success depends."

He and Smathers discussed the possibility of provoking an incident at the U.S. naval base at Guantanamo Bay, "which would then give us an excuse to go in and do the job." They even talked about a Castro assassination: How would the people react? What would it really accomplish?

"What would you think if I ordered Castro to be assassinated?" the President asked *New York Times* correspondent Tad Szulc in the Oval Office. Szulc replied that Castro's removal would not necessarily change the system and that the United States should not be a party to murder.

"Kennedy then said he was testing me, that he felt the same way because indeed the U.S. morally must not be a party to assassinations." Kennedy told Szulc that he raised the question because he was under terrific pressure from advisers to okay a Castro murder. He said he was resisting the pressures. Then he added, "Look, I'd like you to talk to my brother."

"The Kennedys wanted Castro the hell out of there and anybody who says anything different is just plain wrong," said former CIA Director Richard Helms.

Mafia leaders Sam Giancana and John Rosselli were recruited to find Cubans to kill Castro. The assassin was to be promised "everything he needed, telescopic sight, silencer, all the money he wanted." The inspector general of the CIA declared that "it is likely that at the very moment President Kennedy was shot, a CIA officer was meeting with a Cuban agent and giving him an assassination device for use against Castro." The assassination device was a poisoned pen.

A Senate committee later revealed that there had been eight specific plots from 1960 to 1965 by the CIA to kill Castro. There is no record of how many of these John Kennedy knew about— or wanted to know. He seemed to have second thoughts about Cuba. "I don't know why we didn't embrace Castro when he was in this country in 1959, pleading for help," Kennedy told Larry Newman. "That was the time to send him all the equipment, food, and everything else he needed. Instead of that, we made an enemy of them, and then we get upset because the Russians are giving them money—doing for them what *we* wouldn't do." More quietly, he added, "If a man stays in hot politics long enough, he acquires an albatross. I've got Cuba."

* * *

President Kennedy often told his brother and others that a dozen people in the White House who worked under his direction with McGeorge Bundy really performed all the functions of the State Department, that the State Department produced very few policy positions. He estimated the new concepts coming from the White House as eighty percent of our foreign policy.

"The President and I discussed on a number of occasions . . . moving Rusk out, perhaps to the United Nations," his brother said. "Rusk speaks very well, awfully loyal, and a very nice man [but] the State Department wasn't managed properly. It wasn't just a question of bad judgment, but a lack of preparation on major issues, Cuba, or Laos . . . a failure to anticipate, and failure to do your homework."

At the behest of the President, Bobby Kennedy, who took along his dog Bramus, visited Rusk to tell him that Rusk needed "somebody who could organize and pull the place together." President Kennedy had seriously considered making his brother secretary of state. "I talked to Jack about it," Justice William Douglas said. "I talked to Bobby about it. That would get him into the area of where his real interests lay."

The President also talked to Galbraith about replacing Rusk with McNamara saying: "McNamara would be all right. But then, if I don't have McNamara at Defense to control the generals, I won't have a foreign policy."

When Kennedy eased out Undersecretary of State Chester Bowles, Harris Wofford called it "the wrong firing at the wrong time of the wrong view in the wrong department." In a memo to the President, Wofford wrote, "You need someone, from the time he wakes up in the morning until he goes to sleep, who knows that the Cuban invasion is wrong and that our new position on Angola is right. If Bowles goes, I don't know who else you have at the top level ready or able to do this. I do not mean that you should always take Bowles' advice—but it needs to be there steadily, and to be heard."

Bowles was a man of nobility and sweeping concepts, a warm, generous man. In a Kennedy administration of quick answers, he was more inclined to the imprecise long view. Many saw in him "the litmus test" of liberalism in the New Frontier. When Bowles discovered that there was not a single ambassador or career minister under the age of fifty in the State Department, he persuaded 135 older foreign service officers to retire to give a greater accent on youth. He was not, however, the tough organizer that Kennedy wanted. "Chet isn't up to it," Rusk told Ball when he asked Ball to involve himself in more political matters. Bowles accepted the appointment as ambassador to India to replace John Kenneth Galbraith.

"With the Kennedys," Dave Powers had said, "you can't be right ninety-nine times out of a hundred—you have to be right a hundred times."

*   *   *

"People who say that Kennedy didn't accomplish very much as President forget how it was at the end of the Eisenhower administration," Ormsby-Gore remembered. "Here was Eisenhower, one of the most popular American presidents, who couldn't visit Japan because of the expected riots. And here was his vice-president, Nixon, who went to Venezuela and was stoned by the crowds. But two years after Kennedy was inaugurated, this young President was invited by every leader in the world."

In his three years, President Kennedy had seen a dozen more foreign heads of state than President Roosevelt had seen in a dozen years.

When the Kennedys went to Mexico City, the confetti was so thick it looked like a snowstorm. Mexican crowds were delighted with the handsome youth of this couple, and with the fact that Jacqueline Kennedy spoke Spanish everywhere she went. Somebody in Mexico even wrote a song about her. More and more often now, the President called his wife his "number one ambassador of good will"—and he was beginning to believe it.

In the Mexican tradition, when Kennedy admired the unusual watch of President Lopez Mateos, the Mexican president insisted he take it. When Jacqueline appeared in a stunning gown and Lopez expressed his admiration, Kennedy quipped, "You better take back your watch." The Mexican president made a few remarks in Spanish at a joint press conference, and Jacqueline Kennedy scowled perceptibly. She understood Spanish and the remarks were not flattering to the United States.

One of the President's most enthusiastic supporters was Prime Minister Harold Macmillan. Their age difference was so great that their relationship was almost that of a father and a son. Indeed Macmillan said that he not only liked Kennedy but came to love him. Macmillan, after the missile crisis, claimed that Kennedy "did what we failed to do in the critical years before the two German wars. If Kennedy never did another thing, he assured his place in history by that single act."

Kennedy's relationship with De Gaulle was more edgy. "De Gaulle's philosophy," Salinger said, "was that you always supported the person who was weakest in a situation. That way if the weak one wins, you get credit for helping, but if you support the strong contender, he owes you nothing. Esssential opportunism." After one conversation with De Gaulle, Kennedy hung up and said angrily, "totally impossible man." Then he thought quietly for a moment and told Salinger, "Well, he's doing the thing he thinks best for France and I'm doing what I think best for America, and they may not be the same thing."

*   *   *

The pragmatic President was now also more passionate about civil rights. Earlier, he had told liberal Joseph Rauh not to push him on civil rights because his criticism was "quite wrong." Rauh remembered how "Kennedy turned on me with great force." After Birmingham, John Kennedy told Rauh that the civil rights struggle was going to be "a long, tough fight but we have to do it."

What helped change him, what "horrified" him, what made him "sick," was a photograph of a police dog lunging at a black woman. "A snarling police dog set upon a human being," said TV commentator Eric Sevareid, "is recorded in the permanent photoelectric file of every human being's brain." Television amplified the horror, showing Birmingham's police slashing with their nightsticks, using pressure fire hoses, methodically beating people, one policeman even sitting on a fallen woman. Police Commissioner Eugene "Bull" Connor, a candidate for mayor, ordered the arrest of protesting blacks, including a thousand children.

In response to a bombing, the blacks threw rocks, broke windows, burned shops. "Let the whole fucking city burn!" one of them yelled. "I am not asking for patience," the President told black leaders. "I can well understand why the Negroes of Birmingham are tired of being asked to be patient." He startled them by saying they should thank God for Bull Connor because he had helped the civil rights movement "as much as Abraham Lincoln."

One of those arrested was Martin Luther King, Jr.

Black leaders worried that the police would manhandle King in jail, that they might even kill him. Coretta King called Robert Kennedy, who immediately ordered the FBI to check the jail. The next day the President called Mrs. King to say her husband was well and would soon phone her. When King called, his wife updated him about the Kennedy intervention. "So that's why everybody is suddenly being so polite."

The Birmingham mayor contemptuously referred to King as "this nigger who has got the blessing of the attorney general and the White House." The mayor's venom was particularly aimed at the attorney general. "I hope that every drop of blood that's spilled he tastes in his throat and I hope he chokes on it."

Bobby Kennedy and Burke Marshall, his assistant attorney general for civil rights, met with the President for breakfast in his upstairs bedroom. The President was still in his pajamas.

A federal district judge had ordered the University of Alabama to admit two Negroes. Governor George Wallace had declared, "Segregation now! Segregation tomorrow! Segregation forever!" He promised to stand at the college doorway himself to bar their entrance.

The President listened intently to his brother and made "up his mind right away about what we should do. That impressed me," Bobby recalled.

"On the Alabama thing, we were going to wait until the governor moved before calling up the troops . . . then I thought maybe we should call up the troops that morning. So I called him [the President] about doing that and he said, 'Let's just stay with what we decided originally,' which was the right decision."

The confrontation came, the governor standing in the doorway of the college to block the entry of the black students. When the Alabama National Guard arrived, however, the governor quietly left the scene and the students were registered.

A bomb in Birmingham later killed four black children at a Sunday school and one of the picket signs outside the White House read: "MR. JFK, IF CAROLINE AND JOHN JR. HAD BEEN AMONG THE CHILDREN MURDERED, WOULD YOU STILL BE TALKING?"

That was the way to get him—through his children. But there was no more need for "creative pressure." Their cause was now his cause.

Bombs, riots, police dogs, burning, looting in scattered cities. The white South blamed the White House for stirring it all up. Blacks blamed the White House for not helping enough. The rest of the country was torn, with rumblings of conscience, hate, and fear.

Presidential popularity plummeted in the polls, from 76 percent to 59 percent. Attorney General Robert Kennedy offered to resign to minimize the President's political burden in the upcoming election. The President refused, "because it would look as if we were running away from it." The President realized that leadership had to come from the White House, regardless of political consequences.

His decision to talk on television to the American people about this civil rights crisis was impulsive. His aides counseled caution. Only his brother urged him on. He made some notes "on the back of an envelope," then discussed it with Sorensen.

"I remember him sitting there, putting down these notes, without any speech, when he was about to go on television," Assistant Attorney General Burke Marshall recalled. "Five minutes before the President went on the air, Sorensen returned with most of the draft." Even so, Kennedy spoke extemporaneously at the end.

This was not the cool man on the cool medium. This was a speech that burned.

"We preach freedom around the world, and we mean it, and we cherish our freedom here at home, but are we to say to the world, and much more importantly, to each other that this is a land of the free except for the Negroes; that we have no second-class citizens except Negroes? . . . Who among us would be content to have the color of his skin changed and stand in his place? Who among us would then be content with the counsels of patience and delay?

"The fires of frustration . . . are burning in every city, north and south, where legal remedies are not at hand. . . . We face therefore, a moral crisis as a country and as a people . . . [and] those who do nothing are inviting shame as well as violence."

A columnist commented: "There hasn't been a speech like that in a hundred years."

The night of the speech, there was a dramatic, ugly reaction. Medgar Evers, a field secretary of the National Association for the Advancement of Colored People, was killed in Jackson, Mississippi. The President reacted in the swift spirit of his anger. He invited Mrs. Evers and her three children to the White House. They walked in with their pride—a sorrowful but dignified family dressed in black. "I am told that if you sit in the President's chair," Evelyn Lincoln advised them, "and make one wish, it will come true." Each of them solemnly sat in the President's chair. The oldest boy bowed his head. He had wished, he said, that his father had not died in vain.

The President was now ready with his own action, proposing to Congress "the most comprehensive civil rights bill in our history." On June 19, 1963, only eight days after his televised speech, he told Congress, "I ask you to look into your hearts . . . for the one plain, proud, and priceless quality that unites all as Americans: a sense of justice."

In Danville, Georgia, Robert Kennedy pointed out that some accommodations accepted dogs but refused Negroes.

Black leaders no longer wanted to wait for the slow passage of a bill. They wanted action—now. They wanted a massive march on Washington. The President was against it, saw it as an ill-timed big show that might cause congressmen to say, "I'm damned if I will vote for it at the point of a gun."

"It may be ill-timed," King answered. "Frankly, I have never engaged in any direct action movement which did not seem ill-timed. Some people thought Birmingham was ill-timed." Kennedy interrupted quietly, "Including the attorney general."

The President worried that the march might fall flat, that not enough people would come. But the concept had caught the imagination and conscience of a generation. They came from all over America, black and white, young and old, and they all came in peace. The attorney general's office had arranged everything from food to toilets, and had even substituted paper cups for bottles, which could become weapons. No weapons were necessary. For the overwhelming mass of people in front of the Lincoln Memorial on August 28, 1963—more than 250,000—there was the pure fire of a revival meeting. They held hands, swaying to the rhythm of the words of Martin Luther King, Jr.

"I have a dream that one day even the state of Mississippi, a desert state sweltering with the heat of injustice and oppression, shall be transformed into an oasis of freedom and justice . . . when all of God's children will be able to join hands and sing 'Free at last! Free at last! Thank God Almighty, we are free at last!' "

"Fuck that dream, Martin," a black man yelled from the crowd. "Now, goddamn it, NOW!"

FBI Director J. Edgar Hoover watched unmoved. Hoover regarded King as a dangerous degenerate surrounded by Communist advisers. An assistant attorney general reported to Robert Kennedy on how Hoover had fulminated against King. "Oh sure," Kennedy replied, "that's the way it's been for a while." Another Justice aide told the attorney general how Hoover had spent an hour discussing wiretapped bedroom conversations of King in sexual intimacy with various women, some of them white. "Bobby, what is this all about?" the aide asked. Bobby had no comment.

What few knew then was that the attorney general had approved Hoover's wiretap of King. He had done this, friends insisted, because he felt the tapes would prove King innocent of all charges of Communist connections.

The President kept his own list of growing complaints against Hoover. The American consulate refused a visa to a British Communist who wanted to visit his dying sister in the United States. Kennedy ordered the visa issued and asked Abba Schwartz of the State Department to request a twenty-four-hour FBI surveillance while the Communist was in this country. "I want to show how ridiculous the whole business is," the President said.

Hoover refused, claimed he didn't have the money or the staff to do it. Then he told Schwartz, "You know, I have practically financed the Communist Party in order to keep tabs on them."

When Schwartz reported this to the President, Kennedy answered, "Tell it to Kenny; he's keeping a record on all this."

"To me," Schwartz said, "this meant that Kennedy planned to get rid of Hoover after his re-election."

There would be many questions about what President Kennedy would have done if he had been re-elected. Surely, he would not have had to worry about the folder in the Hoover file that connected Kennedy, during the war, with the lovely Inga Arvad, accused of being a Nazi spy.

In terms of domestic legislation, it had not been a good year for John Kennedy. Both his civil rights bill and tax cut bill were stalled in Congress. One-third of his legislative proposals never got out of committee. Nor was he appeased when it was pointed out that Franklin D. Roosevelt never got a major piece of legislation passed in his last seven years in office. His answer to that was to quote Woodrow Wilson, who said that a political party was of no use unless it served a great purpose.

"Perhaps the Kennedy administration changed more than most," Bundy admitted, "possibly because some of us were too optimistic about the uses of vigor in 1961, but quite as probably because a formidable leader had learned so much about his job."

"Jack told Bobby that foreign affairs was a necessity of concentration during his first term," Schlesinger said, "but he wanted domestic affairs to be the main concern of his second term."

When noted liberal economist Robert Nathan pushed an idea about some unemployment legislation that the President felt he could not then accept, he still told Nathan, "I want you to keep this up. It's very helpful now for you to keep pushing me this way."

He borrowed a copy of Michael Harrington's *The Other America: Poverty in the United States,* and publicly mentioned how much sense it made. The book sold over a million copies.

Discussing a voluntary national service corps program at a Cabinet meeting, the President wrote the word "poverty" on a yellow pad and underlined it several times. The domestic Peace Corps idea had been a pet project of his sister Eunice.

One of his growing concerns was the Alliance for Progress. *Alianza para el progreso.* He had made it part of his election campaign and part of his inaugural address. He wanted it compared to Roosevelt's Good Neighbor Policy, combining economic progress and social justice "into a vast crucible of revolutionary ideas." "We are opposed to military coups," he said, "because we think they are self-defeating." Congress had voted funds, and the program had gone into gear. During the fund fight in Congress, Kennedy had said of his opposition, "They try to sound so noble about setting an example with our own people first." To emphasize the desperate need in Latin America, he added, "What does medical care for the aged mean in countries with a life expectancy of forty?"

The *New York Times* had reported that Kennedy's Alliance for Progress was "in a state of crisis," and it was true. Kennedy had recruited Peace Corps Deputy Bill Haddad to go to Latin America and find out what had gone wrong. Haddad soon reported the damning fact that too much American Alliance money had disappeared into too few pockets.

Bartlett summed up Kennedy's mood: "The first term is sort of a tap dance hoping for a second term with a real mandate from the people."

At Burbank, he was scheduled to talk at a Democratic fund-raising dinner when he discovered that a John Burroughs high school class also had a dance scheduled in the same grand ballroom. He had the Democrats re-scheduled to another part of the hotel, and visited the high school dance. "Next to being President," he told them, "I would prefer being a member of this class tonight. . . ."

The way he said it, they almost believed it.

A Rekindled Tenderness

Caroline whimpered because she was frightened. When it came time to get into the motorboat to head out for her first water-skiing lesson at Hyannis Port, she was trembling, and then she cried. Her mother raced to her, hugged her. "Darling, don't be afraid. You don't want others to think you're not brave, do you?"

Caroline—who was not quite six—whispered, "No."

"Now dry your eyes, there's nothing to fear, so come on and let's do it. It will make Daddy so proud when he comes home this weekend."

That weekend the President was standing and applauding as his daughter made her expert turns on the water skis. When it was done, the mother said to her wet, glowing daughter, "Now go to Daddy."

Mrs. Kennedy liked to take her children for a box picnic lunch at Wheaton Regional Park in Maryland, looking at the farm animals with a child at each arm. Perhaps the other mothers with the other children would not have noticed the woman in the orange dress and sandals with the dark glasses and yellow bandanna—except for the Secret Service men in sober blue suits conspicuously at her side as she walked with her children.

Even when they sensed who she was, they thoughtfully let her alone.

Secret Service agents got a special request from the First Lady: In guarding her children, would they please try to be less obtrusive "to avoid a feeling of being in stir."

The cynical said that the Kennedy children were part of the political act, and had to pay their dues. It was true that photographers were often around when the Kennedy children came to call on their father in the Oval Office, crawl into his lap, and hide under his desk. It made popular copy.

But they were not there every morning when the President-father would say to his son, "Come on, let's go to work." And little John—not quite three years old—in his pajamas and bathrobe, would troop along with his father down the White House steps to the Oval Office. Before the Secret Service man took him upstairs again to the family quarters, he would hug and kiss his father.

John, Jr., wanted to fly everywhere with his father. The President gave him a toy plane and said he would get him a real one when he grew up.

"Promise, Daddy, when I grow up? Promise?"

The President held him tight. "I promise. Someday I'll get you a real plane."

When his son visited him during the day, Kennedy held out his arms and John ran to him for his hug and kisses. Then the father grinned and said, "Tell me a secret." John buzzed something into his ear and the father put on an exaggerated look of mock surprise, leaned back in his chair, and said, "You . . . don't . . . tell . . . me!" And his son laughed.

It was something they always did, again and again, and little John never tired of the game. Afterwards, he ran around the desk, pushed against the paneling holding the seal of the United States until it swung inward, and then disappeared inside his private hiding place.

"If you bungle raising your children I don't think whatever else you do well matters very much," Jacqueline had said.

Nancy Tuckerman, who had been her roommate at Miss Porter's School, had replaced Letitia Baldrige as social secretary. Baldrige had quit to go to work at Joseph Kennedy's Merchandise Mart in Chicago in June 1963. Tuckerman and Jacqueline went to see *Anne of a Thousand Days*. Jacqueline whispered how much Caroline would love it, and three days later took her daughter to see it. "If I had a governess, I wouldn't sit through a movie twice," Tuckerman said. "I'd send Caroline with the governess. But that's not Jackie."

If she was not an overly affectionate mother, she was a concerned one. It was not simply a question of practicing French with her daughter, or creating a nursery school in the White House so that her children could have friends their age, but a question of budgeting time every day to give them her undivided attention.

The Kennedys were not permissive parents, but she smiled when John emerged from the bathroom to parade down the hall stark naked carrying an American flag. She sat at the edge of the trampoline, watched them play, and read to them. "John, go down to the fountain and find the goldfish." Away he would race on his little legs and soon return with the report, "Doggies chase all the goldfish away."

They had two dogs, Clipper and Charlie—even though her husband was allergic to dogs—because she felt the children should not be deprived. Her husband agreed. "You be good to those dogs," he told them. "They're your friends."

She worried when they got off a plane somewhere and Caroline asked, "Where are the photographers?" But she loved it when Caroline told a guest that her father was "upstairs with his shoes and socks off doing nothing."

John was an active, inquiring little two-year-old who loved to sing and dance and say no. Visiting heads of state bounced him on their knees or tweaked his cheek. If he wandered into the family dining room while his father had a briefing breakfast, his father usually parked him in his lap.

Caroline occasionally came charging into the Cabinet Room

on her tricycle. When she did, she, too, sat in her father's lap. For a while, there was even a rocking horse in the Cabinet Room. The President told the Cabinet, "We keep that rocking horse in here to remind us of the younger generation and what our responsibilities are in making this country a safe place in which to live."

On Halloween, 1963, the two children arrived at the Oval Office in their costumes and masks and solemnly asked Evelyn Lincoln, "Do you think he'll know who we are?" Mrs. Lincoln assured them that there was no such possibility. As they entered their father's office, he greeted them, "Why it's Sam and Mary." The two were furious until he made them laugh.

One of the games the President played with his son was to say, "Hello there, Sam, how are you?"

"I'm not Sam."

Then the President would say, "OK, I'll race you to the pool." A laughing John always won.

He invited five-year-old Caroline to witness the honorary citizenship ceremony for eighty-nine-year-old Winston Churchill. Her governess was with her and suggested she watch her father.

"My father has told me to always watch the other people," she answered, "because they're the important ones. My father says that I should always keep my eyes open and see other things. My father says I can see him anytime, so today I think I'll watch Mr. Churchill."

On the third floor, the children had a sandbox, cages of rabbits and guinea pigs, and a variety of goldfish and plants. But their greatest fun was in the White House yard. The First Lady had designed a play area for them near the President's office, a place hidden under the trees.

There was a treehouse, a slide, a leather swing, a barrel tunnel, and a rabbit hutch. She later added a snowfence pen for the lambs, houses for the two dogs, and a stable for the two ponies. Then she wanted a trampoline. "They're too little for a high one, so could you place it at ground level so we won't have to climb up to jump. And hide it somehow, *please*." She supervised everything, including the planting of seven-foot holly trees as a screen. "Now when I jump on the trampoline, all they'll be able to see is my head sailing above the tree tops!"

J. B. West, White House chief usher, remembered watching Mrs. Kennedy on the trampoline "so happy, so abandoned, so like a little girl who had never grown up."

"Do you think you could plant some rhododendrons or something along this fence so that everybody can't stare in? I'm sick and tired of starring in everybody's home movies." She also was concerned that her children might be spoiled by too much public exposure.

When thirty large rhododendrons arrived, the President wanted to know why. "Shielding your children," he was told. "I hope it doesn't obstruct the tourists' view of the house," he said seriously. Even the First Lady admitted, "I guess they're entitled to some view of the White House. . . ." The President once came out to inspect the transplanting. "Let me know when you strike oil."

If his son was playing outside nearby, Kennedy sometimes went out to hug him, sometimes waited for him to make appearances. "Isn't he a charge?" the President would ask any visitor who arrived while his son was playing outside nearby. John was an uninhibited little boy with a chipped front tooth who loved the ceremonial parades for visiting dignitaries. "Where's the parade?" he always asked when he heard music. He was proud of his salute, his muscles, and his own model of the Gemini space capsule. He liked to try on the hats of arriving generals, generously handed out chewing gum, and greeted all guests by asking, "What's your name? My name is John Fitzgerald Kennedy, Junior." John also did a very good imitation of a chimpanzee scratching himself.

When the president of the Socialist Federal Republic of Yugoslavia, Josip Broz Tito, walked out of the green helicopter onto the fifty-foot red carpet on the White House lawn, he was greeted by the shrill young voice of John Kennedy, Jr., yelling from the White House balcony, "We want Kennedy. We want Kennedy."

Caroline was almost six when she started to type on Mrs. Lincoln's typewriter. "Which one is the *C*?" she asked. She wanted to type her whole name so she could show it to her father. Mrs. Lincoln also noticed that some of the paper on the President's desk had been initialed "CBK" and then scrawled with "Daddy."

The President was once overheard solemnly asking his daughter: "Have you been eating candy—yes, no, or maybe?"

In one of their discussions on children, Jacqueline said she thought that the ages from eight to eighteen were "useless." Her husband disagreed. He would be happy, he said, to trade places with a teen-ager.

The President greeted a newborn nephew with this letter:

"Welcome, to the youngest member of the clan. Your entrance is timely, as we need a new left end on the team. Here's hoping you do not acquire the political assets of your parents, the prolific qualities of your godfather [Bobby], or the problems of your uncle."

Jacqueline Kennedy's final official appearance before the birth of her third child was a state dinner for the Grand Duchess of Luxembourg, once a long-term guest at the White House and a rumored romance of President Franklin D. Roosevelt's during World War II. Mrs. Kennedy knew that the Duchess was a devotee of Shakespeare and arranged a program of Elizabethan music and poetry. Basil Rathbone recited Kennedy's favorite Shakespearean passage—the St. Crispian speech delivered by Henry V on the eve of the Battle of Agincourt (". . . we band of brothers . . ."). She personally selected the music from tapes sent from the Library of Congress.

The First Lady looked lovely wearing a pale mauve, square-necked evening dress with a gathered empire waistline. Her hair was neatly upswept, and she wore a triple-strand pearl necklace as well as a diamond sunburst pin.

Caroline Kennedy watched the 170 guests from the stairs, wearing a robe over her pink pajamas until she was finally whisked away by her nurse.

Despite her pregnancy, Mrs. Kennedy was in firm control of White House social life planning.

Two months before the State Dinner for the king and queen of Afghanistan in June, 1963, Mrs. Kennedy wrote a memo to Nancy Tuckerman:

This is a final memo. I have discussed it with JFK.

1. He definitely wants tattoo & fireworks—try to have them do the flag of Afghanistan not the King's face as it might not be recognized.
2. Use all the best parts of the Marine Drill but do add the Bagpipes & Drum & Bugle Corps. They add so much—Bagpipes come so romantically out of trees at early part of show—Drum & Bugle—is smashing near finale.
3. I don't think you should have cocktails in East Garden—as so many people will be coming in White House for the first time & that way they will never see State Rooms—& it makes an all outdoor evening so do receiving line as usual in East Room—the dinner &. Also if it rains we would have champagne and music in East Room.

She had later suggestions: "I don't want a lot of photogs milling about guests. . . . Have strolling strings come out at dessert as usual. . . .

With all this, Mrs. Kennedy was in Hyannis Port during the event and her sister-in-law Eunice acted as hostess.

Since she had a traumatic record of miscarriages, Mrs. Kennedy minimized her activities, spending more time on Squaw Island near Hyannis Port doing watercolors, which she planned to make into Christmas cards to be sold for the benefit of the National Cultural Center. Chief Usher J. B. West teased her about the timing of her pregnancy, accusing her of planning her life to avoid campaigning in the 1964 election. "She laughed and gave me a secret knowing look."

The big publicity flap on her pregnancy was Press Secretary Pierre Salinger's statement that the air force was spending a million dollars at the Otis Air Force Base hospital for special facilities for the expected birth. After investigation, it turned out that the money was being used to make the hospital capable of treating atomic war patients—according to a Senate directive.

"Go and tell Pierre that I don't want him opening his goddamn mouth talking about matters he knows nothing about, and to check with the air force or army or navy before he puts out this crap," said an angry President.

*   *   *

The pain was what doctors call "premonitory," a sharp stab. She had been watching her two children taking riding lessons at a barnyard in Osterville, near Hyannis, in August 1963. A farm employee quickly called her obstetrician, while Mrs. Kennedy corralled her children into the family convertible to head home. Both the doctor and the helicopter were waiting when she got there.

The President had been talking to the Citizens Committee for a Nuclear Test Ban when he got the news.

Larry Newman heard the helicopter arrive and he knew it had come to pick up Jacqueline and take her to nearby Otis Air Force Base hospital. Just then the phone rang. It was the President.

"I want you to go over there and just sit in the lobby of the hospital until I get there."

Newman didn't ask him why, he simply said, "I'll go right away."

She was already in the labor room when he got there, and Newman sat in the small lobby and waited.

"How long would it take to fly if I said I wanted to go somewhere?" the President asked.

"Thirty minutes," McHugh, his air force aide, replied.

"I want to fly right now. So get ready."

McHugh called Andrews Air Force Base. *Air Force One* was being tested and couldn't be ready in time. Vice-President Johnson was using the backup plane. They did have several four-engine planes called Jet Stars.

"We'll need three of them. On the ramp within ten minutes."

The President pushed a button on his desk for his helicopter and they were soon airborne. The President suddenly got an idea. There was a famous surgeon in New York. "See if you can get him and tell him to taxi to LaGuardia. We'll pick him up in thirty minutes."

The doctor was traced, found to be on call, and was soon in a taxi to LaGuardia Airport, where the presidential plane landed and picked him up. A helicopter waited at the Boston airport to take them to the hospital.

Within the hour Jacqueline Kennedy was being wheeled into the operating room. This was her fifth pregnancy: the first, a miscarriage in 1955; a stillborn baby a year later by Caesarian; then Caroline and John, Jr., both by Caesarian; and now this one, five-and-a-half weeks early, also scheduled for a Caesarian.

Caesarian section is one of the safest of major operations, and it took only a few minutes to get the baby out. It was a boy, four pounds ten and a half ounces, "a cute little monkey with brown hair," but like one-third of all Caesarian "preemies," he had breathing trouble. A veil-like membrane covered the inside of his walnut-size lungs making it difficult for the cells to exchange oxygen for carbon dioxide in the blood. The condition was called hyaline membrane disease and it killed twenty-five thousand premature babies every year. It was then inoperable.

Newman was still waiting when the President arrived. "He came over and made a move as if he were going to put his arm around my shoulder, then just shook hands and said, 'Thanks for being here. It made me feel so much better knowing you were here.'

"I've never seen him more emotional, and the way he said it, I was very close to tears. And I don't cry very easily."

The baby was in a pressurized incubator when a Catholic chaplain baptized him "Patrick Bouvier." The President was there when the doctors decided to transfer Patrick to the Children's Medical Center in Boston. As they wheeled him outside, a woman made the sign of the cross.

The following day, the President commuted by helicopter from the baby to his wife, then back to the baby again in Boston. For a while, the child began breathing more easily and the father quickly called his wife with the good news. Then the baby again began fighting for breath while the President, in a white surgical gown and cap, watched helplessly through a small porthole in the high-pressure chamber. The antibiotic drugs weren't working. The only hope was that normal body functions would dissolve the membrane.

*   *   *

They were in the plane together later that day, Bobby and Dave Powers, flying to the hospital where the President was watching Patrick die. Bobby wondered aloud what he could possibly say to his brother. He was fingering his rosary beads when he said to Powers, "Why don't we say a prayer? For the baby."

At the hospital, they joined the President, watching the baby struggling to breathe. The doctor noted that the baby seemed slightly better and suggested the President get some sleep. Powers slept in the same room with the President. A Secret Service man awakened him about three in the morning. "Dave, the doctor has told me the baby has taken a turn for the worse."

Dave gently woke the President and the two shuffled into their clothes and walked down the hospital corridor. Along the way, the President noticed a terribly burned baby and asked Dave to call the night nurse. She assured him that the burned baby was getting proper treatment and did not feel any pain.

"Does the mother come every day?" the President asked.

"Yes," the nurse said.

"What's her name?"

The nurse told him. The President then asked Powers for some paper, put it against the glass wall, wrote the woman's name on it, and added, "Keep up your courage. John Kennedy."

Evelyn Lincoln recalled, "I was with him at the hospital when he was holding Patrick's hand and the nurse said, 'He's gone.' And tears came into his eyes. I had never seen tears in his eyes before."

Neither had Dave Powers, who had seen more of him than anyone. Was this the man who aroused so much passion in others without displaying it himself? "He just cried and cried and cried," Powers said.

When his child died—after 39 hours of life—the President said what so many parents had said before him: "It is against the law of nature for parents to bury their children."

"I think this tore him up more than anything," added Newman. "When he came out after the baby's death and got in the car, the photographers were busy as always. 'Larry, the picture they took of me in the car. I don't want to edit anybody but would you please ask them not to run it, not to put it on the wires. I'm asking it as a favor to me. That's just a very personal moment.' "

The picture was never printed.

"But when we got back into the chopper, I had work for him to do, papers to sign, to get his mind away from it," Mrs. Lincoln recalled. "By then he had pulled himself together. We went to Otis Air Force hospital near Hyannis, where he was going to tell Jackie. He went in alone."

They made a poignant picture, the two of them, hand in hand, walking out of wing 2703 of the hospital.

She wore a pink dress, her shoulder-length hair was freshly washed, and her smile faint. The strain was still in her face, and she hesitated at the steps. "Careful," the President murmured, guiding her into the car.

They were going to Brambletyde, their rambling, shingled rented house overlooking the blue waters of Nantucket Sound on Squaw Island near Hyannis. Their two children were there waiting for them.

Jack Kennedy had invited Bill Walton to spend that weekend with them. Walton was almost the only friend equally close to both of them. "It was just the two of them and the kids and me," Walton said. "Probably the most intimate weekend I've ever had with them."

"We were sitting in his office and he was going through the papers on his desk, mostly condolences from the leaders of the world. He'd read them and pass them over to me to look at, and he'd say, 'Look at what the pope said,' or, 'How am I going to answer that one?'

"Then we went swimming and he took off this corset brace, a big contraption for his back, which he didn't even want the Secret Service men to see. He really wanted to bathe in the water rather than swim. While we were out there he unburdened himself of everything that came to his mind, talked about everything from Khrushchev to Berlin.

"The house was full of sadness that weekend and Caroline was being a very bad girl, acting up a lot, and Jack was the only one who could quiet her down by talking to her.

"Jack and Jackie were very close after Patrick's death. She hung onto him and he held her in his arms—something nobody ever saw at any other time because they were very private people."

"He never said so," Jacqueline said, talking about the loss of Patrick, "but I know he wanted another boy. John was such pure joy for him. He was the kind of man who should have had a brood of children. Most men don't care about children as much as women do, but he did. He felt the loss of the baby in the house as much as I did."

"That was the weekend that Jackie got a cable from Lee, inviting her to Greece to go on Onassis's yacht for a trip, and she and Jack were discussing whether or not she should go," Walton recalled. "Jack remembered something hanging over Onassis on some court case and I was instinctively dead set against it. But Jackie didn't want to go back to Washington. The White House was not a real home to her. And, at that time, it would seem more like a prison. Besides, she just wanted to get away. So that weekend it was finally decided that she should go."

Lee had been summering with Aristotle Onassis, the multimillionaire Greek tycoon. She seemed deeply in love and already had asked the Vatican to annul her marriage to Prince Radziwill so that she might be free to marry Onassis. Onassis's own intentions were not clear. He had created an international scandal with his long-lasting affair with opera singer Maria Callas.

Lee telephoned with the Onassis offer of his 325-foot yacht *Christina*, which the First Lady could direct wherever she wanted. The Kennedys had met Onassis some eight years before when they visited Winston Churchill, who had been a guest on his yacht. It came complete with a sixty-man crew, a dance band, two hairdressers, and a Swedish masseuse, and was stocked with all the world's delicacies—from black figs to caviar. A converted Canadian frigate, the yacht had a twin-engine seaplane on the deck; bathrooms with walls of Siena marble and gold-plated faucets; barstools upholstered in the skin of whales' testicles; fireplaces faced with semiprecious lapis lazuli; and walls covered with El Greco paintings.

Jacqueline described Onassis as "an alive and vital person who had started from nothing." "The Golden Greek," one of the world's richest men, who once had been a telephone operator in

Argentina for twenty-five cents an hour, had married the daughter of a powerful Greek shipping magnate. According to Maria Callas, "He's obsessed with famous women." Drew Pearson more bluntly wrote that Onassis wanted to be the President's brother-in-law. Bobby made the suggestion to Jacqueline that Lee's annulment should wait until after the coming election. What concerned the President more was a lingering memory of Onassis's problems with a criminal indictment. The U.S. Maritime Administration had sold Onassis fourteen ships with the understanding that they would remain under the American flag. Onassis made a $20 million windfall by transferring them to foreign registry. To avoid a criminal trial, he paid a $7 million fine.

When Onassis offered to stay ashore during her trip, to minimize unfavorable publicity, Mrs. Kennedy refused to "accept this man's hospitality and then not let him come along. It would have been too cruel."

Jacqueline persuaded Jack to call Franklin D. Roosevelt, Jr., to ask him to accompany her. "I really wanted him as a chaperone," she said. "Poor Franklin didn't want to go along at all. He said he was working on a new image and a trip like this wouldn't do him any good." But FDR's son was undersecretary of commerce and the President persuaded him to go along to add more "respectability" to the trip.

The excited Jacqueline called the forthcoming trip "the dream of her life."

She and Jack celebrated their tenth anniversary shortly before her trip to Greece. The President asked the gardener to pick a bouquet, and asked an antiquities dealer to send a list from which she could pick what she wanted. Her gift to him was a scrapbook of the White House rose garden, made up of headlines and quotations, as well as an excerpt from Joe Alsop's column on gardening. The President once had said drily of the Rose Garden, "This may go down as the real achievement of this administration."

The Bradlees were present for the anniversary dinner. "She [Jacqueline] greeted the President with by far the most affectionate embrace we have ever seen them give each other," Bradlee recalled. As the evening ended, Jacqueline tearfully took Ben Bradlee aside. "You two really are our best friends." Bradlee felt how almost forlorn she sounded.

"They are the most remote and independent people we know," Bradlee said afterwards, "and so when their emotions do surface, it is especially moving." Another friend was there when Mrs. Kennedy visited her husband in the Oval Office. He saw them leave the office together holding hands—which they almost never did in public view.

Before she went on a trip, any trip, she always wrote and preaddressed postcards for John and Caroline, one for every day she would be gone, and asked West to mail them for her because she didn't trust the overseas mail. West found canceled foreign stamps to glue on the postcards.

The last thing she did before leaving for Greece was to have tea with the emperor of Ethiopia.

*   *   *

When John Kennedy was born, Haile Selassie was the Lion of Judah, the King of Kings, and the emperor of Ethiopia. He also claimed to be a direct descendant of King Solomon and the Queen of Sheba. Now he was seventy-two, carried a gold-headed leather swagger stick with a regal air, wore a scarlet-trimmed field marshal's uniform with fourteen rows of ribbons extending almost to his waist, and his people still crawled on their bellies before him.

At the White House, the five-foot-tall Emperor looked more like a little old grandfather while having tea with the First Lady and her daughter Caroline. She chatted with him in French, and apologized for not being able to attend the state dinner for him that night because she would be en route to Greece. He knew about the death of her son, and she explained her need for a holiday.

Before she left, the Emperor had some gifts for her, a gold jewelry box and a full-length leopard coat.

"I am overcome," Mrs. Kennedy told him. Then she took him to the Rose Garden so she could show the coat to her husband. "He brought it for me! . . . He brought it for *me!*"

"I was wondering why you were wearing a fur coat in the garden."

Spotting a reporter in a fake leopard coat later that week, the President quipped, "Everyone's wearing leopard these days."

With Jacqueline gone, Rose Kennedy substituted for her daughter-in-law as the White House hostess in September, 1963, for the Selassie dinner party. Wearing a green satin gown glimmering with gold and crystal beading, she and the small Emperor with the salt-and-pepper beard made an impressive couple. He invited her to come to Ethiopia to visit him, and she later did. Mrs. Kennedy informed some of her guests that she was getting an honorary degree that week from St. Joseph's College in Maryland. "I never did go to college. I was all ready to go to Wellesley when I was sixteen but my father thought I was too young. So I landed in a convent. . . . I've been trying to get a degree ever since." Someone asked her if she would campaign for her son the following year. "No, I'm retiring. I found out tonight I was one year older than Haile Selassie."

She never retired from being the President's mother. "Jack, straighten your tie. . . ."

*   *   *

The yacht went wherever she wanted: to Istanbul to see the Blue Mosque, to Crete to admire the remains of the Minoan civilization, to Onassis's private island of Skorpios—a velvety green place of lovely cypress trees with a rocky hillside where he planned to build a palace. She enjoyed small dinner parties in port, tea with Queen Frederika, midnight bouzouki dances. A *paparazzo* with a telescopic lens took a picture of Jacqueline Kennedy in a bikini that soon flashed onto the front pages of the world. When he couldn't contact her by phone, the irritated President sent her a complaining cable. The press commented that the yacht's parties, often lasting until dawn, did not seem to be fitting for a woman in mourning. Rep. Oliver Bolton of Ohio complained in Congress that the First Lady showed "poor judgment and perhaps impropriety" in accepting "the lavish hospitality of a man who had so defrauded the American public." Why didn't the First Lady see more of her own country instead of traveling abroad so much, the congressman complained.

This country's single biggest deficit in international payments came from the billion dollars our tourists spend abroad annually, the President was told. Couldn't he encourage Americans to stay home next summer? "How on earth can I do that," he answered, "when I can't even keep my own wife from going abroad?"

At the trip's end in early October Onassis gave Jacqueline a diamond and ruby necklace that could be converted into two bracelets. Lee complained to her brother-in-law that Onassis had showered Jacqueline with so many gifts "that I can't stand it." All she got, she said, were three "dinky" bracelets that Caroline wouldn't even wear to her own birthday party.

Jacqueline didn't want it to stop. She felt so wonderfully free and luxurious. Instead of coming home, she accepted the invitation of young King Hassan II of Morocco, who offered her a house of her own in Marrakech as a gift. King Hassan had given the President a gold sword studded with diamonds and Mrs. Kennedy had written him a five-page letter in French.

Informed about the gift of the house to his wife, the President called in his air force aide. "When you get a chance, I want you to go and find out about this house the king gave her."

King Hassan treated her like a desert princess, with her own black and silver sequined tent where she could rest. She had entrée to his cloistered harem, and watched bearded Berber tribesmen play at war for her amusement. The king even flew in a French hairdresser to style her hair like "a Parisian nymph."

Friends felt she was full of guilt feelings when she came home from her two-week trip.

To give her and her husband some undisturbed privacy after her return from Greece, she managed to cancel the visit of a scheduled White House guest by pretending that the rooms were being painted. After Patrick's death and her return from her trip, the two dined alone without guests more often than they ever had. When they did have guests the Kennedys might show a movie as part of the party entertainment, and perhaps sneak away during the movie. "We only have to spend about fifteen minutes of our time," Jacqueline confided gleefully.

"There was a growing tenderness between them," Deputy Defense Secretary Roswell Gilpatric recalled. "It was obvious in the small parties they did have then, something that had not been obvious before. You could see now that he liked being with her. She was more of a challenge to him. She stood up to him. She was no longer the quiet little maid in the corner. He liked that. I think their marriage was really beginning to work out at the end."

"The three of us were at Hyannis one of those days near the end," Spalding recalled, "and Jackie had this smile on her face, and Jack said, 'See that smile on her face? I put it there.' "

He was amused when he was told that Cuba's Ernesto "Che" Guevara had said that the one American he wanted to meet was Jacqueline Kennedy. "He'll have to wait in line," the President replied with a smile.

She had always been so careful not to embarrass the President. The *paparazzo* picture, the midnight parties, the desert adventure all had received prominent publicity. Her husband sensed her disquiet and took advantage of it. "Maybe now you'll come with us to Texas next month?"

"Sure I will, Jack."

Mrs. Kennedy called her former social secretary, Letitia Baldrige, in Chicago. "You're going to be very proud of me. I'm going to start campaigning."

*   *   *

Eleanor Roosevelt, who died in 1962 at the age of seventy-eight, had had kind words to say of Jacqueline Kennedy. Mrs. Roosevelt said Jacqueline was "full of life and so appealing because of her complete naturalness." Her advice to Jacqueline was to "be herself." She added, "I think on the whole the President's wife learns to meet almost any situation she has to meet and not to be annoyed. . . ."

Asked once, "Which do you put first, your husband, your children, or your job?" Eleanor Roosevelt had answered, "My husband. A woman must always put her husband first."

What did he most regret? John Kennedy was asked at a party.

"I wish I had more good times."

Then he became thoughtful, and added, "I've never had a really *unhappy* day in my life."

*   *   *

"Maybe I'm not that religious," Kennedy said. "I feel that death is the end of a hell of a lot of things. But I've got too many things to do. And I just hope the Lord gives me the time to get all these things done."

Rendezvous with Death

You couldn't keep the car window open even a crack in a Kennedy parade in Boston that October of 1963 because fingers would reach in.

Nobody knew it, but it was his last day in Boston. The city saluted him with a tremendous crowd. During the day, he and Dave Powers managed to see half of the Columbia–Harvard football game. They also visited Patrick's grave in Brookline. The next day, "He went to early Mass, then flew to the Cape to spend the day with his father," Powers recalled. "The helicopter landed right where they used to play touch football. The President seemed in good spirits. The first thing he did when he got out of the helicopter was to go over to his father, touch his hand, and kiss his forehead, because his father would always be waiting for him near the landing. His father couldn't move, but oh that *look*!"

They had breakfast together, went for a sail, had lunch, with the President doing all the talking and his father listening intently, seeming to understand all of it, indicating his pride with his eyes.

Earlier, he had asked his father's chauffeur, "Do you think he's getting the best care, Frank?" Then Kennedy added, "I miss him, Frank."

When the President was in residence the presidential flag flew from the tall staff in the front yard. The father would sit there for hours, staring at it.

Powers recalled: "Leaving him that day—and maybe I'm putting something into it because I know it was the last time they ever saw each other—but I remember how moved he was when he said, 'Good-bye, Dad.' "

When the helicopter failed to go on schedule, the father shifted restlessly, wondering what was wrong. He did not see the door open. It was the President returning for a second farewell. The President motioned the nurse into silence, touched his father lightly on the shoulder and said, "Look who's here, Dad." He put his arms around his father, kissed him again, and then walked rapidly back to the door, motioning to the nurse, whispering to her, "Mrs. Dallas, take good care of Dad till I get back."

When he returned to the helicopter, Powers saw tears in his eyes.

*   *   *

Kennedy talked a great deal about death, and about the assassination of Lincoln. A man who lived within a block of the President in Hyannis was caught in Palm Beach with a plastic bomb attached to his body. He was waiting for the President outside the church in Palm Beach on a Sunday and he was going to embrace the President and blow him up. He changed his mind when he saw Kennedy come out with Jacqueline and Caroline, because he didn't want to hurt them, too. And then the Secret Service got him.

Larry Newman had gone with the Secret Service into the man's house in Hyannis and reported to the President that he "was about your size. He had the best-looking shirts, the best-looking underwear, beautiful clothes, and two guns."

"Did you steal the clothes?" Kennedy asked.

"No, I took the guns," Newman said. Kennedy laughed.

When he stopped laughing, he said, "Brother, they could've gotten to me in Palm Beach. There's no way to keep anybody from killing me." Kennedy recalled that President Coolidge had said that any well-dressed man who is willing to die himself can kill the President.

Newman then told him that a call had come to his house the day before from a Secret Service man.

"Larry?"

"Yes," Larry said.

He then told Larry the code name for the President and that he was due at a certain place at a certain time. Larry recognized the man's voice and said, "Look, you're talking to the other Larry Newman. You want Larry Newman, the Secret Service agent."

"Oh, Christ, I've blown the whole cover," the Secret Service man said.

Kennedy listened to this story intently and commented, "This is the way coincidences happen. They fit the things together, and a guy can be shot."

He talked about the deaths of Garfield and McKinley, and how Teddy Roosevelt almost fell down the mountainside because he was in such a hurry to take over the job. "I sort of have the feeling that Lyndon would be running like a son of a bitch to get up there too. I suppose I'd be the same way if I were in the number-two spot. If the President gets knocked off, he's got to have an immediate successor. It's the way our system works."

"The poignancy of men dying young haunted him," Jacqueline Kennedy later recalled. One of his favorite poems was "I Have a Rendezvous with Death," written by Alan Seeger, a young American poet killed in World War I while serving as a French army volunteer. Jacqueline memorized and recited the poem for her husband. Another poem she had memorized parts of for him was "John Brown's Body" by Stephen Vincent Benét.

Isaiah Berlin, the philosopher, dined with the President and came away with the feeling that the President felt he had to make his mark quickly because of the unpredictability of his health. Other friends also felt that the President's restlessness was partly due to his feeling that he would never live out a normal life-span.

"What do you think of the fact that for the last hundred years every President of the United States elected in a year divisible by twenty has died in office?"

The President was talking to his personal physician, Dr. Janet Travell.

"You don't really believe such a coincidence can continue? The odds against it are too great, and anyway, you aren't superstitious," Dr. Travell remembered answering, then added: "He looked at me silently."

                     *   *   *

Some friends wondered why he maintained his friendship with Sen. George Smathers of Florida, who supported him in the Senate so infrequently.

"We both came into the Senate about the same time," Kennedy said. "We both had the same ambitions. And look how it's worked out for me, and look how it's worked out for him. Under the circumstances, I'd hope that I would be as little affected as he was."

"I actually came down here tonight to pay a debt of obligation to an old friend and faithful advisor," he said in Miami. "He and I came to the Eightieth Congress together (1946) and have been associated for many years, and I regard him as one of my most valuable counselors in moments of great personal and public difficulty.

"In 1952, when I was thinking about running for the United States Senate, I went to the then-Senator Smathers and said, 'George, what do you think?' He said, 'Don't do it. Can't win. Bad year.'

In 1956, I was at the Democratic convention, and I said—I didn't know if I would run for vice-president or not—so I said, 'George, what do you think?' And he said, 'This is it. They need a young man. It's your chance.' So I ran—and lost.

"And in 1960, I was wondering whether I ought to run in the West Virginia primary. 'Don't do it. That's a state you can't possibly carry.'

"And actually, the only time I really got nervous at the Democratic Convention of 1960 was just before the balloting; and George came up and said, 'I think it looks pretty good for you.'

"It will encourage you to know that every Tuesday morning we have breakfast together, and he advises with me—Cuba, anything else, Laos, Berlin, anything—and George comes right out there and gives his views, and I listen very carefully."

*   *   *

"I don't know why it was," Smathers said, "but death became kind of an obsession with Jack. 'How do you want to die?' he asked me. 'Would you prefer drowning? Would you prefer strangling? Or hanging? Which way would you rather go?' All that sort of stuff. He talked about that a *lot*. We must have gone through that routine more than a dozen times. He never did say how he'd like to go. I guess he hadn't made up his mind. The last time he talked like that was after a speech he made in Florida on November 18, 1963. We were on the plane flying back to Washington and he said, 'God, I hate to go out to Texas. I hate to go, I just hate like hell to go. I have a terrible feeling about going. I wish this was a week from today. Wish we had this thing over with.'

"He really said that, but something else he said to me, many, many times: 'You've got to live every day like it's your last day on earth and it damn well may be!'

"Well, he lived like that," Smathers said. "Not a day went by that he didn't give it his one hundred percent shot!"

Jack Kennedy also had talked with Peace Corps Deputy Director Bill Haddad about the way he wanted to die. "I'd like to die in a plane," he said.

"Why?" Haddad asked.

"Quick."

"Thank God nobody wanted to kill me today!" he said when he returned from Florida. It was his standard joke to Dave Powers whenever he returned from a trip. The President told Powers that he felt it would be tried by someone with a high-power rifle and a telescopic sight during a downtown parade when there would be so much noise and confetti that nobody would even be able to point and say, "It came from that window."

"Jackie loved the bubbletop because it kept her hair from getting windblown," White House aide Ken O'Donnell claimed. "The President disliked it because it shielded him from the people."

"There's no way to get around it. They put me in a bubbletop thing and I can't get to the people. I want them to feel I am the President of the United States, *their* President of the United States. I belong to *them*—they don't belong to me."

"If somebody is going to kill me," he would say, "they're going to kill me."

"It didn't really concern him," an aide recalled. "He never thought he was going to live to be an old man, anyway."

When Frank Roosevelt, Jr., tried to talk him out of Texas, he answered, "If this is the way life is, if this is the way it's going to end, this is the way it's going to end."

As the Texas trip approached, Mrs. Lincoln passed on to the President her husband's fear. The President merely said as he had said many times before, "If they are going to get me, they will get me even in church."

Kennedy had brought his children to Mass on a hot Sunday morning on the Cape. Not only were the Secret Service men there, as always, but a number of reporters, sitting behind the President. Just before Mass began, the President turned and told the reporters, "Did you ever stop to think that if anyone took a shot at me, they might get one of you guys first?"

The eight Secret Service men who went everywhere with the President were not amused. They were especially watchful when he went to Communion. There was a whole classification of mentally sick killers who would be particularly prone to kill him there.

"You really can't stop a guy, can you?" the President asked.

*   *   *

It was November 13, 1963, and Jacqueline Kennedy would remember what she saw. It was her first White House official function since the death of Patrick three months before. She and her husband were co-hosting a performance by Britain's famous Royal Highland Black Watch Regiment for an audience of seventeen hundred children on the south lawn of the White House. The children were between the ages of six and thirteen, from child-care agencies served by the United Givers' Fund in the greater Washington area. The White House kitchen had provided ten thousand cookies and hot chocolate.

"I don't know when I have seen the President enjoy himself more," Mrs. Kennedy commented.

The major of the Black Watch told the President that their motto was: "Nobody wounds us with impunity."

"I think that is a very good motto for some of the rest of us," he replied.

The weather was brisk but he refused his overcoat as they sat on the balcony with their children and guests. John and Caroline were crawling all over him. At one point, John even had his legs wrapped around his father's neck.

A week later she would call on the Black Watch once again, to perform at his funeral.

*   *   *

Asked to check out the rumor that the Kennedys had sold their Virginia home at Atoka because "it gave the Secret Service nightmares," since a high-power rifle in the surrounding woods could easily pick off the President, *Newsweek*'s Charles Roberts wrote:

"Anyone who wanted to kill Kennedy with a high-power rifle wouldn't have to go to Atoka, Virginia. He could do it in New York, day after tomorrow, in Washington next week, or at any of the hundreds of airports, amphitheaters, coliseums that Kennedy will visit this year and next. The Secret Service does not pretend to screen the President from would-be assassins, but only to deter them with a promise of sudden death."

The date of the Roberts memo was November 7, 1963, two weeks before Dallas.

*   *   *

A few days later, a crisp, sunny afternoon on Armistice Day at Arlington Cemetery, the President said to Rep. Hale Boggs,

"This is one of the really beautiful places on earth. I could stay here forever."

The Armistice Day ceremonies had moved to an amphitheater and the father suddenly noticed his son's absence. "Go get John," he told a Secret Service man. "I think he'll be lonely out there." At the ceremony, the President gave John a playful nudge and his almost three-year-old son hit him back.

"I'm going to tell Mrs. Shaw on you," Kennedy said and playfully hit John again.

"I'm going to tell Mrs. Lincoln on you," his son replied.

Later, that afternoon, Mrs. Shaw brought the children to the Oval Office and he romped with them on the floor.

"What would people think if they saw the President down on the floor?" Mrs. Lincoln asked.

"After all, Mrs. Lincoln, I'm also a father."

*   *   *

John Kennedy and Claiborne Pell had gone to Princeton together, danced on the same debutante circuit, and sailed together at Newport. Both were in San Francisco at the birth of the United Nations. Kennedy once had called Pell the most unlikely political candidate of anyone he knew. Pell became a senator from Rhode Island when Kennedy became President.

During their small suppers at the White House, both men compared notes on their bad backs, and talked about their generation coming out of the war. "We were all pretty young and trying to remake the world," Pell said. Pell felt the President had just a tiny bit of a chip on his shoulder about being Irish, and kidded him about it. And Kennedy asked Pell to check into a house in Newport for summer rental. He wanted it as a surprise for his wife. They both liked the quiet privacy there they didn't get in Hyannis.

The house Pell found for August and September of 1964 was on twenty-three acres behind an 8-foot-high back wall. Annandale Farm, near Hammersmith Farm, was a large white stucco house commanding a spectacular view of Narragansett Bay and Newport Harbor. The President expected to be there when the United States again defended the America's Cup.

The Kennedys also had found a house that they wanted to buy on Squaw Island in Hyannis Port. The President asked Jim Reed to negotiate the final purchase contract. Kennedy was indignant, though, that the seller had asked such a high price. "Imagine the prick charging all that money just because I'm President!"

Kennedy had other long-range plans.

"He said he wanted me to buy a house, a big house, in Washington and keep the house in my name," Walton said. "After he left the presidency, he wanted to settle in Washington. But he wouldn't be there for a while right after he left the presidency, because he didn't want to be in the position of looking over the shoulder of his successor. But he would come to stay at the house from time to time. Meanwhile he and Jackie would travel, and maybe he might lecture at universities and write. Then maybe after three years he'd come back to Washington to live at that house."

*   *   *

On the short range, memories were still sharp.

Jacqueline started talking to the Alphands about some Braque jewelry that André Malraux had sent for their third child, Patrick—before his birth. For a short time she was emotional, close to tears, and then quiet.

The occasion was a small dinner at the White House, and the guests included Franklin D. Roosevelt, Jr., and an Italian couturier. Alphand, the French ambassador, had praised the meal, saying the chef had made progress. Jacqueline promptly gave credit to Alphand's chef, who had advised their chef. The President kidded Alphand because they had both bought the identical shirt, his in London and Alphand's in Paris. Kennedy also teased Roosevelt because they had a bet on who would lose the most weight in a certain period (using White House scales) and Roosevelt had lost. The Kennedy children arrived in their pajamas to say good night, the boy with a lollipop, the girl with a soda.

Talk then turned to the upcoming Kennedy visit to Texas. Jacqueline told Roosevelt that the doctors had told her not to go, but Jack wanted her with him. Roosevelt remembered the unfriendly reception Stevenson had received in Dallas and cautioned Jacqueline on what to expect.

"Well, you're going into a hornet's nest," Congressman Hale Boggs warned him.

"That will make things more interesting," Jack Kennedy replied.

The man with the binoculars watched President Kennedy as he got off the *Honey Fitz* at Newport and walked down the long pier at Hammersmith Farm. Suddenly Kennedy clutched his chest and fell flat on the ground. Walking right behind him was the dignified Countess Crespi and her small son. Both simply stepped over the President's body—as if he were not there—and continued walking toward the shore. Right behind the countess came Jacqueline Kennedy, and she, too, daintily stepped over her husband's body. Behind her was Red Fay, undersecretary of the navy and Kennedy's PT-boat buddy. Fay stumbled and fell directly on the President's body. Just then, a gush of red surged from the President's mouth covering his sport shirt.

It was a grisly kind of humor.

The date of this home movie was Labor Day weekend, 1963.

*   *   *

Asked for his philosophy of life, the President quoted, "Let its report be short and round like a rifle, so that it may hear its own echo in the surrounding silence."

November 22, 1963

"Jack Kennedy would not have gone to Texas," Larry O'Brien insisted, "except that Al Thomas loved him. Al was a very key guy in the House Appropriations Committee and he told me that they were having a testimonial dinner for him in Houston because he was responsible for bringing the Space Center there. I sometimes thought Al had more power than the President. Anyway he told me, 'Gee, I would be so honored if the President would come to my testimonial.'

"Well, I talked about it with Jack in October and he agreed, but he said, 'What's the point of going down there just for the

545

one event? We might as well put a package together.' And that was the start of it."

The advocate of an extended Texas trip was not Lyndon Johnson but Gov. John Connally.

"They'll all think you're coming down here to pick up the money," Connally told him. "We want you to come because we need your help. We gotta win Texas."

As Kennedy told it to Larry Newman, Johnson was miffed, and came to Kennedy and said, "I find you're goin' to my home state." And Kennedy said, "I figured Connally would tell you. John tells everybody everything."

Polls showed that Goldwater was running ahead of Kennedy in Texas. The Gallup Poll put Kennedy's national popularity at only 43 percent. The trip called for five speeches, all supposedly nonpolitical except for a fund-raising Democratic dinner in Austin. Kennedy kidded the Vice-President about that: "Lyndon, I'm always hearing about this Texas money. Hell, it's New England and New York that supports the party, not Texas millionaires."

Since the Austin stop was purely political, the Democratic Party was billed $2,350 an hour for the use of *Air Force One*. The new *Air Force One* had a private living room, a bedroom with two beds, and a dressing room. Jacqueline suggested an overall color blue for the decoration. When Lyndon Johnson wanted to borrow it, the President was indignant, "Under no circumstances. . . . It's *my* airplane!"

Kennedy had been told that the Texas political infighting had been somewhat smoothed out in advance of his trip. "Mr. President, it looks like you're not going to have to wear your bulletproof vest in Dallas."

The logistics were tight. Fly from Andrews Air Force Base to San Antonio, then a motorcade. Back to the plane, fly to Houston, another motorcade. Back again to the plane, fly to Fort Worth, and still another motorcade, all in the same day.

The idea is to hit a city when you can get the largest captive audience. They scheduled Houston at five, when people were leaving work.

Every White House staff member recalled his or her last conversation with the President. For George Ball, fresh from a meeting in Paris, his discussion with Kennedy concerned pending wheat negotiations with the Russians. The President was concerned that a *New York Times* story implied that he might be contemplating a trade offensive against the Soviet Union. The two men arranged to meet after the President's return from Texas.

The President suggested Ball might come down to Middleburg on Sunday and see his new house and brief him for his upcoming meeting with Chancellor Erhard of Germany on Monday.

One of the last bills signed by President Kennedy, on October 24, 1963, was the National Program on Complete Maternity and Infant-Care Services, of which he said, "Programs to combat social and cultural deprivation must at least be on the same scale as the space program."

The last six letters signed by Kennedy, on November 21, 1963, before leaving for Texas, were to the next of kin of servicemen killed in the line of duty.

The night before they left, John was chasing their dog Shannon, and Caroline saw a star.

"Star light, star bright," she recited, then repeated it.

"First star I've seen tonight," Mrs. Lincoln said.

"Up above the world so high," the President added, and Caroline repeated it and he said, "Why don't you go over and say that to Mommy."

Larry Newman's final memory of JFK was his last Hyannis visit, when he dropped in at the Newman house. Newman's daughter Lillie was then five years old, and a presidential favorite. She called him "Mr. Kissable," and he loved it. "Put Lillie on my lap," Kennedy asked, because he couldn't lift her. Just as he left, the President smiled and said, "I'd like to be around when she's about twenty-one."

The last words Jim Reed heard from his friend were, "Jamie, are you getting much?" Then the President quickly added, "Not as much as you deserve."

* * *

The 700 guests were assembled and waiting at the White House reception for the Judiciary, but the President and his wife were late.

When the two came down the stairs to the East Room—almost an hour late—observant reporters made some interesting notes. While the President's hair was never slicked back, it now looked "almost as if somebody had pulled it." His face had an expression one reporter described as "uneasy disgust." Reporter Helen Thomas said of the First Lady, "She looked as if she had been crying." The two moved quickly into the Blue Room for the receiving line and the First Lady disappeared almost immediately afterwards.

Reconstructing the scene, some enterprising reporters discovered that the First Lady had provoked the President by arriving very late from Virginia.

It had happened before. It would not happen again. The next day they were going to Texas.

"No, I don't think the marriage improved at the end," Evelyn Lincoln said. "That's what she wanted people to think. Before he got married he was the gay young bachelor in the *Saturday Evening Post*, and it was too hard to change. He was single for so many years, so independent, and he just didn't want somebody sticking around telling him what to do. And I don't think they were compatible. They were both too independent and neither one wanted to give in. Besides, she was jealous of his celebrity. She was a romantic and he was wholly practical. When he was a senator, I remember she used to draw pictures of a princess falling in love with a romantic prince on a white horse, 'and they lived happily ever after.' That's how she built up this Camelot. It was all fantasy. You know what he would have said about it—'Oh not *that* trash!' She said 'Camelot' was his favorite song. His favorite song was 'Bill Bailey, Won't You Please Come Home?'

"No, I really think that if he had had another term, she would have left him at the end of it. What he should have had was a wife who was brought up in politics."

One of the few and famous flashes of presidential anger happened just before the Texas trip. One weather report predicted chilly weather and suggested warm clothes. Jacqueline packed accordingly. The next day, another weather report said Dallas would be hot, about eighty degrees. The President did not like the idea of telling his wife to repack their clothes—he felt it made him look silly—and he exploded. "He really raved and ranted," Mrs. Lincoln said, "and called the navy man to bawl him out, all very unusual for him. You could tell how edgy he was."

He was also unhappy about the samples of fur in his office. The fur he wanted was for a coverlet, a Christmas present for his wife, and he didn't like any of the samples.

"My daughter Barbara was working at the White House when they went to Texas," Lindy Boggs said. "Somebody from the staff told Barbara that she saw them taking off. 'And just before they got on the helicopter,' said this woman, 'he patted her fanny.' The staff consensus was that it was a way of saying thank you for coming on the trip with him."

Her husband knocked on her door in the plane on the way to Texas. Her secretary answered.

"Yes, Jack, what is it?" she said, brushing her hair.

"Oh, Jackie, I thought I'd check to see if you were all right."

"Yes, Jack, I'm just fine," she said impatiently. "Now will you just go away?"

She had brought along a Spanish teacher to coach her for her speech to the League of Latin American Citizens, and also her press secretary, Pam Turnure. What made Turnure's presence more interesting was a front-page headline in *The Thunderbolt*, a scurrilous sheet published in Texas: KENNEDY KEEPS MISTRESS. The story dealt extensively with his relationship with her.

*   *   *

Thursday was a long day, and it would be longer: Three-and-a-half hours jet flight to San Antonio, another forty-five-minute flight to Houston, a two-and-a-half hour motorcade, a testimonial dinner, and then another flight to Fort Worth.

In San Antonio, Texas, he said, "For more than three years I've spoken about the New Frontier," and he defined it: "It refers to this nation's place in history, the fact that we do stand on the edge of a great new era, filled with both crisis and opportunity, an era to be characterized by achievement and by challenge. It is an era that calls for action and for the best efforts of all those who would test the unknown and the uncertain in every phase of human endeavor.

"Let us not quarrel amongst ourselves when our nation's future is at stake."

In the hotel her secretary saw the thirty-four-year-old Mrs. Kennedy examine her face for some wrinkles and say, "One day in a campaign can age a person thirty years."

For the crowds, the forty-six-year-old President still had his witticisms. "Two years ago I introduced myself in Paris by saying I was the man who accompanied Mrs. Kennedy to Paris. I am getting somewhat the same sensation as I travel around Texas. Why is it nobody wonders what Lyndon and I will be wearing?"

In Houston, Texas Democrat Jack Valenti was no more than a couple of feet from the speaker's platform. He noted that the President read from four-by-seven-inch index cards printed in large type. "I watched his hands," Valenti said. "His hands trembled as he spoke. His hands were shaking as he held those cards. It was curious in a man so used to making speeches. But the ovation was very, very good."

"Dave, how does this compare to our last visit to Houston?" Kennedy asked Powers.

"Well, Mr. President, about as many turned out to see you as the last time. But there seem to be a hundred thousand more shouting, 'Jackie! Jackie!' "

Kennedy turned to his wife. "You see, Jackie, you really are important to me."

Beaming, Jacqueline volunteered, "I'm looking forward to the '64 campaign."

Powers could hardly wait to pass on the good news to O'Donnell.

Powers also observed how much more interested in politics the First Lady suddenly seemed to be. She now asked questions about whether a specific place was Democratic or Republican, and how it had voted in the last election, and who would be in the hall when they got there, and what she should watch for. "She was learning fast," Powers said.

Before going to the testimonial dinner for Congressman Albert Thomas, Jacqueline had learned from Powers that a large group of Latin American citizens was waiting downstairs at the hotel. She asked her husband, "Would it be helpful if I went down and talked to them?"

"It would indeed," he said.

As she talked to them in Spanish, the crowd cheered. A trio of musicians sang a song to her. For someone who supposedly didn't like either politics or crowds, it was an unexpected development. Her feeling was exultant. She had been on the rim of his life, and now she was coming closer to the hub. Reporter Charles Roberts asked how she liked campaigning. They were walking along the chain link fence of the airport, and Roberts vividly remembered how her face literally lit up when she answered, "Oh, it's wonderful, wonderful! I love it!"

At the testimonial to Thomas, Kennedy talked about how the Texas congressman had helped put the United States in a position to fire into space the largest booster rocket, bearing the largest "payroll" in history. As the audience laughed, Kennedy hastily corrected the word to "pay*load*."

It struck Kennedy funny, and he added, "It will be the largest payroll, too, and who should know that better than Houston? We put a little of it right in here."

It was almost midnight when they checked into their Fort Worth hotel. Shortly after they arrived, Dave Powers paged Mrs. Kennedy's personal secretary, Mary Gallagher: "The President wants to see you."

He looked quite disturbed and his message came out in concerned tones. "Mary, Jackie's in the bedroom waiting for you. You'll just have to make arrangements to get to the hotels before we arrive." He suggested she ride in the luggage car. "It takes a different route from the motorcade and reaches the hotel first."

When she got to Jacqueline and apologized, the First Lady said sweetly, "That's OK, Mary." What she had wanted was for

Mary to unlatch her suitcases and put out her things for the morning.

Knowing how much the First Lady liked fine art, some $200,000 worth of paintings, including a Van Gogh, had been collected from Fort Worth citizens for display in the Kennedy hotel suite that night. A special mattress for the President's bad back had been flown in from the White House. The bed was an over-sized twin.

They did not know on November 21, 1963, that this was to be their last night together. That night the First Lady decided to sleep in a small separate bedroom in their three-room suite.

When they awoke for breakfast, there were some five thousand people waiting in the rain in the hotel parking lot chanting, "WE WANT KENNEDY." The President talked to them briefly and then told Powers to "get Jackie." "It was the first time I'd ever seen *women* standing on their chairs to see her," Powers recalled. "Many men, yes, but this was the first time I saw women do that."

* * *

"He reached out to me a lot," Spalding said. "In the twenty-four hours before he was killed, he called me three times. I had the numbers to call back. I think I know what he was calling about. I think he wanted to go down to the country with me that weekend. I've often wondered if that was what he wanted. There was a sort of insistence about those calls."

Dallas was timed for noon and the President showed his wife a black-bordered hate ad somebody had sent from there. The ad vilified him for signing the nuclear test ban treaty. "Oh God, we're really heading into nut country today," Kennedy told his wife. "You know, last night would have been a hell of a night to assassinate a President. I mean it. There was the rain, and the night, and we were all getting jostled. Suppose a man had a pistol in a briefcase. Then he could have dropped the gun and the briefcase, and melted away in the crowd. . . . Jackie, if someone wanted to shoot me from a window with a rifle, nobody can stop it. So why worry about it?"

The Dallas speech he never made warned against "seemingly

swift and simple solutions," confusing "the plausible with the possible." In it, he urged: "America's leadership must be guided by the lights of learning and reason." In another unspoken speech for Austin, he had quoted the Bible, "Lest the Lord keep the city, the watchman watches in vain."

"You two look like Mr. and Mrs. America," Dave Powers said to them, and they both chuckled. "Now, remember," he told them, "when you go down the main street in Dallas, Jackie waves to people on the left side of the street and the President will take people on the right, because if you both wave to the same Texans at the same time, it might be too much for them."

That gave them a real laugh. Just then, the door of the plane opened, and the two of them walked down the steps into history.

VII

The Myth and the Magic

I like the dreams of the future better than the history of the past.
—THOMAS JEFFERSON

AFTERMATH

The third shot tore off the top back half of his head "and we could see the hair and all the stuff go right up in the air," an aide said. Some of the blood seeped onto her pink skirt as the limousine raced for the nearest hospital. The operating room nurse later told her high school friend how difficult it was to remove his back brace, and she wondered how he could make love with that bad a back. Jacqueline Kennedy stayed in the operating room while they split his windpipe to insert an oxygen tube and worked on his chest to get his heart muscles functioning again. She was still there when they put the white sheet over his body, and she slipped her wedding ring on his finger.

In another room, Vice-President Johnson was yelling, "They're going to kill us all! They're going to kill us all!"

A police chief blocked their path as they put the casket into the ambulance. "You're breaking the law. You're breaking the city law and the state law. You can't take his body out of here."

"Get out of the way, you son of a bitch," Ken O'Donnell said grimly, "or we'll run you over."

She sat in the front of the ambulance with the driver. *Air Force One* was waiting. Some of its seats had been taken out to make room for the casket. The air force aide helped lift it into the plane and recalled its being "unbelievably heavy." He also remembered discreetly taking Mrs. Kennedy's hat from her and moving away from her so that she would not see him remove some of her husband's brains, which were still sticking to it. When he brought it back, he stared at the blood on her skirt. "It's his blood. I do not want to remove this," she said quietly to him. "I want them to see what they've done to him."

She asked for a drink and he gave her a Scotch and water. When she finished it, she asked for another. Then she started talking. They were a small group clustered around the casket.

"I should not have allowed him to come here. I didn't want him to come here. And he didn't want to come here. Why on earth did they make him come here?" Then, suddenly, the sad bitterness left her voice as she said, "Oh, we had so *many* good times. . . ."

"She was not a zombie then," the air force aide recalled. "She was logical, as strong as I've ever seen a person. But she never cried. Never."

She seemed to change later when she went to witness Johnson's swearing-in ceremony. A reporter noted a glazed, frozen smile on her face, as if she had fallen into a trance. He felt that if a pistol had been fired right in front of her, she would barely have blinked.

When she returned to the casket, she was talking again, a jumble of scattered memories—the exciting things he told her about Ireland and the name of the person who sang at their wedding. Then she turned to Dave Powers and Ken O'Donnell with a worried question, "What will you boys do now?"

"To think I very nearly didn't go," she said later. "Oh, what if I'd been here, out riding at Wexford somewhere. Thank God I went with him."

*　　*　　*

Sen. Stuart Symington was making a speech before a Senate committe on the balance of payments when the news came that the President had been shot. "Bobby was there and I was staring at him as I heard it," Symington said. "He sat back suddenly in his chair as if he had been hit by a whiplash. Then he very slowly assembled his papers, picked them up, and walked out."

Ted Kennedy was presiding over the Senate when he heard the news. An aide drove him home to Georgetown, racing through the red lights, Ted cautioning him to be careful. The car radio said the President was still alive. Ted's wife was at her beauty parlor preparing for a fifth anniversary party they were having the next day. Ted wanted to call his mother then but the telephones were jammed, so they went instead to the White House.

As they entered, they heard the sobbing and knew he was dead. Eunice and Bobby were already there, and they all spoke to their mother. Somehow they kept their voices calm. They divided assignments. Bobby would take care of Jackie, Ted would go to Hyannis to be with his mother and break the news to his father. Sarge Shriver would handle the funeral arrangements.

Bill Walton called Mr. West on behalf of Mrs. Kennedy: "She'd like the house to be just like it was when Lincoln lay in state."

The end had begun.

* * *

Bobby was there at the airport when the plane arrived with his brother's body. "I don't want anyone to touch him but a navy man," Jacqueline had said. "He loved the navy." A navy ambulance was waiting to take the body to a naval hospital for the autopsy. Jacqueline and Bobby went with the ambulance. She had told his air force aide, McHugh, "Please do not leave him."

They brought a new casket because the other one had a missing handle. The aide stayed through the autopsy, and helped them put the body into the new casket. "His head was too high.

We couldn't get him down. It was terrible. We had to lift him again before we could put him in properly."

When they brought the casket back to the White House, Mrs. Kennedy asked them to open it. Bobby collapsed when he saw his brother. That night, upstairs in the White House, Charles Spalding heard Bobby sobbing. "Why God, why?"

*   *   *

Mike Feldman had been on a plane with the secretary of state and others going to a conference in Japan when they got the news. The plane immediately returned to Washington. That night Feldman was at the White House, and he stopped for a moment to walk into the ghostly Oval Office. "I just about fainted," he said, "because the rug had been green and now it was blood red. I didn't know that Jackie had had it changed while I was away."

*   *   *

Almost everyone remembered where they were when they heard the news.

Six-year-old Tina Martin in East Norwich, Long Island, went down the hill to the store to buy a twelve-inch flag and solemnly marched up and down the street carrying it on her shoulder.

A Georgia farmer—who later became President of the United States—had just finished driving his tractor when somebody told him. "I wept openly for the first time in ten years, for the first time since my own father died."

The people of Copenhagen came out of their homes by the thousands, flowers in their arms, and headed for the American Embassy. By morning, the flowers were piled six feet high, most of them in tiny bunches.

Israel's Prime Minister David Ben Gurion said it was the first world mourning in history.

"Why are you crying?" Sen. Hugh Scott's wife asked. "You didn't have that much admiration for him."

"I'm not crying for him. I'm crying for the American people."

A woman from Louisiana called the White House to order

the networks to stop all the funeral news and resume regular programming. "We want to *see* something," she said.

"Madam," the assistant press secretary said politely, "I suggest you disconnect the set and shove it up your ass, knobs and all."

A six-year-old black boy later said to Bobby, "Your brother's dead . . . your brother's dead."

Bobby picked up the boy and held him close. "That's all right. I have another brother."

*　　*　　*

The crowd parted when they saw him. The long line of people stood aside and the slow shuffling line halted a few minutes while Ted went right up to the casket, knelt, and prayed. In the night light, in the utter silence.

"We must just get through this," Jacqueline Kennedy firmly told the family. Her dignity had a majesty to it. The great of the world had come to pay their respects but she took time out to write a note to the widow of the Dallas policeman who had also been killed that same day. She gave a flower to Charles De Gaulle and he carefully pressed it and put it in his pocket. She excused herself from the grief of her guests because she had promised to attend a birthday party for her three-year-old son. Bobby and Teddy were already there and the three—with their wet eyes—somehow still sang "Happy Birthday."

The grave-digging machine at Arlington National Cemetery digs some twenty graves a day. This one was on top of a hill with a commanding view of Washington. Bobby had found an engineer who spent all night designing the eternal flame that Jacqueline wanted. She also wanted a riderless black horse, just as Lincoln had had.

As the world watched on television, she seemed to have the courage and dignity of the ancient Roman woman. She knelt before the catafalque, and kissed the flag. Then the whole world cried as they watched her three-year-old son salute his father and the flag.

Days later, she and Chief Usher West went down to the Oval Office while the moving men were there, starting to remove things. "Her eyes were like saucers," West remembered, "memorizing the Oval Office—the walls, the desk we found in the basement, the small pictures of Caroline and John."

The two then sat down in the adjoining Cabinet Room, and she looked at his face. "My children," she said. "They're good children, aren't they, Mr. West?"

I don't know what he had. I can't put my finger on it. But he knew how to reach the people and excite them with hope. Whatever he had, it was real, and it was magic. I knew all the presidents from Roosevelt on, and I wasn't overawed by any of them. But I thoroughly loved John Kennedy because he brought his country together in a way I hadn't seen in my time.

—LARRY NEWMAN

REFLECTIONS

"I was there one night when Lerner and Loewe and a half dozen people were at a small White House party and they were playing 'Camelot,' " Spalding said. "He knew Alan very well— they had been at Choate together. Jack asked Alan about the verse and some of us were supposed to write an extra chorus for one of the songs. He liked the *Camelot* music; he liked the concept; he *loved* to play the song. The idea, explicit in the show, could have occurred to him. He might have said, 'Let's do it that way; let's have the brightest people around.' "

Camelot mythology didn't quite fit the Kennedys. The oath of the knights to lead their lives "in purest chastity . . . to love one only, cleave to her," was hardly a Kennedy tenet. The King Arthur tales were among Jack Kennedy's favorites, though, even when he was a boy—the courtliness, the adventure, the search for fame. The part in *Camelot* that now meant the most came at the end when King Arthur told his legends to the young boy so that they would still live even if he were killed in battle.

563

George Ball recalled: " 'You know, I'm only forty-six,' he once said to me. 'If I serve out two full terms, I'll only be in my early fifties. Everything in life then will be an anticlimax.' He said that twice to me."

Joking about his future, Kennedy claimed he would find himself after the presidency "at what might be called the awkward age—too old to begin a new career and too young to write my memoirs."

"I remember him saying to Jackie and me: 'What am I going to do when I get out of here?' " Bill Walton added.

"You're doing so well," a reporter told him, "maybe you should try to repeal the two-term amendment."

"Never, never!" He laughed. "Eight years is enough!"

Then what about his future, after the presidency?

"I would stay on in the Senate, of course," he answered.

Arthur Goldberg, whom Kennedy appointed to the Supreme Court, also asked, "What are you going to do afterwards? You'll be a young fellow."

"Oh, probably sell real estate," Kennedy joked. "That's the only thing I'm equipped to do."

He told different people different things. "He told me that he might be president of Harvard University," Evelyn Lincoln recalled. "Oh yes, I think he was serious." He told an aide that he would work on the history of his administration, hold seminars, talk to students. His problem, he said smiling, was to race two other members of his staff, Bundy and Schlesinger, to the press. Another time he confided that he might buy a newspaper.

"I was older than Jack," Walton commented. "I was the age he would be when he retired from two terms of the presidency. And so he'd often ask me whether everything was still working at my age, and I knew what he meant. He wanted to know what he would be like when he left the presidency."

"The only thing I did feel towards the end of Jack's life," his friend Charles Bartlett said, "a feeling that clouded his last days in office, was the apprehension over the implication of the fact that Bobby had decided to run for president. I think that bothered Jack. The last few times I saw him, Jack talked about how

'68 was going to be a contest between Bobby and Lyndon Johnson, and I don't think he took cordially to it at all."

"I know he felt that Bobby was overly ambitious," Spalding added. "Bobby was hard-nosing it. We talked about that."

The 1964 presidential election was much on his mind. He had asked his brother-in-law Steve Smith to be his campaign manager. Bobby couldn't do it again because he would have had to resign as attorney general. Smith's special concentration was to be New York, Michigan, and Pennsylvania. "The first thing to do with a state is to carry it" was the Kennedy rule. He asked Larry Newman to handle Ohio, West Virginia, and Kentucky in a parallel operation, "but I want you to work directly with *me*." He even worked up a special code with Newman, using certain initials and a Hyannis Port post office box as a return address. "Then Evelyn will know it's from you and she'll give it to me, and nobody else's eyes will get to see it."

Next time, he told Powers, he would win big. Next time he would run ahead of congressmen in their own districts, instead of behind them.

Kennedy wanted to run against Goldwater because he thought he'd be easier to beat. He had given Goldwater campaign advice: "Don't announce too soon, Barry. The minute you do you will be the target. If you give them eighteen months to shoot you down, they'll probably be able to do it."

"He and Goldwater already had agreed to have a series of Lincoln-Douglas debates," Salinger said, "and Goldwater was all for it. Actually, he [Kennedy] liked Goldwater a lot."

"He reminded me of an article I had written on how to be a good opponent," Goldwater said. "Oppose but do not hate, always oppose positively, keep your sense of humor, learn all the tricks of campaigning, applaud your opponent when he's right."

If Kennedy wanted Goldwater as his opponent, his great concern was that it might be Nelson Rockefeller. When Khrushchev had asked Walter Lippmann, "What is the psychology for understanding Kennedy?" Lippmann's answer was "Rockefeller."

"I remember we were on the *Honey Fitz* one day—McNamara, Johnson, a whole group of us," Jim Reed recalled, "and

Kennedy kept talking about one subject during that whole trip —Rockefeller. Everybody there had to tell him everything they knew about Rockefeller. He was insatiable to know absolutely everything—his private world, his techniques, his staff, his philosophy, his women.

"I suppose at the bottom of it all, though, was that Kennedy knew Rockefeller had a certain sense of style that he did not have, that he was a more natural campaigner, more outgoing, perhaps a warmer human being. But they were alike in many ways, too. They both loved politics, both loved fun, both loved their women, although Rockefeller was perhaps more discreet about it."

The President had held his first official strategy meeting for the 1964 election with a small group that included Bobby, Larry O'Brien, Ken O'Donnell, Ted Sorensen, John Bailey, Steve Smith, and several others, with one prominent exception—the Vice-President of the United States was not there.

Did John F. Kennedy intend to dump Lyndon Johnson as his running mate in 1964?

"There was not a chance—ever—that Kennedy was going to replace him in 1964," John Kenneth Galbraith emphasized. "I don't think he had any intention of dropping Vice-President Johnson," Jacqueline Kennedy said. "I don't think he intended to dump Johnson in '64," Arthur Krock added, "but I don't think Kennedy ever would have groomed Johnson as his successor."

Bartlett was swimming with the President in the White House pool and asked, "Why don't you get another vice-president in 1964?"

"Kennedy turned on me and he was furious," Bartlett said. 'Why would I do a thing like that? That would be absolutely crazy. It would tear up the relationship and hurt me in Texas. That would be the most foolish thing I could do.' "

Then *Washington Post* reporter Edward Folliard asked him at a press conference about the rumor that Johnson would not be on the ticket. "He will be on the ticket even if I am not," Kennedy answered.

Evelyn Lincoln insisted she had heard the President say, "We're going to dump Lyndon Johnson and nominate Terry Sanford in 1964."

Kennedy mentioned to Goldberg that Johnson was always threatening to quit. "He won't quit in a million years," Goldberg said. "This is his place in the sun."

Spalding recalled, "He once called me and said, 'I've got the second chapter: Lyndon Johnson has me captured just as I hit the pool.' And then he went into this long bit about what they do to him and how Lyndon behaved. It was a James Bond 007 thriller novel he said he was writing about how Lyndon Johnson was trying to take over his presidency. Every time he got a new idea, he'd call me. 'Now listen to this Charlie—you're going to love it. Lyndon has tied up Mrs. Lincoln and Kenny O'Donnell in a White House closet and he's got a plane ready to take them away. . . . ' In another chapter Lyndon had sealed off the swimming pool and made it a center of operations. I don't know if he ever put any of it down on paper, but he sure had a lot of fun with it."

*   *   *

Sailing on a gray sea on a gloomy day, Kennedy once asked Bartlett, "How do you think Lyndon would be if I got killed?"

The President was conscious of Johnson's gaffes during his goodwill trip to Asia, his drinking, his war whoop in the Taj Mahal. But he also knew Johnson's many assets.

Johnson, less cerebral, less detached than Kennedy, was more concerned with social issues. He could say of a colleague, "That son of a bitch has forgotten he was ever poor."

If Kennedy seemed more concerned with ends, Johnson was more interested in means, making the maximum use of his political power. "If you don't know how to count, you can't be a leader."

As a mutual friend of both put it, Johnson looked towards the mountains and the plains while Kennedy looked towards the ocean.

San Francisco editor Bill Hogan recalled something that stamped Kennedy as a class act—doing something Johnson would never do. It was at the Army-Navy football game and Kennedy tossed a coin in front of live television cameras to determine on which side he would sit first. "If he had dropped that coin before an audience of so many millions, the press and the people would never have let him forget it. That was not only courage, that was style."

*   *   *

He was not a martyr who died for a cause. Did he become a myth mainly because he was killed in his prime?

"What was killed was not only the President but the promise," James Reston wrote.

"I think President Kennedy will be regarded for many years as the Pericles of a golden age," reflected one of his aides. "He wasn't Pericles, and the age wasn't golden, but that doesn't matter—it's caught hold."

Partly it was because the human race has a hunger for heroes. People said he gave the impression of being totally alive, made everyone feel younger, called on the best of us to deal with the worst in us, brought vitality into a time of exhaustion, projected an electricity with a challenging presence. When he called on people to dedicate themselves and make sacrifices, they seemed to listen and believe.

What was it about him? "Oh, it was just the way he *was!* What a joy it was to have him around. Everyone I knew loved him with a sort of possessiveness."

"Was it better, or were we just younger?" one reporter asked another of the Kennedy era.

"Younger."

"I'm not so sure."

Charles Spalding noted: "I think of him when he was getting hold of some of the great things of the world and when he had the wind in his sails."

Laura Bergquist said, "I went to the opening ceremony of the Kennedy Library and they put on a recording of one of John Kennedy's speeches and I found myself crying. After all these years, I found myself crying again. After he was assassinated, I cried on and off for about two months. And the funny thing is that I'm so ambivalent about him.

"My mother told me that she cried as much when he was assassinated as she had cried at my father's death. And my mother was never a real Kennedy fan.

"So I guess that's right: the Kennedy excitement has stayed intact throughout the years for our whole generation."

Years later, the revisionists would come down hard.

Kennedy was no genius. He was not ten feet tall. He was a President of unfulfilled promises. His foreign policy was "quite fumbling." His domestic accomplishments were few, "a very mixed collection of errors and false starts and brilliant illuminations of the future." When all the tinsel was stripped away, "He was a conventional leader, nothing but an enlightened conservative." He would be swallowed up as "a transition figure in history, a footnote, and a flicker." "He didn't leave much of a record," claimed historian John Roche.

His political ability did not equal his ambition, said some, because it was based more on an elite consensus than on mass support. His motto seemed to be, "When in doubt, do something."

Others said he was a good man on the way to becoming a great one, but he lacked the time to prove himself.

Eunice later said it was true that her brother Jack became President "when not a great deal was going on." But he had given her the single sentence that stirred her life's work: "A nation's greatness can be measured by the way it treats its weakest citizens."

★　　★　　★

"They're trying to wipe out the name Kennedy," said the widow in the early months of the Johnson administration.

In reply, Johnson took Walter Lippmann upstairs in the White House to show him a bronze plaque put up by Mrs. Kennedy.

"In this room Abraham Lincoln slept during his occupancy of the White House as President of the United States, March 4, 1861–April 13, 1865.

"In this room lived John Fitzgerald Kennedy and his wife, Jacqueline Kennedy, during the two years, ten months, and two days he was President of the United States, January 20, 1961– November 22, 1963." When Richard Nixon became president, he had the plaque removed.

*   *   *

"I just hope I helped him," Jacqueline Kennedy repeated to friends.

She wrote her own citation for bravery for the Secret Service agent she felt had saved her life. When a Treasury official protested her language, she cut in quickly with, "Are you forgetting who appointed you?"

Money was not a problem. The President had put millions in trust for her and her children and had left an estate of personal and real property worth $1,890,464, including some isolated shares in the Palace Theater on Times Square worth a total of $106.07.

"Honey, you stay as long as you want," Johnson had told Jacqueline Kennedy. One week later, just a few hours before she left the White House, Johnson posthumously awarded the late President Kennedy the Medal of Freedom. As they were leaving, Dave Roberts gave young John a small flag. Walking out of the White House, John carried his father's medal and waved his flag.

An aide insisted that John Kennedy would have smothered the whole idea of the Camelot legend that his wife created. He once told a Yale audience that the greatest enemy of truth was not the lie but the "persistent, persuasive, unrealistic myth."

"God, it's so awful," Bobby Kennedy told an associate. "Everything was beginning to run so well. I thought they'd get one of us, but I thought it would be me. Yes, everything's finished. Everything we hoped for is gone."

"The essence of the Kennedy legacy," said Robert Kennedy of his brother, "is a willingness to try and to dare and to change, to hope for the uncertain and risk the unknown."

"Just as I went into politics because Joe died, if anything happened to me tomorrow, my brother Bobby would run for my seat in the Senate," John Kennedy said. "And if Bobby died, Teddy would take over for him."

*   *   *

For more than a year Jacqueline was in a very deep depression. Her life was very disorganized and she was always breaking appointments. James Reed remembered being with her some four months after the assassination "and Jackie Kennedy suddenly fell sobbing on my shoulder and couldn't stop for a long time."

Roswell Gilpatric, who saw a lot of Jacqueline socially after her husband's death, said, "All the time we dated, she never ever talked about Jack or the White House. It was as if she had put a curtain over the past. A funny thing: Most of the men she dated at that time were older men. After Jack died, she had no relationship with any of the Kennedy sisters, or with the mother. And not even much with Teddy. We even took a trip together to Mexico and Latin America. I remember how interested she was in the Mayan culture, how much she studied and read all about it before we went there. She was very, very bright, very astute, very learned. And she was always talking about Bobby. Bobby was her anchor of strength and security at that time."

She grew to depend on her daily call from Bobby, wherever she was. They saw each other often. What was interesting to friends was that she became intensely involved in politics again because of Bobby. She wanted to know who were the most politically important people in New York, where their power came from, and how she might best approach them. She wanted to help Bobby become President of the United States.

There was little question that Ethel was jealous of their relationship.

Jacqueline was with the family and said, "Won't it be wonderful when we get back in the White House?"

"What do you mean *we?*" Ethel asked sharply.

Jacqueline looked as if she had been hit, then gave an embarrassed smile and left.

"I have no designs on the presidency, and neither does my wife, Ethel Bird," Bob Kennedy joked.

When Bobby declared himself for the presidency, Teddy called him in California and said jokingly, "All of us here are behind you . . . *way, way* behind you."

When Bobby was killed, Jacqueline was shattered. After Bobby's assassination, Dave Powers said bitterly about the Secret Service, "Everytime a Kennedy dies, they improve it."

At Bobby's funeral, Ted said: "My brother need not be idol-ized or enlarged in death beyond what he was in life. He should be remembered simply as a good and decent man who saw wrong and tried to right it, saw suffering and tried to heal it, saw war and tried to stop it."

On a plane back from Alaska in mid-April 1969, Ted had been drinking heavily, and sleeping little. He had a silver hip flask that had belonged to Bobby. "They're going to shoot my ass off the way they shot off Bobby's." And, later, more hysteri-cally, "They're trying to kill me. They're trying to kill me!"

"Chappaquiddick? Jack would never have been caught, be-cause it never would have happened," insisted an intimate. "Bobby? He would have gone to jail. He would have called the cops right off the bat. Teddy missed Jack more than anybody because Jack protected him, would have helped him."

When the Kennedy patriarch died, he still left a son who might be president and a host of grandsons filled with heritage.

Ninety-year-old Rose Kennedy stopped off at the Newman house en route to the airport. She had two taped compresses, which Newman called "back packs."

"Take off your clothes," she told Larry Newman, "you haven't got anything I haven't seen before. I always put these on Jack and I'll always do it for you. They did him a lot of good."

"And every year she brings me these back packs," Newman said smiling, "and she really knows how to put it on. She brings me two, so I'll have an extra one."

*   *   *

Jacqueline Kennedy was now, again, a woman alone, and troubled, wondering aloud to friends what to do with her life. Her main concern was her children.

"Larry, do you have the same problems with your girls as I have with Caroline?" asked Jacqueline some years later. "She knows everything and I don't know anything. I can't do any-thing with her."

"Jackie, you know it isn't going to be any different; it isn't going to get better. What you've got to do is let her grow up

alone. Keep your distance. I'll tell you what I do with my girls
—we have wonderful conversations."

"I can't talk to her," Jacqueline said.

"Maybe you don't talk about the things *she* wants to talk
about."

When she felt a Secret Service agent was getting too attached
to her children as a father figure, she asked that he be replaced,
but first gave him their dog Charlie.

With time, she reassessed John Kennedy, even his womanizing. "There'll never be another Jack," she reminisced to Joan
Braden in Aspen. But she said she now understood so well why
Jack lived the way he did, why he lived every day of his life so
intensely. "And I'm glad he did."

She told a friend she was going to marry Aristotle Onassis,
and was warned, "Jackie, you're going to fall off your pedestal."

"That's better than freezing there," she answered.

Another friend wondered aloud, soon after, "Why did Jackie
always marry men who hurt her?"

"I think she married Onassis because he represented an anchor of security and strength," Gilpatric noted. "He could take
her out of herself, take her away to other places, other life-
styles."

Before the marriage, she had gone to Cardinal Cushing and
he had given her his blessing and approval. In gratitude she had
the National Archives send him a rare papal encyclical that
Pope John had given her.

Teen-age John Kennedy, Jr., was playing one of his father's
recordings when Charles Spalding walked in. It was a tribute
to Mrs. Roosevelt and John was busy taping something from
it. "Listen," he said, "right in here is where I crawl under the
desk and Dad kicks me. It's coming up now. Here it is. He was
talking on the radio and I crawled under the desk and grabbed
him."

Some years later while lunching with Spalding, John, Jr.,
talked about the liberal stands young people were taking, and
asked, "Don't you think that's what you should do when you're
young?"

Bobby's son Joe summed up much of the Kennedy heritage

in a conversation with his grandfather's nurse. "You know, Mrs. Dallas, I can get any girl to go out with me just because my name is Kennedy. But I don't like that. I don't like it at all. It either comes too easy to get what you want, or it comes too hard."

After a moment, he added, "But I guess I better learn to get used to it. Once a Kennedy, always a Kennedy."

The words used most often with the Kennedy children were "keepers of the flame."

Ted Kennedy had become the father figure for all his brothers' children, and the weight was heavy. If his own personal life was torn, his political future was still at the point of promise.

"It was all so brief," Ted Kennedy said of his brother's era. "Those thousand days are like an evening gone. But they are not forgotten. You can recall those years of grace, that time of hope. The spark still glows. The journey never ends. The dream shall never die."

James Reston wrote, "The tragedy of John Fitzgerald Kennedy was greater than the accomplishment, but in the end the tragedy enhances the accomplishment and revives the hope."

What was unexpected was that a 1979 poll of the American people found that the majority considered John Kennedy the greatest president, greater even than Washington and Lincoln.

Jacqueline Kennedy, in her own memorial to her husband, observed, "Someone who had loved President Kennedy, but who had never known him, wrote to me this winter: 'The hero comes when he is needed. When our belief gets pale and weak, there comes a man out of that need who is shining—and everyone living reflects a little of that light—and stores up some against the time when he is gone.'

"So now he is a legend," Mrs. Kennedy added, "when he would have preferred to be a man."

"It's sad to see what's happened in this country," Ted Sorensen commented. "It's as if people don't want to believe in anything today. Sometimes they even turn against John Kennedy because he was one of the last men they believed in."

*   *   *

What then was John Fitzgerald Kennedy?

Not a myth. He was a very real human being full of his own foibles, his own doubts, his own weaknesses.

Not a great president. There was the growth of the man in office, the pragmatism that turned into passion on big issues, the courage that became wisdom. But there was no time to prove his potential.

Still, he *was* a hero for our time. In some mysterious way, he did inspire in so many millions of people all over the world a great excitement of hope. That excitement was real. That excitement still lingers.

To millions, the Kennedy name is still aglow in a gray world, the Kennedy administration's memory, still "a great palace of light," a time of "those who wore their hearts at fire's center."

*　　*　　*

When President Kennedy was killed, columnist Mary McGrory said to Daniel Moynihan: "We will never laugh again."

"Oh, Mary, we'll laugh again," Moynihan replied. "But we'll never be young again."

*　　*　　*

In the Doonesbury cartoon, Mark and Mike roll on the floor with laughter as they recite such phrases from the New Frontier as, "The energy we bring to our endeavors will light a torch, and the fire from that torch shall surely light the world."

As their laughter dies, the two young men look at each other and their expressions change to fear, then to sadness.

"God," said Mark, "what happened to us?"

"I don't know, man," Mike whispers. "I don't know."

CHAPTER NOTES

1 *The Passing of the Torch*

The primary sources for this chapter—as in the rest of the book—come from interviews. Many of these are already attributed in the acknowledgments. The most important source for this chapter was William Walton. Martha and Charles Bartlett and Air Force aide Godfrey McHugh also supplied key material. Others supplying interesting sidelights were Mrs. Kennedy's social secretary, Letitia Baldrige, Edward McLaughlin, Rowland Evans, Jr., and Joseph and Mary Alsop. The Bernstein observations came from the Oral History section of the Kennedy Library. Jacqueline Kennedy's columns in the *Washington Times-Herald* were worth reading. Color and background for the inaugural, aside from interviews, came from the *New York Times* and *Washington Post*, as well as *Time* and *Newsweek*. Hugh Sidey's book, *John F. Kennedy, President* (Atheneum, 1963), was especially good on this period.

2 *Growing Up Kennedy*

The core of this chapter comes from extensive interviews with John and Jacqueline Kennedy and Joseph Kennedy, Sr., made by Ed Plaut and myself in 1959. Among the other pertinent interviews conducted then were with Franklin D. Roosevelt, Jr., and Eunice Kennedy Shriver. Among the key current interviews—made in the last four years—were with Charles Spalding, and Larry and Sancy Newman, who seem to have memories of almost total recall. Among the other more important interviews were with William Walton, David Ormsby-Gore (now Lord Harlech), Sen. Ted Kennedy, Nancy Coleman, Stephen Smith, Ben Bradlee, Alice Roosevelt Longworth, Harvey Klemmer,

Robert Donovan, and Blair Clark. The comments of Clare Boothe Luce were made to a mutual friend. The Kirk Lemoyne Billings remark comes from the Kennedy Library Oral History section. The best and most comprehensive books on John Kennedy, for my purpose, were *A Thousand Days* by Arthur M. Schlesinger, Jr., (Houghton Mifflin, 1965) and *Kennedy* by Theodore C. Sorensen (Harper & Row, 1965). Of the Joseph Kennedy biographies, the best were, *The Founding Father* by Richard J. Whelan (N.A.L.-World, 1964) and *Joseph P. Kennedy* by David E. Koskoff (Prentice Hall, 1974). A valuable book, too, was *Kennedy and Roosevelt*, by Michael R. Bechloss (W.W. Norton, 1980). Rose Kennedy's autobiography, *Times to Remember* (Doubleday, 1974), was particularly interesting about the home and family. I also found some useful information in *The Cape Cod Years of J.F.K.* by Leo Damore (Prentice-Hall, 1967). *Swanson on Swanson* by Gloria Swanson (Random House, 1982) is necessary reading for the relationship with Joseph Kennedy. *The Lost Prince* by Hank Searls (World, 1969) has some value, but John Kennedy's privately printed book, *My Brother Joe* is most revealing.

3   The Playboy Congressman
A good part of Kennedy's early days in Congress comes from interviews made in 1959. David Powers, with his incredible memory, was a prime source. So was Larry O'Brien, John Powers, Gardner Jackson, and Ralph Coghlan. I talked to some of these same people again, particularly Powers and O'Brien. Larry Newman's contribution throughout the book was invaluable, and very much so on this period. Edward McLaughlin also supplied some fascinating material, as did John Sharon. Nancy Dickerson, who dated Kennedy then, had her own illuminating views. Probably the best researched material on John Kennedy's women friends at that time can be found in *The Search for J.F.K.* by Joan and Clay Blair, Jr. (Berkley Putnam, 1974).

Other important stories came from Rep. Frank Thompson, Kay Halle, and Joseph Alsop. David Ormsby-Gore was also important here. The comments of Joan Fontaine and Gene Tierney come from their memoirs. For Fontaine, *No Bed of Roses* (Morrow, 1978); for Tierney, *Self Portrait* (Wyden, 1979).

4   The Luckiest Girl in the World
Jacqueline Kennedy's stepsister, Nina Auchincloss Straight, was most helpful about telling me about their growing-up years. Nina Straight's autobiographical novel, *Arabella* (Random House, 1982), was most revealing. Jacqueline and Lee Bouvier have written a charming book about their trip to Europe, before marriage, *One Special Summer* (Delacorte, 1974). Letitia Baldrige, who went to Miss Porter's school with Jacqueline and knew her in Paris, had some excellent background for me. Her editor at the *Washington Times-Herald*, Frank Waldrop, filled in much detail about Jacqueline's job there. Charles and Martha Bartlett, who introduced Jack to Jacqueline, were both most informative about those days. Martha Bartlett was one of her best friends. David Ormsby-Gore was similarly revealing about his early friendship with them. So were George Smathers, Larry Newman, Charles Spalding, and William Walton. The best newspaper interviews with Jacqueline Kennedy then were in the *Boston Globe*, the best magazine articles in *Life*. Igor Cassini, who dubbed her Debutante of the Year, told me what he remembered and so did Godfrey McHugh, who had dated her. *The Bouviers* by John Davis (Farrar, Straus & Giroux, 1969) supplied some background. Another useful book was *Jacqueline Bouvier Kennedy Onassis* by Stephen Birmingham (Grosset & Dunlap, 1978). Some of Mrs. Kennedy's friends would not be quoted.

5   Scenes from a Marriage
Senator Ted Kennedy was most helpful in recalling these particular days with his brother. Ben Bradlee supplemented in interviews many of the things he wrote in his excellent memoir, *Conversations with Kennedy* (Norton, 1975).

Bill Walton's interviews with me were most valuable for this chapter. Arthur Schlesinger's interviews with Robert Kennedy in the Oral History section of the Kennedy Library were particularly illuminating on this period. The Schlesinger book, *Robert Kennedy and His Times* (Houghton Mifflin, 1978), is the best on the subject. David Powers, James Rowe, Evelyn Lincoln, and George Smathers all added important material, but Charles Spalding was invaluable.

6   A Moment of Magic
I was present at this 1956 convention, edited a convention newspaper, and so was part of the scene. The bulk of the material here comes from interviews made in 1959. Most important of these were with Ted Sorensen, Adlai Stevenson, Eleanor and James Roosevelt, Hubert Humphrey, Robert Sargent Shriver, Jr., Eunice Shriver, Arthur Schlesinger, Jr., Abba Schwartz, Estes Kefauver, Eugene McCarthy, James Farley, William McCormick Blair, Jr., Newton Minow, Dixon Donnelly, John Bailey, Bill Haddad, Thomas Winship, and Stephen Mitchell, among others. I talked to some of these same people again within the past four years to amplify their memories. In addition, I received much additional information from Sen. Ted Kennedy, Arthur Hadley, James Rowe, Nancy Dickerson, and Evelyn Lincoln. Of the newspaper files, the most valuable were in Chicago: the *Tribune*, the *Sun* and the *Daily News*.

7   The Man Who Would Be President
Joe McCarthy's notes and tapes were excellent. McCarthy co-authored *Johnny We Hardly Knew Ye* with David Powers and Kenneth O'Donnell (Little, Brown, 1970). It's a revealing, intimate book. I had interviewed all three co-authors at length before this, but McCarthy's material was a great supplement. Larry O'Brien's memories were also most helpful, and so was his book, *No Final Victories* (Ballantine, 1974). Evelyn Lincoln spoke to me several times at considerable length. Her book, too, is necessary reading: *My Twelve Years with John F. Kennedy* (McKay, 1965). Kay Halle, Joan Braden, and Ormsby-Gore had important comment.

8   The Primaries: The Tide Turns
My interviews with John and Jacqueline Kennedy were the most important for this chapter. I travelled with them during their preliminary sweep before the primaries. I talked to my friend Peter Lisagor a number of times on Kennedy before Peter died, but his oral history report at the Kennedy Library amplified much of what he told me. Similarly, Ken O'Donnell had told me much in 1959, but the McCarthy tapes of his interviews provided much more. Again, the Spalding, Walton, Bradlee, and Bartlett interviews supplemented a great deal. So did Stephen Smith, Arthur Goldberg, Nancy Coleman, Ralph Dungan, and Rowland Evans, Jr. The interview with Franklin D. Roosevelt, Jr., was done in 1959.

9   Winning the Nomination
Merle Miller's taped interviews and notes from his superb book on Lyndon Johnson, *Lyndon* (Putnam, 1980), provided excellent material here. Edgar Ber-

man's *Hubert* (Putnam, 1982), was full of warm, personal anecdotes. The best overall book on the campaign was *The Making of a President, 1960* by Theodore White (Atheneum, 1961). Clark Clifford's detailed memory was invaluable for this chapter. So were Larry Newman and Myer (Mike) Feldman.

Other key interviews here were with Sen. Stuart Symington and his son James, William McCormick Blair, Jr., John Sharon, Bill Haddad, Jim Rowe, and Max Kampelman. The file of the *Los Angeles Times* was most important for detail. Evelyn Lincoln's book, *Kennedy and Johnson* (Holt, Rinehart & Winston, 1968), had some interesting, intimate background.

10   *All in the Family: The Kennedy Campaign*

Nobody had spent more time with John Kennedy than his personal secretary, Evelyn Lincoln, and the same applies to Robert Kennedy and his personal secretary, Angie Novello. My interviews with them were long and detailed. Charles Roberts of *Newsweek* has a full file of notes and papers on the campaign which he made available to me and which were of great value. Lester David, who has written extensively about the Kennedy family, including *Joan* (Warner, 1975) made available some interviews which were most useful. Sen. Ted Kennedy filled in many details about his own work in the campaign, and so did Jim Rowe and others. Blair Clark and Ernest Leiser of CBS had some contributing sidelights.

11   *The Kennedy/Nixon Debates*

Joan Braden, who was National Women's Chairman of the Democratic campaign in 1960, was then the person closest to Jacqueline Kennedy and her memory is excellent. The same applies, as always, to Spalding and Powers. Abba Schwartz and Arthur Schlesinger, Jr., are my main sources on Eleanor Roosevelt and Victor Lasky was my source on Nixon—Lasky's book: *JFK: The Man and the Myth* (Macmillan, 1963). Earl Mazo of the *New York Herald Tribune* was an added source. A number of other reporters did not want to be identified. Harris Wofford wrote an excellent book on the civil rights aspects in *Of Kennedys and Kings* (Farrar, Straus & Giroux, 1980).

12   *You Can Call Him Mr. President Now*

The memory, notes, and papers of John Sharon were most valuable here. So was my interview with George Ball. The McCarthy tapes of O'Donnell and Powers, plus my own interview with Powers offered key material. So did Bill Haddad, and again, as always, Larry Newman. There was excellent material in *Walter Lippmann and the American Century* by Ronald Steel (Little, Brown, 1981). Bartlett and Walton supplemented each other on the story of the selection of a secretary of state. The comment from William Douglas comes from Kennedy Library's Oral History. Chuck Roberts, Clark Clifford, Roswell Gilpatric, McGeorge Bundy, Mike Feldman, Ben Bradlee, and Bill Walton all offered important material. The account of Mrs. Kennedy's White House redecorating is best reported in *Upstairs in the White House* by J. B. West with Mary Lynn Kotz (Coward, McCann & Geoghegan, 1973).

13   *The Pay Is Good and I Can Walk to Work*

In both his interview and in his book, *With Kennedy*, by Pierre Salinger (Doubleday, 1966), Salinger provided considerable insight into the White House scene. So did McGeorge Bundy. Again Evelyn Lincoln's memories were most graphic. Jim Bishop wrote a slim but most informative book, *A Day in* the *Life of President Kennedy*, (Random House, 1964). The Miller material on Johnson, again, was most useful here.

14   *An Elegant First Lady*

The CBS "Tour of the White House" provides an excellent background for Mrs. Kennedy's work there. So does J. B. West's book. *My Life with Jacqueline Kennedy* by Mary Barelli Gallagher (McKay, 1968); *Jacqueline Kennedy, The White House Years*, by Mary Van Rensselaer Thayer (Little, Brown, 1967); and *Of Diamonds and Diplomats* by Letitia Baldrige (Houghton Mifflin, 1968) all have stories to tell about Jacqueline Kennedy. Baldrige told me even more in our interview. Steve Smith had much to add and so did Betty Beale, Helen Thomas, McGeorge Bundy, Godfrey McHugh, Kay Halle, and Dave Powers.

15   *The Men Behind the President*

Robert McNamara told me much of the Hickory Hill seminars, Fred Dutton on Kennedy techniques of creative tension, Gen. Maxwell Taylor on White House teamwork, Evelyn Lincoln on the President's personal traits, McGeorge Bundy on his personality, Robert Manning on his open mind, Blair Clark on his temper, Bob Donovan on his reserve, Nancy Dickerson on his easy boredom, Larry Newman on his humor, Joseph Alsop on his reading, Fred Dutton on his work habits, George Ball on his pragmatism, Harrison Salisbury, Ben Bradlee, and Pierre Salinger on his press relations, and Fred Friendly on his TV awareness.

16   *The Other Women*

This is one chapter in which a great many interviewees would talk, but asked not to be quoted. Nancy Dickerson and Marianne Means had some quotable comment, and George Smathers had more. Smathers was much more voluble with Kitty Kelley in her book, *Jackie Oh!* (Lyle Stuart, 1978). The Blair book retold the Betty Spalding conversation with Jacqueline Kennedy on Pam Turnure. Others with a more printable view included Roswell Gilpatric who has dated her often, James Symington and Bill Walton, who knew her well, and her social secretary Letitia Baldrige. Also most useful here is Nancy Dickerson's book, *Among Those Present* (Random House, 1976), and Paul B. Fay's book, *The Pleasure of His Company* (Harper, 1966).

17   *The Bay of Pigs: An Early Challenge*

General Maxwell Taylor, McGeorge Bundy, and Peter Wyden were the best sources for this chapter. Wyden's book, *Bay of Pigs* (Simon & Schuster, 1979), is the definitive book on the subject. W. W. Rostow told Paul Green his personal observations of the time, supplementing his book, *The Diffusion of Power* (Macmillan, 1972). Chuck Roberts reported the Stevenson-Kennedy conversation and Godfrey McHugh recounted the details of the President's anguish over the mother of a dead pilot. Larry Newman was vivid in describing Kennedy's lonely walks on the Hyannis Port beach during the various crises and Charles Spalding was equally vivid in his memory of the weekend in Glen Ora in the aftermath of the Bay of Pigs.

18   *The Man Who Came with Jacqueline Kennedy*

Ed Welsh was the most important source to me on the story of our space projects. He was the executive director of the National Aeronautics and Space Council. Besides our extensive interview, he provided me with some important relevant documents. The best source on the Kennedy relationship with De Gaulle was former Ambassador to France, Gen. James Gavin. Hervé Alphand was similarly explicit in his book, *L'étonnement d'être: Journal 1939–1973* published in France by Fayard. Alphand is similarly frank about Kennedy's attitude towards women. Pierre Salinger, Letitia Baldrige, Dave Powers, and Hugh Sidey all had pertinent comments on the Kennedy trips to Paris and Vienna. Both Sorensen and Schlesinger have amplified this in their books in detail. Another book that had some interesting background was *To Jack with Love* by Kathleen Bouvier (Zebra, 1979). The book is by Jacqueline's cousin.

19   *Grace Under Pressure*

McGeorge Bundy and John Sharon detailed the Kennedy relationship with the State Department. So did George Ball. The *New York Times* and *Washington Post* had excellent articles on the Pakistan dinner, and J. B. West supplemented them in his book. Gen. Lyman Lemnitzer told Paul Green much of the Berlin background, and Larry Newman and Arthur Goldberg filled in some of the aftermath for me. Bill Walton had a most interesting sidelight, both on Berlin and on the Princess Grace visit. The Baldrige book is also very good on the Pakistan dinner, as are Mary Gallagher and J. B. West.

20   *See the New Frontiersman Run*

The book *Sargent Shriver* by Robert Liston (Farrar, Straus, 1964) has some useful material, but I got much more from Shriver himself, from his wife Eunice, Charles Bartlett, Bill Haddad, and Bill Blair. In the same way, my interview with Larry O'Brien was more valuable to me, on this chapter, than his book. The Morrissey material comes from a variety of sources—the *New York Times* file was particularly good on this, but James Reed was better. The John Glenn comments come from the Kennedy Library Oral History. Kennedy's naval aide, Tazewell Shepard, Jr., wrote an interesting book, *Man of the Sea* (Morrow, 1965), and he amplified much more of it in his interview with me.

21   *The Uncrowned Queen*

A great deal of Jacqueline Kennedy's activities at this time were widely reported in the press and magazines: the *Washington Post*, the *New York Times*, the press associations, all the women's magazines plus many of the general ones. There is a large library of clippings available. Joan Braden, Letitia Baldrige, and Martha Bartlett gave me greater insight than any of the clippings. Of the magazine reporters, Laura Bergquist of *Look* was the most sensitive. She and Mrs. Kennedy became good friends. Betty Beale, who knew the Auchincloss family, provided added insight. Sarah McClendon and Helen Thomas were among a number of women reporters who added much, some of them anonymously. Worth looking at for material was *Dateline: White House* by Helen Thomas (Macmillan, 1975). On White House parties *The Kennedy White House Parties*, by Anne H. Lincoln (Viking, 1961).

22   *A Marriage in Crisis*

The book by Judith Campbell Exner and Ovid Demaris, *My Story* (Grove, 1977) is worth examining despite its sensationalism, simply for personal facts that do check elsewhere. Ben Bradlee's book is much more important and so is the Fay book. *Office Hours: Day and Night* by Dr. Janet Travell (World, 1968) is also worth looking at. So is the *New York Times* index. Blair Clark,

Charles Spalding, and Joan Braden all made important contributions to this chapter.

23 *The Brothers: Jack and Bobby*

Angie Novello's interviews were key to the character of her boss, Robert Kennedy. His deputy, James Symington, was also very important with his memories. Robert Kennedy's own interviews in Kennedy Library Oral History were excellent. But the most moving comment came from Adam Yarmolinsky.

24 *Ambassador Jacqueline*

Jacqueline Kennedy's trips abroad were exhaustively covered in the press, in the greatest detail, but Joan Braden provided me with her personal observations of the trip to India. John Kenneth Galbraith's books, *Ambassador's Journal* (Houghton Mifflin, 1969), and *A Life in Our Times* (Houghton Mifflin, 1981) are also useful references. The best magazine accounts were in *Newsweek* and *Time*. Marianne Means has written an interesting book in *The Woman in the White House* (Random House, 1963).

25 *The Patriarch*

The most revealing material on Joseph Kennedy's stroke comes from his nurse Rita Dallas. Her book, written with Jeanira Ratcliffe, *The Kennedy Case* (Putnam, 1973) is a detailed study, sensitively done. Whelan's book is very good but Koskoff's is more recent and more detailed. David Powers was most important in his recollections of this time.

26 *Teddy: The Godson*

Senator Ted Kennedy provided the most valuable personal material of his own political experience and personal relationship with his brother. Probably the best book source on him is by James McGregor Burns, *Edward Kennedy and the Camelot Legacy* (Norton, 1976). There is, of course, a vast library of newspaper and magazine clippings on Ted Kennedy, but the best such source is the *New York Times* index and the files of the *Washington Post*.

27 *The Missiles of October*

George Ball, McGeorge Bundy, Gen. Maxwell Taylor, and Ray Cline were the most valuable interviews for this chapter. Some of this is in Ball's excellent book, *The Past Has Another Pattern* (Norton, 1982). Ray Cline also has written an interesting book, *Secrets, Spies and Scholars* (Acropolis, 1976). Elie Abel in *The Missile Crisis* (Lippincott, 1966) has written a clear, sharp account. Robert Kennedy's own memoirs, *Thirteen Days* (Norton, 1969), is more revealing and personal. Worth looking at are the personal letters of Dean Acheson, *Among Friends* edited by David S. McLellan and David C. Acheson (Dodd, Mead, 1980). The Alsops' interview on this was the most intimate. The Charles E. Bohlen book, *Witness to History*, (Norton, 1973), is well worth reading on this period. Dave Powers' accounts, again, were most personal and most valuable. Also worth looking at are: *The Making of a Missile Crisis* by Herbert Duerstein (Johns Hopkins University Press, 1978); *The Cuban Missile Crisis* by Abram Chayes (Oxford, 1974).

28 *Goodnight Mrs. Kennedy, Wherever You Are*

Ben Bradlee was the source on the birthday party, and he detailed it further in his book. Laura Bergquist's perspective was most important, and so was

Lindy Boggs and Charles Spalding. The 50-mile walk was best told by Jim Symington and the background by Pierre Salinger. The West book was worth checking here. Another book, with some surprising detail, was by Traphes Bryant with Frances Spatz Leighton, *Dog Days at the White House*, (Macmillan, 1975).

29 *Ich bin ein Berliner*
McGeorge Bundy was the best source on the Berlin trip. The Sorensen and Schlesinger books are both also excellent on this. Godfrey McHugh and Hugh Sidey had interesting sidelights. The Kenneth O'Donnell tapes were most relevant on the trip to Ireland, and my friend Joe McCarthy filled me in with additional stories. A sound book of reference is *To Move a Nation* by Roger Helsman (Doubleday, 1967).

30 *Vietnam: The Looming Crisis*
General Maxwell Taylor, Godfrey McHugh, Ted Clifton, Roswell Gilpatric, George Ball, Robert McNamara, Rep. Frank Thompson, and Larry Newman were all important interviews for this chapter. Cyrus Sulzberger wrote two books of memoirs which are worth examining on this: *A Long Row of Candles* (Macmillan, 1960) and *Last of the Giants*, (Macmillan, 1970). Fred Dutton had some perceptive observations. The *New York Times* file again is indispensable. An interesting book for background was *Politics and Policy* by James L. Sundquist (The Brookings Institution, 1968). An excellent book on this: *The Best and the Brightest* by David Halberstein (Random House, 1969).

31 *Human Rights/Civil Rights*
My interview with Benjamin S. Loeb was a primary source on the Nuclear Test Ban Treaty. Loeb and Glenn T. Seaborg, chairman of the Atomic Energy Commission, wrote a very good book, *Kennedy, Khrushchev and the Test Ban* (University of California Press, 1981). Averell Harriman also told me much of his personal problems in the negotiations, and amplified it in many magazine articles and interviews. Ormsby-Gore revealed to me the private growth of the President on this subject—for which Ormsby-Gore was much responsible. Worth reading is the Chester Bowles memoir, *Promises to Keep* (Harper & Row, 1971). On the civil rights issue, *Kennedy Justice* by Victor Navasky (Atheneum, 1971), is valuable background.

32 *A Rekindled Tenderness*
Larry Newman, Dave Powers, Bill Walton, and Ben Bradlee were the most important sources for this chapter. Letitia Baldrige and Roswell Gilpatric added personal sidelights. The J. B. West observations were also valuable. There are some amusing anecdotes in *White House Nannie* by Maud Shaw (New American Library, 1965). Evelyn Lincoln was also a prime source on the Kennedy children.

33 *Rendezvous with Death*
Again, Larry Newman and Dave Powers were key interviews here. Charles Roberts, George Smathers, Evelyn Lincoln, Bill Haddad, and Sen. Claiborne Pell were all good sources.

34 *November 22, 1963*
William Manchester's book, *The Death of a President* (Harper & Row, 1967) is comprehensively detailed on the subject. On the personal side, in an

interview, Larry O'Brien had some surprising background. Evelyn Lincoln, Larry Newman, and Lindy Boggs all had a contribution here. So did Chuck Roberts. For all speeches and press conferences, *The Public Papers of the Presidents*, three volumes on John F. Kennedy (Government Printing Office), are invaluable.

AFTERMATH

Most vivid were the memories on this from Godfrey McHugh, Dave Powers, Bill Walton, Mike Feldman, and Sen. Stuart Symington.

REFLECTIONS

Some worthwhile books of assessment must include, *The Kennedy Promise* by Henry Fairlie (Doubleday, 1972), and *The Kennedy Legacy*, by Theodore Sorensen (Macmillan, 1969). But the basic content of this chapter, as in the rest of the book, were the interviews.

ACKNOWLEDGMENTS

This book is based primarily on hundreds of interviews that date back to 1959 when Ed Plaut and I were researching *Front Runner, Dark Horse*. That was a book contrasting the political campaigns of Senators John Kennedy and Stuart Symington. In the course of it, we extensively interviewed John and Jacqueline Kennedy, Joseph Kennedy, Sr., Robert Kennedy, and Eunice Shriver Kennedy, as well as other members of the family. We also interviewed all the key members of his staff, particularly Ted Sorensen, Kenneth O'Donnell, Larry O'Brien, Arthur Schlesinger, Jr., Myer Feldman, Torbert Macdonald, and Timothy Reardon, among others. At that time, we also talked to other key pivotal figures such as Adlai Stevenson, Mrs. Franklin D. Roosevelt and her sons James and Franklin, and Hubert Humphrey, as well as many others.

Supplementing those interviews for this current book, I have not only talked again to many of the same principals who are still alive, but to a great many others. Of the Kennedy family, this time, Stephen Smith was again particularly valuable, and Senator Ted Kennedy illuminated more unknown areas for me.

Acknowledgments

My current interviews have stretched over a period of four years with the heaviest concentration on his most intimate friends. The most important, for me, were Charles Spalding, Larry Newman, Martha and Charles Bartlett, Ben Bradlee, William Walton, James Reed, David Powers, and Senator George Smathers.

Of the White House staff, some of the key people for me—besides those already mentioned—were McGeorge Bundy, Robert McNamara, George Ball, Fred Dutton, Clark Clifford, Evelyn Lincoln, Pierre Salinger, General Maxwell Taylor, military aides Godfrey McHugh, Ted Clifton, and Tazewell Shepherd, Ralph Dungan, Arthur Goldberg, Eugene Rostow, General Lyman Lemnitzer, Edward Welsh, Adam Yarmolinsky, and Bill Haddad.

For added information on Jacqueline Kennedy, I am grateful to Letitia Balridge, Joan Braden, David Ormsby-Gore (Lord Harlech), Betty Beale, the Bartletts and William Walton, Frank Waldrop, Blair Clark, Roswell Gilpatric, Nancy Dickerson, Nancy Coleman, Congresswoman Lindy Boggs, William McCormick Blair, Jr., and Nina Auchincloss Straight.

My deep gratitude, as always, to my dear friend Paul S. Green, who acted as my Washington headquarters, arranging interviews for me, checking facts, and doing many of the interviews himself; Ed Plaut, who made available to me his own file of interviews and notes from the book we co-authored; Merle Miller, who gave me his file of pertinent interviews from his book on Lyndon Johnson; Charles Roberts, who had covered the White House during that period for *Newsweek* magazine, for opening his files to me; John Sharon, who made available to me all his papers; Joe McCarthy, who co-authored the book *Johnny, We Hardly Knew Ye*, let me have all his taped interviews; and Lester David, who similarly let me have copies of taped interviews with the Kennedy family and friends.

I am indebted to the staff of the Kennedy Library: Director Dan Fenn, curator of the presidential museum David Powers, chief archivist William Moss, audiovisual archivist Allan Goodrich, research archivist William Johnson, and reference assistant Deborah Greene. The most valuable material in the library for me was the oral history, particularly interviews with those who have since died.

I am grateful for the splendid research of my daughter, Tina, and also Joan Gold Lufrano, Peggy Katzander, and Olga Barbi.

It is not possible to list the names of all those whose cooperation made this book possible, but there are those whom I must name: Harriett and John Weaver, Pearl and Lionel Bernier, Angie Novello,

Acknowledgments

James Rowe, Abba Schwartz, Sidney Shore, Senator Stuart Symington, James Symington, David Hackett, Clare Boothe Luce, Joel Fisher, Peter Wyden, Hugh Sidey, Ernest Leiser, Phoebe and Edgar Berman, Rowland Evans, Kay Halle, Ken Crawford, Sarah McClendon, Harold Reis, Ray Cline, Sam Brightman, Victor Lasky, Charles Tyroler, General James Gavin, Robert Donovan, Theodore White, Eric Sevareid, Michael Straight, Robert Manning, Marianne Means, Joseph Alsop, Susan Mary Alsop, Mrs. William Randolph Hearst, Jr., Sander Vanocur, Ed Morgan, Richard Helms, Cord Meyer, Betty Copithorne, Roscoe Drummond, Paul Nitze, Sancy Newman, Senator Claiborne Pell, Representative Frank Thompson, Edward McLaughlin, Robert Allen, Senator Hugh Scott, Lucius Battle, Laura Bergquist, Marquis Childs, John Gardner, Charles Collingwood, David Acheson, Fred Holburn, Frank Cormier, Alexis Johnson, Jack Raymond, Fred Rosen, David Golding, George Slaff, and Louise Sious among many, many others.

My personal thanks, as always, to my faithful friend and secretary, Mari Walker, who somehow deciphered all my notes and tapes. For their added typing help, I thank Roberta Ginsberg and Barbara Hohol. An added note of thanks for all her help to Andrea Raab. For translating portions of Hervé Alphand's French memoirs, I am grateful to my friend Doris Cramer. For acting as courier aboard the Bridgeport–Port Jefferson Ferry, when I couldn't make it, I thank Palangadan Kunhikannan, and for other extra-special courier service to Lucy and Andrew Ackemann and Phyllis Grann.

I will always be grateful to my publisher Hillel Black, who not only believed in my book, but who made important editorial suggestions; my editor Joan Sanger, who helped structure and shape the book into what it is; Arlene Friedman, who made so many important editorial recommendations; copy editor Dominick Anfuso, who was so patient with me; and Freddie Templeton, who combed my book so carefully. As always I am indebted to my dear friends Ruth and Larry Hall, who come from wherever they are to proofread my galleys—this time helped by Guyo Tajiri.

Finally, and most important, my love and appreciation to my wife Marjorie Jean—always the first to read my manuscript—who filled many many pages with her invaluable comments and criticisms.

INDEX

Index

Index